Rave reviews for James D. Hornfischer and *Neptune's Inferno*

The *New York Times, Publishers Weekly,* and *Boston Globe* bestseller
A main selection of the History Book Club and the Military Book Club
Selected as a Best Book of 2011 by *Military History Quarterly*

"With the publication of *Neptune's Inferno,* a masterpiece of twentieth-century naval history, it's time to declare James Hornfischer a national treasure, a member of the distinguished band of brothers—Stephen Ambrose, Shelby Foote, Ken Burns, Steven Spielberg, and Tom Hanks—whose sacred mission has been vital to America's journey, preserving the stories of our fathers and grandfathers for future generations, before those stories fade forever out of our consciousness and into the shadows of time."

—BOB SHACOCHIS, National Book Award-winning
author of *The Immaculate Invasion*

"An epic work...In *Neptune's Inferno,* Hornfischer deftly captures the essence of the most pivotal naval campaign of the Pacific war....Compiling interviews with survivors, unpublished eyewitness accounts, and previously unavailable documents, [he] skillfully re-creates the bravery displayed by sailors who opposed the Japanese in what could be called America's finest hour of the Pacific campaign. The book is richly supported by meticulous source notes, a concise bibliography, rare photos and campaign maps.... With *Neptune's Inferno,* Hornfischer...has earned his place among the hallowed ranks of military historians....[It] is a literary tour de force that is destined to become one of the most definitive works about the battle for Guadalcanal. It deserves a place of honor on every military bookshelf."

—*San Antonio Express-News*

"*Neptune's Inferno* is well written, packed with scene-setting details and clearly the product of extensive research, including interviews with some of the battle's now-aged survivors.... The author's two previous WWII books, *The Last Stand of the Tin Can Sailors* and *Ship of Ghosts,* thrust him into the major leagues of American military history writers. *Neptune's Inferno* is solid proof he deserves to be there."   —*The Dallas Morning News*

"James Hornfischer's *Neptune's Inferno* contributes a great deal toward balancing the picture...including some firsthand accounts and oral histories that have not been used before....Mr. Hornfischer's focus...is the interplay of character and personality with technology and military doctrine. The result is both analytical and entertaining....Insightful and judicious."

—*The Wall Street Journal*

"Hornfischer (*Ship of Ghosts*) understands the human dynamics of the U.S. Navy in the Pacific war.... [He] gives an empathetic but balanced account ... [reconstructing] the fighting in a masterful synthesis of technical analysis, operational narrative, and tales of courage." —*Publishers Weekly*

"Outstanding ... The author offers balanced assessments of the leaders on both sides, but the real heroes are the American bluejackets, who too often paid with suffering and death for those leaders' slowness to learn. And as in his first two books, the author's narrative gifts and excellent choice of detail give an almost Homeric quality to the men who met on the sea in steel titans." —*Booklist* (starred review)

"This work's major strengths are its careful organization, readable prose, and ... well-reasoned conclusions. Depictions of battles and ships are enlivened with ... apt comments from participants and relevant character sketches of the key figures." —U.S. Naval Institute *Proceedings*

"*Neptune's Inferno* is an exceptional piece of military history. Hornfischer has broadened and deepened our understanding of the U.S. Navy's role in the Solomons campaign in this eminently readable account of the bloody naval battles that doomed the Imperial Japanese Navy to defeat and irrevocably shifted the strategic initiative in the Pacific War."
—Dr. Peter R. Mansoor, Colonel, U.S. Army (retired),
General Raymond E. Mason, Jr., Chair in Military History,
The Ohio State University

"The rich text—augmented by over one hundred illustrations and maps—makes this book one of the precious few that will hold equal appeal to the serious researcher and the general reader.... *Neptune's Inferno* is what every great history book aspires to be: a rollicking great adventure story built on a foundation of tight, precise research. If a reader picks up only one book on the Pacific War this year, *Neptune's Inferno* is the one to read."
—*Armchair General*

"With good maps and extensive documentation, this is gripping and readable, not a dry military report." —*Library Journal*

"The author approaches his subject with the mind of a skilled historian and the heart of a lyrical poet." —Richard B. Frank, *World War II*

"The book's strength is in its dramatic telling of the stories of valiant officers and seamen who persevered in the presence of a ruthless enemy. The stories of sailors' first night battle are so vivid that you can almost see the flashes from the Japanese guns and feel the percussion of shells hitting your hull."

—*The Roanoke Times*

"Hornfischer has produced an account that is visceral yet technical, sweeping yet personal. It's a terrific read, and an important new addition to the literature on this most important naval campaign in the Pacific."

—JONATHAN PARSHALL, co-author of *Shattered Sword: The Untold Story of the Battle of Midway*

"Hornfischer's accounts of naval combat in the Pacific are simply the best in the business."

—IAN W. TOLL, author of *Six Frigates: The Epic History of the Founding of the U.S. Navy*

"With this grand, sweeping, history-correcting book, James Hornfischer takes his place among the elite historians of the United States war in the Pacific during World War II. Like a Curtiss Helldiver, *Neptune's Inferno* catapults the reader high into the skies for a clear perspective on the vast oceanic conflict, then dives relentlessly to propel us right into the smoke and fire and human valor of the brutal inferno known as Guadalcanal. Along the way, and drawing on newly available papers, Hornfischer clears up lingering misconceptions about this battle, including the full extent of the U.S. Navy's role in victory. And in his character portraits of the brilliant, quirky top admirals and generals of the fractious Army-Navy command, Hornfischer offers a worthy counterpart to Doris Kearns Goodwin's *Team of Rivals*."

—RON POWERS, author of *Mark Twain: A Life* and co-author of *Flags of Our Fathers*

"*Neptune's Inferno* is a superb portrait of the U.S. Navy's critical role in the Guadalcanal campaign, both the surface and aerial combat. Comprehensive with much that is new, yet immensely readable, it covers not only the admirals but the junior officers and bluejackets as well. Highly recommended."

—JOHN B. LUNDSTROM, author of *The First Team*

"The star of this year's reading list is James D. Hornfischer, a military historian whose flair for narrative is rivaled only by his ability to organize the sweep of battle and assess strategy and tactics in layman's terms."

—*The Plain Dealer*

Also by James D. Hornfischer

The Last Stand of the Tin Can Sailors (2004)

Ship of Ghosts (2006)

NEPTUNE'S INFERNO

Bantam Books Trade Paperbacks
New York

NEPTUNE'S INFERNO

★ ★ ★

The U.S. Navy at Guadalcanal

JAMES D. HORNFISCHER

2012 Bantam Books Trade Paperback Edition

Copyright © 2011 by James D. Hornfischer

Published in the United States by Bantam Books,
an imprint of The Random House Publishing Group,
a division of Random House, Inc., New York.

BANTAM BOOKS and the rooster colophon are
registered trademarks of Random House, Inc.

Excerpts from unpublished writings by Robert D. Graff
copyright © 2011 by Robert D. Graff. Used by permission.

Originally published in hardcover in the United States by Bantam Books,
an imprint of The Random House Publishing Group,
a division of Random House, Inc., in 2011.

Library of Congress Cataloging-in-Publication Data
Hornfischer, James D.
Neptune's inferno : the U.S. Navy at Guadalcanal / James D. Hornfischer.
p. cm.
Includes bibliographical references and index.
ISBN 978-0-553-38512-0—ISBN 978-0-553-90807-7 (eBook)
1. Guadalcanal, Battle of, Solomon Islands, 1942–1943.   2. World War,
1939–1945—Naval operations, American.   3. United States. Navy—History—
World War, 1939–1945.   4. United States. Navy—Biography.   5. Veterans—
United States—Interviews.   6. Guadalcanal, Battle of, Solomon Islands,
1942–1943—Personal narratives, American.   I. Title.
D767.98.H665 2011
940.54′265933—dc22
2010027231

Printed in the United States of America

South Pacific, 1942 map by Jeffrey L. Ward
All other maps by Lum Pennington

www.bantamdell.com

6 8 9 7 5

Book design by Virginia Norey

In memory:

CHARLES D. GROJEAN
Rear Admiral, USN
1923–2008

Sailor, Leader, Teacher

Never have the gods of all the tribes put upon the seas such monsters as man now sends over them. . . . Their steel bowels, grinding and rumbling below the splash of the sea, are fed on quarried rock. Their arteries are steel, their nerves copper, their blood red and blue flames. With the prescience of the supernatural, they peer into space. Their voices scream through gales, and they whisper together over a thousand miles of sea. They reach out and destroy that which the eye of man cannot perceive.

But . . . all this terribleness will vanish, returning again into the inanimate whenever the capacity and vigor of the guiding mind deteriorates or is worn down by the years that have stolen away the quick grasp of youth.

—Homer Lea, *The Valor of Ignorance* (1909)

CONTENTS

MAPS *xii*
TABLES *xiii*
PROLOGUE: Eighty-two Ships *xvii*

PART I
SEA OF TROUBLES

1: Trip Wire 3

2: A Great Gray Fleet 16

3: The First D-Day 27

4: Nothing Worthy of Your Majesty's Attention 44

5: Fly the Carriers 50

6: A Captain in the Fog 56

7: The Martyring of Task Group 62.6 62

8: Burning in the Rain 80

PART II
FIGHTING FLEET RISING

9: A New Kind of Fight 95

10: The Tokyo Express 109

11: A Function at the Junction 114

12: What They Were Built For   123

13: The Warriors   135

14: The Devil May Care   145

15: The Visit   150

16: Night of a New Moon   157

17: Pulling the Trigger   169

18: "Pour It to 'Em"   179

PART III

STORM TIDE

19: All Hell's Eve   191

20: The Weight of a War   200

21: Enter Fighting   208

22: "Strike—Repeat, Strike"   216

23: Santa Cruz   223

24: Secret History   237

25: Turner's Choice   243

26: Suicide   253

27: Black Friday   263

28: Into the Light   273

29: The Killing Salvo   282

30: Death in the Machine Age   290

31: Point Blank   299

32: Among the Shadows   311

33: *Atlanta* Burning   317

34: Cruiser in the Sky   326

35: Regardless of Losses   335

PART IV

THE THUNDERING

36: The Giants Ride 345

37: The Gun Club 353

38: The Kind of Men Who Win a War 369

39: On the Spot 378

40: The Futility of Learning 385

41: Future Rising 398

42: Report and Echo 409

43: The Opinion of Convening Authority 416

44: Ironbottom Sound 423

Acknowledgments 431

Ships and Aircraft Types of the Guadalcanal Campaign 433

Naval Battles of the Guadalcanal Campaign 435

Total Naval Losses at Guadalcanal 437

Source Notes 439

Bibliography 465

Index 491

Photo Credits 513

MAPS

South Pacific, 1942   *xiv*

Pacific Ocean Area   *xvi*

The Slot   *26*

Battle of Savo Island   *66*

Battle of Cape Esperance   *167*

Cruiser Night Action   *271*

Morning After in Ironbottom Sound   *323*

Battleship Night Action   *351*

Battle of Tassafaronga   *394*

TABLES

The U.S. Navy at Guadalcanal, August 1942   *xxi*

Order of Battle—Battle of Savo Island   *65*

Shipboard Gunnery and Fire-Control Systems   *164*

Order of Battle—Battle of Cape Esperance   *165*

The U.S. Navy at Guadalcanal (as of October 18, 1942)   *214*

U.S. Navy Combat Task Forces in the South Pacific
(as of October 26, 1942)   *225*

The Japanese in the Battle of Santa Cruz   *226*

U.S. Navy Combat Task Forces in the South Pacific
(as of November 12, 1942)   *252*

Order of Battle—The Cruiser Night Action   *270*

Order of Battle—The Battleship Night Action   *350*

Order of Battle—Battle of Tassafaronga   *393*

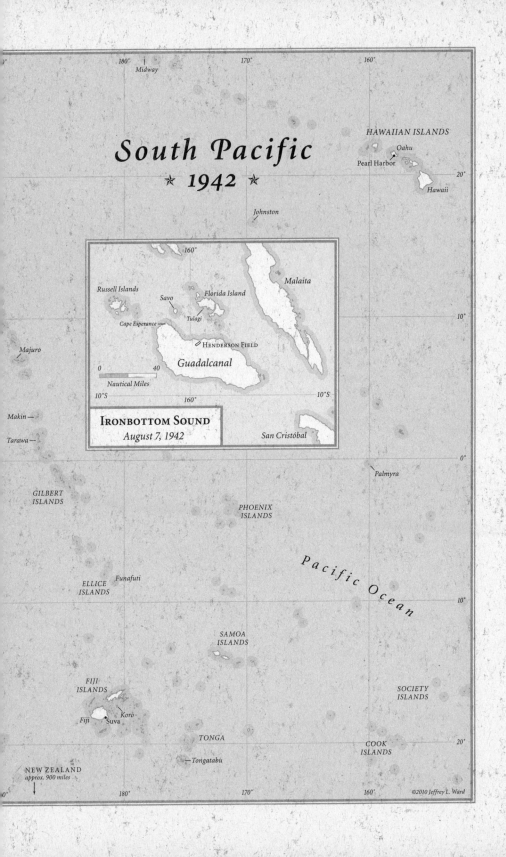

South Pacific

★ 1942 ★

HAWAIIAN ISLANDS

Midway

Oahu
Pearl Harbor

Hawaii

Johnston

160°

Malaita

Russell Islands
Savo
Florida Island

Cape Esperance
Tulagi

HENDERSON FIELD

Guadalcanal

0   40
Nautical Miles

10°S

160°

10°S

San Cristóbal

IRONBOTTOM SOUND
August 7, 1942

Majuro

Makin
Tarawa

Palmyra

GILBERT
ISLANDS

PHOENIX
ISLANDS

Pacific Ocean

ELLICE
ISLANDS

Funafuti

SAMOA
ISLANDS

FIJI
ISLANDS

Koro

Fiji   Suva

SOCIETY
ISLANDS

TONGA

COOK
ISLANDS

NEW ZEALAND
approx. 900 miles

Tongatabu

©2010 Jeffrey L. Ward

Pacific Ocean Area

LEGEND

- - - - - Extent of Japanese control

Eighty-two Ships

ON FRIDAY, AUGUST 7, 1942, EIGHTY-TWO U.S. NAVY SHIPS MANNED by forty thousand sailors, shepherding a force of sixteen thousand U.S. Marines, reached their destination in a remote southern ocean and spent the next hundred days immersed in a curriculum of cruel and timeless lessons. No fighting navy had ever been so speedily and explosively educated. In the conflict that rolled through the end of that trembling year, they and the thousands more who followed them learned that technology was important, but that guts and guile mattered more. That swiftness was more deadly than strength, and that well-packaged surprise usually beat them both. That if it looked like the enemy was coming, the enemy probably was coming and you ought to tell somebody, maybe even everybody. That the experience of battle forever divides those who talk of nothing else but its prospect from those who talk of everything else but its memory.

Sailors in the war zone learned the arcane lore of bad luck and its many manifestations, from the sight of rats leaving a ship in port (a sign that she will be sunk) to the act of whistling while at sea (inviting violent winds) to the follies of opening fire first on a Sunday or beginning a voyage on a Friday (the consequences of which were certain but nonspecific, and thus all the more frightful).

They learned to tell the red-orange blossoms of shells hitting targets from the faster flashes of muzzles firing the other way. That hard steel burns. That any ship can look shipshape, but if you really want to take her measure, check her turret alignments. That torpedoes, and sometimes radios, keep their own fickle counsel about when they will work. That a war to secure liberty could be waged passionately by men who had none themselves, and that in death all sailors have an unmistakable dignity.

Some of these were the lessons of any war, truisms relearned for the hundredth time by the latest generation to face its trials. Victory always tended to fly with the first effective salvo. Others were novel, the product of untested technologies and tactics, unique to the circumstances of America's first offensive in the Pacific: that you could win a campaign on the backs of stevedores expert in the lethal craft of combat-loading cargo ships; that the little image of an enemy ship on a radar scope will flinch visibly when heavily struck; that rapid partial salvo fire from a director-controlled main battery reduces the salvo interval period but complicates the correction of ranges and spots.

In the far South Pacific, you were lucky if your sighting report ever reached its recipient. Even then, the plainest statement of fact might be subject to two or more interpretations of meaning. You learned that warships smashed and left dead in the night could resurrect themselves by the rise of morning, that circumstances could conspire to make your enemy seem much shrewder than he ever really could be, and that as bad as things might seem in the midst of combat, they might well be far worse for him. That you could learn from your opponent's success if your pride permitted it, and that the best course of action often ran straight into the barriers of your worst biases and fears. That some of the worst thrashings you took could look like victories tomorrow. That good was never good enough, and if you wanted Neptune to laugh, all you had to do was show him your operations plan.

This book tells the story of how the U.S. Navy learned these and many other lessons during its first major campaign of the twentieth century: the struggle for the southern Solomon Islands in 1942. The American fleet landed its marines on Guadalcanal and Tulagi in early August. The Japanese were beaten by mid-November and evacuated in February. What happened in between was a story of how America gambles on the grand scale, wings it, and wins. Top commanders on both sides were slain in battle or perished afterward amid the shame of inquiries and interrogations. A more lasting pain beset the living. Reputations were shattered, grudges nursed. The Marine Corps would compose a rousing institutional anthem from the notion, partly true, that the Navy had abandoned them in the fight's critical early going. But the full story of the campaign turns the tale in another direction, seldom appreciated. Soon enough, the fleet threw itself fully into the breach, and by the end of it all, almost three sailors had died in battle at sea for every infantryman who fell ashore. The Corps' debt to the Navy was never greater.

The American landings on Guadalcanal developed into the most sustained and vicious fight of the Pacific war. Seven major naval actions were the result, five of them principally ship-versus-ship battles fought at night, the other two decided by aircraft by day. The nickname the Americans coined for the waters that hosted most of the carnage, "Ironbottom Sound," suited the startling scale of destruction: The U.S. Navy lost twenty-four major warships; the Japanese lost twenty-four. Aircraft losses, too, were nearly equal: America lost 436, Japan 440. The human toll was horrific. Ashore, U.S. Marine and Army killed in action were 1,592 (out of 60,000 landed). The number of Americans killed at sea topped five thousand. Japanese deaths set the bloody pace for the rest of the war, with 20,800 soldiers lost on the island and probably 4,000 sailors at sea. Through the end of 1942, the news reports of Guadalcanal spun a narrative whose twists required no fictionalizing for high drama, though they did need some careful parsing and management, or so the Navy thought at the time. Franklin Roosevelt competed with "Tokyo Rose" to shape the tale on the public airwaves.

In their trial against the Imperial Japanese Navy (IJN) in the waters off Guadalcanal, the Navy mastered a new kind of fight. Expeditionary war was a new kind of enterprise, and its scale at Guadalcanal was surpassed only by its combatants' thoroughgoing deficits in matériel, preparation, and understanding of their enemy. It was the most critical major military operation America would ever run on such a threadbare shoestring. As its principal players would admit afterward, the puzzle of victory was solved on the fly and on the cheap, in terms of resources if not lives. The campaign featured tight interdependence among warriors of the air, land, and sea. For the infantry to seize and hold the island, ships had to control the sea. For a fleet to control the sea, the pilots had to fly from the island's airfield. For the pilots to fly from the airfield, the infantry had to hold the island. That tripod stood only by the strength of all three legs. In the end, though, it was principally a navy's battle to win. And despite the ostensible lesson of the Battle of Midway, which had supposedly crowned the aircraft carrier as queen of the seas, the combat sailors of America's surface fleet had a more than incidental voice in who would prevail. For most of the campaign, Guadalcanal was a contest of equals, perhaps the only major battle in the Pacific where the United States and Japan fought from positions of parity. Its outcome was often in doubt.

This book develops the story of the travails and difficult triumphs of the U.S. Navy during its first offensive of World War II, as it navigated a steeply canted learning curve. It emphasizes the human textures of the campaign and looks anew at the decisions and relationships of the commanders who guided it.

The novelist James Michener wrote long ago, "They will live a long time, these men of the South Pacific. They had an American quality. They, like their victories, will be remembered as long as our generation lives. After that, like the men of the Confederacy, they will become strangers. Longer and longer shadows will obscure them, until their Guadalcanal sounds distant on the ear like Shiloh and Valley Forge." The founders of the U.S. Navy, having faced their own moments of decision, from John Paul Jones off Flamborough Head to Stephen Decatur against the Barbary Pirates, would have felt kinship with the men of the South Pacific Forces. There as everywhere, men in uniform fought like impulsive humans almost always have: stubbornly, viciously, brilliantly, wastefully, earnestly, stupidly, gallantly. At Guadalcanal, so distant on the ear, a naval legacy continued, and by their example in that bitter campaign the long shadows of their American quality reach right on up to the present.

The U.S. Navy at Guadalcanal

Operation Watchtower, August 1942

ADM ERNEST J. KING
Commander in Chief, U.S. Fleet (COMINCH)
Washington, DC

ADM CHESTER W. NIMITZ
Commander in Chief, Pacific Fleet (CINCPAC)
Pearl Harbor, Hawaii

VADM ROBERT L. GHORMLEY
Commander, South Pacific Forces (COMSOPAC)
Nouméa, New Caledonia (USS *Argonne*)

VADM FRANK JACK FLETCHER
Commander, Expeditionary Force
Task Force 61 (USS *Saratoga*)

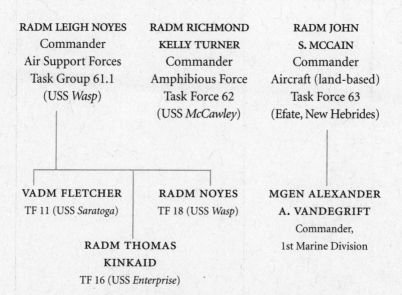

RADM LEIGH NOYES	**RADM RICHMOND**	**RADM JOHN**
Commander	**KELLY TURNER**	**S. MCCAIN**
Air Support Forces	Commander	Commander
Task Group 61.1	Amphibious Force	Aircraft (land-based)
(USS *Wasp*)	Task Force 62	Task Force 63
	(USS *McCawley*)	(Efate, New Hebrides)

VADM FLETCHER	**RADM NOYES**	**MGEN ALEXANDER**
TF 11 (USS *Saratoga*)	TF 18 (USS *Wasp*)	**A. VANDEGRIFT**
		Commander,
RADM THOMAS		1st Marine Division
KINKAID		
TF 16 (USS *Enterprise*)		

RADM VICTOR A. C. CRUTCHLEY, ROYAL NAVY
Commander, Cruiser Covering Force
Task Force 44 (HMAS *Australia*)

PART I

✳ ✳ ✳

Sea of Troubles

"It is better to be bombed into the next world than to live in this one as a slave to anybody or any foreign system. It is that attitude which, we believe, will eventually win this war."

—Collier's, "A United People," January 17, 1942

1

Trip Wire

TWO YEARS BEFORE THE WAR BEGAN, AN OLD SPANISH PRIEST IN A Filipino village said to an American journalist, "The Pacific: Of itself it may not be eternity. Yet certainly you can find in it the scale, the pattern of the coming days of man. The Mediterranean was the sea of destiny of the Ancient World; the Atlantic, of what you call the Old World. I have thought much about this, and I believe the Pacific holds the destiny of your New World. Men now living will see the shape of the future rising from its waters."

The vessel of that ocean held more than half the water on earth, its expanse larger than all the landmasses of the world. Its beauty was elemental, its time of a meter and its distances of a magnitude that Americans could only begin to apprehend from the California, Oregon, and Washington coasts. It was essential and different and compelling and important, whether one measured it by grid coordinates, assessed it by geopolitics and national interests, or sought its prospects above the clouds. And when war came, it was plain to see that the shape of the future, whatever it was to be, was emerging from that trackless basin of brine.

Whose future it would be remained unsettled in the first summer of the war. The forces of distant nations, roaming over it, had clashed briefly but had not yet collided in a way that would test their wills and turn history. That collision was soon to take place, and it would happen, first and seriously and in earnest, on an island called Guadalcanal.

It was a single radio transmission, a clandestine report originating from that island's interior wilderness, that set the powerful wheels turning. The news that reached U.S. Navy headquarters in Washington on July 6, 1942, was routine on its face: The enemy had arrived, was building an airstrip. This was not staggering news at a time when Japanese conquest had been proceeding smoothly along almost every axis of movement in the Asian theater. Nonetheless, this broadcast, sent from a modest teleradio transmitter in a South Pacific jungle to Townsville, Australia, found an attentive audience in the American capital.

The Cambridge-educated agent of the British crown who had sent it, Martin Clemens, had until recently been the administrator of Guadalcanal. When it became clear, in February, that the Japanese were coming, there had been a general evacuation of the civilian populace. Clemens stayed behind. Living off the land near the village of Aola, the site of the old district headquarters, the Australian, tall and athletic, took what he needed from gardens and livestock, depending on native sympathies for everything. Thus sustained, he launched a second career as a covert agent and a "coastwatcher," part of a network of similarly situated men all through the Solomons.

Holed up at his station, he had radioed word to Townsville on May 3 that Japanese troops had landed on the smaller island of Tulagi across the sound. A month later, he reported that they were on Guadalcanal's northern shore, building a wharf.

Then from his jungle hide, Clemens saw a twelve-ship convoy standing on the horizon. Landing on the beach that day came more than two thousand Japanese construction workers, four hundred infantry, and several boatloads of equipment—heavy tractors, road rollers, trucks, and generators. Clearly their purpose was some sort of construction project. Having detected Clemens's teleradio transmissions to Australia, the enemy sent their scouts into the jungle to find him. As the pressure on Clemens and his fellow Australian spies increased, he kept on the move to elude them, aided by a cadre of native scouts, formidable and capable men. The stress of avoiding enemy reconnaissance planes overhead worked on him. He read Shakespeare to settle his mind. "If I lose control everything will be lost," he wrote in his diary on July 23. His radio batteries were nearly depleted, and his food stores thin, when he spotted a gravel-and-clay airstrip under construction on the island's north-coast plantation plain and reported it from his hide in a hillside mining claim. He had sent many reports. This one would bring salvation.

When the commander in chief of the U.S. Fleet, Admiral Ernest J. King, learned from radio intercepts that Japan had sent airfield construction crews to Guadalcanal, a new impetus to action came. He and the Army's chief of staff, General George Marshall, had already struck a compromise that would send U.S. forces into the South Pacific with the ultimate objective of seizing Rabaul, the great Japanese base in New Britain. The first phase of that operation would be the seizure of Tulagi and adjacent positions. With the arrival of the news of Japanese activity on Guadalcanal across the sound, however, the design of America's first major offensive of the war was redrawn, set to begin on Martin Clemens's forlorn hideaway.

It was as if Japan's expansion southeast from Rabaul had struck a hidden trip wire—the lines drawn on Navy charts tracing the paths of sea communication across the South Pacific to Australia. As anyone could see by taking a compass and drawing a 250-mile radius centered on Guadalcanal's airstrip, it would, when operational, enable Japanese planes to threaten the sea-lanes to Australia, whose protection was long one of the Navy's core missions. Construction of the airfield might have been low-order business for Japanese forces spread thinly along a multi-continental oceanic perimeter, but its discovery would draw the fleet straight to Guadalcanal.

The island, shaped like Jamaica, with about half its area, had come to the attention of Westerners long ago. Explorers from the old Spanish priest's homeland, passing through the Solomons in 1568, named it after a town in Andalusia, sixty miles north of Seville. When Captain James Cook arrived 220 years later, he claimed the Solomons for Great Britain, which hung on for another 154 years, until Japanese troops landed. The novelist Jack London visited near the turn of the century and doubted his heart was cold enough to banish his worst enemies to a place so dire, where "the air is saturated with a poison that bites into every pore . . . and that many strong men who escape dying there return as wrecks to their own countries."

A mountain range ran its entire length like a spine, with summits as high as eighty-three hundred feet. On the southern coast, the mountains fell steeply into the sea, making that shoreline a barrier to trade and to war. The north coast's tropical plain was more inviting. Cut through with rivers and forest growth, it was well suited to agriculture—and airfields. The narrow northern beach, guarded by palms and ironwoods and covered in kunai grass, stretched for miles, overlooked by scattered coral ridges, some of them five hundred feet high.

From the British government outpost at Aola to the small Catholic missions in the west, the human settlements were small and prehistoric. The climate, the insects, and the rampant disease made the place hard to tolerate.

A coconut plantation owned by Lever Brothers, the world's largest, drew its employees from the nine thousand resident Melanesians, traditionally divided by culture but now joined imperfectly by one of the few useful things that Britain had brought there: pidgin English.

The U.S. Navy would not have greatly concerned itself with the Solomons, with a census roughly that of Trenton and a population density of ten people per square mile, if not for the accident of its geography, astride the sea lanes to Australia. Tulagi, the British administrative capital, had the best anchorage for hundreds of miles around. On that rocky volcanic islet nestled against Florida Island, huge trees and mangrove swamps lined the shore where they hadn't been cut back to accommodate the trappings of Western empire: a golf course, a commissioner's office, a bishop's residence, a government hospital, a police barracks, a cricket club, and a bar.

Guadalcanal lay about twenty miles south of Tulagi. It marked the southern end of a broken and irregular inter-island corridor that meandered northwest between two parallel columns of islands and dead-ended, about 375 miles later, into the island of Bougainville. As the principal route of Japanese reinforcement into Guadalcanal, this watery path through New Georgia Sound would acquire an outsized strategic importance. It would be nicknamed the Slot.

ADMIRAL CHESTER W. NIMITZ, fifty-six, the grandson of a German hotelier from the Hill Country of central Texas, was born to a rare style of leadership: gentle but exacting, gracious but hard and fearless, like a mailed fist in a satin glove. There was no ruthlessness in him unless one counted as ruthless his willingness to burden the people he relied on with his complete and unfaltering trust. That burden fell heavily upon the men who worked for him, but one of his gifts was an ability to turn the burden into a source of inspiration and uplift for those who shouldered it. The U.S. Navy never needed a leader of his kind more badly than in the months following the treachery of December 7, shortly after which he took command of the Pacific Fleet.

Nimitz's will was ferocious, but held inward and insulated by a kindly temperament that made his ascent to high command a surprise to connoisseurs of four-star ambition. His intensity was apparent only in his close physical proximity, where the heat from his eyes, it was said, could be felt on the skin. Nimitz was an unusually effective organization man, stoic and controlled but demanding. Ascending to theater command had never been his ambition, for ambitions, he felt, were meant not for personal gain but to pursue common goals within the established order of a group. In 1941, a year before circumstances forced him to accept it, he had turned down the appointment to become commander in chief, Pacific Fleet (CINCPAC). He had done so out of respect for the system, unwilling to vault past the twenty-eight officers who were senior to him. But after the attack on Pearl Harbor his own commander in chief gave him no choice. Franklin D. Roosevelt plucked Nimitz from his post as the Navy's personnel boss and installed him as leader of the most important naval theater in the world. It was a call to duty that allowed no humble refusals. The president told Navy Secretary Frank Knox, "Tell Nimitz to get the hell out to Pearl and stay there till the war is won." The Pacific war would be America's war. Running it would be a lonely charge. A commentator for *Collier's* magazine would call the Pacific "an unshared front where America's production, her strategy, her skill and valor must stand the acid test alone.... Our national feeling with regard to the Pacific burns with a purer flame. We seem to realize that here is not a war rooted in the age-old hatreds and grudges of Europe. Here, rather, is a war to resolve new and inescapable problems." Those problems would be many and their owner, as far as the Navy cared, was Chester Nimitz.

Nimitz's chief of staff, Raymond A. Spruance, would call him "one of the few people I know who never knew what it meant to be afraid of anything." His duties were of the kind that exhausted the conscientious and the caring. After the Oahu attack, he had to sort out its myriad administrative consequences—three thousand letters to send to bereaved families, untold gatherings of men and machines to reassign to useful tasks. As head of the Bureau of Navigation, which handled personnel issues, he had tendered the applications of the ambitious and the vengeful, including more than one U.S. congressman who phoned him after December 7 to lobby for an enlistment. Overwhelmed and sleepless, Nimitz was said to have told his congressional supplicants, "Go back and vote us appropriations. We're going to need them."

On December 19, Nimitz left his office on Constitution Avenue and returned to his apartment on Q Street to share the news of his appointment with his wife. Sensing his reluctance, Catherine reminded him, "You always wanted to command the Pacific Fleet. You always thought that would be the height of glory."

"Darling," replied Nimitz, "the fleet's at the bottom of the sea. Nobody must know that here, but I've got to tell you."

He had grown to dread the assignment, and would have even if it didn't entail commanding a wounded squadron, the battleships of Task Force 1, whose lifeblood, their oil, still seeped in rainbow ribbons from their broken hulls off Ford Island. He would have dreaded it because he knew his promotion was a zero-sum transaction; it required the demotion of someone else, and that person happened to be one of Nimitz's closest friends, Husband E. Kimmel. Pearl Harbor had burned on Kimmel's watch, so Kimmel paid the price. If the charge of negligence failed by the standard of a trial court, and if the proceeding that tarred him was driven more by political expediency than by examination of a fuller truth concerning who had what level of warning and when, it was also the verdict that the code of naval leadership required. A captain was expected to go down with his ship; why not an admiral with his base? The principle was clean, simple, and predictable in operation. It was the Navy way.

Within a few short years America's fleet would be more powerful and capable than any before it. The same could be said of Nimitz's superior in Washington, the leading U.S. naval commander of the day. Though he worked in guarded isolation, giving subordinates little direct access, no admiral had ever wielded the same degree of personal influence on wartime policy as Ernest J. King. As the commander in chief of the U.S. Fleet (COMINCH) and chief of naval operations (CNO), he was preeminent in both planning and command. His influence and his formidable personal nature made him a figure to be reckoned with within the Navy Department bureaucracy. Ensconced on the front corridor of the fourth floor of "Main Navy," the large headquarters building on Constitution Avenue, he was memorably unlike Nimitz. "Subconsciously he sought to be omnipotent and infallible," his biographer wrote. "There were few men whom he regarded as his equal as to brains; he would acknowledge no mind as superior to his own." He was abrupt and unyielding, visibly intolerant of those he deemed fools. Though his first reflex was always to reject even the best advice, he did once concede to a staffer, "Sometimes my bark is worse than my bite."

King penalized caution wherever it surfaced. In March, he was outraged to learn that one of his admirals in the South Pacific, Frank Jack Fletcher, had decided to return to base to refuel his carrier rather than stand ready to intercept enemy shipping gathering near Rabaul. During the Battle of the Coral Sea in May, he took a dim view of Fletcher's refusal to release his destroyers to pursue the retreating Japanese carrier force. When Nimitz subsequently recommended Fletcher for both a promotion and a medal—taking pains to defend his judgment to King by pointing out Fletcher's shortage of destroyers to protect his carriers—King refused to approve either.

King reduced all issues to their impact on keeping his fleet ready for war. No other considerations counted. When officials at the Department of the Interior's Fish and Wildlife Service informed him in June that Navy units were targeting whales and other marine mammals during gunnery exercises, King quickly put an end to it, writing Nimitz, "Undoubtedly these acts are committed lightheartedly by the crews without realizing that the killing and injury of whales results in the destruction of valuable war materials of which there is a wholly inadequate supply." King was indifferent to the concerns of marine biologists. To him it mattered only that his fleet needed whale meal and lubricants, resources that the West Coast whaling fleet, thinly drawn by a two-ocean war's demands on shipping, was struggling to provide.

Most people who crossed King's path came to fear him for one reason or another, but the *New York Times* war correspondent Hanson W. Baldwin, no stranger to the COMINCH's high mercury, saw something else in his bluster. "His greatest weakness is personal vanity," Baldwin wrote. "He is terrifically sensitive and in some ways has many of the attributes of a woman." This remark probably revealed more about Baldwin than about King, whose virility was actually a mark against him. Women avoided sitting next to him at dinner parties because, it was said, "his hands were too often beneath the table."

King's personality was famously and not flatteringly likened to a blowtorch. Some people turned that metaphor to his favor, saying he was "so tough he shaved with a blowtorch." That nuance would have been lost on him, for he was never willing to propel his career by cultivating people's favor. After facing off with King at a meeting once, General Dwight D. Eisenhower wrote in his diary, "One thing that might help win this war is to get someone to shoot King. He's the antithesis of cooperation, a deliberately rude person, which means he's a mental bully." King liked his tough reputation. When he was called to Washington to replace Harold Stark as CNO, King remarked, "When things get tough, they call for the sons of bitches." It marked the style of King's intellect and independence, and not necessarily for the better, that he mistrusted the judgment of anyone but himself. Those he deemed lesser minds included some formidable figures, including General Marshall, whom King deemed provincially Eurocentric and ignorant of seapower and the Pacific generally, and the one officer who would prove to have the keenest judgment of all the flag officers in the Navy: Chester

W. Nimitz. King soon learned that he could give his Pacific Ocean Area chief some space to operate, but in the early days he was known to treat Nimitz as he did other subordinates. Of Nimitz he had once said, "If only I could keep him tight on what he's supposed to do. Somebody gets ahold of him and I have to straighten him out." Apparently leery of Nimitz's accommodating way, King sent him unsubtle signals about his expectations. Once he wrote to his Pacific commander, "You are requested to read the article, 'There Is Only One Mistake: To Do Nothing,' by Charles F. Kettering in the March 29th issue of *Saturday Evening Post* and to see to it that it is brought to the attention of all of your principal subordinates and other key officers." So overriding was his will to action that for a time King made a practice of bypassing Nimitz in operational matters. If this was a test of fortitude, Nimitz passed. Finding the discourtesy intolerable, he confronted King during one of their many meetings and told him the state of affairs had to change. King let Nimitz run the Pacific naval war thenceforth with little overt interference.

Fair, gentle, courtly, and vigorous, Nimitz was a match for any of the blustery egos surrounding him. He would emerge in time as the Pacific war's essential man, the figure through whom all decisions flowed, on whom all outcomes reflected, and whose judgment was respected from Main Navy all the way down the line. He lay like a valley of humility between two mountains of conceit: Ernest King and General Douglas MacArthur, the commander of the Southwest Pacific Command and the Navy's stalwart intramural rival. The divided Army–Navy command would be a continuing complication in the war ahead. King and MacArthur had enough weight of will to pull major commanders into their orbits and hold them in place by their gravity. Nimitz, in time, became their fulcrum.

Nimitz generally reserved his thoughts for himself. Complaints he harbored that had no bearing on plans, fruitless reprimands, second and third guesses—he held them within. The emotional pressure they created often left him sleepless. Most nights he awoke at 3 a.m., read till 5:30, then went back to bed. The pace of work at CINCPAC headquarters needed just a few months to exhaust him utterly. By spring 1942 his mind was a turmoil, his spirit gripped by pessimism. The repair of the battle fleet and the reconstitution of Pearl Harbor naval base were moving more slowly than many wanted. He feared his supporters were turning sour. "I will be lucky to last six months," he lamented in a letter to Catherine.

But the season of spring was like a lifetime in that war. Though grievous damage to the fleet was still visible at Pearl, the loss was never as great as it had seemed. All but two of the battleships were sent to the West Coast for repair and modernization and made ready for war within months. The war, of course, did not wait for them. Reconstituted around its aircraft carriers, and under the leadership of new commanders, the Pacific Fleet struck back in the spring.

The carrier fleet's surging esprit de corps, such a novelty for the battered warriors of Pearl Harbor, carried Chester Nimitz through the six months he had most dreaded. The Pacific Fleet's flattops, under Vice Admiral William F. Halsey, Jr., ventured forth and struck targets from the Gilberts to all the way to Japan's home islands. A task force with the carriers *Enterprise* and *Hornet,* the latter playing host to a flight of strangers, twin-engined Army bombers, launched an audacious raid against Tokyo. After Lieutenant Colonel Jimmy Doolittle's B-25s had done their work, the Combined Fleet's commander in chief, Admiral Isoroku Yamamoto, won army backing for his plan to draw out and destroy the nuisance-making U.S. fleet once and for all by seizing Midway and the Aleutian Islands, then targeting Hawaii itself. He also continued the push from Rabaul south toward the stronghold of Port Moresby, New Guinea. He meant to isolate Australia, then continue southeast to threaten U.S. bases as far away as Samoa.

In early May, a carrier task force under Rear Admiral Frank Jack Fletcher intercepted a Japanese invasion fleet bound for Port Moresby. In the Battle of the Coral Sea, the U.S. Navy sank the Japanese carrier *Shoho,* damaged a second, and turned back the invasion. Though the *Lexington* was lost and the *Yorktown* damaged, American pilots relished their victory and soon reformed for another crack at the Combined Fleet. During the first week of June, after Nimitz's codebreakers detected an enemy plan to invade Midway Island, a pair of carrier task forces under Fletcher and Spruance sprang an ambush. By the time fliers from the *Enterprise, Hornet,* and hastily repaired *Yorktown* called it a day on June 4, Japan's thrust toward Hawaii was parried, with losses that included four frontline aircraft carriers and 110 pilots. The victory put the U.S. Navy in position, for the first time, to carry the fight to the enemy.

The old plan for a Pacific offensive envisioned parallel drives toward Tokyo, one running from New Guinea toward the Philippines, the other through the Central Pacific to the Marianas. Which path received priority for supply, equipment, and reinforcement would depend on the outcome of an important battle yet to be fought—between the U.S. Army and the U.S.

Navy. General Douglas MacArthur advocated the New Guinea route; Nimitz and the Navy, the Central Pacific. Though the interservice rivalry was well established, the outbreak of war pitted them in competition for scarce weapons and matériel. As the first American offensive of the war took shape, the warriors in the Pacific would be constantly pleading their cause to those in Washington who rationed the resources. As it happened, King's ambitions faced obstacles from those who outranked even MacArthur. FDR himself was said to favor European operations.

As King saw it, the events of early June provided the longed-for opening for a Pacific offensive. While he knew his president would cherish sending his beloved fleet into action, King also knew what Roosevelt's overriding aim was in the spring of 1941: helping the Russians. In a May 6 memo to the Joint Chiefs of Staff, FDR wrote, "It must be constantly reiterated that Russian armies are killing more Germans and destroying more Axis matériel than all the twenty-five united nations put together. To help Russia, therefore, is the primary consideration." Despite her infamy, Japan was a negligible threat, Roosevelt thought. With Germany knocked out of the fight, Japan could not hold on, he believed. "The whole question of whether we win or lose the war depends on the Russians," he wrote in June. "We can defeat the Japanese in six weeks." King didn't think the Navy's victory at Midway had registered sufficiently with the Allied high command.

As FDR saw it, diverting German forces from the critical Eastern Front and preventing a separate Russian truce with Hitler required a bold American move in Europe. The plan Roosevelt liked best, Operation Sledgehammer, would throw forty-eight divisions, more than seven hundred thousand men, across the English Channel and into France before the end of 1942. The Army's ambitions were constrained by the pessimism of the British and the U.S. Navy's inarguable need to at least hold on in the Pacific. Giving resources to that modest goal, even if it were simply a "maintenance of positions," would compromise Eisenhower's cross-channel plans. An alternative urged by the British, an invasion of North Africa, originally known as Operation Gymnast, then Operation Torch, was less risky from Churchill's point of view, though it still competed for American time, resources, and attention.

From his work with the British, King was aware that, officially, a "Germany first" strategy was operative. But his close involvement in negotiations and personal relationship with George Marshall enabled him to create the leeway to run the Pacific as he saw fit. In many cases he dealt exclusively with Marshall in designing strategy in the Pacific. As far as he was concerned, the strategy all along was "Pacific first." The Navy was clearly most vested there. Four of its five heavy aircraft carriers were in the Pacific, and twenty-seven of its thirty-eight cruisers. "I sent an order to Admiral Nimitz," King wrote after the war, "saying that despite all other orders, large or small, the basic orders are that the Pacific Fleet must, first, keep all means of communications with the West Coast and, second, but close to the first order, to keep all areas between Hawaii and Samoa clear of the Japanese and then as fast as it could expand that area toward Australia." His mandate to Nimitz reflected the clarity of the Navy's self-arranged destiny in the west. King considered "Germany first" little more than a political campaign slogan. Let the Joint Chiefs host their debating society with the British. King's Navy had an ocean to conquer.

For General Marshall, a powerful voice on the Joint Chiefs of Staff, it would take a fully concentrated effort to beat the Axis decisively in either hemisphere. On July 13, he sent Eisenhower a secret telegram stating that an invasion of North Africa would be a fruitless dispersion of force. "We would nowhere be acting decisively against our enemies," he wrote. With North Africa commanding most of its attention, the Army would have few aircraft, so critical to victory, available in the South Pacific. Winston Churchill pressed the case for North Africa, however. He candidly regarded an amphibious assault against France in 1942 and even in 1943 as suicide. Marshall was publicly noncommittal. Fearing a compromise that pleased no one, but wishing to strike effectively against the Axis *somewhere*, Marshall expressed a willingness to entertain the Pacific-first offensive strategy that Admiral King envisioned. The general saw the prospect of a Navy offensive in the Pacific as a lever to budge the intransigent British. If landings in France could not be made by early 1943, Marshall wrote to Eisenhower, "We should turn to the Pacific and strike decisively against Japan with full strength and ample reserves, assuming a defensive attitude against Germany except for air operations."

As King wrote after the war, his idea was to "stop the enemy as soon as we could get the ships, planes and troops to make a stand as far to the westward as possible.... I kept close watch on the area of Guadalcanal and finally decided, whether or not the J.C.S. would agree, I wanted to make some real move.... The Army still insisted that the time wasn't ripe so I answered them, 'When will the time be ripe since we have just defeated a major part of the enemy's fleet [at Midway]?' "

Knowing that he needed King's support in the continuing arguments with the British, even as he feared unilateral Navy initiatives, Marshall agreed to back a Navy-directed plan in the South Pacific. If this was a bluff to cow the Brits, Eisenhower strengthened it by relaying Marshall's suggestion to Roosevelt. Ike, too, thought that if a cross-channel invasion couldn't be launched from England, then America should "turn our backs upon the Eastern Atlantic and go, full out, as quickly as possible, against Japan!"

The president doubted the value of seizing "a lot of islands whose occupation will not affect the world situation this year or next." Still, King knew FDR wanted action and believed he would not likely block a well-considered plan to turn the fleet loose against the Axis. As far back as March, King had urged Roosevelt to approve "an integrated, general plan of operations" based on the idea of holding six strongpoints that spanned the South Pacific from east to west: Samoa, Fiji, New Caledonia, Tongatabu, Efate, and Funafuti. From those bases the Navy could protect the sea-lanes to Australia, then drive northwest into the Solomons and the Bismarcks. The opportunity to do that had finally come.

Neither King nor Marshall seemed to grasp the degree to which politics would compel Roosevelt to veto an express Pacific-first strategy. For reasons of electoral calculation—to preserve his Democratic majorities in a congressional midterm election—Roosevelt wanted American troops fighting Germans before the end of the year. "We failed to see," Marshall would write, "that the leader in a democracy has to keep the people entertained. The people demand action."

Public opinion was increasingly in favor of pursuing the fight in the Pacific. In January 1942, a *Newsweek* editorialist wrote, "Congressmen are receiving a growing stream of mail from constituents condemning the conduct of the war. The writers demand to know why Wake, Guam, and Midway garrisons were neither reinforced or rescued, why the Philippines were left with only a meager force of fighter planes while hundreds were sent to Europe, why the Navy has not laced into the Japanese fleet, etc."

The answer was the political clout of America's Atlantic ally. "King's war is against the Japanese," one of Churchill's advisers had warned him. If London did not commit to Eisenhower's invasion of France, the adviser wrote, "everything points to a complete reversal of our present agreed strategy and the withdrawal of America to a war of her own in the Pacific." On hearing this, Churchill reportedly remarked, "Just because the Americans can't have a massacre in France this year, they want to sulk and bathe in the Pacific." That was a dubious characterization of what his Atlantic cousins really wanted. Because the Japanese had struck them directly, and Hitler hadn't, what many Americans—or the Navy at least—wanted was a massacre in the Pacific. The victory at Midway opened the course.

The Navy would find its war on the boundless battlefield of the western ocean. When Martin Clemens turned on his teleradio in Aola and tapped out news of an airfield in the making, the pattern of the coming days began to take shape in the mind of Ernest King.

2

A Great Gray Fleet

"ON CALM DAYS THE LIGHT BLUE HIGHWAY WITH ITS FROTHY CURB-stones stretches along the great flat ocean to the horizon. This highway needs no signs; it tells friend and foe alike a ship has passed this way. If you follow along this road, your seaman-sharp eyes telling you where we zigged and where we zagged, you will come finally to the thrashing turbulence forced out by our screws; you will have arrived at our fantail, the after limits of a waterborne military community. And should you follow along the welded smooth side of our hull, past the splashing overboard discharges, you will soon come to the swishing white bow-wave, jumping constantly clear, and to the sharp stem cleaving the unmarked sea ahead, these extremities of our life."

The froth of bubbles that the USS *Atlanta* had left behind reached all the way to the northeastern seaboard. The young reservist who wrote these words, a New Yorker named Robert Graff, was new to the fleet but already in its thrall. In the rush of the past year, he had learned what his shipmates were capable of. The good ones on the good days became as brothers. Even some of the bad ones were just the kind of men you wanted on your side in a fight. A ship was a small world and one they came to love, even as its narrow steel enclosure restricted their immediate prospects and carried them, with few diversions, toward a deadly struggle.

The salad days of her prewar launching in New York were a dimming memory. The ceremonial flourish that attended the launch of the ship had been spectacular. The country's most popular purveyor of heavily freighted romance, Mrs. John R. Marsh, better known by her pen name, Margaret Mitchell, had been on hand in Kearny, New Jersey, on September 12, 1941, to celebrate the launching. With a quick two-handed swing, the author of *Gone with the Wind* smashed a bottle of champagne over an after turret housing and christened the lead ship of a new class of cruiser. Moored in the finishing basin at the Federal Shipbuilding and Drydock Company, their decks fouled with electrical cabling and acetylene hoses and pneumatic hardware, unfinished fixtures and unfixed weaponry, two of the new type stood as sisters: the *Atlanta* and the *Juneau*.

Like shipyards coast-to-coast, Kearny, New Jersey, was a festival of naval industry. Half a dozen destroyers and twice that many merchantmen crowded the docks up and down the river. But the *Atlanta* and *Juneau* stood out. What was most noticeable about them, before they were finished out with thousands of fittings, riggings, and shapely facets of superstructure, was the extent of their main battery. The arrangement of the twin-mounted five-inch turrets, three rising forward and three descending aft, with two more in hip positions amidships, helped give them their characteristic lines. The forest of barrels was suited to the mission of the *Atlanta* class: to provide antiaircraft defense for a task force. They had the largest single broadside of heavy antiaircraft weaponry of any vessel in any fleet, nearly half again that of the latest U.S. fast battleships that were five times their displacement. Though antiaircraft cruisers were fitted with the destroyer's traditional armament of torpedoes and depth charges, the *Atlanta* was the embodiment of a navy built for a new kind of war. She was a welterweight ship with a middleweight jab. Her batteries were numerous enough to fend off multiple destroyers in a surface action, and put a dent in the most vigorous air attack as well.

The *Atlanta*'s assistant gunnery officer, Lieutenant Lloyd M. Mustin, showed visitors this thick grove of firepower "with the same pride a mother would introduce her children," said Edward Corboy, another *Atlanta* officer. A new ship was a complex system full of small flaws to fix. Mustin found that the *Atlanta*'s SC radar transmitter couldn't send signals powerful enough to survive transmission through the foremast's eighty-foot run of coaxial cable, bounce off a target, and return back through the receiver and the long cable to the radar room and produce a usable echo. He arranged for preamplifiers to boost the signal and, with adjustments to the receiver's sensitivity, found that he could detect aircraft at fifty to sixty miles and surface ships at fifteen to twenty. He also saw to it that the *Atlanta* was outfitted with the new Mark

37 gun director. Coupled with the new high-frequency model FD fire-control radar, whose narrow beams returned a precise range on a target after it was located by the search radar, and a late-model power-drive gunsight that enabled him to slew rapidly to acquire targets, they were a powerful package. In impromptu training sessions, director crews zeroed their sights on subway trains carrying oblivious commuters across Manhattan's East River bridges.

Three months later, on the day before Christmas, the ship was finished and ready for commissioning into the fleet. Under overcast skies at the New York Navy Yard, Margaret Mitchell was on hand again. As soon as she finished her remarks, the sun broke through over Brooklyn, catching sharply on the swords of officers and flashing on the gray sides of all those gun turrets. "A rather dull tableau suddenly was a scene of splendor," Edward Corboy said. For the plankowners on the first U.S. warship commissioned following the attack on Pearl Harbor, it was an auspicious sign.

Under command of Captain Samuel P. Jenkins, the *Atlanta* shook down in the Chesapeake Bay, ran speed trials off the Maine coast, and was headed for the Pacific before many of her systems were complete. One didn't have to be a veteran, or even a man, to admire her hard, monochromatic elegance. Elizabeth Shaw, the wife of one of her lieutenants, would write, "To my artist's eye she was a thing of beauty and a true oceanic lady." The wives had followed her on the journey from Atlantic to Pacific coast. At each place they were forbidden to board the ship, just as their husbands were forbidden from going ashore. *Secrecy* was the byword of the wartime Navy. Rumors were floated that arctic-weather clothing was due to arrive—"a glorious hoax," Shaw wrote, "to keep the ship's destination a secret even from the officers, for fear someone would tell a wife who would gossip."

When the *Atlanta* arrived at Pearl Harbor on May 6, with orders to join Task Force 16, the *Enterprise* carrier task force, the *Arizona*'s commissioning pennant could still be seen flying above the wreck in mournful defiance. Death was persistent still. A thousand and a half bodies were believed to reside within the sunken battleships. The triumphs of Japanese airpower strongly suggested the need for task force defenses bolstered by ships like the *Atlanta*.

After taking part in the defense of Midway, the *Atlanta* returned to Pearl Harbor and soon found herself with new orders. When Jenkins announced to his crew that their destination was Tongatabu, the Navy's South Pacific fueling base south of Samoa, all hands wondered why. "I think the answer lies in the Solomons," an officer speculated.

* * *

ON JUNE 22, 1942, thousands of well-equipped riflemen of the 1st Marine Division loaded into troop ships at San Francisco, passed Alcatraz, steamed underneath the Golden Gate Bridge, and set out into the Pacific's first long swells. An uncertain future lay dead ahead. The weather decks were packed with men looking back.

The convoy carrying forces from the 1st Marine Division, under Major General Alexander Archer Vandegrift, was three days under way when Ernest King informed George Marshall that these men would be the tip of the first spear he would throw at Japan's Pacific imperium. On July 2, King sent Nimitz a "super secret" dispatch that outlined the Navy plan. Code-named Operation Watchtower, it was an invasion plan whose first stage, known as Task One, was the seizure of the Santa Cruz Islands, Tulagi, and "adjacent positions."

Given a "golden opportunity" by the victory at Midway, King directed Nimitz to begin preparations to go on the attack. No one expected an offensive to begin prior to the late fall of 1942. According to cynics, King believed the surest way to draw more resources to the Pacific was to send thousands of infantry where the prospect of their defeat would be intolerable. But it was clearly a genuine strategic threat that moved him most. According to Vandegrift, "What he jammed down the throats of the Joint Chiefs of Staff, was that just possibly the mighty Japanese had overextended. He saw that just possibly a strike by us could halt their eastward parade."

The signs were clear that the Japanese had their own aggressive designs on the deep South Pacific. There were new concentrations of submarines and air units at Rabaul. But with the airfield project revealed, King considered it "absolutely essential to stop the southward advance of the enemy *at that point and at that time*," and stated his views forcibly to Marshall. Conferring with Nimitz, King accelerated planning and substituted Guadalcanal, an "adjacent position" not mentioned in the original plan, for Santa Cruz. "King's reiteration of *attack, seize the initiative, and do it now* was beginning to take on the throbbing insistence of a war drum."

King deflected General Marshall's attempt to give Operation Watchtower to Army control. On June 25, Marshall had written to King that Guadalcanal and Tulagi fell within the sphere of Douglas MacArthur's Southwest Pacific Command (SOWESPAC), rather than the Navy's South Pacific Area (SOPAC). Recognizing that the key to any such operation would be Marine Corps infantry who would necessarily operate with the fleet, King quashed the idea immediately, responding to Marshall that the operation "must be conducted under the direction of CINCPAC and cannot be conducted in any other way." Marshall conceded to the Navy the responsibility for the first of the three tasks in the seizure of the southern Solomons. He handed the second and third tasks, the capture of the rest of the Solomon Islands and the neutralization and conquest of Rabaul, to MacArthur. Marshall moved the line dividing SOWESPAC from SOPAC, originally drawn to run straight through the southern Solomons, slightly westward to give the fleet exclusive domain over Task One. There were still too many cooks in the kitchen, but the hot appetizer would be the Navy's dish to serve.

Guadalcanal was thirty-six hundred miles from Pearl Harbor. Measuring distance from Pacific Fleet headquarters, an expedition to assault Yokohama would have been just as long. But King and Nimitz would beat Yamamoto to the punch. D-Day on Red Beach was set for August 1.

WHEN GENERAL VANDEGRIFT was at last given the details of Operation Watchtower, several days under way for his staging area in Wellington, New Zealand, he was aghast at the speed required of him. The timetable allowed precious little time for preparation and training: They were to set foot on hostile shores on August 1. His superior, the commander of the South Pacific Forces, Vice Admiral Robert L. Ghormley, joined General MacArthur in Melbourne, Australia, on July 8 to advise a postponement because of a lack of preparation and the inadequacy of friendly air cover over the invasion target. Though MacArthur had been written out of the invasion plan itself, he would still be relied upon to furnish air support to Navy forces with his long-range bombers, useful for both search and attack.

The request, when it reached him, outraged King. He believed the offensive, on the drawing board for months, needed rapid execution. King told General Marshall, "Three weeks ago, MacArthur stated that if he could be furnished amphibious forces and two carriers, he could push right through to Rabaul. He now feels that he not only cannot undertake this operation but not even the Tulagi operation." The admiral thought MacArthur, who was marshaling Army forces to dislodge the Japanese from eastern New Guinea, was pouting over the decision to remove Operation Watchtower from his domain. He was. King had outmuscled him and the first offensive of the war was going to be a Navy and Marine Corps show. The messianic commander of the Southwest Pacific didn't like anything about that.

* * *

THE AMERICAN FLEET supporting the Marines was gathering piecemeal. Dispersed all around the eastern Pacific by the demands of combat operations to date, from the Coral Sea to Midway to the Aleutian Islands, three aircraft carrier task forces were assigned to the operation. The *Wasp* and *Saratoga*, which had missed the battles at Midway and Coral Sea, would join the *Enterprise*, a veteran of Midway and the Doolittle raid, in the Operation Watchtower combat task force. Meanwhile, Vandegrift's amphibious element was scheduled to rendezvous with them in the Fiji Islands to rehearse the landings.

During the last week of June, the *Saratoga* and sixteen other warships— four heavy cruisers, six destroyers, two oilers, and four transports—were under way south for Tongatabu, the fueling base in the Tonga Islands. On July 1, the *Wasp* departed San Diego with the transports *President Adams, President Hayes, President Jackson, Crescent City,* and a surface escort composed of the cruisers *Vincennes, Quincy, San Juan,* and seven destroyers. The *Enterprise* carrier force left Hawaii soon after the *Saratoga* did, conducting gunnery practice on the way. The rigidly programmed exercises, which involved firing on target sleds towed behind slow-moving fleet tugs, and then at sleeves towed by planes, did little to simulate what awaited them in the southern waters. For the gunners and fire controlmen in the cruisers *San Francisco, Portland,* and *Atlanta,* however, the chance to calibrate their radar and check the precision with which their directors aimed their remote-controlled guns was welcome. Everyone knew that a living enemy, long sought, would soon be near.

The streams of combat vessels flowing toward the South Pacific consisted mainly of "light forces," as cruisers and destroyers were known. The battleship fleet was essentially confined to station on the West Coast. Many sailors wondered why eight months after December 7 those battleships, fully repaired and modernized, would have no role in the battle for the South Pacific.

On the eve of the war against Japan, the U.S. fleet had seventeen battleships in commission: fifteen prewar dreadnoughts and two of a fast new breed, the *North Carolina* and the *Washington.* Of the nine assigned to the Pacific, only the *Colorado,* refitting at Puget Sound Navy Yard in Bremerton, escaped December 7 unscarred. Two weeks after the attack, the three battleships whose damage was least, the *Maryland, Pennsylvania,* and *Tennessee,* were under way on their own power for the West Coast. By early March, those three wagons were ready for war again, repaired, modernized, and joined with the *Colorado*. By mid-August 1942, Task Force 1, as the Pacific battleship squadron was known, had been bolstered by three transfers from the Atlantic, the *Idaho, Mississippi,* and *New Mexico*. By any measure this force of seven restored battleships was superior to the one that had been struck at anchor in Oahu.

Their tenure in Hawaii was short-lived. Only four days after arriving, the *Tennessee* was ordered to Puget Sound for more refitting. The *Pennsylvania* followed within a month, and the *Idaho* for gunnery trials requested by Admiral King. They spent the early months of the war running exercises in unthreatened waters. None of the old battleships would reach the Solomons until after the fight for Guadalcanal was settled.

The reason was their vast appetite for fuel. There were limits on the Navy's ability to transport and store bunker oil in the Pacific. The success of Germany's U-boat campaign required a massive redirection of the tanker fleet to the Atlantic to sustain the flow of oil to England. By the time the shuffle was complete, Nimitz had just seven tankers at his disposal. That was crippling to operations, given what fuel hogs the old battleships were. Task Force 1, including its escorts, burned three hundred thousand barrels of oil in a month—the total oil storage capacity of the entire Pacific in early 1942. A carrier task force was almost as thirsty. The Navy had enough fuel available to operate either its carriers or its battleships. As between the two, no combat commander alive doubted which choice to make. Admiral King urged "continuous study" of the problem, but Nimitz vetoed any proposal to operate the old battleships out of Pearl. The math simply didn't work.

The sight of great battleships lolling at anchor in the harbor at San Pedro, south of Los Angeles, deeply chagrined the cruisermen and destroyer sailors who would carry the fight against Japan. "We're up against a navy that doesn't keep its battleships home," the *Atlanta*'s Lloyd Mustin complained to his diary in May. When men from the smaller ships went out on liberty, it was hard to resist raising provocative questions with any battleship sailors they might meet in the bars. The responses were usually fielded with fists. Now the energies of the oceanbound sailors of the *Enterprise* and the *Atlanta* were directed toward another fight.

From Pearl, the route to Tongatabu traced the arc of 160 West longitude. Down this imaginary path went the *Enterprise* and, broad on her bows, the *Atlanta* and the *Portland*. Veterans of the Doolittle raid and victors at Midway, the ships of Task Force 16 were bolstered by the presence of a majestic newcomer churning the seas in the *Enterprise*'s wake. This was the *North Carolina*, the first of a powerful new type of battleship, fast, armed with nine sixteen-inch rifles and a steel forest of twin-mounted five-inch guns. She could keep up with the carriers at cruising speeds and burned 30 percent less fuel than did the older battleships.

But logistics were as important as firepower. As General Dwight D. Eisenhower huddled with his staff in London planning the North Africa landings, half a world away, in Auckland, General Vandegrift was figuring out how to get his ships loaded with men, arms, and two months of supplies, plan landings on a hostile and deeply unfamiliar beach, issue operational orders to his field commanders, and run dress rehearsals. The pressure on American planners to allocate scarce resources effectively was immense worldwide. What little cargo and tanker capacity could be thrown into the southern Solomons operation was a zero-sum deduction from the strength of the Atlantic convoys that kept Great Britain going. In both theaters, the Mediterranean and the South Pacific, America would proceed on a shoestring, and that name, Operation Shoestring, would emerge as Nimitz's joking moniker for the Guadalcanal operation, even as the invasion fleet was being marshaled toward its faraway goal.

WHEN ADMIRAL GHORMLEY received Nimitz's directive to seize Guadalcanal, he summoned a staff officer and asked for charts of the region. "What in the world does this place look like, in the scheme of things?" Ghormley wanted to know. "The knowledge of the geography of the Pacific was hazy to American citizens generally," Ghormley wrote, "and even to many of those in high places who were vitally concerned with the war effort.... We were pioneers, and accepted that fact."

The oldest of six children of a Presbyterian missionary from Portland, Oregon, Bob Ghormley had a knack for going where the action was. On August 15, 1940, he had arrived in London to serve as a "special naval observer" to his president just as Germany's aerial bombing of Britain, the Blitz, began. In October he wrote Secretary of the Navy Frank Knox, "Since my arrival here 2 months ago, I am impressed with the fact that this is a war laboratory which the British Government is more or less placing at our disposal. We are and must take every advantage possible of these facilities for gaining more knowledge and applying it practically to our own Navy."

President Roosevelt was eager for firsthand news on how the British people were holding up under the aerial siege. "Every day I was in London I

felt more and more that England and, in fact, civilization was in great danger, and that the United States was the only country which could turn the
tide," he wrote. His was a diplomatically sensitive position, for Ghormley's
nebulous authority opened FDR to charges that the president was making
"secret treaties" with Britain. In a presidential election year in which voices
favoring isolationism were strong, the merest hint of an undeclared military
alliance with England could have had complicated consequences.

In his personal role as an agent of the White House, Ghormley enabled
President Roosevelt to bypass Ambassador Joseph Kennedy and the State
Department in communicating with 10 Downing Street. Meeting frequently
with the British Admiralty and Air Ministry, Ghormley helped negotiate the
ABC-1 agreement, articulating the Allied grand strategy for confronting the
Axis worldwide. He exchanged candid correspondence with the chief of
naval operations, Admiral Harold Stark, on a wide range of subjects: convoy
routes, Atlantic naval bases, the state of play on the Eastern Front, new war
technologies from magnetic mines to radar, and the efficacy of RAF
bombers and fleet units against German warships. Ghormley was also a
fierce partisan for his own Navy in its intramural wars with other U.S.
service branches. He reported to FDR on the malign machinations of
Hitler—and to Stark on the schemes of the U.S. Army Air Corps to establish
a "United Air Force," which the fleet viewed as a threat to autonomous naval
airpower.

Influential though Ghormley was—some press reports lauded him as
America's premier naval strategist—his selection to command the South
Pacific Forces came as a surprise to his peers. His last sea duty was in 1936,
as captain of the battleship *Nevada*. He had never been to sea as a flag officer. Other admirals had much more experience afloat. Halsey and Fletcher
had been successful carrier commanders. Nimitz's first choice had been
Admiral William S. Pye, the interim Pacific commander in chief after Husband Kimmel's dismissal following the Pearl Harbor investigation, but King
vetoed him. It is possible that Ghormley's highest-ranking admirer, FDR
himself, had a hand in giving him the job.

Ghormley left London in April 1942, stopping over in Washington to
build a staff from the remnants of the dissolved Asiatic Fleet. He had a hard
time finding men with suitable experience. His coding and communications
staffs in particular were either untrained or reservists with no experience
with current fleet procedures and doctrines. He chose as his chief of staff an
officer with political connections, Franklin Roosevelt's former naval aide,
Captain Daniel J. Callaghan.

His appointment to command the South Pacific Forces carried him to the other side of the world with scarcely a week to sit still in one place. On his journey from Pearl through the necklace of South Pacific naval and Army bases—Palmyra, Canton, and Fiji, then to New Zealand and finally Nouméa—the yawning distances between points of strategic interest would unsettle him. East to west, it spanned the same distance as New York to Berlin. Its northern boundary was the equator; to the south, the South Pole. Ghormley hadn't served in the Pacific in thirty years. It was unfamiliar terrain.

From his time at Main Navy, Ghormley was familiar with plans to throw back a Japanese attack. He had no illusions about the nature of his enemy. He saw the Japanese as "dissatisfied, proud, grasping and aggressive. They would stop at nothing to gain their ends." But the South Pacific Area would be a difficult place to fight them. Coming to the Pacific from the confines of London under siege, with scarcely a chance to acclimate, Ghormley would seem overwhelmed from the start by the unbounded expanses of sea. As one of his deputies would discover as a matter of first impression: "Robinson Crusoe should be required reading for anyone who is setting up an advanced base in the South Pacific islands.... There is no such thing as living off the country in the South Pacific, unless you live on coconuts alone."

The Pacific's long swells carried the flotsam of frustrated Western colonial ambitions. The scattered failures of the English, French, Dutch, and Germans were announced by the mélange of place-names woven into the map, from New Britain, Hollandia, and Bougainville to San Cristóbal, Choiseul, and the Bismarcks, and by the lack of civilization, or infrastructure. America's legacy in the South Pacific was unwritten, but those who would begin to write it, for better or worse, were well on their way.

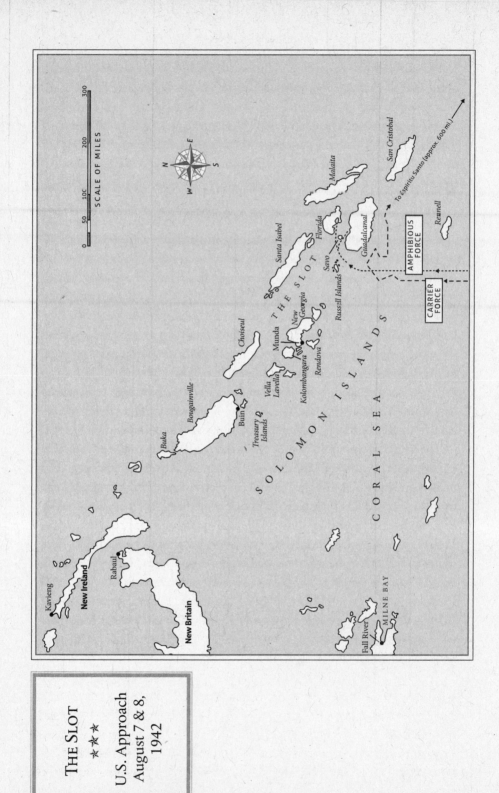

THE SLOT

★ ★ ★

U.S. Approach
August 7 & 8,
1942

SCALE OF MILES

Kavieng

New Ireland

Rabaul

New Britain

MILNE BAY

Fall River

SOLOMON ISLANDS

CORAL SEA

Buka

Bougainville

Buin

Treasury
Islands

Choiseul

Vella
Lavella

Kolombangara

Rendova

Munda

New
Georgia

Santa Isabel

THE SLOT

Savo

Russell Islands

Florida

Guadalcanal

Malaita

San Cristobal

Rennell

AMPHIBIOUS
FORCE

CARRIER
FORCE

To Espiritu Santo (approx. 600 mi.)

3

The First D-Day

ON JULY 22, MAJOR ELEMENTS OF THE OPERATION WATCHTOWER expeditionary force sortied from New Zealand. Rear Admiral Richmond Kelly Turner, whom King had promoted from his own staff, commanded the Watchtower amphibious force from his flagship, the transport *McCawley*. Out of Wellington's Port Nicholson hove the invasion armada in a long single column, twenty-two transports and their destroyer screen, joined by an escort of cruisers, headed north toward the fleet rendezvous in the Fiji Islands. The combined task force's Marine Corps accompaniment under Vandegrift was the largest modern amphibious force yet assembled.

Slugging along at eleven knots, the invasion force needed most of a day to steam beyond reach of the umbrella of friendly aircraft operating from New Zealand. An order went around to all personnel to destroy their diaries. Small things like that tended to work on a man's mind. The frightful possibilities of the experience ahead were beyond what most unblooded marines and sailors could imagine.

From over the horizon came more muscle: two carrier task forces, bringing the *Saratoga* and *Wasp* into the game. The heavy cruisers *Astoria, Quincy, Vincennes,* and *Chicago* joined their Australian counterparts *Canberra* and *Australia.* The *Enterprise* task force was a day late for the rendezvous because Rear Admiral Kinkaid's charts did not accurately show the International Date Line. It was not an inconsequential error. Things like that could keep an admiral from receiving additional stars. "We kept very quiet about it,"

Kinkaid wrote, "and I doubt if Nimitz or Fletcher know it to this day." To make up time and keep pace with the other task forces, Kinkaid's Task Force 16 had one less day in port than it would have had, forcing the *North Carolina* to continue without refueling.

The merger of the far-flung task force in the Coral Sea swelled the order of battle for Operation Watchtower to fifty major ships. It would in the end number more than eighty. By comparison, the carrier groups that had raided Japanese positions on Wake and Marcus islands early in the war each had just ten ships. The Doolittle raid in April sailed with two dozen, as did the Midway flotilla. From horizon to horizon now the Watchtower armada stretched, silhouettes long, gray, cold, and sleek. "We were conscious of the fact that this was one of the largest and strongest groups of war vessels ever gathered, certainly the largest and strongest of this war to date," Richard Tregaskis, a war correspondent, wrote. "The thought that we were going into our adventure with weight and power behind us was cheering. And our adventure-to-come seemed nearer than ever, as the new group of ships and ours merged and we became one huge force."

Experience in wartime Britain made Ghormley wary about the threat of espionage. No doubt mindful of the role that spies played in the surprise attacks at Pearl Harbor and the Philippines, Ghormley wrote his staff, "Loose talk is a stupid habit.... Some would risk the lives of their friends by a silly effort to impress others in public places." There was good reason to fear leaks about ship movements, especially in places like Auckland, where peacetime protocols controlled the movements of merchant vessels into and out of port. The setup was so haphazard that it seemed a miracle operational secrecy was maintained at all. The act of gathering intelligence always came with a risk to the security of planning. Navy intelligence teams were seeking out planters and others who had been evacuated from Guadalcanal to interview for information about the island. Some of those former residents would travel with the invasion force to help identify landmarks.

In Wellington, Vandegrift's intelligence staff had strewn tables in a hotel conference room with sensitive maps, documents, and aerial photographs. One night a drunken civilian reportedly wandered through the lobby and down a hall, passed two MPs at an open door, and blundered straight into Watchtower's intelligence nerve center. "I have smiled many times at reports that only the general knew where we were going," a photographer assigned to the intelligence section, Thayer Soule, wrote. "All headquarters knew. Why the word didn't leak to the enemy, I will never know."

After Midway, when the Japanese began changing their high-level operational code groups, U.S. cryptanalysts were left to deduce enemy movements from the patterns of radio traffic, instead of by deciphering their actual content. On July 30, New Zealand's prime minister, Peter Fraser, was quoted in the Auckland newspaper as saying that an Allied offensive was imminent. Ghormley wrote, "I informed him of how this matter had perturbed me, as I feared it would put the Japs on their guard."

Most of the sailors assigned to Watchtower needed no imagination to envision the destructive handiwork of their enemy. The men of the cruiser *Astoria,* at sea when Pearl Harbor was hit, had come home on December 13 to behold the Pacific battle line laid to waste and the docks of Ford Island lined with caskets. Ruined ships still burned, wreathed in a flotsam of shattered wood and human remains. Men from the battleships, many of them now without stations, were shuffled like spare parts. The *Astoria* filled out her increased wartime complement with these castoffs. Most of them were eager for a lick at the enemy. Some felt they had had enough. "I had experienced what the Japanese could do," said a sailor who transferred to the *Astoria* from one of the stricken battleships, "and I wasn't keen to go out and tangle with them again."

The *Astoria*'s captain at the time took Pearl Harbor's ruin especially hard. When the reality registered with Preston B. Haines about the battle fleet—and about his son, killed on board a destroyer—he was no longer fit for command. Detached for treatment at the naval hospital, Haines was relieved by Captain Francis W. Scanland, recently displaced from command of the battleship *Nevada,* hit in the attack. Another cruiser assigned to Watchtower, the *Chicago,* was commanded by an orphaned battleship skipper. Howard D. Bode was ashore when the end came for the USS *Oklahoma.* His life may have been spared, but the effects of this and coming traumas would weigh heavily on his mind, too.

Captains were fortunate to find help for their troubles. They were given command of a multitude and saddled with fault for their failings. The bargain they made for their privileged place was the right to be last off the ship if the worst came to pass. Burdens grew heavier the higher one ascended in rank. Captains concerned themselves with ships and crews, commodores with squadrons, task force commanders with objectives, and theater commanders with campaigns. The burdens of sailors weighed mostly on the muscles. The weight of leadership was subtler and heavier. It could test the conscience.

The men on the *Astoria* were thrilled, defiant, and unnerved that the Japanese propaganda ministry had expressly marked their ship as a priority target. In April 1939, their ship had traveled to Japan to bring home the ashes of the recently deceased Japanese ambassador to the U.S. Overhauled and freshly painted at Norfolk, with the urn holding the remains of Hiroshi Saito mounted on a special platform in the band room, the *Astoria* spent 158 days crossing the world, more as a gesture of the government's respect to Saito individually than a sign of international rapprochement. Tensions were high from the sinking of the U.S. gunboat *Panay* just seventeen months earlier in the Yangtze River near Nanking. The captain of the *Astoria* on that visit was the man who would command the entire Guadalcanal amphibious force: Richmond Kelly Turner.

Ever since the triumphant visit of Teddy Roosevelt's Great White Fleet to Japan in 1908, almost as soon as Admiral Sperry's squadron departed, attitudes between the Pacific naval powers had hardened. From then on, Japanese naval exercises were predicated on the idea of fighting the U.S. Navy. Soon after the Washington Treaty was concluded in 1922, limiting construction of heavy combatant vessels, the Imperial Japanese Navy began organizing its cruisers and destroyers into special squadrons trained in night combat with an eye toward waging and winning a war of attrition. The Japanese fleet, it was said, adopted a seven-day workweek for training— "Monday, Monday, Tuesday, Wednesday, Thursday, Friday, Friday."

Despite the unpleasantness over the *Panay* incident and the perking suspicions that would be the fuse to war, the diplomatic touches on that 1939 visit were extravagant. The *Astoria* entered Yokohama flying a Japanese naval ensign from her truck. Like the Great White Fleet before her, she traded salvos of greeting with Japanese warships. Though her photographer's mates took furtive shots of naval installations along the way, espionage was not the order of the day. Intimidation always was. From the *Astoria*'s largest men, Captain Turner selected a two-hundred-man landing party. Dressed in shore blues and flat hats—including, to their dismay, some proud members of the shipboard Marine detachment—they provided the escort and funeral party for Ambassador Saito's cortege. At a tea party hosted by the Foreign Ministry, Turner was photographed sitting next to a two-star named Isoroku Yamamoto.

The last U.S. warship to visit Japan before the outbreak of war, the *Astoria* made as strong an impression on the Japanese as the Rising Sun made on her crew. As one of the *Astoria*'s chief petty officers put it, "I never could figure out how one country could produce such nice women and such sons-of-bitches for men." Those men (or their propagandists) would well remember the *Astoria*.

Turner cultivated the *Astoria*'s pride as a fighting ship during his two years as a captain in "the Pineapple Fleet," as the Hawaiian Detachment was known. In peacetime, there were no battles to fight. His crew became connoisseurs of the varied pleasures of international ports of call: In Manila, girls. In Honolulu, girls—and ninety-nine enlisted competitors for every one, or so it seemed. The odds were far better in Hawaii's "happy houses," where the hosts, like their seafaring customers, were known to be safe because every week, until a controversy broke in the papers, it was the Navy's own doctors who examined them.

A ship's history was like a fine wine that gained character with age. The fact that the Great White Fleet had nearly stranded itself at sea for lack of fuel was long forgotten by the time its journey became the emblem of romantic naval adventure. The present was paint-scraping gray drudgery, the future an unguessable puzzle. Captain Turner was a distant memory by the time William G. Greenman took command of the *Astoria* and led her during the Guadalcanal operation.

At sunset, the sailors of the *Astoria,* like every other ship in Admiral Fletcher's expeditionary force, found their gazes drawn high to the starscape that emerged like a field of diamonds on velvet. Enjoyment of such a spectacle required a topside perch, now that all portholes had been welded over in favor of hull integrity. On watch under the stars or secure in their welded-down hulls of steel, sailors had time to indulge in the endless superstitions of the seagoing warrior caste.

The wisdom of higher rank did little to dispel either anticipation or foreboding. On Oahu on a summer evening, where the sunset cast the naval base in red and bronze hues, Chester Nimitz had a direct view of Pearl Harbor's largely vacant dry docks where the cruisers—which belonged to the anachronistically named Scouting Force, once subservient to the battleships of the Battle Force but now powerfully unleashed on their own—had till recently been moored. In the months after the attack, the impression all around the harbor had been of a blooded fleet resurgent: battleships being righted and taken away for repair; carriers, cruisers, destroyers, subs, and auxiliaries coming and going. With the East Loch largely empty now, the fleet under way, Nimitz chafed about the future. He awaited word of the rendezvous in Fiji, and from King the latest news of what reinforcements could be marshaled to support the operation. From MacArthur, no doubt, the next shoe would soon drop in the maverick Southwest Pacific boss's ongoing campaign to claim leadership of the war against Japan.

Two months ago, as his forces approached Midway, Nimitz had told his commanders, "You will be governed by the principle of calculated risk, which you will interpret to mean the avoidance of exposure of your force to attack by superior enemy forces without good prospect of inflicting… greater damage on the enemy." As the day of the invasion came closer, he calculated and recalculated his exposure. What balance needed to be struck between prudent defense and aggressive offense? With three carrier task forces in the South Pacific and just one to protect Hawaiian waters, was he now exposed to another Japanese raid on Hawaii? What were the opportunities, and what were the risks?

With the departure of the Operation Watchtower task forces, Nimitz no longer had enough fighter planes at Pearl Harbor to resist a concentrated air attack. His submarine force was scattered to three horizons. Several more Marine Corps regiments were scheduled to reach the Pacific before year's end, but they hadn't even begun their amphibious training. Given inadequate fuel and a threadbare destroyer force, the battleships would not be sent to the combat theater. At the end of the day Watchtower was all a very big gamble.

Nimitz pondered these and other questions while shooting targets at the pistol range, a diversion recommended by his doctor as a way to channel the mounting stress. He was sociable enough with his staff, always game to swim or run with younger officers who were willing to be outperformed by an old man. Nimitz's competitive instincts ran mostly in another direction. As he diverted his tired mind through the iron sights of a target pistol, he was really only concerned with being outperformed by the Japanese.

ON JULY 26, twelve days out from D-Day on Guadalcanal, the Watchtower amphibious task force arrived in the Fiji Islands for rehearsals. Three years before, in 1939, a similar scene had unfolded off a small Puerto Rican island leased by the Marine Corps. The cast of characters then included several of the principal players now, and they had seen firsthand the possibilities and pitfalls of an amphibious war. President Roosevelt, joined by his naval aide Captain Daniel J. Callaghan, observed from the polished teak deck of the heavy cruiser *Houston*.

Three years later now, at Fiji, it was a misfire. As the landing craft approached their objective, Koro Island, everyone could see that the shoreline was nothing like what was expected. The tide was lower than forecast, and thus the reefs higher. "I saw that its shore was ringed with a coral reef, black and sharp," wrote a transport officer, "like shark's teeth that would have chewed our boats to pieces." The Marines abandoned the exercise. Cruisers practiced their shore bombardment patterns, planes strafed targets. Other than that, the rehearsal in the Fijis bore no resemblance to what had been drawn up on paper. In this respect it may have been the best possible preparation for invasions to come.

While the transports were rehearsing, the senior commanders of Operation Watchtower held a conference on board the carrier *Saratoga*. Later, people would say it was impossible to exaggerate the importance of this meeting, even if one thing that stands out about it was the absence of the theater commander, Vice Admiral Ghormley, who was still preparing to move his headquarters from Auckland to Nouméa in New Caledonia. Chaired by Vice Admiral Fletcher, the expeditionary force commander, the conference included Kelly Turner (commander of the amphibious force), General Vandegrift (the commander of the landing force), Rear Admiral Leigh Noyes (Fletcher's subordinate in the carrier force), Rear Admiral Kinkaid (commander of the *Enterprise* task force), and Rear Admiral John (Slew) McCain (commander of land-based Navy aircraft in the area). Ghormley was represented by his chief of staff, Captain Daniel Callaghan.

Among the challenges the commanders faced was how to get the operation through the blind alley they had entered through haste. "From an intelligence point of view," a Marine Corps historian would write, "the Guadalcanal-Tulagi landings can hardly be described as more than a stab in the dark." When navigators found their charts of the Solomons and spread them across their dead-reckoning tables, they found that the documents had last been updated more than a generation ago, and were drafted on such a large scale as to be useless in operational planning. The direction of magnetic north indicated on them varied from present readings. Nor did they show topography. Sketches hastily produced from recent aerial photographs had large blank areas where clouds had covered the ground on the day the photos were shot.

It was at this meeting, for the first time, that the commanders saw their operation orders. Admiral Kinkaid wrote, "Some of us were until then unaware of the procedure to be followed. Plans had been made hurriedly and many details remained to be worked out." Ghormley hadn't yet seen the orders, either. Owing to the strict radio silence, the area commander would not actually receive Fletcher's detailed operations plan until the campaign was about a month under way, leaving him in the dark about the specifics of the invasion even as he pulled up stakes and relocated to Nouméa.

The hostility that boiled over between Frank Jack Fletcher and Kelly

Turner shocked the other participants. They spoke to each other like enemies. It was well known that Admiral King didn't trust Fletcher's competence. A junior member of Fletcher's own staff had spread unflattering rumors of his intellectual ability. In this assessment, he was "neither sharp nor perspicacious," "uninformed and to a certain extent uninformable," and "antiquated to the extent that he was approaching senility." Seeing as Turner was freshly detached from King's staff, no doubt he shared these doubts about his competence. Fletcher had at least two things going for him that pushed him through the ranks and ensured his place in command: a track record of victory and Chester Nimitz's favor. Nimitz stood against King on the question of Fletcher's role, recommending him for promotion to vice admiral and appointment to task force commander.

The most contentious issue at the conference was the duration of the carrier air support Fletcher would provide the landing force. Nimitz's directive indicated that the *Saratoga, Enterprise,* and *Wasp* would provide badly needed air cover over Guadalcanal for "about three days." A fist-banging argument developed from that lack of specificity. Turner and Vandegrift had said they needed five days of protection to unload their transports and cargo ships at the beach, even though the operations plan called for the supply train to withdraw after three. King and Nimitz reportedly instructed Fletcher not to keep the carrier task force, under the tactical control of Admiral Leigh Noyes, in the area for "longer than two or three days at the most." Forrest Sherman, the captain of the *Wasp,* said after the war, "I am sure that [Noyes] returned with the understanding that carrier air support would be required only two days. That this was unrealistic is now quite apparent, but we had never conducted such an operation before and had much to learn."

Though Turner did believe he could unload his transports in the time offered by Fletcher, he worried about the cargo ships. In New Zealand, there had been no time to reconfigure their loads for combat deployment. They had arrived in Wellington loaded to fill every hold as efficiently as possible. Combat loading was a different art that required the most urgently needed items—ammunition and food—to be loaded last so that they could be unloaded first.

The Marine commanders at the meeting, General Vandegrift and his assistant chief of staff, Lieutenant Colonel Merrill B. Twining, were aghast as Fletcher explained his intention to pull out the carriers after August 9. Vandegrift didn't think Fletcher was well briefed on the landing plan. That plan promised to leave the Marines unprotected against air attack, except for what they themselves could muster from the island. "My Dutch blood was beginning to boil," Vandegrift would write, "but I forced myself to remain calm while explaining to Fletcher that the days of landing a small force and leaving were over. Although Turner heatedly backed me, Fletcher curtly announced that he would stay until the third day. With that he dismissed the conference."

The argument was a product, too, of the unwieldy table of organization. Fletcher, the commander of the whole expeditionary force, was also the commander of the *Saratoga* carrier task force, one of three such groups in the larger force. He was, in effect, conducting a symphony from the second chair in the violin section. His conflicting responsibilities created at least one perverse incentive, and an errant expectation. The expectation was that Fletcher would place priority on what was best for the overall operation. The perverse incentive was that he was and always would be a carrier man whose first thoughts were given to the well-being of his flattops. Thus a certain tension arose whenever Fletcher sought to apply Nimitz's principle of calculated risk. What risks deserved his highest concern: the risks to the expeditionary force (and by extension the landing force, which was the whole outfit's reason for being), or the risks to his carriers, the ships that the Navy valued most?

The Navy had been cautious with its carriers since hostilities began. During planning for the Wake Island relief expedition, which was launched and then abandoned, Admiral Pye decided that the carriers were more important than Wake itself. With that decision, the Navy had won the resentment of every marine in the fleet. Was Guadalcanal any more important than Wake? Presumably it was, for many reasons. But these questions, never addressed authoritatively, were left to surface unbidden at the *Saratoga* conference on July 26.

Fuel was another concern that urged limited exposure in the theater. The heavy ships had fuel to operate for three days at cruising speed, or fifteen knots, and four more days at battle speed, or twenty-five knots. With three days left to travel at the time the estimate was made, the fleet would have just enough fuel for four days of combat operations. For a cautious commander such as Fletcher, whose concern over refueling was well known and had already earned him the wrath of Admiral King, those were numbers worth paying attention to. Turner and Vandegrift would take all the protection Fletcher would give them. Every twenty-four-hour interval was critical. That he insisted on withdrawing after D day plus two was a continuing frustration to them.

In a March 26 memo to King titled "Strategic Deployment in the Pacific Against Japan," Turner had written that any offensive would have to be directed by a local commander "who is closely acquainted with local conditions, and in a position to make decisions on the spot," and supported by enough airpower "to *ensure continuous local naval and air superiority*" (emphasis in original). Fletcher's withdrawal violated Turner's notion of maintaining proper strength—and leadership—at the point of contact.

After the conference, Turner reportedly confronted Fletcher over the withdrawal of the carriers, hissing: "You son of a bitch, if you do that you are yellow." The acrimony would only grow worse. Ghormley wrote Nimitz on July 29 with an update: "I sent Dan Callaghan and LeHardy up to confer with Fletcher. I am enclosing a copy of Callaghan's notes which show some of our problems. The big one right now is fuel. We are working on that as hard as we can.... Some tankers are arriving behind schedule so it is going to be difficult. I fear any chance of advancing dog day is not possible."

At the *Saratoga* conference, Fletcher called aside Captain Callaghan at one point and expressed his thanks that Ghormley had placed him in tactical command of the operation. Fletcher said he had thought Ghormley would exercise that function himself. What Ghormley expected of Fletcher's carriers was unclear. An indication of SOPAC's view of the plan to withdraw might have been a note Callaghan wrote in the margin next to his record of Fletcher's announcement about his plan to leave after three days: a single exclamation point. As Ghormley's representative, he did nothing to challenge this timetable at the meeting.

It was time for the fleet to move again. On July 27, south of Fiji, Turner's amphibians rendezvoused at sea with the battle fleet for the run to Guadalcanal. "At first there was a mast astern of us—then another—and then several," an officer on the destroyer *Sterett* wrote. "Soon superstructures came into view, and we became aware that we were joining a whole fleet of ships: transports, destroyers, tankers, minesweepers, cruisers, a new battleship, and two big carriers."

The scale of the operation was now obvious to all. As various types of major combat ships hove into view with their escorts, captains gathered their crews and informed them of their destination. When skies cleared, the fleet's aircraft resumed flying. Planes from the carriers and cruiser scout planes alike scoured the horizons. When the pilots returned to their ships, they were agog at the extent of the naval power that had been mustered.

* * *

VICE ADMIRAL GHORMLEY arrived in Nouméa, the capital of New Caledonia, on August 1. The French island colony had never been envisioned as a springboard for major military operations. Louis-Napoléon Bonaparte, France's last monarch, wanted it as a penal colony. Even U.S. naval planners didn't foresee its importance until Japan's rise as a power encouraged the development of a secondary path to Asia, across the South Pacific, as an alternative to the newly threatened primary Pacific route passing through Guam.

Named Port-de-France on its annexation by France in 1854, Nouméa featured a spacious inner harbor in Dumbea Bay. It was slow to develop. Nearly a century later, it had but a single large pier, and the marine railway serving it could handle only small vessels. Its yard could not repair damage such as Japanese battleships were likely to inflict. Arriving ships sometimes found no harbor pilots to guide them in, which was unfortunate seeing as the channels into Great Roads, the outer harbor, passed through a treacherous barrier reef ten miles to seaward and old French mines were known to be about. The progress of the world seemed to leave Nouméa behind. The energies of even the most vigorous empires seemed to fade in the fronded South Pacific.

American logisticians came to see that their cargoes would have reached Guadalcanal faster if they were routed through the more capacious facilities in Auckland, more than a thousand miles farther south. Nouméa's principal value lay in its potential. Its location would be the foundation of everything that would follow. If it was located too far south to serve as a staging and support area for operations in the Central Pacific, but not far enough to the rear to be an arsenal secure against all enemy threats, American military surveyors found it was the best place in Oceania from which to manage Operations Pestilence and Watchtower. Reasonably close to both New Zealand and the east coast of Australia, it was a natural way station for flights originating in the eastern Pacific. The island was large enough for several armies to garrison there. Great Roads, well sheltered by reefs, could accommodate almost every U.S. warship in the Pacific.

On arrival, Ghormley found himself in the midst of a near insurrection. The unrest in the French colony was the product of a power struggle between a popular local governor and the man Charles de Gaulle had appointed as his high commissioner in the Pacific. The commander of the U.S. Army garrison nearly had to declare martial law to end their quarrel over imperial administration. The political tension in Nouméa reflected the brittle state of organization in a region that America badly needed to be stable. Without stability, it would be hard to grow a network of self-supporting advance bases from which to generate an offensive. But things could have been far worse than they were: Had the French administration in New Caledonia cast its lot with the Axis, as their counterparts in French Indochina had, America's sea-lanes to Australia would have been closed with or without a Japanese airfield on Guadalcanal.

The Americans made their military headquarters in the optimistically named Grand Hotel, a two-story wooden structure on the waterfront, unpainted and weather-beaten. Next to the fleet landing was the small Hotel du Pacifique, which was soon to become one of the most bustling officers' clubs south of Pearl Harbor. Behind its double wrought-iron gate was a tree-shaded courtyard with a bar said to be the longest in the Pacific. The appeal of the place—beer for fifteen cents, shots for a quarter—would be evident from the condition of the courtyard in time: "pounded flat into baked mud by the dusty shoes of thousands of officers," as a late-coming destroyer officer put it.

When U.S. servicemen first arrived on Nouméa in March, it became clear that the affection of Frenchmen for Americans was inversely proportional to the proximity of an Axis power. In negotiating for use of the island, Ghormley found the colonial administration fearful for its sovereignty. Well seasoned in the sensitivities of European diplomacy, Ghormley assured De Gaulle's man that the United States had no permanent imperial ambitions in New Caledonia. America's intention, Ghormley said, was solely to defeat Japan. When pressed, he pointed to the likely treatment the French would receive after a Japanese conquest. He found the people of the islands considerably more appreciative than their government, if for reasons that hardly seemed helpful in the middle of a total war against world fascism. According to the Navy's official history of the South Pacific Area, "Almost every French civilian hopes America will stay in the area to curb the British; and the British civilians hope we will stay to discipline the French."

For Ghormley and American officers straight down the line, curbing the Japanese with an unprecedented amphibious offensive was the more urgent challenge. It would require innovation across the board. "The war in our area must be considered a warfare under a new name—'Island Warfare,'" Ghormley wrote Slew McCain. "Young U.S. officers and men have many ideas as to warfare.... Encourage new ideas and use the good ones." Ghormley's communications up the chain of command, however, reflected a less hopeful tone. In a secret letter to Nimitz, he wrote, "I think our actual deficiencies are greater than are realized in Washington....I am worried about our deficiencies in port organization at the Bases. These organizations are provided for on paper, but the actual shortage of officers and men to carry out war time port necessities, with nothing to fall back on in the Island bases, is tremendous."

The leading navies of the world were situated in a challenging period between the age of fighting sail and the age of nuclear propulsion when fuel was consumable and therefore a critical limit on their reach. Once the term *steaming* replaced *sailing* in the naval lexicon, the concept of an operating radius took root. "If an enemy lay beyond that radius, the fleet might as well be chained to a post," a maritime historian wrote.

BY DUSK ON AUGUST 5, with a heavy haze saddling the sea and some unlikely escorts, flying fish arcing and splashing amid rainbows in the bow spray, the ships of the Watchtower task force shaped a northward course. By skirting the radius of enemy air reconnaissance, Fletcher aimed to keep the fleet hidden from Japanese snoopers on the final run in.

Shortly after midnight on Friday, August 7, Fletcher's expeditionary force approached Guadalcanal from the west. "God was with us during the approach," the captain of the destroyer *Monssen* said, "because we had a complete overcast of clouds just about five hundred feet above us, complete dense white overcast of clouds, a perfectly calm night, not a ripple on the ocean." To the hundreds of lookouts standing watch, the island revealed itself as a dark-against-dark silhouette, "vague, black and shapeless off our starboard bow," Joe Custer wrote; "like a purple lump in a pool of oil," according to George Kittredge, a turret officer in the *Chicago*. The moon was just rising, a waning crescent only five days to new, but its faint light was enough to make visible the plantation island's interior mountains, and the round mound in the sound, Savo Island, ahead and just to port. The *Chicago*'s bow wave, curling back in a surge of salt spray every time it pressed into a swell, produced a great phosophorescent arrow that receded for miles off either quarter. Kittredge feared it would reveal them to the enemy. But the operation was going like clockwork. After everything—the sonar soundings of fish, the endless refueling, the tense waiting, the failed rehearsals, the massive ocean rendezvous six thousand miles from home—Fletcher's task forces were just fifteen minutes behind the schedule that had been set weeks before.

Two powerful forces indigenous to the island competed to make the first impression on the newcomers: the scent of tropical flora and the stench of a rotted harvest. The abandoned Lever Brothers plantation's fermenting fruits and the tropical vegetation everywhere else made a vivid blend, almost visual in its impact on the senses. En route to this place, the Navy had done well to avoid surprises. The diverse mélange of aromas was the first of many, small and large, that would find them at Guadalcanal.

Because submarine attack was among the worst surprises of all, fighting captains understood the importance of the blackout restriction: lights out, no smoking, exterior bulkhead doors and hatches tightly shut, no exceptions. The *Astoria*'s searchlights were turned in to keep their lenses from reflecting the moon. Turner's transports were exhibiting less discipline. Lazing along off the *Astoria*'s port quarter, they were seen blinking signal lamps at one another. "What the hell do they think this is, Broadway?" someone asked. All nerves were atwitch. A Japanese naval patrol was widely expected to greet their arrival. As the amphibious force approached within three miles of Lunga Point, a strongpoint said by the coastwatchers to house antiaircraft gun emplacements, the commander of the landing force's cruiser screen, Rear Admiral Victor A. C. Crutchley, Royal Navy, ordered his ships to draw a bead while the transports drew past. Shortly after 3 a.m., on all vessels, came the call to general quarters. Bugles blared through intercoms. Synthetic alarm bells summoned the heavy clambering of soles on steel decks and ladders. Then: "All hands man your battle stations! Set Condition One!"

As dawn broke, it was almost possible, from the high perspective of a cruiser's foremast, to comprehend the work of the entire amphibious and bombardment force as one concerted effort, projected by a once-divided nation resolved to fight. In the *Astoria*, Joe James Custer, the war correspondent, lit a match, touched it to his cigarette, and looked down from the director platform at the showers of sparks shooting from the cowling of a scout plane throttling up on an amidships catapult. With a muffled blast the canvas-winged biplane was shot wobbling into the sky. It turned and headed for the island to serve as eyes for the guns. No sooner had the journalist stuffed a wad of cotton into each ear and slackened his jaw against the thunder he expected than he was lifted by a great concussion and thrown against a splinter shield that was draped with charts and posters showing Japanese aircraft silhouettes. A cruiser's broadside did things like that. His helmet knocked askew, Custer was swallowed by a cloud of gray-white smoke from the *Astoria*'s nine main guns. Ahead, the *Vincennes, Quincy,* and *Chicago* were salvoing, too, tongues of yellow-green flame lashing out sudden and staccato from their eight-inch batteries. Seen from a distance, their projectiles lofted slowly, like lazy red flares, through the lightening predawn sky.

When the red lines descended into the dark island, they split into shallow V's, ricocheting through the hillsides and jungles, tearing up tree trunks, and repulverizing sand.

Distance was a cleansing agent for everything. "The pervasive mud, and jungle gloom and tropical sun, when they are not all around you smothering you, can have a haunting beauty at a far remove," wrote an infantryman who would arrive at Guadalcanal later, James Jones. "When you are not straining and gasping to save your life, the act of doing so can seem adventurous and exciting from a distance. The greater the distance, the greater the adventure. But, God help me, it was beautiful."

No one found the sunrise of August 7 more beautiful than the stranded British-colonial-agent-turned-spy, Martin Clemens, hiding out in Guadalcanal's eastern hills. He was napping, having spent the previous night reporting to Townsville on the locations of Japanese troops and facilities, and making plans for his own escape. The deep concussion of the naval bombardment awakened him. Looking out to sea, he made out the dark forms of American cruisers low on the water. Overhead, gray-blue aircraft streaked by.

As Clemens's heart surged, he tuned his teleradio to a frequency that was full of urgent chatter: aviator lingo, cast in a distinctive American twang. When one of his operatives, a Melanesian sergeant major named Jacob Vouza, found him, Clemens was in rapt bliss listening to the pilots' voices. Off the beach near Lunga Point flowered a sight he had dreamed of: a friendly fleet drawing near, and landing craft churning toward his liberation. An "amazing panorama laid out as far as the eye can see, from Savo to Rua Sura, from Lunga to Tulagi—ships everywhere." He made out fourteen troopships and half a dozen cruisers. He found the scene so surreal that he was moved to invoke the spirit of Lewis Carroll's Jabberwock. "Calloo, callay, oh what a day!!!" he wrote. Flash. Salvo. *Thrump.* The guns of a friendly squadron were trained in anger on his miserable island.

As the American cruisers moved in closer, from ten thousand yards to four, and the destroyers closer still, the pilots Clemens had heard on the radio droned into view. The carrier planes split into elements and dove on their targets. Bob Ghormley did seem to appreciate the critical role the planes would play in the first days of the landings. On August 2, having debriefed Dan Callaghan after the *Saratoga* conference and learning of the argument between Fletcher and the others over the withdrawal of the carriers, Ghormley sent Fletcher a dispatch that read: "UNDER INFORMATION YOU PLAN TO WITHDRAW CARRIER SUPPORT FROM TULAGI AREA PRIOR TO DOG

PLUS 3 DAYS. NECESSITY EXISTS OF PROVIDING CONTINUOUS FIGHTER COVERAGE FOR AREA." General Vandegrift, for one, might have wondered why Dan Callaghan hadn't emphasized this on Ghormley's behalf at the conference.

If Ghormley's message itself was unemphatic and less than specific, he offered some alternatives for accomplishing that goal, including ferrying squadrons of planes from the departing carriers to Guadalcanal, or stocking rear-area bases with external fuel tanks so that their fighters could grow longer legs and fulfill the mission. Fletcher was still weighing his options as the landing boats reached the line of departure off Guadalcanal, bound for the beach whose boundaries were marked off by colored smoke pots.

Across Savo Sound, the four transports assigned to Landing Group "Yoke" were already disgorging their marines for the assaults on Tulagi and Gavutu. Resistance there would be sharp. The delicate crack and stutter of small-arms fire was soon audible in the sound. The *Chicago,* joined by the antiaircraft cruiser *San Juan* and the destroyers *Monssen* and *Buchanan,* roamed offshore, main batteries flashing. Eight Japanese flying boats, caught at anchor in a bay south of Tulagi, went up like matchsticks under concentrated naval fire and air attack. Ashore, the last dispatch that the Japanese headquarters managed to send to Rabaul—*"Enemy strength is overwhelming"*—barely preceded the salvo from the *San Juan* that wrecked the station. So completely did these ships, under Rear Admiral Norman Scott, toss up the Gavutu waterfront that an element of the first wave had to be diverted from its original landing site, a seaplane ramp that was shattered by the fury of five-inch thirty-eights. A Lever Brothers' dock nearby, somehow still intact, was used in its stead.

It was 9:10 a.m. when the marines of Landing Group "X-Ray"—assigned to seize Guadalcanal—prepared to embark in their landing boats. As the morning wind rose there came from the transports the slow grind of chains on davits as the landing craft settled into the sea. Streaming over the gunwales and crabbing down the nets draped overboard went the marines. The novel sights and sounds of amphibious war would become common: the throaty hum of aircraft streaking through the morning sky; diesel motors gurgling and swelling as the boats readied to make the run to shore; munitions depots and assorted flammable stores on shore blossoming bright within churning plumes of smoke; and then that smoke, dissolving and dispersing, becoming a gray haze that covered the area like dirty gauze.

Despite the ill omens of the rehearsals in Fiji, the actual landings on Guadalcanal were an anticlimax. When the marines hit Red Beach, five miles east of Lunga Point, they found an almost complete lack of opposition. Near the airfield, they gathered the spoils that the enemy workers left behind: meals still on the table, personal gear tossed in all directions, valuable equipment intact. They found ammunition, guns and artillery, fuel, radio equipment, trucks, road graders, refrigerators, and electrical generators. To keep watch over the area, they erected bamboo platforms on either side of the Lunga River, with views commanding Savo Sound as far west as Cape Esperance, and out to Koli Point in the east. Phone wires were unspooled from the platforms to General Vandegrift's command post, and another line went to an Australian intelligence officer who monitored the network of coastwatchers in the Solomons chain.

The first wave made quick work of Guadalcanal's beachhead, penetrating a mile and a half inland to the most prominent overwatch in the sector, the rocky fifteen-hundred-foot summit of Mount Austen, six miles south of the airfield site. On August 8 Vandegrift's men would set up a defensive perimeter around the gravel-and-clay airstrip that was the objective of the whole operation. Seeing no enemy fire meeting the marines, Kelly Turner elected to anchor his cargo ships close in, just two thousand yards offshore, the better to unload them quickly.

Then on that morning, harbinger of things to come, the colors flew. The first American flag to be raised over conquered Japanese territory in this war was a scrap of bunting, six inches by eight, purchased by Lieutenant Evard J. Snell, USMC, in Vineland, New Jersey, on Memorial Day 1934. Faded and frayed by eight years of travel, it was run to the top of a captured Japanese flagpole at Kukum, eight months to the day after the attack on Pearl Harbor. A detachment of leathernecks pushing inland paused briefly to give it a cheer. It was a modest display, but it made its point.

4

Nothing Worthy of
Your Majesty's Attention

WHEN WORD OF THE AMERICAN LANDINGS ON GUADALCANAL reached Japan, Emperor Hirohito, vacationing at the imperial villa north of Tokyo, told his advisers he would return to the palace immediately to consider the implications. Admiral Osami Nagano, the chief of the Naval General Staff, went to him first. "It is nothing worthy of Your Majesty's attention," he said. An intelligence report from the Japanese military attaché in Moscow reported that only two thousand American troops were on Guadalcanal. The number suggested that American ambitions were modest: merely to raid the installation, destroy the airfield, and withdraw. Imperial intelligence was expecting a major Allied attack elsewhere, on Papua, where Japanese troops were advancing through a treacherous mountain jungle toward Port Moresby. The attack on Guadalcanal was thought a diversion.

Other officers were less blasé. Admiral Matome Ugaki, the Combined Fleet's chief of staff, fumed at the totality of the surprise. He saw the landings as a threat to Japanese operations in New Guinea, and even to Rabaul. At the very least, Ugaki surmised, this was good reason to postpone pending operations in less critical areas such as the Indian Ocean, much as the June defeat at the Battle of Midway had forced the cancellation of Japanese plans to attack New Caledonia and Samoa.

Ugaki's superior, Admiral Yamamoto, felt that Guadalcanal had little strategic value. Though the Americans saw it as a threat, the Japanese had no plans to develop it as one. Its seizure had been dilatory, the construction of an airstrip a halfhearted half measure. He had no planes ready to base there in any event. Its real importance, Yamamoto would come to see, was America's interest in it. Imperial Navy planners had long espoused the "decisive battle" that would allow them to break the U.S. fleet after a prolonged campaign of attrition. Perhaps the enemy could be lured to the South Seas. If so, it would be a chance to concentrate Japan's naval forces and redeem the disaster of June.

At the end of July, senior Japanese commanders had held a conference at Truk, the great naval base that served as headquarters for the Southest Area Force. This meeting, like the American gathering on the *Saratoga,* brought to light important divergences of interest among the services. The Southeast Area Force consisted of the 8th Fleet, headquartered closer to the front, at Rabaul, the 17th Army, and a flotilla from the Navy's 11th Air Fleet. Throughout the critical early weeks of the Guadalcanal campaign, the commanders of the 17th Army were mostly concerned with the fight for Port Moresby and had, according to a high-ranking Japanese naval officer, "absolutely no concern with the Solomons."

An agreement between the services had made the defense of the Solomons the IJN's responsibility. But the gravity of that task was not fully appreciated. When the commander of the 8th Fleet, Rear Admiral Gunichi Mikawa, later expressed concern that the U.S. landings at Guadalcanal might represent a major operation, he was dismissed by headquarters staff as an anxious arriviste. Even after Midway, American forces were lightly regarded by naval commanders. Army commanders were confident they could recapture Guadalcanal at their leisure and disdained cooperation with the Navy.

Japanese failures of intelligence would become a pandemic. The Army's unbridled optimism—it had urged war against the United States on the assumption that a German defeat of Russia and a Japanese defeat of China would free up forces to use against America—was matched only by its paranoia concerning the Imperial Japanese Navy. The Army did not share its advanced codebreaking techniques with the Navy and, worse, neglected to reveal to the Navy the fact that American codebreakers had succeeded in decrypting the Navy's operational code prior to Midway. If the Japanese military was deficient in interservice cooperation, the schism was equally bad within each of the Army's and Navy's operations and intelligence sections. Operations staffers fancied themselves the best and the brightest and seldom consulted with intelligence specialists, whom they regarded as politically minded. Japan had no central, cabinet-level intelligence organization.

Operating in that vacuum of knowledge and understanding, Japan's combat commanders relied on their warrior instincts. Even on that score, senior officers lamented what they found in the Southern Area. Admiral Mikawa was surprised by the complacent spirit that had prevailed among his peers. He was a sea dog of the old school, the most experienced combat commander in the IJN, and widely recognized for his judgment and courage. Third in his class of 149 at the naval academy at Eta Jima, he was known for a quick mind and a gentle spirit. Eight months into a war that had given them no reversals, the Japanese were showing symptoms of a contagion soon to be given a mordant diagnosis, "victory disease."

Mikawa was taking nothing for granted. He decided to use his forces for a counterattack, and quickly. At noon on August 7, the 8th Fleet commander sent a dispatch to his cruiser captains outlining his plan to run south and strike the U.S. invasion fleet by night. He would make do with what he had: his flagship, the heavy cruiser *Chokai*, plus four other cruisers, the *Kinugasa*, *Kako*, *Aoba*, and *Furutaka*, based in the rear area at Kavieng, beyond range of air attack. Admiral Nagano considered the plan reckless and ordered it stopped immediately. After consultation with his staff, however, he decided to approve Mikawa's plan and turn the cruisers loose.

Japanese forces at Rabaul would respond by air, too. Mere hours after the first word of the landings arrived from Tulagi, fifty-four Japanese planes of the 11th Air Fleet were aloft, including twenty-four twin-engine Betty bombers. Early in the afternoon of the seventh, Mikawa took the *Chokai* out of Rabaul's Simpson Harbor, joined by the light cruisers *Tenryu* and *Yubari* and the destroyer *Yunagi*. The next morning, he ordered the four other cruisers to sortie from Kavieng and rendezvous with him by sundown. American radio intelligence intercepted his plan, but would not decode it for more than two weeks.

ON TULAGI, JAPANESE TROOPS put up a determined fight. On the smaller island of Tanambogo, several Marine Corps tanks were stalled at the water's edge. As Ghormley saw it, though, the greatest risk to the success of the landings in their early phases was not ground resistance, but the threat of air attack. Cloud cover had protected his task force during the approach. On August 5–6, gray weather had suspended Japanese air searches from Rabaul and given the amphibious force the advantage of surprise. It was during the landings that the enemy fliers found their first opening to attack.

The aviators of the 11th Air Fleet arrived shortly after 1 p.m., sweeping in low from the east. The raid, numbering twenty-four twin-engine Mitsubishi G4M Betty medium bombers and sixteen Aichi Val dive-bombers, escorted by seventeen Zeros, came buzzing over Florida Island then dropped down low to the sea, the planes holding a tight formation with their shadows bounding over the wave tops. A timely warning from a coastwatcher had enabled Turner's amphibious force to get under way before the planes arrived. The cruisers and the destroyers were fanned out in an antiaircraft disposition that placed the cargomen at the center of a great circle of warships. Overhead, eight Wildcats from the *Saratoga* piled in, joined by ten more from the *Enterprise.* Their combined fire was too much for the attackers. Just one Allied ship was damaged, the destroyer *Mugford,* hit in the after deck house with a bomb that took nineteen lives.

At noon the next day, the Japanese naval air corps staged an encore. Once again, given advance warning from an alert coastwatcher, the transports and their screen were maneuvering at battle speed when the air strike arrived. Approaching from the northwest in a loose, diamond formation, skimming over Florida Island and Tulagi, they hedge-hopped over the transports and broke up into smaller groups, looking for targets. Their orders were to strike the American carriers, suspected to be operating east of Tulagi. Their secondary target was the landing force. The latter was all they could find, and more than they could handle.

Kelly Turner's fleet, maneuvering in four columns abreast, led by his own flagship, the *McCawley,* offered its assailants few opportunities except to die. Admiral Crutchley marveled at how the "magnificent curtain of bursting high explosive was put up and enemy aircraft were everywhere crashing in flames." Rear Admiral Norman Scott's flagship, the antiaircraft cruiser *San Juan,* a sister of the *Atlanta,* was built for the job, with a battery of sixteen five-inch guns arrayed in eight twin turrets. Her officers got good solutions and had plenty of time to train and aim. The heavy cruisers, including the *Astoria,* worked over the incoming planes with their older batteries. Planes with red meatball insignia plummeted to the sea, pancaked in single forward flips, caught wing to wave and cartwheeled into pieces, or struggled on by, drawing black contrails in steepening downward arcs.

While under attack, the *Astoria*'s gunnery officer, Commander William H. Truesdell, found some time to explain the fine points of antiaircraft fire control to the journalist Joe James Custer during this live demonstration of the state of the working art. Technology was part of it, but the unpredictable way of the human heart was part of the system. Hearing one of his gunner's mates wheezing into a harmonica as the bullets flew—*Be it ever so humble, there's no place like home*—Truesdell chuckled and asked, "How can you beat those kids?"

The impact of the ship's defensive gunfire was terrific. When Custer returned to his stateroom, he found it a wreck: the telephone torn from the bulkhead, lightbulbs popped, personal effects scattered across the deck, including his chief weapon, his typewriter. The performance of the gunners was redeemed by the fact that most of the Japanese bombers ended their missions rather worse off than the journalist's cabin. Only five Bettys returned to base. It was a far cry from their devastating turn against the Royal Navy's heavies, the *Prince of Wales* and *Repulse,* eight months before.

Even with reliable warning, it was still a considerable trick to launch and vector fighter planes from aircraft carriers to intercept at the right place and time. As a result of the difficulties of communication and coordination among the carrier groups, the combat air patrol was paltry on the second day. A dozen and a half Wildcats, ten from the *Enterprise* and eight from the *Saratoga,* belatedly intercepted the Japanese and harassed them halfway back to their base in New Georgia. For the Japanese, the returns of their second air attack were meager: The destroyer *Jarvis* was hit by a torpedo and the transport *George F. Elliott* crash-dived by a damaged bomber, scuttled and left burning in the shallows off Tulagi.

The first two collisions of the Watchtower fleet with Japan's world-beating naval airpower punctured the impression of invincibility the latter had earned over the past year. A number of Japanese bombers were seen to break off their attack and fly away to the north. "Either these are Army pilots, or the Japs are down to their second team in the Navy," scoffed an *Astoria* officer. "I've never seen them that bad before. Those crack Jap Navy pilots—the ones we tangled with in the Coral Sea, and at Midway—they don't let up. Never. They come right at you, and they keep on coming until you get them or they get you. These punks—running away . . ."

Joe Custer got a close look at their kind when he found himself appraising five enemy aviators in the water near the ship. Through a telescope he could see their husky forms, heads shaven, wearing ribbed inflatable life jackets. As the *Astoria*'s sailors jeered them—"How do you like that, you Jap bastard!"—the skipper, Captain William G. Greenman, refused a request to turn the ship's twenty-millimeter guns on them. When a U.S. destroyer moved in to attempt rescue, the Japanese aviators pulled their sidearms and did it themselves.

At sunset, with the excitement of D-Day-plus-one waning, Task Force 62 reconfigured itself to confront the night. The carriers withdrew to their night patrol area south of Guadalcanal, out of range of enemy aircraft. At six thirty, Admiral Crutchley directed his heavy cruisers to take station guarding the two avenues into Savo Sound, on either side of Savo Island. The heavy cruisers *Vincennes, Quincy,* and *Astoria,* escorted by three destroyers, patrolled the entrance east of Savo Island, under command of the *Vincennes* skipper, Captain Frederick Riefkohl. The *Chicago,* joined by the HMAS *Australia* and the HMAS *Canberra,* watched the approach southwest of the island. The route into the sound from the east, through Sealark and Lengo channels, was defended by the *San Juan,* Australian light cruiser *Hobart,* and two destroyers. Closer to the transport anchorage, destroyers and destroyer-minesweepers guarded against incursions by submarines and torpedo boats. The destroyers *Blue* and *Ralph Talbot* were ordered to patrol north of Savo Island as early-warning radar pickets.

It was in the anticlimax of Saturday, August 8, less than forty-eight hours after the first contact of American boots with enemy-occupied Oceania, that the most potent Japanese threat would become manifest. Even as Admiral Fletcher prepared to execute the most controversial decision he would make as commander of the Operation Watchtower expeditionary force, a flashing Imperial Japanese Navy sword was sliding out of a scabbard just over the horizon.

5

Fly the Carriers

KELLY TURNER, THE COMMANDER OF TASK FORCE 62, THE AMPHIBIOUS force, was forged from the same hard brass as his mentor, Ernest J. King, whom he had served as director of war plans in the war's first months. Turner was hard on subordinates, and carried himself with an edgy intensity. "Whenever he became disgusted," a sailor who knew him wrote, "he would emit a small spitting sound, stamp his foot lightly and say 'Balls!'"

But he could show warmth when he needed to. "I have seen him 'blow up' a junior officer and I was taken in," a magazine reporter said, "till I saw the look in his eye and the smile that finally came.... He is aware of men's sensitivities and he recognizes their abilities even when they occasionally annoy him. His men admit he is tough—he admits it himself—but they love to work for him."

Given the problems that plagued the supply effort at the beach, Turner was fortunate that ground resistance was so light. His cargo ships did not have enough men embarked to haul crates and equipment for forty-eight hours straight. Without the benefit of docks, cranes, or other cargo-handling facilities on the virgin beach, it was impossible to unload directly to shore. Small boats had to ferry the cargo in, and when they reached the beach, hundreds of them gunwale-to-gunwale, human hands did the heavy lifting. Beyond the backbreaking nature of the work itself was the problem of organization and triage. According to the commander of the transport

Hunter Liggett, "After dark, conditions reached a complete impasse." It took waiting boats up to six hours for a chance to land.

The tremors of the interservice argument that would define the first two weeks of the operation arrived quickly. "No small share of the blame for this delay," the commander continued, "which prolonged by nearly twenty-four hours the period when the ships lay in these dangerous waters, would seem to rest with the Marine Corps personnel and organization. The Marine Corps Pioneers, whose function it was to unload the boats and keep the beach clear, were far too few in numbers." An officer from the transport *Barnett* described men "lounging around under the palm trees eating coconuts, lying down shooting coconuts from the trees; also playing around and paddling about in rubber boats. All of these men were Marines that should have been unloading boats." Even Kelly Turner, whose fondness for his seagoing infantrymen was peerless, pointed to "a failure on the part of the First [Marine] Division to provide adequate and well organized unloading details on the beach. The Marine officers on my staff feel very strongly on these matters—as strongly as I do."

Time was of the essence, but speed faced many obstacles. Many of the small craft used to bring in supplies were loaded so deeply by the head that they couldn't make it all the way up the beach. When their ramps were lowered, they filled with water and their straining engines drowned. Compounding the trouble was the way the big transports offshore had been loaded in Wellington: for commerce, efficiently and in volume, not for combat, enabling quick access to food and ammunition. In the Chesapeake Bay area and on the West Coast, the Navy was still establishing specialty schools to teach these skills to their beachmasters. At Guadalcanal, on-the-job training would have to suffice.

Early in the evening of August 8, in his flagship *McCawley,* Turner was wrestling with these frustrations, minding the possibility of further attacks, when Frank Jack Fletcher did what Turner had been dreading for two weeks. In a message to Admiral Ghormley, Fletcher was requesting permission to withdraw his three aircraft carriers, now serving as Task Force 62's umbrella and shield, from their supporting positions near Guadalcanal.

The reasons Fletcher cited were various—that his F4F Wildcat fighter force had, after two days of action against Japanese bombers, been whittled from ninety-nine planes to seventy-eight; that his ships' fuel reserves were dwindling; and that the presence of torpedo-armed enemy aircraft posed a threat to his carriers. Fletcher's reasoning was never clear or consistent.

When he asked Admiral Noyes, the tactical commander of the carrier force, for his opinion about a withdrawal, a shortage of fuel was not among his expressed concerns. But when Ghormley notified Nimitz of the decision, fuel was the only concern he mentioned.

Turner never forgot the contentious planning conference on the *Saratoga*, where he and General Vandegrift pushed for the carriers to remain on station through August 9. Fletcher's defenders say he only ever promised two days of air support—through August 8. Either way, the argument continued. Passions about the use of the carriers ran so high that they even got to the gentlemanly Marine commander. Vandegrift would be moved, in his memoirs, to accuse Fletcher of rank cowardice: "This was the Koro [*Saratoga*] conference relived, except that Fletcher was running away twelve hours earlier than he had already threatened during our unpleasant meeting. We all knew his fuel could not have been running low since he refueled in the Fijis."

Though Ghormley approved his request solely on the basis of a fuel shortage, Fletcher's carriers had enough fuel for several additional days at cruising speed. His destroyers were at about half capacity, with enough fuel for about thirty-six hours of high-speed operation. The larger ships on hand could have topped them off. Since he had yet to receive Fletcher's final operations plan, Ghormley had no independent knowledge of the actual risks to the carriers and felt bound to take Fletcher at his word. "All knew that the enemy could arrive in force and catch our Task Forces short of fuel," Ghormley wrote. "This had to be considered very seriously. When Fletcher, the man on the spot, informed me he had to withdraw for fuel, I approved. He knew his situation in detail; I did not."

Weeks earlier, in joining MacArthur's call to delay the invasion, Ghormley had expressed the need for a continuous presence by carrier aircraft. As MacArthur put it to King, "It is the opinion of the two commanders, arrived at independently and confirmed after discussion, that the initiation of this operation at this time without a reasonable assurance of adequate air coverage during each phase would be attended with the gravest risk as has been thoroughly demonstrated by the Japanese reverses in the Coral Sea and at Midway." The Navy's successes were also cautionary tales. If "assurance of adequate air coverage" was indeed essential, one might wonder why Ghormley did not more closely monitor the carriers' actual fuel needs or simply insist they stay on hand, within range of shore.

Fletcher was the most battle-seasoned senior officer in Operation Watchtower. The experience of combat had taught him its costs. At both Coral Sea and Midway he had had a great carrier, the *Lexington* and then the *Yorktown*, sunk from under him. At a time when the Pacific carrier fleet numbered just four, three of which were assigned to Watchtower, he was fearful of further losses. During the day, the *Enterprise, Wasp,* and *Saratoga* operated from a position about twenty-five miles south of the eastern end of Guadalcanal. From there, naval aircraft on patrol were but a quick few minutes from the beaches. Though Japanese planes from Rabaul six hundred miles away would have little capacity to strike them even if they could find them, the danger posed by the Japanese carriers and submarines was considerable. The paramount question was whether the carriers were foremost in Fletcher's mind, or the overall operation.

In his original July 2 operational order to Nimitz, King had specified the conditions under which the Joint Chiefs of Staff (JCS) could order the carriers withdrawn. "The withdrawal of the naval attached units of the U.S. fleet may be ordered by the U.S. chiefs of staff *upon completion of any particular phase of the operation* in the event that (1) conditions develop which unduly jeopardize the aircraft carriers (2) an emergency arises in other Pacific areas which dictates such withdrawal" (emphasis added). In King's view, completion of a particular phase of the operation—for instance, the landings—was a necessary precondition to a high-level decision to remove the carriers. Not even a serious threat to the carriers themselves excused their departure prior to the completion of a phase. Though it is unclear exactly what constituted a "phase," and while the criteria for a withdrawal ordered by the JCS were not the same as for one ordered by the tactical commander, it does seem unlikely that Admiral King ever envisioned a withdrawal before the initial unloading of supplies was done. The second precondition allowing the carriers' withdrawal—undue jeopardy to them—required that Fletcher view his losses of fighter planes and consumption of fuel, both rather predictable outcomes of operations, as excessive.

Fletcher was said to be the only U.S. flag officer who understood that Watchtower would provoke the Japanese to a major naval counterattack. "His major job," wrote author Richard B. Frank, "was to win the carrier fleet action that would decide the fate of the Marines." If that was the case, it would have been reckless to risk his carriers before that threat actually appeared. He knew he would have to win that battle without ready reinforcement to make up his losses. No new carriers were due from the shipyards until late 1943.

A well-situated referee to the controversy over Fletcher's decision making was Marine colonel Melvin J. Maas. If his position on Fletcher's staff makes his sympathy for his boss unsurprising, his status as a leatherneck inclined him to balanced perspective. He believed the only way the Japanese could retake Guadalcanal was through a major amphibious counteroffensive. "Marines cannot be dislodged by bombers," Maas wrote. Because he saw the carriers as the key to preventing an enemy landing, he favored a withdrawal of the carriers, even at the expense of his brothers.

"To be able to intercept and defeat [Japanese troop landings], our carrier task forces must be fueled and away so as not to be trapped here. . . . By withdrawing to Nouméa or Tongatabu, we can be in a position to intercept and pull a second Midway on their carriers. If, however, we stay on here and then, getting very low on fuel, withdraw to meet our tankers, *and* if *they* should be torpedoed, our whole fleet would be caught helpless and would be cold meat for the Japs, with a resultant loss of our fleet, 2/3 of our carriers, and we would lose Tulagi as well, with *all* the Marines there and perhaps all the transports.

"It is true, Marines will take a pounding until their own air gets established (about ten days or so), but they can dig in, hole up, and wait. Extra losses are a *localized* operation. This is balanced against a potential *National* tragedy. Loss of our fleet or one or more of these carriers is a real, worldwide tragedy." There is little doubt Fletcher's view of the situation off Guadalcanal took a serious accounting of the strategic significance of this scarcity of carrier power.

So would go the debate. The amphibious commanders met on the evening of August 8 to discuss what to do, Kelly Turner summoning Vandegrift and Crutchley to his flagship, the *McCawley*. Vandegrift arrived by launch from the beach. Shortly after 9 p.m., Crutchley, the cruiser force commander, pulled his flagship, the heavy cruiser *Australia*, out of formation in the southwestern covering force and set course for Lunga Point. This left the other two cruisers in that force, the *Chicago* and the *Canberra*, to guard that entrance to the sound. Crutchley left the commander of the *Chicago*, Captain Howard D. Bode, in interim command of his group.

The *Australia* anchored off Lunga Point, and Crutchley took a whaleboat to the *McCawley*. During the meeting, Vandegrift was struck by both Turner's and Crutchley's absolute physical weariness. There had been no break in the pressure they faced. Two days of air attacks and continuous difficulties with logistics ashore had worn them down to the threshold of exhaustion. Turner announced a tentative decision that he had been reluctant to make: In view of Fletcher's withdrawal, he would remove the transports and all of the cargo ships from the area, too. They would leave at sunrise on the ninth. Turner asked Vandegrift if enough stores had been unloaded to last his forces for a while. He asked Crutchley whether the cruiser screen could hold for a day or two without the protection of carrier-based fighter planes. Turner heard their grumbling affirmations and let's-hope-sos and adjourned the meeting at eleven forty-five.

As the commanders took leave of Turner's flagship, the enemy's torpedoes were already in the water.

6

A Captain in the Fog

IF COMMAND IS A LONELY MOUNTAIN, THERE WERE FEW PEAKS MORE desolate than Howard D. Bode, the captain of the *Chicago*. Largely, it seemed, he liked it that way. It was common practice for a skipper to take all his meals alone in his cabin. This suited the ship's officers, because Bode's manner was insulting and intimidating when he was not entirely aloof. He visited the wardroom only for meetings, and his presence always chilled the company.

Bode could wield the chilling power by proxy. "His officers were scared to death of him," said his Marine orderly, Raymond Zarker. "The minute I would walk in there they would freeze, like a bunch of frightened rabbits." According to an officer who knew him on another ship, "he was short and stocky and to a young ensign the most staggering thing about him was that he let his hair grow long enough so that it hung down over the collar of his service dress whites. He used to stick one of his hands in his blouse in front and he postured a little like Napoleon postured and looked a little like I thought Napoleon was supposed to look."

On the *Chicago*, officers who stood by their captain on watch and tried to be helpful did so at their peril. To give advice to a tyrant was to suggest his fallibility and offer oneself as a scapegoat should things go wrong. There were a few senior officers whom Bode outwardly respected, but he treated most of them in line with his whispered nicknames, "Captain Bligh" and

"King Bode." Of the Pacific Fleet's eleven heavy cruisers, the *Chicago* ranked lowest for engineering performance, a fact that may have arisen in part from the unwillingness of his engineers to fudge fuel records—a technique sometimes used to mask actual consumption but which might well have invited a stickler's wrath. He was bound for flag rank, had shaped his career toward that goal ever since he had survived some unpleasantness as a senior midshipman at the Naval Academy: a disciplinary proceeding for hazing, all of it duly reported on the front page of the Sunday *New York Times*. It was mortifying, but it didn't hold him back. He was a star, bound to command task groups and wear gold stars.

The scuttlebutt on the *Chicago* had it that Bode was from money. The son of a Cincinnati judge, he had married into the Dupont family and thus would have known the glamour of overseas capitals even had his prewar service as a naval attaché not taken him around the world. In that capacity, and later as a section chief in the Office of Naval Intelligence, he had become an expert in foreign intelligence. When Bode urged the disclosure to Pearl Harbor's commander of certain evidence that the berthing locations of vessels within the base were under scrutiny by Japanese agents, he reportedly clashed with Admiral Turner—a gambit for only the stoutest of heart. Turner, it was said, shut him down. His next assignment was to command the battleship *Oklahoma*. On December 7, it was only through chance that he was ashore when Mitsubishi crosshairs found his ship. The *Oklahoma* was heavily hit and capsized, killing almost half of her 864-man peacetime complement. Bode's absence spared his life. He and ten other men from the battleship transferred to the *Chicago*.

On the night of August 8, when Admiral Crutchley took the *Australia* out of the southwestern screening force to confer with Turner, he signaled the *Chicago* by light, "TAKE CHARGE OF PATROL. I AM CLOSING CTF 62 AND MAY OR MAY NOT REJOIN YOU LATER." With mere hours between the end of the conference and the rise of dawn, when the *Australia* and the other cruisers were supposed to go south to protect the transports, Crutchley saw no point in returning to his nighttime patrol station. And so Bode was alone again, in temporary command of a two-cruiser squadron guarding one of two routes into Savo Sound. The elevation to commodore-for-a-night was, he no doubt thought, a foretaste of duty to come.

Bode had reckoned with the possibility of a ship-to-ship fight against the Japanese on the night of August 8. According to a sighting report from an Australian plane out of Milne Bay, New Guinea, the Japanese fleet was on the move. Recorded at ten twenty-five that morning but delivered near dusk, the report read: "AIRCRAFT REPORTS 3 CRUISERS 3 DESTROYERS 2 SEAPLANE TENDERS OR GUNBOATS 0549 S 15607 E COURSE 120 TRUE SPEED 15 KNOTS."

It was a curious report, vague as to ship type. When the *Chicago*'s navigator plotted the coordinates of the enemy naval squadron, Bode's executive officer, Commander Cecil Adell, determined that it was too far away to reach the *Chicago*'s patrol area before midmorning on the following day.

So it will be a quiet evening after all, Bode thought.

Because the narrow waters between Guadalcanal and Savo Island were poorly charted, Bode had elected not to take the lead as befitted his command. Bringing his six-hundred-foot-long heavy cruiser to the head of the truncated column would have required him to conduct a minuet of giants in perilously confined waters after dark.

The *Chicago*'s crew was on the brink of exhaustion after several days at battle stations. As soon as one attack ended, a warning of the next one usually followed. There would be a warning this night as well, or a hint of a warning, but it would be cried only faintly, and no one would seem to hear it, or fathom it, until it was too late.

ADMIRAL MIKAWA WAS AWARE he had been spotted. One of his lookouts saw the plane that had betrayed him. Its appearance in the cloud gaps overhead persuaded him to reverse course in order to deceive the pilot that he was en route to Rabaul or Truk. But there was no need to fool an aviator who was already fooled.

The pilot of the plane, a New Zealander named William Stutt, reported to his base at Milne Bay that the ships scribing white lines in the waters of New Georgia Sound might include two seaplane tenders, or gunboats. These references to disparate ship types bewildered those receiving the report. Gunboats were not a recognized class of modern warship, though the term might suggest a small combatant such as a PT boat. Seaplane tenders were rarely mistaken for surface combatants of any kind. The ambiguity served to mask the actual lethal nature of Mikawa's striking force. Knowing nothing of Operation Watchtower in any event, Stutt was not predisposed to alarm. His report languished for hours at his base, and then for hours more at Brisbane, and finally reached Turner and Crutchley between 6 and 7 p.m. With its reference to seaplane tenders, it failed to arouse the suspicions it ought to have. Turner surmised that the enemy's mission was to establish a seaplane base near Rekata Bay, off the northern tip of Santa Isabel Island.

Continuing to vary his course to mask his purpose, Mikawa ordered his cruisers to launch search planes to survey the waters ahead. Within a few hours their reports would come back. Off Guadalcanal: fifteen transports, a battleship, four cruisers, seven destroyers, and an "auxiliary carrier"; off Tulagi: two heavy cruisers, twelve destroyers, and three transports. At a quarter to five, Mikawa signaled the battle plan to each of the ships: "WE WILL PENETRATE SOUTH OF SAVO ISLAND AND TORPEDO THE ENEMY MAIN FORCE OFF GUADALCANAL. THEN WE WILL MOVE TOWARD THE FORWARD AREA AT TULAGI AND STRIKE WITH TORPEDOES AND GUNFIRE, AFTER WHICH WE WILL WITHDRAW TO THE NORTH OF SAVO ISLAND."

Mikawa knew nothing of Fletcher's plan to withdraw. His only sure evidence of the threat posed by U.S. carriers was the chatter of American pilots that his radiomen were intercepting. To avoid that threat, he would have to strike under cover of darkness. He calculated that as long as the fight began before 1:30 a.m., his force, on withdrawal, would be outside the range of U.S. carrier planes come daylight.

On came Mikawa's column at twenty-four knots, the flagship *Chokai* in the lead, followed at thirteen-hundred-yard intervals by the heavy cruisers *Kako, Kinugasa, Aoba, Furutaka,* then the smaller *Tenryu, Yubari,* and *Yunagi.* Preparing his lunge into the American anchorage, Mikawa ordered his commanders to jettison all flammables. From the signal yards of each ship rose long white battle streamers that whipped the air. Back at Truk, Admiral Ugaki spent the day relishing the thought of what was coming: "The Eighth Fleet is going to surprise the enemy in Guadalcanal tonight. Come on boys! Do your stuff!"

THE HMAS CANBERRA led the *Chicago* in column with the destroyers *Bagley* and *Patterson* along a northwest-to-southeast patrol line, reversing course by a column turn every forty-five minutes. To give the weary crews some relief, the ships were in what was known as Condition Two, a state of partial battle readiness that kept one of the cruisers' two forward turrets fully manned, and the after turret half manned. Bode was reassured to know that both Crutchley and Turner had received the same contact report he had. In Turner's judgment, the reference to seaplane tenders suggested the ships were bound for a quiet anchorage north of Guadalcanal where the Japanese had a seaplane base. As for the threat of enemy surface ships, Turner was unconcerned. He had told Crutchley that he was comfortable with the disposition of the cruisers to protect the anchorage. "I was satisfied with arrangements, and hoped that the enemy would attack," Turner later wrote. "I believed they would get a warm reception." While Turner was with Crutchley and Vandegrift, a Japanese aircraft—a floatplane from one of Mikawa's cruisers—revealed itself to spotters on the *Ralph Talbot*, running low, flying east over Savo Island. The destroyer announced, "WARNING— WARNING—PLANE OVER SAVO ISLAND HEADED EAST." The message was repeated on several radio frequencies. It shouldn't have been news. Word had arrived hours before from the *San Juan*, leading three destroyers on patrol off Tulagi, that an unidentified plane had been sighted over Savo Island. The picket destroyer *Blue* saw it, too. That ship's gunnery officer asked his captain for permission to open fire, but since the plane was displaying running lights, it was deemed a friendly. The *Blue*'s skipper feared that if he reported the plane by radio, he would only risk the Japanese detecting his ship's location by radio direction finder. Fear of using sensors and communications was widespread in the screening force. When Captain Bode retired to his cabin behind the pilothouse for a nap, confident no attack could come that night, he ordered his radar officer to turn off the *Chicago*'s search radar for fear that Japanese ships might detect and trace the beams.

Rains were moving over the cloistered waters around Savo. Lightning flickered sporadically. It was 1:42 a.m. when the *Chicago*'s lookouts reported orange flashes of light against Savo's shadow. To Bode and the men of the bridge watch, they looked like fires on the beach. A minute later, the plane that was lazing in circles overhead began dropping flares. Five blinding orbs burst well astern, near the transport anchorage off Tulagi.

From the destroyer *Patterson* ahead came a blinker signal, "WARNING— WARNING—STRANGE SHIPS ENTERING HARBOR." Out in the storm-lit sound, the forms of unidentified ships were dimly visible, approaching nearly head-on. The *Patterson*'s battery barked, lofting star shells, aiming to backlight the bogeys. The *Chicago* followed suit, but her phosphorous candles failed to light. Critical minutes passed in the dark. The *Bagley* swung left, drew on the enemy, and fired four torpedoes from her starboard battery. Seeing targets against the glow of his star shells, Commander Frank R. Walker ordered the *Patterson*'s helm left and shouted an order to launch torpedoes, but the crashes of her gun battery swallowed it. Then Bode heard a report of torpedoes in the water, inbound on several bearings.

Ahead, the *Canberra* was seen turning sharply to starboard when a cry came of a torpedo wake headed for the port bow. Bode ordered his rudder hard to port as the *Chicago*'s engineers, deep in the ship, labored to answer the bell to make full speed. Noticing a quick, bright exchange of gunfire to the west, Bode steered the *Chicago* on what he thought was "a good course for engaging both turrets and broadside." As his ship came to twenty-five knots, Bode was still seeking his enemy when, without fanfare or forewarning, the *Canberra* was savaged by a concentrated barrage. More than thirty Japanese shells struck the Australian heavy cruiser, killing her commander, Captain Frank E. Getting, and other senior officers. Almost at once both of her boiler rooms were destroyed, and with them died all power and light throughout ship. She was a floating nest of flame.

In this fleeting moment of contact, the *Chicago* never did fire her main battery. A shell struck the leg of her mainmast, killing two sailors, including the chief boatswain's mate, and wounding thirteen, including the exec, Commander Adell, who was hit in the throat. A torpedo fired by the *Kako* struck the ship from starboard, clipping off part of the bow and vibrating the rest of the ship hard enough to disjoin the main battery director. Gunners on her five-inch secondary battery managed to train on and hit an enemy ship, the *Tenryu*, killing twenty-three men. But the darkness hid the larger targets. Of the forty-four star shells the *Chicago* lofted, all but six failed to light. As Bode struggled to decide what to do next, he neglected to report the encounter either to his absent superior, Crutchley, or to his colleague who would be up next in the shooting gallery, Captain Riefkohl in the *Vincennes*, flagship of the northern cruiser group.

As the Japanese column steamed by, rounding Savo Island in a counterclockwise course and approaching Riefkohl's squadron, Bode continued west toward what he thought would be the arena of the principal fight. Afterward, the track charts of the battle would show with cruel clarity that this is not at all what Bode was accomplishing. The record would even suggest, to the uncharitable eyes of inquiring superiors, that the star skipper of the cruiser *Chicago* was in the grip of an emotion quite distinct from courage.

On a night when the American fleet would need all the best virtues of its commanders, officers, and men to join together, Bode had committed the first in a swift accumulation of errors. Admiral Mikawa had won the draw and, continuing to the east, found Frederick Riefkohl's cruisers, majestic on patrol but no more alert than the wayward watchdogs of the southwestern force had been despite the spectacular catastrophe of the preceding four hundred seconds.

7

The Martyring of
Task Group 62.6

EAST OF SAVO, TWENTY MILES ASTERN OF CAPTAIN BODE'S WESTWARD-charging warship, the nighttime cloud cover was cast into gray relief by intermittent lightning and the distant flashing of gunfire. On a calm sea, the cruisers *Vincennes, Quincy,* and *Astoria* were tracing the northwesterly leg of a box-shaped patrol pattern five miles on a side. Their officers were alert to the light but unaware of its source. They did not know that a critical alarm had already been raised.

Captain William Greenman of the *Astoria* was steaming as closely as he thought prudent to the *Quincy* ahead, in order to get maximum protection from his threadbare anti-submarine screen. With only two destroyers, the *Wilson* and the *Helm,* leading them in the van, his greatest fear was submarine attack. On August 6, Nimitz had sent "ultra secret" warnings to all his Operation Watchtower commanders regarding the submarine threat. On the evening before the battle, Turner had instructed Crutchley to discontinue using his shipboard floatplanes to search the Slot for enemy ships. The undersea menace loomed largest.

Now came a radio warning delivered by a destroyer from the southern screening group, the *Patterson,* "WARNING—WARNING—STRANGE SHIPS. . . ." What to make of this?

Transmitted at 1:47 a.m., the warning had been missed altogether by Captain Riefkohl in the *Vincennes.* The TBS frequency was clogged with commanders exchanging the administrivia of the midwatch. It had been burdened most of the night by the chatter of destroyer officers wondering how to approach the task of scuttling the transport *George F. Elliott,* hit in the afternoon air attack. Though the bridge watch on the *Quincy* received the warning and sounded general quarters, the reason for the alarm was not immediately conveyed to the ship's gunnery-control stations.

In the *Astoria,* a petty officer named George L. Coleman, stationed in the plotting room beneath the bridge, trained his search radar to the west and reported a bogey approaching on the surface at twenty-nine miles. Though Savo Island's mass blocked the radar's field of vision within a twenty-five-degree arc off either shore, Coleman registered contacts and reported them to higher command. The fire-control radar was out of order at the time, but Coleman had faith in his longer-range search set. "The search radar was operating as well as it ever had," Ensign R. G. Heneberger, the *Astoria*'s radar officer, would write. When the officer-of-the-deck refused to sound general quarters, Coleman pressed his case. "The more I insisted that the enemy was out there, the more I got excited," Coleman wrote.

Still, the unfamiliar power of a new technology was seldom a match for a complacent human mind bent on ignoring it. "The OOD and the other officers tried to tell me that I had a double echo on my scope and that we had a destroyer in that area," Coleman said. He made such a nuisance of himself after his relief by the midwatch that someone finally threatened to send him to the brig if he didn't let the next watch settle in and do their jobs.

The first irrefutable sign that enemy ships were near came when searchlights fixed on Riefkohl's slumbering formation and a heavy salvo raised the seas just short of the *Vincennes.* No one, not even the officer whose duty it was to expect the worst, Riefkohl, believed a Japanese fleet could reach them before morning.

Sweeping the horizon through his glass, the executive officer of the *Vincennes* spotted a glow of light and silhouettes on the water, about four miles on his port beam. The "great display of light" blooming in the haze was the product of the high halo of a star shell. The gunnery officer believed it was from the flash of American gunfire bombarding shore. The *Astoria*'s captain, Greenman, too, was fooled by the evidence before his eyes. When he was roused to a view of Bode's southern group dying in the dark, he said, "I didn't know they were shelling the beaches tonight," and returned to his cabin. But even when the shock of heavy underwater explosions came, the throes of Bode's squadron could too easily be dismissed by the most plausible explanation: the detonations of depth charges dropped by destroyers hunting submarines.

Captain Greenman was unaware of the discord in his pilothouse concerning purported radar contacts. Had he been awake, he might have heard through the open hatch the argument between one of the two quartermasters of the watch, Royal Radke, who heard a plane overhead and asked permission to pull the general alarm, and the officer-of-the-deck, a young lieutenant, who declared such an action the captain's prerogative. Radke wasn't standing on ceremony when a decision might determine life or death. Without further deliberation or entreaty, he pulled the red lever. Some would say that this act of insubordination ended up saving more than a few American lives.

Having dealt with Bode's force in summary violent fashion, the four Japanese cruisers—the *Chokai* leading the *Aoba*, *Kako*, and *Kinugasa*—swept along to the northeast. The *Kinugasa* was still dealing fire at the ruined *Canberra* when the *Chokai* ahead fixed her searchlights on the *Astoria*, last in Captain Riefkohl's column, and eighty-two hundred yards, or four and a half miles, to the northeast. The *Aoba* lit the *Quincy*, and the *Kako* took the *Vincennes*.

Mikawa's gunners were turning their batteries on the American column when the lieutenant in the *Astoria*'s main battery director, Carl Sander, found himself studying a strange cruiser through his spotting glasses. Recognizing foreign architecture, he shouted into the phones, "*Action port! Load.*" As Sander coached the boxy bulk of his gun director onto the target, his gunnery officer, Lieutenant Commander Truesdell, in Sky Control high in the foremast, saw searchlights probing out of the darkness to port. He shouted, "Fire every damn thing you got!"

Awakened, Greenman reached the bridge shortly after *Astoria* had let loose her first salvo. "Who sounded the general alarm?" he demanded to know. "Who gave the order to commence firing?" Greenman thought the worst—not an enemy attack, but a blunder of fratricide. When the second salvo blew, the captain feared his gunners were firing into friendly ships. The quartermaster, Radke, was still catching hell from the skipper when a report came that the five-inch-gun deck was on fire. Only when an experienced voice such as Truesdell's had confirmed that the ships illuminating them were hostile did Greenman let his gunners do their work. From that moment on, the *Astoria* roared.

Feeling the lurching of the ship and watching yellow light flash through the slats of the porthole to his sleeping compartment, Joe Custer knew suddenly that he would not escape the battle unhurt. "It was there, as vivid and clear as though someone had told me," he wrote. For a moment he was frantic to know where the injury would strike him, but then he understood there was little use fretting over what he couldn't control. "I was suddenly cool and calm: What is to be, is to be."

Running to the weather deck, a radio department officer, Lieutenant Jack Gibson, was "surprised to see that we were fixed by a searchlight like a bug on a pin." Like her two consorts, the *Vincennes* and the *Quincy*, the *Astoria* seemed to come to fighting life when her guns opened up. But enemy gunners were several turns ahead of the Americans in the cycle of loading, fire, and correction of aim. Two hundred yards ahead of the *Astoria* and five hundred yards to port, a tight group of splashes rose, short. The next group fell a hundred yards closer ahead, five hundred short. The *Astoria* responded,

---

Order of Battle—Battle of Savo Island

Allied	Japan
TASK GROUP 62.6	**STRIKING FORCE**
Rear Adm Victor A. C. Crutchley, RN	Vice Adm Gunichi Mikawa
	Chokai (CA)
Radar Pickets	*Aoba* (CA)
Blue (DD)	*Furutaka* (CA)
Ralph Talbot (DD)	*Kako* (CA)
	Kinugasa (CA)
Southern Cruiser Group	*Tenryu* (CL)
HMAS *Australia* (CA)	*Yubari* (CL)
HMAS *Canberra* (CA)	*Yunagi* (DD)
Chicago (CA)	
Bagley (DD)	
Patterson (DD)	
Northern Cruiser Group	
Vincennes (CA)	
Quincy (CA)	
Astoria (CA)	
Helm (DD)	
Wilson (DD)	

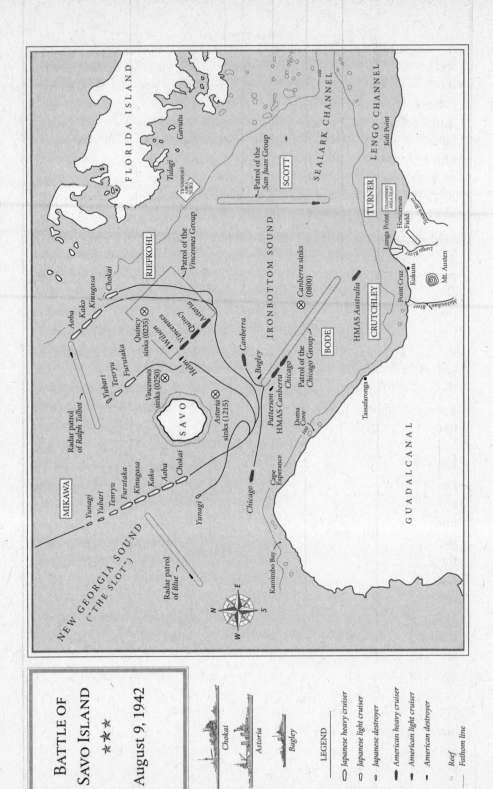

BATTLE OF
SAVO ISLAND
★ ★ ★
August 9, 1942

LEGEND

Chokai   *Japanese heavy cruiser*

Astoria   *Japanese light cruiser*

   Japanese destroyer

Bagley   *American heavy cruiser*

   American light cruiser

   American destroyer

   Reef

   Fathom line

FLORIDA ISLAND

Tulagi   Gavutu

TRANSPORT AREA YOKE

Patrol of the San Juan Group

SCOTT

SEALARK CHANNEL

LENGO CHANNEL

Koli Point

TURNER

TRANSPORT AREA XRAY

Lunga Point   Henderson Field

Lunga River

RIEFKOHL

Patrol of the Vincennes Group

IRONBOTTOM SOUND

Canberra sinks (0800)

HMAS Australia

Point Cruz   Kukum

Mt. Austen

Matanikau River

CRUTCHLEY

Chokai

Kinugasa

Aoba

Kako

Quincy sinks (0235)

Wilson

Vincennes

Quincy

Astoria

Canberra

Bagley

Chicago

BODE

Patrol of the Chicago Group

Helm

Vincennes sinks (0250)

Radar patrol of Ralph Talbot

Yubari

Tenryu

Furutaka

Patterson

HMAS Canberra

Doma Cove

Tassafaronga

S A V O

Astoria sinks (1215)

Furutaka

Kinugasa

Kako

Aoba

Chokai

Cape Esperance

Chicago

GUADALCANAL

MIKAWA

Yunagi   Yubari   Tenryu

Yunagi

Radar patrol of Blue

Kamimbo Bay

NEW GEORGIA SOUND ("THE SLOT")

N
E
S
W

and then a third salvo fell, directly abeam to port but still five hundred yards short. Tracking targets that were running on a course opposite her own, the *Astoria*'s director-controlled turrets swiveled aft until they hit the stops that kept them from blasting her own superstructure. The fourth salvo from the Japanese reached out three hundred yards closer aboard. Finally, after the fifth enemy salvo, Admiral Turner's old ship took one square amidships, in the aircraft hangar.

There was a sublime absurdity to the process by which a U.S. warship roused itself to action. When the general quarters or battle stations alarm rang, men assigned to a particular station on routine watch were replaced by men assigned to that same station to do battle. The replacement of watch personnel by general quarters personnel was wholesale, including key people such as the supervisor of the watch, the officer-of-the-deck, the junior officer-of-the-deck, the helmsman, and all the talkers assigned to the phones on the bridge. Every one of these people changed stations when the general alarm sounded. Though a well-drilled crew could complete the scramble within short minutes, the procedure ensured that officers and crew spent precious, perhaps decisive minutes scrambling, not fighting. It was like a game of musical chairs, begun precisely in that critical moment when seconds weighed most heavily and the marginal cost of a lapse was highest.

A gunner's mate standing watch in the forward antiaircraft director, known as Sky Forward, had a difficult course to run after the alarm sounded. He had to scramble down a warren of ladders and passageways to the armory, retrieve the key to the five-inch magazine, run to the magazine, unlock it for the handling crew, then run back up to the flight deck and stand by to launch aircraft from the catapult. All of this had to be done in three minutes—"a stupid set up," an *Astoria* sailor would say. "By the time I started my descent, the ship had been hit by several salvos and was on fire below."

Surprise was lethal to a ship that operated under such a system. When ladders between decks were blown away, crews had no way to reach their stations. Lieutenant Jack Gibson, the radio officer, was witness to this absurd and tragic chaos. He was climbing from his watch station on the weather deck all the way up to the main battery director while the first blows landed. "The *Astoria* was shuddering from heavy hits and the repercussion of her own gunfire," he wrote. "The air was filled with shrapnel that was clanging against the bulkheads, and the well deck, as I passed over it, was strewn with bodies of fallen men. I crouched down to the level of the metal railing, then clambered up to the hangar deck. Up there I was struck by the full glare of the Jap searchlights—and between that and the whizzings and ringings of metal all around me, I suddenly felt as if the fury of the whole war had been turned on me."

Gibson bucked up his courage and continued to climb. "One more crossing, another ladder, and I was at my station and out of the light. A burst of shells followed me through the door. They pierced the hangar deck and set the launches on fire. Then the planes began to burn. Their gas tanks caught fire and spread the flames." Another shell hit the base of the starboard aircraft catapult, plowed across the well deck, and exploded in or under the galley, setting afire the starboard side of the well deck and igniting the plane on the starboard catapult.

A hard lesson came now: The Achilles' heel of a cruiser in battle was the highly flammable realm of her shipboard aviation division. In modern navies, cruisers carried catapult-launched floatplanes for reconnaissance and gunfire spotting. The traditionalists bemoaned the oil stains the aircraft left on their ships' polished teak. Untended planes could do far worse under fire. They made their hosts into tinderboxes. Hangars were rich with flammables: spare wings, drums of lubricating oil, gasoline, and ordnance. The simple act of launching the aircraft unmanned into the sea, and jettisoning their combustibles as the Japanese had already done, would have paid a great dividend. Pacific Fleet headquarters had considered the risks and left the decision to discard the planes to the personal discretion of commanders.

The hangars were fuses to countless other flammables: paint, paper, furniture, and exposed crates of ready-service ammunition in nearby gun mounts. Steel and wire and cork and glass—all of it burned readily. The heat of the fires was sometimes intense enough to ignite paint on bulkheads two compartments away. The burning paint ferried flames through the compartments. Vital sprinkler systems were distributed by long runs of piping, exposed and vulnerable to shellfire, shock, and shrapnel. Fire mains, centrally fed and routed, could fail shipwide with a single hit in the wrong place.

High-velocity fragments ignited the crates of powder and ordnance stacked on the gun deck. Five-inch shells were set off like rockets or sat there and burned, igniting other charges or causing the projectiles themselves to explode.

Custer was watching one of the boxes burn as a sailor played a stream from a fire hose over it. "In a few minutes the stream grew feeble, stopped altogether; the power was off. The sailor moved away with the hose, and I edged forward for a better view of the flaming gun deck below. . . . There was a tremendous white flash—a huge sheet of flame—then crimson spurts flaring in all directions. I heard the whir-whir of shrapnel on all sides...and suddenly I felt a hot, piercing stab of pain in my left eye...shooting stars sprayed in violent streaks." Feeling for his wound and smearing red streaks across his cheek, he thought, *I'll never see Hawaii again.* Squinting through the blood, he groped toward a cluster of sailors sheltered under an overhang in the superstructure. Custer's thinking ran to distraction—*So this is how it feels to die,* he thought—even as he rebuked himself for his dramatics.

Robert E. Riddell, a gunner's mate, was awakened by flares as he slept near his station, a 1.1-inch quad mount forward on the port side. He told his trainer, F. C. Loomer, to train on a searchlight to port. Coaching onto his target, Riddell pulled the firing lever and rattled away for a while. The light went out, another appeared, and he had no sooner nudged Loomer's shoulder to change targets when time stopped and the world went black. When Riddell came to he found that his legs wouldn't take his weight, and that whatever had taken out his legs out had drilled Loomer straight through the torso.

As the *Astoria* shuddered, the *Vincennes* took several devastating shell hits from the *Kako*. These first hits were critical, striking the bridge on the port side, killing the communications officer and two men in the pilothouse. Hits came by the dozen now, the price of being enveloped after Mikawa's single column of ships separated into two parallel columns during the rush of battle maneuvers. The Americans were caught in the crossfire by gunners who could see their every burning move. Somewhere between seventy-five and a hundred medium-caliber shells found Riefkohl's ship.

The Japanese eight-inch projectiles were set to explode after traveling an average of sixty feet following penetration. Grievous as those internal wounds were, torpedoes were far worse. Hitting below the waterline, they turned the pressure of the heavy sea itself into a lethal weapon. The quick use of torpedoes was a signature Japanese tactic. IJN torpedo officers were taught to hold their fire until everything, slow fish and fast shells, could hit all at once. According to Raizo Tanaka, a rear admiral who pioneered the proactive use of destroyers in night combat, "An ideal torpedoman is full of aggressive spirit and has a strong sense of responsibility and pride in his work." IJN destroyer commanders were skilled shiphandlers all—"the Navy's crack night combat force" and "brilliant torpedo experts." According to Tanaka, "From top to bottom the training and discipline of the crews was flawless. Operational orders could be conveyed by the simplest of signals, and they were never misunderstood."

Several torpedoes hit the *Vincennes* from the port side. The blasts, amplified by the weight of the water, struck at the vital innards of a ship. When inrushing water killed the electrical system feeding the *Vincennes*'s main battery and silenced her circuits of internal communication, Captain Riefkohl was unable to talk to his engine room, to the officers in Central Station, or the gunnery team in Main Battery Control. He could not signal his following ships. In the course of the short twenty-minute contest, the flagship would manage just two nine-gun salvos, both to port, and two six-gun salvos to starboard. Her battle was quickly and mercifully over. The gunfire of Mikawa's turret captains was aimed with uncanny accuracy. Six of the nine eight-inch turrets on the three U.S. cruisers were disabled by direct hits. Though Riefkohl must have known that his enemies lurked on all bearings, in the disbelieving first minutes he never quite shook the belief that he was under attack by friendly ships. He blinkered entreaties to them, and hoisted colors, bright in the glare of hostile searchlights, meaning to suggest that this was all a mistake. It all was a mistake, but not the kind the commodore imagined.

From the perspective of Toshikazu Ohmae, Mikawa's chief of staff in the *Chokai,* the Americans were like targets in a gallery. "There were explosions everywhere. Every torpedo and every round of gunfire seemed to be hitting a mark. Enemy ships seemed to be sinking on every hand!" About eight minutes after landing their first hits on the *Vincennes,* the *Kako* and *Kinugasa* shifted to the *Astoria,* last in the staggering American line. The *Furutaka* and *Yubari* picked up the *Vincennes* by the light of her fires and the *Furutaka*'s searchlight.

Riefkohl's destroyers, the *Wilson* and *Helm,* could do little to save her. When the *Wilson,* riding on the starboard bow of the *Vincennes,* turned left to close with the enemy, she found the U.S. cruisers blocking her approach. Tactical prudence kept her from firing torpedoes in the proximity of friendly ships, and their flames blinded her to any targets. With the nearby mass of Savo Island lying in the line of sight behind Mikawa's ships, the *Wilson*'s radar could not register accurately. She fired her four five-inch guns in a rocking ladder, back and forth over the range that was shown by her stereoscopic rangefinder: about twelve thousand yards. Most of the rounds the *Wilson* fired—more than two hundred of them—were antiaircraft rounds with fuzes set on safe. Time rushed by to the point of vertigo, and even the *Wilson*'s clocks surrendered to the chaos. "Times in the above narrative are approximate," the captain wrote after the action, "for the hands on the bridge clock fell off on our first salvo and it was not realized that the quartermaster was not making exact time records of the occurrences until some time later." The *Helm,* steaming on the port bow of the *Vincennes,* fired just four rounds at the Japanese for want of visible targets.

Several fires were already burning on the *Quincy,* courtesy of the *Aoba*'s third salvo. The ship's after turret took a hit in the faceplate, dislodging a large piece of armor and jamming the turret in train. An aircraft on the port catapult ignited. Her two forward turrets got off three salvos each before turret two was hit and burned out, killing everyone inside. Some of the fires on the ship were the product of incendiary shells that exploded without penetrating and cast flammable pellets all over.

On the *Astoria,* Keithel P. Anthony, a water tender, was racing through the machine shop, aiming to reach the ladder that descended to the number three fire room, when a powerful kinetic force seized the whole bulkhead in front of him and swung it into his path. He was standing there perplexed, his way blocked, when a lieutenant named Thompson found him and said, "There are men in the forward mess hall who need help. Will you go with me?" Anthony assented and, strapping a gas mask over the top of his head, was preparing to venture forward when another explosion bedazzled him. "The lights went out and there were millions of sparks everywhere—like electrocution. I was knocked out and don't know how long I laid there on the deck. When I came to, there wasn't a soul moving in the compartment."

When Anthony saw Lieutenant Thompson again, he was dead, "blown clear through a wire mesh and his body wrapped around the main steam stack." His left arm and leg useless, bleeding and in severe pain, Anthony entered the machine shop and found bodies two-men deep. He wondered how he had survived, and soon found that it was only because he had somehow managed to snap the chinstrap of his gas mask that he would live with the curse of being a sole survivor. Poisonous gases killed everyone else. Anthony pulled himself through an escape hatch to the main deck by the starboard side galley. "I sat there and listened to hits coming in left and right overhead. Everything was burning."

Lieutenant Jack Gibson described "a roar like an express train in a tunnel" as a Japanese shell hit the main battery director's control station. "It came right through it, clipping off the steel stem of the sight-setter's stool and dropping him swearing to the deck. In the half-dark I could see him clawing at the rear of his pants to find out if he was all there." A voice with a Tennessee twang drawled, "That'll teach you not to be settin' when yo' betters are left standin' up."

"We didn't have long to laugh," Gibson wrote. "Our director was so jammed we couldn't move it."

Bathed in the glare of the enemy's carbon arcs, Joe Custer was lazily aware of men huddled around him. From them came "an overtone of muffled sounds, like mumbled prayers," he wrote. "There was a crash of an exploding shell right around my ears, and the sudden rat-tat-tat of unseen fragments ricocheting all about me, like steel popcorn sprayed up against the inside walls of a cage. I couldn't see them, but I could hear them whistling by and spattering off the overhead."

He remembered his premonition that he would be wounded, but realized then, too, that he would not die. The chief radioman guided him past a large gash in the deck and seated him behind turret two, which provided a loom of shelter even as it shattered his world now and then with blasts from its three muzzles. Then the chief led him down a boom to the main deck, but then turret two raged again, producing "a crushing explosion" right above him. The deck heaved as Custer shuffled down the boom, using his hearing to gauge his progress. "Look out for my leg," a sailor nearby said. Custer forced his good eye open and saw through his own blood a chubby sailor in dungarees, his right leg hanging by a shred below the knee. As the sailor sat down on the forecastle, soaked in gore, Custer wondered how the end would feel. *If I have to go,* he thought, *let it be quickly.*

Lieutenant Gibson, stationed in the main battery director, could scarcely stand from the slippery blood on the metal deck. "In flashes of light I could see some of my men, dead with their earphones still on. They had stepped to the door to see what was happening and had taken shrapnel through the chest. The smoke and heat were unbearable in our iron box, but we still tried to get our guns into play. First-class fire controlman Wade Johns reported huskily, 'I can see 'em, sir!' It was more than I could do. My gun pointer and gun trainer were at their places straining to get their cross wires lined up, and my sight-setter sat on his metal stool. I noticed wounded men on the floor trying to drag themselves up to their posts."

The sixth salvo hit *Astoria*'s turret one, forward-most on the forecastle. It absorbed three projectiles, including two to the barbette below the gun house, and one straight through the eight-inch-thick Class B armor on the faceplate, killing almost everybody inside. The hits came fast and furious for the next few minutes, slowly disabling the ship's fire-control apparatus. When turret two jammed in train, Captain Greenman found he could only direct his guns by turning the ship's rudder. As he ordered the helm around to enable the jammed battery to match bearings with the director, the *Astoria*'s twelfth and final salvo was fired, rather futilely, by local control.

The *Astoria*'s engineers struggled to coax full battle speed out of the besieged ship. The chief water tender, Milton Kimbro Smith, had just lit off the two standby boilers in the number three fire room. He was still looking to bring them online when an explosion rocked the compartment. Shrapnel rained down through the gauges of a control panel. Smoke washed over him, funneled down through the ventilation blowers.

At the main generator board in the forward engine room, chief electrician's mate Gilbert G. Dietz heard scuttlebutt that the topside decks were awash with flames. The compartment directly above him was trembling from repeated impacts. The blowers were fighting a losing battle to bring breathable air below. Sparks showered around him, and circuit breakers jumped out. The engineering spaces, fully dependent on forced ventilation, were choked from above. The *Astoria* had reached fifteen knots when her power plant began to fail.

Men without masks gasped and fell to the deck grating, struggling. Smith cut the supply of fuel oil to the burners and sounded the emergency alarm. Crew in the number two fire room succumbed to waves of smoke. Shrapnel rained in a hail down the blower trunk. The heat forced the crew in the after engine room to abandon station. When a shell penetrated a kerosene tank en route to exploding in the after mess hall, the combustible liquid leaked all over the well deck. It caught fire and flowed through a hole in the main deck, spreading below. A fire room, an engine room, two more fire rooms, and another engine room—they died in that order. Soon the *Astoria* was coasting to a tortured stop.

Matthew J. Bouterse, the *Astoria*'s junior chaplain, described a din of "steel piercing steel in a shower of fire and lightning bolts and the groans of a great ship in her death throes. . . . The steel bulkheads were alive with that lightning as they bled streaks of fire." Smoke was everywhere, and it overcame him. "I became aware I couldn't hold my breath any longer," Bouterse recalled.

By 2:08 a.m. Greenman's ship was down to seven knots. He could see the *Vincennes* in the lead, brightly ablaze amidships, just as bad off as his ship was. On the port bow, swinging right, appeared the *Quincy*. A wholesale mass of fire, Captain Samuel N. Moore's ship was still firing intermittently. Greenman could see that as the *Astoria* drew ahead of the *Quincy*, he was at risk not only of moving into her line of fire, but of a collision, too. He ordered a hard right turn to let the *Quincy* draw ahead. With the turn, the Japanese ships the *Astoria* was firing on passed astern. Tracking them, Commander

Truesdell in the forward main battery director found he couldn't see past the large fire amidships. He ordered control passed to director two aft, but they were blind as well.

Just as the *Astoria* passed the *Quincy* to starboard, a salvo struck the *Astoria* on the starboard side of the bridge superstructure, hitting the pelorus. Quartermaster Donald Yeamans was thrown ten feet and hit the deck with his right eardrum blown out. The blast felled the entire bridge watch to their knees, killing the navigator and several others. The ship careened for a time, guideless. Then the boatswain's mate, dizzied, regained the helm, turning left on orders from Greenman, trying to find the *Quincy* and re-form the column. When the boatswain told his captain he was feeling weak and could not hold on, Greenman ordered steering control shifted to Central Station and tried to conn by telephone. He wanted to order a southerly zigzag course toward the transport anchorage, but Yeamans, his talker, found that the phone line was dead.

The officer in command of Central Station, far belowdecks, Lieutenant Commander James Topper, felt a heavy vibration and a sickening rattle of metal. Blind to it all, connected by wires and tubes and voice lines, he tried to direct the fight to save stations he could not see. As thermostats in the fire alarm systems went out and alarm bells began ringing, electricians moved about, shifting circuits to determine which were working and which were gone. Topper heard a series of grim announcements. The boat deck: an inferno. Wounded men on the bridge. Turret one: hit heavily with few if any survivors. Three more explosions and Radio One was out. Another shattering hit and the number one fire room was gone. An engine room was full of smoke. The after control station commanded by the ship's executive officer, Battle Two, was threatened by fires.

Topper ordered a crew from the forward repair party to go topside and join the fight to save the ship. Then a shell came rattling down the armored escape trunk that reached from the foremast to the hull bottom. It exploded atop Central Station's armored hatch. The watertight seal, flash-fired, flinched. A metal seam opened up, admitting a gust of toxic smoke. Pieces of sparking metal, burning rubber, and debris rained down from above. All hands put handkerchiefs to their faces and stuffed rags into ducts, to little avail. When their request to abandon station was denied, all hands put on gas masks. The chief electrician, Halligan, grabbed a fire extinguisher and played it upon the debris. Then another projectile penetrated the ship's port side and exploded against the barbette to turret two, giving them other things to worry about. As the *Astoria* slid to a stop, her bow reaching for the new course, a searchlight appeared on the port beam. Lieutenant Commander Davidson climbed up to trainer's window of turret two and coached the damaged triple mount onto the tormenting light.

As far as Greenman knew, it was the last turret he had. The large fires amidships kept him from being able to see whether the after main turret was still firing. But Greenman could follow his shells as they flew, and could see them hit. One of the *Astoria*'s salvos missed its target, the *Kinugasa,* and struck another cruiser, the *Chokai,* on her forward turret. The momentary suppression of the Japanese flagship's fire did the *Astoria* little good. When Greenman asked what speed the ship could make, the answer from what was left of his engineering division was, "None." She was dead in the water.

At about two fifteen, the avalanche of shellfire engulfing the *Astoria* relented. The flashes receded and the roar of shelling died. Splashes became intermittent. Then the gunfire ceased. Further shooting at the *Astoria* would have been gratuitous on the part of the Japanese. Fires were eating her, within and above. Her engineers advised Greenman that the choked and burning engineering spaces should be abandoned. On board the two other American cruisers, similar discussions were taking place.

At two thirty, with his port side opened up to the sea, Riefkohl passed the order to abandon ship. Shortly before 3 a.m., the *Vincennes* turned turtle. The captain was nearly felled by the mast of his capsizing ship smacking the water. In an unceremonial plunge, the *Vincennes* went down by the head.

For the *Quincy,* like the *Astoria,* a sudden violent crash of enemy steel into the hangar deck had been the inciting catastrophe. She carried five airplanes aboard: one SOC Seagull mounted on each catapult, another floatplane secured on the well deck, and two more parked in the hangar. All of them should have been somewhere else, if not airborne on patrol then at the bottom of Savo Sound, flung away as a safeguard against fire. It was unfortunate that the rolling steel curtain that enclosed the *Quincy*'s aircraft hangar had been removed the previous day, damaged by the shocks of her shore bombardment. The price of this accident was paid as soon as the *Aoba*'s first shells hit: a contagious wash of fire over the well deck, and four of the five Seagulls brightly aflame. They could not be jettisoned while burning. By the time the fire hoses were rigged, there was no pressure left on the line.

The fires, unchecked, were a gift to the Japanese. Their spotters and fire controlmen could switch off their searchlights, hide in the dark, and train on the illumination offered by the *Quincy* herself, as they did with the other U.S. cruisers as well. The flame and the smoke flowing over the amidships gun deck blinded the surviving gunners in turn. In the struggle to continue, they could not see their targets, and it was impossible for most of them to know that their foundering ship had taken a decapitating blow.

When the hit came to the *Quincy*'s bridge—probably from the *Aoba*—most of the men on watch were killed at their stations. The *Quincy*'s exec, Lieutenant Commander John D. Andrew, moved forward as soon as the fires aft allowed. He wanted to find his captain. He needed new orders to help direct the ship's gunnery and helm. He was stunned by what he discovered. "I found it in a shambles of dead bodies with only three or four people still standing. In the pilothouse itself, the only person standing was the signal-man at the wheel, who was vainly endeavoring to check the ship's swing to starboard and to bring her to port. On questioning him I found out that the Captain, who was at that time lying near the wheel, had instructed him to beach the ship and he was trying to head the ship for Savo Island distant some four miles on the port quarter."

Andrew tried to get a fix on the island as the helmsman sought to avoid a collision astern. "At this instant," Andrew wrote, "the Captain straightened up and fell back, apparently dead, without having uttered any sound other than a moan." Shortly before he fell, Captain Moore had ordered control of the ship transferred to Battle Two, the battle station of his executive officer, high in the tripod mainmast aft. When Andrew heard that Battle Two had been hit and destroyed, he knew it was time to abandon ship.

All life in two of the cruiser's fire rooms had been extinguished by a single torpedo. By two twenty, the fireboxes in a third fire room were swamped. One of *Quincy*'s engine rooms never got the abandon-ship order. The final act of the chief engineer was to order a sailor forward to inform Captain Moore that the power plant was nearly inoperable. By then, the captain was already dead, and minutes after the messenger left, two torpedoes from the *Tenryu* struck the compartment, leaving that sailor as its sole survivor. As the *Quincy*'s port rail touched the sea, the five-inch-gun deck was engulfed. Floodwater partly quenched the fires that blazed belowdecks. But the mercy of this happenstance was useless. At about 2:35 a.m., the *Quincy* rolled on her port beam ends and sank by the bow.

BEREFT OF THE COMPANY of her sisters, the *Astoria* faced a terrible struggle after the Japanese melted into the night and the encounter off Savo Island was left to reverberate in the memories of a thousand lives lost. Like the *Vincennes* and *Quincy,* she had been gutted before her officers knew what was happening. Though some foresighted aviation machinists had drained the gas lines of her Seagulls the night before, there was no shortage of things to explode. When the valve heads on some gas cylinders stored in the aircraft hangar became superheated, they blew spectacularly, and "gas jetted high in the air, igniting as it went up 'like Roman candles,'" one sailor recalled. As an *Astoria* marine recalled, "Our ship was blazing like a straw stack on a summer night."

In the northern cruiser force on its night of doom, a hundred small dramas played out. As the *Astoria*'s executive officer, Frank Shoup, ordered Battle Two abandoned, he saw that the fire on the boat deck had spread to the legs of the mainmast and was greedily climbing, devouring its smooth gray veneer. Battle Two was the last refuge now of several dozen trapped sailors. On all sides, the ladders down to the main deck were blocked by the rising flames. "All communications were shot away," Jack Gibson wrote. "Our eyes were burning with smoke, and we were choking in the fumes of flaming diesel oil."

Leaving the director and going out to the machine-gun platform, Gibson found seven dead men "all heaped together behind the torn splinter shield in a jumble of arms, legs and broken bodies." They included Ensign McLaughlin, the machine-gun control officer, killed with his crew before they ever got off a shot. Puzzlement, anger, and frustration, not fear, were the predominant emotions of the moment. Gibson saw a fire controlman named Dean pull a large hunk of steel out of his thigh and throw it disgustedly to the deck.

Gibson recalled, "We salvaged the first aid kit from the control room and gave the wounded shots of morphine. Then I called down to the fantail for a fire hose." With help from sailors who had climbed onto the roof of turret three, a hose was attached to a light line and tossed up to the platform. It didn't carry much water. It sputtered and went dead.

"Without a word," Gibson wrote, "Seaman Barker went down the hot ladder to the flaming launches and hacked off a heavy coil of rope. Machine-gun ammunition exploded around him, but he got back up with only minor burns." The improvised zip line had been singed badly enough to call its utility into question. Unsure of its strength, they puzzled how best to test it and finally settled on a coldly pragmatic method underwritten by a difficult moral calculus: They decided to try it on the worst of the wounded. An unconscious sailor was attached to the line and sent on his way, sliding down toward the roof of turret three. "He could not have been more than ten feet down," Wade Johns recalled, "when the line went slack in our hands and we heard the crunching sound of his body after he fell that last forty feet.

"We checked every foot of the remaining line. We knotted it around the burned segments, checked again, and then began the successful lowering of the wounded, one by one."

The *Astoria* was divided in two by a valley of fire amidships. About 150 men were trapped on the fantail. They could get no word of their shipmates in the forward stations. With the fires amidships walling them off, they doubted there could be any survivors. "We sat there while the fire roared amidships and our ammunition was blowing up," Gibson wrote. "We were sure all hands forward were dead, while they never dreamed that anyone could have survived the fire aft." Wounded men were being saved in unlikely ways, in some cases delivered topside through large gashes opened up by the impact of enemy shells.

The *Astoria's* bridge had an enormous section shot away, and her scorched hangar area was blackened. Her most threatening wounds were eight large shell holes located just above the torpedo belt on her starboard side. She was holed but seaworthy, and though many of her rivets were weepy, the larger penetrations were well plugged from within. As long as the port list could be controlled, the volume of water shipping in would not be fatal.

Chaplain Bouterse, seated on the fantail, was dangling his legs over the side and resting them on the welded letters spelling the name of his ship. There came a drizzle of rain and he welcomed its coolness. The water below his feet was obsidian and foreboding, lit only by the flicker of flames and the little splashes of light that came whenever debris, cast by explosions into the sea, disturbed the plankton and stirred them to a momentary green glow. Here and there fuzzy iridescent streaks were swirled up by the baleful wakes of shark fins.

Contemplating a world without a USS *Astoria,* Bouterse found he could not take his eyes from a ghastly sight. "One of our crew had been killed at his battle station at After Control, the tall superstructure just abaft the hangar, which contained some of our fire control equipment. His body had caught on the rail and was hanging there. The fire from below was coming closer and closer to him as I watched transfixed.

"I know I wasn't the only one of that group of dazed survivors who noticed our shipmate's body slowly shrinking as the flames consumed it. The thought never crossed my mind that I should try to climb up and pull that body down, and no one else moved either . . . a funeral pyre seemed symbolically appropriate in the last moments of our ship's existence, and, for all we knew, ours. One must only watch in dignified silence and say farewell."

One sailor who was sent below to find some life jackets returned with a box of cigars. Bouterse knew the kid. He had been trying to teach him to read and write. As he offered smokes to men clustered around turret three, the kid swelled a little, as if he knew he had won a small battle. He shouted to the chaplain, "Hey, man, I just made chief the hard way!" The sight of this sailor, cocky despite the circumstances, struck Bouterse in the heart. "I was back in a more familiar world where sailors could do crazy things like that, throwing the butchery of battle right back into the face of the enemy. . . . The bitter laughter tasted good."

8

Burning in the Rain

IT WAS ABOUT 2:40 IN THE MORNING WHEN ADMIRAL CRUTCHLEY, from the bridge of the *Australia*, observed a trio of objects burning on the sea between Savo and Florida islands and wondered what calamity he had missed. The muzzle flashes he had seen earlier had stopped. His commanders had reported no victory, yet no attack on the anchorages had ensued. The pieces of a strange puzzle floated all over the sound.

To his interim squadron commander, Captain Bode in the *Chicago*, the British officer sent a terse imperative: "REPORT SITUATION."

Bode was quick with a reply: "CHICAGO SOUTH OF SAVO ISLAND. HIT BY TORPEDO, SLIGHTLY DOWN BY BOW. ENEMY SHIPS FIRING TO SEAWARD. CAN-BERRA BURNING ON BEARING 250 FIVE MILES FROM SAVO. TWO DESTROYERS STANDING BY CANBERRA."

Crutchley pondered this incomplete report and passed what he could to Kelly Turner: "SURFACE ACTION NEAR SAVO. SITUATION AS YET UNDETER-MINED."

Among the transports off Tulagi, nerves were tight as tow cables. The *Hunter Liggett* went to general quarters at about 2 a.m. at the first sign of trouble. Her skipper, a Coast Guard captain named Lewis W. Perkins, leaned on the front rail of his bridge and peered into the night, studying the flashes of gunfire. Then he heard the uneven gurgling of an aircraft engine, and suddenly it was like daytime as a flare popped overhead. "Its searing light revealed the transports and destroyers, grotesquely naked. On the horizon, firing began again." Perkins shouted, 'Hold on! If we're going to get it, this is it!'

"We stood breathless, gripping the rail. The shells, if they were coming, were on the way. The white light glared down on us. Our ships just sat there: fat, stupid ducks in the blinding glare."

Mikawa's arrival had been a surprise to all. Joe Custer, who interviewed several of the observers, recalled their confusion and fear. There was no comprehending the horrible truth behind the pyrotechnics that flashed in the night. "Huge balls of red fire would leave one ship; they could watch them winging in an arc straight for the other ships, then the spurting of flames as they hit. Then, answering balls of fire would retrace the arc, and explode in flaming geysers."

"We'd automatically move our heads from left to right, from side to side, at the exchange," the navigator on one of the transports said. "It was like watching a tennis match—in hell." That officer made out one large ship in particular, very possibly Mikawa's *Chokai,* throwing salvos so swiftly that they appeared to be chasing one another through the air. In the direction of their arc, flames were towering in the black sky. Some distance still farther away, the bottoms of clouds were warmed by a red glow. The *Canberra* was in her final throes.

The destroyer *Patterson* came alongside the burning Australian cruiser, only to be driven away by the detonations of ordnance. She tried again and stayed, passing over pump and fire hoses. The rains were driving then, extinguishing smoldering debris but doing little against deeper conflagrations.

Bad as it looked for the *Canberra,* the plan to abandon her was delayed when it became clear that she would not be left until all the wounded were removed. The destroyers turned to the task, with the *Patterson* taking four hundred survivors on board, including seventy wounded, and the *Wilson* rescuing more than two hundred more. A call came then to aid the *Astoria.*

But the tin cans could only accomplish so much. At four fifteen, with the *Canberra* suffering from internal explosions, her starboard list growing to almost thirty-five degrees, the *Patterson*'s deck force threw their hoses off, helped the wounded to settle in, and then passed the order for the stricken cruiser to abandon ship.

Kelly Turner had always intended to withdraw most of his amphibious and supply ships from Guadalcanal and Tulagi forty-eight hours after the landings. Fletcher's removal of his carriers was pending—they would spend the night and predawn morning in a "night retirement station" southwest of San Cristobál. If the *Canberra* could not be righted and made seaworthy in

time to join the fleet's exit, planned for 6:30 a.m., she would have to be scuttled. The *Patterson* relayed Turner's grim order to the *Canberra*.

It was about five fifteen when a strange ship, presumably a hostile one,
appeared on the *Canberra*'s port quarter. Seeing the threat, the *Patterson*
blinkered the *Canberra*: "OUT ALL LIGHTS." It was not a moment too soon,
for the approaching ship immediately took the *Patterson* under fire. The
destroyer replied in kind. The good news was that none of the shells the
strangers traded hit. The bad news was that the ship firing at them proved to
be Howard Bode's *Chicago,* returning from her solo foray into the west. The
Patterson turned on her identification lights and Bode checked his fire.

THE PYRES OF THE *Vincennes* and *Quincy* were not long below the waves,
and the *Canberra*'s and *Astoria*'s bouts with fire only beginning, when Rear
Admiral Gunichi Mikawa took on his next challenge—deciding how to
exploit his stunning rout. At issue was whether he would carry out his principal mission and attack the transport anchorages. Mikawa and his chief of
staff, Toshikazu Ohmae, knew that the landing areas off Guadalcanal and
Tulagi were vulnerable. They also understood their own exposure. The *Aoba*
had already escaped catastrophe during the battle when an American shell
struck her port side torpedo mount. Because thirteen of her sixteen fish had
been fired already, the explosion did not produce the devastating secondary
blast it might have. A shell from the *Quincy* that destroyed the *Chokai*'s chart
room struck five yards aft of the bridge, just a hairbreadth from killing the
admiral and most of his staff. As was always the case in a high-speed action
at night, a few minutes' notice either way could have changed the outcome.
"I was greatly impressed by the courageous actions of the northern group
of U.S. cruisers," Mikawa would comment. "They fought back heroically
despite heavy damage sustained before they were ready for battle. Had they
had even a few minutes' warning of our approach, the results of the action
would have been quite different."

Frayed by the confusion of battle, Mikawa's formation re-formed northwest
of Savo Island. The *Chokai* took the lead in column ahead of the *Furutaka,*
Kako, Kinugasa, Aoba, Tenryu, Yubari, and *Yunagi.* The ships were all low on
torpedoes—fully half of them had been launched in the preceding hour—
along with as much as a third of their main-battery ammunition. Chief among
the admiral's worries was the question of time and daylight. If he pressed on
into the American anchorage, he doubted he would escape before daylight. He
estimated it would take half an hour to finally reassemble his force, another

half hour to close up into battle formation, and still another half hour to regain battle speed. From there, the anchorage was a sixty-minute sprint at high speed. The total time of those processes, two and a half hours, meant that Mikawa's task force would hit the anchorage just an hour before sunrise; it would be impossible to escape under cover of the night.

The shadow cast by naval aviators was long and dark. The outcome at Midway, like Coral Sea before it, had taught Mikawa that land-based air-power was usually the master of its surrounding seas. "To remain in the area by sunrise would mean that we would only meet the fate our carriers had suffered at Midway." It was six hundred miles from Rabaul to Tulagi, and the 11th Air Fleet was having trouble finding planes to commit to Guadalcanal in any event. Trouble loomed. From intercepted radio traffic, he knew Fletcher's carriers were out there somewhere. He lacked friendly air cover to save him from American planes in a daylight sprint back to base.

En route to surprising Bode and Riefkohl, it had been keen navigational skill that enabled Mikawa to hug Savo's black coast. Proceeding into the littorals of an anchorage without good charts—incinerated when his flagship's chart room was hit—would have been perilous. Besides, what was the hurry? Victory had been easy. Other opportunities would come. The Army had long been saying it would be no great chore to unseat the Americans from their small beachhead.

Eight months earlier Mikawa had been second in command to Vice Admiral Chuichi Nagumo, commander of the Pearl Harbor strike force. Mikawa had command of Battleship Division 3, the mighty *Kirishima* and *Hiei*. When a decision loomed then about whether to retreat or attack again, Mikawa had urged further attacks against Oahu's oil storage and repair facilities. Now he evaluated similar if smaller risks and chose discretion—and withdrawal. The irony of that decision was considerable: As Mikawa departed to the north, the U.S. aircraft carriers whose wrath he feared were preparing to get under way in the other direction.

"We were all shocked and disconcerted momentarily," wrote Ohmae. "We were still absorbed with the details of the hard fight just finished and had lost track of time. I was amazed to discover that it was just shortly after midnight, and then we were headed in a northerly direction. As we continued northward, we ran the risk of going ashore on Florida Island, so a change of course was made to the left. I asked the lookout if there was any sign of pursuing ships. There was not."

* * *

THE FIGHT TO save the *Astoria* was at a fever pitch. With hundreds of sailors marshaled as a bucket brigade, heaving water with buckets and spent eight-inch shell casings, many of the fires raging throughout the ship began to yield. Countless small acts of gallantry marked the morning. A lieutenant, Walter Bates, dove overboard to push a life raft containing a portable pump closer to the ship. When he noticed a shark trailing him, he leaped into the raft, grabbed an oar, and splintered it over the predator's skull. Then Bates was in the water again, pushing the raft into position. The pump coughed to life and water flowed for a brief while. When it died again for good, Bates climbed up on deck and joined scores of others removing wounded. "He was everywhere, working feverishly," Joe Custer reported. "And he came out with only a sprained ankle." A first-class petty officer named C. C. Watkins had the kind of commanding presence that rallied the bucket brigade. "Men naturally responded to his confidence, actions, and commanding voice," wrote Lieutenant Commander John D. Hayes, the engineering officer. When Frank Shoup, the exec, first noticed a sailor trapped between a whaleboat davit and a gash in the starboard side of the upper deck, he thought the man was dead. He had only a moment to register the slight wave of the hand the sailor gave before Watkins, joined by two other sailors, Wyatt J. Luttrell and Norman R. Touve, were picking their way through the flames to bring him down. The rescuers found two other sailors while saving this first man, including one who was clinging to the bulge in the cruiser's torpedo belt as the ship was threatening to capsize. "The rescue of these three men," Shoup wrote, "was a heroic action, and was the finest deed I witnessed in a night when high courage was commonplace....I would not have ordered anyone in to make this rescue, as I did not think it could be done."

When Shoup heard a pump motoring in the forward part of the ship, beyond the no-man's-land of the amidships fires, it was his first indication that people were alive on the other side of the hangar deck. Within an hour the persistent labor of the bucket brigades had quenched the fires as far forward as the well deck. Only a stubborn lube-oil fire in the starboard forward corner of well deck was evidence of the great conflagration that had been.

Shoup and Hayes were optimists. But a hotter blaze was worming its way deeper in the *Astoria*'s belly, a severe fire in the wardroom that was unapproachable by hand or by hose. Notified of it, Greenman ordered the forward magazines flooded to prevent an explosion. Enterprising sailors tossed a couple of preventive bucketfuls down the ammunition hoists, then turned open the seacocks. As the powder bags were swamped, one danger vanished and another rose in its place. The weight of the water accumulating below threatened to increase the modest port-side list.

It was around 3:30 a.m. when the rain came, and for about an hour it fell, heavy and cold. Custer remembered some folklore he'd heard that said rain always came after a big naval battle because the concussion of big guns unhinged the equilibrium of the atmosphere.

Topside the rains fell hard. Though they did little against the blaze in the well deck, the superstructure cooled, steamed, and smoked. The blackened foremast turned to solid steel again after buckling under the heat. Hoses lay about, withered down to their coils like discarded snakeskins. The forward turrets, manned now by corpses, were still trained in the direction of the last known target. The ship, coughing flames from her belly, shook occasionally from the muffled thump of five-inch projectiles exploding in superheated hoists. In the midst of it all, men were nearly stuporous. "I stood for a moment of silence in memory of the men I had known," Jack Gibson said. "Then voices roused me. They came from a destroyer coming up alongside."

When the *Bagley* first appeared ahead at around four o'clock that morning, the ship was blacked out and identification impossible. The *Astoria*'s survivors mistook the flashes of her signal lamp for the muzzle of an enemy rifle firing into their shipmates adrift. Captain Greenman ordered a signalman to climb atop turret two and challenge the newcomer with a blinker gun. "Shaking with cold and fright," recalled signalman Vince Furst, "I sent out *AA* and the familiar *SOS*."

The voice that came in reply was unmistakable, the New England twang of the *Bagley*'s skipper, Lieutenant Commander George A. Sinclair, well known in the *Astoria* from his recent tenure as her engineering officer. His destroyer approached bow-to-bow in a well-executed "Chinese landing" and held fast to the vastly larger cruiser. The wounded were taken from the *Astoria*'s forecastle by triage, stretcher cases first, crews working in the darkness by voice and touch. When Joe Custer's turn came, he began descending to the destroyer's deck, then heard Greenman call from the bridge, "Able-bodied men stay aboard! We are not abandoning ship!" A spontaneous cheer went up.

The effort to save the *Astoria* called Kelly Turner's battered screening group to a proud new purpose. The *Bagley* took aboard seventy of her wounded. Playing searchlights on the water, looking for more, Sinclair's tin can shoved off and drew alongside aft. She took off more wounded and sent aboard a salvage crew of several hundred men. As the sun rose low over Florida Island, the destroyer-minesweeper *Hopkins* approached and backed up to the *Astoria*, fantail-to-fantail. Captain Greenman, blood all over him, arm in a sling, asked for a tow. A cable was tied to the base of the smaller ship's towing winch and fastened tight. A 120-volt electrical lead and a fire hose followed. Shoup and Hayes were glad for the help. If power could be restored, steam might be raised, too.

Then the *Wilson* came alongside, sidling up on the windward beam to starboard, pumping water into the fires forward. The work never proceeded without thought of a renewed enemy attack. The destroyers were repeatedly called away to investigate sonar contacts.

With the *Hopkins* towing from astern and the *Wilson*'s deck force hosing fires in the wardroom, the list steadied. Bucket brigades redoubled their back-straining labors. It was not enough. When fires below reached the shell hoists, seized by shell damage and full of ordnance meant for enemy targets, a series of explosions began weakening the ship from within like small strokes. As several of these breached the hull, the *Astoria*'s list slowly grew more serious. At ten degrees it was difficult for men to walk on deck.

Further on into the morning, the *Astoria* suffered a particularly heavy explosion deep within, probably in the forward five-inch magazine, which precautionary flooding never reached. From a deep and inaccessible void, its detonation was felt more than heard. There was a muffled cacophony of collapsing bulkheads. Bubbling to the surface on the port side came an exhalation of yellow gas, detritus of a burned-out powder magazine. Sailors on the other ships could see tendrils of smoke leaking from nearly every rivet on the ship, thousands of them. When the list grew to fifteen degrees, the shell holes above the waterline started shipping water. The makeshift bandages of mattresses and pillows shored up with timber could do only so much. When the list reached thirty degrees, all her sailors could do was watch the *Astoria* yield.

Shortly after noon, the port side gunwales were awash. The bucket brigades stood down as all hands were ordered aft. The *Buchanan,* alongside to fight fires, secured her hoses and began taking off survivors. Sailors without life jackets floated on the sea gripping discarded powder cans. Destroyers stood by to retrieve them. A survivor of the *Astoria*'s forward turrets, Charles C. Gorman, saw a man in the water near the fantail of a destroyer screaming for help. The deckhands threw him a line, but as they did so, the destroyer accelerated, evidently called away to pursue a submarine contact. The man grabbed the line but missed, and the sharks were soon on him. Gorman called it "one of the most horrible sights of all the wars I have been in."

Many more-fortunate souls were already aboard the tin cans, lying prone on their steel decks. The decks of the *Bagley* were filled with *Astoria* wounded; limbs, heads, and torsos wrapped in bandages and gauze. On the *Bagley,* those who could manage it stood at the rail, attention fixed on the floundering carcass of their onetime home. The *Astoria* was rolling to her port side, bow deep and stern raising high. On the afterdeck, a sailmaker and a special working party wrapped bodies for burial at sea until the list forced them to disband.

"Off her slanting side, men were walking slowly, deliberately, into the calm water," Joe Custer observed from the *Bagley.* "Some of them went into shallow dives, like kids off a raft. Others just walked off the edge and started their arms in motion. Some wore life jackets, others didn't. Officers' khaki mingled with seamen's dungarees. There were hundreds of heads bobbing in the water. And now the great group went into a mass crawl, like so many porpoises, toward the destroyers and lifeboats hovering nearby."

"The day was beautiful, the sea like glass and the ship was slowly overturning and sinking," a sailor on the transport *Alchiba* wrote. "Men were in the water, boats were picking them up. It would have made a gripping picture." It was just past noon on the ninth when the *Astoria* began settling by the stern. Then she was gone. The inventory of enshrouded dead piled on the afterdeck entered the sea without ceremony. For the third time within twelve hours, the temperate waters of Savo Sound absorbed the heat of an American man-of-war's incandescent ruins.

AT HIS HEADQUARTERS in Nouméa, Vice Admiral Robert Ghormley was awaiting news of the landings, about which he knew nothing, nor about the explosive events that followed. "These were endless hours and days for us," the commander of SOPAC wrote. Evidently, however, he felt no urgency to end them. He did not ask his commanders for updates. "I did not want to interfere with the operations by demanding reports when I did not know the local conditions as to ability to send dispatches," he would write. Ghormley was wise to assume the worst of his patchwork radio setup. But it would strike some as curious that he, a theater commander, equated inquiry with interference and used his unfamiliarity with the forward area to justify his continuing detachment from it.

When news of the disastrous fate of the cruisers filtered down to the landing area that morning, unloading accelerated to a frantic pace. Turner's plan was to withdraw his troop transports and cargo ships on August 9, getting them under way at first light. That decision looked more urgently necessary than ever. Already they were unguarded by carrier planes. Now their cruiser screening force had been wiped away, too.

Supplies were needed ashore, and shipboard deck space was in demand for the wounded. As stores and arms flowed to the beach, the vacated stowage was used to accommodate casualties of battle. A transport officer recalled, "Most of them were young kids sitting numbly, their semi-naked bodies black from burns and the oil of sunken ships. I doubt I will ever forget that sweet smell of burned flesh."

Before sunrise on Sunday morning, August 9, the remnants of Task Force 62 gathered for their march of shame. The antiaircraft cruiser *San Juan*, Rear Admiral Norman Scott's flagship, used her new surface radar to form up in the dark. If the new equipment was useful in retreat, there was no telling how it might have performed in battle. As the battle raged the *San Juan* stood idle, several miles to the southeast, patrolling outside the Tulagi transport anchorage. "If the *San Juan* had been up there," said Lieutenant Commander Horacio Rivero, her assistant gunnery officer, "we would have picked up [Mikawa's] ships coming down. . . . We had the only radar that could do that. And we weren't in the area where it could be used. They didn't realize what it could do." Turner was indeed unaware that the equipment in the destroyers on picket duty, the *Blue* and *Ralph Talbot*, was inadequate to cover the breadth of their patrol line. Though Admiral Ghormley had questioned the idea of using just two destroyers as pickets, he was assured that they would detect the approach of any enemy ships within twelve to fourteen miles with their SC search radar. Its range was just five thousand yards, or about half of what Crutchley believed it was, and half of the "conservative estimate" given to Admiral King by the commander of the Pacific Fleet's destroyer force, Rear Admiral Walden L. "Pug" Ainsworth.

As the sun rose, Task Force 62 steamed eastward through Lengo Channel, older, smaller, and, soon enough, wiser for the disaster of the preceding six hours. The broken-bowed *Chicago* led the *Patterson*, *Mugford*, *Ralph Talbot*, *Dewey*, and five destroyer-minesweepers along with several transports. In the second group went the rest of the transports, with the *Australia*, *San Juan*, and *Hobart* escorted by the destroyers *Selfridge*, *Henley*, *Helm*, *Bagley*, *Blue*, *Ellet*, *Wilson*, *Hull*, *Monssen*, and *Buchanan*. Shortly after the first dog watch (i.e. 1600–1800), the amphibious force, unloaded to the degree possible, got under way for Nouméa, too.

Officers on all ships struggled to comprehend what had transpired the previous night. The skipper of the *Monssen*, Commander Roland N. Smoot, saw the missed opportunity as a disgrace. "I couldn't help but keep saying to my gang around the bridge, 'Why in the devil don't we get into this? What are we doing down here waiting to be picked off one at a time? What's the matter with us?'" Smoot's comments had hindsight's clarity. As the battle raged, the only American flag officer within range of the scrap, Norman Scott, believed he was watching the two American cruiser groups firing on each other. Scott's thinking appears to have mirrored that of the five heavy cruiser commanders, four of whom, all but Captain Bode in the *Chicago,* were asleep in their sea cabins when the bugles rang. Despite the revolutionary radar eyes available to him, Scott was, according to Rear Admiral Thomas Kinkaid, "without information except for what he had seen indistinctly." As Mikawa's cruisers were rounding the bottom curve of their counterclockwise circuit of Savo Island, Scott's group had just reversed its patrol course to the south and was only fifteen thousand yards south of Mikawa's fast-firing *Chokai.* Opportunity arrived at twenty-four knots and soon was gone again.

Combat readiness simply wasn't the order of the day. Captain Riefkohl would acknowledge that he had received reports of an approaching Japanese force on the afternoon of the battle, and that he had even calculated it could well arrive that night. If that was the case, it is hard to explain why, after noting this in his night order book, he retired to his cabin.

The commanders on duty that night would have years to sort out the questions of culpability and innocence. Those whose ships had gone down fighting at least had that much honor left to hold on to. Captain Bode of the *Chicago* wasn't given such a reprieve. Had the *Chicago* been sunk, leaving him a gallant survivor, it might have discharged some of the shame. Payment for his sins of omission and commission would come due in time.

ADMIRAL KING WOULD CALL it the "blackest day of the whole war." More than a thousand Allied sailors died on the night of August 8–9. The tally grew every hour through the day on the ninth as the badly wounded succumbed. Reporting the disaster to his president, King promised that the new battleships *South Dakota* and *Washington,* as well as the light cruiser *Juneau,* would help make up for the shortage of surface combatants. They were due to arrive at Tongatabu the first week of September. King asked Nimitz to send three to five of the repaired older battleships to shore up the battered South Pacific surface fleet. Nimitz, always a serious student of costs and benefits, was eloquent by his inaction. In the meantime, Vandegrift and his men stood essentially alone.

Turner knew that the most essential need for the invasion force ashore was food, followed by land-based aircraft, ammunition, antiaircraft guns, barrage balloons, and radio construction personnel. Turner planned weekly convoys from Nouméa to keep them supplied. Running the convoys without air cover would be an unavoidable risk.

Recuperating in the *President Jackson* en route to Nouméa, Captain Greenman was surprised to find two familiar faces from the *Astoria,* his executive officer, Frank Shoup, and the newsman Joe Custer. Lying on his back in his bunk, the skipper gestured to Custer and said to his exec, "Look what we've got here!"

"A ghost!" said Shoup. The exec's entire face was thick and black with burn jelly, as were his forearms and hands, except for his fingertips. "Well, aren't we a lovely looking pair of sailors?"

"We've just been discovering we still belong to the living," Greenman said. As they lit smokes, Shoup found he couldn't bend his middle three fingers. He held the butt with his pinkie and thumb. For a week he would be under medical orders to keep his arms high, to prevent blood from flowing into the burned flesh of his hands and forearms. Greenman had eleven pieces of shrapnel in him, including one that had struck in the small of his back and missed his spine by less than an inch. While the doctors took X-rays and picked shrapnel, he began reconstructing events to prepare his after-action report, making a list of the dead, the wounded, and the living and interviewing his officers and men.

At Nouméa, Greenman forgot his own wounds and checked on his orphaned crew, asked after them, concerned himself with their mental state. He attended many of their burials at sea. As a chaplain intoned the Lord's Prayer, two men would lift the cot with crisp ceremony. The hiss of the shroud sliding over canvas was "a sound that I felt go through my bones," Joe Custer wrote. "This was the memory, I knew then, that I would never forget: the sound of bodies sliding on canvas.... The battle itself didn't convey the despair, the hopelessness of this sound, for in the turmoil and the thunder of that battle night there were sounds of life all about, of men's voices, of leather pounding steel decks: There was Life—and here was Death."

The *Astoria*'s junior chaplain, Matthew Bouterse, was haunted ever afterward by one corpse in particular: the one he had seen suspended in the mainmast, cooking above the flames. "That body burned in my dreams for weeks and it was almost completely consumed both in my dreams as it was in reality, and it came near consuming me with it."

Army personnel were generous, giving rescued sailors new shoes and olive drab fatigues. The crew of the transport *American Legion* would raise a fund to provide each survivor with a carton of cigarettes with matches, a toothbrush and toothpaste, and a dollar's worth of coupons to the ship's store.

One of the high-ranking naval officers in the area paid a visit to the hospital ship *Solace*. Walking between bunks, he talked quietly with every sailor he saw, many of them from his old ship. "When he got to me," said Keithel P. Anthony, a water tender, "he knelt down and asked, 'What ship, sailor?'

"I said, '*Astoria*.'

"And he asked, 'Were you on there when I was captain?'

"Then I saw his name and said, 'Oh, Captain Turner. My God, yes. You were the captain when we went to Japan.'"

The Savo disaster struck him personally. He grabbed Anthony by the hands, tears rolling down his cheeks, and said, "This should never have happened. If I had been aboard that ship it would never have happened." And Anthony believed him.

The Navy would do its best, for a time, to pretend it hadn't. When transports carrying survivors of the Battle of Savo Island finally returned home, the men were sent to quarantine, removed from public circulation. They had stories to tell that Admiral King would be quite happy not to see in the newspapers. Some five hundred survivors of the *Astoria, Vincennes,* and *Quincy* were held under virtual house arrest in a barracks that had been constructed on Treasure Island for the 1939 World's Fair. Marines were detailed to prevent the sailors from leaving. "Don't you say one word about the battle," they were told.

When rumors reached the detainees that their officers had been allowed to go home, they rioted. After the sacrifice they had given, it was intolerable to be treated as security risks. And so the chairs flew. According to *Astoria* survivor John C. Powell, it took more than a hundred guards to settle them down. Stories about the August 9 defeat would not hit the papers until the middle of October. It could be said that the naval high command was still learning how to calculate its risks.

THE UNITED STATES finally drew blood in the opening chapter of the Guadalcanal naval campaign when the submarine *S-44* torpedoed the heavy cruiser *Kako* as she was returning to Kavieng.* The loss of the ship did noth-

---

* Given Nimitz's fear of submarines, and the *S-44*'s success here, it is mystifying why U.S. submarines were not more aggressively deployed in the Slot. As Admiral William S. Pye, the president of the Naval War College, noted, "It would seem that this would have been an ideal area for such operations. It was like a well-baited trap. We knew the Japanese were determined to reinforce their troops and try to recapture the island. They had to come to us, and they did come, again and again, from the very beginning of our occupation. They had to traverse narrow waters" (W. S. Pye, President, Naval War College, "Comments on the Battle of Guadalcanal, November 11–15, 1942," June 5, 1943). Ghormley wrote Samuel Eliot Morison in 1950, "No submarines were under my command. After I was detached, it is possible that Halsey had some assigned to him, but I doubt it.... I asked CINCPAC for submarines once or twice, but none were made available" (Ghormley to Morison, November 15, 1950, Ghormley Papers).

ing to dim the mood at Truk. Yamamoto's chief of staff, Admiral Ugaki, was filled with a sense of prideful vindication. He would write in his diary that "the conceited British and Americans who regard the battles of the Coral Sea and Midway as supreme victories cannot say anything now. . . . The enemy must be feeling the autumn in the fortunes of war." Such verdicts were always debatable. By leaving the area, Mikawa would allow the U.S. Navy to say that the defeated American cruisers had, at the end of the day, kept the enemy from his objective.

In early August, autumn had arrived for no one quite yet. The campaign for Guadalcanal had only begun. All the same, the first battle between major naval forces in the South Pacific left no doubt whose navy was master and whose was student. For Ernest King, Chester Nimitz, and U.S. commanders all the way down the line, the residual sweet smell of the victories of spring had been borne away on a fell new breeze.

Dead sailors rose from out of the deep,
Nor looked not left or right,
But shoreward marched upon the sea,
And the moon was a riband of white.

A hundred ghosts stood on the shore
At the turn of the midnight flood.
They beckoned me with spectral hands,
And the moon was a riband of blood.

—from "Iron Bottom Bay" by
Walter A. Mahler, chaplain, USS *Astoria*

9

A New Kind of Fight

ON AUGUST 10, AT HIS HOUSE NEAR PEARL HARBOR, ADMIRAL NIMITZ hosted a dinner party with his staff in honor of a visiting dignitary, the commander of the New Zealand Air Force. He would not learn until much later that the inefficiencies of his guest's own service branch contributed to the bloody fiasco in the Battle of Savo Island. Even if there were cause to blame him, the toast Nimitz lifted that evening to the common cause would probably have sounded the same. As the Pacific Fleet commander related it to his wife, Catherine, "We drank a cocktail toast to our Marines in the Solomons, who despite losses have done magnificently. I can sleep better tonight than I could for several nights past, although I am well aware we are not out of the woods yet."

After the debacle off Savo, Nimitz was showing his knack for understatement. What Admiral Turner would call "a fatal lethargy of mind" still gripped his fighting surface fleet. After eight months of war, in which his carrier fleet had enjoyed striking successes learning its trade under fire, the surface forces still were not battle-ready. Cruiser captains were not focused on the kinetic realities of wartime. So long as the carriers were deemed too precious to risk, the campaign would hinge on getting the surface forces of the Pacific Fleet ready to win battles. Paradoxically, the problem was their overconfidence. According to Admiral Turner, the surface forces at this time were "obsessed with a strong feeling of technical and mental superiority over the enemy. In spite of ample evidence as to enemy capabilities, most of our officers and men despised the enemy and felt themselves sure victors in all encounters under any circumstances." Complacency and timidity were first cousins as contributors to defeat.

And the problems were not just psychological. They were systemic as well. The radio links between units and commands were almost always unreliable. The fruits of the wide web of air searches, performed by PBY Catalinas and B-17s operating from bases on New Caledonia, the New Hebrides, Santa Cruz, and Malaita, withered under pressure from bad weather, the shortcomings of human senses, poor coordination, and the vagaries of radio reception. Though the physical reach of the search planes was impressive— PBYs from Malaita could easily reach Rabaul, 650 miles away—aircraft from MacArthur's Southwest Pacific Command could not communicate directly with South Pacific Area naval units.

Coverage of the Slot on the afternoon of August 8 was a particularly egregious failure. Turner had asked the commander of land-based area air forces, Rear Admiral John S. McCain, to supplement MacArthur's patrol coverage of the critical waterway. As it happened, McCain's aviators were blocked by bad weather from flying the missions, but his message to that effect did not reach Turner until nearly midnight on the ninth. Had he known that his eyes in the sky could not fly, he might have alerted Crutchley, Bode, and Riefkohl to the possibility of a naval attack that night. He might also have requested that Fletcher use his carrier planes to fill the gaps in the search net.

Too often, fighter pilots could not communicate with the ships vectoring them, nor sometimes with one another. Bomber pilots couldn't contact the troops they were flying to support. Search aircraft could not communicate with ships. Squadron commodores could not reach the ship captains under their command. There was no network. In the narrow windows of time in which ignorance was costliest, all too often the components of SOPAC were fatally out of touch.

As his screen was dying off Savo, Turner found he was unable to reach directly the only flag officer on screening duty that night, the capable Norman Scott. The TBS radio in Turner's flagship, the *McCawley,* was partially shorted, and was effective only to about eight miles. Getting to Scott required him to go through Riefkohl on *Vincennes.* Turner couldn't raise Ghormley, either. According to Ghormley, Turner's radio frequency "could not be heard by the Commander of South Pacific Force. It is doubtful if all unit commanders of Task Force 61 could hear more than fragments of the blind transmissions on that frequency." Ghormley could not hear Fletcher, either, and though the *McCawley*'s communications suite had been bolstered with the addition of sixteen field radios, Turner could not regularly monitor Fletcher's frequency.

Plain bad luck joined wholesale system failure in plaguing the Americans. When the New Zealand Air Force search plane transmitted its sighting report at 10:25 a.m. on August 8, the radio station at Fall River was shut down, under air attack. After the pilot, Bill Stutt, landed the plane, he learned that his transmission had gone unreceived. He sped by jeep to the operations hut and delivered it in person. It sat there for nearly two hours before being sent to Southwest Pacific headquarters in Brisbane, and languished there for another three and a half hours before being routed to Canberra for area broadcast, and to Pearl Harbor for relay to the fleet. Turner did not learn of this important sighting of unidentified ships until the evening of the attack.

Waiting for Ghormley to approve his request to withdraw, Fletcher was still standing by with the carrier task force, some 150 miles from Savo Island and well within striking range of Mikawa. When the approval came and the carriers finally did turn south at 4:30 a.m. on the ninth, Fletcher knew nothing of the opportunity. Long into the morning as his carriers withdrew, Admiral Fletcher "was completely uninformed regarding the surface actions in Ironbottom Sound during their progress," according to his subordinate Kinkaid. "Had timely and accurate information of the surface actions been received," Kinkaid wrote, "it is possible that the carrier air groups could have made the dawn air attack on the Japanese cruiser force which Mikawa so greatly feared." The carriers hadn't yet flown. They simply never learned that an enemy was near. Mikawa got away with his kills.

Among Vandegrift's men on Guadalcanal, adverse assessments of the Navy's fighting spirit were not hard to find in the coming weeks. It wasn't just marines who had doubts. Few were satisfied with the way the carriers were being employed. "The way these carriers operate seemed chickenhearted as hell to me," the *Atlanta*'s Lloyd Mustin, now a lieutenant commander, wrote on August 8. "Ended the day down off San Cristobal, pretty goddamn far from Tulagi for fighter support, if you ask me. I wonder when we will ever get the nerve to really *go after* these bastards, seek them out to destroy them." A line lieutenant from the *Wasp*, Thomas R. Weschler, said that his captain, Forrest Sherman, "was always trying to get Admiral Noyes's attention about the kinds of things Admiral Noyes ought to be thinking about"—including reversing Fletcher's decision to withdraw from Savo Sound after the battle of August 9. As the tactical commander of the carrier force, Noyes held an almost superfluous position given that Fletcher flew his flag in a carrier, too. Noyes seemed hesitant to embrace a leadership role. According to Weschler, "Three times during the night, Captain Sherman said to Admiral Noyes, 'I recommend you tell Admiral Fletcher that we should turn around and go back in there. They need our support.' But Admiral Noyes never sent a single one of those messages forward." Weschler, who would serve as an aide to Vice Admiral Arleigh Burke and ascend to three-star rank himself, was unimpressed with Fletcher's deputy. "I always thought Admiral Noyes was sort of afraid of his own shadow. . . . He'd walk up and down the quarterdeck, in greens, wearing his aviation pigskin gloves, and that's really the only time I ever saw him. I always had the impression of him as being sort of a mannequin, rather than really being a flesh-and-blood naval officer who was in the thick of decisions and ready to take over and set the course."

It was clear how far the fleet needed to go to beat the Japanese at a game the Americans thought they owned. The Navy entered the war with a xenophobic professional chauvinism prevailing at almost every level. They would have to overcome it in order to learn how to fight: to exploit new technologies; to change the way crews lived and worked aboard ship; to procure ordnance that actually exploded. More fundamentally, a spirit of "battle-mindedness" was needed in its commanders. Those who had been born with a fighter's instinct would need little help. But for the majority of officers and men who had never experienced the sudden violence of ship-to-ship combat before, the Battle of Savo Island was a deeply unsettling lesson.

The U.S. Marines had won the initial draw at Guadalcanal and strung a tight defensive perimeter around the airfield. A thousand miles to the west, the Japanese had beaten MacArthur to New Guinea. With the parallel Navy and Army campaigns now joined in earnest, the critical points of contact with the enemy were established along 9 degrees South latitude. The lines of battle in the South Seas had been drawn.

FOR SOME OFFICERS, the hurdles to clear en route to getting their ships ready to fight were quite simple. One was no more complicated than getting the kids from Georgia off the battle telephones. The terse lingo of command had to run smoothly through a ship's lines of communication. Regionally accented speech could block the instant recognition that a fighting crew needed in a scrap. Commander Joseph C. Wylie, the executive officer of the destroyer *Fletcher,* recalled that after the influx of patriotic volunteers to the fleet had taken place, only one in five of his men had ever been to sea before. Among them was a group of kids from the backwoods of the Peach State who had managed to sidestep boot camp altogether. They were fine and useful behind a squirrel gun, hunting in their native swamplands. In fights on larger waters, they were liable to foul things up. "We had to be very careful to have all or none of the Georgia boys on the telephone circuit, so that they could understand each other and we could understand them," Wylie said. "There were a lot of special arrangements we had to make."

One of them involved the communication of relative bearings. Typically these are given in terms of an imaginary compass circumscribing the ship. Zero degrees is dead ahead, 180 degrees astern. "These kids had never heard of that and we didn't have time to teach them. So we used clock bearings like the aviators had adopted. . . . If it was out on the starboard side, three o'clock, do you see?"

One winter in Manila in the mid-1930s, Wylie walked into the wardroom of his ship, the heavy cruiser *Augusta* (Captain Chester W. Nimitz commanding), and encountered a "fist-banging argument" between two of the ship's up-and-coming young officers. At issue was what it took to become skilled at rifle or pistol marksmanship. One officer, Lloyd Mustin, said that only someone born with a special gift could learn to do it well. The other, a marine named Lewis B. Puller, said, "I can take any dumb son of a bitch and teach him to shoot." Mustin would go on to become one of the Navy's pioneers in radar-controlled gunnery. Puller would ascend to general, the most decorated U.S. Marine in history. Gesturing to Wylie standing in the doorway, Chesty Puller declared, "I can even teach him."

A ten-dollar bet ensued. The next time the *Augusta*'s marine detachment found time to do their annual qualifications at the rifle range, Wylie was Puller's special guest. And by the end of the experiment, he was the proud owner of a Marine medal designating him an expert rifleman.

The experience helped Wylie understand both native gifts and teachable skills and predisposed him to work with the rural kids under him. Now he could smile when the sighting of an aircraft approaching at a distant but undetermined range came through the *Fletcher*'s bridge phones as, "Hey, Cap'n, here's another one of them thar *aero*-planes, but don't you fret none. She's a *fur piece* yet." Wylie was a good enough leader to appreciate what the recruits from the countryside brought to the game. "They were highly motivated," he said. "They just came to fight."

Back home, a great gathering was still under way. The stately pace of a global war allowed time for the majesty of a mass mobilization to build. Few of the untraveled young men who made their first venture west ever forgot its impressions. A Pullman car clicked and rolled through the slash pine and swamps of the South, and then into other terrain. "The moon rose, but still there were only the pines, a light here and there, a crossing bell, headlights of a car, then darkness again," a new second lieutenant with the 1st Marine Division wrote. Bored but too anxious to sleep, recruits in dining cars played cards into the night. Others, foreheads leaning on windowpanes, watched the nighttime landscape roll unendingly past. From Augusta to Atlanta, then Birmingham, St. Louis, to the high plains, across the Rockies, and toward the Pacific's great frontier.

Nimitz's successor as chief of the Navy's personnel office, Rear Admiral Randall Jacobs, lamented that "The Nation has passed through an era of soft living and rampant individualism" that resulted in a "staggering" rate of rejection among new recruits for physical shortcomings. But the flood tide was rising. On December 7, the Navy had 325,095 personnel, plus more than 70,000 marines. Two years later the fleet's muster rolls would carry more than 2,250,000 names, and the Marine Corps 391,000 more.

Routed to training centers in San Diego or Michigan, finding their ships at Norfolk or Mare Island, shaking down and running speed trials off Maine or Puerto Rico, the new recruits made their homes in ships that would steam to victory, and carry kids and men and admirals alike to their death. A navy was still in the making, its day of triumph unknown, the men who were forming it yet unformed themselves, but motivated and carrying west. As Marine Corps aviator Samuel Hynes would observe, "They go to war because it's impossible not to. Because a current is established in society, so swift, flowing toward war, that every young man who steps into it is carried downstream."

Standing in its rolling surge, directing traffic, was Bob Hagen. A newly minted ensign himself, Hagen was assigned to duty as a service school selection officer at Great Lakes Naval Training Station. He and his enlisted helpers sorted wheat from chaff, assigning recruits to advanced training based on their tested aptitudes. Giving six lectures a week to thousands of boots, he explained what water tenders did, and gunner's mates, and yeomen. The tests would determine whether a kid saw colors well enough to be a signalman, or discerned tones sharply enough to be a radioman. Hagen and his staff collated the results and reviewed each applicant's preferences. Those with the highest scores were routed to specialty training that filled the Navy's most acute needs. Now and then a mandate would come down from on high. Once Hagen was told to find men to be pharmacist's mates. Then the call came to fill out some newly forming construction battalions. Kids who had come of age on farms driving trucks found themselves in demand and quickly wore the chevrons of senior petty officers.

Hagen's commanding officer was out of the office on the day that five tall youngsters were ushered in before him. "I thought I was in a forest," Hagen said. "These big oak trees, they were all over six feet, probably." They told him they had all been promised duty in the same ship. Their names rang a bell with Hagen, because the paper in his hometown of San Francisco had carried news of their enlistment. The five boys were from Waterloo, Iowa, the sons of Alleta and Tom Sullivan. George and Frank were four-year veterans already. Discharged before Pearl Harbor, they reenlisted after the attack and lobbied to serve together with their three younger brothers, along with two pals from their hometown motorcycle club. Ahead of their arrival at Great Lakes in January, George wrote the Navy Department, "As a bunch, there is no-body that can beat us.... We would all do our best to be as good as any other sailors in the Navy.... We will make a team together that can't be beat."

Five brothers serving on the same ship seemed like an awful idea to Hagen. With all the finesse of a twenty-two-year-old who was quite sure of his judgment, he sent the Sullivans away, saying he couldn't help them. "I didn't think much of it," Hagen said, "but a couple of days later my boss came up with smoke coming out of both ears." The commander told Hagen that the Navy's well-publicized promise would be honored. All branches of the service were hungry for recruits. The Sullivan boys held all the cards.

"Well, this doesn't make very good sense to me," Hagen said. The commander turned on his uppity ensign and said, "Hagen, do what you are told to do in the Navy. You are twenty-two years old and you don't have to think."

The Sullivans were mediocre students, standing apart in Iowa's Protestant cornrows largely by virtue of their Catholicism. But with their wicked talent for pranks and an untroubled outlook that seemed out of step with the Depression that had limited their prospects, they were more at home at the pool hall than in catechism. At home they were toughs, sons of a hard-pressed Irish railroad worker. They kept the east side of Waterloo "straight and clean," said one resident. "Police didn't go in our area much, but the boys took care of everything." Their impulse to enforce justice had been triggered anew by the attack on Hawaii. The Japanese had killed one of their own there: a kid named Bill Ball from Fredericksburg, just forty miles up U.S. 63. Every family had its Bill Ball, a personal loss inflicted by an alien enemy an ocean away. The Sullivans resolved to deal with the Japanese like they had their rival thugs on Adams Street. "I guess our minds are made up, aren't they fellows?" the oldest brother, George, said. "And when we go in, we want to go in together. If the worst comes to worst, why we'll all have gone down together."

At Pier Two in the New York Navy Yard, they found their new home, the USS *Juneau*. She was a sleek light cruiser of the new *Atlanta* class, lightly armored but fitted with a formidable array of antiaircraft guns. The first four *Atlanta*s would all fight in the Solomons. At the commissioning, the Sullivans were celebrities, posing for the wire services in buttoned-up peacoats and flat caps. On liberty at Jack Dempsey's lounge on Broadway, they were photographed with the heavyweight champ. The *Juneau*'s captain, Lyman Knute Swenson, was ambivalent about the publicity, the benefits of which were fleeting and dwarfed by the risk of a concentrated tragedy. But celebrity was an intoxicant, for the brothers and the armed service alike.

Departing the Navy yard, the camouflage-dappled *Juneau* steamed around the Battery and headed up the Hudson River for the Iona Island ammunition depot, where she would load her magazines for battles unknown.

BOB HAGEN'S OWN first shipboard assignment after his tour at Great Lakes was over was the *Aaron Ward,* a new destroyer headed to the Pacific. Commander Orville F. Gregor was reputed to be the dictatorial type. Hagen's new duties as assistant communications officer included filling a new job that few officers, not even the *Aaron Ward*'s captain, yet understood—the job of radar officer.

The idea of aiming a pulse of radio energy at a target and measuring its range and compass bearing by the nature of the echo had the potential to revolutionize the ancient art of ships putting ordnance on target. Radar, or "radio detection and ranging," was first put into practice by the Royal Navy. The technology came to the United States eventually through the Naval Research Laboratory and the Massachusetts Institute of Technology, in partnership with engineers in private industry, Bell Labs and RCA earliest among them. Two opposite misconceptions impeded its introduction. The fleet's Luddites clung to the idea that because radar had not figured in World War I's Battle of Jutland, which was the textbook case study at the Naval Academy and the war colleges, it must not be terribly important. Against them railed evangelists who believed radar was, as a historian of the technology put it, a "magic box on which one need only press the button and the battle was won."

The first officers to be selected for MIT's fire-control course had helped design the technology for naval use and knew its potentials and limitations. Alfred G. Ward, who would join the battleship *North Carolina,* had helped develop electric-powered, servo-controlled guns. Lloyd Mustin, the debate opponent to Lewis "Chesty" Puller and range instructor to Joseph Wylie, had conceived of gyro-stabilized antiaircraft guns. As a graduate student in MIT's electrical engineering program, he and Lieutenant Commander Rivero of the *San Juan* helped develop the computer that calculated how far an antiaircraft gunner had to lead his target to hit it. As the assistant gunnery officer on the *Atlanta,* Mustin would have ample time to refine his theories. As the first radar officer at the Bureau of Ordnance, Rivero had the job of routing new radar sets from the factory to whichever ship was on hand, in port for overhaul or repair, to receive it.

Installing technology was one thing. Encouraging warriors to discover a second-nature knack for using it was another. The Navy was slow to move beyond the period of high secrecy that surrounded the research. "There wasn't any real training program," Rivero said. "That's one mistake we made. We didn't think that far ahead."

In 1942, the attitudes of most line officers toward this fledgling technology spanned the full range of know-nothingdom, from raw ignorance to well-considered dismissal. Hanson Baldwin regarded the typical naval officer of the day as "a narrow man, with fixed and unassailable ideas of politics, life, and society; too often—though master of the details—he cannot see the woods because of the trees." The problem ran straight to the top. "Our flag officers and senior captains are old compared with those of other navies; far too many of them suffer from nervous or heart disabilities; to stand the great strain of heavy responsibilities they should quite clearly be ten years younger." As Kelly Turner admitted, "Neither I nor any of my staff knew anything about radar, except by reputation." By the time the technology reached the fleet, a more capable version, the SG or "Sugar George" microwave surface-search radar, was already making it obsolete and ensuring the continued puzzlement of officers responsible for tactical action. The SG's shorter wavelength—10 centimeters as opposed to 150 in the SC search set—gave it better resolution. Coupled with a motorized rotating receiver and a new cathode display known as a Plan Position Indicator (PPI), it generated a more visually intuitive, 360-degree overhead view centered on the transmitting ship. But technology advanced much faster than training or tactical doctrine did.

The officers in Bob Hagen's ship, the *Aaron Ward,* were slowly learning the foibles of the strange new piece of equipment in their chart room. The destroyer's SC radar required its operator to point the antenna manually by turning a hand wheel. Its "A scope" displayed any contacts located on that particular bearing as spikes on an x–y axis, where x denoted range and y the strength of the signal and hence the size of the object. If there were many targets to track, the radar officer would be a busy man, slewing the transmitter back and forth to acquire them and plotting the data by hand. When the machinery failed, it required an inordinate amount of time for radiomen and electricians to put it back in order. In one respect it outperformed hopes: Because the boxy receiver-indicator console drew a lot of power and accumulated its heat, it offered a handy surface on which to keep a coffeepot warm.

Untroubled with new technology to master, the Japanese had refined the task of optical target spotting to lethal effect. After Mikawa's masterly performance in the Battle of Savo Island, Admiral King's staff could do little else but marvel: "It is to be hoped that we will profit by their example and in the future turn against them the lessons they have so ably taught us."

Admiral King saw the need to relearn his trade from the ground up. He understood that in the art of war, amateurs talk tactics but professionals talk logistics. Ernest King was a professional. "The war has been variously termed a war of production and a war of machines," he wrote. "Whatever else it is, so far as the United States is concerned, it is a war of logistics. The ways and means to supply and support our forces in all parts of the world—including the Army of course—have presented problems nothing short of colossal and have required the most careful and intricate planning. The profound effect of logistics on our strategic decisions are not likely to have full significance to those who do not have to traverse the tremendous distances in the Pacific. It is no easy matter in a global war to have the right materials in the right places at the right times in the right quantities."

The path from Nouméa northward into the southern Solomons had an important waypoint in the New Hebrides, at the base of Espiritu Santo, about 625 miles south of Guadalcanal. On August 10, Ghormley designated it as a strongpoint for the support and reinforcement effort. Espiritu Santo, even less developed than Nouméa, offered plenty of space for expansion: wharves, cargo piers, airstrips, and anything else the 6th and 7th construction battalions would find the means to build. Rear Admiral McCain immediately saw its value as an airfield site; he directed the construction and ordered a five-thousand-foot runway cut ino the coconut plantation and jungle. Ghormley rerouted to Espiritu all of the equipment—a tug, two barges, a pontoon wharf, and ship-mooring buoys—once earmarked for the occupation of Santa Cruz, an original objective of Task One that was canceled in favor of landings on Guadalcanal. He directed construction of a large wharf with a timber crib sturdy enough to support a heavy crane, several piers for the rapid handling of light cargo, and a second channel nearer the airfield. The focal point of the entire logistical apparatus, of course, was the island that was the newest and most hazard-ridden property of the U.S. Marine Corps.

On August 12, a McCain staffer landed on Guadalcanal in a PBY Catalina patrol plane, went ashore for an inspection, and declared the unimproved twenty-six-hundred-foot airstrip on a broad grassy savanna fit to receive fighter aircraft. Later that day, the airfield was named in honor of the well-loved commander of a Marine bombing squadron, Major Lofton R. Henderson, shot down and killed while attacking the carrier *Hiryu* on June 4, the decisive day off Midway. Without carrier aircraft to cover them, and with the airdrome at Espiritu Santo still just "a gleam in Ghormley's eye," the men on Guadalcanal would have to establish their very own air corps to defend themselves. It would soon be known as "the Cactus Air Force."

Marine engineers co-opted steamrollers, tractors, and other abandoned Japanese assets to make the airfield serviceable for heavier strike aircraft such as Dauntless dive-bombers and Avenger torpedo bombers. Caches of ordnance and ammunition were buried along the perimeter of the strip. The violently variable weather made it difficult to operate. "It was dry and would raise a cloud of dust that you could see a mile," Ernest M. Eller, one of Admiral Nimitz's staffers, said. "It would block out any other plane coming along. An hour later it would rain, and you would sliver in just as if you were in a mud hole. Then the hot sun would dry the field within another hour or two." As often as not in the early days, pilots would have to contend with Japanese sniper fire as they taxied or made their approach.

They were bitter about the Navy's abandonment of them, and would tell stories ever afterward about how they persisted despite it. Well within extended range of the Japanese base at Rabaul, the marines had to contend daily with raids by Japanese bombers. The harassment did not end, not by day or by night. Japanese mortarmen and the odd artillery piece, too, worked long hours making their lives miserable. The small contingent of Japanese on Guadalcanal had fled to the hills when the Americans landed. They would serve mainly as a harassing force while awaiting reinforcements from Rabaul.

The pattern of fighting through June 1942 had suggested that carriers would play the deciding role in the naval war against Japan. What kind of fight this South Seas campaign would become remained an open question. Carriers would be important, but after the Battle of Savo Island it was clear that the "gun club" didn't need disbanding yet. Admiral Ghormley knew in his bones the power of the battleships. His career was rooted in the big-gun fleet. He had served in the *Nevada,* the *Oklahoma,* in a prominent staff job in the Battle Force, and then in the *Nevada* again as her commander.

The fight that was taking shape in the southern Solomons was going to be neither a single, climactic World War I–style daylight slugfest nor a repeat of Midway, a dance of search planes and long-range naval air strikes. The South Pacific Forces would draw strength from a foundation of supply and re-inforcement built far south of the point of contact with the enemy. And the point of the spear that dueled with the enemy would be the surface fleet—destroyers, cruisers, and battleships, aided by aircraft, whose job would be to seize control of the seaways from the enemy. Neither the Navy nor the Marines had fought a war like this before. Its finer points would be developed, tested, and adjusted on the fly over time.

On August 12, Captain Samuel Jenkins, skipper of the *Atlanta,* called together his officers and shared the story of what had happened four nights before, of how in the fog-swaddled night near Savo Island, flares, then search-lights, then plunging fire left a powerful squadron of U.S. heavy cruisers burning and helpless. As the *Atlanta* made circles with the carriers north of Nouméa, the inactivity bothered those who felt the ache for revenge. The fight for Guadalcanal had only begun. At least one report reached SOPAC suggesting that as many as forty Japanese destroyers were based at Rabaul. "There is going to be a bitch of a night session up here, some dark night, with torpedoes in the water as thick as flies," Lloyd Mustin confided to his diary.

It was intolerable to battle-minded men that the aircraft carrier task force that was ostensibly covering the landing force and its escorts should forgo a sunrise counterattack on Mikawa on August 9. With more tempting targets available to the Japanese—transports and cargomen vulnerably shuttling between the Solomons and Nouméa—Mustin considered the idea "completely fantastic" that Japanese planes would be able to fly all the way down from Rabaul for a long-shot strike against carriers that were well defended and seldom precisely located. He didn't think much of the fighting spirit of his superiors. "They're so goddamned scared their lousy carriers will get hurt that the whole effective Pacific Fleet hauls ass at the mention of a few Jap planes," Mustin wrote. "We have no high commanders capable of playing ball in the same league with many of the Japs," he continued. "I wish to God Wild Bill Halsey were back here to put a little fire, drive, and action into things."

The *Enterprise, Saratoga,* and *Wasp,* each of them irreplaceable in the near term, spent several days cruising the Coral Sea, four hundred miles southeast of the Solomons, taking turns drinking from the oilers *Platte* and *Kaskaskia.* Their screen, including the *Atlanta,* stayed faithfully by in their defense.

Wags in the Royal Navy were said to joke that if they ever came to blows with their cousins on the other side of the Atlantic, "all their fleet would have to do to insure victory would be to remain safely at ease in port for six weeks; at the end of that time they could sally forth to find an American Navy exhausted by its own frenetic maneuverings." The frenetic idling was never greater than in the early days off Guadalcanal. As Admiral Ghormley occupied himself with the puzzle of supplying Vandegrift's men, and as the carriers burned fuel and refueled north of Nouméa, a week passed then another without further appearances by the Imperial Japanese Navy.

Finding planes to send to Henderson Field had been no easy thing given the jealous way Fletcher's carriers and Ghormley's island bases husbanded their aircraft, but on August 20, word spread through General Vandegrift's perimeter that air reinforcements were finally on the way. Nimitz directed their deployment to the South Pacific as soon as the pilots designated to fly them finished their training. Ferried from Fiji by the escort carrier *Long Island,* two squadrons of Marine Corps pilots made a short two-hundred-mile hop to the island and landed amid cheers. Fresh from flight school and with scarcely a carrier landing among them, they included nineteen F4F Wildcats under Captain John L. Smith (Marine Fighting Squadron 223), and a dozen SBD Dauntlesses under Major Richard C. Mangrum (Marine Bombing Squadron 232).

Marines driving jeeps raced the planes down the runway as they arrived. "Our planes had come at last!—only thirty-one, but in that joyful moment they seemed to darken the sky," a photographer, Thayer Soule, wrote. General Vandegrift, a reserved, even-tempered southern gentleman, was giddy. The arrival of the planes rated as "one of the most beautiful sights of my life." With tears welling in his eyes, Vandegrift greeted Mangrum as he climbed down from the cockpit of his Dauntless, saying, "Thank God you have come."

"That night we went to bed early and slept well," Soule wrote. "The fleet that had sailed away so long ago had not forgotten us after all." The preceding two weeks had seemed long indeed. The coming twenty-four hours would be longer still. For the Japanese chose that moment, the night after the pilots landed, to make their first concentrated stab at evicting the defenders of Henderson Field.

10

The Tokyo Express

CABLING JOSEPH STALIN TO APOLOGIZE FOR MISSING A CONFERENCE in Moscow, President Roosevelt acknowledged the urgency of the Eastern Front and declared, as politics seemed to require, that "our real enemy is Germany." As Soviets reeled before the assaults of the Wehrmacht, and the transatlantic convoys meant to save them withered under U-boat attack, FDR made the case for hope in the Pacific. "We have gained, I believe, a toehold in the Southwest Pacific from which the Japanese will find it very difficult to dislodge us." The Japanese Army's first concentrated attempt to do so began taking shape on the night of August 19, when a detachment of shock troops under Colonel Kiyonao Ichiki snuck ashore some fifteen miles east of Henderson Field.

The commander who carried Ichiki's men to the island was a destroyerman who would become famous for running Japan's fast resupply and reinforcement missions by cover of night, soon to be referred to as the "Tokyo Express": Rear Admiral Raizo Tanaka. He had studied the difficult novelties of amphibious operations. Without either surprise or a strong softening-up by naval or air bombardment, he "foresaw grave difficulties in my task and knew that we would suffer heavy losses." He deemed his orders to bring down the Ichiki detachment "utterly unreasonable." But he was underappreciating the extent of the Japanese command of the night. Under cover of darkness, Tanaka arrived with six destroyers off Taivu Point and put Ichiki ashore with nine hundred men.

Once assigned to seize Midway Island, Ichiki's 28th Regiment was a veteran outfit whose experience and success would work against them now. As a company commander serving in China, Ichiki had helped instigate the infamous Marco Polo Bridge Incident in July 1937, a clash between Japanese and Chinese troops that some historians would identify as the first hostility of World War II. His intelligence service had warned him that frontal attacks on Guadalcanal might be costly. But Ichiki's reputation preceded him, and that reputation, and the recklessness it inspired, would lead to his fall. Some called it "victory disease." Ichiki expected a quick victory. As he advanced boldly on the Marine positions, he regarded them as easy marks.

Vandegrift knew enemy reinforcements had landed after one of his patrols routed an enemy probe and recovered their documents and diaries. Where their main strength lay no one knew, but the appearance of Japanese first-teamers was an alarming sign. Until Colonel Ichiki's arrival, the marines had contended in most instances with poorly equipped labor battalions, or "termites" as they called them. Now experienced Japanese assault troops were out there somewhere. It worked on men's nerves.

The night had a hundred ways to provoke a sentry to a startled fusillade: the rustling of lizards and crabs through the undergrowth; the birds whose calls sounded like wood blocks smacking together. Vandegrift's largely unseasoned men had to cure themselves of the impulse to promiscuous firing. To keep their positions concealed, they learned the rigors of field discipline: discipline with their triggers, with their mess equipment, with their sanitation and patrol doctrine. They cultivated the patience to remain still and silent until the need came to uncork a sudden, lethal attack.

Late in the night of August 20, near a tidal lagoon that Martin Clemens and his scouts had christened Alligator Creek, Marine sentries heard movements, a buildup of some kind. Soon thereafter, in the first dark hours of the following day, a green flare burst overhead, then, spilling out of the brush and across the sandbar in Alligator Creek, came an assault force of two hundred Imperial Army shock troops.

Vandegrift's riflemen were ready. Supported by well-placed anti-tank guns firing exploding canister rounds, and with carefully drawn lines of interlocking fire, Colonel Pollock's 2nd Battalion, 1st Marine Regiment, stopped Ichiki cold. The Japanese assault faltered then collapsed as artillery and mortar fire ripped into them. Admiral Tanaka likened the attack on the fortified position to "a housefly's attacking a giant tortoise." A counterattack by Colonel Clifton B. Cates's 1st Regiment reserve began the rout. Lieutenant Colonel Lenard B. Cresswell's 1st Battalion led the destruction of the trapped Japanese unit. Enveloped near the mouth of the lagoon, Ichiki's men died by the score under attack by four Wildcats from Henderson, whose machine guns were a welcome addition to the order of battle for the marines. A trio of Cates's tanks rolled in that afternoon. "We watched these awful machines as they plunged across the spit and into the edge of the grove. It was fascinating to see them bustling amongst the trees, pivoting, turning, spitting sheets of yellow flame. It was like a comedy of toys, something unbelievable, to see them knocking over palm trees, which fell slowly, flushing the running figures of men from underneath their treads, following and firing at the fugitives," the correspondent Richard Tregaskis wrote. By 5 p.m., about sixteen hours after it had started, most of the Japanese force, more than eight hundred men, lay dead, for thirty-four marines killed and seventy-five wounded. Japanese prisoners numbered just fifteen. Only a few escaped back into the jungle, no doubt to tell sober tales of the Marine Corps' proficiency with massed defensive firepower. Observing vacantly as the disaster unfolded, Ichiki himself appears to have been a suicide, last seen by one of his men walking straight toward the American lines.

At first Major Mangrum, the dive-bomber squadron commander, missed the significance of the affair. "We thought it was just a Fourth of July celebration about a mile and a half from us, and went on to sleep. We found the next day that our Marines had killed some 830-odd Japs over there, and then we figured that it was really somebody shooting at somebody!" The stout performance of Vandegrift's men enabled Mangrum to get about his own work without delay. His pilots flew four-plane patrols all the next day to acquaint themselves with the area. August 20 and 21 were a boost to marines who had been largely unsupported by U.S. airpower for two weeks. Boasting their first victory in close-quarters fighting and now in possession of an air force all their own, they readied themselves for the struggle ahead with hopeful and defiant hearts.

When news of the Army's failure reached Truk, it "shook Yamamoto," wrote one of his destroyer captains, Tameichi Hara. Meeting in his cabin aboard the super battleship *Yamato* with task force commanders Vice Admiral Chuichi Nagumo and Vice Admiral Nobutake Kondo, Yamamoto directed the Combined Fleet to gather its considerable assets and head south to confront what was clearly a significant commitment of American force. He drew up a complex and powerful order of battle. Down from Truk, into the seas east of the Solomons chain, would steam four separate combat task forces: a Striking Force under Nagumo with the large carriers *Shokaku* and *Zuikaku* and their escorts; Rear Admiral Hiroaki Abe's Vanguard Group, with the battleships *Hiei* and *Kirishima,* three heavy cruisers, a light cruiser, and six destroyers; the Diversionary Group, consisting of the light carrier *Ryujo,* a cruiser, and two destroyers; and the Support Group, with the old battleship *Mutsu,* a seaplane tender, and four destroyers.

Clinging to an unrebuttable belief that the destroyed landing force under Colonel Ichiki would somehow yet seize the airfield, the 17th Army decided to send down the remaining fifteen hundred men of Ichiki's regiment. An additional thousand Japanese marines—a Special Naval Landing Force— were embarked in three transports escorted by eight destroyers of Admiral Tanaka's Destroyer Squadron 2. The Japanese carriers would operate east of the Slot, sweeping the seas of their American counterparts, then turn in support of Tanaka's landing force. This Japanese force nearly rivaled in combat power the group sent to seize Midway. Neither side had a firm idea where the other's carriers were. Fletcher and his flattops were steaming about 250 miles southeast of Guadalcanal, staying beyond range of enemy air attack, where they could refuel when necessary and send air search patrols over the Slot to supplement the work of the longer-range PBYs and B-17s. Scout pilots flying from Henderson Field faced maddening technical difficulties. One day their radio communications were in perfect tune two hundred miles out from base; the next day they were utterly garbled or silent within twenty miles.

Effectively, two parallel but separate naval campaigns were developing. The seas immediately around Guadalcanal would be the setting for a campaign of surface fights between light forces for control of the seas. Farther out to sea, generally to the north and east of the Solomons, a less geographically constrained campaign would be fought as the roaming aircraft carrier forces made themselves selectively available to duel, striking with their planes but never coming within sight of each other.

On the night of August 21, the marines on Guadalcanal were witness to a quick, fiery encounter between light naval forces in Savo Sound. On that night the destroyers *Blue* and *Henley,* having brought two cargo ships into Guadalcanal, caught an enemy destroyer, the *Kawakaze,* bent on intercepting the U.S. cargomen, which had been sighted that afternoon. Before the American duo knew anything was awry, the *Kawakaze* had put six torpedoes in the water. The radar set on the *Blue* had only just revealed the enemy's presence about three miles away when the American ship was racked by a torpedo. The blast removed most of her stern, killing nine men and leaving her to be scuttled the next night.

But Admiral Yamamoto had much more than destroyer skirmishes to worry about. The assignment to send his carriers against a U.S. island air-drome when the American carriers were unaccounted for must have given him an unsettling flashback to June, when he had tackled a similar dual threat, Midway and three enemy carriers, and paid a heavy price. If Yamamoto's carriers met the Americans again, it would be a rematch between the commanders Fletcher and Nagumo, who had traded blows eleven weeks earlier off Midway.

11

A Function at the Junction

GHORMLEY SUSPECTED YAMAMOTO WAS SENDING A POWERFUL welcoming party to greet the newly ensconced aviators at Henderson. An intelligence report from Nimitz's headquarters ventured a "rough guess," based on aircraft and submarine reconnaissance, that a heavy Japanese striking force of carriers and battleships could arrive in the area around August 24. This guess had the virtue of being right on the money. Ghormley warned Fletcher, "Indications point strongly to enemy attack in force on Cactus area 23–26 August. From available intelligence...presence of carriers possible but not confirmed.... Important fueling be conducted soonest possible and if practicable one carrier task force at a time retiring for that purpose."

On the morning of the twenty-third, a search plane flying from Ndeni, in the Santa Cruz Islands, sighted Tanaka's southbound transports. Pilots from Henderson Field and from Fletcher's flagship, the *Saratoga*, winged out to intercept but failed to find them. With this, Fletcher thought that the momentum toward battle had dissipated. That evening, with no targets in sight and with the fleet intelligence summary misleadingly placing Nagumo's carriers at Truk, he followed Ghormley's recommendation and sent the *Wasp* and her escorts south to refuel. Hundreds of miles to the north, the powerful Japanese task forces were making tracks in his direction.

The next morning, McCain's PBY Catalinas found what they were looking for: Japanese carriers. The light carrier *Ryujo* was 280 miles northwest of Fletcher's position. Although he was deprived of the *Wasp*, Fletcher would have his rematch with Nagumo. More than two weeks after the disaster of August 9, the third major aircraft carrier battle of the war was in the offing.

The Americans and the Japanese were well practiced in the new business of carrier combat, from the tricky dance of reconnaissance to the difficult choreography of flight and hangar deck operations, with ordnance gangs and plane handlers muscling their planes into the cycle: load, spot, launch, strike. When planes were fortunate enough to find targets, attacks succeeded or failed on individual pilot skill, the effectiveness of defenses and fighter interception, shiphandling, and, always and ever, luck.

Fletcher deployed his two carriers in separate groups ten miles apart. The *Enterprise* steamed at the center of a protective circle four thousand yards across that included the battleship *North Carolina,* the heavy cruiser *Portland,* the *Atlanta,* and six destroyers. The *Saratoga* was screened by the heavy cruisers *Minneapolis* and *New Orleans* and five destroyers.

A large burden of any carrier commander was deciding when to strike. At 9:35 a.m., having *Ryujo* but suspecting larger quarry in the area, Fletcher declined to launch his attack. At 11:28 a.m., a second sighting of the *Ryujo* arrived. Only two hours later, when aircraft from the *Ryujo* appeared on the *Saratoga*'s radar, bound to strike Guadalcanal, did Fletcher order the flagship's strike planes to launch. He threw most of his air group after the *Ryujo,* thirty SBD Dauntless dive-bombers and eight TBF Avenger torpedo bombers. Soon the Catalinas were reporting more carriers, sixty miles northeast of the *Ryujo.* Thereafter a flood of sighting reports deluged Fletcher. There were three distinct groups of enemy ships within 225 miles—two carrier groups and a cruiser vanguard. Fletcher knew Japanese snoopers had likely sighted him. Nagumo received a sighting report just after two, and an hour later his aviators from the *Zuikaku* and *Shokaku* were loaded and airborne. On the wing, in reciprocal directions, flew the opposing strike groups that would decide the outcome of the day.

After 3 p.m., fliers from the *Enterprise* found the *Shokaku* and delivered a hit and a near miss: minor damage. Less than an hour later, planes from both U.S. carriers located the sacrificial lamb, the *Ryujo.* They dove down and struck. When they departed, the Japanese carrier was heavily damaged and stuck circling, a mass of flames.

The counterstrike arrived quickly. Just past four, the *North Carolina*'s air-search radar detected bogeys at 180 miles. The new sets indicated not only the range and bearing of targets but also their altitude. The arrival of the enemy provoked a general scramble of all available F4F Wildcats. After the loss of the *Yorktown* at Midway, each carrier's allotment of fighters was upped from twenty-three to thirty-six, at a corresponding cost to torpedo bomber strength. And so Fletcher's two carriers put fifty-three Wildcats into the skies. "Old *Lexington* and *Yorktown* had never been half so well protected," Samuel Eliot Morison wrote.

The Japanese formation absorbed the first runs from the American fighter planes, then bore in against the *Enterprise* and her escorts. A twenty-millimeter gunner on the *Enterprise* saw a glint of sun on a metal wing and indicated the direction of the plane with a torrent of tracers.

The radio frequency used by the combat air patrol was a frenzy of voices. American pilots hadn't learned to separate the urgent from the merely important, and with everyone transmitting on a single channel the vital instructions from the shipboard radar controllers were so many whistles in the wind. Down upon the *Enterprise* fell rivulets of dive-bombers, the Vals peeling off and dropping as if following a spout, down and down, one following the other every few seconds, through dense hanging fields of black smoke stains from flak. "First ones spotted were just on our port bow, diving in," wrote Lloyd Mustin of the *Atlanta*. "The sky was just a solid sheet of tracers and shell bursts—impossible to tell your own." Reaching the release point, the planes let go their explosives, then pulled out or failed to pull out and plunged into the sea.

The blasts of five-inch guns on the collected ships of the task force had risen in seconds from a scattered staccato to the roll of heavy timpani. "Men on other ships said the *Atlanta* seemed to burst into flame from bow to fantail and from mast tip to water line," Edward Corboy wrote. She rode off the *Enterprise*'s starboard bow. Each turret in the antiaircraft cruiser's main battery could put out a two-gun salvo every four seconds; fifteen salvos and thirty shells a minute, with eight turrets so engaged. The ship's mascot, a dog named Lucky, was yapping in full voice, running around the decks seeking out his favorite person, the assistant medical officer. "Lieutenant Commander C. C. Garver of Atlanta would cover Lucky's ears until the action was over," Corboy wrote, "but the pup would yap furiously all the way through it." The flak from the U.S. task force was furious and effective. Mustin wrote, "First plane missed and flew off. Second and third missed and crashed. Some came apart in mid-air, some fell wildly out of control, some came down burning, and some just flew on into the water in various stages of pullout. Majority of all that attacked was shot down." Of eighty incoming planes, it was estimated that fewer than ten escaped. American pilots entered that buzz saw at their peril. When the *Enterprise* air group commander, Lieutenant Commander Maxwell F. Leslie, flew past the *North Carolina*, his

Avenger took several hits but his relief at his luck was sufficient to keep him good-humored about it. He congratulated the battleship's gunners for shooting well.

The Val pilots who lined up on the *Enterprise* were a persistent group. Enough of them survived to deal her six damaging blows: three bomb hits, and three near misses. The first hit the after elevator near the starboard gun gallery, penetrated five decks, and exploded deep within the ship. Half a minute later, a second bomb hit just fifteen feet from where the first one had, exploding instantly and igniting powder bags that started deck fires. The third bomb hit just aft of the island, on the number two elevator. Though it only partially exploded, it was enough to tear a ten-foot hole in the flight deck and disable the critically important elevator.

As bombs lanced down into and around the carrier, Admiral Kinkaid and his staff were tossed around the flag bridge by the shocks. Seventy-four *Enterprise* men would die, but it could have been far worse. The ship was saved by a little luck, and a lot of determination by her firefighters. The small blazes throughout the ship were quickly conquered; it was the timely work they did just minutes before the attack, draining and venting the gas lines and filling them with carbon dioxide, that prevented a far worse result. The flagship would live to fight again. With holes in her flight deck patched with sheet metal, she turned into the southeasterly wind to begin recovering aircraft.

Ninety minutes after the last Val had departed, the helmsman noticed a serious and potentially fatal problem: The carrier had lost steering control. A flood of water and firefighting foam had swamped the steering engine room, disabling the engine that moved the rudder and freezing the ship in a starboard turn. Recovery of aircraft ceased as the ship circled out of control. While she sheered through the formation, her officer-of-the-deck blasted her whistle in warning to smaller ships in her path.

On a PPI scope in the pilothouse, Captain Arthur C. Davis watched as the next wave of Japanese aircraft inched toward his wounded carrier. The southeast-bound gaggle of enemy planes passed just fifty miles to the *Enterprise*'s southwest. The reprieve gave the crew time to make critical repairs. Aiming to restore steering, a chief machinist named William A. Smith strapped on a rescue breather and, joined by one of his division mates, Cecil S. Robinson, ventured belowdecks, where temperatures surpassed 170 degrees. Finding the steering engine room through the suffocating heat, Smith managed to start a standby motor, restoring steering control to the bridge after thirty-eight minutes. The *Enterprise* air group was flown off to the *Wasp,* the *Saratoga,* and area islands. Freed from duty to the departing aircraft carrier, the *North Carolina,* the *Atlanta,* and two destroyers were sent to join the *Saratoga* group.

After absorbing the brunt of the U.S. carrier strikes and seeing one of his two large carriers damaged, Nagumo decided he had had enough. He ordered a withdrawal to Truk. As Nagumo's carriers turned away north, Tanaka's transport force was left to joust unprotected with Major Mangrum's dive-bombers on Henderson Field. The aviators of Marine Fighting Squadron 223 had turned in a brilliant performance on the afternoon of the twenty-fourth, intercepting a strike of fifteen bombers escorted by Zero fighters from the carrier *Ryujo.* They repelled the raid before it ever darkened Henderson Field's gravel runway, shooting down six Zeros and ten Betty bombers.

On the morning of August 25, after a PBY relocated Tanaka's transports, now about 150 miles north of Guadalcanal, the Cactus Air Force threw itself into the fray again. Joined by planes from the *Enterprise,* the land-based Dauntless dive-bomber jockeys bombed and strafed two transports and worked over Tanaka's flagship, the light cruiser *Jintsu.* When a flight of B-17s from Espiritu Santo arrived overhead at ten thirty, they found a destroyer, the *Mutsuki,* tending to a damaged transport. In a rare feat of high-level marksmanship against a naval target—the Flying Fortresses had a poor record hitting ships—the bombers sank the stationary tin can.

Knocked briefly unconscious in the air attacks, Tanaka arose and ordered a withdrawal. If the August 24 carrier clash, soon to be christened the Battle of the Eastern Solomons, had been a tactical draw, Tanaka's failed reinforcement run transformed it into a U.S. victory. Fletcher, whatever people would say about him later, had helped thwart Japan's first determined effort to reconquer Guadalcanal. "My worst fears for this operation had come to be realized," Tanaka would write. It was clear to him that without an explicit plan to coordinate the naval groups or provide the transports with air cover, "it would be folly to land the remainder of this battered force on Guadalcanal."

A severe judgment would fall on Nagumo for his timid way with his carriers. He had allowed a numerically inferior U.S. force to turn him back. The Americans lost the services of the *Enterprise.* She, with the heavy cruiser *Portland* and four destroyers, set course for Pearl Harbor by way of Tongatabu. As the carriers of both nations made tracks for safer waters, a wag in General Vandegrift's force was said to remark, "Everyone is withdrawing but the Marines."

* * *

ON AUGUST 25, Ghormley wrote Nimitz, more than a little alarmed. He recounted the matériel deficiencies of his command and requested more bombers—fifty more B-17s and forty B-25 Mitchells—and crews. "CONSIDER SITUATION CRITICAL." Nimitz absorbed Ghormley's alarm and processed it into an optimism that he relayed up the chain of command. He wrote to Admiral King, "WE HAVE MADE GOOD START IN OUR OFFENSIVE. WE HAVE SUFFERED MODERATE LOSSES AND DAMAGE WHICH CAN BE ACCEPTED IF REPLACEMENTS ALREADY REQUESTED ARE IMMEDIATELY SENT." Then he added an uncharacteristic flourish of evangelism, perhaps not wanting King to get too bright a notion of the immediate future: "LET'S NOT LET THIS OFFENSIVE DIE ON THE VINE."

Four days later, Ghormley's mood brightened. Notwithstanding the shortages of combat power that had bothered him the day before, now he declared his readiness to parry all threats. "UNTIL THE STRENGTH OF THE HOSTILE MAIN EFFORT IS DETERMINED AND IT HAS BEEN COMMITTED TO A DEFINITE LINE OF ACTION," he wrote Nimitz on August 29, "I SHOULD KEEP MY CARRIER TASK FORCES CENTRALLY LOCATED, PREPARED TO OPERATE ANYWHERE ON THE FRONT SAMOA—MILNE BAY."

It was a tall order for his remaining carriers, the *Wasp* and *Saratoga*. Holding them in reserve, Ghormley promised to let others worry about the daily business of Guadalcanal's defense. "FOR THE PRESENT, HOSTILE INFILTRATION TACTICS AND INITIAL SHOCK OF A HOSTILE MAIN EFFORT MAY HAVE TO BE BORNE BY GROUND TROOPS AND LAND-BASED AVIATION. LAND-BASED AVIATION ATTACK AGAINST JAPANESE INFILTRATION MOVES SHOULD EXTRACT A CONSTANT TOLL OF TRANSPORTS AND ESCORTING COMBATANT SHIPS, WHICH THE JAPANESE CANNOT LONG SUSTAIN. SHOULD JAPANESE CARRIER-SUPPORTED MAIN FORCES MOVE TO ATTACK, OUR LAND-BASED AVIATION SHOULD BE ABLE TO EQUALIZE THE OPPOSING CARRIER STRENGTH. IN SHORT IT IS HOPED THAT THE RESULT OF USE OF OUR DEFENSIVE POSITIONS AND LAND-BASED AVIATION MAY CREATE A FAVORABLE SITUATION WHEREIN I CAN DECISIVELY EMPLOY THE CARRIER TASK FORCES, WHETHER ON MY EXTENDED FRONT OR TO THE WESTWARD. IT IS HOPED THAT MY FREEDOM OF ACTION WILL NOT BE CIRCUMSCRIBED BY RESTRICTIVE TASKS OR MISSIONS."

Nimitz and his staff read these words in bewilderment. Just four days earlier, Ghormley deemed his situation "critical." Now he was requesting "freedom of action" and professing not to see the direction of the Japanese thrust. Retiring his carriers—and with the *Enterprise* ordered back to Pearl

Harbor for repairs—he was promising to stand ready to defend a twenty-five-hundred-mile front, and assuring high command that the threadbare Cactus Air Force—which by Ghormley's own count at month's end had just eight fighters capable of intercepting Japanese bombers and which was struggling to fend off destroyers, much less the entire Combined Fleet—could hold off Nagumo's still-potent carrier force. In London he had learned, following British operations off Norway and in the Mediterranean, that "surface craft, unless heavily protected by fighters, cannot stand up against shore based aircraft." But now he was expecting far more than the gallant fliers and ground crews of Henderson Field could deliver.

As it happened, the Japanese had newly settled on the thrust of their "main effort." With their traditional invasion convoys unable to land by day in the face of American air attacks, and too slow to sneak in and out by night, Yamamoto abandoned sending reinforcements via troopships altogether. As his chief of staff, Admiral Ugaki, wrote, "It is apparent that landing on Guadalcanal by transports is hopeless unless the enemy planes are wiped out." A new way to bring troops to the embattled island would have to be found. Raizo Tanaka would be asked to repeat his exploit delivering the Ichiki detachment again and again, using not slow transports but swift destroyers and other fast combatants to carry the Japanese Army south.

Several days before the Japanese reinforcements began running, Ghormley wrote MacArthur to state his preferences as to the types of ships he wanted the Southwest Pacific Command's pilots to strike. Ghormley reckoned that the "greatest immediate threat to success" came from the Japanese surface fleet, and that the highest-priority targets should be aircraft carriers and troop transports. Destroyers were last on his list. Ghormley was not alone in underrating the value of enemy destroyers. That he expressed the thought so clearly on the very day the Japanese settled on them as their principal means of carrying arms and men to Guadalcanal was no small irony.

On the evening of August 28, seven Japanese destroyers approached the island. Sallying within range of Henderson, their vanguard was greeted brutally by the Cactus Air Force's dive-bombers, who exacted a steep price: the *Asagiri* sunk, the *Shiratsuyu* rendered unnavigable, and the *Yugiri* badly damaged with her commander mortally wounded. It was a remarkable performance against the small, difficult-to-hit ships. The rest of the Japanese flotilla turned back after the grim news was reported. A "perfect failure," Ugaki called it. But in the week that followed, bad weather prevented the boys from Cactus from blocking the Tokyo Express. Stubbornly maintaining his pace of nightly runs from Rabaul, Tanaka finally landed the last of

Ichiki's and Kawaguchi's forces—more than five thousand men. Through piecemeal assembly, the Japanese had at last marshaled enough men to undertake their first general counteroffensive on Guadalcanal.

Yamamoto now resolved officially to make Guadalcanal, not New Guinea, the "principal operational zone of the Southeast Area" and postponed the drive to capture Port Moresby. On Guadalcanal, General Kawaguchi's troops had gathered and, fading into the jungle near Lunga, began planning a renewed assault on Vandegrift's perimeter.

On August 29, as the bomb-damaged *Enterprise* steamed toward Pearl Harbor, Admiral Ghormley ordered his remaining carriers, the *Wasp* and the *Saratoga,* to take turns reprovisioning at Tongatabu. Until the Japanese fleet made another appearance, the carriers would remain on station in their usual position, 220 miles southeast of Guadalcanal, flying their planes in protection of convoys traveling from Espiritu Santo to Guadalcanal. A third carrier, the *Hornet,* was under way south from Pearl Harbor.

Because of the submarine threat, the carrier task force made a practice of steaming at just thirteen knots in order to optimize the efficiency of the sonar gear on their escorting destroyers. But that slow speed increased the ability of submarines to intercept and target them in the first place. On the morning of August 31, Commander Minoru Yokota, captain of the submarine *I-26,* stalked the *Saratoga* east of San Cristobál. When he chose his moment to attack, he closed so aggressively that his periscope scratched the hull of a destroyer in the U.S. screen. The Americans spotted his incoming torpedo wakes, but too late to evade. Shortly before 7 a.m., the carrier shook "like a house in a severe earthquake" as a torpedo struck her. The shock wave whiplashed the hull from below the sea to the flag bridge, tossing Admiral Fletcher up into the overhead and inflicting a forehead wound that would make him—much to his embarrassment—the highest-ranking U.S. naval officer to date to receive the Purple Heart. The blast tripped circuit breakers in the *Saratoga*'s turboelectric drive system, leaving her dead in the water.

The *Saratoga* was an exceptionally stout ship, built originally as a battle cruiser and converted after the conclusion of naval treaties. Her engineers righted the starboard list by transferring fuel between tanks. Then the cruiser *Minneapolis* took her in tow, gingerly bringing her along at seven knots. With a stiff headwind, Captain Dewitt C. Ramsey's flight crews were able to perform the remarkable feat of conducting flight operations while under tow. Twenty-nine of *Sara*'s strike aircraft got off the deck and flew to Espiritu Santo while their ship was in this infirm condition.

The waters southeast of Guadalcanal would earn the bitter nickname

"Torpedo Junction." Whenever the sound of gunfire or the basso thudding of depth charges were heard, someone would inevitably remark, "Sounds like there's a function at the junction." With the *Saratoga* out of action for three months, Fletcher could no longer survive Ernest King's acid mistrust. Fletcher's caution paid no dividends now that his carriers' favorite haunts, outside range of enemy air attack, were infested with submarines. His reward was a recall to Pearl Harbor in his damaged flagship and, before the year was out, to have his career as a carrier task force commander terminated by the COMINCH. When Leigh Noyes assumed command of Task Force 61, the U.S. Marine Corps no longer had Frank Jack Fletcher, the victor at Midway, to kick around anymore.

But they got plenty more planes. After the *Saratoga*'s disabling, her valuable air group, like that of the *Enterprise,* found temporary homes—on the *Wasp,* on Espiritu Santo, and on Guadalcanal as well. A Marine general with a keen sense of the absurd was said to remark, "What saved Guadalcanal was the loss of so many carriers."

12

What They Were Built For

IN THE WEEKS AHEAD, THE MOMENTUM OF ATTACK AND DEFENSE would swing daily, diurnally, as the Americans commanded the skies and seas by day, and the Japanese regained them by night. Neither side could effectively fight on the other's terms. Whipped by Mikawa at Savo Island, the warriors of the U.S. Navy's surface force would continue to spend much of the month screening carrier task forces or escorting convoys, not roaming the seas as the predators they were meant to be. "It seemed we were on the fringe of battle for months," Richard Hale of the destroyer *Laffey* said. "I felt uneasy knowing the real war was only five hundred miles north of us in the Solomons, and we could have run up there in a day's steaming."

Ten days before the Battle of the Eastern Solomons, a plan circulated briefly, never to be executed, providing for the creation of a "surface attack group" under Fletcher's cruiser boss, Rear Admiral Carleton H. Wright, drawing the battleship *North Carolina*, the heavy cruisers *Minneapolis*, *San Francisco*, *New Orleans*, *Portland*, and *Salt Lake City*, the *Atlanta*, and four destroyers into a single fighting force should the Japanese fleet come within gun range. Those ships were finally reckoned too valuable to spare in missions other than antiaircraft defense.

The cruiser and destroyermen circling with the task force relished the idea that the surface Navy might one day reassert itself in its traditional role. Japanese destroyers ferrying supplies and men to Guadalcanal disgorged their cargoes mostly unopposed, took potshots at Henderson Field with their main batteries, and headed home. Much as the Japanese 17th Army's senior leadership hated traveling light, without the heavy weapons and equipment that a transport could have accommodated, but not a destroyer, the activity of the fleet emboldened Japanese artillery crews and mortarmen hidden in the surrounding hills. Their sporadic barrages, along with nightly visits by aircraft that dropped small bombs haphazardly around the island's northern plain, were a malicious nuisance that kept the marines sleepless.

The principal reason Admiral Yamamoto was hesitating to mount a general attack on the island was his respect for U.S. airpower. Henderson Field was an unsinkable aircraft carrier, host to an interservice brotherhood of aviators whose bonds were strengthening under the test of fire and loss. With the arrival of more Navy pilots and planes, including twenty-four well-seasoned Wildcat jockeys from the *Saratoga*, the shoestring holding together the American position on Guadalcanal was cinched a little tighter in early September.

Japanese pilots had their own shoestrings to worry about. When the 8th Fleet chief of staff, Toshikazu Ohmae, arrived at Rabaul from Truk in late August, he was appalled by what he saw as a lackadaisical approach to harbor defense, and the evident vulnerability of the whole place. The stronghold at New Britain had just nineteen fighters, twenty-nine medium bombers, and four flying boats at the time. With the Cactus Air Force getting stronger on its feet every day, Imperial pilots suffered worse for the geographic disadvantage. Taking off at first light so that they could strike and return before sunset, at the edge of their fuel envelope, they were bound to a schedule that put them over their target during the same midday window and from the same northwesterly bearing. With forewarning by coastwatchers, Cactus Air Force Wildcat pilots usually had the forty minutes they needed to scramble and reach interception altitude before the enemy planes arrived. Battling close to their base, with fuel tanks full, they had the flexibility to engage, maneuver, and fight that the Japanese lacked. Though many Zero pilots were no novices in long-range missions—the December 8 raid against MacArthur's airfields on Luzon, launched from Formosa, was a fine example—sustaining daily operations indefinitely over great distances was a steep challenge.

Because the Japanese kept their ships clear of the outer reach of U.S. search planes until late afternoon, Mangrum's dive-bomber pilots seldom could hit them before dark, even when the weather cooperated. The Marine aviators did their best after nightfall, depending on the elevation of the moon, the position of the clouds, and the light cast by stars. But there were only four or five days a month when the lunar phase permitted nighttime attacks. Bad weather reduced that number. Even by day, dive-bombers could not reliably hit the agile thirty-four-knot Japanese destroyers steered by Tanaka's veteran shiphandlers. Their skill was impressive. They seemed to know well Guadalcanal's northern coast, where they usually landed their men and supplies. Despite the hazards of night navigation, the Cactus Air Force's dawn patrols never found them grounded or struggling in the shallows. "They come right up to the beach . . . and get them right out. They don't lose any time," said Lieutenant Colonel Charles L. Fike, the exec of Marine Air Group 23. "Certainly the means we had at our disposal were not enough. Control of channels of supply there were always in dispute, and the Japanese were more often in control of them than our own Navy. Under those circumstances, we were reluctant to build up the force on Guadalcanal because of the possibility that we wouldn't be able to meet the supply requirements."

The rising strength of the Guadalcanal-based aviators taxed the morale of the IJN, too. On the night of August 29, one of Tanaka's captains refused a direct order to take his four destroyers and attack an inbound American convoy. On a clear night with a full moon, Captain Yonosuke Murakami explained, U.S. planes would have a clear shot at his ships. Tanaka found the explanation "so dumbfounding . . . that I could not even think of words to reprove him. Blame attached to me, of course, for having such a man in my command." The next day, physically exhausted and in a fury about the continuing resistance of 17th Army officers to using destroyers for transport, Tanaka found himself done in by his rival service branch. He was relieved of command of the Reinforcement Unit and returned to Truk to rejoin the 2nd Fleet as a destroyer squadron commander.

But Major Mangrum grasped airpower's limits. "It was difficult for us to understand, while sitting in a foxhole, without adequate surface [ship] support, that we could be expected to maintain the peace and quiet of Guadalcanal," he said. Nimitz was pressing King for more aircraft of any and all types. Late on the night of September 1, from his headquarters at Pearl, he implored his superior, "Let's give Cactus the wherewithal to live up to its name. Something for the Japs to remember forever." But two legs of the air–land–sea tripod weren't going to get the job done, no matter how stout they were. As Nimitz was beseeching King for more hardware, Vandegrift weighed in with Admiral Turner, copying Ghormley, on what it would take to hold the island.

"Appears enemy is building up striking force by continuous small landings during darkness," Vandegrift wrote. "Due to difficult terrain areas are beyond range of land operations except at expense of weakened defenses of airfield. We do not have a balanced force and it is imperative that following measures be taken: *A*. Base planes here capable of searching beyond steaming range during darkness. *B*. Provide surface craft DD's or motor torpedo boats for night patrolling. *C*. Provide striking force for active defense by transferring 7th Marines to Cactus. If not prevented by surface craft enemy can continue night landings beyond our range of action and build up large force." In other words, the Marines needed the Navy.

On September 3, Rear Admiral Leigh Noyes, Fletcher's replacement as carrier commander, proposed that the cruisers and destroyers of the disbanded *Saratoga* group be used much as Vandegrift had suggested—to add muscle to the surface Navy in direct support of the Marines. A few days later, Ghormley revamped the task force assignments to provide for a separate "surface screening and attack force" of cruisers and destroyers, known as Task Force 64. It was a humble flotilla, far less powerful than the *North Carolina*–led force envisioned earlier. To be based at Espiritu Santo and placed under temporary command of Rear Admiral Carleton H. Wright, the new surface attack force was made up of the heavy cruiser *Minneapolis,* the light cruisers *Boise* and *Leander,* and four destroyers. Still, the unit's designation as Task Force 64 was an organizational signal that these ships had a vital mission and deserved stature on par with the carrier task forces (Task Force 61), Turner's amphibs (Task Force 62), and McCain's land-based air command (Task Force 63).

No longer under a foreigner's flag, as Crutchley's cruiser screen had been, or linked by a decimal to the amphibious fleet, as Riefkohl's martyred Task Group 62.6 had been, Task Force 64 were their own warriors. Given nominally to the operational control of Kelly Turner, they had an essential mission that "leaves much to the initiative of Task Force Commanders," Ghormley wrote. "Keep in mind that there is no quicker means to ultimate victory than the sinking of enemy ships."

Only the ships of the surface fleet could hold safe the nighttime supply lanes and finally ensure American control of the island. Only surface ships, the mobile heavy armor of the seaways, could stop the Tokyo Express after dark and hold control of the seas. All that remained was for the Navy to find the will and the opportunity to send them into action again against the reigning masters of the old way of naval war.

Thus far in 1942, six of the seven Allied heavy cruisers that had ventured forth and fought Japanese surface ships muzzle-to-muzzle lay at rest beneath a blood-warm sea. The *Vincennes,* the *Quincy,* the *Astoria,* the HMAS *Canberra,* and, four months earlier and far from the Solomons, the *Houston* and the HMS *Exeter,* had all been overmatched and destroyed by their counterparts. All seven might have been lost had Howard Bode's *Chicago* entered battle on the night of August 9. This record was doubtlessly on the minds of all the skippers of the fast, multi-role ships that the Navy had long assumed would prevail in any direct action with Japanese surface ships. In the cold trade of naval warfare, such preconceptions held no value. There was but a single axiom that counted (now confirmed and amended by Gunichi Mikawa): Victory flew with the first effective salvo, and a second and a third didn't hurt the cause either.

Training courses in evolving disciplines such as fire control were under furious revision. Certain courses, for radarmen for instance, were being designed from scratch. All these changes, the growth of manpower and the evolution of doctrine, were aimed at one thing: knocking Japan to the mat in what was shaping up to be an epic oceanic brawl. In the sweltering South Pacific, the hardware needed to do that was plowing relentlessly south, fresh from the proving grounds.

On the morning of September 6, the men of the light cruiser *Atlanta,* en route to Hawaii with the damaged *Saratoga,* arrived at Tongatabu and beheld a heartening sight. Two powerful new ships were in the harbor, the battleship *South Dakota* and the antiaircraft cruiser *Juneau.* News came that the mighty *North Carolina*'s sister ship, the *Washington,* was seven days out of the Panama Canal, due in the theater the following week.

The coming of the powerful (and more fuel-efficient) fast battleships raised hopes at a time when naval planners were intensely aware that Japan's great 69,000-ton *Yamato* and several of the heralded 36,600-ton *Kongo*-class battleships were at Truk. No U.S. ship in the area could match them. "I cling to the fond hope that some one of our admirals, some day, will force the fight—will go after these bastards at a time of our choosing, and with forces arrayed to our satisfaction, and will blow the bloody bastards clean to hell. And the *North Carolina* and *Washington* are some of what it takes to do that job," Lloyd Mustin wrote.

Lieutenant Commander Edwin B. Hooper, the alumnus of MIT's fire-control course and an assistant gunnery officer in the *Washington,* proclaimed the fast battleships "a tremendous step forward in technology, orders of magnitude over the old battleships, even with their modernization." The most dramatic improvement they offered over the older battleships was their high-frequency SG radar, the existence of which was still secret. The *North Carolina* had had her new apparatus installed at sea instead of within view of prying eyes in the shipyard. The ship's Marine detachment stood armed guard over the newly equipped fire-control and plotting rooms. The *Atlanta*'s sailors had hardly gotten the dope on the *South Dakota* or greeted their counterparts on their sister ship, the *Juneau,* when the two newcomers were under way again. Then, oddly, just a few hours later they were returning to port. Misfortunate had struck the *South Dakota.* She had run aground on an uncharted coral head.

Reputations form fast in the cloistered passageways of the fleet. The *South Dakota* was already known as a hard-luck ship. Some ascribed it to the state of South Dakota's failure to follow the tradition whereby states presented their namesake dreadnoughts with a handmade silver service. The governor didn't deliver, and the consequences were inevitable. During a shakedown run in the Chesapeake Bay, she went aground and lost electrical power. In speed trials off Casco Bay, Maine, the *South Dakota* collided dead center with a whale. Unable to slow down during the stringently prescribed test of the power plant, the ship ground the hapless mammal in half. Some of the chief petty officers said this heralded, somehow, good fortune. If good fortune was to be had, it belonged to Captain Thomas Gatch, for he might have been relieved of command on the spot had any of this made the papers. Now he had done it again, and his reward for putting an eighteen-inch-wide gash the full length of her underside was to be ordered back to Pearl for two weeks of repairs. It was a serious setback for the reconstitution of SOPAC's surface striking force.

ON SEPTEMBER 7, Admiral Nimitz flew to San Francisco to meet with Admiral King and Secretary Forrestal at the St. Francis Hotel. On the agenda was a review of the state of the South Pacific command, partly occasioned by the defeat in the Battle of Savo Island. It would be more than a month yet before such matters became fodder for headline writers.

On that same day, on board his flagship *Argonne* at Nouméa, Admiral Ghormley composed a letter to Nimitz that he knew he had no business writing. He was in the grip of an exhaustion that seemed to color everything. It might have been cabin fever; he hadn't left his flagship since his arrival on the first of August. He couldn't stop himself from unburdening himself. "I have to spill this to somebody," he wrote, "so I am afraid you will have to be the goat, but I hope you will burn this after it is read."

By the time this reaches you, Mr. Forrestal will have seen you. I think for the time he was here, he got an eyeful and an earful. Whether he can do anything about it, I don't know. Somebody said the last day or two, on the British first visit to Washington they burned it, on the second visit they occupied it. It looks so to me that we are doing their job all over the world and the Government is not backing us up down here with what we need, why, I don't know. I feel sure that you have the picture completely, but I am very surprised from one or two of King's dispatches, that I do not believe he appreciates it.

As between King and Ghormley, the doubts were mutual. King was growing skeptical about his SOPAC commander's fitness for command. King asked Nimitz whether Ghormley could stand up physically to the strain of South Pacific duty. Nimitz had no way to know. He knew his friend was a seadog, a strategist, a diplomat, and a gentleman. But he would soon wonder if he had the one thing that was needed most in the South Pacific in 1942: a fighter's heart.

"Our carrier situation at present is precarious," continued Ghormley's letter to Nimitz of September 7. "Some people are probably saying why don't I send surface forces in strength to Guadalcanal at night. The simple reason is, it is too dangerous to suffer possible loss under the present conditions where they have submarines, motor torpedo boats, surface forces and shore based aircraft to aid them in restricted waters."

The last sentence revealed that Ghormley didn't really understand what confronted his men in the combat theater. If Japan's change in radio codes left Navy intelligence snoopers poorly apprised of movements, it should have been clear by the second week of September that Japanese motor torpedo boats were not a major threat in the Slot, nor did they fly land-based attack aircraft at night. As for the restricted waters, they were, of course, no less restricted for the Japanese than they were for the Americans, who enjoyed the significant advantage of defending those waters instead of attacking them. While the Navy's conservatism with its carriers was well justified, the same could not be said of the light forces. If the gunslingers of the fleet were too valuable to risk now, when would they be risked?

Ghormley was of mixed mind regarding the appropriate range of his command authority. He wrote Nimitz in that same letter, "A recent dispatch from Washington told me of several ships that had P-38's on board, but they have never given me authority to divert a ship. I do not want that authority, for in diverting a ship in order to get an airplane, I might divert the very ship that had the critical ammunition in the hold to tide over a tough situation in Australia." The pressures of command were clearly weighing on him. He had insufficient authority, but he was no longer sure he wanted more of it.

At the St. Francis, Nimitz acknowledged to King and Forrestal that the problems in the South Pacific were grave. While he was glad to have three battleships in his theater—the *Washington, North Carolina,* and *South Dakota*—they were poor replacements for the heavy cruisers lost at Savo because their ravenous appetite for fuel limited their deployability. Nimitz didn't yet have enough tankers to keep them operating. Forrestal promised he would do what he could.

But the question of Ghormley's fitness for command was a far more perplexing problem. Nimitz knew then, faced with Ernest King's inquiry, that he had no other choice: He would hop on a Coronado patrol plane and fly to Nouméa to see his old friend personally. He would order Ghormley to undergo a physical examination. Then he would let King know what he found.

Ghormley had long complained that Washington had little interest in or sympathy for his problems. What he didn't know was that Forrestal, based in part on impressions formed during his own recent trip to Nouméa, was going powerfully to bat for him. Forrestal had visited hospitals where badly burned sailors from the Battle of Savo Island were still fighting for their lives. "What could I say in the face of such heroism and such suffering except to bow my head," Forrestal said. The Navy secretary would find tankers for Nimitz and urge Roosevelt to speed up reinforcements. He was so vocal in his entreaties on Ghormley's behalf that Secretary of War Henry L. Stimson, by now occupied with planning the invasion of North Africa, thought Forrestal had been unduly influenced by his personal impressions. "Jim," Stimson said, "you've got a bad case of localitis." Forrestal replied without a lost beat: "Mr. Secretary, if the Marines on Guadalcanal were wiped out, the reaction of the country will give you a bad case of localitis in the seat of your pants."

Before adjourning at the St. Francis Hotel, the three leaders settled on a personnel move that would send electricity through the carrier fleet and beyond. It was agreed that Vice Admiral Halsey would return to Pearl Harbor with Nimitz and eventually take over his old billet as commander of the *Enterprise* task force as soon as repairs to the battle-damaged carrier were complete in mid-October.

Shortly after they returned to Pearl, Nimitz took Halsey to visit the *Enterprise.* On board the weathered and battle-worn ship, competing with the pneumatic and hydraulic clangor, Nimitz awarded decorations to the crew. Then he announced, "Boys, I've got a surprise for you. Bill Halsey's back!" There were cheers. Then he told them, "I know that you have been promised a rest and God knows that you deserve it, but you also know that we have lately suffered severe losses in ships and men. I have no recourse but to send you back into battle." That statement received a courteous silence, and they would have five more weeks to think about it.

IN HINDSIGHT IT was unclear which of the opposing fleets was less prepared for the fight that lay ahead. As the American brain trust was conferring in San Francisco, Yamamoto held a series of conferences in the flag quarters of the *Yamato* at Truk. According to Tameichi Hara, a destroyer captain who participated in the meetings, his commander in chief's agenda was trivial next to other pressing issues. When would the world-beating Combined Fleet summon the will to gather, coordinate, and smash the upstart Americans? Where was the fuel going to come from that would enable the great Imperial battleship force to churn south? A culture of deference kept tough questions from being addressed. "Criticism of basic concepts in the Imperial Navy would have impugned the top-level admirals, and brought instant dismissal of the critic," Hara wrote.

The problems Yamamoto faced were those that plagued every commander in the machine age, when ships were more powerful than they had ever been before, but were effectively tethered to bases by their insatiable need for fuel. Situated much like the Americans were, waging war six thousand miles from home, the Japanese struggled all the more because of the large investment of pride they had made in the ships that were least amenable to operating at high tempo. That pride manifested itself in doctrine that vested supremacy in battleships: The Japanese fleet had been created under the idea that it would win a decisive battle over the Americans, at a time and place of its choosing. The pieces were in place. The battleships *Yamato, Mutsu, Hiei,* and *Kirishima* were all in the theater at Truk, backstopping Nagumo's roaming carriers. If the idea of sidelining their heaviest naval armor was dismaying to the Americans, it was downright intolerable to the Japanese, who counted on them to win the "decisive battle."

The Japanese Army's hubris and ambition were part of the problem. Famed for its iron discipline, it failed to discipline its ends to its means. The 17th Army stubbornly refused to abandon its failing bid to cross New Guinea's central range and seize Port Moresby. This strained both resources and attention. The Imperial Japanese Navy saw the limitations more clearly. "Unless Guadalcanal is settled," Ugaki wrote, "we cannot hope for any further development in this area." A continuous realignment of means with shifting ends took place as both sides wrestled with complexities of the battlefield that were seldom apparent at the game table.

On September 11, Turner and McCain met with General Vandegrift to plan their resistance to an expected Japanese attack that the U.S. fleet would be in no position to stop. Early that morning, Ghormley wrote Nimitz again to recount the deficits and laxities of the various components of SOPAC, "SITUATION AS I VIEW IT TODAY IS EXTREMELY CRITICAL." Not wanting the carriers to seek battle unnecessarily, Ghormley ordered Noyes to keep them south of 12 degrees South latitude, about 150 miles south of Henderson Field. With land-based air strength on Guadalcanal down to eleven Wildcats and twenty-two Dauntlesses, once again the marines were left to their devices to endure air attacks, bombardment by naval gunfire, and seaborne landings of enemy reinforcements. On the night of September 13, the defenders of Henderson Field faced their most serious test yet.

That night—just as, on the other side of the world, the earth shook from the German assault on Stalingrad—Vandegrift's marines faced some seventeen hundred Japanese troops charging their positions about a mile south of the airfield. Skillfully dug in on a high ridge soon to be named in his honor, Lieutenant Colonel Merritt Edson mounted a determined defense, coordinating artillery and mortars with the close-in work of his riflemen. The tenacity of the Japanese was unnerving, their nearness to victory harrowing. They briefly overran a second airstrip under construction east of Henderson Field, named Fighter One. A patrol of infiltrators was killed within fifty feet of General Vandegrift's tent. Though the casualties of this battle were poorly recorded—the Japanese lost around eight hundred men, as against a hundred or so for the Americans—the Battle of Edson's Ridge was another resounding victory for the marines. Nevertheless, the savagery and determination of the Japanese attack suggested grim things to come if the nighttime reinforcements were allowed to flow. American reinforcements were on the way. A regiment of the 1st Marine Division, the 7th Marines, was at last under way from Nouméa to join Vandegrift.

The *Wasp* and the newly arrived *Hornet* were assigned to provide air cover to the transport force. En route north to their operating area on the afternoon of September 15, the carrier task force got its hardest shock yet. Admiral Noyes was turning the *Wasp* out of the wind as flight operations ended for the day. She was making sixteen knots, about 150 miles southeast of San Cristóbal, when a periscope broke the water and crosshairs settled on the carrier. The Japanese submarine *I-19* maneuvered, lined up on the carrier, and loosed six torpedoes.

It would go down as the single most devastating torpedo spread of the war; the *I-19*'s torpedoes struck three ships. The *Wasp* absorbed two of them, producing a series of blasts fed by aviation fuel and stored bombs. In minutes the carrier was a pyre, her pall visible for miles. The torpedoes that missed boiled onward, toward the *Hornet* task force six miles away. The destroyer *O'Brien* was struck, too, and lost part of her bow. The battleship *North Carolina* was the third victim, taking a torpedo forward on the port side that opened a thirty-two-foot-wide hole in her hull, buckled two decks, and disabled her number one turret, killing six.

The dying *Wasp* drew in her escorts in a feverish rescue effort. It was the way of the South Seas that episodes like this were well attended by sharks. As the escorting vessels moved in with cargo nets thrown over the gunwales, the sailors were horrified. "Sharks were everywhere," wrote Ford Richardson, a sailor from the destroyer *Farenholt*. "Dozens. Hundreds. A shark would catch a man by an arm or a foot and pull him under, cutting off his screams. The poor devil would pop up again, and again, like a cork on a fishing line. Each time his scream would be weaker than before. Finally, he would come up no more. Sometimes the shark would grab a poor man in the middle and shake him like a dog shaking a rat. Then the shark would back off, dragging the dying man's entrails behind him. The water would turn milky with blood." The rescuers worked until nightfall shrouded the scene of the horror. The ordeal was never more luridly horrifying than for a pair of brothers whom the deck force of the *Farenholt* tried to rescue. "Just at dark, a sailor came drifting by just out of range of a heaving line. He was holding up another sailor, but that man's head was drooped over and his face was under water. He was dead. We shouted to the sailor, 'Turn him loose and swim to us. He's dead!'

"'He's my brother,' he replied.

"'He's dead, Let him go and swim closer!'

"'He's my brother! He's my brother! He's my brother . . . !'

"Helplessly we watched as the current swept him by us, and on into the darkening gloom. The last we saw of him, he was still holding onto his dead brother. The last we heard faintly 'He's my brother.'"

Although her escorts pulled aboard more than four hundred survivors, jamming them into all available spaces and passageways, the *Wasp* went down in the Coral Sea with 173 men. Though quick work by her damage-control crews kept her at full speed, the *North Carolina* would need six weeks at Pearl Harbor for repairs. The *O'Brien* was patched up, too, but she sank when her hull buckled en route to the West Coast.

Next to the loss of the *Wasp*, the costliest casualty of the *I-19*'s attack was the Navy's confidence in its commanders. Nimitz took a dim view of how Leigh Noyes had handled the carriers, operating at speeds that CINCPAC believed too slow to stay clear of prowling submarines. (Destroyer commanders preferred to operate below thirteen knots to enable best use of sonar.) Noyes was quietly removed and returned to the States to take a shore command, and placed before a board of inquiry that explored the culpability for the loss of the carrier. He was exonerated by a 1943 inquiry into the loss of the *Wasp*, but was never recognized for his combat service.

The loss of the ship was kept a closely guarded secret. "They didn't want anybody to know the *Wasp* was lost," Thomas Weschler said, "just as they didn't want anyone to know the *Lexington* had been lost at Coral Sea.... The Japanese would have had a heyday if they really knew how close to the end we were." The *Wasp*'s survivors, like the survivors of the Battle of Savo Island, were hidden away—quarantined—in Nouméa. The news of the carrier's sinking would not be released until December, by which time the survivors, sworn to secrecy about the reason for their leave, were finally allowed to tell family and friends the rest of the story. Stories of unmitigated disaster were never helpful to morale. While the *South Dakota* was under repair at Pearl Harbor, her skipper, Thomas Gatch, tried to use the story of the Battle of Savo Island as a teaching opportunity, inviting the captain of one of the sunken cruisers to visit his wardroom. Telling of the disastrous battle against Mikawa's cruisers, his guest spoke in tones that fell from solemn to dire. "I guess he and Captain Gatch were old friends, and I am pretty sure Captain Gatch didn't know in advance what this captain was going to say. His talk was very pessimistic," recalled Paul H. Backus, a junior-grade lieutenant on the battleship. "At the end, Captain Gatch had to get up and say, in front of this officer, that nothing like that was going to happen to the *South Dakota*, that our best defense against this kind of nonsense was our nine sixteen-inch guns—cut and dried—and then he escorted the officer out of the wardroom. It was kind of sad, because this guy had lost his ship, and the way he lost it had left a very discouraging impression on him." That mood would persist until the fleet got off its heels and did something to turn around morale. Admiral Wright, with Task Force 64, had under his command the tools to do the job. But the tools are not the craftsman, and they would be of little productive use until the right men showed up to do the job.

13

The Warriors

IT TOOK CONSIDERABLE FORCE OF WILL TO OVERCOME THE PARALYSIS of the routine, the heavy inertia of predictability that almost every aspect of Navy life promoted, from the plan of the day to the formation plans drawn on the navigation board. It was easy not to notice how tiny elements of routine fused into a culture and made every day reassuringly like the last. The rhythm was made possible through a professionalization of the business of naval service that would never have existed but for previous great victories. In war, those comfortable rhythms needed to be violently overthrown if further victories were to be possible. Fast-thinking, quick-acting men would be needed to overthrow them.

The awareness that one was in the presence of such an insurgent came at a pheromonal level. He didn't have to be brash or intimidating. If he had the right qualities, they carried through the air around him despite his quietude. Some men were fiery and motivational, leading with a barely restrained recklessness and a demeanor of perpetually fresh anger. Others were intellectual warriors, brains in circuit with the matrix in space where vectors flew toward other vectors and the results of battle followed from the nature of their intersections. The fighter's way was elemental. It was not possible to cultivate it reliably in an academic meritocracy, or to gauge it by class rank. The woodsmen with their squirrel guns who beat the British at New Orleans rallied to Andrew Jackson's readiness to fury, a scent that inspired fear, his instinct to abandon prudence and seize a sudden opening to kill. Such a man knew that a warship was not a lady but a platform of systems that fire projectiles that kill. Having tasted defeat, the Navy was starting to come back to appreciating the unpolished strengths of the Georgia farm boys who found themselves under gentle persecution on board Commander Wylie's *Fletcher*. A rebel yell and a blast of powder. That and a little planning and technical proficiency would carry the day.

Rear Admiral Norman Scott was one of them. A 1911 graduate of the Naval Academy, he was known as "one of the best-liked men in the class," in part no doubt because of his prowess in a hand-to-hand fight. An expert fencer, he had won "immortal fame," as the irrepressible yearbook scribes wrote, by beating West Point en route to becoming an intercollegiate champion. He was a warrior; he always wanted his sword in the fight. According to Admiral Raymond Spruance, Scott's tour of duty in the CNO's office was an unhappy one. Sent there after commanding the heavy cruiser *Pensacola*, Scott "made things so miserable around him in Washington that he finally got what he wanted—sea duty." Robert Graff of the *Atlanta* thought Scott was "kind of like a junior Halsey." But fighters don't always find their fight. It had been Norman Scott's fate to sit idly by in the antiaircraft cruiser *San Juan* off Tulagi as the Japanese sliced through Captain Riefkohl's cruiser screen on the night of August 9. Scott spent the next day, his fifty-third birthday, reflecting on what little he had seen of the Battle of Savo Island. He could claim some prescience for the screen's unpreparedness for combat. He had warned Crutchley about the "grave inadequacies" of Condition Two, the state of partial battle readiness whose circuitous personnel shifts underlay the slow-footed response to Mikawa's appearance.

When he was named as Carleton Wright's successor as commander of Task Force 64 in mid-September, one of his first acts was to return to tradition. In the late thirties, the U.S. Navy borrowed a training regimen from the Royal Navy, the so-called offset gunnery exercise. In these drills, ships squared off as they would in battle, fixing their gun directors on one another but setting off the alignment of the turrets by several degrees. As the guns fired askance, a second director measured the precision of the offset. Any shot that landed a calculated distance behind the ship, projected in accordance with the range and the degree of the offset, was deemed a hit. Such drills were generally more orderly affairs if one ship did the firing and another served as target, rather than having both duel and maneuver simultaneously at full battle speeds. Precautions notwithstanding, the exercises were acts of faith: With fears of a catastrophic accident always present, they were conducted with a flinching caution that could keep officers up the rest of the night.

Greater cause for insomnia lay in not knowing the proficiency of one's crew. Admiral Ghormley had been hampered by this uncertainty. He didn't know what his ships and commanders were capable of. He hadn't spent time with them, or among them; hadn't been physically present to assess critical variables, from their intangible esprit to the physical soundness of their machinery. He was candid about this. "I did not know, from actual contact, the ability of the officers, nor the material condition of the ships nor their readiness for battle, nor did I know their degree of training for warfare such as was soon to develop in this area. Improvement was acquired while carrying out combat missions," he would write. This was a startling admission of a leadership failure. Norman Scott wasn't about to emulate it, and certainly wasn't satisfied to leave the education of his men to the enemy.

After the damaging of the *South Dakota, North Carolina, Enterprise,* and *Saratoga,* the U.S. Navy had more capital ships on the sidelines than it had in the forward area. The loss of the *Wasp* left just one carrier, the *Hornet,* in the entire South Pacific. Battleships would find their moment, when fortune and necessity conspired. Until then, the "light forces"—cruisers and destroyers—would hold the line. The Slot would be their battlefield. "It was the way the Japs would come. We talked about it constantly," wrote the *Helena*'s Chick Morris. "The talk was always of the impending clash with the enemy's warships. Were we good enough? None of us knew. We had never been through the real thing."

In the last two weeks of September, during moments stolen from the drudgery of escort duty, Scott arranged for his cruisers to practice their craft. Determined to make his own force a match for the Japanese, he had studied the recent night surface actions carefully and instituted what a Marine gunner on the *San Francisco,* Clifford C. Spencer, called "Night Fighting Course 101." No peacetime moonlight excursion this. "For the next two weeks we held daily gunnery practice and high speed night tactical maneuvers, every night, all night," Spencer wrote. "We were at general quarters every night and had mock battles with opposing ships, all moving at flank speed. Some fun! The object of the practice was to have everyone sharpen their night vision and spot the enemy before he saw you. With training, helmsmen were able to maintain ship intervals with more expertise and direct more energy to finding the enemy ships, allowing you to get off those very important first salvos." Floatplanes towing target sleeves. Flash cards with ship silhouettes.

Competitions were instituted to determine the fastest gun crews. "In Texas the battle cry had been 'Remember the Alamo!' Here the rally cry was 'Remember Savo Island!'" Spencer wrote. "Fatigue melted away when you thought of the slaughter of friends in the now infamous August 9th 'Battle of the Sitting Ducks.'"

The exercise Norman Scott led on September 22 was the first time some of his heavy cruisers had fired their big guns at all in five months, and the first offset practice they had done in more than a year. Trying to draw a bead on a highly maneuverable destroyer, the gunners of the heavy cruiser *Salt Lake City* learned the value of alert observation, and of close cooperation between the spotter and the rangekeeper or radar operator. Her officers called it "the best simulation of action it had thus far in target practices." A few nights later the *Salt Lake City* was out again, on orders from Scott to duel the *Helena*. Parameters were loosened, the band of permissible speed widened to fifteen to twenty knots. The *Salt Lake City* pushed the limits, charging the *Helena* at twenty-four knots and landing a first-salvo offset straddle from 23,500 yards, more than thirteen miles away. Doctrine called for heavy cruisers to open fire in good weather from twenty thousand yards. Radar could bring even better results, allowing engagements to begin at ranges as great as thirty thousand yards.

In June, after the Battle of Midway, radar was being touted as "the outstanding development of the war in fire control." In a night exercise, a cruiser drawing ranges with the new high-frequency, magnetron-powered FD fire-control set landed eleven successive straddles on its target. Nimitz's people looked at those results, studied the reports of battle coming back from the front, and drew the only conclusion: "We are still not getting all that we should out of this splendid instrument." When his ships were firing on towed sleds, Scott ordered the sleds wrapped with metal and wire mesh, to provide a crisper radar return.

Captain Small of the *Salt Lake City* knew that technology itself took you nowhere. Understanding and application were everything. Small had made it the "basic radar policy" of the ship that radar was the domain of the gunnery department. Data from the radars was transmitted not only to the bridge and Central Station, as on other ships, but straight to all gun director and control stations as well. This was no trivial modification to standing doctrine. According to the *Atlanta*'s Lloyd Mustin, there was "quite a lot of technique involved in transferring a radar target from detection by search radar to acquisition by the fire-control radar." The search radar's readings, so laboriously gotten, had to be manually plotted on the bridge before they could be conveyed by telephone to the gun directors. Small's approach saved critical time by letting the gunnery team do its own plotting and get a direct picture of the situation.

With enough practice, even liabilities could become strengths. Through the drills ordered by Scott, the *Salt Lake City*'s fire-control teams discovered that faulty circuitry was causing cross-talk between the circuits used by the main and secondary batteries. This defect would have confused an unpracticed crew, but Small's men turned it into a strength. Overhearing the communications of their counterparts, the two teams came to recognize each other's voices and in time enjoyed a productive cooperation.

Good commanders helped their men get past their limitations, be they mechanical or psychological. The lessons Scott's fighters learned were duly circulated fleetwide in bulletins. The problem of "buck fever"—the initial overeagerness of gun crews, firing before solutions were ready—had only one cure: the sobriety that came with experience. Special effort had to be made to keep fire controlmen informed of radar readings whenever a ship began the game of musical chairs that was going to battle stations. As key people changed stations, the flow of critical information could freeze. On some ships, including Scott's flagship, the *San Francisco,* the first salvo from the main battery reliably knocked the delicate instrumentation of the FC radar out of operation. The shock of the main battery could jolt the foremast hard enough to throw the man aiming the director off his target, sometimes carrying the aim of the searchlight operator with him. In a light rain, those searchlights were ineffective beyond five thousand yards, like automotive high beams in a fogbank. Cold guns were full of surprises with their quirky ballistic properties. And as always, a ship-to-ship shootout after dark was a harrowing affair that confounded the senses, like riding a galloping bronco through a foggy night while aiming a rifle at a target that lies beyond a burning building. Simply put, there were no panaceas to defeat the sailor's age-old foe, Murphy's Law, and the universal problem of entropy.

Their sheer terror was never greater in exercises than on the night of September 30. The *San Francisco* was shooting at a target towed by the minesweeper USS *Breese* when that small vessel sent word that the towline had parted. Targets drifting loose at night presented a danger to navigation. Sometimes the targets weren't small sleds but derelict ships or large barges on which façades had been built to provide realistic silhouettes. To locate the wayward hardware, Scott's ships began circling, searchlights reaching out into the darkness. No sooner did word come that the target had been found than gunners in one of the *San Francisco*'s starboard mounts were gripped by the sight of a ship bearing down on them fast, her bow to their starboard beam. When the crew alerted the bridge, the *San Francisco* went into a hard port turn and the *Breese* swung her rudder to the right. The minesweeper's momentum carried her into the *San Francisco* starboard quarter, delivering a severe but glancing blow that collapsed the *Breese*'s bow and tore a thirty-foot gash in the cruiser's side. As the ships turned, their sterns clapped together in a second collision. Physically, it was a mismatch. When the minesweeper's stern struck the high wall of gray steel that was the *San Francisco*'s stern, it was forced underwater, subducted by the cruiser's bulk. "With a sickening *thump thump thump* our outboard screw passed across *Breese*'s stern deck and quickly cleared her," Clifford Spencer, the *San Francisco* marine, wrote. "Her stern popped up in the water like a cork. I never heard if the *Breese* had any fatalities, probably a few, but life was cheap in those days and soon it, the collision, was only a memory."

The vigilance required to avoid such mishaps took a toll. Spencer wrote: "In trying to give you an idea of the strain put on everyone from the Admiral on down to the lowest ranks during this period, I am at a loss, but try this: Imagine your living room is made of steel, the windows are your lookout posts and you have been there for two weeks. With very little rest and less sleep, you stare out day and night for an attack from the air, from across the street, or up from your basement, that you know will destroy your home and probably take your or your family's life. This might give you a small idea of what the mental and physical conditions are like in sea warfare. This was maneuvers, but we knew that the real thing was just ahead. Grueling, yes, but Admiral Scott had to instill behavior into his ships and crews that the Japanese had perfected over many years. The Admiral had days, or at best a few weeks. We bitched and probably whined a lot, but by God, we learned!"

The *Helena*'s turret crews learned as rapidly as any in Scott's task force. They were "quick and slick as precision machinery," Chick Morris wrote, "swinging their arms with the grace of ballet dancers to maintain the flow of ammunition from magazines to guns." They got good. They expected to hit, every time. The gunnery department acquired, Morris wrote, a "bull's-eye complex." Against Mikawa's sharp-eyed shooters, they would need it.

The light cruiser had recently taken aboard a new skipper. When Captain Gilbert C. Hoover was swung over in a canvas bag from a destroyer to the larger ship, the crew liked what they saw. Waving to his crew, the forty-eight-year-old native of Bristol, Rhode Island, wore an aviator's leather jacket and a jaunty overseas cap. He had a Navy Cross, too. The consensus was, "He'll be a *Helena* man the minute he puts a foot on our deck," Chick Morris recalled.

Hoover had smarts and sophistication—he had been an aide to President Herbert Hoover (no relation), and served on the first government committee formed by Franklin Roosevelt to study nuclear fission. Those qualities were evident in his bearing and attitude. "They liked the way he came over the side. They liked his looks and his grin. They liked the cut of him. His expression plainly said he was proud to be coming aboard, and that was all they needed to know," Morris wrote.

At the change of command ceremony, a culture shift became apparent. His predecessor was dressed in the traditional whites. Hoover was ready for work, wearing slacks and short sleeves. "We knew things were going to be different aboard ship," a *Helena* sailor named Robert Howe said. "Captain Hoover had been overseas since the war had started. We didn't know it then, but he knew how to handle a fighting ship."

When Morris saw Hoover poring over the ship's blueprints in his sea cabin, he noted that he wasn't a big man. Neither short nor tall, stout nor slender, he seemed measured and balanced; smart, reliable, and steady in every respect. "In his leather jacket he looked a little like a middle-aged suburbanite about to go for a walk in the woods, with a trout rod tucked under one arm. But that room was a calm and confident place, mellowed already by the captain's personality." It was just what the *Helena* would need in the days ahead.

After the loss of the *Wasp,* the *Helena,* one of her escorts, took aboard some four hundred survivors. It was not her crew's first encounter with a capital ship loss. They had had nine months to process the events of December 7 into a righteous and productive brand of anger. Their ship had been berthed at Pearl Harbor right where Japanese agents had reported the battleship *Pennsylvania* would be. Pier-side at the 1010 Dock, the *Helena* took the first torpedo of the war. Dropped from a plane, it burrowed through the sea, passed underneath the shallow-draft vessel moored alongside the *Helena,* and smashed into the cruiser's forward engine room. The blast killed forty and wounded one hundred. But it completely did in the *Helena*'s berth-mate. The old wooden-hulled minelayer *Oglala* was lost to the underwater detonation close aboard. Her crew would say she was the only warship ever to sink from fright.

Whether they arose at Pearl Harbor or off Savo Island, the debilitating effects of defeat had a certain half-life and it took special measures to exorcise them from the bilges. Repaired at Mare Island as the carrier battles of May and June were fought, the *Helena* left San Francisco on July 23, 1942, escorting six supply ships for the South Pacific. As the deep swells took hold of her en route again to Pearl, a desire for revenge animated her crew. "The *Helena* craved action," one of her officers, C. G. Morris, wrote. "Her men talked of little else and prayed for the day when the ship's guns would set their words to music."

Designed exclusively for gun engagements, with five triple turrets mounting six-inch, forty-seven-caliber guns, the *Helena* had a full-load displacement of fourteen thousand tons—two thousand tons greater than that of a heavy cruiser. It was only her main battery that could be called light. Her six-inch projectiles, 130 pounds apiece, were half the weight of a heavy cruiser's eight-inch ordnance. What her battery lacked in weight it made up for in rate of fire. Firing "semi-fixed" ammunition that held the powder charge with the projectile in a single case, the *Helena*'s fifteen guns were rated for ten rounds per minute, as against three or four for a heavy cruiser. The only factor that limited this furious pace, aside from the possibility that her magazines might become exhausted, was the risk that the gun barrels would warp from the heat.

The *Helena*'s gunnery officer, Commander Rodman D. Smith, built on the strong foundation of his predecessor, Irving T. Duke, who had told his crew on commissioning day at the New York Navy Yard in September 1939, "We want to be consistent. Not sensational, but consistent. All I ask—all I insist upon—is that we get a better than average percentage of hits every time. And to do that, we must know our guns." Duke left the ship before she ever saw action, but his legacy endured. "The *Helena* never lost the inspiration he so gently pressed upon her in those early days of her schooling," Chick Morris wrote.

Morris and two other ensigns, Ozzie Koerner and Sam Hollingsworth, joined the *Helena* at Espiritu Santo, their final stop on a month-and-a-half journey to the South Pacific in nine different ships. Coming aboard, they were so awestruck that they hardly noticed the assistant gunnery officer standing at the top of the brow, expecting a salute. Lieutenant Warren Boles caught the single-stripers gaping at the ship's triple turrets, three forward—low, high, low—and two more aft. "Have you ever heard fifteen six-inch guns go off in unison?" he asked. The newcomers shook their heads. "It's something to hear for the first time. Just be careful which way you jump."

Veteran sailors worked hard to be nonchalant about the noggin-rattling impact of the *Helena*'s batteries, but a man's nervous system couldn't be rewired by will alone. "The whole ship is enveloped in one shattering blast of noise, and you jump like hell," wrote Morris. During gunnery exercises, the crew in the radio shack learned to transcribe the five-character blocks of the encoded fleet radio broadcasts while leaning down on their typewriters, the better to keep them from jumping off their desks.

For the *Helena* and her cohorts in Task Force 64, there was little time for rehearsing combat. Single-day exercises were "too short a time to justify any hope of obtaining adequate tactical unity in a newly organized force," Admiral King wrote. Gunnery exercises were dangerous business. Accidental explosions of mishandled powder in turrets and hoists took a fearful toll in life. To minimize the risks during peacetime, the drills were carefully scripted, from the number of firing passes each ship made, to which batteries fired and when, to what speeds the ships made. In night exercises, ships towing the target sleds obligingly kept their searchlights trained on the firing ships, just so there were no tragic mistakes. With the location of targets brightly revealed at all times, the potential for confusion—and realism— was written right out of the script.

Eliminating confusion and danger in peacetime exercises was understandable. Eliminating realism and danger during wartime exercises was unforgivable. A low-order schism had developed on Admiral Nimitz's staff centered on this divide. "His training section was constantly fighting the operations section," one of his staff officers, Ernest M. Eller, recalled. The goal of the training section was to maximize the proficiency of crews in battle. "Operations," on the other hand, "saw the world as a series of times of departures and times of arrivals," Eller said. "Training was something that sailors should know already." What they didn't yet know about the art of fighting would be learned finally in action against a living, death-dealing enemy.

Commanders did what they could with local incentives. On the destroyer *Sterett,* the gunnery officer held a contest to see which of his mount crews was fastest in loading four hundred rounds into the practice-loading machine. The winning crew did it in less than thirty minutes, about four seconds per load, and their reward for their hustle was a four-thousand-dollar cash prize. In Task Force 64, much remained to be done. While it was running with the carriers, training for a surface fight "had practically lapsed," Admiral Ghormley wrote. What was needed was an overhaul in readiness and spirit. And on both of those counts, Norman Scott, taking command of the flotilla in September 1942, was just the man for the job.

WITH THE ARRIVAL in the South Pacific of commanders such as Norm Scott, Gil Hoover, and Captain Edward J. "Mike" Moran in the *Boise,* and with the crown prince of shipboard gunnery, Rear Admiral Willis Lee, awaiting the arrival of the *Washington* at Tongatabu, the Navy was reshuffling its decks and getting the footing it needed for a new kind of fight. Distinctions were being drawn between officers who were battle-minded and those whose savage instincts were reserved for advancing their own careers. Qualities that got you ahead in peacetime were yielding to skills equally ageless, but prized only in desperate times: a glint in the eye, a forward-leaning, balls-of-the-feet bearing, a constitutional aspect of professionalized aggression.

The reach and impact of individual leadership was in flux in the machine age. According to legend, the eleventh-century Spanish general El Cid had such a powerful command presence that it survived his own death. With his corpse secured in his saddle, riding in the lead position, his army was said to have routed a foe by the mere illusion of his leadership. Innovations in the art of war could on one hand extend the reach and power of individuals. The commander of the carrier *Enterprise* pointed to a new dynamic in the age of airpower. "It is continually proved that the ability of a single individual can make or break the entire situation," he said. Planes individualized war. The pilot at the stick was the guidance system of his ordnance. But teamwork had not gone out of fashion within the hull of a ship. Men who were battle-minded would win the day so long as their spirit had a contagious strain. Careerists would climb as they usually did: with or without the glory of victory. Though deciding who belonged to which camp was often a matter of private controversy—in 1942 the carrier commanders were the principal case studies in that debate—one thing was clear. The street fighters were coming into play in the South Pacific.

With his return to basics and a regimen that left little time for idle watch standing, the commander of Task Force 64 was winning over his men. "Scott had balls," Robert Graff of the *Atlanta* said. "He was smart. And he was shrewd. Those three things usually make a fighter."

His mission as September drew to a close: bow up to the Tokyo Express and give it its first bloody nose.

14

The Devil May Care

FROM EVEN A SHORT DISTANCE OUT TO SEA, THE FIGHTING ASHORE seemed remote, aseptic. As his destroyer, the *Monssen,* prowled the northern shore of Guadalcanal, Roland Smoot found himself thinking: *So this is war. It's nothing.* It was, of course, hardly that. A captain's thoughts seldom wandered far from the fact that the surface fleet was almost ten months into a war and had yet to win a significant battle.

The carriers and their pilots were proven winners. American submariners were emerging as world-beaters. The surface Navy—the battleships, cruisers, and destroyers of the traditional black-shoe fleet—would have their day. At Guadalcanal as ever, it was the most expendable members of the deep-sea combat fleet, the destroyers, that made first contact with the enemy and carried the fight to him. While Norman Scott was getting his legs under him as commander of Task Force 64, the destroyer Navy was called to turn its guns in support of their ground-pounding brethren ashore.

Destroyer captains were known for their esprit. Off Balikpapan, Borneo, in January 1942, the old four-stack tin cans of the now-disbanded Asiatic Fleet had made the first offensive surface-ship foray of the war. In a quick nighttime raid against Japanese shipping at rest in an anchorage, a quartet of destroyers pressed in, turned out, and left several cargomen ablaze. For the first time, the night had been seized from the victory-sotted empire.

Chester Nimitz was well acquainted with this spirit. In 1907, as an ensign in command of the destroyer *Decatur,* he ran his ship into a sandbar off

Bataan. After turning himself in like the George Washington of legend, he faced a court-martial for incaution and negligence. His defense turned on his observation, calmly articulated during the proceedings, that the commander of a destroyer was supposed to have a devil-may-care attitude and that was precisely what he had given his Navy. In view of his spotless (if thin) record, and the handicap of having outdated charts, he was forgiven the offense and his path to the stars remained open.

It was in this tradition that the *Monssen* went hunting on the morning of September 27. Smoot's ship had been shepherd to a large cargo ship, the *Alhena,* on a run from Nouméa to Guadalcanal. As the *Alhena* was being unloaded, the Marine command decided to take advantage of having a modern destroyer in the area. A 1,630-tonner of the *Benson* class, the *Monssen* was ordered to cruise along the western shoreline and bombard targets of opportunity. She was a veteran of the North Atlantic convoy runs, of Jimmy Doolittle's Tokyo raid, and of Coral Sea and Midway, but Smoot had never been involved in something like this, where the enemy was standing so near, taunting him with his proximity.

The Japanese garrison had been making good use of the reinforcements the Tokyo Express was bringing them. They no longer underestimated the Marines. As they learned to fight smarter, U.S. patrols into the jungles and hills near Henderson Field found their days becoming increasingly dangerous. When the Marines asked the *Monssen* for a hand, Captain Smoot gladly answered the call.

The *Monssen*'s patrol line took her close to the mouth of the Matanikau River, the western boundary of the beachhead, about three miles west of Lunga Point. For several hours, the *Monssen*'s gunners fired on small Japanese landing craft on the beach, suspicious structures that might shelter the enemy, and anything resembling a fuel or ammo dump.

Then, cruising off Lunga Point, Smoot spied through his binoculars an American tank climbing a hill and a small group of Japanese soldiers emerging from a cave nearby. For a warship on a fire-support mission, the margin of victory in an encounter like that was defined by the flight time of a salvo to the beach. As far as the men in that tank were concerned, the gulf separating them was unbridgeable. The soldiers began running toward the tank. They climbed atop it and doused it with gasoline. Then a torch was produced and that was that. But the exchange was a total loss for the Japanese, too. "My gunnery officer saw those Japs running back," Smoot said, "and he turned the whole broadside of the ship on that cave and blew it to smithereens." Everybody burned.

Overhead, a high-flying V of Betty bombers arrived and began a run on the airfield. The *Monssen* pointed her batteries high and engaged them until several Marine Wildcats arrived. Smoot and his men watched as the last Betty in the formation was assaulted by the fighters, began falling, and exploded. One of its wings struck the water just a hundred feet from the ship. Ashore, the bodies of the Japanese dead could be seen wasting in the sand at the mouth of the Matanikau River. This was not distant. It was personal.

Late in the morning, as sounds of battle echoed through the coconut groves, the *Monssen* was ordered to escort several landing craft bearing two hundred Marine riflemen who were to be landed behind enemy lines. Four Higgins boats carrying them followed the destroyer to a projection of shore about a mile west of the river. The *Monssen* shelled the jungle behind the beach as the marines went ashore and vanished into the jungle.

At that point, another wave of Bettys arrived. They were promptly met by the Cactus Air Force's fliers. "The sky was soon crisscrossed with dozens of white streaks, which seemed to persist for many minutes from high altitude to sea level," a *Monssen* sailor, Chester C. Thomason, said. "Perhaps a dozen planes—friend and foe—were seen to plunge into the sea. The *Monssen* did not attempt to fire, as individual dogfights were too confusing." Afterward, once the surviving aircraft had dropped their bombs and departed, a group of men, apparently Americans, appeared on an open grassy hillside about half a mile inland. They seemed to be surrounded. Mortar rounds were bursting among them. Evidently the landings that the *Monssen* had accompanied hadn't managed to encircle and destroy the Japanese.

It was then that Smoot noticed a lone figure on another hill waving signal flags. His signal read: SEND BOAT ASHORE. The captain was wary of Japanese trickery. The figure was dressed in what he called "army drill," but from this distance the man could belong to either side. "We didn't know who it was and I wasn't going to take any chances." Smoot asked a signalman if there were a way to verify his identity. The signalman had an idea, and flagged a question to their mysterious correspondent: WHO WON THE WORLD SERIES IN 1941? The answer—YANKEES IN FIVE—decided the issue.

The deck force lowered a whaleboat over the side, and it motored in to the beach. When it returned, it was carrying the commander of the 1st Battalion of the 7th Marines, his aide, and two other marines. Coming aboard, Lieutenant Colonel Lewis B. "Chesty" Puller, age forty-four, saluted Smoot. "I doggone near lost my life getting down to the beach. I've got a whole group of my men up there in the hills. I've got to get them out of trouble."

Puller told a grim story. His marines, landing at Point Cruz and attempting to join up with Colonel Merritt A. Edson's 1st Raider Battalion, were in the midst of a faltering effort to dislodge Japanese forces from the Matanikau village area. When Puller's battalion got ambushed and pinned down by the well-entrenched units of General Kawaguchi's 17th Army, they were effectively cut off. By day's end, two dozen men would be dead and that same number wounded. They needed evacuation. Puller arranged for a couple dozen Higgins boats to do the job. The *Monssen* would lend fire support. "They are trapped up there," he told Smoot. "Let me tell you where to shoot."

Puller conferred with the destroyer's gunnery officer, and in short order the ship's four five-inch guns were trained inland again and set to barking. "We just ploughed it with bullets, straight up and down the middle," Smoot said. "Then we spread the firepower up two sides." Several Higgins boats, crewed by volunteers, motored in under fire to evacuate the trapped marines.

Wielding her main battery like a long-armed plow, Smoot's gunners blew open a path through the jungle. "As the first marines appeared on the beach," Chet Thomason wrote, "heavy enemy rifle and machine gun fire commenced from both sides. After a few minutes, the landing boats retreated back alongside the *Monssen*." Getting the men to the beach was much easier than retrieving them from it. When Puller thought that the boat crews hadn't committed themselves fully to the evacuation, he was furious. He stepped on Smoot's toes by yelling at the coxswains, telling them to drive back to the beach and not come back until all the survivors had been retrieved.

"Four marines had managed to scramble into one of the boats earlier," Thomason said. "They were lying down exhausted in the bottom of the boat. When they realized that the boat was being sent back into the beach, they scrambled up and jumped for the *Monssen*. Three managed to grab the lifelines and were pulled aboard. The fourth marine missed, and he disappeared beneath the water under the weight of his equipment. Two of the *Monssen*'s sailors quickly stripped off their clothes and dived into the ocean in an attempt to locate him, but they failed, and he was not seen again."

A Marine Dauntless pilot who had been strafing Japanese positions, Lieutenant Dale M. Leslie, guided the boats to the landing area. As the *Monssen*'s brain trust peered out through the clearing smoke through their glasses, the boats closed the beach. The coming of darkness would soon give them cover. With the setting of the sun, bright red slashes of tracer bullets could be seen reaching out from the jungle, splashing all around the departing vessels. One of the coxswains of the landing party, a Coast Guard signalman named Douglas A. Munro, lingered during the evacuation to support his mates with his craft's light machine gun. A Japanese machine gunner drew a bead on Munro's boat and opened fire, killing him.

After Puller and the marines rescued from the island were dropped off in a waiting boat at Lunga Point, Smoot took the *Monssen* away from Guadalcanal. The destroyer joined the *Alhena* for the nighttime run out to sea, away from the threat of nighttime surface attack. The next day the two ships returned for a final day of unloading, and the *Alhena* evacuated many of the wounded rescued the previous day. With a lull in the fighting ashore and the skies free of air raids, the day was quiet and the ships retired again late that afternoon for Espiritu Santo.

Their traditional griping could not mask the fact that the marines needed their fleet for much more than just transportation. The *Monssen*'s display of fighting spirit restored some of their faith. And many had had enough of a taste of life at sea to know they wanted no part of it. After Smoot had given Puller his parting gift the day before—a steak dinner in the wardroom, a hot shower, a seabag full of clean clothes, and a stash of cookies and cigarettes—the infantryman took his leave from the ship. Smoot was glad to be of some help to the Marine Corps. "Everything we could do to help in their rugged life ashore, we did." Puller thanked him, then said, "God, I wouldn't have your job for anything in the world."

At this, Smoot raised an eyebrow. "You mean to tell me you'd go back and go into that messy stuff over there and get yourself filthy and live on c-rations? You've come to see the kind of life I lead out here and you prefer yours?"

"I sure do. When you get hit, where are you? When *I* get hit, I *know* where I am."

Like most of the other commanders in Operation Watchtower, Roland Smoot could not know where getting hit would leave him. For the time being, the storm of war had settled its eye on the fetid island. It had not yet come directly for him. When it did, as would almost always be the case, the little tin cans would take its brunt.

15

The Visit

SEPTEMBER WAS A MONTH OF PREPARATION, OF CONSOLIDATION, OF preliminary reckoning. "Today," Admiral Matome Ugaki wrote in his diary on the thirtieth, "September is going to pass. Looking back, I find nothing has been accomplished this month." That judgment may have been just deserts for being slow to grasp the significance of the American move into the Solomons. The Japanese were finding themselves outgunned at the point of contact and hamstrung by the geometry of the inter-island campaign. A shortage of fuel at Rabaul forced them to be sparing and selective in the use of their major warships.

The Americans had their own problems, some of them similar, but they were confronting them with active, troubleshooting minds. The fleet's Service Squadron, the command that operated the tankers and transports and tenders and supply ships, had moved its headquarters north, from Auckland to Nouméa. The Navy was solving the algorithms that would determine how many tons of supplies, ammunition, fresh water, and food were needed per capita to keep an operation going. When the destroyer *Laffey* left the shipyard for war, she carried 103 pounds of beef liver, 280 pounds of cabbage, 400 pounds of carrots, 418 pounds of bacon and 499 pounds of pork loin, 36 pounds of chili powder, and nine gallons of ice cream—and that was just for her own men. Her inventory was typical, and delivering the calculated sum was a challenge to planners.

One of Nimitz's staffers, visiting to investigate and report on the state of the supply chain, found Nouméa's harbor a choked bottleneck of fully loaded cargomen waiting for dock space. The trouble ran all the way from San Francisco, where few seemed to know about the problems confronting SOPAC's stevedores, to Wellington, New Zealand, where an untimely long-shoreman's strike was looming. Though Nouméa's facilities could handle only twenty-four ships per month, often as many as eighty or more awaited unloading. The cranes in the harbor weren't stout enough to haul away heavy loads such as PT boats. Serious thought was given to a crude remedy: sinking the merchantmen so that the Elco motor torpedo boats, eighty feet long and fifty tons each, could simply float free.

Admiral Nimitz had long been worrying about the chemistry of the SOPAC command. He decided to visit the theater personally to size up not only its materials but also its state of mind. On September 28, his seaplane set down in Nouméa harbor and he was promptly taken to the *Argonne* for an afternoon meeting of area commanders.

On his first arrival, Nimitz was disappointed to learn that the battleship *Washington* was still at the Navy's fueling base at Tongatabu, eighteen hundred miles from Guadalcanal, "so far removed from the critical area," he would scold Ghormley, "that she might as well have been in Pearl or San Francisco, insofar as taking advantage of favorable opportunities is concerned." Nimitz also thought Ghormley was keeping Admiral Scott's striking force on too short a leash, holding them too far south "to do much about visiting enemy ships."

At 4:30 p.m. Nimitz sat down in the flagship's ward room with a gathering of brass that included Ghormley, the SOPAC chief of staff, Dan Callaghan, Kelly Turner, Major General Richard K. Sutherland from MacArthur's headquarters, and General Henry H. "Hap" Arnold, the commanding general of the Army Air Forces.

Arnold, a four-star, was Nimitz's only equal in the room. Arnold was no friend of the Navy's ambitions in the Pacific. Before leaving, he sought General Marshall's advice on dealing with the rival service branch. Marshall's advice was basic Dale Carnegie: Listen to the other fellow's story. Don't get mad. And let the other fellow tell his story first.

"We recognized the fact that the Navy was hard-pressed at Guadalcanal," Arnold wrote. "They did need a 'shot in the arm'—and needed it badly; but I was not sure that the way to give it to them was by sending airplanes that might better be used against the Germans from England." He viewed the Navy's demands for aircraft as a "separate intramural war" that was driven by "uninformed pressures" arising from public interest in the Pacific war.

Arnold had been shocked by President Roosevelt's posturing on the question of which theater should have priority. In private, FDR affirmed a Europe-first strategy. In public, he made statements that Guadalcanal had to be "held at all costs." While Arnold didn't argue with the idea that Guadalcanal should be held, he noted, "A natural word of encouragement from the President was at once seized upon as proof that he had changed his mind" about theater priorities. As Arnold would write, "It was obvious that the naval officers in this area were under a terrific strain. It was also obvious that they had chips on their shoulders." Ghormley said that the pace of work had been such that he hadn't left the *Argonne*'s flag quarters in about a month. When Arnold told him "that probably was the cause of some of his troubles, because no man—I don't care who he is—can sit continuously in a small office, fighting a war, with all the complicated problems that come up, without suffering mentally, physically and nervously," he received a quick comeuppance. "Admiral Ghormley lost no time in telling me that this was *his* theater and that no one could tell him how to command it. I assured him all I wanted was information; I was not trying to tell him in any way how to run his command. Things smoothed down after that, but it was clear that Ghormley and the other naval officers in that area—Admiral John S. McCain and Admiral Daniel Callaghan—were very worried about the situation there. . . . It looked to me as if everybody on that South Pacific front had a bad case of jitters."

The logistical bottlenecks Arnold found at Nouméa appalled him. He found the practice of rerouting ships to New Zealand for unloading and reloading inexcusable given the shortages everywhere else. "At that moment the planners of Torch were going nearly crazy in their search for ships," he wrote. In view of the accumulations of crated aircraft that he found at Nouméa, Arnold said that no more planes ought to go to SOPAC until the inventory had been unpacked and sent forward. The Navy's principal problem, he told Admiral King, was a shortage not of planes, but of airfields.

Ghormley disagreed. "I presented the need for aircraft of all types, especially Army fighters. . . . I felt that our emergency needs should be met even if our commitments to allied nations, on lend-lease and our commitments to the African Campaign, which had not yet commenced, had to be slowed down somewhat." Alas, the Army planners who allocated the service's planes worldwide made decisions based on projected U.S. and Japanese air strength six months out, in April 1943. Since the planners estimated that the U.S. would have five thousand planes in the Pacific then, and the Japanese only four thousand, the more immediate needs of SOPAC were immaterial. The Cactus Air Force would have to make do in '42.

Even though the U.S.–British Combined Chiefs of Staff had specifically agreed to divert fifteen Army air groups from Britain to the South Pacific, General Arnold successfully contrived to cancel it by arguing that any such reallocation, no matter how specific, was void because it jeopardized the "agreed strategic concept" of going on the offensive in North Africa.

As of September 1942, there was only one Allied offensive that stood in actual jeopardy, and it was far from the beaches of Casablanca. American forces on Cactus, Ghormley said, were "under constant pressure. Logistics supply is most difficult. We can send only one ship at a time and from the eastward there is only one channel.... The Japs are still getting in despite our air activity. Nobody knows exactly how many are on Cactus right now." Ghormley made a worrying impression on his superiors. Nimitz took note of the discrepancy and the awkward second looks it caused around the room. Watching closely as Ghormley spoke, Nimitz found him worn, weary, and anxious. He couldn't estimate enemy troop strength in part because he hadn't visited the island himself to talk with the marines. Vandegrift's intelligence section based their numbers on actual contact and behind-the-lines reconnaissance. When Ghormley mentioned that the island's supply of aviation gas was down to just ten thousand gallons, Turner pointed out that the supply had actually been as low as half that volume.

After Arnold remarked on the pressing need for aircraft worldwide and observed that the South Pacific already had all the planes its airfields could effectively handle, Nimitz asked Ghormley a pointed question: Why hadn't SOPAC's naval forces been sent out at night to sink the Tokyo Express? The answer came when staffers interrupted the meeting twice to deliver priority radio dispatches to Ghormley. When he read them, his reaction both times was to say, "My God, what are we going to do about this?" In his voice were the echoes of the defeat at Savo, a generalized dread that manifested itself in defeatism. Ghormley saw the whole operation as standing on a precipice. As he later recalled, "If the Japanese desired to take a chance, with the major portion of their fleet supporting a large landing force, they could retake Guadalcanal and break through our lines of communication."

As it happened, what Ghormley feared was exactly the plan then being devised by Yamamoto and his staff at Truk. On the Imperial Navy's drawing boards was an ambitious schedule of sustained reinforcements, to be coordinated in October with another major naval push.

* * *

THE DAY AFTER the conference of high commanders on the *Argonne*, Chester Nimitz stepped into a B-17 Flying Fortress and flew to Henderson Field to tour the island battlefront. General Vandegrift was there to greet him. Nimitz promptly reaffirmed to him that his primary mission was to hold Henderson Field, as opposed to dislodging the Japanese garrison from the surrounding jungles and hills. Vandegrift had understood this well from the beginning, when he drew up his landing plan.

In the bamboo grove outside Vandegrift's headquarters, Nimitz decorated several men. Colonel Merritt Edson, commander of the 1st Marine Raider Battalion and victor in the early clash south of Henderson Field, received the Navy Cross, as did the Marine Corps fighter ace Captain Marion Carl and Vandegrift himself. As Hal Lamar, Nimitz's chief of staff, read the citations, Nimitz pinned them on each recipient. Among them was a tall sergeant who had captured a Japanese tank and blown up a couple of machine-gun nests. As Nimitz reached up to pin him with the Navy Cross, the sergeant fainted. "I never saw an admiral before," he offered later.

When Nimitz returned to Nouméa, he met again with Ghormley and told him exactly what he wanted. He wanted all-weather airfields, more storage facilities for aviation gas, and Quonset huts, not tents, to shelter his pilots. He wanted better cargo-handling facilities, better roads, and more attentive aircraft repair services. "Planes are too expensive and too hard to get to let only minor damage render them permanently unserviceable," he said. Nimitz wanted a salvage tug in the area, and improved radio procedures and better equipment. He wanted new doctrine for communications and more efficient distribution of mail.

In cataloging these things, Nimitz was showing Ghormley how he wanted leadership exercised. It would not prove helpful to Ghormley's career that Nimitz visited Guadalcanal before Ghormley himself did. Gracious and subtle as ever, CINCPAC calmly told Ghormley something that might have been tinged with hellfire coming from a different commander: "I want you to go up and see conditions for yourself."

At their second meeting, Nimitz learned that Ghormley had not responded to a request from the Joint Chiefs of Staff for a schedule of planned offensive operations up the Solomons toward Rabaul. Ghormley said he had not responded because "I feel that our present operations have not yet reached a point where such a plan and schedule would be worthwhile."

Ghormley's failure to propose the requested schedule of future operations was a command failure of a high order. Nimitz was suspicious of commanders who found reasons to stay out of harm's way. Typically he kept his judgments of people to himself, but after two months of fighting and no victories to show, he was in a mood for accountability. He instructed Ghormley to include in his final report on the Battle of Savo Island his view as to the responsibility for the results that night. "Such a blow cannot be passed over, and we owe it to the country to do our best to fix the responsibility for that disaster, and to take the action necessary to prevent a recurrence," Nimitz said.

Back at Pearl Harbor, Nimitz would give a *New York Times* reporter a sunny assessment of his trip. He professed himself "satisfied in every way with what I saw." His other remarks, artfully innocuous, sent a warning shot over his South Pacific commander's bow. Nimitz told Trumbull, "It was just the kind of trip you would expect a senior officer to take from time to time to see what's going on."

Late one evening on Guadalcanal, Nimitz had said to General Vandegrift over a drink, "When this war is over we are going to write a new set of Navy regulations. So just keep it in the back of your mind because I will want to know some of the things you think ought to be changed."

"I know one right now," the marine said. "Leave out all reference that he who runs his ship aground will face a fate worse than death. Out here too many commanders have been far too leery about risking their ships."

Nimitz said nothing but smiled, perhaps recalling his tenure in command of the *Decatur* and of the court-martial charges that he had so audaciously defeated. Somehow that spirit had to be made to prevail here and now. There was little doubt that he meant to send his friend Bob Ghormley a message: Know your theater, know your command, then find those aggressive captains, the fighters, who would win the day.

Off Tassafaronga and Cape Esperance, night after night, Imperial Navy cruisers and destroyers landed troops and supplies with scant interference. Between the end of September and the first week of October, Admiral Mikawa made eight runs after dark with fast destroyer-transports, delivering virtually without incident ten thousand troops of the Imperial Army 2nd Division, a veteran unit that had won infamy for its work during the murderous occupation of Nanking.

To Norman Scott and his cruiser captains—Gilbert Hoover in the *Helena,* Mike Moran in the *Boise,* Charles H. McMorris in the *San Francisco,* Ernest G. Small in the *Salt Lake City,* and soon enough many others—a terrible burden was about to be passed. They would confront the Japanese at night and try to reverse their momentum after dark.

Probably encouraged by Nimitz, Ghormley ordered Scott on October 5 to "HAVE STRIKING FORCE OPERATE IN POSITION OF READINESS TO ATTACK ENEMY VESSELS LANDING REINFORCEMENTS AT CACTUS." Scott was the author of a new night battle plan that attempted to apply the lessons of the previous months. Flying his flag in the *San Francisco,* he accompanied the escort carrier *Copahee* within range of Guadalcanal and stood by on the sixth as air reinforcements flew off to Henderson Field. Then he joined the *Salt Lake City,* the *Helena,* the *Boise,* and five destroyers east of Rennell Island and prepared to seize his opportunity.

16

Night of a New Moon

WITH GHORMLEY'S BATTLE ORDER IN HAND, NORMAN SCOTT WASTED no time departing Espiritu Santo. Task Force 64 arrived south of Rennell Island on October 9. There he ran them through a series of intramural scrimmages, pitting his cruisers against one another in offset gunnery exercises. That same day, two transports, the *Zeilin* and *McCawley,* departed Nouméa carrying a regiment from the U.S. Army's New Caledonia–based "American" Division— the 164th Infantry with 2,837 men under Colonel Bryant E. Moore—as well as 210 ground crewmen from the 1st Marine Air Wing, eighty-one jeeps and trucks, heavy guns, and forty-two hundred tons of supplies and cargo. Scott's cruiser force joined them at sea for the journey to Guadalcanal.

Scott had chosen as his flagship the heavy cruiser *San Francisco,* commanded by Captain Charles H. McMorris. As one of two such ships in Task Force 64, she was a traditional if not an ideal choice from which to command this particular battle force. Even among the heavy cruisers, she was a black sheep. After she performed poorly in gunnery exercises off Hawaii early in the year, the *San Francisco* found herself assigned to escort convoys rather than sailing with a combat task force. To equip her for an escort role, the shipfitters at Pearl had fastened to her fantail a depth charge rack. This hardware, customarily found on a destroyer, was of dubious value in a heavy cruiser, insofar as those ships had no sonar equipment with which to locate submarines. Cruisers were meant to fight surface actions, in which depth charges were decidedly unhelpful things to have aboard. The unusual fitting was a shameful "scarlet letter" that brought derision from other cruiser sailors.

Though the twelve-thousand-ton heavy cruisers *San Francisco* and *Salt Lake City* were the largest and most heavily armed ships in Scott's force, as well as the two highest-rated cruisers in the fleet in terms of the efficiency of their overall engineering performance, they were not necessarily the most technologically capable or most powerful in combat. That honor belonged to his light cruisers, the *Helena* and the *Boise,* which were equipped with fast-firing six-inch main batteries and the new microwave-frequency SG surface-search radar, far superior to the SC sets carried by most heavy cruisers. But radar was a newfangled complexity. Almost all admirals of the World War II era were more comfortable with mechanical-optical fire control, based on direct observation and visual adjustment. This and other factors, including considerations of onboard living space for an admiral's staff, recommended the heavy cruisers as flagships.

As October settled in, quickening radio traffic continued to suggest a surge in enemy naval activity in the northern Solomons. Admiral Ghormley queried MacArthur and Rear Admiral Aubrey W. Fitch, who on September 21 had replaced Rear Admiral John S. McCain as commander of SOPAC's land-based air forces,* whether their search pilots had seen any of the "new-type heavy units" that he believed the Japanese were operating in the area. He mentioned sightings of an "extra large cruiser, *Mutsu* type," as well as some kind of a "mystery ship." Perhaps scorning his South Pacific commander's foggy notions of the Japanese Navy's generally familiar ship classes, Nimitz replied dismissively: "No mystery ship known here." But as ever in war, the faster information flowed, the more the questions proliferated.

On the morning of October 11, the sense of pending action was well apparent to anyone with access to a radio. In the *Helena,* encoded blocks of text dashed through the foremast antenna into Chick Morris's radio room, "a steady, chattering stream that kept the typewriters hopping," he wrote. There were reports of sightings, requests for information and clarification, questions from pilots on patrol. The latest was that a pair of Japanese cruisers and six destroyers were southbound from Rabaul. This report was rather innocuous on its face, and not entirely accurate. The Japanese force that was sighted, commanded by Rear Admiral Aritomo Goto, consisted of two separate groups. The cruiser force, which Goto personally commanded from his flagship, the *Aoba,* actually included three heavy cruisers, the *Aoba, Furu-*

---

* McCain returned to Washington to serve as chief of the Navy's Bureau of Aeronautics.

taka, and *Kinugasa,* and two destroyers. The Reinforcement Group, steaming separately, contained the fast seaplane tenders *Nisshin* and *Chitose* and five troop-carrying destroyers.

Goto's cruisers were dispatched to bombard Henderson Field on the night of October 11–12. The two tenders, meanwhile, were scheduled to anchor off Tassafaronga and send ashore heavy artillery, ammunition, and equipment as well as a battalion of troops. Powerful as Goto's combined group was, it was but the vanguard of a much larger force that Admiral Yamamoto was gathering at Truk, soon to flatten Henderson Field and destroy the U.S. Navy forces protecting them once and for all. Under the overall command of Vice Admiral Nobutake Kondo, this force included all five of Yamamoto's carriers. A force that included the carriers *Junyo* and *Hiyo,* with the battleships *Kongo* and *Haruna* and four heavy cruisers and the ten ships of Raizo Tanaka's Destroyer Squadron 2, sailed under Kondo's direct command. Vice Admiral Chuichi Nagumo's fast carrier striking force, with the *Shokaku, Zuikaku,* and *Zuiho,* steamed separately. Rear Admiral Hiroaki Abe would command the rest of the combined task force's heavy surface forces: the battleships *Hiei* and *Kirishima* and three heavy cruisers, escorted by fifteen destroyers. Sixteen submarines advanced in a skirmish line ahead of the surface task forces.

This tremendous gathering of naval power would unleash itself on Guadalcanal and its neighboring seas in coordination with an assault on Henderson Field by the 17th Army, tentatively set to step off on October 22. Yamamoto would await the Army's signal. Meanwhile, Goto's force would serve as the spearhead of the counteroffensive.

SCOTT PREPARED TO enter battle on the basis of partially correct and incomplete information. American search planes found the Reinforcement Group but mistook the tenders for cruisers—a near-perfect reversal of the error made by the New Zealand scout pilot back in August, who reported tenders or gunboats, thereby masking the identity of cruisers. Now Goto's cruisers approached undetected, and behind the Reinforcement Group. The manner of approach suggested the Japanese had no fear of an American surface fleet. On October 11 and 12, attacks by the planes of the 11th Air Fleet would suppress Henderson Field and enable the tenders to reach Tassafaronga, while the cruisers struck the airfield.

In the *San Francisco*'s flag quarters, Scott studied the charts with his staff and did the math, figuring the approaches his enemy was most likely to use and planning his own countermoves backward from the point of optimum contact. His designation as "Commander, Night Screening and Attack Force," suggested the approach he would use in defending Savo Sound. There was nothing attack-oriented about Admiral Crutchley's approach back in August. Scott intended to choose the circumstances of first contact. He seemed to appreciate something a surviving officer of the *Quincy* wrote regarding the disaster of August 9—that "Battles can only be won by ships engaged in *offensive actions*. . . . In spite of the fact that we had numerically superior forces in the area, a bold attack by the enemy was partially successful. Doubtless a similar attack by our own forces on a Japanese stronghold would have been equally successful." In an evaluation released by Admiral King's headquarters, it was urged, "Surface ships should be employed as striking forces. So far the war in the Pacific has been featured by long-range carrier air duels. We have, however, suffered equal if not greater losses from submarine and surface ship attacks. We must use our surface ships more boldly as opportunity warrants." Scott saw the night patrol as a hunt. He would remain hidden, and set out to intercept when the moment was right, seeking the enemy. At a conference at Espiritu Santo, he discussed the new mission with his commanders and formulated the doctrine that would give them a chance to beat the Japanese at their own game.

Doctrine, simply put, is an agreed plan of action that clarifies who will do what, how, and when. Existing tactical instructions for combat commanders emphasized major actions between capital ships fought at long range. According to *General Tactical Instructions*, formulated in 1940, any firing that took place below seventeen thousand yards was considered "close range." The light forces that engaged at those close ranges had no standardized doctrine at the fleet level; squadron and division commanders had the responsibility to devise their own doctrine and battle plans. Norman Scott's plan for Task Force 64 on the eve of battle would go like this: On the night he planned a sortie, Scott would keep his nine ships south of Guadalcanal near Rennell Island, outside the range of enemy bombers, until about noon. He would begin his run after the open window to air attack had closed. Moving north during the midafternoon, with his cruisers' aviation divisions stripped to a single floatplane, he would accelerate to battle speed—twenty-five knots— when he was about 130 miles south of Savo Sound. As his task force made its five-hour sprint toward the battle zone north of Guadalcanal, friendly search planes would confirm the enemy's position by last light. Once the battle area was reached, he would form into a single column with the destroyers *Farenholt, Duncan,* and *Laffey* in the van, followed by the flagship *San Francisco, Boise, Salt Lake City,* and *Helena,* with the destroyers

Buchanan and *McCalla* bringing up the rear. He would then launch his float-plane for tactical spotting leading up to the engagement. Radio silence on the talk-between-ships frequency would be broken only to report actual contacts.

If the timing worked out, Scott would intercept the Tokyo Express west of Savo in accordance with its faithfully kept delivery schedule. His destroyers would illuminate the enemy ships immediately upon radar contact and attempt a torpedo attack. His commanders would be free to open fire on first contact, without requesting his permission. *Fire first and ask questions later* would be the order of the day. His leading cruisers would close rapidly and fire at short range in continuous-fire rather than salvo mode. The two rear cruisers, the *Salt Lake City* and the *Helena,* and the rear destroyers would keep watch on the formation's disengaged side. A particular challenge for the leading destroyers would be to stay alert for course changes blinkered from the *San Francisco* behind them. Improvised maneuvers were likely to be frequent once the action started.

Unlike the Navy brain trust in the campaign's inaugural days, Scott based his doctrine not on sunny assumptions, but on grave possibilities. Whereas Kelly Turner and his commanders had once assumed the Japanese could not reach Savo Sound before morning on August 9, Scott set himself to face the worst. His plan was no stroke of brilliance, nor was it even American in origin—he was more than willing to learn from the success of his enemies. His approach resembled nothing quite so much as a defensively oriented version of the one that Admiral Mikawa had prevailed with two months earlier.

One thing Scott's tactical instructions didn't adequately clarify was how his destroyer captains would bring their torpedoes to bear. Torpedoes were the killing weapons of naval war, and much easier to aim than guns were. The art of gunnery, of firing projectiles at a moving target, entailed difficult calculations, including the problem of physically stabilizing guns on a rolling sea and the vagaries of three dimensions. Torpedo solutions were expressed in just two dimensions. If you knew your own torpedo's speed, it was a simple matter to trace the enemy's crossing angle and estimate the intersection point. "Any qualified watch officer accustomed to maneuvering a destroyer in formation can estimate the lead angle accurately enough to produce a collision course [for a torpedo]," an experienced destroyerman wrote. "At the short ranges of engagement being reported, a destroyer's hull length would cover almost any error in estimate." Aside from that over-sight—Scott intended to rely on his guns—he had ably applied common sense, and the standard tactics for surface battle that every professional graduate of the Naval War College should have known well.

IN THE *HELENA,* as in all the ships of the SOPAC force, runners hustled decoded message traffic to Captain Hoover and his department heads. Three or four times an hour, Ensign Morris ran to Hoover's cabin behind the bridge with messages and battle plan dispatches from Scott. There was no doubting the pace of activity within the skipper's mind. His bulkheads were papered with charts of the southern Solomons area, marked in red where enemy submarines and ships had been reported. Whenever Hoover received a new dispatch, he studied it quietly then turned to his chart, tracing his finger over the track marking the progress of the Japanese ships. "The two lines on the chart were twin fuses, smoldering toward each other," Morris wrote. "When they met there would be an explosion."

Despite that, Hoover "was without question the calmest man on the *Helena,*" Morris continued. "It was, in fact, something more than simple calmness. On entering that cabin from the feverish bustle of the ship, you sensed a kind of loneliness. You felt the pressure of the responsibility upon the man who sat there hour after hour, thoughtfully planning the attack of his ship—our ship. . . . Her officers and men were already waging that battle within themselves, measuring their mettle, wondering how they would shape up in action." Hoover told Morris that he expected action that night and asked him to show the reports to all the *Helena*'s department heads.

Commander Rodman Smith, Hoover's gunnery officer, was tall and husky and not given to pleasantries: "as grim as his guns." When Morris found him he was poring over gunnery charts, ordnance data, and hundreds of other technical matters that determine a ship's ability to land salvos on target. When the ensign handed him the dispatch board, Smith initialed it without comment and gave it to his assistant, Warren Boles.

"Captain seem to be worried?" Lieutenant Boles asked.

"Not a bit," Morris said.

"Are we going in?"

"He says it looks like it."

"I hope so. The men need something to shoot at."

The prospect of a small steel-enclosed world crashing in around a man has a useful way of concentrating the mind. Men whose stations were in belowdecks compartments, situated below the waterline and sealed in at battle stations by watertight doors, were keenly aware that they already lay in their tombs should a torpedo hit. On untested ships especially, people tended to fidget. The *Helena* had a fire controlman named Samuel Maslo who reliably predicted the worst. Whenever talk of intercepting the Tokyo Express came up, which was always, he would say things like, "We'll catch it sure. They got twenty ships to our one. They'll murder us." They called him "Sobbin' Sam the Fire Control Man." Fretting like that was easy to laugh off, but the echoes tended to linger. Still, one learned through the strenuous pace of shipboard life not to dwell on remote possibilities. Nimitz had found that confidence grew and pessimism waned the closer one got to the combat front.

To sailors and officers whose knowledge of war had come in school, as opposed to the crucible of the actual thing, there was comfort in numbers—and in the open air. On the *Helena*, Chick Morris and his fellow ensigns and j.g.'s (junior grades) made a habit of gathering on the forecastle. They called themselves the Junior Board of Strategy. Until sunset left them sitting in darkness, they studied the flag hoists by which Admiral Scott sent messages to the squadron, then discussed and analyzed the implications. On the moonlit nights, beautiful to a layman's eye but fraught with danger for sailors in a war zone, the creamy light was bright enough to play cards by. But it was another kind of contest that held their imaginations captive.

What would it feel like when it finally came? "The Japs would strike—they had to strike—but when?" Chick Morris wondered. "The ship's officers talked of nothing else." The young could be forgiven their nerves. Experienced officers would be given less latitude to indulge themselves.

Morris never forgot the otherworldly serenity of the tropical evening of October 11 as the Junior Board of Strategy stood in session, watching the *San Francisco*'s flag hoists raise the orders for the night. "We were moving west, straight into the sun," he wrote, "the air so clear and still that the whole visible world seemed splashed with sunset colors. It was good to stand there and watch the ships of our formation steaming through that placid sea. And I was not alone. Other men were thinking the same thoughts. Some were sitting around anchor windlasses. Others were parked on the bitts, quietly 'batting the breeze.' One man was asleep on the steel deck, and another, nearby, was deep in a magazine of Western stories."

With the four cruisers in column and five destroyers arrayed in an antisubmarine screen ahead, the formation covered nearly three miles of ocean. The men in the task force stood in the place that separates the boundless tedium of being under way from the freeze-frame intensity of action. The physical magnitude of what was coming was beyond the ken of everyone except the crew who operated the SG search radar's graphical scope. The

Boise's rangekeeper operator swept his parabolic transmitter through a continuous 360-degree arc, generating a map-like visual display on the PPI repeaters and distinguishing ship from shore so sharply as to reveal inaccuracies in the ancient charts. The search radar scanned for targets. When they were found, the narrower beams of the ship's fire-control radars would zero in. The fire-control radars could also be used for search. Moran's FD operators probed for targets through a quarter-circle arc pointed east. Not fully trusting radar, Scott had ordered his commanders to refrain from using their older SC sets during the run-in, lest their transmissions be detected by the enemy much as the beam of a lighthouse could be seen from beyond its effective range. A man's eyes could reach only from the churning wake of the ship ahead to the flaring bow wave of the one behind. Everyone in the force, from the admiral down to the loaders on the powder hoists, had his senses heightened by his ignorance.

In the *Boise,* some turret crewmen breathed a soft chant over the battle telephones: *Pass the word from gun to gun: This won't be a dummy run.* Captain Moran's ship had compiled a far-flung war record. Fresh from an audacious solo raid on Japanese shipping in their home waters, conceived as a diversion to assist the Guadalcanal landings, "Iron Mike's" men redeemed what had been a frustrating deployment with the Asiatic Fleet in January. Off Timor, they had met the same fate the *South Dakota* did off

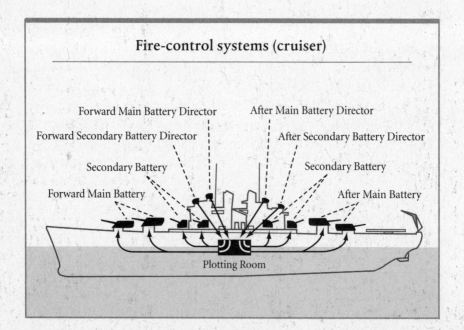

Fire-control systems (cruiser)

Forward Main Battery Director

After Main Battery Director

Forward Secondary Battery Director

After Secondary Battery Director

Secondary Battery

Secondary Battery

Forward Main Battery

After Main Battery

Plotting Room

Tongatabu—grounding on an unfortunately situated coral head. The *Boise*'s withdrawal from the Asiatic theater for stateside repair had earned her the nickname "the Reluctant Dragon." Having missed battle, Moran's gang were just like the others in Task Force 64: eager for a scrap but awaiting the measure of their worth that only the actual thing can provide. No officer could have burned with anticipation more than Norman Scott himself.

Shortly after 6 p.m., the Japanese ships spotted by the patrol planes that morning were reported again, 110 miles north of Guadalcanal, heading down the Slot at twenty knots. Exactly what their mission was—bombardment or reinforcement—continued to be anybody's guess. The evening call to general quarters was pre-climactic. Hours would pass with Scott's crews in that ready state, and the heavily fraught tedium mounted. "There was little to do," Chick Morris said. "Our search planes had returned to their bases and had nothing more for us." Despite Scott's order to muzzle the search radars, the

Order of Battle—Battle of Cape Esperance
(October 11, 1942)

U.S.	Japan
TASK FORCE 64	**BOMBARDMENT GROUP**
Rear Adm. Norman Scott	Rear Adm. Aritomo Goto
San Francisco (CA) (flagship)	*Aoba* (CA) (flagship)
Salt Lake City (CA)	*Furutaka* (CA)
Boise (CL)	*Kinugasa* (CA)
Helena (CL)	*Fubuki* (DD)
Farenholt (DD)	*Hatsuyuki* (DD)
Duncan (DD)	
Laffey (DD)	**REINFORCEMENT GROUP**
Buchanan (DD)	*Nisshin* (CVS)
McCalla (DD)	*Chitose* (CVS)
	Asagumo (DD)
	Natsugumo (DD)
	Yamagumo (DD)
	Murakumo (DD)
	Shirayuki (DD)
	Akizuki (DD)

Salt Lake City began radiating with its SC unit as the projectilemen loaded star shells into the fuze pots.

The moon was new behind the abundant cirrocumulus, the seven-knot wind scarcely rippling the moderate swells as they blew from the east-northeast, when Task Force 64 rounded the northwestern coast of Guadalcanal and turned north to intercept.

But there was a watcher in the sound: a Japanese submarine riding on the surface in Kamimbo Bay, a landing area near Cape Esperance that was favored by the Tokyo Express. Scott had no inkling the *I-26* was there. The same boat that had torpedoed the *Saratoga* on August 31, she may have been too close to the coastline for radars to discern. The American presence so startled Minoru Yokota that he ordered an emergency dive before he could send a sighting report. By the time he surfaced again two hours later and transmitted it, the events of the evening were too far along for it to matter.

Rear Admiral Goto's three heavy cruisers and two destroyers churned south toward Henderson Field. On came the heavy cruisers *Aoba, Furutaka,* and *Kinugasa,* all veterans of the Battle of Savo Island, with the destroyers *Fubuki* and *Hatsuyuki* riding off their bows.

On the *San Francisco,* a marine assigned as a loader on a five-inch gun, Clenroe W. Davis, overheard a radarman in the radar room report to the bridge unidentified blips on his scope. The radarman listened to what the officer had to say in return, then replied, "Well, sir, these islands are traveling at about thirty knots."

In the *Helena,* at the rear of the cruiser column, the men on the bridge were hard to recognize through the layers of their protective clothing. "Dumpy and fat in fireproof goggles, steel helmets, mae wests and gloves, they resembled visitors from Mars," Chick Morris wrote. In the humid confines of the ships, sailors innocent of combat often resisted donning the protective garb. Those with a better idea of what battle could bring pulled on the heavy clothing, or unrolled their shirtsleeves at least.

At ten, Scott ordered each cruiser to send aloft a search plane. When the *Salt Lake City*'s crew flung their plane off the catapult, it caught fire almost immediately, courtesy of a flare on board the plane. The aircraft hit the sea in a mass of flame, searing the dilated irises of the lookouts and stiffening everyone's nerves with the fear that they had declared their presence to an unseen enemy. The plane burned like a pyre for what seemed like hours.

Per the battle plan, Scott ordered his destroyers to re-form in a single column with the cruisers. The *Buchanan* and *McCalla* heeled out of formation,

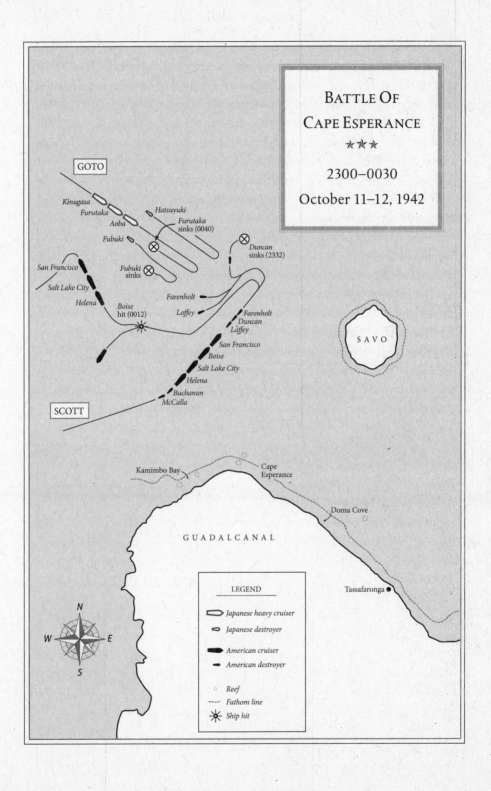

BATTLE OF CAPE ESPERANCE

★★★

2300–0030
October 11–12, 1942

GOTO

Kinugasa
Furutaka
Aoba
Hatsuyuki
Furutaka sinks (0040)
Fubuki
⊗ *Duncan sinks (2332)*
San Francisco
Fubuki sinks
Salt Lake City
Helena
Boise hit (0012)
Farenholt
Laffey
Farenholt
Duncan
Laffey
San Francisco
Boise
Salt Lake City
Helena
Buchanan
McCalla

SCOTT

SAVO

Kamimbo Bay
Cape Esperance

Doma Cove

GUADALCANAL

Tassafaronga

LEGEND

N
W E
S

⬭ Japanese heavy cruiser
⬬ Japanese destroyer
▬ American cruiser
– American destroyer
○ Reef
---- Fathom line
✳ Ship hit

let the rest of the column overtake them, and took station at the rear. When the search plane from the *San Francisco* checked in, reporting *"One large, two small vessels, one-six miles from Savo off northern beach, Guadalcanal. Will investigate closer,"* Scott turned to the northeast, looking to pass Savo Island, darkly visible ahead, five miles off his starboard beam. "The only indication of impending battle was the speed at which the fleet was traveling," remembered Ensign George B. Weems of the *McCalla*. "We would step up our speed a couple of knots at frequent intervals, till we were boiling along."

It was almost eleven thirty when the *Salt Lake City*'s search radar painted three distinct clusters of steel on the water to the west and northwest. Captain Small ordered his fire-control radar operators to seek targets on that bearing. The returning echoes conveyed valuable particulars: bogeys at sixteen thousand yards, on course 120 degrees true, speed twenty knots.

As it happened, the Americans were tracing the same track of sea that the picket destroyer *Blue* had on the night Admiral Mikawa came calling. If the station was familiar, Scott's use of it had an entirely different posture now. Running northeast, perpendicular to the axis of the enemy approach, his nine ships were buttoned up for battle. As the pilot relayed further details on the warning net, Scott radioed his commanders: "EXECUTE TO FOLLOW— COLUMN LEFT TO COURSE 230." Task Force 64 had finally found its fight.

Admiral Ernest J. King: "He would acknowledge no mind as superior to his own."

Admiral Chester W. Nimitz: the Pacific War's essential man.

Vice Admiral Robert L. Ghormley wasn't Nimitz's first choice to command South Pacific naval forces. His remote leadership style and tight nerves would lead to his relief by Halsey.

Rear Admiral Frank Jack Fletcher, victorious at Coral Sea and Midway, took heat for his cautious employment of his carriers off Guadalcanal.

Rear Admiral Richmond Kelly Turner, commander of amphibious forces, had a virulent disagreement with Fletcher over how Operation Watchtower should be run.

Rear Admiral John S. McCain, commander of land-based naval air forces in the South Pacific.

An F4F Wildcat prepares to launch from the *Wasp* in support of Watchtower, August 7, 1942.

Before dawn, the heavy cruiser *Vincennes* opens fire on Japanese positions on Guadalcanal. She went down in glory two nights later.

Captain Frederick L. Riefkohl, commanding officer of the *Vincennes* and Task Group 62.6.

The *Astoria*, in the early days of Operation Watchtower.

Astoria gunners in drills, spring 1942.

Captain William G. Greenman commanded the *Astoria* before her loss, then ran Guadalcanal's makeshift naval base.

The *Astoria*, shown in Hawaiian waters in July 1942, prepares to recover a floatplane using her starboard-side crane.

The last photo of the *Quincy*, caught in the glare of Japanese searchlights, down by the stern in the Battle of Savo Island.

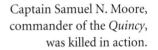

Captain Samuel N. Moore, commander of the *Quincy*, was killed in action.

Rear Admiral Gunichi Mikawa, victor in the Battle of Savo Island.

The *Quincy* in the South Pacific, August 1942.

Chicago sailors cut away bow plating damaged by
a Japanese torpedo, August 10, 1942.

Captain Howard D. Bode of the *Chicago* was
among many who performed poorly at Savo Island.
He would bear more than his share of the blame.

Two U.S. destroyers, the *Blue* (left) and the *Patterson*, assist the burning HMAS *Canberra* on the morning of August 8. She could not be saved.

Lloyd M. Mustin (shown here as a rear admiral), served as assistant gunnery officer in the *Atlanta*.

Admiral Isoroku Yamamoto, commander of the Imperial Combined Fleet, believed he would find his decisive battle off Guadalcanal.

Rear Admiral Norman Scott (shown here as a captain) taught the Navy's light forces how to fight.

The light cruiser *Boise* in a South Pacific port, late August 1942.

Captain Robert G. Tobin (right)
commanded Scott's destroyers in the Battle
of Cape Esperance. Here he receives the
Navy Cross from Admiral William F. Halsey.

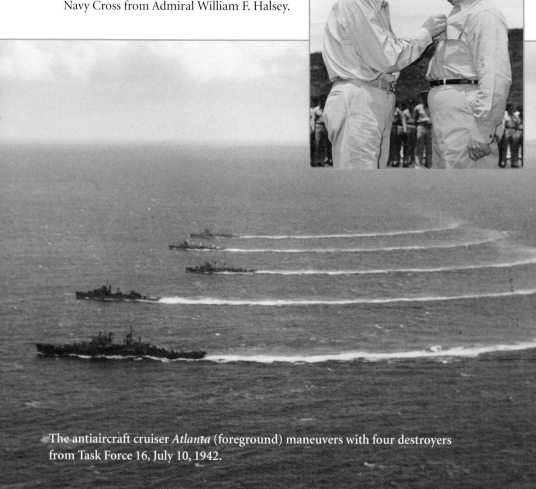

The antiaircraft cruiser *Atlanta* (foreground) maneuvers with four destroyers
from Task Force 16, July 10, 1942.

The destroyer *Farenholt*, shown here in August 1942, took a beating from friendly fire on October 11.

Radar first came to the fleet in 1941. Once the fighting sailors learned how to use it, the new technology would change everything.

YOUNG MEN WANTED IN
NAVY RADAR

BE A RADIO TECHNICIAN

- Enlistees and inductees both eligible
- You start as a Seaman First Class
- Ten months of specialized training
- You earn a Petty Officer rating
- One of the war's most exciting fields
- Insures your postwar future

INQUIRE AT NEAREST NAVY RECRUITING STATION

The SG radar, with its 48-inch by 15-inch parabolic transmitter, was the first to employ the familiar circular display. Used for search, fire control, or navigation, it gave commanders an unprecedented picture of the enemy at night.

Major Joseph Foss, the executive officer of VMF-121 at Henderson field, arrived in October and became the USMC's leading fighter ace of WW2.

Major General Alexander A. Vandegrift, USMC, paid all costs to hold Henderson Field against repeated Japanese assault from air, land, and sea.

Marine tanks prowl the killing field near Alligator Creek, where Colonel Ichiki's detachment was slaughtered on August 21.

Lieutenant Colonel Lewis B. "Chesty" Puller (shown here, second from left, in January 1944 with his regimental staff on Cape Gloucester) worked closely with the Navy in defense of Marine positions on Guadalcanal.

Nimitz with Vandegrift. Nimitz boosted morale with his September visit to Guadalcanal.

The SBD Dauntless served as the principal ship killer of the Cactus Air Force while Henderson Field's Wildcats controlled the skies of the Slot by day.

As the *Wasp* burns in the background,
the destroyer *O'Brien* is rocked by a torpedo
from the submarine *I-19*.

Rear Admiral Raizo Tanaka
led the Tokyo Express, as the Japanese
seaborne reinforcement runs to
Guadalcanal became known.

The *Wasp* sank quickly. Japanese submarines were nowhere more
effective than off Guadalcanal.

The destroyer *Laffey* brought hundreds of *Wasp* survivors home to Espiritu Santo. An *Atlanta*-class AA cruiser is in the background.

In the Battle of Santa Cruz, the *South Dakota* (left) churns a heavy wake. A Japanese plane takes the plunge while the *Enterprise* takes a bomb.

The damaged *Hornet* under tow from the *Northampton*, October 26, 1942. Another Japanese air strike is inbound to finish her.

Chaplain James Claypool (facing camera, at left) presides over burials at sea on the *South Dakota* after the air battle off Santa Cruz.

Daniel J. Callaghan, shown here as a captain, served on Robert Ghormley's staff before returning to the fighting fleet.

Many argued the newly outfitted *Helena* should have served as Callaghan's flagship.

Captain Gilbert C. Hoover

The *Atlanta*: a welterweight ship with a middleweight's jab.

The *Portland* paid her freight on Friday the 13th.

Captain Samuel P. Jenkins, shown in 1946.

Captain Laurance T. DuBose, shown here as a rear admiral in 1943, maneuvered the *Portland* out of a jam.

Lieutenant Robert D. Graff, signal officer in the *Atlanta*.

17

Pulling the Trigger

NORMAN SCOTT, DESPITE HIS PAINSTAKING ATTENTION TO DETAIL, nearly threw away the game board before the match had even begun. His orderly march toward battle ended as soon as the task force executed his latest order, "COLUMN LEFT TO 230 . . . EXECUTE."

In a "column turn," ships turn to the designated heading upon reaching a fixed point in space. The leader turns, and each successive ship follows as soon as she reaches the leader's rudder kick—the visible swirl in the sea produced by rudder movement. In such a maneuver, each ship retains her place in the column, following in her predecessor's wake. If visibility is good, it is a simple matter to verify one's proper position in the formation: The wake of the ship ahead is a ready visual reference. The disadvantage is that the turn takes a while to execute, its total duration being the time it takes the last ship in column to reach the spot where the leader first turned.

A very different type of turn is known as a "simultaneous turn," in which each ship within the column executes the turn immediately. A single column of ships ordered to turn ninety degrees ends up steaming in line abreast on the new heading. A 180-degree turn serves to reverse the column's heading, with the former lead ship bringing up the rear and the original tail-end Charlie serving as the new column leader. A simultaneous turn is quicker to execute than a column turn, but because the conning officer in each ship lacks the visual reference point provided by the stern of the ship in front of him, careful plotting is needed, especially in conditions of poor visibility.

It was on this basic curriculum, elementary to any course in naval shiphandling, that Scott's battle plan foundered. As the SG radar showed, a well-executed reversal of course would have brought his column right across Goto's—a perfect "crossing of the T"—allowing his formation to rake the Japanese column with their full broadsides and leaving Goto to reply with only his forward batteries. But Scott's notion of the timing of the engagement and the spacing of his ships was thrown into disarray as soon as his van destroyer, the *Farenholt,* threw her rudder over.

Quite unexpectedly, the conning officer of the *San Francisco* turned simultaneously with the *Farenholt.* This error threw a hot potato to Captain Moran in the *Boise.* Following astern of the *San Francisco,* he faced a critical decision that had to be settled in a snap: Should he continue as ordered and make a column turn, holding his rudder until he reached the spot where the *Farenholt* turned? Or should he turn immediately and stay with his flagship? Either choice would have sundered Scott's column in two. The first would leave the *San Francisco* on her own. The second would cut loose his vanguard destroyers. Perhaps realizing that keeping the cruisers together was the more urgent priority, Moran chose the latter course. As the *Boise* turned, and as the *Salt Lake City* followed her, Scott's leading trio of destroyers forged out into the night alone.

As the cruisers settled into their southwesterly course, the order passed for the turret crews to match up with the bearing of the turret directors as they sought to pin down targets broadly located by the search radar. On the secondary batteries, star shells were locked into their breeches. The SC search radar of the *Salt Lake City* was the first to make contact with the Japanese. The *Boise*'s radar picked them up soon afterward, sketching their approach in electron beams, the vertical stem of the T just fourteen thousand yards to the northwest. When Moran's talker reported these contacts as "bogeys," some listeners wondered whether he might be referring to aircraft.

Scott had instructed his commanders to open fire as soon as they had a confirmed fix on the enemy. With the destroyers lost in the night, nothing could be confirmed now. Flying his flag in a ship that had no SG radar and was forbidden from using its SC set, Scott certainly had no ready picture of the unexpected geometry of the fight. The contact reports he was hearing from the other cruisers might well be Captain Robert G. Tobin's destroyers, spun off from his column by the *San Francisco*'s error. His fears were firmly underscored when the *Boise* reported a cluster of ship contacts bearing sixty-five degrees. Moran meant to report contacts at sixty degrees *relative* to the *Boise*'s own course heading. Standard tactical doctrine, however, required ships to report contacts as *true* bearings, with 0 degrees indicating the north and 180 the south.

The difference was critical to Admiral Scott. A report of strange ships at sixty-five degrees true would have been consistent with his notion of where he believed the *Farenholt, Duncan,* and *Laffey* were located. Captain Tobin, dismayed to find himself separated from the battle line, somewhere off the starboard quarter of the cruisers, ordered his tin cans to ring up flank speed. As the commanders in the cruiser line prepared to open fire, the *Farenholt* was steaming about nine hundred yards abreast of the *Boise;* the *Laffey* was following, even with the *Helena.* At eleven forty-five, Scott didn't have a clear picture. He radioed Tobin, *"Are you taking station ahead?"* Tobin replied, *"Affirmative. Moving up on your starboard side."*

In his battle plan, Scott allowed for the possibility that his ships might wander from his grasp. His plan, which called for any stragglers to fall out on the column's disengaged side, presupposed there would be an orderly engagement and that the stragglers would know where the American column was in the first place. The perils of ambiguous identity were severe. "Do not rejoin," Scott wrote, "until permission is requested giving bearing in voice code of approach." That was more or less what Tobin had just done— except that Scott's ships had no way of knowing at exactly what bearing to starboard the friendly destroyers would appear. The Japanese ships they were tracking were to starboard, too.

As the ten-centimeter waves radiating from the *Boise*'s and *Helena*'s parabolic antennae pulsed along, their operators watched as the range between Scott's broken column and Goto's onrushing T closed to three miles. But still the muzzles were silent. When a *Helena* lookout reported to Captain Hoover, "Ships visible to the naked eye," the ship's young radar officer remarked to the navigator, "What are we going to do, board them?" A chief wondered aloud, "Do we have to see the whites of the bastard's eyes?"

Hoover, the commander of the *Helena,* didn't know what the problem was. He had commanded destroyers once. In May, he led Destroyer Squadron 2 in the Battle of the Coral Sea and later served in the *Yorktown*'s screen at Midway. From his time at the Bureau of Ordnance, he had learned about the Navy's experiments with radar and knew the importance of drilling with his destroyers to get the most out of the new tool. He fully appreciated now, as the pips on his scope blinked toward each other, that a critical advantage was being frittered away by indecision.

The *Helena*'s skipper instructed his talker to raise the *San Francisco* and make a request to open fire. The transmission, per the fleet's General Signal

Procedure, went out as *"Interrogatory Roger,"* with "interrogatory" indicating a question, and "Roger," code for the letter *R*, the signal for opening fire. This brought from Admiral Scott a quick affirmative response: *"Roger."* Hoover repeated the request, just to be sure. And again came *"Roger."*

But Scott thought he was answering a different question altogether. Captivated by his concern for the whereabouts of his destroyers, he was not ready to open fire yet. As he would explain afterward, he misinterpreted Hoover's message as a request that he acknowledge *Helena*'s last transmission of a radar contact. Hoover, of course, was beyond caring whether Scott was receiving him. If Scott wanted to rely on what the radar was showing, he would have made the *Helena* his flagship. Hoover interpreted Scott's response, *"Roger,"* in accordance with its standard meaning in the General Signal Book: as a code to commence firing.

With this critical exchange, which prompted the immediate and ferocious discharge of the *Helena*'s fifteen six-inch guns, a miscommunication compounded a previous miscommunication and the engagement that would be known as the Battle of Cape Esperance spun into chaos, beyond the control of any single commander.

Throwing gunfire against surface targets was what the *Helena* and her class did best. It was a light cruiser's first and only business, and so it went, muzzles roaring, spent brass tubes kicking out to the turret deck, projectile hoists whining, shell trays loading, breeches slamming and spinning shut, and the turrets salvoing again. Fire-control doctrine prescribed a more deliberate cadence of salvo fire—all fifteen guns discharging at once—when targets were beyond twelve thousand yards from the ship. At closer ranges, the ship switched to automatic-continuous mode. The experience was elemental. "The night had been still and inky black a moment before," Chick Morris wrote. "Now suddenly it was a blazing bedlam. The *Helena* herself reared and lurched sideways, trembling from the tremendous shock of recoil. In the radio shack and coding room we were sent reeling and stumbling against bulkheads, smothered by a snowstorm of books and papers from the tables. The clock leaped from its pedestal. Electric fans hit the deck with a metallic clatter. Not a man in the room had a breath left in him." If this was the effect of the ship's gun work on the men who were practicing it, one can imagine what life might have been like on the ships they were hitting.

The *Salt Lake City*'s heavier guns lashed out to starboard, planting a straddle just short of what was identified as a cruiser, probably Goto's flagship, the *Aoba*, four thousand yards away. The director was ranged up three hundred yards and another salvo went out. "The second never touched the water," the cruiser's action report declared. "All hits."

As the night blossomed in flames, Captain Moran of the *Boise*, wired for sound wearing headphones and a steel helmet, shouted to his gunnery officer, Lieutenant Commander John J. Laffan, "Pick out the biggest and commence firing!"

The *Boise*'s directors were fixed on the same ship the *Salt Lake City* was targeting, the leader of the Japanese column, the *Aoba*, a mere forty-five hundred yards distant, forward of the starboard beam. In the *Boise*'s depths, in Central Station, the damage-control officer, Lieutenant Commander Tom Wolverton, decided it was time to relieve the tension. Recalling his four-year-old son's panicked response the first time he rode on a roller coaster and clanked his way to the summit, he gathered his deepest baritone and shouted so that everyone could hear him: "Daddy, I want to go home now!" The effect worked magic as grins spread over a dozen faces and his crew settled back and relaxed. When Captain McMorris in the *San Francisco* saw a destroyer-sized target to starboard and persuaded himself that the ship could not possibly belong to Tobin's squadron, he opened fire, too. Task Force 64's cruiser column was fully engaged, opening fire from rear to fore.

In the aborning age of radar, the stately traditional method of firing ranging salvos first, then walking shells to their target by progressive correction was a thing of the past. In Mikawa's blitz against Riefkohl, the Japanese performed the old ritual well. Four salvos were fired short of the *Vincennes* and *Quincy* before blood was finally drawn. Now, with microwave radar laying the guns, fire controlmen tapped the power of Newtonian physics. With electron beams cleansing their equations of errant human perception, opening salvos usually yielded immediate straddles and hits. Several outlying shells from the *Boise*'s first broadside were seen to hit a heavy cruiser. After a correction of "up one hundred" was dialed in to the rangekeeper, extending the reach of the guns by a football field's length, the next salvo registered more heavily and the Japanese ship was soon buckling and burning under a radar-controlled barrage. It happened so fast, the Japanese never knew what hit them.

Variations in the efficiency of individual gun crews soon turned the structured cadence of full-salvo fire into a continuous staccato as single guns waged their own fights in parallel trios from turret to turret. When the firing cycle reached full tilt, Moran's and Hoover's capacity to monitor the action with their own senses was obliterated by their ravenous muzzles, turned out and blasting away just forward of their bridge stations. When Scott led his cruisers in an unsignaled turn to the northwest, Moran's conning officer could make out the *San Francisco* ahead only by the flashes of her gunfire and the periodic blinking of her fighting lights.

Ensign Weems in the destroyer *McCalla,* at the end of the American column, mistook the output of the cruisers for machine-gun fire. The rolling stream of six-inch tracers looked like the fire from the 1.1-inch "Chicago pianos." The Japanese, witnessing this from the business end, would discuss the appearance of these "machine-gun cruisers." Through the flash and concussion of the *McCalla's* number three gun, firing directly over him, Weems had fleeting glimpses of the enemy. "I felt a wildly exultant joy in watching us let them have so much at such murderous range. If you stop and think— 2,500 to 3,500 yards is point-blank range for big guns. You can hardly miss even if you wanted to!"

The burning enemy ships looked to him like "the most dramatic Hollywood reproductions.... I saw two that worked about like this: 1) pitch darkness, 2) stream of tracers from our ships, 3) series of flashes where hits were scored, silhouetting of ships by star shells, 4) tremendous fires and explosions, 5) ship folds in two, 6) ship sinks. All in all, a much better performance than Hollywood's very best."

This was pure burning savagery, a Marine Corps attitude, the spirit of Colonel Chesty Puller brought to sea. Now staccato, parsed with short pauses, then overlapping and simultaneous and cacophonous, like the mistimed pistons of a gigantic combustion engine, the continuous cycling output of cruiser gunfire gave no break to the eardrums. Any sailor sprinting past a turret was likely to get his ears deafened or his hide scorched.

Four minutes after the *Boise* opened fire, the ship had put out three hundred rounds from her main battery. Out in the dark to starboard, Moran could make out a trunked forward stack and a latticed tripod mainmast close to the after stack, the architecture of a cruiser. This ship was ready for action and returned fire. There came the whistling of "overs" as the *Boise* was straddled fiercely. Reports of the death of the Imperial fleet would be greatly exaggerated that night. More Japanese destroyers were reported sunk in official U.S. records than Admiral Goto actually commanded. But there was no questioning the vector of the outcome. The throw-weight of Scott's line was beginning to tell. At least three enemy ships were burning in the *Boise's* immediate vicinity.

The *Aoba* was hit no fewer than twenty-four times in the battle's first twenty minutes, knocking out two main turrets, her main gun director, several searchlight platforms, her catapults, and several boiler rooms. Her foremast toppled down and demolished a starboard antiaircraft mount. The flagship veered out to starboard, signaling earnestly, "I AM *AOBA*," as if her assailants were friendly. In the early going, it seemed Goto was unaware that the ships he was closing with were hostile. The Japanese commander's final thoughts as American projectiles shattered his world, claiming the lives of seventy-nine men, including his own, were apparently that a Japanese force, his own reinforcement group, was firing on him. As his ship absorbed the blows of the U.S. cruisers, he shouted in frustration, *"Bakayaro!"*—idiots! Captain Yonejiro Hisamune ordered a smoke screen, and the *Aoba* vanished from view.

In those same tumultuous minutes, Norman Scott was seized by a corresponding fear: that the ships he was hitting were his own. The admiral was apoplectic as he climbed the ladder from the *San Francisco*'s flag bridge to the main bridge. He shouted an order that astonished everyone.

"Cease firing, all ships."

Scott was gone as quickly as he had come, as the cease-fire order was relayed to the task force. It no doubt came as a relief to men on both sides when the firing slackened, but the *Boise* among others never relented, even as Scott repeatedly ordered Moran to check fire. Captain McMorris kept firing, too. He raised the microphone to his mouth and addressed the whole crew with the order he gave his gunners. *"Rapid fire, continuous..."* Then, in apology, he leaned over the rail of the bridge wing and added, "Begging your pardon, Admiral." McMorris knew well who and what he was shooting at. Ceasing fire preemptively could get men killed.

As Tobin, the destroyer commander, radioed Scott, saying, *"We are on your starboard hand now, going up ahead,"* the firing continued, all the while Scott futilely repeating the cease-fire order on the TBS. Buck fever was rife, and spreading. "It took some time to stop our fire," Scott wrote. "In fact it never did completely stop."

The strains on discipline reached down to the enlisted ranks. A gun captain in the *Farenholt* by the name of Wiggens couldn't bring himself to obey the order, even when his own captain, Lieutenant Commander Eugene T. Seaward, repeated it. An old hand from the Asiatic Fleet, he had been forced to leave his wife, a Chinese national, behind in Singapore in December when the British stronghold fell to the Japanese. He learned later that she had been killed by the occupiers. "Every time he could train on that huge Jap battle-cruiser (at point-blank range) he would let go with another round," wrote Ford Richardson, a talker for the *Farenholt*'s gunnery officer. "Wiggens went wild. Crazy wild. He hated Japs with a passion." He never stopped shooting.

The *San Francisco*'s errant turn had been a mystery to the officers in the lead destroyer. As the *Farenholt*'s executive officer, Lieutenant Commander Alcorn G. Beckmann, watched the flagship lead the other three cruisers in a turn inside the *Farenholt*'s own, he wondered at his ship's own lagging pace. Scott's cruisers, it seemed, were outrunning some of his destroyers. He had heard Captain Tobin respond to Scott's query, *"Affirmative. Moving up on your starboard side."* They would need to hustle to avoid getting caught in the crossfire between the American and Japanese lines.

Settling into a westerly course as the *Farenholt* led the destroyers in their separate column, the destroyer *Duncan,* commanded by Lieutenant Commander Edmund B. Taylor, plotted an unidentified radar contact eight thousand yards to the west and rang up flank speed to pursue it. The U.S. cruiser line was in full voice now, and by the light of the fires they were planting on his target, Taylor could see it was a cruiser. Soon another enemy ship appeared, following close behind the first. As Taylor brought the *Duncan* broadside to the enemy ships and prepared to launch torpedoes to starboard, he found himself in the difficult position of standing between Scott's cruisers and their prey. To port, he saw the familiar silhouette of the *Helena.* As he overtook the light cruiser, he steered right standard rudder, looking to stay clear of the light cruiser's line of fire.

Knowing that he had lost control of events, Scott tried to raise Tobin on the TBS. *"How are you?"* Scott asked the commander of Destroyer Division 12. *"Were we shooting at Twelve?"*

Tobin replied, *"Twelve is okay. We are going up ahead on your starboard side. I do not know who you were firing at."*

Scott then ordered Tobin's ships to display their recognition lights. They flashed momentarily in a proscribed pattern of green and white. With friends having declared themselves to friends, Scott directed his group to open fire again to starboard. Tobin would soon know all too well which ships Scott's cruisers were targeting.

Ford Richardson, stationed in the *Farenholt*'s main battery director, "stood there transfixed watching the pyrotechnics. Our cruisers on one side of us were firing at the Jap ships on the other side of us." Standing out of the hatch of the gun director, Richardson's gunnery officer steered the fire of the forward five-inch battery into an enemy ship that had been brilliantly illuminated by star shells. When he dropped back down inside the director, Richardson, as his talker, followed him. "At that *very instant*," Richardson recalled, "we were hit by a six- or eight-inch shell at the cross arm of the foremast, some twenty-five feet over my head!"

Tobin had just ordered his squadron to fire torpedoes at targets of opportunity when the airburst rattled the *Farenholt*'s decks. Shrapnel cut down several men in exposed topside stations. The heavier shards penetrated the rangefinder, slicing through a man standing forward of it. The wounded man was passed down from the rangefinder to Richardson. With a penlight he saw that the shrapnel had entered the man's body behind the collarbone, exited below his arm, and reentered his body near the groin, leaving a big hole in his upper leg. Then it went through the deck. Richardson stopped the heavy bleeding by stuffing a T-shirt into his shipmate's gaping wound and using his belt as a compress.

The hit sliced the *Farenholt*'s radar antenna from the foremast, exploding spectacularly and sending a shower of fragments that pierced the air flask of a torpedo loaded in the ship's quintuple mount, which was aimed on the centerline straight ahead. With a hiss of compressed air, liberated by the penetration, the missile launched itself from the tube and wedged in the base of the destroyer's forward stack. The impact tripped the starter that sparked the torpedo's motor to life. The motor screamed for a while before burning itself out without exploding. Another shell hit the waterline on the port side, knocking out all power and communications in the forward part of the ship. Water rushed in, and she took a list to port. Altogether Captain Seaward's tin can was holed at the port side waterline by four American shells. The hits on the *Farenholt* most likely came from one of Scott's own heavy cruisers, the *San Francisco* or the *Salt Lake City*. Friendly ships shot up the *Duncan,* too. The destroyer had turned her forward batteries on a Japanese cruiser thirty-three hundred yards off her starboard bow when she took a hit to the bridge that knocked out fire control and set afire the handling room beneath the number two gun. The *Duncan*'s skipper, Commander Taylor, had no sooner managed to steady on a torpedo firing course and release his first fish when another shell burst forward of the director platform, disabling the director and seriously wounding the torpedo officer, Lieutenant (j.g.) R. L. Fowler. The chief torpedoman fired another torpedo by local control at a target that already had the attention of Scott's cruisers. "Almost immediately she was observed to crumble in the middle, then roll over and disappear," Taylor wrote. The *Duncan* would share her fate.

Another salvo floated in, blasting the chart house, killing the two men on the *Duncan*'s SC radar, a sonar operator, the bridge radioman, and the yeoman keeping the record of the battle. The main radio room was a total loss with no survivors, the fire there having merged with the blaze from the number one fire room, fed by fresh air pouring through a rent in the overhead. Taylor lost steering control and found himself circling helplessly in a left-hand turn. When the forward portholes were opened to vent the smoke and steam washing into the pilothouse, they served not as an exhaust, but as an intake for flames and smoke coming from the burning number two gun. Trapped in the asphyxiating cloud, Taylor could see little of the battle now but sensed that his circling had carried him out of the line of fire of the American cruisers. But the ship would not be saved. When the boilers in the after fire room lost their supply of feed water, the fire main pumps failed, too, and the flames spread, punctuated by detonations of five-inch projectiles. The crew fought a brave rear-guard action with handy-billy pumps, but Taylor could see it was futile. He helped lower wounded from the bridge level to the deck and then into the water. Then, with flames enveloping the pilothouse on all sides, he found his only route of escape was by jumping from the starboard bridge wing.

The gunfire from Scott's cruisers was prodigious, and when their lines of fire got clear of the obstruction presented by the van destroyers, they did far worse to intended targets than accidental ones. Tracked by all four American cruisers as she advanced along the axis of Scott's column, the *Furutaka* took a series of heavy hits that would prove to be mortal. The Japanese cruiser was hit in her number three turret and in the port torpedo tubes. Several of her Long Lances caught fire, and the flames drew more fire.

It was just a few minutes past midnight when the *Salt Lake City* swept the beams of her fire-control radar through a wide arc to the engaged side. The extent of destruction wrought by Scott's ships was reflected in these high-frequency microwaves. All of the ships the radar found were marked in the visible wavelength by fires.

18

"Pour It to 'Em"

AS THE LAST HOUR OF OCTOBER 11 EXPIRED INTO A NEW DAY, GOTO'S squadron awakened to the reality that it faced a formidable enemy battle force. The Japanese cruisers had spent the first minutes of the battle with their turrets turned in. Originally loaded for shore bombardment, hoists filled with time-fuzed shells designed to explode short of impact and throw burning fragments over a wide area, they were finally alive to the challenge of Scott's group. Shortly before midnight, the *Salt Lake City* was on the wrong end of an anti-personnel airburst that exploded high amidships. That shell sprayed her topsides with steel, cutting down twenty sailors on starboard gun mounts, four of them dead.

The *Boise* was struck by an eight-inch shell that dented and ruptured her side plating above her waterline armor belt, shattering the sleeping compartments used by the ship's junior officers. A minute later, two or three smaller rounds registered, blasting Captain Moran's cabin and leaving it a wreck of twisted metal. A clock was knocked from the skipper's desk and shattered on the deck, frozen at five minutes to midnight as the flames spread.

Tom Wolverton, the *Boise*'s damage-control officer, was providing a play-by-play to crew belowdecks that was "getting hotter than a Joe Louis fight broadcast." Up to then, Wolverton had little to do in his assigned capacity. Scott's fast-firing cruisers had been delivering an overwhelming one-way barrage. But in battle, circumstances are usually temporary and perception almost always fragile. A short lull followed in which Scott tried to reassemble his straggling line behind the *San Francisco*. As he called course changes over the radio, the Japanese used the reprieve well. They continued removing bombardment rounds from their hoists, replacing them with armor-piercing rounds engineered to kill ships.

As the *Boise* plunged along in the *San Francisco*'s wake, Moran found that his radars were becoming almost as badly impaired as his own vision. It was hard to pick out targets in the abundant intermingling of ships. Many shell splashes were large enough to return an echo to his scopes. Though other ships made good use of star shells to silhouette their targets, Moran chose to use his searchlights now. Locating a target off his starboard beam, he ordered his searchlights on. As his turrets raged out at what he thought was a light cruiser, fires sprang to life on that ship. The *Boise* was revealed in bright relief by her own mirrors. The Japanese ship returned fire and scored at least four times.

Ahead, on the *Boise*'s starboard bow, there appeared a larger ship whose directors pegged Moran's ship cold. This vessel, probably the heavy cruiser *Kinugasa,* "fired at *Boise* unopposed," Moran would write in his action report, "shooting beautifully with twin eight-inch mounts. She straddled us repeatedly along the forward half of the forecastle, and made two known hits." The first struck the barbette underneath turret one, crashed through a deck, and lay in a compartment near the turret stalk, an explosive-laden steel time bomb with a defective fuze fizzing along. Alive to the pending catastrophe, the turret officer, Lieutenant Beaverhead Thomas, pushed open the turret's small escape hatch and ordered the crew to exit. As he guided the gun house gang to safety, he reported to Commander Laffan, his gunnery officer, that he had abandoned station. He said, "The fuze hasn't gone off yet. I can still hear it spluttering." They were his last words. The muffled blast of the 250-pound projectile vented through passageways, hatches, and vents, incinerating or asphyxiating a hundred men in a flash.

The survivors of turret one, eleven men, exited to the deck just in time to be batted down by two more hits. One plastered the faceplate of turret three, just forward of and below the bridge, gashing the barrels of its trio of rifles and spackling the superstructure with shrapnel. Another shell from the *Kinugasa* entered the water short of the *Boise,* precisely as intended. This projectile was designed with a protective cap that broke away on impact and enabled it to retain its ballistic properties underwater. It hit close enough aboard to swim downward and penetrate the hull nine feet below the waterline. Bursting through the hull and exploding in the forward six-inch magazine, it sent a wash of flame through the forward handling rooms and up the stalk of the two forward turrets, roasting the entire crew in turret two and several of the escaping survivors of turret three.

Mike Moran noted proudly that the men on the port side five-inch battery were keeping their backs turned to the fiery spectacle unfolding to starboard. Their duty was to watch for threats on the disengaged side. A spout of flaming gases shot into the air from the *Boise*'s forward turrets and a jolt threw men to their knees. The eruption reached as high as the flying bridge and set much of the forecastle deck ablaze. It was followed by a torrent of hot seawater, debris, smoke, and sparks. A storm of sparking splinters and smoldering leather and burning bits of life jackets and life rafts blew across the superstructure. Struggling against fumes, firefighting teams dragged out heavy hoses, fed by mains in the after part of the ship.

In the *Helena*, high up in Sky Forward, an antiaircraft director station, Lieutenant Jim Baird held a stopwatch and a clipboard, keeping a record of the gunners' performance. Counting salvos and tabulating hits, he shook his head in disbelieving admiration at what the new light cruisers could throw. His colleagues in Control were coaching the ship's batteries onto a target to starboard, and splashes landed all around the ship, when a burning vessel was sighted in the U.S. column ahead. Word spread quickly that it was the *Boise*. As the *Helena* moved past her burning cousin, a flurry of salvos straddled her. Hoover's men had gotten to know Moran's crew at Nouméa, had gone head-to-head with them on the baseball diamonds there, bound by a pride that only the sailors of a fistfighting light cruiser could know. In the exercises under Norman Scott, their sense of squadron identity grew stronger. "The battle had been a game until then," Chick Morris wrote. This put some fire in their fight. As Moran shouted, "Cruiser to starboard. Shift target!" Lieutenant Warren Boles in Spot One relayed the order coolly: "*Set 'em up in the next alley. Pour it to 'em.*" Noticing that one of the talkers with him on the fighting bridge was visibly jittery, Captain Hoover put a hand on his shoulder and said, "Take it easy, son. We'll get you out of this."

In the *Boise*, a gunner's mate named Edward Tyndal pleaded with his superiors to allow him to enter one of the turrets to look for survivors. He refused to believe his younger brother, Bill, was not alive in there somehow, needing his help. When the firefighters tried to play their nozzles into the turrets via the hatches, they found several of them blocked by a grotesque clotting of charred bodies, men who had given their last while trying to escape. The stymied firefighters inserted their nozzles through the case ejection scuttles in the bottom of the turrets instead, and quenched their burned interiors.

As the HMS *Hood* had learned in her duel with the *Bismarck,* and as the *Arizona* had discovered in the sights of Nagumo's Pearl Harbor bombers, an explosion in a powder magazine was the gravest calamity a warship could suffer. Moran knew he had to flood his forward magazines, but when he issued the order he found that the men assigned to the remote valve-control station were not alive to carry it out. The *Boise* was spared from disaster by the collateral effect of her gutting: Waves of seawater let in by the underwater hit flooded all the forward hull spaces, including the magazine. The water's weight on the third deck imparted a wave motion to the long, slender hull that was strong enough to make some of the crew believe a torpedo had struck.

As smoke spread below, men wearing rescue breathers shored up bulkheads against the flood and set submersible pumps to race the waters flowing in through the breached hull. The medical department decided to move the sickbay from the wardroom to the battle dressing station. One of these patients, wearing a cast on his broken leg, limped quickly along on crutches. A sailor who had had his appendix removed several days earlier rose from his bunk and told the corpsmen converging on him with a stretcher, "Outta my way! I'm getting the hell out of here!"

Observers throughout Scott's task group believed the *Boise* was doomed. But despite the evisceration of her forward stations and the pyrotechnic display that bloomed overhead, her boilers and engines were intact. Moran's engineers responded quickly to his order to flank speed. Down by the bow and listing to starboard, the ship sheered out of line to port, accelerating to thirty knots, just as another salvo from the *Kinugasa* raised a cluster of splashes right where the *Boise* would have been had Moran not changed course. All the while, her after turrets kept up the cadence in continuous fire. Soon her expenditure of six-inch ordnance topped eight hundred rounds.

To avoid the *Boise* ahead, Captain Small ordered the *Salt Lake City*'s rudder hard right and threw the starboard engine into reverse to sharpen the turn. This placed Small's ship between the Japanese and the burning *Boise.* Silhouetted by the ship he was thus shielding, Small paid the price almost immediately. An eight-inch shell struck the *Salt Lake City*'s starboard side and exploded, dishing in the plating of the armor belt. Another penetrated the hull, passed through the supply office, and settled with a heavy clang on the deck plating of the fire room before exploding with a muffled, low-order blast. Though several men standing just six feet from the point of impact were uninjured, saved by untold failures of mechanics or chemistry within the powder charge, this explosion still managed to sever electrical cables, disable a boiler, and start a fire in the bilges that, fed by twenty-six thousand gallons of fuel oil leaked from a ruptured transfer line, grew hot enough to warp one of the ship's heavy longitudinal I-beams and buckle the armored second deck.

As the *Salt Lake City* came clear of the burning *Boise*, which was falling out of line and limping away from the action, Small rang up full speed again as his battery trained on an enemy heavy cruiser forward of his starboard beam. The amidships secondary guns coughed a spread of star shells to a perfect bursting point beyond their target, a Japanese cruiser, three miles distant. The heavy cruiser's searchlight shutters opened, shone briefly, then closed, and a ten-gun salvo roared out. When it landed—straddle, over—a correction was dialed into the rangekeeper, and the next four salvos touched nothing but steel. But for the *Salt Lake City*'s gallant interposition, the *Boise* might have been finished. The *Boise* would remain a burning beacon, and a pyre for more than a hundred dead, visible for miles, until her firefighters finally prevailed over the turret fires. At that point the ship, alone, seemed to vanish into the night.

On the *Salt Lake City*, circuits failed throughout the ship as the salvos hit. Captain Small lost steering control from the bridge. Receiving a mistaken report of fires forward, he preventively flooded his forward magazines. As steering was transferred to the after emergency steering cabin, the *Salt Lake City*'s engineers, bereft of steam from the forward fire room, closed the throttles to the outboard engines, leaving the two inboard screws to carry her load.

WITH THE FURUTAKA and the *Aoba* rent by shattering blows, Admiral Goto dead, and the sharpshooting and undamaged *Kinugasa*, too, turning a course north, the Japanese force began its retirement. At 12:16 a.m., Norman Scott brought the *San Francisco* onto a northerly heading as if to pursue. Wondering how many ships would be in a position to follow, he then thought twice about it and decided to retire. He recalled later, "The enemy was silenced and our formation at the time was somewhat broken." A clear recognition of who was friend and who was foe had been the first casualty of battle, and from that followed much of the tragedy of the night. The Battle of Cape Esperance ended as if by tacit mutual assent.

It seemed that at least one Japanese captain was looking to exploit the confusion. From the flying bridge of the *San Francisco* the shout went out that an unidentified destroyer was approaching. A mysterious ship came rushing in on the flagship's starboard bow, displaying an unfamiliar pattern of recognition lights—white over red. Her gambit was overly bold. Recognizing the improper signal, the *San Francisco* opened fire, then the destroyer's signalmen doubled down on their deception, flashing in Morse code: "D491 v D456," indicating with the respective hull numbers a call from the *Farenholt* to the *Laffey*. Captain McMorris interpreted this as a legitimate query and promptly ordered his cruiser to cease fire. Other American observers recalled seeing the ship up close, and recognizing the telltale white striping painted on a Japanese destroyer's stack. The opponents exchanged fire—what hits might have been registered is lost to history—and the destroyer was soon gone.

The *Helena* had come through the gauntlet unscathed except for a small fire ignited astern by a hot shell casing and a close call with a hang fire in turret four. The *Salt Lake City* was badly bruised but soon fulfilled the expectations held of the top-rated engineering department in the Pacific. Captain Small signaled Scott that despite the damage to his fire room, his engineers had steam to make twenty-five knots.

Nothing had been heard from Mike Moran and the *Boise*. Scott ordered Captain Tobin via the TBS: "*Detail one of your boys to stand by* Boise." Told that the ship's location was unknown, Scott queried Small in the *Salt Lake City* and was informed she was last seen twelve miles west of Savo Island, heading west. That ship soon became the object of a concentrated search in the dark.

Scott prepared a quick dispatch to Admiral Ghormley in Nouméa, summarizing the night's events. "ENGAGED ENEMY WEST OF SAVO ABOUT MID-NIGHT. AT LEAST FOUR ENEMY DD'S BURNING AND PROBABLY ONE CA HIT BADLY. BOISE BURNING BADLY WHEN LAST SEEN. FARENHOLT NOT YET LOCATED. MCCALLA SEARCHING. REQUEST AIR COVERAGE. AM PROCEEDING TO POINT CAST [50 MILES SOUTH OF CAPE SURVILLE, SAN CRISTOBÁL], SPEED 20."

Then, attempting to gather his scattered task force via the radio, Scott ordered all ships to switch on their emergency identification lights for ten seconds. On *San Francisco,* Lieutenant Commander Bruce McCandless noticed that the flagship's port side bulbs did not come on. Soon thereafter, two star shells burst overhead, illuminating the night and possibly heralding hotter fires. Aware that the threatening ship was friendly, a *San Francisco* signalman lofted three green flares. "And the navigator pushed the buttons even harder," McCandless wrote. "This time both sides lighted up. This seemed to satisfy the fire control teams in the *Salt Lake City*, 3,000 yards to port. One of the operators on her main battery director had already sounded two stand-by buzzers and was about to ring the third and turn loose a salvo when the flares ignited. "Hold it! It's the *'Frisco!*" someone shouted, knocking the man out of his metal seat. "For this we will eternally be grateful," McCandless wrote.

IN THE SHATTERED heavy cruiser *Furutaka*, shortly after midnight, Captain Tsutau Araki passed the order to abandon ship. He ordered the ensign pulled down and the emperor's portrait salvaged, but the man assigned to the task was killed by American shellfire before he could retrieve it. Araki went to his cabin on the bridge to end his disgraceful ordeal, but found that his revolver and his sword had been taken away from him. When he returned to the bridge to strap himself to the compass mount, he could find no fasteners right for the job. The possible culprit confronted him there: his executive officer, who pleaded for his captain to survive. As the two officers argued, the rising sea engulfed the deck of the bridge, and as the *Furutaka* foundered Araki found himself floating alongside the bow, disgracefully alive.

The idea that a captain should die with his ship, so central to the Japanese Navy's code of ethics, was opposed by Admiral Yamamoto. Concerned about the high command's tendency to be "rather too sensitive in punishing commanders for their incapability in carrying out operations," Yamamoto conferred with his chief of staff, Matome Ugaki, and the two composed a letter to the chief of the personnel bureau: "If we do not approve of the skipper surviving when his ship goes down after hard fighting, we shall not be able to carry through this war, which cannot be settled soon. There is no reason why we should discourage their survival, while we are encouraging the fliers to survive by means of parachute. In a war which must be carried out against tremendous odds, I, as commander in chief, could not help feeling reluctant in issuing orders if I had to ask our skippers not to return alive when their ships sink." A modern fleet, he felt, could go nowhere but down in the grip of such primitivism. The Imperial Navy would improve through experience and prevail over the decadent Americans only if its delicate sense of honor was kept somehow intact and experienced commanders were not required to immolate themselves on the dubious altar of pride.

Twenty-two miles northwest of Savo Island, the *Furutaka* went down stern-first. Thirty-three officers and crew went down with her, with 225 more missing in action. The two other heavies, the *Aoba,* badly mauled, and the *Kinugasa,* scarcely scratched, set course for Shortland Island with their destroyers.

IT WAS NEARLY 3 A.M. when the *Boise* was finally located again. Captain Moran's battered light cruiser fell in with the *San Francisco, Salt Lake City, Helena, Buchanan,* and *Laffey* and headed south. Off the western end of Guadalcanal, heading for his own preset rendezvous point, Admiral Scott wanted to ring up maximum speed to elude the radius of enemy bombers and pull his ships farther under the covering shelter of the aircraft of the South Pacific Force. But the *Boise* was nearly a cripple. Rescue and recovery crews were exploring the burned-out forward turrets. Scores of men had been trapped in those flames. A few were revived with artificial respiration, but nine in ten were dead of asphyxiation or concussion. Mike Moran slowed to twenty knots to reduce the sea pressure on his shored-up forward bulkheads. The *Farenholt* survived her bashing by American cruisers. She extracted herself from the vacated and bloodied battlescape with some deft and rapidly applied damage control: tossing heavy gear—whaleboat, depth charges—over the listing side, transferring fuel from port to starboard, and running portable pumps and a bucket brigade to lighten the load till her waterline holes were dry. She trailed the cruisers by fifty miles but reached Espiritu Santo under her own power.

Lingering behind while a repair party went aboard the *Duncan* in a futile attempt to salvage her, the *McCalla* searched Savo Sound for survivors and recovered 195 of them, nearly the entire crew of the wounded ship. When a dawn patrol of Wildcats from Henderson Field found the *Duncan* abandoned near Savo, her entire topsides melted by the fires, the flight leader noticed two big holes in her hull and remarked that her "bow end looked cooked." With the arrival of dawn, American planes found the rest of Task Force 64 by its trail of bunker oil and followed it all the way home to the anchorage at Espiritu Santo.

Despite the carnage, much of it self-inflicted, Scott's task force had plenty of cause for celebration, and that was just what the veterans of the battle did after they returned to Espiritu Santo on October 12. "As we pulled into harbor, we were a cocky bunch," *Laffey* signalman Richard Hale recalled. "We wanted to paint a couple of cruiser and destroyer symbols on the side of our mount to let everyone know that the *Laffey* was a real fighting ship. We lost all fear of battle at that point, and getting away without a scratch while pounding the enemy meant that we were ready to win the war." As turret crews mustered to clean powder residue out of their barrels, with two pairs of sailors, one inside the turret, the other out, pulling hard wire back and forth to scrub them clean, they relived the battle and recalled its highlights and sidelights—"little things, remembered now in detail and passed from group to group, often distorted beyond recognition before they got very far," Chick Morris wrote. "But it was good for the ship's morale. Anything was good that contributed to the story of the enemy's defeat."

Scott credited his "crude night firing practices" for the success. Mike Moran was so pleased with his ship's performance that he overlooked the fact that some of his zealous gunners had continued firing despite Scott's orders to cease. According to Moran, "The rapidity and accuracy of fire, fire discipline, and absence of material casualties were all without precedent in target practice. Perfect fire discipline was an especially conspicuous feature. At the orders of 'Commence Firing' continuous fire began instantaneously. When ordered to cease or check fire the batteries responded at once. In an action involving relatively brief bursts of fire and frequent target shifts, the importance of such positive control can scarcely be overemphasized." Sailors of the *Farenholt* and *Duncan,* of course, thought the cruisers' fire discipline left plenty to be desired. Captain McMorris paid the *Farenholt* a traditional tribute and fee. When they reached Espiritu Santo, the flagship sent over twenty gallons of ice cream—"reparations," Ford Richardson called it. But there was no making light of the tragic mistake. Gunfire from friendly ships had killed three of the *Farenholt*'s men and wounded forty-three.

There was nothing sweet about the Japanese experience in a battle that in many ways resembled the American ordeal in the Battle of Savo Island: a rout by a battle-ready cruiser force over a complacent one. If Admiral Scott didn't exact the same punishing price from Goto that Mikawa took from Bode and Riefkohl, the effect on American morale made the difference a matter of accountancy. "Throughout the 'Night Battle off Savo Island,'" an official Japanese source wrote of the engagement that Americans would call the Battle of Cape Esperance, "providence abandoned us.... The future looked bleak for our surface forces, whose forte was night warfare." For U.S. sailors who had been overawed by the Japanese prowess in night battle, here was reason to believe that the IJN was run by mortals after all.

Captain Small's staff in the *Salt Lake City* drew a wide range of lessons, cataloging them in thirty-nine numbered paragraphs in the ship's action report, covering everything from gunnery and fire control to shiphandling, repairs, and communications. Most of them could be learned only in battle:

"Restrict telephone circuits to the business at hand. Do not permit uncertainty or panic to creep in on circuits either by tone of voice or context of message."

"It is the function of Control to search for targets. Never require the director to do so when engaged."

"In a short-range night action, shift targets during the loading interval."

"Stretcher bearers should remain in a darkened compartment or wear dark adaptation goggles during night battle to preserve their night vision."

THOUGH THE U.S. NAVY had a victory to celebrate, its immediate benefit to the men on Guadalcanal would be negligible. The Reinforcement Group that had sailed ahead of Goto benefited from Scott's preoccupation with the cruisers. Eluding detection, it reached Doma Cove on Guadalcanal's north coast, unloaded its cargo of artillery, vehicles, men, and supplies, and escaped before the rise of morning.

And as the events of the next forty-eight hours would show, the marines of General Vandegrift's garrison and the airmen at Henderson Field had yet to experience their most trying hour. Scott's victory, though an invigorating boost to the spirits, would do little to stop the coming rain of fire.

"The regular Navy enlisted man is today the highest type in our history; he is intelligent, aspiring, and has initiative, albeit a ready and cheerful susceptibility to discipline.... Properly handled, he will go through fire and water. He is not always properly handled."

—Hanson W. Baldwin, "The Naval Defense of America,"
Harper's, April 1941

19

———

All Hell's Eve

WHEN THE SOUTH PACIFIC AREA HEADQUARTERS RECEIVED NORMAN Scott's dispatch about the battle that took place the night of October 11, Admiral Ghormley was hosting lunch in his flagship, the *Argonne,* with his chief of staff, Dan Callaghan, and an old friend from his days in London, Donald MacDonald. "Admiral Ghormley treated me like a son," said Mac-Donald, then serving as the exec on the destroyer *O'Bannon.* "We had a nice lunch, and we talked about what was going on. Ghormley wasn't exactly depressed, but he just thought he was trying to hold the line with very little strength. He said he wasn't getting enough support, having to fight on a shoe string." Among the problems the SOPAC commander articulated to his guests was one of combat leadership. "You know, Donald," he said, "I don't have any fighting admirals out here." The statement seemed self-indicting. Until Scott took station off Cape Esperance, no U.S. admirals in Ghormley's theater had been given an opportunity. Scott's battle report provided an immediate rebuttal to Ghormley's lament.

It has been said that an army is as brave as its privates and as good as its generals. In a navy, the dynamics are different. On a ship bound for battle, admirals and seamen alike stand equally exposed to the hazards of combat. Admirals must have the same degree of physical courage. "The ship and crew members will go where he directs them—discipline and training will guarantee that—but his is the choice of the hazard that all will incur," a naval strategist wrote.

Historians like to tally victories for their own sake, like league standings or stock market prices. Combat commanders have a more pragmatic perspective on the consequences of battles. It is not the volume of the enemy's hardware destroyed nor the number of his men killed that matters. What makes the difference is a battle's impact on the will to fight, and on the ability to impose one's will on an enemy in the future. Victory is in the mind, not the metal.

While the Battle of Cape Esperance was a U.S. win in terms of ships sunk and immediate objectives realized, its actual impact on the larger fight for Guadalcanal had yet to be determined as the battered ships of Task Force 64 returned to Espiritu Santo.

The future would belong to the side that most tenaciously maintained its will to fight. The Cactus Air Force at Henderson Field now boasted forty-five Wildcats, including the recent arrivals from the *Saratoga;* twelve Army Airacobra fighters of the 67th and 339th fighter squadrons; sixteen Dauntlesses organized into three bombing squadrons, two Navy and one Marine; and six Avengers of the *Hornet*'s Torpedo Squadron 8. Fighting within a comfortable radius of their home base, they held their own against the Japanese air forces opposing them from Rabaul, Buka, and Buin. The Japanese Navy's 11th Air Fleet fielded a powerful armada of fighters and bombers: eighty-six Mitsubishi A6M Zeros and sixty-three Mitsubishi G4M Bettys, plus a handful of Aichi Val dive-bombers and Kate torpedo bombers. But the Cactus Air Force held the line.

Defeated on the ground and stalemated in the air, Admiral Yamamoto was enacting an ambitious plan to hammer down on Guadalcanal from the sea. Goto's defeat at the hands of Norman Scott was a small setback. The rest of the big push he was preparing against the island continued on schedule. As Scott was finishing his scrape with Goto's cruisers, two Japanese battleships, the *Kongo* and *Haruna,* were pressing down through the Slot toward their objective: bombarding Henderson Field.

NEAR MIDNIGHT ON October 13, the warning horn mounted in Henderson Field's Japanese-built pagoda tower began sounding its forlorn, winding wail. A single-engine plane was heard overhead, and lightning was seen to flash. For half a second the grassy plain around the airfield's perimeter was visible in bright relief. Then everything was black again. None of these events was remarkable. Nuisance artillery fire and petty air raids were nightly occurrences. An officer with the Marine intelligence section, Thayer

Soule, lay in his bunk counting off the interval from flash to thunder. Hearing the drone of the Japanese aircraft overhead, he thought, *Damn that plane, keeping us awake.*

Then an escalation, and the arrival of a waking nightmare:

"Outside, a thousand rockets burst in the sky. The tent snapped taut. The blast blew me from my bunk. I groped for my shoes. This was a shoes-off night, the major had said. The light died out in a shower of sparks. Somebody shouted, 'Star shell!' Another crushing blast! A heavy salvo landed on the other side of the ridge. Trees snapped. Men up there cascaded off the cliff. Major Mather in pajamas. We hit the hole and sat, eleven of us, in a nine-foot-square hole."

The alert to Condition Red sounded. Henderson Field's defenders poured from their mosquito-netted tents into a battlefield of biting malarial insects. On instinct and reflex, a thousand combat-seasoned men were racing for cover.

A gunner's mate assigned to the Naval Operating Base, Bill Kennedy, recalled the night of October 13 the way everyone would, as a terrifying holocaust. "The exploding gunfire from the ship was so loud and the concussion so great that we were literally blown out of our bunks. Shaving mirrors and what little glass we had around was broken. Running from tent to foxhole was like running a new kind of obstacle course; when a salvo was fired, the concussion threw you to the ground. Then when you got up, the concussion from the exploding salvo on the airstrip threw you down again."

The unseen ships that were hitting them were unnervingly close to shore. The trajectory of their gunfire was tellingly flat. The marines could feel on their skin the heat of the projectiles ripping by overhead, trimming the fronds from the tops of palm trees and blowing coconuts loose from their high groves. Fear paralyzed even the most proven veterans. "The air was filled with a bedlam of sound: the screaming of shells, the dull roar of cannonading off shore, the whine of shrapnel, the thud of palm trees as they were severed and hit the ground, and in the lulls from the big noises, the ceaseless sifting of dirt into the foxhole."

Soule scrambled into a shelter roofed with logs and steel plates and sandbags, smartly sited in the defilade of a ridge. "Our single light bulb swayed as salvos shook the ground.... Wham! Another salvo close by, then silence. There we sat—the colonel, the major, all of us—sitting on palm-log seats, staring at the too-low ceiling. Nobody spoke.... The plane was overhead now, and there was that flash again, red and fiery. I saw it out of the corner of my eye. Let's see. Count to twenty-eight. We waited and counted. My knees wouldn't stop shaking. . . . The earth heaved. Heavy pieces thudded on the roof. My stomach caved in. My head swam. The light went out. Or was I blind? I choked on the dust now thick in the air. We all coughed, gasped, coughed again, and sat there dazed."

Someone tried to light a lamp. The phone rang and someone moved to answer it. "Again the earth heaved. The roof bounced. The steel plates rang. One of the logs cracked but didn't give. Dirt crashed into the entrance behind me. A tinkle of glass got through the blast. I smelled kerosene. Because we were in the center of the impact area, there was no whine, no shriek, no sound like a train, just the blast. It came all at once—the noise, the punch of wind, the dust. I guess we all blacked out."

The terrible march of the naval bombardment proceeded away from them now, having spared neither enlisted man nor general officer. No shelling they had ever taken came close to this. Japanese field artillerymen suffered from a serious shortage of ammunition that limited their output to less than a dozen rounds per day. Many of their guns were worn from prior service in China and Manchuria. Their Navy was another story. The battleships' enormous guns were well maintained and well within their range. The Marine fighter ace Joe Foss found himself seized physically by the experience. "It seemed as if all the props had been kicked from under the sky and we were crushed underneath," he said. One salvo came perilously close to decapitating the leadership of the 1st Marine Division, knocking Arch Vandegrift himself to the dirt in his shelter.

Then, somewhere offshore, fire was checked. The great armored turrets were brought in to the centerline, hoists stopped, and rudders turned so that the marauders could escape the coming of daylight. Morning revealed the results of the bombardment. In the foxholes and tents and covered pits around Henderson Field, forty-one men lay dead.

Littering the torn earth were hundreds of small tubes. The length of a finger, an inch in diameter, they were innocuous enough when inspected up close. Packed in large projectiles and showered in from a few miles out to sea, designed to fall at a certain angle and burst at the height of a telephone pole, their incendiary and fragmentation payloads dismembered aircraft and men within a wide radius of the airfield and its dispersal areas. The storm over the airfield played havoc with the camp and its infrastructure.

"Daylight disclosed what we had feared but dared not say," Soule remembered. Tent camps shredded, gear ruined, and large holes scooped from the ground all across the encampment. "Atop our shelter were two big pieces of shrapnel, three inches thick, two feet long. Two men could barely lift them.

A little jigsaw work showed that they were parts of one shell fourteen inches in diameter! Whole salvos had landed around us. The airfield had been clobbered." Just one of the coastwatcher station's three aerial masts remained standing, an Australian coastwatcher named MacKenzie wrote, "but luckily the teleradio transmitting aerial, in falling, had caught up in the head of a palm. We called 20J for a test report on our signal strength and readability. The answer came back at once: 'Seems much improved. Have you been making adjustments?'"

Still, the raking that the battleships *Kongo* and *Haruna* delivered that night was no laughing matter. Until then, young marines had learned to strut with disregard for the Japanese howitzers hidden in the hills. Their shells seldom reached the airfield. A journalist assigned to the area wrote, "The Marines at the airport treat its shells the way city-wise pedestrians treat taxicabs—with caution, but without nervousness." But these same men were thunderstruck by the heavier throw-weight of fourteen-inch guns. It wasn't the weight of steel that got under their skin. "It was the hopelessness, the feeling that nobody gave a curse whether we lived or died," said Lieutenant Commander John E. Lawrence, one of the Cactus Air Force's air combat information officers. "It soaked into you until you couldn't trust your own mind. You'd brief a pilot, and no sooner had he taken off than you'd get frantic, wondering if you'd forgotten to tell him some trivial thing that might become the indispensable factor in saving his life." The physical and emotional penetrations of the 973 large-caliber projectiles would be felt for a long time to come. Some would call this bombardment "All Hell's Eve." It was the heaviest and most concentrated artillery shelling a fighting man had to that time ever endured.

The use of battleships in direct support of the Army was a rare departure from the typical Imperial Japanese Navy way. Guided by its old doctrine of seeing a decisive battle against the enemy fleet, it preferred to hoard its heavy combatants until they could be loosed for the lethal, war-ending blow. Rear Admiral Takeo Kurita had protested his orders to bring the two 762-foot-long monsters into Savo Sound so vehemently that Yamamoto had to threaten to lead the mission himself before he finally relented.

Covered by fighters flying from Buin, an airfield south of Bougainville, the battleships arrived in an audacious gamble. And it paid off. Up in smoke went all of Henderson Field's Avenger torpedo bombers, a dozen of its forty-two fighter aircraft, and all but seven of its thirty-nine dive-bombers, along with nearly all of its aviation fuel. The only defense offered by the U.S. Navy that night consisted of four PT boats sortieing from Tulagi and skirmishing fruitlessly with Kurita's destroyer screen. The mighty *Washington* was not far away, having just escorted a convoy carrying Army reinforcements to a point just south of San Cristobál. In the company of the *Atlanta* and two destroy-ers, she parted ways with the convoy on the evening of October 12, and was en route south to Espiritu Santo when Kurita's biggies came calling.

The Japanese tide was so high, their appetite for bombarding U.S. shore targets so strong, that even Espiritu Santo was not safe. On the morning of October 14, a Japanese submarine surfaced off Segond Channel and opened up on the airfield with its deck gun. That day Yamamoto declared Hender-son Field "suppressed."

In the days following Admiral Scott's return to base after the Battle of Cape Esperance, U.S. naval forces were largely powerless to challenge what seemed an unceasing tide of Japanese ships. Pilots of American patrol planes were reporting more enemy vessels carving southerly wakes. On the morn-ing of the fourteenth, two groups were spotted heading toward the island. One was especially foreboding: a force of six troop transports escorted by destroyers. The other was a pair of heavy cruisers and an escort of two destroyers.

The only available U.S. carrier, the *Hornet,* was far from the theater of action, fueling northwest of New Caledonia. The *Washington* and the *Atlanta* were en route south, a day from reaching Espiritu Santo.

On Guadalcanal, a lieutenant colonel from the headquarters of the Marine air commander on Guadalcanal, General Roy Geiger, paid a visit to one of his squadrons and described a dire and potentially disastrous situa-tion. In the midst of intermittent Japanese artillery fire from the hills, he told them, "We don't know whether we'll be able to hold the field or not." He said another task force of enemy warships and troop transports was headed their way. "We have enough gasoline for one mission against them. Load your air-planes with bombs and go out with the dive-bombers." If on their return to base they landed in the midst of a pitched battle against newly landed Japa-nese troops, the pilots were told they would no longer have the luxury of fighting with wing-mounted machine guns, thousands of feet above their targets. "After the gas is gone we'll have to let the ground troops take over," he said. "Then your officers and men will attach themselves to some infantry outfit. Good luck and goodbye."

As instructed, the pilots flew off under the bright South Seas sun. As it turned out, speeches were speeches and their momentous mission was no Hollywood film. Planting a thousand-pound bomb with a delayed-action fuze into a speeding, veering destroyer was difficult even for a pilot who was not strung out after sleepless weeks of air attacks and artillery bombardment. Though even a near miss that fell seventy-five feet away could inflict damage, the Dauntless dive-bomber pilots, flying in pickup squads that sometimes numbered as few as two to four planes, were seldom effective. The two waves of air attacks the Cactus Air Force sent out on the fourteenth damaged only a single enemy destroyer. Meanwhile, the six heavily laden Japanese transports, with major elements of the Combined Fleet standing off far to the east, plunged toward Guadalcanal.

ON THE AFTERNOON OF October 14, Ghormley informed Nimitz that the Japanese transports would land on the island that night, that enemy carriers and cruisers were on the move, and that he had no carriers to intercept. "THE SITUATION IS CRITICAL AND ENEMY REINFORCEMENTS MUST BE STOPPED IF OUR POSITION IN CACTUS IS TO BE HELD."

That night, the defenders of Henderson Field were given no peace for rest. Admiral Mikawa, in his flagship *Chokai,* with the heavy cruiser *Kinugasa,* accompanied a convoy to its unloading point off Tassafaronga, then detached the two cruisers to roam off Henderson Field. As the transports anchored offshore and began disgorging troops to the beach, the two cruisers lit up the sound for the second consecutive night, firing more than seven hundred eight-inch shells into the airfield without challenge.

At dawn, the unloading of Japanese transports continued within plain sight of the besieged Marine detachment but outside the range of their artillery. The Cactus Air Force cobbled together an attack from available aircraft, fueled by dribbles of remnant aviation gasoline salvaged or brought in to the airdrome via emergency means, and damaged three of the transports badly enough that their captains chose to beach them. Protected by an umbrella of fighter planes from Nagumo's carriers, the Japanese beachmasters still unloaded forty-five hundred men and two-thirds of their cargo and supplies from the grounded ships.

The tenacity of the Japanese reinforcement effort and the power of its air cover compelled Ghormley to turn back one of his own convoys, scheduled to arrive that morning. On the morning of October 16, he ordered three tugs towing barges loaded with urgently needed gasoline to reverse course and leave the area. The destroyer that accompanied them, the *Meredith*—she towed a barge as well—was sent forward to Guadalcanal, only to be set upon by planes from the *Zuikaku* and quickly sunk. Her survivors, adrift for three days, lost well over two hundred of their company to sharks.

The success of the enemy landings underscored an undeniable truth. In the words of the coastwatcher MacKenzie, "It became immediately obvious that to hold Guadalcanal it was essential for the U.S. Navy to gain control of the sea." Looking at his roster of ships after the Cape Esperance battle, Nimitz wrote to King, "SECURITY [OF] OUR POSITION CACTUS DEPENDS UPON ADDITIONAL FORCES NOT NOW IN SIGHT." Vandegrift's marines, he noted, had taken a heavy pounding from air and sea and "CANNOT REMAIN EFFECTIVE INDEFINITELY UNDER SUCH CONDITIONS."

Despite the victory, Yamamoto, too, was feeling the despair of attrition. "I have resigned myself to spending the whole of my remaining life in the next one hundred days," he wrote to a friend.

Nimitz wrote, "It now appears that we are unable to control the sea in the Guadalcanal area. Thus our supply of the positions will only be done at great expense to us. The situation is not hopeless, but it is certainly critical." As if to underscore his point, on the night of the fifteenth the heavy cruisers *Maya* and *Myoko* arrived off Lunga Point unopposed and turned loose on Henderson Field with more than a thousand shells. After this, the third consecutive night of naval bombardment, the Cactus Air Force found itself in possession of just nine Wildcats, eleven Dauntlesses, seven Airacobras, and no Avenger torpedo bombers—barely a third of its previous strength. Though the fuel needs of this diminished contingent weren't what they once were, there was a desperate shortage of avgas as well. Rear Admiral Fitch, the new commander of SOPAC land-based air forces, delivered a grim assessment to Ghormley. The Marines, Fitch wrote, "CAN USE NO MORE AIRCRAFT UNTIL THE AVGAS SITUATION IMPROVES AND UNTIL DESTRUCTIVE ENEMY FIRE ON AIRFIELD FROM BOTH LAND AND SEA IS HALTED. SO LONG AS ENEMY SHIPS PATROL THE SEA AREA OFF LUNGA DAY AND NIGHT I CANNOT SEE HOW [DESTROYERS OR BARGES] CAN BE BROUGHT IN WITH REASONABLE CHANCE OF SUCCESS AND UNTIL THIS IS CHANGED, THE AVGAS SITUATION CANNOT BE IMPROVED TO ANY EXTENT. OFFENSIVE AIR OPERATIONS NOW LIMITED TO STRIKES FROM BUTTON [ESPIRITU SANTO]."

The delivery of fuel would proceed on the backs of some unlikely beasts of burden: submarines, barges towed by tugboats, and cargo planes. Ground crews picked through the skeletal remains of the planes destroyed in the bombardment to drain the last of their tanks.

With the service fleet, submarine force, and cargo aviators extending themselves to help supply the island, it was easy for the riflemen to wonder about the combat fleet. "The Japs have the run of the waters around Guadalcanal," Marine intelligence officer Herbert Merillat wrote in his diary on

October 15. "Where is our Navy, everyone wants to know. I still have confidence in them, and feel sure they are doing something to counter this threat. If not, we are lost." Surveying the grassy expanse of the Fighter One airstrip, half a mile from Henderson Field, General Geiger said to one of his squadron commanders, "I don't think we have a goddamn Navy."

20

The Weight of a War

AFTER THE GREAT CARRIER DUELS IN THE FIRST HALF OF THE YEAR, the obituary of the surface fleet had been prematurely written. Even if Scott's victory did nothing to stop the earth-shattering bombardment that swallowed Henderson Field the next night—he parried the jab, but never saw the roundhouse coming—he had put a dent in the notion of Japanese invincibility and given some swagger to the American light forces.

Admiral Ghormley's conservatism would continue to keep the battleship *Washington* chained to a carrier task force. But the *Atlanta*, which was designed for a defensive role in a carrier task force, was now thrown into Scott's fighting line with her eight destroyer-sized turrets.

The *Atlanta*'s men understood the practical tradecraft of combat. The ship's newsletter contained exhortations on various matters of fighting efficiency. During gunnery operations: cotton in the ears. At night on deck: all cigarettes out. At battle stations: watertight doors shut. When a sailor had nothing else to do, he could make a mental map of the locations of fire extinguishers. If your six hundred shipmates all improved the way they performed a single small task, the collective benefit could be large.

Lloyd Mustin, the deputy boss of the guns, knew what the score was against the Japanese fleet. He vented to his diary, "Call it what you will, their navy is exercising every function of control of the sea and every single resultant advantage is accruing to them. . . . The usual indecision, fear of a surface fight, trying once more to do it all by plane in the teeth of steadily repeated proofs that it couldn't be done that way, has now brought us to this. We are forced into a surface fight." The officers of Samuel Jenkins's ship took every opportunity to learn from what their counterparts in the *San Francisco* and the *Salt Lake City* had experienced against the Japanese. *What does it look like when everybody opens fire? What range do you pick them up with the radar? What speeds are they using? What are their reactions?* Mustin said, "There were lots of lessons to be learned, and we sought them out eagerly and got the information."

The *Atlanta* had spent the first half of October steaming with Willis Lee's flagship, the *Washington,* in defense of the *Hornet* task force, the only carrier in the theater. When Lee was around, Mustin noticed, the air vibrated differently. "He was the perfect example of an officer who made sure everyone knew what he wanted done." This knowledge clarified people's purpose and gave shape to their plans.

Mustin had the kind of garrulous personality that recommended him for liaison work. The *Atlanta*'s exec, Commander Dallas Emory, sent him over to the *Washington* to share stories with her unbloodied gunnery department about the carrier battle in the eastern Solomons and the surface battle off Savo. Mustin found the *Washington*'s crew "magnificently trained with just a gorgeous morale," in part because of the intensity of their recent deployment to the Atlantic. There the possibility of an encounter with the German battleship *Tirpitz* had concentrated their minds. In offset gunnery exercises with the *Atlanta,* the *Washington* put on a show.

With the battleship firing from thirty-five thousand yards, far over the horizon and out of sight except for the top of her mast, Mustin stationed himself on the *Atlanta*'s fantail with an apparatus to measure and report where the battleship's projectiles landed. When the *Washington* let loose, a gout of yellow-brown muzzle smoke would blot the horizon. Then, after a certain lapse of time, came a crash of heavy shells in the sea, followed by a supersonic crack and the rippling roll of the guns from below the horizon. The shells landed smack in the middle of the *Atlanta*'s wake, raising columns of seawater, closely clustered. Mustin knew the discipline that underlay not only the accuracy but also the tightness of the pattern. Willis Lee and Captain Glenn B. Davis knew what they were doing. "They didn't come down over and short. They came down right on, meaning that the *Washington*'s battery was beautifully aligned and beautifully calibrated. Those 2,700-pound armor-piercing projectiles were going to be very bad news for anybody they were ever aimed at."

The men on Henderson Field no doubt would have passed the night of

October 13–14 very differently had the Navy's leadership been willing to turn loose the *Washington* from convoy escort and send her into Savo Sound.

EVER SINCE HE RETURNED from his visit to SOPAC in early October, Chester Nimitz had fretted over the type of leadership being exercised by his old friend Bob Ghormley. Nimitz had put a sunny face on things for the benefit of the press, telling *The New York Times,* "The Japanese must not be underestimated. They are brave, resourceful and, for the most part, experienced fighters. But now they are meeting people with those same characteristics and are suffering losses accordingly." His real feelings were reserved for private conversations with staff. What troubled Nimitz most was something that General Arnold had noted: The closer one got to the fighting front, the higher the level of confidence one found. Defeatism was nowhere more pronounced than in the rear areas.

When Hanson Baldwin flew into the theater in late September, the *New York Times* man received a powerful impression of Ghormley. "He was almost despairing. He was heavily overworked and he said, 'This is a shoestring operation, we haven't got enough of anything. We're just hanging on by our teeth.' He was very frank about this. Here was a time when you needed tough, hard, almost ruthless men. He was a miscast, in my opinion. He should never have been in that job. He was a superb planner and he should have been kept as a planner, but I don't think he was a good operator.... The staff didn't share these impressions entirely, but they were becoming infected. So the whole thing was very unpleasant."

One of the few failures of leadership that Admiral Nimitz might be accused of was his failure to make sure Ghormley exerted personal command over his South Pacific naval forces. Admiral King's original directive to Nimitz had stated, "Assume you will make Ghormley Task Force commander at least for Task One [the seizure of Tulagi and Guadalcanal], which he should command in person in the operating area." Though it was far from clear exactly what this should have meant, it was initially interpreted to be the New Caledonia–New Hebrides area. Ghormley never ventured north of Nouméa.

In these difficult days, Ghormley summoned one of his operations staff, Lieutenant Charles W. Weaver, and asked him to start keeping a personal log of events. As Weaver explained, "I think he had a premonition then that he was going to have to make an accounting later."

In the early hours of October 16, General Vandegrift radioed Ghormley as follows: "THE SITUATION DEMANDS TWO URGENT AND IMMEDIATE STEPS: A: TAKE AND MAINTAIN CONTROL OF SEA AREA ADJACENT TO CACTUS TO PREVENT FURTHER ENEMY LANDINGS AND ENEMY BOMBARDMENT SUCH AS THIS FORCE HAS TAKEN FOR THE LAST 3 NIGHTS. B: REINFORCEMENT OF GROUND FORCES BY AT LEAST 1 DIVISION IN ORDER THAT OFFENSIVE OPERATIONS MAY BE INITIATED TO DESTROY HOSTILE FORCE NOW ON CACTUS."

Ghormley read the message and a few hours later sent a dispatch to Nimitz, King, and all the ships under his command, informing them that part B of the request, which would have stripped area bases of their small garrisons, was not possible with the current troop levels in the theater. "URGENTLY NEED THIS AREA 1 ADDITIONAL ARMY INFANTRY DIVISION. PRESENT FORCES.... INSUFFICIENT TO GARRISON PRESENT BASES AND THEREFORE OBVIOUSLY INADEQUATE [TO] SUPPORT OFFENSIVE OPERATIONS. HAVE NEITHER ON HAND NOR IN SIGHT SUFFICIENT FORCES TO RENDER CACTUS SECURE AGAINST PRESENT INFILTRATION TACTICS."

The next message Ghormley sent to Nimitz would be the final straw. Referring to aircraft sighting reports from Canberra indicating the presence of a Japanese aircraft carrier west of the Santa Cruz Islands, he wrote, "THIS APPEARS TO BE ALL OUT ENEMY EFFORT AGAINST CACTUS POSSIBLY OTHER POSITIONS ALSO. MY FORCES TOTALLY INADEQUATE [TO] MEET SITUATION. URGENTLY REQUEST ALL AVIATION REINFORCEMENT POSSIBLE."

Lieutenant Ernest Eller was with Nimitz at Pacific Fleet headquarters on the night this message arrived. The mood was already tense. Nimitz was preparing, among other things, to inform his commander in the Aleutians that his roster of warships was to be stripped to fulfill the "overwhelming need for strength in SoPac." His intelligence section, fresh from predicting one of the Japanese bombardments of Henderson Field, learned from radio intercepts that two enemy carriers were close by, north of the island. Eller called it "one of the few times that I really saw Admiral Nimitz excited, emotionally. He wasn't demonstrative. But you could see it in his face and his eyes."

Late one night Eller overheard a discussion that began behind the closed doors to Nimitz's office and suddenly swelled and spilled out into the hall. Some members of Nimitz's staff were speaking to their boss in vehement tones. "The situation looked very dark on Guadalcanal. It looked like the Japanese were about to overrun the airfield," Eller said. "We'd had heavy ship losses. I guess it was toward midnight. I was still in the office working and came out to listen." Nimitz's staff, it seemed, was on the verge of insurrection.

There was a sense that the fleet was laboring under a hesitating, passive hand. As Nimitz's intelligence officer, Edwin T. Layton, wrote, "It was evident to all of us at Pearl that Ghormley was faltering. His actions—or lack of them—had abdicated command of the sea to the enemy." That difficult reality put Nimitz in a bind. Though "it was obvious that [Nimitz] felt that Ghormley had handed over command of the sea to the Japanese," Nimitz told his staff that he wouldn't tolerate gloom and defeatism. He certainly didn't like their suggestion that Ghormley be relieved. This last recommendation, he said with uncharacteristic overstatement, was "mutiny."

In fact, the possibility of Ghormley's relief had come up at staff meetings as early as the first week of September. There were concerns about his health; candidates for his replacement were discussed. Nimitz was said to prefer Kelly Turner for the job, but a certain stigma had attached to the commander of the amphibious force following the early losses in his cruiser force.* At the time, Nimitz deflected the conversation, saying he would visit Nouméa himself and check on Ghormley's condition. Now, after long consideration of the style of his leadership and the content of his dispatches, Nimitz concluded not only that Ghormley was "too immersed in detail and not sufficiently bold and aggressive at the right times," but that he was on the verge of an actual nervous breakdown. Nimitz was no clinician, but he was a perceptive reader of people. If his conclusion was too stark for him to record in its own day, many years later he would state this opinion in no uncertain terms.

A few days after Nimitz had decried their "mutiny," Layton and some other staffers decided they needed to see their commander in chief again to press their earlier recommendation. Though the admiral was preparing himself for bed, he agreed to see them for five minutes. "We wasted no time spelling out what was on our minds," Layton wrote. "The situation was so grave that he could not allow any thought of kindness or sympathy for a brother officer to stand in the way. Nimitz thanked us. He said he understood entirely why we had spoken so frankly. There was no further discussion of the painful issue."

Nimitz had burdened Ghormley with his complete and unfaltering trust. It was painful to see his friend waver under it. Nimitz suffered a sleepless night on October 15 before notifying King of his doubts about his SOPAC commander the next morning. "IN VIEW GHORMLEY'S [LATEST DISPATCH]

---

* The notion would arise that the defeat at Savo was the reason for Ghormley's removal. Ghormley had no hand in the tactical dispositions that night.

AND OTHER INDICATIONS INCLUDING SOME NOTED DURING MY VISIT I HAVE UNDER CONSIDERATION HIS RELIEF BY HALSEY AT EARLIEST PRACTICABLE TIME. REQUEST YOUR COMMENT."

"It was a sore mental struggle and the decision was not reached until after hours of anguished consideration," Nimitz wrote Catherine. "I feel better now that it has been done. I am very fond of G. and hope I have not made a life enemy. I believe not. The interest of the nation transcends private interests."

When Nimitz's message was decoded in Washington that afternoon, the COMINCH was preoccupied arguing with General Arnold about fifteen groups of Army planes that King believed had been earmarked for the Pacific. His terse reply seemed more like a response to a recommendation than an exchange of views on a tentative idea. Addressed to Nimitz marked, "Personal and Secret / Most Secret," it contained a single operative word: "APPROVED." With that, Robert L. Ghormley's career as a leader in the war zone was over.

AFTER SCOTT'S VICTORY at Cape Esperance, the Navy made its first public release of details about the sea battles of the previous two months. The public hungered for news of the war's first American-led offensive. A dispatch went out detailing Scott's victory over Goto. With this good news cushioning the blow, it also acknowledged the defeat at Savo Island. On his visit to Henderson Field, Hanson Baldwin of *The New York Times* had sniffed out the latter story, as well as the torpedoing of the *North Carolina*. Though he itched to file stories, he saw a larger need. American readers certainly deserved to know the truth about Savo. The question was whether it put sailors at risk in the continuing fight. Baldwin wrote a series of stories, including an account of Savo as he had learned it on the beaches of Guadalcanal and the decks of warships. His eventual accounts withheld the number of ships sunk, their names, and the vulnerabilities that resulted in their loss. "I fudged this very carefully because I realized it was very important that the Japs not know exactly how damaged we were."

At Espiritu Santo, Norman Scott's healthy ships scavenged from the wounded. The *Salt Lake City,* still seeping water through stressed rivets, and the *Boise,* damaged to within three degrees of her life, were ordered home for repair. Before leaving for Nouméa on October 15, the two cruisers gave up the dregs of their magazines to the *San Francisco* and the *Helena*, respectively. The admiral himself visited a hospital ship and paid tribute in the sickbay. "Not once during the entire visit was I answered with a grumble or a bellyache or a whine, but invariably with a grin or at least with an attempt at one," Scott wrote to his wife, Marjorie, at their home in Washington. "Sometimes the answer would be low, and I would lean well over to make the conversation easier going. It might take a few seconds, and then I would hear, 'I'm doing pretty well, thank you, sir.' One like that, and your heart goes right out to him. It is the custom in the Navy to remove one's cap in the sick bay. Mine will always be off to those men."

Scott doffed his cap, too, to his old friend of a quarter century, Bob Ghormley. "Dear Ghorm," he wrote him, "Going back to our old days of friendship—twenty-four years—I do not feel like saying that I am sorry about this situation of yours. That doesn't express it. It seems to me, if what you say is literally true, that the change was inevitable. I doubt if many people can really appreciate the endless difficulties you ran up against, beginning with the Cactus show before the 1st of August, when you came into the South Pacific. It is too much to expect that you would not run into a dead end eventually.

"Now that you have scrapped a good scrap give the guilty ones one more good stiff punch—where it will do our mail the most good.

"If and when you reach Washington please phone Mrs. Scott. We will both appreciate it.

"Best luck as ever, Sincerely, Norm."

AMONG GHORMLEY'S LAST ACTS as theater commander was to order the still-viable ships of Task Force 64 back into the fray for Savo Sound. The *San Francisco, Helena,* and *Atlanta,* joined by the heavy cruiser *Chester* and eight destroyers, refueled and departed at daybreak escorted by six destroyers. This powerful squadron was soon augmented by a true heavyweight. The 44,500-ton battleship *Washington,* Admiral Lee's flagship, joined them under way. Plans had been drawn up for the *Atlanta* to go as well, but she received other last-minute orders. She drew an assignment to bombard Japanese positions off Lunga Point, in support of infantry operating behind enemy lines. When Captain Jenkins's ship arrived on station, Marine officers motored out to her with field maps marked with Japanese troop areas and supply dumps. In just under two hours the *Atlanta* liberally salted the jungles of northern Guadalcanal with quick-fuzed anti-personnel projec-tiles that detonated on impact with treetops or the ground; with timed shells that sprayed airbursts across the jungle and fields; and with star shells that coughed burning magnesium that stuck to and scalded everything it touched. By the end of it, the antiaircraft cruiser's decks fore and aft were blocked by piles of empty brass shell cases, more than four thousand of them all told.

The crew gave the visiting marines cigarettes and parted as brothers in arms. "They were just delighted at what we had done, and as far as they were concerned it didn't matter whether we hit one single Jap in there or not," Mustin said. "It had let the Japs know that there were other people to contend with than just the few marines on the island."

21

Enter Fighting

WHEN ADMIRAL HALSEY BOARDED A BIG CORONADO FLYING BOAT on October 16 and took off from Pearl Harbor, bound for Nouméa, his orders were to take command of the task force that included his old ship, the *Enterprise,* now fully repaired and ready to rejoin the fight. With him in the four-engine aircraft was Nimitz's chief of staff, Rear Admiral Raymond A. Spruance, who was under orders to inspect conditions at headquarters and report to his boss on, among other things, the readiness for command of one William F. Halsey, Jr. The hero of the early-1942 carrier attacks on the Marshall and Gilbert islands as well as the Doolittle raid in April, Halsey had missed the chance to serve in the Battle of Midway because of a viral skin condition: herpes zoster, or shingles, a malady that was thought to have a psychosomatic component. Before he saddled him with a theater command, Nimitz wanted reassurance that Halsey could be depended on to reenter the war as his old effective self.

Gauging Halsey's mood and temperament on the flight, Spruance liked what he saw and reported it to Nimitz. And so the final piece of Nimitz's command reorganization was set into place. When Halsey's flying boat touched down in Nouméa's glistening harbor on the afternoon of October 18, a whaleboat came alongside. Admiral Ghormley's flag lieutenant stepped out, saluted, and handed Halsey a sealed envelope. Opening it, he found another sealed envelope. Inside was a memo from Nimitz.

"You will take command of the South Pacific Area and the South Pacific Forces immediately," it read.

The first words the "utterly surprised" admiral spoke in response were, "This is the hottest potato they ever handed me!" When Halsey boarded the *Argonne* and finally located his old friend and Naval Academy football team-mate in a cramped cluster of steel compartments, hot and oppressive, he understood right away the need for his relief. Ghormley, to Halsey's eye, was "burdened beyond my own personal capacity," swamped in reports and data and plans, assisted by a single staffer in the massive task of overseeing operations. "I have always insisted on comfortable offices and quarters for my staff," Halsey would write. "Their day's work is so long, their schedule so irregular, the strain so intense, that I am determined for them to work in whatever ease is available." Why were the headquarters so meager? Ghormley told Halsey he had been unable to find space ashore. The French, it seemed, had been intransigent.

The day before Halsey's plane splashed down in Nouméa harbor, Ghormley received notice from Nimitz that Halsey was en route to relieve him. Ghormley acquainted Halsey with the facilities of his operations before taking his leave and boarding a plane for Pearl Harbor, then on to Washington.

The word that a new boss was in town passed quickly through the loudspeakers of every ship in SOPAC, and from tent to Quonset hut to tent ashore. Halsey's arrival was electric. Ed Hooper, an assistant gunnery officer in the battleship *Washington,* said, "We were absolutely elated when we heard the news. It was a shot of adrenaline for the whole command; things had been getting pretty wishy-washy down there." Even the junior officers had been fidgeting under the absence of inspiring leadership. "During wartime it's important how the leadership, starting with the Chief of Naval Operations, gets a message across to everybody in every ship, submarine, airplane and shore station. You need to hear it said that this is an extraordinary moment in your life and in the life of the country, and that you're not going to let it down," the *Atlanta*'s Robert Graff said. "Until that day, we had received no such message."

When Halsey had taken the *Enterprise* to sea in late 1941, he issued Battle Order Number One, which read: "The *Enterprise* is now operating under war conditions. . . . Pilots will sink anything they sight." The declaration was unremarkable except for the fact that it was issued more than a week before the strike on Pearl Harbor. When Halsey was barely into his twenties, his Annapolis classmates referred to him as "A real old salt. Looks like a figurehead of Neptune." His men liked his style. He had once said he was perfectly willing to divide the Pacific Ocean with Japan. "We would take the top; Japan would take the bottom."

From a seagoing family, Halsey had sailed with Teddy Roosevelt's Great White Fleet as an ensign on the battleship *Kansas*. While that experience had taught him to appreciate the symbolism of naval power, he did not generally speak the language of the diplomat. "He was a fighting man, sans fancy trimmings," the journalist Joe James Custer wrote. "He slipped in deftly, and he hit and he hurt. He was adept and clever, and he packed a terrific wallop: he was the Jack Dempsey of the Pacific raiders, he poled the Japs for a goal, and he swung from the floor."

Back in January, commanding the *Enterprise* during the raid on Japan's Marshall Islands bases, he taunted the base commander over the radio: "From the American admiral in charge of the striking force, to the Japanese admiral on the Marshall Islands. It is a pleasure to thank you for having your patrol plane not sight my force." Halsey's public tauntings of the Japanese were so aggressive and frequent that a rumor spread that they had vowed to capture him and torture him to death. His colleagues Aubrey Fitch and William Calhoun reportedly embraced and gleefully spread this rumor. Sometimes when they saw Halsey they would mimic stirring a large cauldron, intoning, *"Boiling oil . . . !"* Halsey's inevitable reply—"You go to hell!"

Halsey was neither a genius nor even a working scholar in any academic or technical field, but he had a quality of brilliance that may have been even more important in a combat capacity. He was, it was said, "brilliant in common sense." He knew that battles and wars were won not principally with well-drafted paperwork or subtle diplomacy or high materials and engineering ratings aboard ship, but by something quite simple and direct: placing ordnance on target. He knew, working backward from there, that the quality of the mind and spirit of the men distributing that ordnance was at least as important as the mechanical state of the weapons themselves. And he knew that small and simple acts, trivial in themselves but intangibly powerful, raised and perfected that quality; sometimes those things were as prosaic as showing up and listening to people.

In the new South Pacific headquarters, a culture of informality reigned. Halsey rejected the new gray uniforms mandated by Washington. He favored working khakis. "The officers and chiefs of my command are wholly at liberty to wear the damn things—if, that is, they are so lacking in naval courtesy and have such limited intelligence as to prefer dressing differently from the commander of the force," he wrote. Halsey's approach to dress wasn't dogmatic or dictatorial. A verse graced a plaque in the front hall of the headquarters: "COMPLETE WITH BLACK TIE / YOU DO LOOK TERRIFIC, / BUT TAKE IT OFF HERE: / THIS IS STILL SOUTH PACIFIC!"

The casual ethos helped promote something else Halsey thought important: eliminating the distinctions among the services. His men were not marines or sailors or soldiers, but warriors of the South Pacific Fighting Forces. Halsey's all-service *esprit de guerre* was relentlessly practical. Interservice tribalism was always costly, and all costs paid to the enemy's cause. Halsey wasn't shy about drawing from the Department of the Army's budget. Under the principle of a united SOPAC team, he drew in Army welders, electricians, and mechanics to service the fleet—and asked that the cooperation be loudly touted. "I would like to see it widely advertised that the army is helping us here. I have never seen anything like the spirit there is in this neck of the woods. It is a real United States service."

Taking in the breadth of his duties, Halsey quickly sympathized with his predecessor. "As I dug into my new job, I realized that the tremendous burden of responsibility that Bob Ghormley had been carrying was far beyond my own capacity." No matter how brilliant or hardworking a man was, he couldn't do it himself. Halsey would lean on his staff. "There's a lot to be done," he told them. "Look around, see what it is, and do it." Halsey had once begged off from an assignment to command the Norfolk Navy Yard. His reasoning, as he told the Navy's personnel chief at the time, Chester Nimitz, was that he didn't feel suited to administering an industrial establishment. That, of course, was precisely what he had signed on for now.

Halsey continued Ghormley's effort to clear the cargo logjam at Nouméa. He expanded the plan to increase covered storage from 200,000 square feet to a million, then brought in hardware for a new 160-by-600-foot pier and tools to equip three new construction battalions. Since forceful leadership always seemed to be in short supply, he asked for a captain or commander from the Civil Engineer Corps to command the Seabees. "The maximum possible urgency must be assigned to the development of this base," he wrote King's office. When Halsey invoked urgency and immediacy, he did it not in complaint but in affirmation, on behalf of specific tasks and challenges. The long memorandum he sent to Nimitz demanding more of everything (above all "tankers and more tankers and more tankers") was detailed and straightforward but did not suggest "or else disaster will follow," as Ghormley's sometimes did. "You are well aware of our needs and this is not offered in complaint or as an excuse but just to keep the pot boiling," he wrote to Nimitz.

His manner of securing a new headquarters from the French administration at Nouméa reflected his action-minded personal ethos. One day he sent his intelligence officer, Marine Colonel Julian P. Brown, to discuss his headquarters accommodations with the Free French governor. Wearing his best dress uniform, pinned with decorations dating to the First World War, Brown presented himself and began pressing the case for a new American facility ashore. When the governor asked, "What do we get in exchange?" Brown replied with the same ordnance-on-target forthrightness that Halsey was known for, if with some uncharacteristic sobriety: "We will continue to protect you as we have always done." This somehow failed to impress the governor, who in grand diplomatic fashion took the matter under advisement. It required little more of such treatment before Halsey went volcanic. He rode ashore with a contingent of marines, marched to the headquarters of Admiral Thierry d'Argenlieu, the surly *haut commissaire,* posted the U.S. colors, and, finding the Frenchman absent, took over his office and set out his guard. For his personal quarters, Halsey seized the former Japanese consul's residence, a brick house with a view of the harbor. As construction battalions broke ground for new recreational facilities—until then strictly forbidden by the Free French—it was clear whose well-being Halsey was committed to, and whose loyalty he was out to win.

AS HALSEY WAS taking SOPAC's reins in Nouméa, U.S. naval intelligence concluded that Admiral Yamamoto had assumed direct command of Japanese naval forces in the area. On October 19, radio snoopers noted something else that seemed ominous: High-precedence traffic had dropped to a level suggesting that the Combined Fleet was in "the final period of adjustment and preparation for action on a major scale." The nightly runs of the Tokyo Express through the Slot had boosted the Japanese garrison on Guadalcanal from six to twenty-two thousand men, nearly a match for the twenty-three thousand Americans there. Several hundred miles north of Guadalcanal, the main elements of the Japanese carrier and battleship fleet were marking time, preparing for a new assault on the island, coordinated with an attack by Japanese troops ashore.

Under pressure from the Joint Chiefs to lend more support to the Guadalcanal operation, Douglas MacArthur foresaw a dark future if the Navy did not meet Yamamoto's challenge. "If we are defeated in the Solomons, as we must be unless the Navy accepts successfully the challenge of the enemy surface fleet, the entire Southwest Pacific will be in gravest danger." MacArthur continued, "I urge that the entire resources of the United States be diverted temporarily to meet the critical situation." The fleet would be left to exert itself piecemeal. On October 20, the *San Francisco* and *Helena,* joined by the heavy cruiser *Chester* and six destroyers, entered Savo Sound to throw shells into the jungle near Cape Esperance. The mission came at a prohibitive price when a Japanese submarine put a torpedo into the *Chester,* forcing her removal for repair.

As Imperial ground forces on Guadalcanal marshaled for a new assault near the Matanikau delta, Halsey decided to move his carrier task force into waters east of the embattled island. The *Enterprise* and the *Hornet,* escorted by the *South Dakota,* steamed northwest of Santa Cruz, casting search planes around the compass. At midday on October 25, a PBY Catalina spotted the vanguard of a large Japanese battle group. The return of two patched-up capital ships, the *Enterprise* and the *South Dakota,* and the arrival of a fiery new theater commander, put American forces in a position to be aggressive again. The rumblings of these events reached all the way to Pearl Harbor. "Today—our Saturday, 24 Oct—Halsey's Sunday 25 Oct—will be a memorable day," Nimitz wrote Catherine. "It is the start of the big long-expected push and we are as nearly ready as it is humanly possible to be.... Tonight and tomorrow will be critical in our history—and pray God they will be successful for us."

WHEN GHORMLEY ARRIVED at Pearl Harbor with Spruance, they were, as Nimitz wrote, "tired, hungry and much in need of baths, which they had missed for several days while in our island staging points." They soon got a bath: in the bright light of publicity. They arrived at Nimitz's headquarters almost simultaneously with the morning paper announcing the change of command. "The view expressed in informed quarters here," read Charles Hurd's page-one story in *The New York Times,* "was to the effect that the new Solomons commander would be expected to turn that venture from a currently defensive operation into an aggressive fight.... Very little informed analysis of the basic meaning of these changes was possible here...in view of the complete silence on the part of the men best qualified to explain them."

Sitting down with Nimitz, Ghormley asked, "What did I do that was wrong?" Nimitz produced a sheaf of the dispatches Ghormley had sent him. Nimitz said that if things were as dire as the dispatches indicated, "we needed the very best man we had to hold down that critical area. And then I asked him whether he was that very best man." Ghormley told Nimitz he could make no such claim.

Ghormley was a talented and decent man, but the war had outgrown his gifts. Writing Nimitz, Secretary Frank Knox was critical of the outgoing commander, referring to his "complete lack of offensive use of our surface

---

The U.S. Navy at Guadalcanal

Operation Watchtower (as of October 18, 1942)

ADM ERNEST J. KING
Commander in Chief, U.S. Fleet (COMINCH)
and Chief of Naval Operations (CNO)

ADM CHESTER W. NIMITZ
Commander in Chief, Pacific Fleet (CINCPAC)

VADM WILLIAM F. HALSEY, JR.
Commander, South Pacific Forces (COMSOPAC)

RADM RICHMOND KELLY TURNER
Commander, Amphibious Force
Task Force 62 (later 67)

RADM AUBREY W. FITCH Commander, Air (land-based), SOPAC Task Force 63	**MGEN ALEXANDER A.** **VANDEGRIFT** Commander, 1st Marine Division
RADM THOMAS C. KINKAID TF 16 (*Enterprise*)	**RADM GEORGE D. MURRAY** TF 17 (*Hornet*)

RADM WILLIS A. LEE
Task Force 64 (*Washington*)

RADM NORMAN SCOTT
Task Group 64.4 Cruiser Striking Force (later 67.4) (*San Francisco*)

craft until Norman Scott's very successful raid north of Savo Island." Knox thought the early days of the Pacific campaign resembled the start of the Civil War. "I presume most of us, if we had been required to choose at the beginning of the war between the brilliant, socially attractive McClellan and the rough, rather uncouth, unsocial Grant, would have chosen McClellan, just like Lincoln did." As Ghormley's staffer Charles W. Weaver would write, "When history is written, the good admiral will have his place in it, *if* the account faithfully records the true facts of the Admiral's great burden in the early days of the Pacific War."

As Ghormley returned to Pearl Harbor to take the post of commandant of the 14th Naval District in Hawaii, President Roosevelt was watching events in the South Pacific with something more than a commander in chief's typical remove. After standing forcefully for the idea that aid to Russia was essential to defeating the Axis, and supporting a Europe-first strategy, his interest in the Solomons campaign was vigorous. His oldest son, James, was serving on Guadalcanal. Despite the potentially disqualifying handicap of being handed, at age twenty-eight, a reserve commission as a lieutenant colonel, which in time he rejected, Major James Roosevelt set himself to emulating the example of his father's rough-riding fifth cousin. A capable and popular officer, he urged the creation of a new type of commando unit, Marine Raiders, which under the leadership of Evans Carlson and Merritt Edson would go on to distinguish themselves at Guadalcanal and elsewhere. James served as the executive officer of the 2nd Marine Raiders on Guadalcanal despite chronic physical ailments.

On October 24, FDR wrote to the Joint Chiefs of Staff, "My anxiety about the Southwest Pacific is to make sure that every possible weapon gets into that area to hold Guadalcanal, and that, having held in this crisis, that munitions and planes and crews are on the way to take advantage of our success. We will soon find ourselves engaged in two active fronts and we must have adequate air support in both places, even though it means delay in our commitments, particularly to England. Our long-range plans could be set back for months if we failed to throw our full strength in our immediate and impending conflicts."

Roosevelt's urgent sense of events in the South Pacific developed not a moment too soon for King, Nimitz, and Halsey. On the very day he urged his Joint Chiefs to redirect their energies westward, and seven days into Halsey's tenure in command of the theater, the Japanese turned loose what would be their most ferocious and concentrated attack yet on America's island foothold.

22

"Strike—Repeat, Strike"

ON GUADALCANAL, "SOMETHING IS IN THE AIR," HERBERT MERILLAT wrote. "I am not sure what it is but can make the obvious guess. All signs point to increased Jap activity, and soon. I expect it will be a pretty mighty blow—the climax of their efforts to retake this place. They have powerful naval forces to the northwest and have been building up a reserve of planes for more than two weeks. So look out for bombs and fourteen-inch naval shells and artillery. I'll bet they open up with field artillery from the hills. In short, it looks like a very hot time for the next few days. Operations officers and the command have suddenly become very secretive. There is an undercurrent of excitement in the CP."

The new theater commander did not long ponder how he would use the discretion Nimitz had allowed him. Just six days into his tenure as South Pacific commander, his desk covered with sighting reports of enemy ships in the waters northeast of the Solomons, Halsey ordered the *Enterprise* and *Hornet* to venture farther north than they had gone since August and seek battle. Doubling down on his aggressive willingness to take risks, he stood ready to send Rear Admiral Willis Lee's force, the battleship *Washington* and his cruisers, all the way up the Slot to bombard Japanese harbors south of Bougainville.

Lee, commanding the surface striking force from the flagship *Washington*, with the cruisers *San Francisco, Helena, Atlanta,* and ten destroyers, operated separately from the two carrier groups. Cruising south of Guadalcanal and east of Rennell Island, he prepared to sortie at sunset and enter Ironbottom Sound from the west. His force would sweep the area off Cape Esperance and around Savo Island and—as the *Atlanta*'s Lloyd Mustin put it in his diary—"smash anything we find.... Maybe a close-range, shotguns-across-the-dinner-table sort of affair." The convoys would get whatever rag-tag escort Turner's staff could manage. The fleet's heavies had at last been unleashed to go hunting.

They didn't catch any prey on their first run, but they made their presence felt hundreds of miles to the north. Word that an American battleship was in Savo Sound led the 8th Fleet's planners to cancel the Tokyo Express bombardment run scheduled for the night of October 25–26.

The naval forces the Japanese were bringing down from Truk dwarfed anything the Americans had seen in the South Pacific to date. It was the full-scale seaborne counteroffensive that the 17th Army headquarters at Rabaul had been envisioning since the failures of September: an Advance Force under Vice Admiral Nobutake Kondo, including battleships and cruisers earmarked to support the Army's triumphant capture of Henderson Field, and the aircraft carrier *Junyo*. (Another carrier, the *Hiyo*, should have been with Kondo, too, but she had suffered an accidental fire on October 22 that forced her return to Truk.) With them, steaming two hundred miles to their east, came Chuichi Nagumo's Striking Force, comprising the carriers *Shokaku*, *Zuikaku*, and *Zuiho*. South of Nagumo plowed Rear Admiral Hiroaki Abe's Vanguard Force, including the battleships *Hiei* and *Kirishima* and three heavy cruisers.

Imperial plans were better coordinated than they had been two months ago leading into the Battle of the Eastern Solomons, the campaign's first clash of carriers. They called for a bold combined assault: the heavy combatants descending on the island while the Army mounted an assault on Henderson Field, and the carriers sweeping the seas of American naval power. The fleet would move south and engage as soon as the Army sent word that it had seized the airfield. Yamamoto and his staff relished the thought of avenging Midway and luring the elusive American carriers to their destruction.

The commander of the 17th Army, Lieutenant General Harukichi Hyaku-take, had planned to launch a multipronged assault on Henderson Field on the twenty-second. Personally commanding the Japanese forces there—consisting of the 2nd (Sendai) Division, two battalions of the 38th Division, some survivors of Ichiki's and Kawaguchi's forces, as well as a regiment and three batteries of heavy field artillery, two battalions and one battery of field antiaircraft artillery, one battalion and one battery of mountain artillery, a mortar battalion, a tank company, and three rapid-fire gun battalions—Hyakutake began assembling his units and preparing to send them into position as soon as they piled ashore from the transports.

The assault would begin with a diversionary artillery barrage from forces massing in the west, across the Matanikau River. The main assault, undertaken by the Sendai Division marshaled in the tangled jungle south of Henderson Field, would follow. Still underestimating U.S. troop strength on the island—an intelligence report in late September pegged Vandegrift's garrison at seventy-five hundred men, well below half its actual number—Hyakutake apparently remained as cocksure of his success as he had been on the day he ordered Colonel Ichiki's detachment to its slaughter.

From their positions on the west side of the Matanikau River, Japanese heavy artillery began firing on Henderson Field, and the diversionary infantry regiment tried to make its presence known to the Americans. With the preliminaries still under way, Hyakutake's staff radioed a confident message to 17th Army headquarters at Rabaul: "The victory is already in our hands. Please rest your minds." He instructed his aides to begin planning for an American surrender.

Words were words. The Japanese Navy wanted deeds. Frustrated by the Army's delays, and with Yamamoto threatening to haul the fleet back to Truk to refuel if ground commanders didn't get on with things, Kondo and Nagumo maintained course.

As the Imperial Japanese Army was stalking the jungles surrounding Henderson Field, torrential rains engulfed the island. And then it was over—or so claimed a dispatch that reached the *Yamato,* moored at Truk, that night. It was after 1:30 a.m. on the twenty-fourth when the telegram was given to Admiral Ugaki as he was meditating by moonlight on the weather deck. It was a dispatch from the 17th Army, proclaiming, "2300 BANZAI!—A LITTLE BEFORE 2300 THE RIGHT WING CAPTURED THE AIRFIELD." "This settled everything," Ugaki wrote. He exhorted to his diary, "March, all forces, to enlarge the result gained! Hesitation or indecision at this moment would leave a regret forever."

And so the fleet pressed on. The announcement of the airfield's conquest led Vice Admiral Mikawa to send in the light cruiser *Yura* and several destroyer divisions to blockade the shore and bombard in support of the advancing Imperial Army. Later that morning American planes from Henderson set upon the *Yura,* the 17th Army's claim to have captured the airfield notwithstanding. The ship took a bomb from an SBD, as did a destroyer.

Later that afternoon another flight of dive-bombers, joined by half a dozen B-17s, let fly against the wounded ship, which had to be scuttled.

Though the Americans had little sense of where the Japanese ground forces were located—the mustering of the Sendai Division had gone undetected by U.S. ground patrols and search planes in the thick jungle south of Lunga Plain—American units were well positioned, with a perimeter divided into five regimental sectors.

General Vandegrift would not be present for the coming assault on his perimeter. Urged by General Thomas Holcomb, the commandant of the Marine Corps—who had picked an inopportune time to inspect Cactus—Vandegrift had traveled to Nouméa to confer with Halsey. General Geiger, Vandegrift's aviation deputy, took temporary command of U.S. forces on the island.

On the night of October 23–24, the Japanese offensive began with a diversionary attack from the west, across the Matanikau River. American artillery smashed up the leading wedge of tanks. The next night, south of the high ground recently named Edson's Ridge, just half a mile from the airstrip, elements of the Sendai Division sent two powerful forces at Henderson Field. Each consisted of three rifle battalions, and with three more in reserve, the Japanese plan envisioned a powerful two-pronged surge toward the airfield. Owing to fatigue, confusion, and poor communications, the attack was launched piecemeal. Conceived in general contempt for their enemy, the Japanese attack followed the same routes of the disastrous September assault. On toward Edson's Ridge the Japanese charged now, poorly coordinated and straight into a murderous enfilade of artillery and rifle fire. Colonel Chesty Puller's seven-hundred-man battalion from the well-seasoned 7th Marines, joined with a battalion of the newly arrived 164th Infantry under Lieutenant Colonel Robert Hall, put up a stout defense despite their lack of advance warning on enemy preparations. When the *pup-pup-pup* of small-arms fire finally faltered and died in the predawn hours of October 25, the first assault had failed.

The 17th Army's announcement that it captured the airfield might have been a deep misapprehension. It might even have been a lie. But on came the Japanese fleet. Encouraged by false reports of the Army's progress, Kondo and Nagumo kept their prows aimed south, searching for Halsey's fleet while standing by to hit Henderson Field, too. Their carrier planes were reporting nothing but empty expanses of ocean. The land-based planes of the 11th Air Fleet, flying from Buin and Rabaul, made several sightings of Admiral Lee's *Washington* task force near Rennell Island, but the American heavy was too far away for Japanese aircraft to reach her. A superior Japanese force was advancing on bad intelligence. What result would flow from it was an imponderable that only another deadly trial by fire would solve.

CHESTER NIMITZ HAD developed a general approach for confronting a superior enemy. "Having inferior forces," he wrote early in the campaign, "we must count heavily on attrition, but losing no chance to come to grips with the enemy under the principle of calculated risk." Still, the principle's requirements were far from clear. How does one calculate, and what does one risk?

A doctrine so subjective offered little decision guidance at all. Its spirit was not prescriptive; it was merely advisory. But this seemed to be the American way of war. Commanders since the Revolution had enjoyed the freedom to act on their best personal initiative. This flexibility and discretion was the gift—and the burden—that Nimitz always bestowed upon his commanders. Admiral Halsey was free to act on his instinct now.

While Japanese scout pilots were revealing to their astonished command that Henderson Field, contrary to dispatches, had not been seized, Willis Lee's surface striking force, including the *Washington* and the heavy cruiser *San Francisco,* marked time about thirty miles east of Rennell Island, ready to run north for a sweep of Savo Sound. On the twenty-fourth, Rear Admiral Norman Scott was transferred from the *San Francisco* to the antiaircraft cruiser *Atlanta.* His new flagship would soon be detached from Lee's Task Force 64 and, leading a striking force of destroyers, be thrown directly into the fight for Guadalcanal.

Meanwhile, Halsey's two carrier groups—Task Force 16, with the *Enterprise* and *South Dakota,* and Task Force 17, with the *Hornet* and a quartet of cruisers—under the overall command of Rear Admiral Thomas C. Kinkaid (who flew his flag in the *Enterprise*), moved toward the suspected location of the Japanese carrier fleet as if by the attraction of gravity.

LATE IN THE NIGHT of October 24, in his cabin in the *Argonne* in Nouméa harbor, Halsey prepared to adjourn his conference with General Vandegrift, Kelly Turner, and senior Army and Marine officers. The ground commanders articulated the woes of the long-suffering garrison on Guadalcanal. They said morale was deteriorating under constant attacks and a sure, intuitive sense that more enemy forces were massing at Rabaul and Truk. According to Halsey, "They began to echo the question that the public had asked in the weeks following Pearl Harbor, 'Where is the Navy?'"

It was late by the time the litany of the riflemen ended. Halsey asked Vandegrift and Major General Millard F. Harmon, the senior U.S. Army officer in the South Pacific, "Are we going to evacuate or hold?"

Vandegrift responded, "I can hold, but I've got to have more active support than I've been getting." To this, Kelly Turner reacted defensively, pointing to difficulties of defending shoal-cluttered waterways with a fleet that was attriting as surely as the garrison was. Knowing no choice remained but to hold fast, Halsey took Vandegrift's statement differently. According to the historian Richard B. Frank, "If Vandegrift had fired an arrow into Halsey's chest he probably could not have wounded him more. It was simply unacceptable to Halsey for the Navy to be viewed by the Marines as not carrying its end." He told Vandegrift, "All right. Go on back. I'll promise you everything I've got."

For starters, Halsey reconsidered a plan, long on the boards, to use Army troops to occupy Ndeni in the Santa Cruz Islands. Ghormley had authorized the operation even though General Harmon, the Army's SOPAC chief, considered it a wasteful diversion. So Halsey canceled it, redirecting the soldiers earmarked for it to Guadalcanal.

Halsey's more immediate task was deciding what to do about the threat from the Combined Fleet. Surveying intelligence and reconnaissance reports suggesting the approach of a Japanese carrier force, he concluded that "action was obviously a matter of hours." He took stock of the needs of the Marines and the capabilities of his naval force. He liked his chances a great deal better now that two carriers were on hand. "Carrier power varies as the square," he wrote in his memoirs. "Two carriers are four times as powerful as one." In a two-carrier task force, one carrier could be designated as the "duty" carrier, sending out air searches and providing combat air patrols and anti-submarine patrols, while the other carrier held a fully armed and fueled strike ready on deck. One carrier operating alone could do none of those things very effectively, and her crews were especially hard-pressed to switch between roles. "Until the *Enterprise* arrived, our plight had been almost hopeless. Now we had a fighting chance," Halsey added.

Determined to intercept Nagumo, Halsey ordered Kinkaid to ring up twenty-two knots and take the *Enterprise* and *Hornet* task forces northwest from their patrol position east of Santa Cruz. A reprise of Midway, a curtain call for Coral Sea, the next collision of American and Japanese carrier airpower would go down as the last aerial engagement between the fleets until

U.S. troops were on the beaches of Saipan and in the hedgerows of Normandy.

Ashore, the Japanese hammer had struck the American anvil. It was the hammer that would crack. The fleets, meanwhile, prepared for their own reckoning.

Just before midnight on October 24, as his marines ashore were battling the Japanese assault, Halsey radioed his principal naval commanders, Kinkaid and Lee, with a galvanizing message that would echo through the passageways and compartments of every ship in the South Pacific Force. The four syllables, bereft of any operational specificity or doctrinal nuance and apropos of no particular target, placed a clean vector through everyone's mind that ordered and oriented their next moves.

"Strike—Repeat, Strike."

23

Santa Cruz

EVEN WITH KNOWLEDGE THAT AN ENEMY FLEET WAS NEAR, LOCATING and attacking it effectively was no small challenge for a carrier commander. Aircraft fuel was dear, range limited, weather variable, and intentions of opposing commanders ever unknowable. The doctrines that governed the mechanics of carrier operations—how many planes to send out searching, how many to retain in reserve for a strike, and how many to keep aloft nearby as a defensive umbrella for the fleet—were in a state of constant experiment and evolution. Then there was nature to contend with: Given that strikes had to be launched into the wind to get heavy airplanes aloft, which compass heading did one need to pursue, and was the day too far gone to retrieve the aircraft during daylight?

The Americans had a considerable advantage in Admiral Fitch's land-based PBY Catalina patrol bombers and B-17 Flying Fortresses operating out of Espiritu Santo and other area island groups. They had the ability to fly at night and their range, at up to eight hundred miles, was peerless. On the morning of October 25, a flurry of sighting reports reached American commanders. At nine thirty, a B-17 spied the *Junyo* northeast of Malaita. Mere minutes later, a PBY spotted the battleships and cruisers of Abe's vanguard. This was followed by a third sighting ten minutes later, reporting three Japanese carriers. At the time of these sightings, the Japanese were about three hundred miles northwest of the Santa Cruz Islands. Kinkaid's and Murray's task forces were about an equal distance east of the islands.

Realizing he had been discovered, Admiral Nagumo, furious that his scouts hadn't yet found the U.S. carriers, decided to reverse course to the north, taking his three valuable carriers out of range of potential attack. It was a wise and fortuitous move. A flight of B-17s was summoned from Espiritu at first contact, and the *Enterprise,* too, launched a strike. Nagumo knew all too well that the first carrier to be seen was usually the first to be sunk as well. The fact that the American strikes missed him was testimony to the value of caution. The pilots from the *Enterprise,* meanwhile, encountered the terror that beset even the most experienced pilots returning to their ship after dark. Attemping to land on the small flight deck at night, eight aircraft were lost, either forced to ditch or suffer damage on hard landings. Two pilots were killed.

Through the night, Fitch's snoopers kept up a determined effort to relocate the Japanese carriers on the night patrol. On Guadalcanal that night, the Japanese Army renewed its assault on Henderson Field, using the same general approach for a similarly grim result. General Hyakutake's infantry, blistered by machine-gun, mortar, and canister fire, was forced to retreat. Japanese deaths were as many as thirty-five hundred. American fatalities in what would be known as the Battle for Henderson Field numbered around ninety.

As Vandegrift's men held again, the first report from the PBYs reached Kinkaid around midnight and passed to Halsey. Dispatched shortly after 3 a.m. on the twenty-sixth (by a courageous Catalina pilot who doubled down on his luck by trying to bomb the *Zuikaku*), the report did not reach Kinkaid for two hours. When it finally did, the vintage of the news persuaded him to hesitate. He would not launch his attack until fresher information came.

The *Enterprise,* as the duty carrier, sent up the dawn patrol to resume searches to the west and north of the task force. At 6:17 a.m., two Dauntlesses working the western search sector spotted battleships, Abe's Vanguard Force, about eighty-five miles out. But it was the carriers that were prized most highly. Less than thirty minutes later, two other *Enterprise* aviators hit pay dirt, spying Nagumo's carriers to the west-northwest of Kinkaid, about two hundred miles away.

Unfortunately for Kinkaid, his decision to await better information before striking took place just as one of Kondo's scout planes finally located him. As a consequence of the American commander's delay and his bad luck in being spotted, the Japanese launched their principal attack about twenty minutes ahead of the Americans. At seven thirty-two, the *Hornet,* operating about ten miles from the *Enterprise* task force, began launching her first deckload of aircraft.

Because Kondo was heading southeast, directly into the wind, whereas Kinkaid's carriers were steaming with the wind and thus had to reverse course into the wind in order to launch or recover aircraft, the Japanese were

---

U.S. Navy Combat Task Forces in the South Pacific (as of October 26, 1942)

Carrier Task Force (Task Force 61)
Rear Adm. Thomas C. Kinkaid

TASK FORCE 16	TASK FORCE 17
Enterprise (CV)	*Hornet* (CV)
(Rear Adm. Kinkaid)	(Rear Adm. George D. Murray)
South Dakota (BB)	*Northampton* (CA)
Portland (CA)	*Pensacola* (CA)
San Juan (CLAA)	*San Diego* (CLAA)
Cushing (DD)	*Juneau* (CLAA)
Preston (DD)	*Morris* (DD)
Smith (DD)	*Anderson* (DD)
Maury (DD)	*Hughes* (DD)
Conyngham (DD)	*Mustin* (DD)
Shaw (DD)	*Russell* (DD)
Porter (DD)	*Barton* (DD)

Battleship Task Force (Task Force 64)
(off Rennell Island)
Rear Adm. Willis A. Lee

TASK FORCE 64

Washington (BB)	*Aaron Ward* (DD)
(Rear Adm. Lee)	*Benham* (DD)
San Francisco (CA)	*Fletcher* (DD)
(Rear Adm. Norman Scott)	*Lansdowne* (DD)
Helena (CL)	*Lardner* (DD)
Atlanta (CLAA)	*McCalla* (DD)

quicker on the draw by about thirty minutes. By seven forty, sixty-four Japanese planes—a nearly even mix of Kate torpedo bombers, Val dive-bombers, and Zero fighters from the *Shokaku, Zuikaku,* and *Zuiho*—were airborne and outbound.

The American scout pilots who spotted Nagumo's carriers were quickly intercepted and driven into the clouds by the enemy combat air patrol. Two other *Enterprise* Dauntlesses heard the sighting report, navigated to locate the enemy fleet, and winged over into steep dives. Targeting the light carrier *Zuiho,* Lieutenant Stockton B. Strong and Ensign Charles B. Irvine planted a five-hundred-pound bomb into the after part of her flight deck. The fifty-foot hole would knock her out of the fray, but her strike pilots were already aloft, winging toward Kinkaid's carriers.

The two American carriers embarked 137 operational planes between them (64 fighters, 47 dive-bombers, and 26 torpedo bombers). Their four Japanese counterparts carried 194 (76 fighters, 60 dive-bombers, 57 torpedo

---

The Japanese in the Battle of Santa Cruz

Support Force
Vice Adm. Nobutake Kondo

ADVANCE FORCE	STRIKING FORCE
Vice Adm. Kondo	Vice Adm. Chuichi Nagumo
Junyo (CV)	*Shokaku* (CV)
Kongo (BB)	*Zuikaku* (CV)
Haruna (BB)	*Zuiho* (CVL)
Atago (CA)	*Kumano* (CA)
Takao (CA)	8 destroyers
Myoko (CA)	
Maya (CA)	
10 destroyers	

VANGUARD FORCE

Rear Adm. Hiroaki Abe	*Tone* (CA)
Hiei (BB)	*Chikuma* (CA)
Kirishima (BB)	*Nagara* (CL)
Suzuya (CA)	7 destroyers

bombers, and a reconnaissance plane). But more important than numbers was the speed with which planes could locate and strike their targets. With this small but telling first blow, which destroyed the *Zuiho*'s arresting gear and robbed her ability to recover aircraft, the Battle of Santa Cruz was joined.

For commanders making split decisions amid great uncertainty, it was far from clear which approach prudence urged: sending out planes to strike as quickly as they left the carrier deck, or having them gather in strength near their carriers before turning out after the enemy. With the two U.S. task forces operating independently, separated by about ten miles, it was not easy to combine the aircraft formations in any event. The pilots on the *Enterprise* received conflicting instructions on that score. What ensued was far from an orderly affair.

With the Japanese two hundred miles distant, fuel was too precious to burn circling to rendezvous. The principal strikes from the *Hornet* and *Enterprise* were hastily launched and ordered to seek the Japanese as soon as they were airborne. An *Enterprise* flight deck crewman held aloft a sign— "PROCEED WITHOUT *HORNET*"—indicating that each carrier's strike group was on its own. By eight twenty, a gaggle of twenty-seven Dauntlesses, twenty Avengers, and twenty-three Wildcats, loosely organized in three groups, was winging after Kondo.

The leading American planes were airborne for barely thirty minutes when the Japanese strike came within view on a reciprocal flight path. Thus began an impromptu melee as nine Zeros peeled off from escort duty and dove down on the American flight about sixty miles northwest of the U.S. carriers.

The commander of Torpedo Squadron 10, Lieutenant Commander John A. Collett, flying in the leading four-plane section of Avengers, felt his aircraft shudder and his starboard wing dip. As the turret gunner opened up with his fifty-caliber machine gun, Collett's radioman, Thomas C. Nelson, Jr., got no response from his pilot over the intercom. Collett, forced to abandon his burning cockpit, threw back his canopy and crawled out onto the starboard wing. As Collett was whisked away into the airstream, never to be seen again, Nelson abandoned the radioman's compartment in the belly of the plane. He was the only survivor. The aerial scrimmage cost the *Enterprise* air group four Wildcats and four Avengers shot down or forced to turn back. The babel of voices on the pilots' radio frequency told Admiral Kinkaid in the *Enterprise* of the fracas that developed as the outbound American and Japanese air strikes ran into each other. Connecting the dots, he sketched a picture of an inbound attack and ordered his carriers, still steaming about ten miles apart, to hustle the rest of their planes into the air.

Shortly before nine o'clock, the inbound Japanese strike was bathed in the transmissions of the air-search radar of the heavy cruiser *Northampton,* assigned to escort the *Hornet* in Task Force 17. Somehow neither the *Hornet*'s nor the *Enterprise*'s electronic eyes ever saw the bogeys. The *Northampton*'s skipper, not knowing this, relayed word to the *Hornet* in a leisurely way, by signal flags rather than by a faster but less secure radio broadcast. As a result, the *Enterprise* never received word at all. Worse, the *Enterprise*'s inexperienced fighter director officer, responsible for guiding the combat air patrol to its targets, whiffed completely. He reported the angle of approach of the Japanese strike with reference to the relative heading of his ship. Such a pole star was of little use to any pilot who couldn't see the reporting vessel. And so on that cloudy day most of the thirty-seven Wildcat jockeys flying combat air patrol failed to intercept the attack before it was already over their carrier. Fortunately for the *Enterprise,* she found concealment in a rain squall. As a result, the first Japanese air strike fell on the perpetrator of the Doolittle raid, the *Hornet.*

As the *Hornet*'s outbound strike group left its task force behind, some of the pilots saw the black puffs of flak dotting the skies behind them. That's when they knew the Japanese had found their ship. A flight of twenty-one Val dive-bombers from the *Zuikaku,* under command of Lieutenant Sadamu Takahashi, were the first to attack the *Hornet.*

To the dismay of the carrier's crew, half of her powerful five-inch antiaircraft battery was effectively disabled when the young officer who supervised the after five-inch battery "drove the guns into the stops," freezing them in a horizonal elevation just as the first enemy dive-bomber appeared overhead. "Believe you me, the gun captains took this very, very personal. All his training, everything, right out the window," gunner's mate first class Alvin Grahn remembered. "Five of our most lethal guns now sat with their barrels locked in place. They would have made mincemeat out of that plane."

As the Wildcats on combat air patrol tangled with the escorting Zeros, the Japanese dive-bombers concentrated on their target, hitting the *Hornet* with three bombs. A Val struck by antiaircraft fire fell burning and crashed into the island superstructure in a wash of flames. The plane penetrated several decks, spreading fire as it went, straight down into a squadron ready room one deck below the flight deck. Its five-hundred-pound bomb was found later, unexploded and rolling around in a passageway outside. As the Vals were doing their work, torpedo bombers from the *Shokaku* were down low on the water, closing on the *Hornet* from two directions, off the starboard bow and the port quarter. The textbook "anvil" attack would expose the carrier to torpedoes from one group of Kates or the other, no matter which way she turned. In short minutes, two torpedoes were crashing into the carrier's starboard side, flooding both fire rooms and snuffing out her propulsion and power. The time was 9:15 a.m.

Several hundred miles to the north, Admiral Nagumo was in no place to celebrate. Overhead, pilots from the *Hornet's* two Dauntless-equipped squadrons had found his carriers.

As the commander of Scouting Squadron 8, Lieutenant Commander William "Gus" Widhelm, surveyed the fleet below, four Zeros from the *Shokaku* piled in to intercept. Cagey and determined, the American dive-bombers, no match for Japanese fighters in air-to-air combat, avoided the slashing head-on passes and high-side runs of the Japanese combat air patrol. When the leader of the Japanese fighter section dove on Widhelm from twelve o'clock high, the American pulled back his stick and turned loose with his fifties. If a dive-bomber seldom beat a fighter in an aerial duel, a veteran could occasionally pick his spot. The converging planes were just a short football field apart when the Zero's engine caught fire and exploded. Widhelm flew through the debris and continued closing with the *Shokaku* ahead.

As Zeros and Dauntlesses engaged in their murderous dance, a Japanese pilot lined up Widhelm's plane and pulled a burst from his twenty-millimeter cannons. As Widhelm's squadron mates were hurtling down upon the *Shokaku* in seventy-degree dives, heads hunched forward peering into their bomb sights, dive brakes gripping the air, it was a sure mark of their spirit that as Widhelm's engine coughed smoke and died, his comrades found their hearts on fire listening to his Navy-grade cussing about the lack of effective help from the *Hornet's* fighters as he guided his smoking aircraft into the sea. Surviving the crash landing, Widhelm would be left to observe the exploits of his comrades from a bobbing yellow life raft.

It wasn't long before Lieutenant James E. "Moe" Vose, the leader of the *Hornet's* second flight of Dauntlesses, from Bombing Squadron 8, found Nagumo's carriers. Radioing a sighting report, they pushed over on the *Shokaku* and piled in. Dauntlesses flying search or "scouting" missions carried a half-sized five-hundred-pound bomb, the better to extend their range. Dauntlesses armed for strikes carried a thousand-pound egg. Vose's aviators were loaded for bear. As they dove down on the speeding, swerving *Shokaku*, the veteran of the Pearl Harbor attack gamely skidded out of the path of the first three or four big bombs. The next few, all of them thousand-pounders, scored heavily, shattering the carrier's flight deck and destroying her center elevator. By nine thirty, with fires sweeping through her hangar deck, the *Shokaku* was no longer capable of flight operations. She could still make thirty-one knots, but she, like the *Zuiho* before her, was out of the fight.

The heavy cruiser *Chikuma*, less valuable than the *Shokaku* but an important naval asset nonetheless, took a couple of bombs from *Hornet* Bombing Squadron 8 aviators, and two near misses from *Enterprise* Dauntless jockeys, and was left battered and burning but navigable, with almost two hundred dead.

Thirty minutes after the U.S. attack pilots first set upon their targets, they were finished with their attacks and bound for home.

DURING THE LULL that followed the first attacks on the *Hornet,* the *Northampton* maneuvered to take the crippled carrier under tow. Several miles away, in Task Force 16, Admiral Kinkaid learned of the *Hornet*'s ill fortune when the word reached him that his flagship, the *Enterprise,* was to land all returning planes, including those from the *Hornet.* The Big E was preparing another air strike at the time, her ordnancemen loading bombs onto racks, pulsing fuel hoses everywhere. If an enemy attack arrived in that vulnerable window, it could be disastrous. As it happened, it was an American plane that drew first blood from the *Enterprise* task force.

It was the fluky kind of thing that only seems to happen in wartime. Just before 10 a.m., the pilot of a damaged Avenger was waved off from his first approach on the *Enterprise.* Unable to circle for another landing attempt, he ditched near the destroyer *Porter.* As he and his crew scrambled into the life raft, the destroyer approached them and stopped. The deck force was preparing to take the flight crew aboard when a lookout yelled, "Torpedo wake on the port bow!" Pilots overhead spotted the missile, tracing a counterclockwise circle ahead of the *Porter.* They dove down and made two strafing passes in an effort to detonate the weapon short of the ship, but onward it churned, finally striking port side amidships. The blast killed fifteen sailors and left the ship fit only for scuttling. Though another destroyer would report a suspicious periscope as she was maneuvering to recover survivors, in fact the torpedo had come from the very plane that the *Porter* was racing to save. It jarred loose on impact with the water.

Just minutes later, the Japanese strike reached the *Enterprise* group. From high above the six-thousand-foot cloud ceiling, from astern the *Enterprise*, fell a waterfall of Vals, unopposed by U.S. fighters.

The newly outfitted *South Dakota*, the heaviest ship in the *Enterprise*'s screen, joined by the antiaircraft cruiser *San Juan* and the heavy cruiser *Portland*, put up a staggering volume of fire. "As each plane came down," an American pilot reported, "a veritable cone of tracer shells enveloped it. You could see it being hit and bounced by exploding shells."

Radar-directed five-inch gunfire was lethal. The *South Dakota* and the *San Juan* led the screen in downing a total of thirty-two enemy planes bearing down on Task Force 16. An officer on the *Junyo* was stunned by the paltry number of aircraft that returned. "The planes lurched and staggered onto the deck, every single fighter and bomber bullet-holed. . . . As the pilots climbed wearily from their cramped cockpits, they told of unbelievable opposition, of skies choked with antiaircraft shell bursts and tracers." A bomber squadron leader would return to the *Junyo* "so shaken that at times he could not speak coherently." But no defense could be perfect. Between ten seventeen and ten twenty, the *Enterprise* took three bombs through her flight deck. It was only by deft shiphandling that her new captain, Osborne B. Hardison, who had replaced Captain Arthur C. Davis just three days before the battle, evaded the deadlier missiles released by the torpedo planes. Good work by firefighting and damage-control crews prevented the bomb explosions from burning the carrier beyond salvation.

At ten twenty, a pilot returning from attacking the Japanese fleet crash-landed his damaged Avenger near the *South Dakota*. Mistaking the aircraft's stout, cylindrical fuselage for a surfacing submarine, gunners on the battleship and nearby destroyers took the plane under fire. The destoyer *Preston*, maneuvering to rescue the pilot and his crew, had to veer away to escape being raked by fire from the battleship's secondary guns.

No feat of shiphandling that day surpassed the one turned in by the captain of the destroyer *Smith*. During the air attack, a stricken Japanese torpedo plane, hotly pursued by a Wildcat, fell smoking toward the ship and crashed into her forecastle. As the flames engulfed the entire forward part of the destroyer, her skipper, Lieutenant Commander Hunter Wood, steered his burning vessel into the voluminous spray thrown up by the wake of the fast-stepping *South Dakota* ahead of him. The cascades of froth washed over the decks, bringing the fires under control.

The stricken *Hornet*'s chances were not helped by a signal that her captain had issued around noon via blinker light: "GO TO ENTERPRISE." Her commander had intended the signal for the many American pilots overhead who were looking for a place to land. When the *Northampton*'s signal department repeated the signal, the *Juneau*'s commander, Captain Lyman K. Swenson, believed the message was meant for him. At once the antiaircraft cruiser turned out of formation and rang up full speed to join Task Force 16 over the horizon. Task Force 17 badly needed the *Juneau*'s heavy antiaircraft battery. In the thirteen-minute-long air attack that morning, her gunners claimed credit for a dozen of the many Japanese planes that were seen to fall around the task force.

The American command's insistence on operating its carriers separately doomed the *Hornet* to a lonely death. At 1:35 p.m., having recovered his returning strike aircraft, Kinkaid elected to withdraw south with Task Force 16. The *Enterprise,* with the *South Dakota* and her other escorts, turned southeast. This was bad news for the *Hornet,* for nearly an hour ago, Japanese pilots had spotted her and reported a target of opportunity. The *Enterprise* departed the scene, taking her protective umbrella of fighter aircraft with her; another Japanese strike, this one launched by the *Junyo,* arrived later. With the appearance of more enemy planes, the *Northampton* cast off her towing wire to the *Hornet* in favor of renewed evasive maneuvering. With a fifteen-degree list and a rudder jammed to starboard, the *Hornet* was a poor candidate for salvage in any event. Adrift, she faced yet another attack.

"With our air cover gone, the Japs had it pretty much their own way," gunner's mate Alvin Grahn recalled. "Dive-bombers and torpedo planes, like I say all mixed up. There were destroyers and cruisers zig-zagging all over the place and firing their guns like mad, and the Jap torpedo bombers had trouble trying to line up on the *Hornet* with so many other vessels in the way. The torpedo planes finally were able to find an opening along our starboard side and that's when we really caught hell. One of them dropped a torpedo and then swooped up and over the flight deck. Somebody hit him good and he caught fire. Just a mass of flames, with the landing gear falling off and all. The pilot layed his plane right over and made a tight circle and came back and smashed into the port side.... The plane's engine and fuselage penetrated four or five staterooms and kept right on going and ended up in the forward elevator pit. All this punishment left us without power or water pressure, dead in the water and fighting fires with bucket brigades."

The *Enterprise* task force came under a final attack, too. For all the withering resistance their brothers had met over the American carrier task forces, the pilots who flew on Kondo's final strike of the day, launched by the late-arriving *Junyo,* braved the gauntlet once again. They put a five-hundred-pound bomb into the *San Juan* that penetrated her thin decks and exploded beneath her, wrecking her rudder. Another bomb hit the forward turret of the *South Dakota*. Exploding atop the heavily armored roof, this blast had nowhere to go but up and out.

Every officer on the battleship's bridge except one hit the deck. That officer was Thomas Gatch. The ship's captain was standing on a catwalk forward of the conning tower, watching the *Enterprise* ahead of him through the evening mist. The popular commander, who prized a certain kind of honor from studying Napoleon's wars, the literature of Shakespeare, and the history of the War Between the States, would say later that "it was beneath the dignity of a captain of a U.S. man-of-war to duck for a Japanese bomb." The reward for his bravado was a spray of shrapnel that nicked his jugular vein. As the chief quartermaster hastened to pressure the wound, the ship's doctor made his way to the bridge. Rumors flew that Gatch was near death. For him, readiness to do battle put everything else belowdecks. Spit and polish—out. Regimentation for its own sake—out. Discipline as a means of encouraging anything other than fighting efficiency—out. His medical condition was the chief topic among the crew for days.

As the *Hornet* foundered and listed, her fires out of control, carrying 111 dead, two American destroyers were detailed to ease her into death. The *Mustin* and the *Anderson* trained out their torpedo batteries on the carrier and fired, but each failed to put her under. The destroyers then turned to their guns, popping five-inch rounds into the *Hornet*'s waterline. After several hundred rounds, her fires were all the hungrier, but still she refused to go. It was after the Americans had left her to the night—around 1:30 a.m., with fires raging so badly that she would be of little use even if the Japanese seized her as a war prize—that Kondo's men-of-war closed with the hulk. It was Japanese destroyers that finally put the *Hornet* under with their torpedoes.

The foregoing, evidently, was enough drama for one day. Disliking his chances with one damaged flattop against two unscarred enemy carriers— the *Zuikaku* and *Junyo* were at large and dangerous, and he knew nothing of the shredded state of their air groups—Kinkaid continued retiring. He would face stern second-guessing for his decision to abandon the *Hornet*.

Rear Admiral Hiroaki Abe, the commander of the Vanguard Force, would be censured for caution, too. He elected not to pursue Kinkaid's withdrawing *Enterprise* task force as night fell on October 26. The decision couldn't have been for lack of motivation. He had been present at the Battle of Cape Esperance, where his lifelong friend Aritomo Goto had fallen. He had heard tell of Goto's dying profanities—"*Bakayaro!*" (idiots!)"—as the cruiser *Aoba* was smashed by forces he had believed were friendly.

AS THEIR SHIP SLUGGED SOUTH in the company of the battered *Enterprise,* the crew of the *South Dakota* turned to the ceremonies by which they honored their dead. After dark, Captain Thomas Gatch ordered the engines slowed and came to a stop so that a proper burial at sea could be conducted for her first two dead. The night was black, and a feeling of gloom pressed down like a weight. The chaplain, Commander James V. Claypool, kept a strong grip on the belt of the nearest pallbearer, lest he stumble and fall overboard as he intoned the words. "Forasmuch as the spirit of the departed has returned to God who gave it, we therefore commit his body to the depths of the sea. . . ." Captain Gatch was belowdecks and for all the celebrants knew he might well be next off the slab. Untold hundreds of men lay dead on other ships or were already within the sea's embrace. As the *South Dakota*'s attending crew performed the committal, raising one end of the burial slab so that the bodies could slide into the sea, Claypool read the benediction. "May the Lord bless thee and keep thee. . . ." As he spoke, the moon shone through a break in the clouds, illuminating the decks of the great ship. Claypool thought it was a signal of immortality awaiting all who believed.

The *South Dakota* had taken aboard the survivors of the *Porter,* the destroyer lost that day to the crashing Avenger's wayward torpedo. The survivors were given clothes, smokes, bedding, and anything else they needed. Several of that ship's engine room crew, badly burned in the fire from the torpedo, died in the battleship's sickbay. The captain of the *Porter* asked Claypool to do the rites as the destroyer's crew gathered aft. "In their borrowed clothes they stood in a horseshoe on the fantail of our ship, listening to the words of hope and love spoken by our Lord Jesus Christ. They wiped away tears with the sleeves of their dungarees, but they left the burial service with shoulders straightened and heads high. Watching them, I thought I heard a bugle sounding the thrilling Navy call, 'Carry on!'" Claypool wrote.

When the ship returned to Nouméa after the October 26 battle, the wounded men sent away to hospital ships begged to be allowed to return, but only if Gatch remained in command. Was he alive? they wanted to know. All too well, the SOPAC medical corps would tell them. He was said to be a difficult patient. Chaplain Claypool kept him on the straight and narrow. Gatch followed a British tradition that required the captain to read the Scripture lesson at Mass. The captain's faith no doubt empowered his chaplain, who thought that organized religion was a natural thing for a Navy to promote. "Men have to have something in their heads," he would write. "If they don't have religion, superstition rushes to fill the vacuum....They don't stand up under fire. In the Navy, we take along religion as we take along ammunition." The *South Dakota* had loaded that particular magazine to capacity while en route to the theater. Crossing the International Date Line, Claypool was pleased to find himself with back-to-back Sundays, thanks to the change in time zones.

THE JAPANESE WASTED no time making the most optimistic claims about the performance of their fliers that day. "I wish we had as many carriers as they claim to have sunk," Nimitz wrote to Catherine the following day. But no tall tales were needed to claim a material victory. "Numerically or tactically, it was a Japanese victory," Tameichi Hara, an IJN destroyer captain, would write, echoing American opinion at least with respect to ship losses. "The enemy [the Americans] had entered the fray with a tactical and psychological advantage, but complacence had cost them a high price. The enemy was able to strike at times and places of his choosing. To his surprise, the head and tail of the Japanese opponent were versatile and flexible— contrary to Midway—and they struck back effectively with what force they had."

Though the losses of aircraft were about equal—ninety-seven Japanese planes were lost against eighty-one U.S.—it was in personnel casualties that America gained its most striking if seldom-appreciated victory. In Japan's first concentrated exposure to state-of-the-art antiaircraft fire, 148 pilots and aircrew died—a third more than at Midway (110). Fully half of Nagumo's dive-bomber flight crews were lost. American squadrons suffered twenty dead on the day, plus four more rescued by the enemy and taken prisoner. The leadership in the IJN's squadron ready rooms took a severe blow; twenty-three squadron and section leaders were lost. By sundown that day, more than half of the pilots who had hit Pearl Harbor on December 7 had been killed in action. The carriers *Zuikaku* and *Junyo*, though not seriously damaged, were forced home to Japan for want of men to fly their planes. With the evisceration of its naval aircrews, the Japanese suffered a critical deficit that they would never make up. Captain Hara's assessment was a profound understatement: "Considering the great superiority of our enemy's industrial capacity, we must win every battle overwhelmingly. This last one, unfortunately, was not an overwhelming victory."

The battle took a heavy toll from the Japanese carrier force, and also from its longtime commander, Chuichi Nagumo. Haggard and old, appearing to friends to have aged twenty years in less than a year of action, Nagumo was relieved in command of the carrier striking force by Jisaburo Ozawa, a destroyerman whose abilities as a task force commander were unknown to his peers.

After the Battle of Santa Cruz, the United States would have not a single operable carrier task force in the South Pacific until the *Enterprise* could be repaired at Nouméa and placed back into service. Task Force 17 was dissolved with the sinking of the *Hornet*. And with the *Enterprise* going to the yard for repairs, the *South Dakota* was sent to join the *Washington* in Task Force 64.

Having exhausted their carrier forces in the seas east of Guadalcanal on October 26, the opposing fleets returned to their bases to regroup. With Halsey's and Yamamoto's carriers sidelined for now, the question to be answered in the parry and thrust of the coming weeks was: Which side's surface combat fleet would step up and control the seas by night? No matter how gallantly men might fight on land, they would not hold on long if their Navy finally failed them. In a few short weeks, the greatest challenge yet to the American position on Guadalcanal would loom in the dark waters of Savo Sound.

24

Secret History

THE LULL IN THE LAST DAYS OF OCTOBER WAS A TIME FOR LICKING wounds. Following the collision of carrier forces off Santa Cruz, the tempo of action slowed to a pace that suited the languid tropical breeze. The flat-tops withdrew to their bases to tend to their many lacerations. Ashore, the infantry had fought to a standstill as Vandegrift's men repulsed Hyakutake's haphazardly executed assaults. Still, the persistence of the Japanese pressure on the airdrome from air, land, and sea exacted a toll from body and mind.

By the end of the month, every one of the nineteen Dauntless pilots from the *Saratoga*'s Scouting Squadron 3—which had relocated to the island after their carrier was torpedoed on the last day of August—was a casualty, removed from the flying rotation because of illness, fatigue, health-threatening weight loss, or "nervous condition." For these same reasons squadron mechanics had lost the handle on record keeping and couldn't perform basic preventive maintenance on planes. They applied themselves only to actual malfunctions, but little could be done for their own break-downs. The island made short work of all who were sent there, man and machine alike. General Geiger, the commander of Guadalcanal's air units, gave way to the strain, too. His chief of staff, Brigadier General Louis Woods, would replace him in a changing of the guard that saw the arrival of several new Marine air squadrons as well.

On October 27, Halsey ordered the *San Francisco* and the *Helena*, escorted by several destroyers, to leave Task Force 64 and set course for

Espiritu Santo, where they would escort three transports carrying reinforcements to Guadalcanal. Kelly Turner, having promised Vandegrift that the Marine commander's requests for support "have received most earnest attention," dispatched the fast transports *Fuller* and *Alchiba* from Nouméa to ferry a load of heavy artillery, ammunition, and stores. The 155-millimeter guns, set to arrive on November 2, would boost the infantry's ability to counter the Japanese artillery that threatened Henderson Field from the surrounding hills. Another convoy carrying reinforcements from the 8th Marine Regiment would bolster Vandegrift's order of battle and enable him to take the offensive ashore.

The detachment of these ships coincided with the dissolution of Admiral Ghormley's staff. Halsey's arrival at Nouméa meant the replacement not just of Ghormley, but also of everyone else in his headquarters. Given the idiosyncrasies of Halsey's style, it was important for him to work with a hand-picked team. It had been said only partly in jest that it took a certain type of sailor to serve well with Halsey: He didn't want anyone who didn't smoke, drink, or run around with women. Even if that were just playful rhetoric, it must have given a smile to Admiral King, whose wandering hands and eyes were well known to his peers. It certainly suited the first man from Ghormley's headquarters, Dan Callaghan, his gregarious chief of staff, to find a seagoing combat command under Halsey. Promoted from captain to rear admiral just days before Operation Watchtower began, Callaghan was a seadog at heart. Halsey sent him back to sea in the *San Francisco,* which Norman Scott had until a few days before made his working home.

Writing the commanders of his surface units on October 30, Halsey observed that "enemy offensives since September 15 have followed the same general pattern"—the carriers operating within a rectangle of sea northeast of Malaita and their reinforcement convoys tracking in through the Slot, descending from the north-northwest. He pointed out that two or three days' warning of an enemy naval force's approach was usually available, thanks to the combined efforts of coastwatchers, submarines, and long-range air search. He emphasized the importance of coordinating search efforts with follow-up air and naval attacks. "Submit comment and proposals by earliest air mail," he wrote.

Halsey had no way to know the full extent of the Japanese quandary. Increasingly, they were operating in a straitjacket zipped tight by the limitations on their supply and oil lifeline. The destroyers of the Tokyo Express made an average of six runs a month to ferry men, arms, and critical consumables to Guadalcanal's northern coast, the typical run consisting of six destroyer-transports and two destroyers as combat escorts. Their capacity was entirely inadequate. The 17th Army required far more than thirty-six destroyer loads a month. General Hyakutake's staff calculated its needs as 5 loads of supplies per night, or 150 every month. If the reinforcements of heavy weapons and supporting equipment were added to this, the necessary portage increased to eight hundred runs per month, plus twenty more from fuel-hungry seaplane tenders. As the historian Jonathan Parshall has calculated, that level of effort would have taken half of the Imperial Navy's monthly allotment of fuel. Measured in terms of tonnage delivered per unit of oil burned, cargo ships were thirty times as efficient as destroyer-transports. But use of the slow ships was fruitless as long as U.S. pilots controlled the skies of the Slot. It was a difficult problem: Without the heavier capacity of those larger vessels, Imperial ground forces would be unlikely to take the airfield.

The only feasible way the Japanese had to deprive their enemy of air superiority was to destroy Henderson Field's air group with bombardment from the sea. And by that same reasoning, the only way the Americans could prevent a repeat of the devastating nighttime ordeal of mid-October was by pressing their surface forces into the fight and seizing control of the night. The wartime "food chain" circled right back to the ancient art of ships grappling with one another on the sea.

Halsey continued to reshuffle his decks as October wound to a close. On the thirtieth, he ordered Norman Scott to take his small task force—the *Atlanta* and four destroyers—and shell Japanese positions near Point Cruz in support of Marine units that were crossing the Matanikau River to secure Henderson Field's western flank. The fleet had to get its guns into the fight one way or another.

IN A NOVEMBER 1 ARTICLE headlined, "Navies Manoeuvre for Big Stakes in Solomons," *New York Times* reporter Charles Hurd wrote, "In the end, one side or the other of the Guadalcanal contestants will be cut off from supplies.... They now look toward the sea for the next great phase in the contest. That sea and air battle may be fought at any hour or it may not occur for weeks. In any event, we probably will not know about it until the issue has been decided."

Certainly they wouldn't if Admiral King had his way. He was no friend of the fourth estate. Hanson Baldwin, covering fleet maneuvers in Panama before the war, was chagrined to find the censors butchering one of his *New*

York Times dispatches because it reported a commander's golf score. Now that a war was on, restrictions were far more severe. It had been said that King's preferred approach to press relations would be to remain silent until it was over, then announce, "We won." "So far as I'm concerned," King told a correspondent for *Collier's* magazine, "information given the public is information which will almost certainly reach the enemy.... I have no intention of giving the enemy anything from which he can derive a shadow of aid and comfort. That's the way I am, that's the way I have always been, and that's the way I always will be." The secrecy was so tight that *The New York Times* made it front-page news in mid-October when the Navy officially acknowledged having bases in the New Hebrides and the Fiji Islands.

A *Chicago Tribune* reporter named Stanley Johnson learned one of the war's most closely guarded secrets: the breaking of the Japanese code and the Navy's ability to follow Japanese fleet movements. In an account of Midway appearing in his paper, he revealed the names of participating enemy ships—information that only Tokyo would have. Certain that this would betray the secret of its code-breaking success, the Navy brought charges against the paper, but didn't seem to have considered the consequences. When the *Tribune* began editorializing about its persecution by the government—a complaint made plausible by the fact that Secretary Knox had been the publisher of its rival daily before the war—the Navy was unable to reply, since the grounds of its suit were sensitive state secrets. The possibility of a courtroom circus vanished when a grand jury refused to indict.

A fog lay low over fleet operations for the first two months of the South Pacific campaign. Chester Nimitz was a master of showing grace and easy hospitality to reporters who visited him without revealing actual newsworthy information. The Navy insisted that everything was progressing well toward a major U.S. offensive that would push the Japanese back north. When news of the Battle of Savo Island finally broke in mid-October, and word followed a few weeks later that the carrier *Wasp* was lost, the Navy's credibility suffered. "So mismanaged was the Navy's handling of news releases, both as to timing and candor, that according to one informed source the American public grew to believe that the Japanese version of the Pearl Harbor story was more accurate than our own, making Tokyo's subsequent claims of success all the more plausible," wrote the historian Lloyd J. Graybar.

Baldwin's October reporting got him invited to a November meeting of the Joint Chiefs of Staff Joint Strategic Survey Committee, a "solemn conclave" held in the U.S. Public Health Service Building, across from the Navy

Building on Constitution Avenue. Baldwin was asked to take a seat at a long table with twenty-five or thirty officers of all services in dress uniforms and testify secretly to what he had seen on Guadalcanal. The hitch was that he could not tell his bosses at the *Times* about it. He agreed and entered the large meeting room as a witness to events at the front.

"I spoke more frankly, of course, than I was able to do in the pieces I'd written," Baldwin said. He described how the *North Carolina* had been torpedoed and how, with but one battleship and one carrier in the theater at the time, "we were just hanging on by our teeth. When I said this about the ship damage and about the cruisers that had been lost at Savo, and I gave them the names of the cruisers in this secret meeting. A Navy captain stood up, violently angry, and said, 'I object to that, I object to that. This is top-secret information! Admiral King has given the strictest orders that no one is to know about this!'

"Well, of course," Baldwin told his antagonist, "I understand it's top-secret information. I haven't published the names of these ships or the exact losses or details and I don't expect to. I was asked to come down here in top secrecy and not even tell my paper about it, and I've done so." As the captain kept pressing his case, Baldwin gathered the impression that many of the officers who were there that day, sitting on a committee charged with advising the president on military matters, had no idea what had actually happened in the waters off Guadalcanal back in August. "That," Baldwin would say, "is a hell of a way to run a war."

Change was already in the air. When Admiral Spruance first laid eyes on a copy of the *Boise*'s after-action report from the Battle of Cape Esperance, air-couriered to Pearl Harbor from Nouméa, he gave it to Nimitz, who gave it to King, and all understood what a publicity bonanza it was. So began the process of legend building that would make some ships famous for things they never did, and leave others unknown despite their great deeds. A statement in the report that "the *Boise* fired on six targets" was conflated in the press to the *Boise* sinking six ships. A Navy publicist referred to the *Boise* as a "one-ship task force." As a result of this hype, few would ever hear of Captain Hoover and the *Helena,* whose barrels flaked as much paint as the *Boise*'s had that night off Guadalcanal. When the *Boise* reached the Philadelphia Navy Yard for repairs in late November, the public saw a living, breathing man-of-war baring her scars—and the accuracy of history was quickly a casualty.

News of the *Boise*'s performance at Cape Esperance was released simultaneously with, and perhaps as an antidote to, the darker tale of the Battle of

Savo Island. As reporters began to challenge the Navy Department's manip-
ulations, King, in spite of himself, took a page from Nimitz's book. He began
hosting meetings with newsmen at the Virginia home of his attorney and
friend, Cornelius Bull. At the first such gathering, on November 6, King circulated among eight reporters, addressing rumors that operations at
Guadalcanal were foundering and rebutting the accusation that the Navy
was stonewalling press inquiries. He defended his silence during the early
phase of the operation on grounds of operational security. "There was every
reason to believe that the Japanese did not know the extent of their success,"
he said. Breaking a personal oath, he drank alcohol with reporters. The four-
hour soirée won them over. "They were for him 100 percent by the time they
said good-bye," one participant said. These "Sunday vesper services," as the
scribes began calling them, would continue at Bull's home until 1944.

Elmer Davis, the head of the Office of War Information, felt it was essential to publicize the pathbreaking effort in the Solomons, but lamented,
"There was no one in Washington who was seeing that the Navy got any
credit for what it did, or telling the story in any way, shape or form." Soon,
however, the pubic appetite for tales from the combat zone would be too
strong to ignore. If the press had to learn to stay out of the Navy's way and
let it win a war, in time the Navy would learn to stay out of its own way and
let its story be told.

25

Turner's Choice

LEAVING THEIR DAYS AS A CARRIER TASK FORCE ESCORT IN THEIR wake, relieved to be out of the submarine-haunted waters of Torpedo Junction, the men of the antiaircraft cruiser *Atlanta* entered Sealark Channel, approached Lunga Point, and laid eyes on a new battlefield ashore. "In the half dawn," Edward Corboy wrote, "we could see our planes landing and taking off with their lights on. Flashing shell bursts lighted the scene at intervals as the Marines and the Japs traded early morning punches."

A Marine major came aboard by motor launch to aid in gunfire spotting. When the *Atlanta* cruised within range of enemy territory, she opened fire, aided by an Airacobra pilot, who circled overhead, diving to point out targets and radioing corrections to the ship. Norman Scott's squadron worked over the coastline from the Matanikau delta up to Tassafaronga Point. By the time they were finished, the gray paint was peeled back from the *Atlanta*'s rifle bores, her fantail littered with five-inch shell cases and spent powder cans, and the known artillery emplacements and supply and ammunition dumps considerably less useful to the Japanese. As the deck force broke out the fire hoses to cool down the barrels, the major boarded a launch to return to shore. Tears welled in his eyes. "He couldn't thank us enough," Corboy said. "The raking we gave that coast made history in the Solomons."

Promised help by Halsey and expecting further reinforcements, General Vandegrift had issued an operation order on October 30 calling for an offensive push west of Henderson Field. Rising out of their defensive crouch and venturing into the west, his men would try to drive the Japanese beyond artillery range of the airfield and encircle any units dug in on the Matanikau River delta. On November 1, two battalions of the 5th Marines, well supported by artillery, crossed the Matanikau and tore into enemy positions. Thoroughly exhausted and beset by malaria, the Japanese melted against the onslaught. Vandegrift lacked the men both to hold his airfield perimeter and sustain a serious offensive, and that spared the remnants of the 2nd (Sendai) Division from a far worse fate.

The fleet, for its part, had multiple roles, each challenging in its own right: to cover and protect the supply lines to Guadalcanal, to throw gunfire in support of Marine positions ashore, and to counter the expected thrust by enemy combat ships, submarines, or aircraft. Halsey gave Turner overall command of naval forces in the Guadalcanal area, and Callaghan and Scott command of the cruiser task forces that were haphazardly assembled from them. Kinkaid was replenishing in Nouméa with the wounded *Enterprise,* while the battleships of Lee's Task Force 64 lurked south of Guadalcanal, out of range of Japanese air attacks.

Still recovering from the carrier battle and pressured by the need to assign combat vessels to escort duty, Halsey did not concentrate his major surface warships in a striking force. He made do with what he had, peeling off the cruisers and destroyers escorting convoys as they came north and sending them out hunting. On November 4, as Vandegrift was pushing west along the coast, Turner ordered the *San Francisco,* the *Helena,* and the destroyer *Sterett* to lash at Japanese positions. In four passes along the shore, the *Helena* put out more than twelve hundred rounds of six-inch fire, and four hundred rounds of five-inch. It was little more than a live-fire exercise, but it sufficed to get Dan Callaghan, in his flagship, the *San Francisco,* acquainted with his tools.

The Japanese seemed unnerved by this aggressive use of U.S. naval might. The Tokyo Express, stretched as it was, did not have the stomach to confront American cruisers without heavier support from the Combined Fleet. According to Turner, captured documents and diaries suggested that the presence of U.S. warships at this time deterred the IJN from bringing in thousands more reinforcements for an attack on Henderson Field.

Its desperate position on Guadalcanal led the 17th Army to beseech the IJN for emergency reinforcements and support from the 11th Air Fleet. At first light on November 5, Admiral Tsukuhara's aviators swarmed aloft. The twenty-seven Bettys and two dozen Zeros were foiled from attacking by heavy cloud cover over the airfield. Naval forces had better luck. That night the light cruiser *Tenryu* led fifteen destroyers to their unloading points off Tassafaronga and Cape Esperance, where they dropped a regiment of troops, which promptly rallied to confront Vandegrift's advance. These men were just the first wave of a far more ambitious effort. U.S. snoopers monitoring radio transmissions from Truk and Rabaul had hints of a scheme that entailed forces much larger than the Tokyo Express runs did. Yamamoto was marshaling resources to deliver an entire division to the embattled island.

The next day a coastwatcher in southern Bougainville reported thirty-three Japanese vessels off Shortland Island. Two days later, on November 8, another coastwatcher warned of a dozen transports steaming southeast through Buka Passage, on the northern tip of Bougainville.

On November 8, Halsey landed on Henderson Field for a tour of ground zero in the ongoing campaign. He knew that an all-out enemy attempt to retake the island was near. As he considered his own next move, it was time for him to confront the consequences of his gamble off Santa Cruz a few weeks earlier. The decision to throw his only two carrier groups at a superior Japanese force had cost him the *Hornet* and made the damaged *Enterprise* too valuable to lose. The inestimable value of that lone remaining carrier would keep Willis Lee's battleships, the *Washington* and the *South Dakota*, the most powerful available surface unit in the entire Pacific Fleet, tethered to the *Enterprise* for protection. Once again, the marines ashore would be left exposed for lack of robust carrier support. And once again, it would be the Navy's light forces that mustered to their defense.

Receiving Halsey for dinner, Vandegrift instructed his mess attendant to serve his superior the best meal possible. "I know we haven't got much, but make it good for the Admiral," he told them. On a disease-ridden mud pit of a battlefield, a can of Spam is four-star cuisine. Vandegrift's cook took some beans and dehydrated potatoes and added chunks of the canned meat to make a salty gray stew. He followed that coarse course with slices of cooked Spam with boiled beans. A peach cobbler made from soggy canned fruit was dessert.

As the plates were cleared, Halsey said, "I'd like to compliment the cook on our dinner." So Vandegrift summoned a big, red-faced sergeant who appeared to have been pulled from the front lines for this special duty. Halsey said to him, "Son, I want to compliment you. That's as fine a dinner as I could have got in the Waldorf-Astoria. That soup was out of this world. I've never had Spam or meat cooked like that. And those beans were just right on the spot. That pie you had, that cobbler, why even my mother couldn't have made that." The sergeant grew redder and redder in the face as Halsey spoke, and finally all he could say was, "Aw, Admiral, horse . . . *stuff.*"

That night a Japanese destroyer approached Guadalcanal's shoreline and gave the South Pacific boss a sterner rebuke. Without any protection from his own fleet, Halsey found himself first embarrassed, then gripped by rank fear as Henderson Field absorbed the barrage. "It wasn't the noise that kept me awake; it was fright," he would write. "I called myself yellow—and worse—and told myself, 'Go to sleep, you damned coward!' but it didn't do any good; I couldn't obey orders."

Three U.S. convoys were en route to Guadalcanal. Having returned to Espiritu Santo, where they hauled aboard new stocks of five-inch ammunition to replenish their depleted magazines, the men of the *Atlanta* found themselves ordered back to sea. At 8:30 a.m. on November 9, with Norman Scott aboard as task force commander, the *Atlanta* led four destroyers, the *Aaron Ward, Fletcher, Lardner,* and *McCalla,* out of Espiritu Santo escorting three cargo ships. Before dawn on the tenth, another group left Espiritu Santo—the *San Francisco,* embarking Rear Admiral Callaghan and commanded by Captain Cassin Young, who had relieved Captain Charles H. McMorris with the heavy cruiser *Pensacola,* the *Helena,* and the destroyers *Cushing, Laffey, Sterett, Shaw, Gwin, Preston,* and *Buchanan.* Admiral Turner himself was under way from Nouméa leading a group labeled Task Force 67. His flagship, the transport *McCawley,* led the transports *President Jackson, President Adams,* and *Crescent City,* escorted by the cruisers *Portland* and *Juneau* and the destroyers *O'Bannon, Barton,* and *Monssen.* After the transports had safely reached anchorage, Turner decided to assemble the cruisers and destroyers into a single striking force.

On the morning of the eleventh, Scott's *Atlanta* task force reached Guadalcanal, and its three transports started unloading troops near Lunga Point. After dark, Scott's warship escort joined Callaghan's. Turner's amphibs landed six thousand men, bringing the U.S. garrison on Guadalcanal to twenty-nine thousand. Halsey ordered the *Pensacola* and two destroyers, the *Preston* and *Gwin,* to return and fortify the *Enterprise* task force. That night the combined cruiser force swept Savo Sound but found nothing. At dawn on the twelfth, another group of transports arrived and anchored off Kukum. As these vessels came under fire from a Japanese shore battery after sunrise, the *Helena, Shaw,* and *Barton* silenced it.

The quiet of early morning was a surreal time, the sea glassy calm, the clear sky warmed by a bright sun. Inbound Japanese planes were still hundreds of miles away. On the *Helena,* blasting unseen targets ashore, "The gunners fired as though at rehearsal—as though Guadalcanal were a target being towed past for their convenience," Chick Morris wrote. "For more than an hour our bombardment mowed down the island's coconut trees and drilled tunnels in the jungle. Seabee bulldozers might have done the job as well, but hardly with such fantastic speed. As the shells burst upon impact, spraying shrapnel for yards around, we watched enemy troops scrambling in panic up the hillsides. We watched them die." The destroyers *Buchanan* and *Cushing* razed the shoreline westward, destroying several dozen small barges lying along the beach and enemy ammunition and supply dumps farther inland.

Valuable though this work was for the infantry, the Navy's greatest challenge lay at sea. And in Norman Scott, the fleet had the right man available to meet it. In the Battle of Cape Esperance, he had stared into the void of night, squinted at the flash of enemy powder, studied the silhouettes of unknown ships, and carried his force through to a victory. Though it wasn't a resounding victory, it had put vital seasoning into a man who was by nature already a fighter. Afterward, Scott had the sole claim to status as a victorious surface-force commander. He had absorbed the lessons of his experience and acted on them with a focused seriousness.

One lesson arrived swiftly: that war is the craft of putting ordnance on target decisively, and it is really nothing else. This lesson was being learned the world over in more than a dozen languages. The rigmarole of military life, after all, was designed in part to shape the character of men to respond effectively in that half second where a vital decision must rise instantly from habit. A ship full of pilothouse philosophers, sailors' lieutenants, and colorful China hands who inspire great fiction will lose a fight in an eye's blink to a quick, tight, fast-firing crew who snaps their weapons on target and delivers direct fire by the express route. The victors in every battle from Pearl Harbor to El Alamein to Stalingrad had learned this important truth, and now Admiral Scott was among them. On the other side of the world, the Wehrmacht was locked in a death grip with the Russians at Stalingrad. In North Africa, British forces were winning a decisive victory over the Afrika Korps at El Alamein. Such a turning point was soon to be at hand in the South Pacific.

Seasoned under fire and wise to how he might have won previous fights still more convincingly, Scott knew what tools worked best. Like Turner, he had had time to think through the lessons of experience against the Tokyo Express. "FOR OPERATIONS AGAINST JAP LIGHT FORCES," Scott wrote Halsey on the eighth, "SUBMIT NECESSITY FOR GUNS LARGER THAN FIVE-INCH. JAP STRENGTH IN TORPEDOES NECESSITATES EARLY EFFECTIVE HITS WHICH CAN ONLY BE MADE BY LARGER GUNS. EFFECTIVENESS OF FIVE-INCH AA FOR SINKING DD IS DOUBTFUL. ATLANTA CARRIES ONLY ABOUT 10 PERCENT COMMON MARK 32. IN ORDER MAKE BEST USE OF OUR DOUBTFUL TORPEDOES DDS WITH TWO OR MORE MOUNTS SHOULD BE ASSIGNED STRIKING GROUPS."

Good men had died for Scott to gain these insights. Given his emphasis on larger guns, he must have lamented the order that detached *Pensacola* from the area. Having won at Cape Esperance largely on the blowtorching output of the *Helena*'s and *Boise*'s six-inch batteries, he preferred heavy-gunned ships to antiaircraft cruisers. But the *Pensacola* had her problems. The first of the new eight-inch-gunned cruisers built to treaty restrictions, she had a tendency to roll even in moderate seas, which compromised the accuracy of her guns. Her seams tended to pop whenever a full salvo was fired. So while the *Juneau* or the *Atlanta* might have seemed better suited to protecting SOPAC's last aircraft carrier, the *Pensacola* got that job and the antiaircraft cruisers were thrown into the line despite Scott's wishes.

The *Atlanta* didn't have the additional space that other flagships had for an admiral and his staff, but Scott didn't mind. "He spent a great deal of time on the bridge just as a unit commander does in a destroyer flagship," Lloyd Mustin, the *Atlanta*'s assistant gunnery officer, said. "The captain's chair was in the traditional starboard corner of the pilot house. There was a similar chair on the port side. Admiral Scott inhabited that through many long hours, day and night. The officers of the deck spent hours with him in the pilothouse. Sitting inside the door to the bridge wing, feet up on a chair, he was accessible, friendly, and conversational. He discussed anything and everything." Typically an admiral kept his own staff apart from the captain's wardroom. But Scott didn't mind mingling with the leadership on his host flagship. "We were the eyes and ears of the captain of the ship. We were also Admiral Scott's eyes and ears when he was not on the bridge," Mustin said.

Then a dispatch came down from Kelly Turner's headquarters. It was a shocker. It said, in effect, that when Callaghan's and Scott's forces merged into a single force, to be designated Task Group 67.4, Scott would take second seat to Callaghan. Halsey was personally close to Scott. But because Callaghan had held the rank of rear admiral for fifteen days longer than Scott, tradition forced an absurd result: Callaghan, the chief of staff to a theater commander who had been removed for his lack of battle-mindedness, was relieving Scott, the only proven brawler in the American surface fleet admiralty, as officer in tactical command of the striking force.

When Callaghan served in the heavy cruiser *New Orleans*, he befriended a medical officer named Ross McIntire. When McIntire became President Franklin Roosevelt's personal physician, he recommended Callaghan as the president's naval aide. Receiving the assignment to shore duty at a point when his advancement depended on gaining command of a major warship distressed Callaghan deeply, but he tried to make the best of it. In the spring of 1941, he pleaded for sea duty, and the president released him to command the *San Francisco*. A year later, he was ordered to serve as Ghormley's chief of staff. In October, the cycle seemed to repeat itself when Callaghan was cast loose after Halsey's arrival, and the best billet available to him—the nearest hull in the storm—was, once again, his old ship.

The news of his return to sea was met with joy in the *San Francisco*, where he had earned the nickname "Uncle Dan" for his collegial way. The men of Task Force 67's other heavy cruiser, the *Portland*, were pleased, too, for Callaghan had once been their exec, a role in which he had achieved the nearly impossible: becoming popular in the always-difficult position of the captain's stern right hand. Oakland-born and San Francisco–educated, Callaghan had turned prematurely gray, it was said, after a court-martial in 1915 (fully acquitted) for allegedly mismanaging some engine room equipment while serving as the engineering officer in the destroyer *Truxtun*.

The news of his elevation now hit the *Atlanta* hard. The crew, overjoyed when Scott came aboard with his flag, was deflated by his relief. The prestige of serving as flagship to a victorious admiral had been considerable. Now, though he would remain aboard, Scott would have nothing of substance to do but advise and consult (if ever asked) and follow Callaghan's orders. It would strike more than a few fighting sailors as a shame that the Navy was taking Scott's expensively earned curriculum of experience effectively out of circulation.

What didn't change as a result of Scott's replacement was the *Atlanta*'s assignment to roam with the street fighters. Ironically enough, Scott himself probably wouldn't have kept her in the task force had he been in charge of its composition. In this stout company, an antiaircraft cruiser was as out of place as a fox in a pack of wolves.

AS THE AMERICANS were gathering, U.S. radio intelligence learned of large enemy naval forces gathering in the north. Back at Nouméa after his visit to Henderson Field, Halsey studied the briefings of CINCPAC radio cryptanalysts. Nearly foiled because of changes the enemy had made in their code groups and call signs, they still made a fair appraisal of the naval forces Yamamoto had ordered into action at virtually the same time Halsey was dining with Vandegrift on November 8. In the coming days, the enemy's order of battle would be appraised in the aggregate as having two carriers, four battleships, five heavy cruisers, and about thirty destroyers. This assessment was mostly accurate, though it overestimated the carrier power available to the Japanese and did not reveal the complicated deployment plan that Admiral Yamamoto had settled on.

Issued to his fleet on November 8, the Japanese operation order was designed to bring the eleven troop transports under Admiral Tanaka to unloading points off Tassafaronga and Cape Esperance. Carrying seven thousand troops, twenty days of supplies for thirty thousand men, and loads of artillery ordnance, they were escorted by a dozen destroyers. Much farther to the east, standing sentinel for the transports, was a powerful element of the Combined Fleet known as the Advance Force, under Admiral Kondo. It contained the battleships *Hiei*, *Kirishima*, *Kongo*, and *Haruna*, three heavy cruisers, three light cruisers, and twenty-one destroyers. Separately, Admiral Mikawa commanded a striking force with four heavy cruisers, the *Chokai*, *Kinugasa*, *Kumano*, and *Maya*. Owing to battle damage and severe attrition to air groups, only one aircraft carrier, the *Junyo*, was available to lend air cover to this major operation. The report also indicated a massing of air strength at Buin, which would launch concentrated attacks three days before the landings. Though their troops were starving and their pilot ranks thinning, the Japanese had by no means given up on Guadalcanal. The heavy striking power of the Japanese battleship force was still to meet its match.

In the second week of November, the Guadalcanal campaign entered a kinetic new phase. In a letter to Callaghan concerning the future operations of Task Force 67, Turner had forecast the nature of the coming Japanese assault like a meteorologist: air attacks beginning on the tenth and continuing daily with increasing strength; the departure of a troop convoy from Buin with escorts; a separate sortie by battleships and cruisers to bombard Henderson Field; a strike by enemy carrier planes; and then the crowning blow, an amphibious landing near Cape Esperance or Koli Point, supported by another naval bombardment. The Japanese were a day or so behind the initial reports of this cycle, but they were coming, like a violent storm front that would not be turned aside.

How to array his available forces against the oncoming heavy surface group, arguably the most dangerous threat, was the most pressing decision Turner faced. Since no enemy transports had yet been sighted with it, he saw two possible purposes as to the Japanese mission: to attack his transports during the night, or to bombard Henderson Field and Vandegrift's infantry positions. Turner's options, then, were to keep his combatant ships close to the anchorage in order to guard his transports, or send them out to do battle in the open sea and keep the IJN's guns away from Henderson Field.

Seeing that control of the nighttime sea was vital, Turner made the latter choice. Rather than see to his own immediate safety, he detached Task Force 67's entire supporting cruiser force, stripping the transport anchorage of the major ships of its screen, and gave it all to Callaghan. This was a significant gamble, for Turner could well have kept the warships close to the landing area, protecting his anchorage. Clearly he had had time to consider the errors of the campaign's early days, when divided cruiser forces, deployed piecemeal in Savo Sound, had been dispatched with ease by a concentrated enemy flotilla. Improvision was always the order of the day. But the convergence of three separate convoys into the area all at once now offered an opportunity to concentrate. Turner wrote Callaghan, "It looks this time like the enemy is finally about to make an all-out effort against Cactus. . . . If you can really strike the enemy hard, it will be more important for you to do that than to protect my transports. Good luck to you, Dan. God bless all of you and give you strength."

Halsey was painfully aware that his only carrier, the *Enterprise,* would be without the use of her forward elevator until near the end of the month. Nonetheless, he knew that whatever airpower she could throw into the coming fight would be indispensable. Accordingly, on the morning of November 11, Halsey ordered the *Enterprise* task force to get north from Nouméa with instructions to take positions two hundred miles south of San Cristóbal and strike Japanese shipping near Guadalcanal. Given the poor state of repair of her forward elevator, it was risky to commit the *Enterprise* into battle again, and this may be why Halsey's decision to send her north was too late to allow the carrier to be in position to strike enemy forces then en route south. He had briefly considered detaching her air group to Espiritu Santo. But could not afford to throw the dice as aggressively as he had at Santa Cruz, and he knew it. He held Admiral Lee's battleship group in the south with the *Enterprise* for the time being, too. They were a powerful reserve.

Turner's election to commit his entire combatant force for an open-sea encounter was the only practical possibility under the circumstances. As Hanson Baldwin informed the readers of *The New York Times* as the lead-up to the Santa Cruz carrier battle, "We must establish local naval superiority around Guadalcanal. . . . This can be done only by the continuous use of sur-

U.S. Navy Combat Task Forces in the South Pacific
(as of November 12, 1942)

TASK GROUP 67.4
(Cruiser Support Group)
Rear Adm. Daniel J. Callaghan

San Francisco (CA)	Sterett (DD)
Portland (CA)	O'Bannon (DD)
Helena (CL)	Aaron Ward (DD)
Atlanta (CLAA)	Barton (DD)
Juneau (CLAA)	Monssen (DD)
Cushing (DD)	Fletcher (DD)
Laffey (DD)	

TASK FORCE 16	**TASK FORCE 64**
(Carrier Task Force)	**(Battleship Support Group)**
Vice Adm. Thomas E. Kinkaid	Rear Adm. Willis A. Lee
Enterprise (CV) (damaged)	Washington (BB)
Northampton (CA)	South Dakota (BB) (damaged)
Pensacola (CA)	Preston (DD)
San Diego (CLAA)	Gwin (DD)
Morris (DD)	Benham (DD)
Hughes (DD)	Walke (DD)
Russell (DD)	
Clark (DD)	
Anderson (DD)	

face craft; air power is also absolutely essential to this end, but, as we have seen, alone it is not enough, alone it cannot prevent the Japanese from constant nightly infiltration by sea into Guadalcanal." There was no other way to deflect an enemy surface force at night than to go all-in with the surface forces, whose "smashing offensive spirit," Baldwin wrote, was key to everything. If they prevailed, and if the destruction of the airfield was thereby prevented, the Cactus Air Force would be free to strike the stragglers at will during that morning sanctuary when even the earliest-rising Japanese planes would still be hours away.

Now it would be Kelly Turner's turn to be a riverboat gambler. On Dan Callaghan's untested shoulders he would gamble his entire command.

26

Suicide

ON THE *SAN FRANCISCO*, IT WAS LIKE OLD TIMES AGAIN. DAN Callaghan, the ship's former skipper, was aboard wearing the two stars of a rear admiral. Just as in old times, a *San Francisco* sailor named Eugene Tarrant found that he occupied the ideal place from which to observe Callaghan at work and in repose: right in his shadow.

No men on a ship were wiser to the way things worked than the sailors who stood invisibly in the wardroom's midst. The white-jacketed mess attendants and cooks—a lowly caste within S Division, which saw to the supply and sustenance of the crew—mostly were black enlistees. Like all enlisted men, they cultivated what scraps of control and power were left to them. The ladder of ranks and ratings had its peculiarities, with voids on middle rungs and true power residing at the bottom and the top.

Battleships and carriers had separate dining facilities for junior and senior officers. On cruisers, all the officers dined together except for the captain, who had his own cabin. When he was in command of the *San Francisco*, Callaghan made a practice of eating with his men. He used the wardroom to break down barriers and accelerate the growth of his young officers. The mess attendants and cooks had as good a view of the goings-on as anyone.

On duty in the officers' galley, Tarrant found that he could raise the pantry door, which was designed like a dumbwaiter, and hear Callaghan talking with his staff in the next compartment. With access to high-level scuttlebutt, he sometimes found himself as well informed as the intelligence analysts at headquarters. "I heard about all the plans," Tarrant said. "They'd talk about what forces they were going up against, when they expected contact with the enemy, how they planned to deploy the fleet."

In the after-midnight morning of November 12, Admiral Turner informed Callaghan that patrol planes had reported two battleships or heavy cruisers, one cruiser, and six destroyers southbound at twenty-five knots, and within a day's run of Savo Sound. Tarrant was on duty when Callaghan received Turner's order to gather the disparate cruisers and destroyers from three task forces and take them into action against this threat.

At the news that a fight with battleships was brewing, Callaghan began pacing his flag bridge. He was heard mumbling that it was a fool's errand to take on ships three times the *San Francisco*'s size, and that it was a shame there was no time to confer again with Admiral Halsey. When the moment presented itself, Eugene Tarrant exercised the cook's prerogative and asked Callaghan if he really thought the mission was hopeless. As Tarrant recalled, the task force commander was candid. "He said to me, 'Yes it may be that. But we are going in.'"

The officer-of-the-deck for the first dog watch, Lieutenant Jack Bennett, listened to the admiral conversing with Captain Cassin Young as they stood on the starboard bridge wing. "The wind carried their voices to me as I paced the deck and I was able to clearly observe the demeanor of each," Bennett said. "They were discussing the unannounced fact that there were battleships in the Tokyo Express.... Captain Young... was in an understandably agitated state, sometimes waving his arms, as he remarked 'This is suicide.' Admiral Dan Callaghan replied, 'Yes I know, but we have to do it.'" As Bennett saw it, Callaghan was "calm, unemotional, resolute and perhaps resigned to his fate."

Rumors had a way of sweeping a ship like wildfire. Word spread through the *San Francisco* that Callaghan deemed his orders a death sentence. "We were all prepared to die. There was just no doubt about it," said Joseph Whitt, a seaman first class whose battle station was in turret one. "We could not survive against those battleships."

Callaghan was fifteen years old when, three days after Easter in 1906, the great earthquake struck San Francisco. In the chaos and wreckage, he had done what a teenager could to help the injured. His prep school, St. Ignatius, was destroyed. As the fires consumed the school and its church, one student thought that "all hell seemed dancing with joy." For the rest of the term Callaghan was left to study Virgil and Dante in a makeshift classroom amid the city's ruins while the Jesuits rebuilt their school. For the men of the *San*

Francisco and the rest of Task Force 67, it would begin that afternoon. Inbound now at twenty thousand feet, moving swifly toward the island, came a wave of twin-engine Betty bombers and thirty Zeros, fuel burning fast on half-empty tanks.

BELIEVING THAT U.S. CARRIER STRENGTH had been eliminated entirely in the Battle of Santa Cruz, Yamamoto planned to neutralize the last bastion of U.S. airpower in the theater, stubborn Henderson Field, with a one–two punch of air attack and naval bombardment. The Bettys were first spied by a coastwatcher near Tonolei, on Buin, around 1 p.m. The air-search radar on Guadalcanal registered the bogeys when they were still more than a hundred miles out. That was enough time for Kelly Turner to get his transports under way in Savo Sound, where they could maneuver and make themselves much harder targets, and for Callaghan to herd his cruiser task force into a protective antiaircraft ring around them.

Hiding above the cloud bottoms, the torpedo-armed bombers revealed themselves at the last minute, dropping down and buzzing Florida Island, throttles firewalled, descending steadily until they were right down on the water. U.S. fighter pilots were close in pursuit. Captain Joe Foss, leading a flight of eight Marine Wildcats and eight Army Airacobras, pushed over on them from twenty-nine thousand feet. The speed of his dive ripped loose the cockpit hood of Foss's Wildcat. The Bettys divided into two groups and came in from the starboard beam of Turner's northerly oriented formation. Unmindful of the heavy five-inch airbursts and twenty-millimeter tracer fire thrown up by the ships, which turned to present their sterns to the attackers, Foss and his boys chased the Japanese bombers right down to the deck, fifty feet above the water.

The Bettys fanned out wide, approaching in line abreast to avoid suffering multiple casualties from flak bursts. Lieutenant Commander Bruce McCandless in the *San Francisco* thought the twenty-one planes looked like "an old-time cavalry deployment." The skies were filthy with the bursts of antiaircraft fire. When the planes were within five thousand yards, the *San Francisco* and the *Helena* turned out their main batteries and walloped the sea in front of the planes, intending for the tall splashes to force the pilots to veer away or stop them with a wall of water. This technique seldom if ever worked. Mainly, all the big guns accomplished was to interfere with the aim of the other antiaircraft gunners with the blast and smoke.

The *Atlanta* steamed on the far side of the formation, away from the planes. Lloyd Mustin's practiced gunner's eye told him there was a high risk of hitting friendly ships if his ship fired too soon. The gun elevation needed to target the low-flying planes was virtually flat. "With this beautifully clear view of these planes coming in, in a position where the entire *Atlanta* broadside could have engaged them, we really were unable to open fire," he said. According to Mustin, neither the Navy nor the local commanders had issued a doctrine for distributing antiaircraft fire against a large aircraft formation. When the bomber line flew across their stern, Mustin's gunners opened fire.

Confronted with the savage defenses, many of the Japanese pilots flinched. Failure to hold formation was the kiss of death. As they reached the crucial moment of decision—push ahead and drop the torpedo, or lose nerve and turn away—most chose the latter. Turning, they lost airspeed and showed their bellies to the hungry Navy gunners, and that was it. The twenties and forties lit them like fuses. The five-inch guns "seemed to literally hammer them down," Captain Hoover of the *Helena* remarked.

On the *San Francisco*, Lieutenant (j.g.) John G. Wallace was looking out to starboard from the after main battery control station when he observed a Betty release a torpedo toward the ship from just forward of the beam. The twenties mounted around the mainmast barked out. A gray tendril of smoke trailed from the bomber's starboard engine, dissipating in its airstream. On it came, closer and closer, and as it did so it became clear that the pilot, if he was alive, had terminal intentions. Though the torpedo somehow missed, the plane itself did not. To those watching helplessly from other stations, the ship's antiaircraft gunners, in their final moments, were an inspiration: eyes focused through iron sights on the plane as it sped at them, weapons hot, going cyclic, hunched down and never flinching until the Betty struck high on the mainmast, killing them all. The plane jackknifed around its own blunt nose as it hit, each heavy engine tearing away from its wing and hurtling past the director platform to either side. A wash of gasoline enveloped the area and ignited at once.

"I just had time to duck inside the outer door," Wallace wrote, "when a tremendous explosion knocked me all the way up to the forward side of secondary conn." When he regained consciousness, the back of his trousers and shirt were on fire, and his hair and face burned. "I looked around and found myself all alone. I jumped into a nearby motor launch and rolled out my flames on the tarpaulin covering."

Joined by another element of Marine Wildcats under Major Paul Fontana, Joe Foss and his boys were viciously in pursuit. They were daredevils, constrained by long training to operate their war machines as a cohesive band. That mix of spirit and discipline paid handsome returns now. "We heard them yelling and cussing as only fighter pilots know how to cuss," Chick Morris in the *Helena* recalled. "*Watch it. He's coming in on your port quarter!*" "*He's on the run. He's baggin' ass. Get on top of the bastard and finish him!*" One pilot did just that. Lieutenant Pat McEntee in the *Atlanta* witnessed it: a Wildcat closing fast on a Betty from behind. The fighter was evidently out of ammunition, for its driver resorted to an unusual tactic. Down came his landing gear. Down went his airspeed. It looked to McEntee as if he was trying "to set his ship down on the bomber's broad back. And he did—again and again, and again, with sledgehammer impact. He literally was pounding the enemy into the sea with his wheels." The bomber pilot had no escape. If he tried to pull up, it only increased the force of the impacts. Any evasive turn was easily matched by the agile fighter. "The only course open led down. But before the Jap could make a decision, something snapped under the pounding and the bomber plunged beneath the waves of Savo Sound."

The bomber formation was largely shredded in its five minutes over the task force. Its survivors winged out to the west. Just two of them would return to Rabaul. None of their torpedoes found the mark. The *Atlanta* found a solution on the departing planes and two more fell. Most of the damage Task Force 67 took from direct fire came from their own muzzles. The destroyer *Buchanan*, steaming ahead of the *Atlanta* and *San Francisco*, was hit in the after part of her stack by a five-inch shell. Excited gunners on the *Helena* briefly squirted their own superstructure with a twenty-millimeter cannonade, busting up a smoke generator and showering a gun crew with its noxious mix.

The seas around Task Force 67 were a junkyard of broken wings and parts of fuselages and motionless forms of enemy airmen held afloat by their torched life jackets. There was at least one surface engagement that afternoon—a ridiculous duel between a top-turret gunner in a downed Betty and the gunners on an approaching destroyer. It was over in a hurry for the defiant airman.

The *Barton* passed a downed Betty just as its pilot was climbing out on the wing. The destroyer's skipper instructed his crew not to shoot, wanting to recover the aviator for interrogation. A chief petty officer ended the discussion by fixing a Thompson submachine gun at his hip and squeezing out a few bursts. "There was no comment from the bridge," a witness said.

Not far from the *Helena*, two Japanese hung onto the wing of their plane. The younger of the two, evidently a teenager, was willing to be rescued. As an

American boat approached, "almost pathetically he held out his hands," Chick Morris said. But the boy's companion, much older, "seized him angrily by the neck and yanked him back, slapping his hands down. When the boy struggled to free himself, the big fellow produced a pistol and shot him. Then, swimming away from the rescue boat, he turned defiantly and shot himself. We saw it very clearly."

Turner's transports escaped damage, but the *San Francisco*'s fire aft was serious. Flames were coming out both doors leading into Main Battery Control, incinerating its critical instruments. Hearing cries for help, Jack Wallace went in and nearly stepped on a man lying on the deck, moaning. It was one of his fire controlmen. "I got him over my shoulders with his clothes still smoldering and I half fell, half climbed down the port ladder and left him on the top of the hangar deck. Then I ran back up the ladder into main battery control and saw a man standing there with his clothes on fire and he couldn't seem to walk. I led him into secondary conn, and stripped him of all his burning clothing. I asked him if he could walk and then pointed him out the door on the port side to the ladder. I made one more trip into Main Battery Control and picked up a young small kid about seventeen years old named Posh. He was burned horribly. His face was blackened. I carried him down to the deck below and got back to secondary conn just in time to get trapped when more fire came pouring out of both doors leading to Main Battery Control. So, I jumped out of the window in the forward part of secondary conn onto the top of the hangar deck. It was a long drop."

On the hangar deck, Wallace was assisting some firefighters when he heard a feeble cry coming from a motor launch on the port side. He lifted himself to look over the gunwale and into the boat, where he saw the fire controlman he had rescued from Main Battery Control lying prone wearing nothing but shorts. "How he got into the boat I'll never know. Large pieces of skin on his back were peeled half off. I yelled for him to climb out, which he did, into my arms, and I half carried, half dragged him to a stretcher out on the forward part of the hangar deck. I gave him a shot of morphine." He then found several men lying in a passageway near the ammunition clipping room. One of them was Posh, "blackened and burned from head to feet."

"He must have crawled in from the port side when I left him at the foot of the ladder. I asked 'How are you doing Posh?' He said, 'I'm dying, but I sure don't want to. I breathed in the flames.'

"I lied to him: 'You're too young and too healthy. Here, let me give you a shot in the arm so you'll go to sleep.' At first he wouldn't let me but with the

help of a couple of men we peeled some shirt off his arm. Jabbing the morphine needle in his arm was like jabbing a board. There was no skin—just
muscle—and none of the morphine went in. It just oozed back out. I tried
three times with the same result. A stretcher finally arrived and we got Posh
on with quite a bit of trouble. He was in agony. They carried him off to the
mess hall where a temporary sick bay had been set up." Among the casualties
was the ship's executive officer, Commander Mark H. Crouter, who had both
of his legs seriously burned up to the knees. The young kid, Posh, didn't
make it.

In the carnage that took place on Callaghan's flagship, twenty-two men
died, and twenty-two more were wounded. The casualties were taken to the
transport *President Jackson*. Commander Crouter remained aboard. He
insisted it was his duty to stay and coach the newly elevated exec, Commander Joseph C. Hubbard, and to make himself useful to another recent
newcomer to the ship, Captain Young. Though Young had received a Medal
of Honor for his heroism while commanding the repair ship *Vestal* at Pearl
Harbor on December 7, the *San Francisco* was his first major combat ship.
He needed the experienced guidance of his executive officer. Crouter was
escorted to his cabin to recuperate while Hubbard replaced him as exec and
Lieutenant Commander Herbert E. Schonland, the assistant first lieutenant,
replaced Hubbard as the damage-control officer.

As terrible as the afternoon was for the *San Francisco,* it was a fine one for
the task force as a whole. The air attack had cost Turner's transports just a
few hours of unloading time. As soon as the surviving planes disappeared,
the transports returned to the anchorage and resumed debarking troops of
the U.S. Army's 182nd Infantry Regiment till sunset.

A submarine contact, pursued vigorously but inconclusively by Callaghan's
destroyers, caused a ruckus before dark. At six fifteen, Turner ordered his
transports to depart for Espiritu Santo with five destroyers. Callaghan and
Scott steamed in the opposite direction, passing through Sealark Channel
and assembling for a sweep of Savo Sound. A SOPAC staff historian of the
campaign would impose a master plan on these movements, suggesting that
Callaghan was moving to fight "a delaying action so that Admiral Kinkaid's
battleship-carrier force could intercept the anticipated landing forces
believed to be enroute." But there is no evidence of such a design. In that
moment Kelly Turner knew nothing of the movements of Task Force 16. For
all he was concerned, the entire might of the South Pacific force sailed with
Callaghan, and it would be they who determined his fate.

* * *

TASK GROUP 67.4 went to general quarters at 8 p.m. The sea rolled easily under a ten-knot southeasterly wind. The moon had set, leaving the squadron in the dark. The destroyer *Cushing* led the way, leading the van with the *Laffey, Sterett,* and *O'Bannon.* They were followed by the *Atlanta* (the flagship of the idle Norman Scott), the *San Francisco* (Callaghan's flagship), the *Portland,* the *Helena,* the *Juneau,* and the rear quartet of destroyers. Hot soup and coffee were served to the crews at their stations as the six-mile-long column entered Sealark Channel.

As the column passed through the channel, sailors on the *Atlanta* noticed an unsettling omen, the appearance of the electrical phenomenon known as St. Elmo's fire. The mysterious incandescence, manifesting itself in their rigging, was widely thought to be a sign of trouble, its reputation well established in literature a century before. In *Moby-Dick,* when the *Pequod* was touched by these coronal discharges, Ishmael called it "God's burning finger laid on the ship." As he described it, "All the yard-arms were tipped with a pallid fire; and touched at each tri-pointed lightning-rod-end with three tapering white flames, each of the three tall masts was silently burning in that sulphurous air, like three gigantic wax tapers before an altar." Coleridge called it "death-fire."

Naval tradition is ever rife with superstition, but sometimes the ill signs are so powerful that they operate in the other direction. In Callaghan's force, the number thirteen was so prevalent—thirteen ships from Task Force 67 were headed to tangle with the Japanese on Friday the thirteenth—that the tide of superstition shifted. When the commander of the *Portland,* Captain Laurance T. DuBose, read the instructions Turner had given Callaghan, he showed them to his exec, Commander Turk Wirth, who made virtually the same remark Callaghan had on receiving them: "This is suicide, you know." Talk of battleships inspired that kind of thinking. DuBose called Wirth's attention to the date, November 12, and added, "If we can get across midnight into tomorrow, we may make it." Wirth got what his captain was driving at. DuBose had been president of the Naval Academy class of 1913 and considered thirteen a lucky number.

The last ship in Callaghan's column had additional cause for concern as Friday the thirteenth approached: the USS *Fletcher* was the thirteenth ship in line, named in honor of Frank Friday Fletcher, and had the hull number 445, whose sum was 13. But the destroyer's Georgia boys weren't spooked. The signs were so luridly ominous as to become a source of general amusement.

The *Fletcher*'s exec, Commander Wylie, referred to the giddy hilarity that accompanied their anticipation as "triskaidekaphilia." Let the night come, whatever it may bring. They were U.S. Navy sailors and the 91st Psalm was their shield: "You will not fear the terror of night.... A thousand may fall at your side, ten thousand at your right hand, but it will not come near you." More worrisome than numerical coincidence was the sense Wylie was getting that Callaghan didn't seem to know fully what he was doing. At least he didn't seem to appreciate what the newest tools of his trade could do. The *Fletcher,* the *O'Bannon,* the *Helena,* the *Juneau,* and the *Portland* all had the new high-frequency SG search radar. Callaghan's flagship, the *San Francisco,* had not yet been modified. Wylie tried to point out the need for the flag commander to have access to an SG, but never got a response.

"If Callaghan had had any understanding of things, he would have given fairly serious thought to moving over to the *Helena,*" Lloyd Mustin said. "There had been opportunities for Gil Hoover to make known to Callaghan that he had this capability and give him some outline of what it amounted to.... But if any such exchange had occurred it was not known to us in the *Atlanta....* If he really had stopped to recognize what he had there in his SG radar capability, he would indeed have given important thought to transferring his flag." Just as Callaghan had ascended to command—by tradition— he selected his flagship the same way: Tradition held that the heaviest ship in a force serve as its flagship. Norman Scott had made the same decision in October, riding in the *San Francisco* in the Battle of Cape Esperance. Having served as Scott's flagship recently, she was fitted with a complete flag suite. These factors encouraged her selection now, even though another heavy cruiser in the group, the *Portland,* had the SG radar, too.

As Lieutenant (j.g.) Bennett left the *San Francisco*'s bridge at the end of his watch, he recalled that exactly a year ago, on November 12, 1941, Bruce McCandless had led a clinic for officers in the gunnery department. The handout he prepared analyzed matchups between the *San Francisco* and various enemy ship types. A *Kongo*-class battleship was included "only to show disparity of their fighting strength," Bennett said. "It was considered an unlikely encounter" and scarcely worth game-boarding, for the weight of a full salvo from such an opponent was five times that of an American heavy cruiser.

Callaghan and Captain Young were hunched over the chart desk with the navigator, Rae Arison, when Bennett joined them. The appearance of the junior officer led them to change the subject, but that was easy enough. Callaghan recognized Bennett from the ship's basketball team. Callaghan, a fan, had attended the team's every game at Honolulu's Aiea High School gym. The skipper was their only spectator, and his boosterism helped them battle to a first-place tie with the team from the battleship *West Virginia,* whose officers, Bennett contended, arranged with friends in the Bureau of Navigation to have the best athletes assigned to their ship. As the two recalled old times, Young noticed blood leaching through the sling on Bennett's elbow, a minor wound inflicted by a wingtip of the Betty that hit them. "You're in no condition to stand a watch," Young said. "Go on below and get it looked at." Bennett protested briefly that he'd just stood a watch, but orders were orders. According to Bennett, "I went below but I didn't stay below. Having heard about the battleships, there was no way was I going to be in my bunk when this went down. I took a lap around the wardroom, then reported to Willie Wilbourne." The gunnery officer told Bennett to take over a 1.1-inch mount on the fantail.

When the moon set, the starscape swelled. "I was praying to God to watch over us," said Robert Howe in the *Helena.* "It is hard to explain how you feel looking out over the water into the dark of night knowing soon you would hear the report from the radar room, '*Contact, ships....*' It was hard to keep from shaking."

27

Black Friday

THE JAPANESE FAILURE TO DESTROY THE U.S. BEACHHEAD HAD BEEN
worrying the emperor. Though he had recently praised his Navy's efforts in
an Imperial Rescript, a newer telegram told of Hirohito's anxiety concerning
this place, Guadalcanal. "A place of bitter struggles," he called it. According
to Matome Ugaki, "He expressed his wish that it be recaptured swiftly."

Swiftness was certainly Raizo Tanaka's style. The destroyer commander
didn't enjoy being a hostage to the squat, slow troop carriers. A destroyerman, he had pioneered the use of swift escorts as transports. Because they
had the speed to approach, unload, and depart under cover of night, their
use kept American pilots from blocking the reinforcement effort all by
themselves. But the architect of the Tokyo Express no longer enjoyed the
freedom to do things his way. The payloads carried by the small ships
weren't large enough to satisfy the ravenous needs of the Army. That was
why now, churning south in the destroyer *Hayashio*, Tanaka sailed with the
sows. His slow-footed transports were assured of facing air attack come
morning if the infernal U.S. airfield was allowed to remain in business. The
only way they would make it through was if the Combined Fleet's heavy
units could deliver more of what the *Haruna* and *Kongo* had given the American aviators less than a month ago.

Accordingly, Rear Admiral Hiroaki Abe, in command of the battleships
Hiei and *Kirishima,* had been detached from Kondo's Advance Force with
orders to deluge Henderson Field with incendiaries again on the night of

November 13. The idea of repeating Rear Admiral Takeo Kurita's performance of October 13 made Abe nervous. He didn't believe the Americans
would allow the same plan to succeed twice. Like Tanaka, he was a destroyer
specialist, but Abe was not dashing and audacious. Some thought it was
telling that Abe's task force was named the Volunteer Attack Force, a usage
that seemed to suggest a change of psychology in the Combined Fleet. Prior
to this, victory was generally assumed. Now, as momentum shifted in the
southern islands, sailors were being asked to step forward and offer themselves to the flames. There had to be a way to neutralize the airfield. Soldiers
on foot had failed to breach its perimeter. Pilots by wing had failed to beat its
fliers in the sky. Ships, too, had failed thus far, but ships would try again. The
Combined Fleet's strategists had never envisioned the decisive battle looking
like this.

   By midmorning on November 12, three hundred miles north of Guadalcanal, Abe arrayed his force into battle formation. The light cruiser *Nagara*
led the two battleships, with destroyers arrayed like shields off each bow. By
4 p.m., cruising at eighteen knots, they were within two hundred miles of the
island. Abe's flagship, the *Hiei,* catapulted a floatplane to explore the sound
ahead. As dusk fell, Abe's force pressed ahead into a heavy bank of storm
clouds. Then the rain began. Hara, commander of destroyer *Amatsukaze,*
would write, "In all the years of my career, I never experienced such a rain. It
was completely enervating." One of Captain Hara's ensigns said he would
rather fight the Americans than the rain. For a time, the storm drifted south
with the task force, concealing it from snooping eyes. Abe dismissed the concerns voiced by his staff that poor visibility would make stationkeeping difficult and risk the integrity of his formation. Abe had confidence in Rear
Admiral Susumu Kimura, flying his flag in Destroyer Squadron 10's lead
ship, *Nagara.* He was reputed to be one of the Imperial Navy's top navigators. Abe's vindication came when the floatplane pilot reported more than a
dozen enemy warships off Lunga Point—Callaghan's force. If the rains
cooperated, the Japanese force might avoid detection altogether. "This
blessed squall is moving at the same speed and on the same course we are,"
Abe said. "If heaven continues to side with us like this, we may not even have
to do business with them."

   There were practical problems posed by the rain, however. Since Japanese
gunnery was optically controlled, Abe would have to be clear of the storm
before he opened fire on the airfield. His cloak would soon be a blindfold.
The rain on the pilothouse windscreen was almost loud enough to drown
out thought as Abe puzzled over what to do. Near midnight, he ordered his

ships to stand by to reverse course to get clear of the storm. Normally the order to execute such an order followed within thirty seconds or so, after each ship had acknowledged it was standing by. But two destroyers that should have been on his starboard bow, the *Yudachi* and *Harusame,* did not reply. Had they veered from their stations to avoid running aground somewhere? Abe repeated the standby order on a medium frequency. At this Captain Hara shouted, "Has *Hiei* lost its mind?" He knew the medium-frequency radio band was vulnerable to enemy snooping.

Slowing to twelve knots as a precaution, Abe turned north and held that course for some thirty minutes, until the storm's cover lifted. As he reversed course again and resumed the approach to Guadalcanal, free of the storm, he knew that he had paid for that freedom in two equally valuable and irreplaceable currencies: time and fuel. And after seven hours of blind steaming and a pair of 180-degree turns, Abe's once-tight formation was in ragged threads. The battleships still occupied the center of the southbound formation behind the *Nagara,* but the destroyers to either flank had become scattered.

On the *Amatsukaze,* the middle ship in a column of three destroyers riding on the *Hiei*'s port beam, a lookout shouted, "Small island, 60 degrees to port!" Another called, "High mountains dead ahead!" The two islands, Savo and Guadalcanal respectively, were like sentinels standing astride Savo Sound. The Japanese Army observer on Guadalcanal reported that the rain had cleared and no enemy ships were visible off Lunga Point. Twelve miles out, Abe ordered the *Hiei* and the *Kirishima* to fill their main-battery hoists with Type 3 incendiary projectiles. They would close with the beach and give the Cactus Air Force another fireworks show.

Captain Hara was looking forward not to bombardment duty, but to a collision with the American fleet. A trembling took hold of him as he peered into the shroud of Guadalcanal's black mass. The destroyer skipper called to his weaponeers: "Prepare for gun and torpedo attack to starboard! Gun range, 3,000 meters. Torpedo firing angle, 15 degrees." He was ready for whatever might come.

A SAILOR IN THE *JUNEAU,* Joseph Hartney, would recall the darkness that night as "a blackness so thick, so heavy, so velvety, you felt you could take the night in your hands and wring it like a rag." Over the mountains of the islands nearby, flashes of lightning made the clouds jump. From the black curve of Guadalcanal, Hartney heard the soft ringing of gongs and suspected it was marines signaling a warning of a naval bombardment. As he sat at his gun mount in the *Juneau*'s superstructure, he sympathized with his ground-fighting naval cousins. "'Where in the hell is the fleet?' they were asking in that hour," he said. "We were the fleet and we were going out to show them that the navy, too, could face overwhelming odds. We were going to repay them for those weeks of courage when they lay in their foxholes and beat back the enemy." The scent of gardenias wafting out from the island struck him as funereal.

The eighth ship in Callaghan's line, the *Helena*, was buttoned down and restive. Her navigator was practicing shooting stars with his sextant, a couple of young officers on watch were talking Georgia Tech football, and a rummy game was quietly in progress in the coding room. As Callaghan's thirteen ships passed Lunga Point in single file and turned north, there had been little traffic to report in the radio shack. Ashore, tracers could be seen whipping back and forth as infantrymen shot it out in the dark. When the first sign came of an enemy presence on the sea, it was almost an hour and a half after midnight on November 13. For Lieutenant (j.g.) Russell W. Gash, the *Helena*'s radar officer, all mystery evaporated as the number, formation, and bearing of the Japanese force appeared in bright relief on the PPI scope of his search radar. The light-echoes registered with metric precision: one group of vessels at 312 degrees true, range 27,100 yards, a second group at 310 degrees, range 28,000 yards, and a third at 310 at 32,000 yards. Judging by the relative brightness of the lumens, Gash believed that the two nearest groups were composed of smaller ships—probably escorts for the farthest group. The *Helena*'s five triple turrets turned out to port and were raised to their maximum elevation. As Callaghan's and Abe's forces advanced toward a collision, the speed at which their separation closed could be gauged by the whirring of the turret motors when the guns lowered to stay on target.

The radio logs documenting the approach showed Callaghan torn between his competing senses, querying his destroyers ahead about what they were actually seeing while the *Helena* dutifully weighed in, reporting contacts from the radar, which Callghan seemed to ignore. Nearly every question he asked the *Cushing,* leading the van two miles ahead of him, could have been answered almost instantly by the *Helena,* following half a mile behind. Callaghan placed his faith in people, not technics, a preference that was expressed by his selection of the ship that led his column. The *Cushing*'s skipper, Lieutenant Commander Edward N. "Butch" Parker, was a veteran of the Asiatic campaign of early 1942, where he had fought in several battles in the Java Sea as a destroyer division commander. This made him one of the only destroyer officers in the Navy with experience in the type of close-range night battle that Callaghan sought. It didn't seem to bother Callaghan that the *Cushing*'s fire-control radar hadn't worked reliably since installation. The cost of that handicap was well compensated for by having a salt like Butch Parker at the head of his line.

In possession of an electronic picture, the *Helena*'s captain, Gilbert Hoover, and his gunnery officer, Commander Rodman D. Smith, chafed at Callaghan's evident lack of interest in their electronic scouting. As he watched the wake of the *Portland* ahead, Hoover did not relish waiting to open fire. At Cape Esperance, Scott delayed until the enemy was a mere four thousand yards away. The fact that only one person at a time could send messages over the talk-between-ships radio made it impractical for Hoover or anyone else to raise questions.

The way Callaghan had arranged his column minimized the value of their most advanced sensors. In the four-ship van, only the last vessel, the *O'Bannon,* had an SG set. So, too, with the trailing group of destroyers, where the *Fletcher,* bringing up the rear, was SG-equipped. Among the five cruisers in the "base unit," the two leaders, the *Atlanta* and *San Francisco,* were the only ships not to have it. Still, the *Atlanta*'s older-model SC search radar caught Abe's scent at twenty-two thousand yards.

As time passed, the advantage Callaghan could have seized from the radar faded toward a vanishing point. "When we finally had the whole formation in view, they were about ten thousand yards," Graff said. "Pretty soon they were within five thousand yards. Then three thousand." As Chick Morris in the *Helena* saw it, Callaghan drove ahead in a manner "as uncomplicated as that of a train rushing headlong into a tunnel. Callaghan and his staff had decided to do the unexpected and to do it quickly, and so we steamed into the dragon's mouth with every man at every gun on every ship holding his breath and waiting for the inevitable eruption."

AS RANGE DIALS spun downward, destroyermen up and down the line wondered why they hadn't been released to make a torpedo attack. In the *Aaron Ward,* the radar officer, Lieutenant (j.g.) Bob Hagen, expected the commander of Destroyer Squadron 12, Captain Robert G. Tobin, to order his tin cans to prepare their undersea missiles for use. "We knew the bearing, speed and range of the enemy. But I don't think we ever moved our torpedoes," Hagen said. "It never occurred to the captain, but this is what destroyers were *for* in a surface action."

In the Battle of Cape Esperance, Tobin had served in the *Farenholt,* as the destroyer squadron commander. That night, both his ship and the *Duncan* had suffered heavily from friendly fire. The experience might well have made him cautious about the risks of operating destroyers independently of the line. In the gun director of the *Sterett,* the third ship in the van, Lieutenant C. Raymond Calhoun heard his chief fire controlman call out: "Solution! Enemy course 107—speed twenty-three knots!" From there it would have been simple trigonometry to set a spread of torpedoes on an intersecting course. Calhoun called the solution to the bridge and received silence in return. According to Calhoun, "There was no order from the OTC [the officer in tactical command—Callaghan] to do anything but move right down the middle, between the two Japanese forces." Destroyer crews at this time were more thoroughly drilled in gunnery than torpedo firing. The Navy had never really urged or rewarded anything else.

Bill McKinney, the *Atlanta* electrician's mate, served on a damage-control party belowdecks. His job was to stand by within reach of a large steel locker full of damage-control and rescue equipment: ledges, chocks, lines, rescue breathers, oxygen masks, hoses, lanterns, and flash-protective clothing. He checked in with Central Repair—"Manned and ready"—then dogged the hatches and sat tight as the vibrations of the accelerating engines seized the deck, the bulkheads, the entire ship. When the ventilation system shut down, the predominant sound in McKinney's space was the metallic whining of the two ammunition hoists that ran from the magazine below him to a five-inch twin mount directly above him. "I said a short prayer and waited," he wrote.

IT WAS ABOUT 1:40 A.M. when lookouts in the *Cushing,* leading the American column, saw a strange ship slide past. Captain Parker radioed Callaghan this first visual contact with Abe's van. *"There is a ship crossing bow from port to starboard, range 4,000 yards, maximum."* Another ship appeared, followed by a larger one.

The destroyers *Yudachi* and *Harusame,* way out in front of Abe's formation after the two course reversals in the rain, were the first of Abe's vessels finally to emerge from the dark. The Japanese destroyers were widely dispersed around the core of the flotilla, the *Hiei* and *Kirishima,* led by the light cruiser *Nagara.* The third and largest of the ships that the *Cushing* spied was most likely the *Nagara.*

While the *Helena* continued to report its radar readings over the jammed TBS radio frequency, Callaghan kept his eyes forward and ears closed. He asked Parker, "*What do you make of it now?*" Gil Hoover was trying to tell him. "*We have a total of about ten targets. Appear to be in cruising disposition.*" Behind the *Cushing* and the other three van destroyers followed the *Atlanta,* the *San Francisco,* the *Portland,* the *Helena,* the *Juneau,* and the rear destroyers. They plunged toward enemy contact in silence, their reservoirs of potential energy stored deep within, their steel enclosures tense with superheated steam, churning and roaring but held in, like a hidden passion.

When the range had closed to two thousand yards, Captain Parker turned the *Cushing* to port, to bring his torpedo batteries to bear. The commander of Destroyer Division 10, Commander Thomas M. Stokes, who also rode in the *Cushing,* requested permission to make a torpedo attack on what were very plainly hostile ships. "*Shall I let them have a couple of fish?*" he radioed Callaghan. Callaghan denied his request, instructing the destroyers to remain in column, on course 000 true—straight north. The torpedo officer in the destroyer *Laffey,* Lieutenant (j.g.) Thomas A. Evins, was denied his request, too.

Captain Parker was instructed to maintain a course heading north, but abruptly had to veer to port to avoid hitting the Japanese ships in front of him. So did the *Laffey,* following five hundred yards astern, and the *Sterett,* and then the *O'Bannon,* rushing fast into this mess, turning even more sharply left to prevent a telescopic buckling of the entire front of the line. It was now, at about 1:45 a.m., that some fifteen minutes of electric and uncertain silence ended with the blast of guns from the leading units of the opposing task forces.

The fire-control officers in the *Atlanta* were the first of the cruisers to glimpse the chaos at the intersection of the vans. Lloyd Mustin said, "There in the starlight, that dim light in which you can see a great deal when you are fully dark-adapted, I saw the target." Through his binoculars, he made out the silhouette of a light cruiser crossing ahead of the *Atlanta* at six thousand yards. Close ahead, and startlingly so, the four van destroyers were broadside to his ship's course, making emergency turns to avoid running into their enemy. Captain Samuel Jenkins swung the helm sharply left. When Callaghan saw the ship heeled over and veering away to the west, he radioed, "*What are you doing, Sam?*"

"*Avoiding our own destroyers,*" was the reply.

At 1:46 a.m., Callaghan said, "*Come back to your course as soon as you can. You are throwing whole column into disorder.*" But the disorder was not Jenkins's doing. The disorganization of Task Force 67 was irreversible now. It was forced upon it by geometry, by Callaghan's belated perception of his tactical situation, and by the imperatives felt by individual commanders toward survival of their ships.

Coordinated task force navigation was growing difficult when the American task force commander issued his last meaningful command to his column as it moved north. It was an order to change course ninety degrees to the left—directly into the midst of Abe's widely dispersed force. The *Portland*'s quartermaster logged the order with some uncertainty. Other ships did not log it at all. It is possible the order reflected Callaghan's recognition that, confronted with battleships, cruisers could prevail only at point-blank ranges, where a battleship's heavier armor was no proof against eight-inch fire.

REAR ADMIRAL ABE'S first indication of an enemy presence came from the destroyer *Yudachi*. Unsure of his own location, her captain, Commander Kiyoshi Kikkawa, reported an enemy force in the direction of Lunga Point. A

Order of Battle—The Cruiser Night Action

U.S.	Japan
TASK GROUP 67.4	**BOMBARDMENT FORCE**
RADM DANIEL J. CALLAGHAN	RADM NOBUTAKE KONDO
San Francisco (CA) (flagship)	*Hiei* (BB) (flagship)
Portland (CA)	*Kirishima* (BB)
Helena (CL)	*Nagara* (CL)
Atlanta (CLAA)	*Akatsuki* (DD)
Juneau (CLAA)	*Ikazuchi* (DD)
Cushing (DD)	*Inazuma* (DD)
Laffey (DD)	*Amatsukaze* (DD)
Sterett (DD)	*Yukikaze* (DD)
O'Bannon (DD)	*Teruzuki* (DD)
Aaron Ward (DD)	*Asagumo* (DD)
Barton (DD)	*Harusame* (DD)
Monssen (DD)	*Murasame* (DD)
Fletcher (DD)	*Yudachi* (DD)
	Samidare (DD)

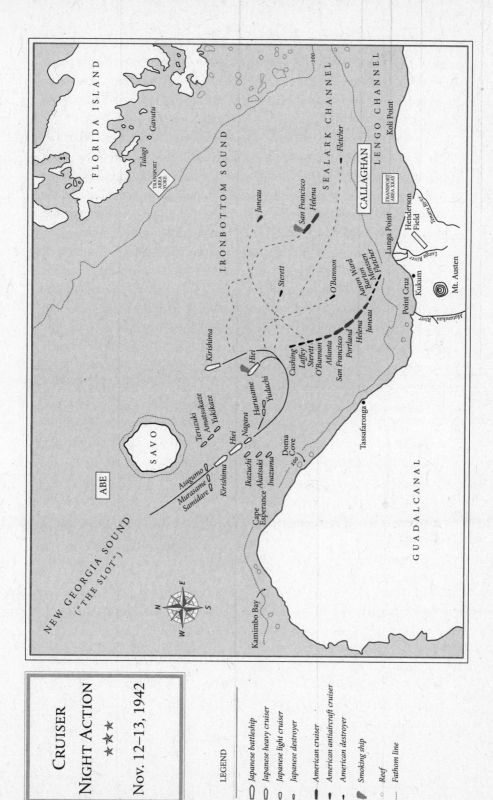

CRUISER
NIGHT ACTION
★ ★ ★
Nov. 12–13, 1942

LEGEND

Japanese battleship
Japanese heavy cruiser
Japanese light cruiser
Japanese destroyer
American cruiser
American antiaircraft cruiser
American destroyer
Smoking ship
Reef
Fathom line

minute later, the *Hiei*'s lookouts reported four enemy cruisers at nine thousand meters (ninety-eight hundred yards). Abe sent a blinker message to his Bombardment Unit: "PROBABLE ENEMY SHIPS IN SIGHT, BEARING 136 DEGREES."

On contact with the Americans, "pandemonium" broke out within the chain of command of the Japanese force, according to Captain Hara of the *Amatsukaze*. In the *Hiei*, Captain Masao Nishida and his gunnery officer debated what type of ordnance the flagship should be loading. Prepared for a bombardment mission, the gunnery officer had Type 3 incendiary and high-explosive projectiles loaded in his hoists. They settled in favor of armor-piercing ammunition. But as crews in the shell decks and turrets of both the *Hiei* and *Kirishima* scrambled to remove bombardment rounds from the hoists and ready storage execution, it was clear that execution was more difficult than decision. "There was a stampede in the magazines, men pushing and kicking to reach the armor-piercing shells stored deep inside," Hara wrote. Evidently the Japanese were unsuccessful switching out their projectiles, judging by the volume of pyrotechnics that burst over Callaghan's formation that night.

For the leading ships, the shooting would begin at a range so close that mechanical sensors were altogether unnecessary. The Battle of Friday the 13th would go down as the first naval engagement in the steam age to begin with a nearly blind head-on collision in the dark.

28

Into the Light

THE HELENA'S GUNS WERE LAID ALMOST TO THE HORIZONTAL—AND still no order to commence firing had come—when a piercing beam of light stood out in the darkness to port, artificial and startling, stinging the night-adjusted eyes of every American sailor manning a topside station. "The light seemed high, as though shining down on us from a higher elevation than our own fighting bridge," wrote Ensign Bin Cochran. "There was a shocking moment when, staring into that light, all seemed completely silent. Everything around us in the night was quiet and black and here we were standing out for all to see." On the lightless nighttime sea, the flare of a match could be seen for miles around; the searchlight was overwhelming in its brightness.

"There was a feeling, one that you knew was without logic, that there was protection in getting out of the direct glare of that light," Cochran continued. "Everybody I could see crouched into a shadow." It was while squatting in that undignified position, stooping behind the four-foot-high sides of the *Helena*'s open bridge, that Rodman Smith decided he'd had enough and hustled over to his skipper. "Permission to open fire, Captain?"

Hoover, ducking out of the light himself, shouted back to his gunnery officer, "Open fire!"

The *Atlanta* was swinging through her own turn to avoid a collision with the van when the searchlight, probably from the destroyer *Akatsuki*, lit upon her from abaft the port beam. Captain Jenkins reacted as commanders had been trained in peacetime: "Counter-illuminate!" he shouted. His gunnery officer, Lieutenant Commander William R. D. Nickelson, Jr., preferred to respond with other hardware. At once he shouted into his headset mike: "Fuck that! Open fire!" His assistant, Lloyd Mustin, was recording accurate ranges from the narrowcasting fire-control radar and didn't need help from other wavelengths. *"Action port. Illuminating ship is target,"* he instructed his gun captains. Mustin, controlling the after trio of five-inch mounts, and Nickelson slewed their directors onto the lights and opened fire immediately.

As Abe's battleships lofted star shells high in the air, which burst behind the American cruisers, the Japanese destroyers hit Commander Stokes's destroyer van with terrific fire. The *Atlanta* came under fire now, too. Captain Jenkins had just ordered the antiaircraft cruiser's torpedoes fired—she was basically an oversized destroyer—when small-caliber projectiles from the *Akatsuki* plowed into her port torpedo director. The officer assigned to that station, Lieutenant (j.g.) Henry P. Jenks, was one of the first casualties. With the loss of automatic control, the bulky torpedo mount, loaded with four big Mark 15s, was too heavy to operate manually with sufficient speed.

But guns were the USN's weapon of choice. By the white light of his carbon-arc fixtures, Mustin could see his own salvos hitting the water just short of the *Akatsuki*'s searchlight. He called corrections to his spotter, who upped the pointer elevation and walked the next one right in. As their target, followed by another destroyer, crossed *Atlanta*'s bow heading north, "You couldn't help but see our projectiles were just tearing into it," Mustin said. "Shooting into a destroyer-size hull from six hundred yards, you just don't miss. You just don't miss."

The *Akatsuki* paid the price of all vessels that uncloaked themselves first in the night. Gunfire from the *Atlanta,* the *San Francisco,* the *Helena,* and several destroyers converged on her. Soon she was wrecked and afire, her steering, power, and communications gone, her deadly torpedoes still in their tubes.

The destroyers *Inazuma* and *Ikazuchi,* trailing the *Akatsuki* just ahead of the *Hiei*'s starboard beam, exited the rain squall and took over the lead. Japanese naval doctrine generally dictated the firing of torpedoes prior to the opening of bright, position-revealing gunfire. Conning his ship past the battered *Akatsuki,* Commander Masamichi Terauchi, captain of the *Inazuma,* saw silhouettes of American ships ahead, blinking with flashes of gunfire. He had had no instructions from Abe. The first signal that came from the *Hiei* conveyed not orders, but requests for information. In the absence of orders,

Terauchi and his torpedomen would do what they did best. Launching at angles to lead the American line, they were as prodigious as ever. Each of the destroyers loosed six torpedoes toward the *Atlanta,* their closest target, before the *Ikazuchi* was hit hard, taking at least three eight-inch shells around her forward gun mount. The burning ship was forced to retire.

Soon after the shooting started, Callaghan ordered, quite superfluously, *"Odd ships commence fire to starboard, even to port."* Given that steel was already flying, and that the American column was in the midst of executing a sharp turn, the use of a command based on ships' relative headings—starboard and port—was "a display of futility," Mustin thought. "Starboard was north with us and port was south, but it was east for other people and so on." Though Callaghan was trying to avoid wasteful concentrations of his gunfire, micromanaging a captain's decisions in battle was risky business. A ship's own officers usually knew what they should be shooting at, especially after the shooting had started.

Commander Jesse Coward, the captain of the destroyer *Sterett,* third in line, had all guns and his torpedo tubes trained on an approaching target to port. But when Callaghan's order came, requiring odd ships to fire to starboard, he complied begrudgingly, swinging his weapons to the opposite beam. Lieutenant Cal Calhoun, the gunnery officer, ordered his fire control-men to seize hold of the closest enemy target to starboard. A light cruiser, the *Nagara,* filled that bill.

Several of the *Sterett*'s mounts were loaded with star shells. From four thousand yards their effect was spectacular if ineffective, detonating on contact and enveloping the light cruiser's forecastle in magnesium-phosphorous pyrotechnics. The next four-gun salvos from Coward's tin can were common projectiles. These packed a harder punch, and *Sterett* fired a dozen such salvos at the *Nagara* as she passed by. Life and death had been set loose on their own schedule, and task force commanders no longer had much to say about it.

When the *Cushing* opened fire on a destroyer skitting away to the east, probably the *Yukikaze,* Captain Parker lost use of his voice radio from the concussion. Mute now and blind without fire-control radar, Parker would fight without the benefit of hearing Callaghan's course and speed orders. He had rung up twenty-five knots after opening fire, but was able to hold it only briefly. Just a couple of minutes after opening fire, the *Cushing* was hit hard by shellfire and began losing power. Enveloped by enemy ships and raked by lighter weaponry, the destroyer slowed and lost steering control. And then a new threat appeared on her starboard hand.

The large vessel's dark form was massive, eldritch, as it loomed off the *Cushing*'s port bow in the flash-lit darkness. This was the *Hiei*. The recognition of the battleship spread down the van, from the *Cushing* to the *Laffey* to the *Sterett* to the *O'Bannon*. Parker came right, with his crews swinging the rudder by hand, and fired six torpedoes by local control. The range to their big target was about twelve hundred yards—too close to miss, but also too close for the torpedoes to arm themselves en route. A destroyer's life expectancy within hailing distance of a battleship was short. The *Hiei*'s secondary guns and several destroyers tore into the *Cushing*, landing accurate fire on each of her gun mounts, and blasting her engineering plant with medium-caliber ordnance. She shook from the impact of hits from ships all around her, and very quickly her loss of steam power was complete. The other ships of the van, passing her on both sides, carried the battle forward, moving in and among Abe's ships. Lieutenant Julian Becton, the executive officer of the *Aaron Ward,* wrote, "It was disorganized. It was individual, with every ship for herself. Perhaps if Tennyson had seen it he would have called it magnificent."

The *Laffey* now found herself leading the American van. Tom Evins, her torpedo officer, was deafened by the ship's battery as it fired on a destroyer ahead—"a roar so constant as to create the impression that there was no noise at all." Though the ship had ridden in Scott's van at Cape Esperance, each battle seized the mind in unique ways. For the sailors in the *Laffey*, that signature image was the *Hiei*, closer to hand now than anyone might ever have wished. The great vessel's proximity registered stunningly on Evins through the time-slowing numbness of five senses strained by overload. "There, bearing down on us on a collision course from the port side, was what seemed to be the biggest manmade object ever created," he said.

Richard Hale, the pointer in gun two, was startled to see the battleship's bridge and superstructure through his pointer's scope. "It was so close we could throw hand grenades and hit it." The five-inch guns trained out and started a brisk cadence, joined soon, Hale recalled, by the chattering twenties. "The flight of our shells to the target was instantaneous," he wrote. "We saw them penetrate their bulkheads and explode inside."

"She was only about a thousand yards away, and there was clearly not a second to lose," said Tom Evins. "It seemed like an eternity before I was able to launch our single spread of five gas-operated steel fish. Meanwhile the great battleship came relentlessly on, as if to crush us." The effect from the destroyer's point of view was like the head of a great ax slicing toward them through the water.

The *Laffey*'s captain, Lieutenant Commander William E. Hank, rang emergency full astern. Cross-connecting his engine and fire rooms, with burners full open, he then signaled emergency full ahead. The captain's shiphandling had been a source of consternation and embarrassment to the crew when he showed a willingness to use emergency engine orders during routine docking. Now the circumstances required it. The destroyer leaped forward as her screws bit into the seas. Surging just past her fantail went the *Hiei,* "so close Hank could have hit her with a slingshot," Julian Becton wrote. The destroyer's gunners riddled the Japanese ship with guns of all calibers. A sailor named John H. Jenkins, impressed with the opportunity at hand, ran to a twenty-millimeter mount whose operator was hanging lifeless in the harness. Wrapping his arms around the corpse, using it as a shield, he raised the barrel and fired a clip into the battleship's portholes. As fire from the *Laffey* and the other three destroyers raked the *Hiei*'s bridge, Admiral Abe took shrapnel to the face, and Captain Masao Nishida fell wounded, too. Abe's chief of staff, Commander Masakane Suzuki, was a fatality. As heavier blows fell, delivered by American ships farther away, flames and smoke washed through the pilothouse. Jenkins saw pieces of the superstructure falling onto the great fourteen-inch turret below it.

Having momentarily "blinded the Cyclops," in Becton's words, the *Laffey* pulled away to the north, under heavy fire but opening the range. Her narrow escape from a collision with a ship eighteen times her weight was only the first of her hurdles. As the ship headed for Savo Island, looking to use the island's silhouette as camouflage, the trio of destroyers on Abe's northern flank of his van, the *Asagumo, Murasame,* and *Samidare,* began crossing ahead of her from port to starboard and took the *Laffey* under fire. "The whole world suddenly seemed to burst into the brilliance of an eerie blue midday as the star shells exploded over our heads," Tom Evins recalled. "The *Laffey* was designed for 37.5 knots but we were making in excess of forty," wrote Lieutenant Eugene A. Barham, her engineering officer.

The battleship *Kirishima,* steaming on the *Hiei*'s port quarter, fired on the *Laffey.* Two shells bit into her bridge and her number two gun mount. According to Evins, "The next second I was hanging onto a stanchion, trying to keep myself from being thrown from the ship. She seemed to pitch herself into the air and then nosedive for the bottom. Tons of water poured down over our superstructure; it was difficult to stand under the weight of it and every man topside was drenched to the skin." This particular excitement—a straddle by a fourteen-inch salvo—was followed by a shell that penetrated the deckhouse below his station in the torpedo director, passed through the ship, and hit the water, exploding in a mess of blue dye.

Around this same time, a torpedo hit the fantail. The explosion ripped loose fifty feet of the *Laffey*'s stern, all the way forward to gun number four, which was folded up onto the mount located just forward of it. The destroyer's after fire room and electrical workshop were a gutted shambles. Up from within this deep wound swirled a terrible oil fire. Just forward of the blast, in the machinery spaces, the ship's propeller shafts began spinning wildly as her screws, along with her rudder, were shorn away. According to Richard Hale, "I could see that a fire of that magnitude meant the magazine could blow at any time. I went back up to the bow to get as far away from that fire as I could."

The crew of the *Laffey*'s gun number four were dead at their stations. Sailors looking to rescue them found a fuze setter still alive in his seat, but trapped by the shell hoist, which had been bent in over him. The smoke was overcoming him, and he was nearly unconscious. According to Ensign David S. Sterrett, only a skilled shipfitter with a blowtorch could have cut him out of the metal prison. "The air was full of thick, dark smoke," Sterrett said. "There was nothing we could do. We handed him a gas mask so he could have a few more breaths of air."

THROUGH THE SPRAY kicked up by his bow wave, Captain Hara in the *Amatsukaze,* advancing with Abe's left-hand vanguard, saw five or six American ships 5,000 meters (5,450 yards) away on his starboard bow. They were silhouetted in the yellow-white light of airborne flares. "I gulped. My heart bubbled with excitement," he wrote. Most likely these were Callaghan's rear echelon: the *Juneau* leading the *Aaron Ward,* the *Barton,* the *Monssen,* and the *Fletcher.* Lieutenant Masatoshi Miyoshi, his torpedo officer, shouted, "Commander, let's fire the fish!" Hara ordered, "Get ready, fisherman!" Ordering the helm left, he let fly with eight of them.

The Savo Sound fireworks show commanded a large audience ashore. Searchlights stabbed and intersected, playing briefly on their targets then blinking out when the opposing gunners caught on. From on high floated star shells and flares. There were moments when the men in the ships, too, indulged themselves as onlookers and marveled. Commander Coward of the *Sterett* noted that the Japanese were firing "a form of firecracker or sparkle effect with brilliant white flashes fired low between the two forces with the apparent intention of blinding our cruisers." These were surely the airburst incendiaries loaded in the hoists of the battleships and meant for the men of Henderson Field.

At the start of it, the exec of the *Sterett* had told his gunners not to bother manning their weapons, as he didn't think a destroyer's small guns would have any work this night. But this battle had no precedent in their experience. Ahead, they could see the *Nagara* delivering a beating to the *Cushing*, whose engineers were trying to use the lull to get her engines going again. The *Laffey* was in a crossfire, too. The *Sterett*'s gun crews concentrated on the *Nagara* for a while, until they found a larger target, the *Hiei*, within range. Looming to port, the great ship drew their fire in to two thousand yards, by which time the battleship underwent a sudden transformation from "a ghostly gray" to "a brilliant orange" as flames seemed to take hold of her from stem to stern.

While the formations surged through one another, a Japanese destroyer, possibly the *Harusame*, appeared a thousand yards on the *Sterett*'s starboard bow. Coward launched two torpedoes at this vessel, and his gunners turned loose several full salvos at eight hundred yards. Though the torpedoes never could have armed, somehow the enemy ship was seen to rise from the water by her stern. This gut punch, probably landed by another ship, left the enemy's after mounts swallowed in flames and her stern glowing a cherry red. Watching from the director, Lieutenant Calhoun found himself shouting, "Oh, you poor son of a bitch!" As he recalled, "The water around her seemed to boil, and her hull threw off steam with a hiss that we could hear aboard the *Sterett*." Calhoun passed news of this to his gun captains over the phones. "I told them to send their powder monkeys up the ladder to the main deck so they could see what they had just done." But there was little time to celebrate.

Around this time the *Sterett* fell into a withering enemy crossfire from her port side. "It was as if a huge star shell had burst and illuminated the sea. It was like noon on a bright sunny day," Perry Hall recalled. The *Hiei* and other ships were focused on her. The foremast buckled as radar and radio antennae were carried away. Shrapnel peppered the gun director, felling most of the fire-control team. Cal Calhoun took a shower of steel into his kapok life jacket and battle helmet but emerged, improbably, no worse for the wear.

As fires ignited and began to spread, the firefighters discovered that the mains lacked pressure. Shambling about in their flashproof clothing and asbestos pullovers, they played weak streams from torn hoses on the conflagration aft. Keeping a good footing on decks slick with blood was difficult when the ship was veering to and fro. A shell slammed into the galley locker, scattering potatoes about. The screams of the wounded pierced the night and mingled with more sober voices directing the firefighting. "The number-four handling room was a near holocaust," Perry Hall said. "Bits of burning bedding smoldered on the bunks, burnt bodies were scattered about the decks, and water poured into a shell hole, just above the waterline, whenever the ship wheeled to port or starboard.... The stench of burning flesh and powder made breathing difficult."

The *Sterett* took eleven direct hits, all on her port side, all above the waterline, and sustained severe shrapnel damage from many near misses. Her after deck house and number three gun, an unshielded open mount back aft, were engulfed by flames that brightly illuminated the flag on the small ship's mainmast truck. Her after handling rooms were set afire, causing powder in ready service storage to ignite. Though the fires were horrible, it was the crew's great good fortune that the ship's engines were undamaged. With just two guns operable and a pair of torpedoes stuck precariously in damaged tubes, Captain Coward found he had to slow occasionally to lighten the breeze stoking the topside fires, which were threatening to rage out of control. Twenty-eight of his men were dead, another thirteen seriously wounded. Four leaped overboard to extinguish their burning clothes. Those who stayed aboard and saved the ship braved burning compartments to turn flood valves and remove wounded from impossible places. They defied smoke to soak powder, gird bulkheads, patch holes, fix pumps, run hoses, and keep electricity flowing. They allowed their hands to melt while connecting superheated brass hose couplings to fight fires. Braving flames that would not otherwise have been beaten, they threw well-baked projectiles overboard and lowered rafts to save their brothers.

They were cool, efficient, leaderly, and unselfish, according to those who saw them and wrote the reports. "The following men are deserving of commendation"—and this would be written many times in the coming days and weeks—"for the accuracy of his control of the gun battery... at great risk he entered the smoke filled handling rooms #3 and #4... and directed the damage control parties... for his courage in personally supervising the fire fighting below decks... without thought to his own safety... worked continuously all night and the next day reinforcing shores and operating pumps... it is recommended that this man be advanced to chief... for his heroic action in entering the flames... when after being struck in the neck by shrapnel, although he could in no way determine the extent of his wounds except to feel blood soaking his shirt, calmly identified silhouettes as they appeared... and removing casualties from gun #3 and getting #7 life raft into the water... for his tireless effort and continued excellent performance of duty... directing the fire party to successfully extinguish the fire which helped the ship continue fighting...and rendered valuable aid putting out a fire in compartment C-203-L...for fine assistance in handling casualties of gun #3...and for helping extinguish fires on clothing...."

Feats like these would be easily lost, along with the names of their authors, men like Byers, Burris, Morris, and Lovas; Keenum, Kozak, Conn, and Hammack; Kelly, Wholley, Fray, and Mayefsky; Lastra, Dean, Weller, and Talbot; Seymour, Boudreaux, Blankenship, Spence, and Shelton; Hall, Hanna, Hodge, Homer, and Robinson. They were men without rank to have monuments but whose names shine out from the haze of reports and deserve to be held up for notice. Not just the men of the *Sterett,* but all of them, American and Japanese, striving and desperate and frightened and riled and tender and human, in fateful collision on Friday, the thirteenth of November, 1942.

29

The Killing Salvo

CALLAGHAN'S SINGLE COLUMN RESEMBLED A WORLD WAR I–VINTAGE battle line of yore. But it echoed a weapon more ancient still as it thrust into the body of Hiroaki Abe's force: a piercing long sword, or perhaps a lance. The American commander might have employed it as an archer firing arrows, standing off, using his advanced sensors, killing by surprise out of the dark. Instead, he ran straight ahead, blade fixed, and plunged straight in. The delicate tip of his sword broke on first contact, the van destroyers penetrating momentarily before fracturing, and throwing reverberations back toward Callaghan, riding in the hilt. What followed was a melee, Colosseum-style, with the lights out, and a heavy fog blown over the fighting arena. What can be settled and known is the time of first contact, and the time, ultimately, of disengagement. The terrible middle became a swirl of slash and thrust, ship against ship, captain against the enemy of the moment, which, battered then vanishing, was replaced by a new enemy who delivered or received the next blow unwitting. The records muddle the precise sequence of things. Individual memories are indelibly vivid but pointillistic, dead certain to the beholder but seldom tracking with anyone else's and unhelpful to the big picture. The events of November 13, 1942, in their chaotic simultaneity, defy the benign lie that is narrative. But the big picture is as simple to understand as a precise 360-degree portrait is difficult: On that night, two groups of powerful steel machines surprised each other on the sea in the dark and, blundering and veering in a manner unworthy of the elegance of their design, grappled bodily, delivering hammer blows until death.

It was a mystery to participants then and to analysts in decades to come why Callaghan never issued a written battle plan to his commanders. As Bruce McCandless, the *San Francisco*'s officer-of-the-deck, saw it, a slight turn to the right at the outset, away from the oncoming Japanese swarm, would have "crossed the T" of Abe's force, bringing the American formation on a course perpendicular to that of the Japanese. This textbook naval maneuver, performed by Norman Scott at Cape Esperance, would have enabled all the U.S. ships to fire full broadsides and the destroyers at either end of Callaghan's line to attack with torpedoes on the bows. It "should have sufficed to derail this Tokyo Express," McCandless would write. This was the clarity of hindsight. In the present, there had been no tactical planning. There is no evidence Callaghan ever communicated his expectations to his subordinates. At the moment of contact, he ordered his column left, steering it directly into the enemy's midst, on a path that the laws of the indifferent universe always seemed to urge, as inertia devolved into entropy.

After the bloody encounter of the van destroyers with the leading elements of Abe's force, and after the early battering of the *Atlanta,* the next ships into the maelstrom were Callaghan's cruisers. When the *Portland* made her turn to the west, following the *San Francisco,* Captain Laurance DuBose saw five evenly spaced searchlights ahead and to starboard, stabbing across the water toward the American line. His five-inch batteries lofted star shells, aiming to shed light on the situation. Then, at murderously close range, sixty-two hundred yards, his main battery lashed out. Though the forward fire-control radar was out, a casualty of short circuits, the "Sweet Pea" scored a first-salvo hit with eight-inch fire. "At least four bursts of flame leapt from the enemy vessel," wrote the gunnery officer, Lieutenant Commander Elliott W. Shanklin. After the second salvo, the target, a destroyer, blew up and was left sinking. It was probably the *Akatsuki.*

Astern of the *Portland,* the *Helena* was worked up to a servo-mechanical rage with her six-inch main battery, targeting a searchlight just forty-two hundred yards to her west. It must have belonged to the *Hiei;* it appeared too high and large to belong to a destroyer. The officer in a spotting station high overhead reported that the tracers were perfectly aimed in deflection and that "practically all of our shots appeared to hit." One of her turret officers, Lieutenant Earl A. Luehman, observed, "The tracers from fifteen guns looked like a swarm of bees heading for a target you couldn't see." Cycling rapidly with the firing keys closed, the ship's broadside was like a gigantic combustion engine with mistimed pistons. Nodding up and down, driven by their director-controlled motors, the guns laid a "rocking ladder" of fire across a two-hundred-yard-long path centered on the range given by the radar. No ship, no matter how stout its armor, would want to be in the path of what she was sending out: more than two hundred 130-pound shells per minute, according to Bin Cochran. As the *Helena* reached the turning point for the left column turn, the light that her gunners were shooting at faded to black. The superstructure of the enemy ship was a "smoky orange bonfire," Chick Morris recalled. "How high into the sky that tower of flame extended, no one can say, but the brightness of it was unbelievable."

Farther ahead, the *Atlanta* turned to port to avoid the traffic jam in the van. The *San Francisco* was riding on the *Atlanta*'s port quarter. Bruce McCandless at the flagship's conn called to Captain Jenkins, "*The* Atlanta*'s turning left. Shall I follow her?*" Back came the reply, "*No. Hold your course.*" Then, a few seconds later, "*Follow the* Atlanta."

McCandless recalled: "First I had to swing the *San Francisco* slightly right to clear her, then use full left rudder; this resulted in our paralleling the *Atlanta* on a northwesterly course with her slightly on our port bow. As we started to swing in astern of her, enemy searchlights came on, one illuminating her from port. The *Atlanta* then swung back across our bow from left to right, firing rapidly to port as she went."

The heavier *San Francisco* took wider turns than the *Atlanta* and swung outboard of her both times. As a result, Callaghan's flagship, instead of following the antiaircraft cruiser, ended up steaming on her port hand. The *Atlanta* "swept out of line, her five-inch guns spitting a giddy pattern of fireworks," wrote Chick Morris on the *Helena*. "The rest of us stayed in line, led now by the *San Francisco*, and as we continued at high speed through the tunnel, Jap ships were afire on both sides of us. We were silhouetted like witches speeding across a Halloween moon."

Suddenly the *Atlanta*'s 541-foot length was gripped from below and shaken violently. Robert Graff felt "a tremendous *piiing*. The ship lurched, like when you hit a heavy pothole." The word went around immediately: A torpedo had struck on the port side. Two of them, actually. One Long Lance hit the ship between the forward fire room and forward engine room and exploded powerfully. Though magnified by the ocean's pressure, the blast of the thousand-pound warhead, which seemed to have been delivered by the destroyer *Ikazuchi*, did not rip the ship apart completely. It was contained within the airtight enclosure formed by the 3.75-inch armored belts on the sides of the hull below the waterline, and by the 1.25-inch armored deck above. But the violent discharge had to go somewhere. According to Lloyd Mustin, it rushed fore and aft, rupturing the after bulkhead of the forward engine room and letting seawater into the machinery spaces. "A monstrous column of water and oil rose on our port side and cascaded down all over the ship, drenching all of the topside. People were thrown to their knees, including me, by the shock of the explosion." A second torpedo penetrated the hull and stuck fast without detonating.

Raymond E. Leslie felt the *Atlanta* move "like a pendulum" and feared he would be flung overboard from the searchlight platform by the elastic swinging motion. "The torpedo created a heavy downpour of seawater on top of us and filled our searchlight platform like a bath tub." The plotting officer, Lieutenant James C. Shaw, stationed five decks below, was thrown into the bulkhead by the blast, smashing his right hand. As water swirled over the deck, he called Commander Nickelson, the gunnery officer, told him of the flooding, and asked for orders. Nickelson replied, "Stick a pillow in it," and then the phones went dead.

When the boilers were secured and a safety valve opened, pressurized steam gusted upward through an exhaust vent in the number two stack, right near the after air defense station, where Mustin and the exec were stationed. "It was absolutely deafening," Mustin said. "It was impossible to communicate by voice, even by putting your mouth to someone's ear and shouting. You couldn't communicate above the sound of that escaping steam."

In the dark, groping for a way topside with the help of a battery-powered lantern, electrician's mate Bill McKinney heard a rending and tearing of metal, as if the ammo hoists that were routed through his compartment had suddenly gone off their tracks. The radio was out. The ship's lights and engines and gun turrets were dead. The chief engineer was, too.

When the power died, the final range reading shown by the fire-control radar in the forward main battery director, which electrician's mate Bob Tyler saw on a plotting board in the interior communications room, was shocking. The distance to the director's last target was just 450 yards.

Pounding on the forward bulkhead, McKinney got a return knock, and by shouting found out that several of his shipmates were in the dark as well. Damage-control doctrine forbade them from opening the hatches. Doing so could compromise the watertight integrity of the gravely damaged ship. The question, as on all dying vessels, was whether the doctrine still applied— whether the collective enterprise of fighting as a crew had given way to the pursuit of individual survival. It was anybody's guess whether Captain Jenkins had ordered them to abandon ship. Through the thin steel overhead, McKinney could hear men choking and coughing and more undetermined noises, and he would have many measureless moments in which to think about such things.

Around this time, the foundering *Atlanta* was taken under fire by a heavy cruiser, about thirty-five hundred yards abaft her port beam. Mustin attempted to return fire with the only turret that was responsive on the intercom, turret seven aft, which had to be fired manually. But her crew stood down when the light of their target's own gun discharges revealed her to be a friendly vessel. Lloyd Mustin recognized the flash of her smokeless powder and the deliberate cadence characteristic of American eight-inch gunfire. The U.S. cruiser's gunners were all too adept. A series of heavy hits shivered the *Atlanta*'s forward superstructure and decks.

Jenkins was with Admiral Scott, standing on the starboard bridge wing looking north, where the battle seemed to have drifted, when there was "some alarm on the port side," Lloyd Mustin said. "Captain Jenkins went around the catwalk to the port side to see what was going on. When he came back, there was no starboard bridge wing." Seven large shells had pierced the *Atlanta* just below the bridge deck. The four-inch armor plating protecting the pilothouse couldn't stop them. They penetrated and exited forward. The bulkhead door flew from its hinges and slammed into Jenkins from behind, but he was spared the worst of this violent shock to the pilothouse, which killed sixteen of the twenty men stationed there.

Robert Graff, riven with shrapnel in his legs, hips, arms, hands, and face, the biggest of the pieces about the size of a walnut, crawled from the port signal bridge into the pilothouse, over innumerable bodies, and continued through to the starboard signal bridge. There was a huge hole in the bulkhead there. Graff thought he might climb through it and let himself down to a gun platform, then the main deck. He didn't remember how he got there, but he would never forget something he realized in the pilothouse along that way: that one of the officers he had crawled over was high ranking and familiar.

My God, they got Scott, Graff thought.

"I remember a quick twinge of sadness as I crawled by him. I remember thinking, *Oh, shit, that's a terrible loss.*"

Lieutenant Stewart Moredock, Scott's operations officer, saw his admiral take his last steps. He would dredge up this memory later, after his recovery from his injuries, recalling how Captain Jenkins had approached him, saying, "Let's get below. There's nothing we can do up here." Unable to find a ladder to the main deck, Moredock, the only one of Scott's staff to survive, hugged the bridge railing and swung his body over. With his right hand broken he found he couldn't hold his entire weight with his left, and he plummeted down, falling some twenty feet into a gun tub. "I hit, I'm pretty certain, a bunch of dead bodies on that gun emplacement," Moredock said. "I heard the noise of their, you know, their lungs, whatever. It was a shattering kind of feeling."

The dead were everywhere but they registered only faintly, the sight of their scattered remains too horrific to bear, though indelibly seen in the periphery, like dim stars. Robert Graff, in a state of shock as he sought a way down to the main deck, said, "I don't know where I thought I was going. Talk about being on autopilot. What did I think I was going to gain by going to the main deck? Maybe to find a live human being." As the thought continued to reverberate with him—*My God, they got Scott*—he felt the need to express it to someone, but found nobody left alive to talk to.

For years no one would speak comfortably about what had happened that night, or how. Lloyd Mustin was among the first to suspect it. He saw it as it was happening in a blinding incandescent flash of nitrocellulose powder. This "illuminated the firing ship brilliantly and unmistakably," Mustin said. "It was as easy to recognize the *San Francisco* in the flash of her own guns as it would have been at high noon in San Francisco Harbor."

Norman Scott and his staff and so many men had been cut down by Callaghan's flagship, which was, it seems, firing on an enemy target beyond the *Atlanta*. Scott had learned in the Battle of Cape Esperance what happens when ships get caught between friends and enemies at night and lose track of each other with no ready means of identification. Visibility was poor owing to the heavy smoke. Flames and the flashes of muzzles constricted the pupils.

According to a *San Francisco* signalman, Vic Gibson, watching from the signal bridge, the *Atlanta* was caught in a crossfire. "We were firing at such close range that the shells leaving our guns were going right through the superstructure of the *Atlanta* and the Jap shells were doing the same from their direction." In the confusion, the *San Francisco* had simply lost track of her. "Probably she drifted into our line of fire—an almost perfectly flat trajectory at that range," Lieutenant Commander Bruce McCandless wrote. "Perhaps something like that was inevitable in the wild, free-swinging brawl that resulted when the two formations merged."

The best evidence of whose shells hit her lay spattered around the *Atlanta*'s boat deck: a mess of green dye powder, the telltale color that

Callaghan's flagship used to aid in spotting her shell splashes. Mustin found that another salvo from the *San Francisco* had struck the port side five-inch waist mount, still trained forward from its engagement with Abe's lead destroyers. That salvo penetrated the mount from left to right, smashing the breech, slicing one of the guns away, and killing nearly everybody inside. The back was blown loose. It stood leaning against the superstructure. There was no doubt these were eight-inch shells. "You could measure them with a ruler," Mustin said. The only other ship firing eight-inch ordnance that night was the *Portland,* but her dye loads were orange. In the *Atlanta,* from behind the hatchway that led forward from his damage-control station, Bill McKinney, the electrician's mate, heard banging and shouting. Men were saying that their belowdecks compartment had been breached, that flames were visible, and that blood was running down into it. They needed to get out fast. "I continued to try our phones without success," McKinney wrote. "Our very large compartment was a factor in the ship's buoyancy, and I did not dare open the watertight door forward. I did take a peek through the escape scuttle in the large double hatch covering above and leading to the sick bay passageway immediately above us. The space above was full of thick, yellow smoke."

Donning a rescue breather, McKinney left through the topside hatch and, joined by a sailor named Daniel Curtin, climbed the ladder into the scuttle above. "The smoke was so thick that the beam of our battle lantern did not extend for more than two feet. We stumbled over the body of the sailor who had been coughing and choking earlier. I wondered if we could have saved him."

AS THE BATTLE LOST coherence in the minds of its participants, an order came over the TBS that left Laurance DuBose in the *Portland,* his gunnery officer, Commander Elliott Shanklin, and every turret officer and gun captain mistrustful of their own ears: *"Cease firing own ships. Cease firing own ships. Cease firing own ships...."*

The message was from Callaghan. The *Portland* had just fired a pair of nine-gun salvos at a cruiser that could not be positively identified when the perplexing order came. Captain DuBose asked his admiral, *"What is the dope, did you want to cease fire?"*

From Callaghan came, *"Affirmative."* That response, documented in the *Portland*'s radio log, seemed to refute the idea, floated later, that an order meant only for the *San Francisco* got accidentally transmitted to the whole group. Clearly the flagship, like the *Portland,* had just fired on a ship of uncertain nationality that made the order necessary. It was identified in records only as "a small cruiser or a large destroyer." Murky identifications were unavoidable in the night and smoke. It very well could have been the *Atlanta.*

The gunners on the *San Francisco* were firing at shadows. Said Edgar Harrison, a fire controlman on a five-inch director, "We fired at so many targets, what I was doing was have my trainer train on shadows. I'm running the range dial on the computer, and I could see the red-hot bullets go out, then I changed the range up and down until the bullets were disappearing into the shadow. Then I'd check fire and find another target."

In the *Helena*'s chart house, Ray Casten kept a close eye on the PPI scope as he did navigational piloting and managed the dead-reckoning plot. "I watched, almost transfixed, as our ships interleaved with those of the enemy," the young officer would write. "I actually counted a total of twenty-six blips within the 5,000-yard sweep radius on our PPI scope. Would anyone, could anyone, ever believe this? Even when Captain Hoover asked where our ships were, I was only able to inform him of apparent concentrations." Amid the confusion of the interlaced formations, it was left to individual captains to decide who was friend and who was foe. Most of Callaghan's captains, if they ever heard the cease-fire order, ignored it, having arrived at their own diverging views of the priorities of life and death.

30

Death in the Machine Age

HE MUST HAVE SMOKED TWO PACKS OF CIGARETTES THAT NIGHT. Pacing the decks of his flagship, gray brows beetling, nerves afire, he found himself hardly able to stand it, knowing that his fleet was in action and he was not. The bustling pace of Nouméa by day had quieted down, leaving Halsey's imagination in overdrive as his watch officers in the *Argonne* brought him the radio intercepts. There would be little or no sleep for him or his staff that night.

To be a commander in the machine age was to suffer the barrier of distance and live in immediate ignorance of the outcomes of battle. With the *Enterprise* in the war's early months, he had awaited the returns of his air groups in the Marshalls and the Gilberts and off Honshu. The stakes then were nothing like they were now. He passed the time poring over charts in Flag Plot, walking the decks, and smoking, and conferring with his staff, and diverting himself, when he could stand no more, with the trashiest magazines in the wardroom, and smoking, always smoking. "I drank coffee by the gallon," he wrote. The men of his South Pacific Forces were at a moment of decision. All that the dispatches could tell him, again and again, was that another battle was under way. Which way it was going was anyone's guess.

The action was more cinematically enthralling for the young men watching from Guadalcanal's northern shore. It was a diversion from their life in a diseased, death-ridden combat zone. As far away as Aola Bay, almost fifty miles east of Savo Sound, "The concussion could be felt as it came in on the airways, and the explosions seemed to rock the ground under our feet," recalled a U.S. Army infantryman on Guadalcanal. "One could see the bellows of black smoke over the battle scene, shooting high into the air; at night these smoke clouds were capped with red flames."

A marine, Robert Leckie, wrote, "The star shells rose, terrible and red. Giant tracers flashed across the night in orange arches.... The sea seemed a sheet of polished obsidian on which the warships seemed to have been dropped and been immobilized, centered amid concentric circles like shock waves that form around a stone dropped in mud." From Tulagi's hills, "all you could see were the tracers and the muzzle flashes, and the hits. But you didn't know who was getting hit," a sailor wrote. Tracers looked like glowing red blobs, moving slowly through space to their target, then crashing into larger flashes and fires when they struck. There was a three-beat delay before the wave of thunder arrived over the water.

Infantrymen who had fought bitterly for months were often callous. The novelist James Jones, an Army soldier who arrived later, developed a perverse outlook. Having resolved that he would die, he could root for death's reign everywhere. "Consciously or unconsciously," Jones would write, "we accepted the fact that we couldn't survive. So we could watch the naval battle from the safety of the hills with undisguised fun. There was no denying we were pleased to see somebody else getting his. Even though there were men dying. Being blown apart, concussed, drowning. Didn't matter. We had been getting ours, let them get theirs. It wasn't that we were being sadistic. It was just that we had nothing further to worry about. We were dead."

CALLAGHAN'S AND ABE'S heaviest ships, the "base units," came to grips just before 2 a.m. Tracking four enemy ships in column to her northeast, the *Helena* asked Callaghan, *"Can we open fire if we have targets?"* The task force commander replied, *"Advise type of targets. We want the big ones."* That's exactly what he got. According to John Bennett, the *San Francisco* was closing with three formidable opponents: a cruiser abaft her starboard beam, the *Hiei* approaching forward of her starboard beam, about twenty-two hundred yards away, and the *Kirishima* about three thousand yards sharp on the starboard bow. According to Bruce McCandless, "The duel about to begin in which flagship fought flagship was like something out of the past.... The action was brief but violent," as the *Hiei* and *San Francisco* approached on opposite courses.

With Cassin Young designating targets for the gunnery officer, Lieutenant

Commander William W. Wilbourne, McCandless swung the helm left to unmask the after turret. As the *San Francisco*'s eight-inch turrets roared, the *Hiei*'s great turrets answered in kind. "Two four-gun salvos hit the water short of us, bursting on impact and projecting vivid greenish pyrotechnics—incendiaries," McCandless wrote. Wilbourne had little more to do than close his firing key and pray. In close and brutally fast was his only chance, given that his salvos had 20 percent the throw-weight of her enemy. "Had anyone timed our loading crews that night, he doubtless would have seen some new records set." The crew of the *San Francisco*'s turret three was operating in local control after the destruction of the after control station by the Betty that afternoon. From twenty-two hundred yards, it was hard to miss. The *San Francisco* lashed out with all three turrets, battering the *Hiei* all along her length. The turret officer in turret one shouted over the voice tube to his crew, "We just put a nine-gun salvo into the side of a Jap BB!" At this range not even a battleship's armor was proof against cruiser fire. The *San Francisco* would claim "at least eighteen hits" on the *Hiei*. From amidships, near the *Hiei*'s waterline, came a blast that "caused plates and wreckage to fly about," the *San Francisco*'s action report would state. Stationed on a five-inch mount on the starboard side of the *San Francisco*, Cliff Spencer was awestruck. "With a pagoda-like superstructure, the big ship was so close she looked like the New York skyline. As our stream of shells hit, you could see men or debris flying off the [searchlight] platform, it was that close.... When my vision returned I looked out upon the battle scene to starboard.... The magnitude of the battle was almost unbelievable."

As the time approached 2 a.m., life in Savo Sound was a violent blur, with ships up and down the line fighting for their lives. To the northwest, beyond the maelstrom's center of gravity, the battered *Cushing* endured another blizzard of steel as Abe's rear destroyers, the *Asagumo, Murasame,* and *Samidare,* swung past her. The *Cushing*'s skipper, Butch Parker, would describe this night "just like a barroom brawl with the lights out."

Despite some claims to the contrary, the U.S. destroyers likely never got their torpedoes effectively into play. Opportunities to fire them occurred at such close range that the weapons seldom had time to arm. The destroyer *O'Bannon*, last in the van, spied the *Hiei* close on her port bow, burning but still roaring salvos over the mast of the American destroyer at unknown targets behind her. Commander E. R. Wilkinson loosed four torpedoes, the third of which coincided with the battleship's complete envelopment "from bow to stern in a great sheet of flame." The *Sterett* claimed a pair of torpedo hits on the *Hiei* as well, but Japanese records, which chronicle gunfire damage in detail, suggest that the damage went unnoticed. Very possibly these claims arose from the battering the *Hiei* was taking from the *San Francisco* around this time.

As burning particles from the *Hiei* fell on the *O'Bannon's* forward decks, Captain Wilkinson, deeming the Japanese battleship "killed" and finding that no further targets offered, ordered the rudder right until his destroyer was on an easterly course. Swinging the helm again to avoid the shattered *Laffey*, the *O'Bannon* passed through waters dotted with U.S. sailors. Wilkinson's crew tossed life vests, some fifty of them, to the men in the water as they passed. As the *O'Bannon* steamed away to the east, "attempting to locate either definite targets or definite friends," five unidentified vessels— probably the *Cushing, Sterett, Atlanta, Hiei,* and *Akatsuki*—were seen burning or exploding in her wake.

It was the *San Francisco* that had the full attention of the Japanese heavy ships now, the *Hiei* to starboard and the *Kirishima,* less vividly noticed, moving across to port. It would be estimated that the *San Francisco* took some forty-five shell hits, twelve of them major-caliber. One fourteen-incher struck the barbette of turret two, opening its seams, and shattered the flood-control panel. This activated the flooding system in the forward magazine and the lower handling room. The crew in the turret stalk, believing the ship was sinking, began pouring out of the top of the turret, into the open air and a storm of flying metal. Airbursts from fourteen-inch anti-personnel and incendiary rounds were shattering. What they did to people in topside stations was unspeakable. Wherever a shell struck armor, the projectile broke up, denting the plating and smoking up the paintwork. The airbursts hurled incendiaries and fragments in all directions. "Seemingly everywhere," Bruce McCandless wrote, "we found short lengths of what looked like gas pipe about an inch in diameter. A few contained unburned incendiary, a mixture of powdered aluminum and magnesium, with fuzes at both ends.... This stuff was responsible for many of our casualties and much of our damage." The crews on the starboard secondary battery were cut down virtually to a man. "The smell of burning flesh.... These are recollections that will last my life," Bennett said. "That's something you don't get over."

An armor-piercing projectile bulled into wardroom country, where the ship's executive officer, Mark Crouter, was convalescing after his legs had been burned in the afternoon air attack. He had insisted on remaining on board. This decision cost him his life. The shell killed him where he lay. This third-hitting salvo from the *Hiei* was costly. Four fourteen-hundred-pound projectiles crashed into the *San Francisco's* bridge and forward superstructure, smashing the chart house and propelling the navigator, Commander Rae Arison, over the port side of the superstructure. He made two complete turns in the air before crashing three decks below onto the barrel of a five-inch mount. The impact broke both of his legs. The gun captain, to the considerable surprise of both men, caught Arison and pushed him aside— toward a ladder that led downward. Helpless now, Arison slipped down the ladder and fell onto the deckhouse, facedown in a sizable puddle of water that had welled in a dished-in section of the deck. From his new vantage point, through the tears of pain in his eyes, Arison could see that everything above him was on fire. He struggled to reach a morphine ampule on his belt but discovered he couldn't bear to use his fractured right arm. "That failure," he wrote, "kept me alive, for had I reached it and taken an injection I would have most likely passed out and would then have drowned in the water in which I sat." The constant struggle to reach that ampule kept him conscious and, he thinks, saved his life. Twice he tried to hail passing crew for aid, but couldn't make a sound, because a fragment in his neck was pressing on his larynx.

This blast caught hold of Cliff Spencer, too. "One instant I was fine and the next I was blasted through the air for about twelve feet, fetching up on the amidships ladder rail, hanging head down, draped over the railing," he wrote. "Groggy, and disoriented, my first thought was, 'I'm hit.' I tried to right myself and as I did I felt a sharp blow as shrapnel from below hit me in the lower back. When I put weight on my right foot, the ankle wanted to turn. I reached down and felt that a portion of my right heel had been sliced away as if with a large knife." He moved numbly forward toward the radar room, was hit again, then found a shipmate from the Marine detachment, Allen B. Samuelson, calling for him from within the wreckage of a gun mount. Spencer saw that a gun recoil spring had impaled him through the neck, "giving the impression of a grotesque bow tie." Samuelson asked him for a life jacket. "I reassured him we were not sinking and told him that I would be right back with a life jacket."

On the bridge, Bruce McCandless, stunned, ears ringing, wondered where everyone had gone. Quartermaster Harry S. Higdon called out from the helm, "I've lost steering control, sir!" and spun the useless wheel to demonstrate. Making eighteen knots, the heavy cruiser, the helmsman found, was locked into a left turn. The new exec, Joseph Hubbard, contacted Central Station and instructed his first lieutenant, Lieutenant Commander Herbert E. Schonland, to shift steering and engine control to Battle Two, the after control tower that had been soaked in flames when the Betty bomber struck it that afternoon. "Hardly had this been accomplished," McCandless wrote, "when a shell plunged through the roof (overhead) of Battle Two, laying waste to this place for the second time in twelve hours, killing Hubbard and the men around him." Schonland ordered the ship's steering and engine control shifted to the conning tower.

Concussed and in shock, McCandless managed to tell Schonland that he didn't know where Captain Young and Admiral Callaghan were. He said he appeared to be the only officer alive on the bridge. That meant Schonland was the ship's senior officer. McCandless asked, "What are your orders?" As damage-control officer, Schonland had plenty to do belowdecks. Several holes in the hull were shipping water, flooding the second deck, located near the waterline. The valves that were used to flood the magazines were a problem, too. A shell hit up forward had killed the damage-control party and ruined the control panel used to open and close the valves. Stuck open, the valves let the water flow. The magazines filled and kept on filling. Soon water was pouring through the ventilation system and flooding other forward compartments. Additional water pumped aboard by firefighting crews added to the problem.

The *San Francisco* had at least twenty-five fires, but the remedy was shaping up to be worse than the disease. The ship faced a serious stability issue. Every time she turned, the water on board rushed the other way, throwing a massive amount of weight into the side of the ship on the outside of the turn. The "free-surface effect" of all this water could capsize the ship. Schonland realized that if he went to the bridge to take command, there would be no officer below who understood the delicate flooding situation. He instructed McCandless to "carry out the admiral's orders." If McCandless needed help, he said, he would come as soon as he had the stability problem in hand.

McCandless went down to the heavily armored enclosure below the bridge, joining two quartermasters, Higdon and Floyd A. Rogers, who took turns going aft to the smoke-filled central steering compartment to relieve the faltering steersman, whose job was physically onerous. Through the horizontal slits in the eight-inch armor of the conning tower, McCandless kept a close lookout ahead, keeping the ship in the open water between Savo Island and Guadalcanal. Spying the coast near Lunga, he decided that if it became necessary to beach the ship, he would be sure to do so in the American-controlled sector. As he proceeded along, he imagined himself to be straightening out his battle line, re-forming the assembled power of Task Group 67.4 behind the flagship. Behind the *San Francisco,* the *Portland* was advancing into the mix with Abe's battleships, too. The light cruiser *Helena* was blasting away at anything her gunners could find. The *Juneau,* behind her, leading the rear destroyers, lashed into targets near and far with five-inch fire. For all practical purposes, though, the task force had ceased to be a cohesive unit.

CLIFF SPENCER, having promised Allen Samuelson a life jacket, went to a life jacket locker, opened it, and found a man hiding inside. "This locker is too thin to protect you!" he hollered, and the marine displaced, only to be killed elsewhere minutes later. Retrieving a pair of life jackets, Spencer went to find Samuelson, stepping around the dead. When Spencer found him again and handed him the jacket, the marine clutched it to his chest and, as Spencer put it, "quietly passed from this vale of tears." Standing over the dead man, experiencing his first twinges of survivor's guilt, Spencer wrote, "In his final moments he was not in pain. The life jacket I gave him gave him comfort, and he just slipped away."

Then his right hand took an impact that felt like a baseball bat. Spencer saw that his thumb was blown back, leaving "mangled red meat where my hand attached to the wrist." A sergeant in his detachment, John Egan, was rallying survivors to get the silenced five-inch guns back into action. Seeing that Spencer would be of little help, Egan directed him to sickbay. As Spencer descended several ladders, the last one was ripped away and he fell in a heap to the quarterdeck. When he recovered his senses, he looked around and saw that all but one man from the gallery of five-inch mounts had been cut down. The lone survivor was a chief fire controlman, wounded but still standing. "His headset wires were cut off just below his chin and he was bleeding from the ears and nose," Spencer wrote. "He shouted the order repeatedly for his non-existent crews to 'fire.' He appeared to be dying on his feet and I knew he could not even hear me, let alone help me."

Lurching aft on one good leg over razor-edged debris, Spencer stepped over and around the human forms, careful to soften his path by treading on their sleeves and pant legs. One fallen sailor, thus disturbed, shouted, "Get off of me you SOB. I ain't dead yet." Spencer hid behind a searchlight platform as a Japanese destroyer appeared to port, firing with small arms. As tracers and small rounds ricocheted off bulkheads, he was hit again. He cried and tried to pray. From a dark corner of the ship, he heard another sailor sobbing. Recognizing the voice, he found it was someone he knew well and hailed him by name. "I'm no coward," the sailor said. "I just don't know what to do!" Spencer gave him a job. "He cut off most of my undershirt and wrapped it around my right hand.... He then half carried me down to the mess hall for treatment, talked to me while we sloshed our way forward through the starboard passageway, giving me encouragement every step of the way. Let me tell you, that sailor was no coward." In sickbay, a corpsman patched his hands and feet with large wound compresses, gave him two morphine syrettes, and sent him to the machine shop to convalesce. "I hobbled and waded through water and over fire hoses to the shop and went through the metal screen door. I hobbled over behind a large lathe, thinking it would protect me from any shell blast to port, and popped myself with a syrette." Under the influence of the morphine, named after the Greek god of dreams, Spencer laid his head on a life jacket and escaped from the nightmare.

WHEN JACK BENNETT reported to the *San Francisco*'s bridge, having seen most of the gun crews he was supervising cut down by gunfire, McCandless departed the conning tower. "Leaving Higdon at the forward slit and Rogers steering, I went back up to the navigation bridge to have another look for Captain Young and get him into conn where he could exercise command of his ship if he were still alive."

To a young officer whose training had never prepared him for the vertigo and shock of this butchery, restoring his captain to command must have seemed like a sensible way to set right a careening universe. McCandless found that his head had stopped a few small pieces of shrapnel. The ringing in his ears would not quit, but he was crisply alert to his surroundings. "Against a midnight-blue backdrop brilliant starshell flares drifted down to go out in the sea," he would write. "Red, white and blue tracers interlaced. Searchlights stabbed the darkness; the *Hiei* put a cluster of three on us, only to have them shot out by a hail of automatic weapons fire from half a dozen ships. Guns flashed yellow flame. Shell hits kicked up hot red sparks, often a flash; misses threw up splashes. Aboard the *Hiei* a shower of luminous snowflakes rose above her masthead and fell like a waterfall.

"The navigation bridge was a weird place indeed in the intermittent light of gunfire," McCandless continued. "It had been hit several times more during my brief absence. Bodies, helmeted and life-jacketed, limbs, and gear littered the deck. The siren was moaning and water was raining down through holes in the deck above from the ruptured water-cooling system of the forward 1.1-inch quads. I could not identify Captain Young in my hasty search of the navigation bridge, but left convinced that neither he nor anyone else up there would take further part in this action." He would not. Nor would Admiral Callaghan or any of his staff. On the starboard side of the flag bridge, McCandless found all of them. A battleship projectile had struck the underside of the navigation bridge from slightly abaft the beam and burst directly overhead. Littering the deck were the bodies of Callaghan and three lieutenant commanders on his staff, Louis M. LeHardy, Damon M. Cummings, and Jack Wintle. A fourth, Emmet O'Beirne, was unconscious but alive, the only survivor among the senior staff.

While making this grim discovery, McCandless stepped into a jagged hole in the deck, fell through, and stuck fast. As he wriggled free, he found himself looking out through another shell hole in the port bridge screen. Through it he could see a Japanese destroyer just a few hundred yards away, racing down the port side on a reverse course, firing into his ship. "Her first shots hit the forward part of the bridge just as I arrived on its after end, but she conveniently shifted to our port five-inch battery, which had taken her under fire. In this mutual mayhem one of our open mounts was hit directly, the others were swept by a storm of fragments. But one gun, firing in local control under chief boatswain's mate John McCullough, with the last round it got off, caused a large explosion on the destroyer's stern that looked like depth charges going off."

Around this time McCandless reached Schonland on the battle telephone and confirmed that Schonland was the senior surviving officer. With this fragile chain of command, the ship was, according to McCandless, "fighting by departments, each headed by a lieutenant commander. Schonland, in command, would keep us afloat and right side up; Rodney B. Lair would run the engineering plant, which was virtually intact; Wilbourne and Cone controlling our main and antiaircraft batteries, respectively, would engage any enemy ships they could identify; I would essay the role of navigator; and Dr. Edward S. Lowe would attend to the wounded.

"We had good interior communications (despite a shortage of talkers) over the sound-powered battle telephones, but because of indoctrination and training, little coordination between departments was necessary: officers and enlisted men assumed leadership, saw things that needed to be done and got about doing them without waiting to be told. This is not the best way to run a ship, but it is surprising how far the momentum of a well-trained outfit will carry when its leaders are cut down."

31

Point Blank

THAT NIGHT THE TORPEDO MARKSMANSHIP OF THE JAPANESE HAD been practiced to the usual high professional standard. Long Lances gutted the *Laffey* and the *Atlanta*. Now the hull-busting weapons found the middle of the American line.

It was nearly 2 a.m., barely fifteen minutes since first contact. Captain DuBose of the *Portland* had settled on a northerly course. He was blowing salvos at a target on his starboard beam when a torpedo, probably fired by the *Yudachi*, bubbled in and struck aft on the starboard side. The blast chewed into the cruiser's fantail, leaving a rough, semicircular bite about sixty feet in diameter. The blast destroyed eighteen compartments, sheared off the inboard screws, and disabled turret three by heaving it from its roller path. A large piece of hull plating, torn out, extended into the sea and scooped a cataract of water, forcing the ship into a sharp right turn that the jammed rudder was helpless to correct. As the ship began circling, nothing the helmsman did with the rudder or the engines could straighten her course.

After the *Portland* finished staggering through her first clockwise circle, the *Hiei* appeared at four thousand yards dead ahead. As his ship came right, Lieutenant Commander Shanklin's forward eight-inch turrets engaged, firing four salvos as they trained left through the cruiser's swing to the right, planting an estimated ten to fourteen hits into the ship. As flames washed through her superstructure, the *Hiei* boomed in return, hitting the *Portland* with a pair of fourteen-inch bombardment projectiles that squandered most of their force by exploding on contact with the armor instead of penetrating.

An exact chronicle of events was beyond anyone's reach now, although a collage of impressions was indelible and immediate to all within the tempest. DuBose saw an unidentified large ship sundered by a great blast. He saw the *San Francisco* burning. The *Helena* steamed by close aboard to starboard, drawing clear, her six-inch batteries fast-cycling at targets in the dark. Chick Morris was caught in the spell of what the engines of naval war had wrought. "Other ships, blazing just as brilliantly, rushed through the night like giant torches held aloft by invisible swimmers. It was a picture too vast for the imagination, and even when it was over no man could quite put the flaming bits of the puzzle together or be sure of what he had seen."

The *Hiei*, fires raging all through her now, drew abeam the *Juneau*. The Japanese battleship was "wallowing there like a wounded monster, spouting a hell of flame, but still very much in action," the *Juneau*'s Joseph Hartney would write. "Her searchlights flashed on, fingered across the 2,000 yards of water and seemed to waver and then clamp down on us." Hartney swiveled his fifties at the light. "I felt nothing now. I was just part of the gun that was bouncing in my hand." The antiaircraft cruiser's five-inch batteries slashed into the enemy warship. The tracers looked from afar like "a bridge of red-hot steel between us and the target."

The trio of Japanese destroyers from the disengaged side of Abe's formation entered the mix after the *Hiei* and *Kirishima* cleared their lines of fire to the south. The *Asagumo*, *Murasame*, and *Samidare* sighted strange ships burning everywhere. The *Murasame* jabbed with the *Juneau*, trading salvos and loosing a spread of eight torpedoes.

A torpedo caught the *Juneau* in the belly, on the port side near the forward fire room. Joseph Hartney felt his ship leap and shake in the air and fall back down, heavier on the water than before, listing to port. The explosion ruptured internal bulkheads and buckled the deck. The fire-control system serving her eight twin five-inch turrets failed. Oil fumes leaked up from within. Her chief engineer thought her keel was broken.

The stricken cruiser veered toward an unidentified Japanese ship whose duress was similar. Seeing her sailors leaping from her burning decks and struggling to escape her fire-eaten passageways, Hartney called it "a weird, unforgettable pageantry that Dante himself could not have dreamed up." When a lookout shouted a warning of a collision, the quartermaster in the after control station, on a quick order from the exec, evaded in time. The *Juneau*'s reward for ducking the impact and opening the range again was another fusillade of gunfire into her superstructure. One of her stacks took a hard hit, casting the ruins of its searchlights from their platform onto the deck below. A fourteen-incher smashed into the mess hall triage, killing all the wounded there and their attendants. In the tangle of remaining steel plating, it was difficult to distinguish bulkhead from deck from overhead.

Throughout the American squadron, a hundred small catastrophes played out. The *Portland,* torpedoed and circling; the *San Francisco,* shattered but game. The *Atlanta,* a leaking, burning wreck; the *Juneau,* torpedoed and drunk in the keel; the *Laffey* sinking; the *Cushing,* still afloat but a lost cause; the *Sterett,* in a crossfire and burning. On the *Laffey,* whose propellers had been shorn away with the rest of her fantail, her hull nearly broken in two, a brief argument ensued between Captain Hank and his engineering officer, Lieutenant Barham, about whether the ship could be saved. "Chief, just get me going and I'll get you out of this," Hank said. But the engineer recommended abandoning ship. Barham asked for permission to let boats over the side, the least he could do for crew who had already gone over the rail. The captain approved. As Barham left to see about that task, Hank passed the order to abandon ship. Soon thereafter the fires reached a powder magazine. The eruption tore loose the deck, and shattered steel filled the air. "My first reaction was one of surprise—it was as if an old and trusted friend had suddenly hit me with a baseball bat," Tom Evins remembered. This catastrophe was the last the ship would suffer. Hank was never seen again.

Such catastrophes were often private experiences for their victims, unwitnessed by ships even in close proximity. As Bruce McCandless would write, "That these disasters could occur within such a short distance of the flagship and not be observed from her bridge seems incomprehensible; that this was the case testified to the intensity of the firestorm about the flagship herself." Whenever things looked bad, the one thing Admiral Nimitz liked to remind his staff was that "the enemy is hurting, too." And he was.

Once the *Hiei* finished her pass against the *Helena,* Abe's flagship had grappled with virtually the whole American line. Her entire superstructure was a conflagration, fiercely lit from within. That vast steel complex, towering over the two sleek and angular twin-mounted fourteen-inch turrets on her forecastle, looked to Jack Cook, one of Captain Hoover's Marine orderlies, "like a huge apartment building completely engulfed in flames. It was the most amazing sight I ever saw." Any number of U.S. ships could take credit for the result. Enough of them had crossed the battleship's path to make most all claims plausible. Among witnesses the predominant emotion seemed to be awe, not joy. These molten ruins had recently been proud, striving, and human. On a night like this, it was difficult not to relate to the enemy's plight, even as one celebrated it. In the midst of his 1898 victory at the Battle of Santiago de Cuba, the U.S. admiral Jack Philip said: "Don't cheer, men. Those poor devils are dying." Such a situation called for the right combination of satisfaction and solemnity.

The idea that fast battleships like the *Hiei* and the *Kirishima* would sweep the seas of heavy cruisers like the *San Francisco* and the *Portland*, one-third their size, turned out to be unfounded, at least in a battle fought at hull-scraping ranges where heavier armor was no significant advantage. It was probably the *San Francisco* that inflicted the *Hiei*'s most consequential wound, a two-meter-wide hole in her starboard quarter that quickly flooded the steering room and shorted the steering engine. With generators short-circuited, the Japanese battleship lost use of her turrets and her hydraulic steering. The secondary battery was disabled by the destruction of its control tower. Despite the battering the *Hiei* took from some fifty eight-inch and eighty-five five-inch hits, there was little underwater damage and not much flooding aside from the breach of the steering room.

Around this time, Admiral Abe, struck in the face by shrapnel and probably concussed, must have been operating on reflexes and adrenaline, for he would remember nothing of the battle after he was hit. Sometime around 2 a.m., distracted by his wounds and flinching at the ferocity of the American gunfire, and perhaps even believing he was facing a superior force, Abe decided to cancel the bombardment of Henderson Field. He ordered a general withdrawal.

In their flooding compartment, the *Hiei*'s steersmen labored by hand and muscle to keep the ship navigable. Because they could not turn as sharply as the *Kirishima*, which started her reversal of course from a position on the *Hiei*'s port quarter, the *Kirishima* turned inside the flagship's arc, remaining concealed behind Abe's burning ship while she came to a homeward course at high speed. As the action drew away from the *Portland*, Captain DuBose was disoriented. "In the confused picture of burning and milling ships it became impossible to distinguish friend from foe." Gunners on the destroyer *Samidare* mistook the *Hiei* for a U.S. ship. Her commander was preparing a torpedo spread when a correct identification was made, but not before the battleship had fired her secondary battery at the *Samidare* in turn.

Callaghan's ships never drew a good front-sight bead on the *Kirishima*. Her only damage by direct fire was a single eight-inch hit on the quarter-deck. In parting, the Japanese battleship's after turret lofted a last salvo at the *San Francisco*, a pair of fourteen-inchers fired straight back over the fantail.

The *Kirishima* would escape to fight another day. The *Hiei* would have a longer residence in Savo Sound.

AS THE HELENA PASSED the circling *Portland* and raced after the *San Francisco,* her main battery directors located a target to starboard, receding at about nine thousand yards. Less than half a minute later, the unidentified vessel opened fire on the *San Francisco.* It was a destroyer. Instantly, Hoover turned slightly to bring his five turrets to bear. The object of the light cruiser's continuous-automatic fury was Captain Tameichi Hara's *Amatsukaze.*

Hara had committed a cardinal sin of naval tactics. "Shell drunk," as he described himself, he neglected to order his searchlight off after taking the *San Francisco* under fire. Suddenly under a terrible barrage, Hara's ship reeled. He ordered his gunners to check fire, his searchlight operator to douse the light, and his deckhands to lay a smoke screen. "I hunched my back and clung to the railing. The blast was so strong, it almost threw me off the bridge. The detonations were deafening. I got sluggishly to my feet, but my mind was a complete blank for several seconds. Next, I felt over my body, but found no wounds." Hara was a lucky one. His ship took some three dozen hits from the *Helena,* almost all of them blasting holes a meter or more wide in his ship. The *Amatsukaze*'s hydraulics failed, freezing the gun mounts and the rudder. A warrant officer on the rangefinder had his skull split by a sliver of steel. That same hit tossed Hara's gunnery officer over the side. In the radio room below him, everyone was dead. Gil Hoover's gunners had about ninety seconds to batter the *Amatsukaze*—firing 125 six-inch rounds—before the *San Francisco* interfered with their line of sight and Hoover ceased fire. The only damage the *Helena* suffered in the exchange appeared to have been a five-inch hit on her high-mounted after turret, which blew away the leather bloomer from the center gun and gouged its bronze chase so that it could not recoil. The next time the gun was loaded, Lieutenant Earl Luehman, the turret officer, found it would not fire. Confronted with a hot, live round in his breech, he quickly ordered it ejected. When the six-inch round hit the deck, its powder scattered and caught fire, raging briefly until a firefighting team mustered.

In the *San Francisco,* damage-control parties were working furiously to keep the floodwaters from overturning the ship. No pumps were available to fight them. There were no drains on the ship's second deck, where the flooding was worst. With free surface water sloshing back and forth with each rudder movement, changing the ship's center of gravity unpredictably, the water level was rising by the minute. There was nowhere to send it. The first challenge was to stop the inflow. A crew led by Ensign Robert Dusch crawled forward through the flooded passageways and compartments, feeling for the valves that controlled the magazine flooding and groping with reach rods to turn them shut. They struggled like run-blocking offensive linemen to prop mattresses against holes in the hull, no small task on a ship maneuvering at battle speed.

When Schonland climbed out of Central Station to see what could be done, the water was threatening to spill over the top of the hatch coaming that led down to his belowdecks compartment. His men, trapped in the dark and relying on handheld lanterns for light, were sorry to see the popular officer leave them. When some water came sloshing over the coaming, they feared they might be drowned by a deluge from above.

To get rid of the water, Schonland and Ensign Dusch directed the crew to position mattresses in the port passageway from the Marine compartment to serve as a sluice gate. Then they opened the door and opened the hatch to the air lock leading down to the number one fire room. Warning the men below that "We're going to take water down there, a lot of it, and fast," he proceeded to drain the second deck compartments into the lower decks of the ship, to serve as ballast. From there bilge pumps could begin discharging water out of the ship.

Noticing his ship's drunken gait as she turned in a lazy circle, Lieutenant (j.g.) Jack Bennett returned forward and found Bruce McCandless lying unconscious outside the conning tower. A large shell had struck atop it, about two feet over McCandless's head. The thickly armored overhead held fast, but flames roared in through the viewing slits through which the lieutenant commander had been peering with his binoculars. The device probably saved McCandless's eyes, but the concussion laid him out flat. How long the quartermaster, Floyd Rogers, had been conning the ship alone, passing orders (his own) to the after steering station, was impossible for Bennett to tell. "Rogers couldn't see the compass and the gyro was fifteen degrees out anyway. He couldn't see. It was pitch black, and with a headset on he couldn't hear. But he kept his cool," Bennett said. Callaghan and his staff lay scattered around the deck, their bodies without a mark of violence on them, soaked by water leaking from a cooling tank on a 1.1-inch mount.

Since the loss of electrical power had disabled the flagship's sprinkler system, bucket brigades went to work battling the two dozen fires within the ship. All the water they might have needed was sloshing around in the ship three decks underfoot, but with the pumps and mains out of order, they had to lower buckets into the sea on lanyards made from telephone wire.

The flooding was serious, but it would have doubtlessly been fatal to the flagship had Abe's battleships used armor-piercing ordnance instead of high-explosive and incendiary rounds meant for bombardment. If this was a gift to the *San Francisco* as far as her hull integrity went, it extracted a steep cost in casualties topside. Eugene Tarrant, the captain's cook, was a standby fuze setter on one of the five-inch gun mounts. He was also detailed, as many in S Division were, to assist the ship's two doctors and four pharmacist's mates in tending to the wounded. Early in the battle, the call went over the loudspeakers for all medics to report to the well deck on the double. Their workload did not relent.

Assigned to work with a pharmacist's mate, Tarrant treated and bandaged those he could, gave morphine to those who needed it, and put tags on the rest. If someone needed a tourniquet, or an emergency procedure that was painful or invasive, it was Tarrant who held him down and tried to settle him while the pharmacist's mate went to work. He quickly ran out of syrettes, so he started taking them from fallen officers, each of whom carried six on his belt. When Tarrant ran low again, he started splitting them two ways, then three. He wondered if the lower dosages did any good.

Tarrant helped lead a fire hose around turret three into the burning aircraft hangar, set afire by enemy gunfire. The planes had been catapulted away, but plenty of flammable things remained: fabric parts, textiles, gasoline, and stored aerial depth charges. A pile of kapok life jackets was burning fiercely. When that fire was suppressed, the remains of one of the ship's floatplane pilots were found underneath. He had died where he tried to hide. A first-class boatswain's mate, Reinhardt J. Keppler from Wapato, Washington, fought the fires in the hangar and elsewhere and ministered to the injured despite his own severe wounds. They were mortal. Before he finally collapsed from blood loss, he saved several others from the same fate.

Leonard Roy Harmon, a mess attendant first class, was a genial kind of guy, big, tall, and, according to Tarrant, fun to be around. Hailing from Cuero, Texas, he was clean-cut and very country. He didn't drink and didn't smoke and was awkward on the dance floor. He had a girl back home whom he planned to marry. Until then, he bided his time in the fleet and made friends where he could find them—among the cooks and mess attendants. "We were the only game in town," Tarrant said. "If we didn't get along together, we were in terrible shape. All we had was each other. We went ashore together, went to dances, picked out our girls."

Tarrant and Harmon were called topside, given stretchers, or "metal baskets" as Tarrant called them, and assigned to help the pharmacist's mates locate and rescue wounded from lower decks. The work would have been strenuous even if the ship hadn't been maneuvering under heavy fire. Ladders were blown away throughout the ship, hatches jammed, and the threat of shrapnel, fire, and flood all-encompassing. Moving up and down from below to the boat deck, and then carrying the wounded back to fantail, was exhausting, even for a muscular sailor.

Tarrant had never felt closely attached to the ship. He was willful and not shy about meeting the gaze of those who had been raised not to like him. Even if the shipboard culture hadn't been one of exclusion, it was usually hard for a man who had his own mind to feel part of the team. But now, moving around the ship tending to the *San Francisco*'s wounded, Tarrant found the alienation washing away. His ship dying. Everyone at risk. Common cause under a buffeting of explosions. A burning in the shoulder and legs, the clatter of a metal stretcher going up a ladder. Blood on his sleeves. The sound of a shipmate's moaning.

"You move like you're moving in a dream," he said. "You're trained to do this. And you reach a point where you're going like a robot." In the dark, on the quarterdeck, near the ruins of an antiaircraft mount Tarrant heard: "*Help* me." Dimly he saw a figure slumped in the mount's steel trainer's seat. He grasped the man's shoulder in order to assess his wounds, and the shoulder and the arm, all of it, came off in his hand. A spray of warm blood splashed across his face and spread down the front of his shirt. He reacted as all medics were trained. He made a fist. He stuck it into the hole above the armpit. With the bleeding stanched, the pharmacist's mate went to work wadding and wrapping the wound. "I dreamed about that for nights and days and years."

Elsewhere on the ship, Leonard Roy Harmon was helping a pharmacist's mate named Lynford Bondsteel. Harmon's numerous small acts of duty and mercy included pulling the unconscious navigator Rae Arison out of the puddle in which he lay, saving him from an unlikely drowning. Harmon had comforted the executive officer Crouter as he lay dying in his stateroom. He took him out into the passageway and stayed by his side as he passed. Harmon was on the well deck, heading with Bondsteel to the aid station in the hangar, when a burst of tracers began snapping into the bulkheads around them. Harmon interposed, pushing Bondsteel down so hard he almost fell down a ladder as he himself was engulfed by the swarm. Tarrant would find Harmon later, unconscious with a wound in his head. He spoke to his friend, urging him to fight. "Harmon suffered for quite a while before finally letting go. It seemed to me to last forever." Tarrant found another friend from the wardroom mess, Charles Jackson, on the deck near the officer's galley, his abdomen opened by a blast. Herbert Madison, too, Tarrant's partner during countless sparring matches on the quarterdeck, with a body so beautifully chiseled and heroic, was dead but without a cut on his body, slain by shock.

There were many men to tend to, of all rates and races and regions, but never did one of them say to Tarrant, "Take your hands off me. I don't want to be saved by your kind." Men like the Georgia boys in the *Monssen* who couldn't be understood over the battle telephones, or the aggressively unsu- perstitious backwoods souls on the *Fletcher* who had laughed at the ill omens of so many thirteens—not one of them ever called Tarrant the name that would have been routine for the times under ordinary circumstances. "They'd look at me and they'd thank me," Tarrant said. "Some of them, while they were dying, were delirious. They called me 'mother,' or 'brother,' or something like that. They'd say, 'Hold me mommy,' and I'd hold them. We all bleed, we all grieve, we love, we hate, we do all the things that any other human being does. We all learned that, and it really applied, on that night."

THE CHALLENGE FOR VESSELS in the rear of the American and Japanese lines, the last to make contact, was to make sense of the chaos that churned the seas in front of them and to do something useful in confused close com- bat. "I am reluctant to compare what happened next to a land battle," wrote Julian Becton, the exec of the destroyer *Aaron Ward*, "yet in this case the con- fused drive of our ships right into the middle of the Japanese formation did somewhat resemble the charge immortalized by Tennyson. Every American ship took the bit and raced at Admiral Abe's forces. We were in among them before they knew what was happening, firing every gun that would bear, launching torpedoes port and starboard."

From the bridge of the *Amatsukaze,* just a few hundred yards away, Cap- tain Hara saw the *Yudachi* ahead, guns blazing, cutting in front of the Amer- icans and nearly colliding bow-to-bow with the *Aaron Ward,* which was following the *Juneau,* and leading the four rear destroyers. The second U.S. tin can, the *Barton,* had to reverse her engines to avoid colliding with the *Aaron Ward* from astern. Less than a minute had passed when, with the *Bar- ton* lagging about a thousand yards off the *Aaron Ward*'s starboard quarter, two Long Lances struck the *Barton,* producing a monstrous explosion and an incandescent ball of fire. In the *Aaron Ward,* Bob Hagen had a close-up view. Commander Wylie, the exec of the *Fletcher*, bringing up the rear, wrote that the ship "exploded and simply disappeared in fragments." Tameichi Hara rubbed his eyes in disbelief, believing his torpedoes had done this lethal work. "The ship, broken in two, sank instantly. I heaved a deep sigh. It was a spectacular kill and there was a roaring ovation from my crew."

The *Barton*'s survivors, a mere 42 of her complement of 276, were splashing into the sea even before they could grasp what had happened. Only two officers survived, and just one man from the hundred-odd men stationed belowdecks, a radioman named Albert Arcand, who narrowly escaped the after radio compartment through a surge of seawater that plunged through the overhead hatch as he spun it open. They were soon set upon by the *O'Bannon,* speeding east, away from the battle zone and right into their midst.

The experience was terrifying for the survivors in the water. The bow wave tossed them up and away, then the suction of the passing hull, clearly emblazoned with the number 450, drew them back in toward her, the wake marking the path of the churning twin screws. There followed an explosion, probably caused by depth charges detonating. The blast lifted the *O'Bannon*'s stern out of the water as she steamed by, leaving untold casualties among the men in the water.

Bob Hagen was still thunderstruck by the demolition of the *Barton* off his starboard quarter, helping Captain Gregor distinguish friend from foe, when the *Aaron Ward* made the passing acquaintance of an enemy destroyer, probably the *Yudachi*. The American ship got the better of the fierce, brief exchange, leaving the *Yudachi* dead in the water. A few minutes later, the *Aaron Ward* caught a big one. A fourteen-inch bombardment round tore a thirty-inch hole in the bulkhead outboard of the galley on the port side and exploded, swirling up a gust of shrapnel that flew in all directions. Hagen was cut down by a concussion that burst upward at him, suffering multiple wounds from fragments of silverware and shards of glass. His left bicep was minced. A four-inch-long bolt stuck in his thigh. Dazed and bleeding badly, he tried to turn away the pharmacist's mates who tended to him, but both put a syrette into him. One of them fixed him a tourniquet around his left arm, and before long he was in "la la land," asleep in his own blood.

Steaming behind the *Barton*, second to last in line, the destroyer *Monssen* loosed five torpedoes, one at a time, at a battleship off her starboard beam. A few minutes later, after counting several hits on that target, Lieutenant Commander Charles E. McCombs, her captain, fired five more torpedoes in succession at a destroyer. Ahead to port, he could see a U.S. destroyer, probably the *Aaron Ward,* getting the worst of an exchange with a Japanese ship at close range. His gun boss turned the *Monssen*'s four guns in the American ship's defense and let loose until the enemy ceased firing.

As star shells popped overhead, McCombs turned his rudder full right and saw a destroyer ahead to starboard, less than a thousand yards away, unmistakably Japanese with double white bands painted around her stack. The *Monssen*'s starboard twenties laced into her, throwing a thousand rounds into her topside stations. McCombs's after five-inch gun added half a dozen more. McCombs cursed the illumination from the star shells fired by what he suspected were friendly ships. As a precaution, he switched on and off the trio of colored lights on his superstructure that signaled his identity as an American vessel. And that was when a wave of hellfire washed over the small ship.

At around two twenty-five, the *Monssen* absorbed a fusillade. A five-inch shell hit the forward gun, killing the entire crew. The handling rooms serving guns two and three took hits that put them out of action. Another shell struck the *Monssen* in the engineering spaces, cutting steam lines and rupturing a throttle manifold. Off the starboard bow, a larger enemy ship was letting go in a deeper, statelier rhythm. One of these heavier projectiles seems to have been an incendiary. The oversized Roman candle hit the *Monssen*'s superstructure and turned it into a bonfire. The smaller shells hitting the ship all along her length became too numerous to count; McCombs would estimate them at forty.

The man who had captained the *Monssen* at the start of the Guadalcanal campaign, Commander Roland Smoot, had fallen ill and was hospitalized at Nouméa. When Smoot's replacement was killed in a plane crash en route to the theater, fortune arranged for Lieutenant Commander McCombs, Smoot's exec, to ascend to command. McCombs might have pondered this conspiracy of fate as he stood in the midst of the blaze on his bridge, his escape aft blocked by fires eating up the passageway, and his route out and down blocked by the sudden absence of ladders, torn from the bulkheads by the gunfire. With all of officers' country afire, with the ship's power dead, all guns silent, all fire mains without pressure, both battle dressing stations hit, and virtually every soul on the ship, including McCombs, wounded by shrapnel or worse, the captain passed the order to abandon ship. A torpedo, a white track lit by star shell light, broached and porpoised fifty yards ahead. Two more passed underneath the ship. A fourth buzzed astern on the surface, its propeller kicking up a spray.

As the *Monssen* slowed and settled, the *Fletcher* passed her to port. By the time the *Fletcher,* the last ship in Callaghan's column, entered battle, the outcome had been decided, the worst damage inflicted. The destroyer's executive officer, Joseph Wylie, could hear metal fragments from the *Barton* raining down on the deck as he watched the SG radar in the chart house aft of the bridge. His skipper, Commander William Cole, appreciated the value of the advanced equipment even if Admiral Callaghan hadn't. Cole broke with traditional practice by putting his senior subordinate, Wylie, in the chart house instead of in the after control station. Wylie was sketching the radar readings, but the effort was superfluous now that the principal opposing ships had spent themselves and were looking to regroup and withdraw. Cole conned the *Fletcher* to a southerly course toward Guadalcanal, then swung east to run parallel to shore. The destroyer was near Lunga Point when lookouts spied a large ship shooting at something in the north. Recognizing an enemy vessel, Cole turned to unmask his torpedo batteries and launched a spread. Seeing explosions, he claimed several hits on the distant target. Wylie and his captain had been speaking through a ventilation port in the bulkhead between the chart house and the bridge. Through it now, Cole hollered to Wylie, "Hey, Joe, aren't you glad our wives don't know where we are right now?"

32

<hr/>

Among the Shadows

GUN BARRELS COOLED AS THE NIGHT PULLED ITS CURTAIN CLOSED again, leaving the world dark, quiet, and small. The senses of men throughout the task force had withstood a ferocious assault. But the peace had a wounded character, and men found it discouraging. As the *Helena* continued along, heading toward Savo Island, Gil Hoover worried that he had heard nothing from the *San Francisco*. The *Portland* checked in, requesting a tow, but Hoover decided now was not the time for that. The flagship had gone off the air at the height of the engagement, shortly after the base units met. Where had she gone?

It was around 2:30 a.m. when Hoover decided, in the apparent absence of Callaghan and Scott, that he had in all likelihood ascended to officer in tactical command. His first task was to contact surviving ships and arrange a rendezvous. From the *Helena*'s navigation bridge, he called all ships over the TBS. "*Form 18. Course 092. Speed 18. Don't answer.*" The message instructed the task force to head east at eighteen knots. Hoover didn't want everyone to break radio silence now, but over the TBS came a voice from the *O'Bannon*, asking him to repeat the course heading. Hoover did so, adding, "*Unable raise other big boys.*" In the indeterminate distance, he saw ships believed to be Japanese firing at each other.

There came a cry as a lookout spotted a large ship ahead, off the port bow. Hoover started following it about eight hundred yards astern. "That sure looks like a battleship," Robert Howe said to another sailor. He surmised that it had to be friendly or they never would have gotten so close. "We didn't know where it could have come from, but we were sure glad to have a battleship on our side."

Then a flare popped overhead and began swinging down on a parachute. It was "like sitting under a big streetlight," Howe said. Studying the ship more closely, he noticed sailors in foreign white uniforms. "We had no trouble telling that it was a Japanese battleship," he said.

After a few minutes following astern the enemy monster—likely the *Kirishima,* scarcely damaged at all and withdrawing at high speed—Hoover broke away and turned east. His PPI scope showed a scattering of green blips sliding north. Abe's force was withdrawing in disarray.

Soon another phantom loomed in the night, pressing in on the starboard bow. Bin Cochran identified it as a cruiser of the *Atlanta* class, knifing straight for the *Helena*'s midsection. Since the *Atlanta* lay dead in the water, this had to have been the *Juneau.* Hoover ordered a hard right rudder, and as the stern started swinging left, Cochran tensed for an impact on the starboard quarter. Somehow the blow never fell, and soon the *Juneau* was gone again in the night.

That ship was consumed with her own problems. The *Juneau* had no fire control to her turrets. Her fantail was broken and buckled all the way forward to the hip-mounted five-inch gun on the starboard deck. Her electrical devices were subsisting on thin gruel from the emergency diesel generator. Several large belowdecks compartments were full of the dead, snuffed out by the blast of a torpedo in her engineering spaces. Having lurched through the enemy formation with a broken keel and a crippled main battery, the *Juneau*'s sailors came out badly shaken. They were no more rattled and no less gallant than any other men in the task force, but under fire, men could feel the impulse to claw at the steel decks with their hands to escape the killing hail, or vomit on deck, or weep.

According to Allen Heyn, a gunner's mate stationed on the *Juneau*'s fantail near the depth charge mount where the oldest of the five Sullivan brothers, George, stood watch, "It seemed like everyone was giving it to us, you know. There was a big flash, and the salvos would hit the water on one side of the ship and splash all over and then they would hit on the other side.... Then something hit up forward. I don't know what it was because it hit again and the ship shook all over. The ship seemed to be out of control kinda." With most of that behind them, they found refuge in the night. The *Juneau*'s skipper, Lyman Swenson, thought he might find shelter near Malaita, hole up to see about repairs.

The majority of Callaghan's ships—now Hoover's ships—had taken as heavily as they had given, but the *Helena*'s own damage was slight: just five hits, none of serious consequence. With a single man killed and two hospitalized, she was deeply lucky. Slugging through two first-order nighttime brawls in two months, she had taken scarcely a scratch. Smart reliance on SG radar had allowed Hoover to refrain from the standard but generally suicidal act of opening searchlight shutters within gun range of an alerted foe. He wisely chose to illuminate his targets on invisible frequencies, with his radars.

At length, late in the night, the *O'Bannon,* the *Fletcher,* and finally the *Sterett* checked in on the radio. The *Sterett*'s captain, Jesse Coward, bristled at first when he was asked if he intended to retire. "We'll fight her until we sink!" he said. He had two torpedoes left in the tubes. When his torpedo officer informed him the mount was inoperable, Coward turned to his exec, Lieutenant Frank Gould, and said, "Frank, let's get the hell out of here." As the destroyer left the area, six or seven burning pyres dotted the sea behind her.

Belowdecks, firefighting crews played their streams over smoldering bedding and red-hot shell cases, stuffed the holes in the hull with mattresses, and shored them. "Bodies, mattresses and other debris sloshed back and forth with the movement of the ship," Perry Hall said. "Footing was difficult and battle lanterns provided the only light. I had no idea what time it was or where the ship was. I knew we were maneuvering using the screws because I couldn't hear the rudder."

Ahead lay the outline of Florida Island. "We had not seen an American ship for a long time, and I began to wonder if we were the only one left," the *Sterett*'s gunnery officer, Lieutenant Cal Calhoun, wrote. Surveying the wreckage of his ship, which held the remains of twenty-eight men, Calhoun felt "strangely detached, as if I were on another planet surveying the earth in miniature." The feeling persisted till the ship reached Lengo Channel, where she would eventually catch up with Captain Hoover's survivors.

STILL TRYING TO GATHER his surviving vessels, Hoover sent the instruction *"Answer"* to the *San Francisco,* but none came. Where was Callaghan? Norman Scott and the *Atlanta* were unaccounted for, too. Finally a lookout announced the sighting of yet another unidentified ship on the port bow. The *Helena*'s killing train was set quickly rolling. Hoover ordered, "Shift target!" and Rodman Smith, the gunnery officer, coached his turrets on the new bearing. This ship, spectral and suspicious, had been shattered. Not a pane of glass remained in her. Fires glowed in several places on deck.

The officer-of-the-deck of the damaged mystery ship was studying the *Helena* through his binoculars as she overtook him to starboard. From about two thousand yards away, he could make out her twin stacks and five sleek turrets—all trained right at him. Then, in the *Helena*'s superstructure, a light signaled the letters "H-I-S H-I S." An encoded challenge signal required a prompt reply, but neither of the two officers up forward on the battered vessel's navigation bridge, Bruce McCandless nor John Bennett, knew what reply to give to this challenge. The dispatch containing the reply codes assigned for use that day had been lost in the fires. Though the codes had also been scrawled with chalk on the bulkhead of the flag bridge, the metal where they had been recorded was thoroughly punctured and scorched. Any attempt to memorize the codes had been "driven from my mind by the events of the last hour," McCandless wrote. "In seconds, unless the correct reply was given, fifteen six-inch and four five-inch would fire into us." Virtually all of the principal means of communication—TBS radio, searchlights, signal flags and halyards, fighting lights—had been destroyed or made inoperable. The steam line to the flagship's siren and whistle had been punctured by splinters. The signalmen had a blinker light, but they hesitated to respond because they knew something their officers didn't: that the three-letter reply code specified for that day was "J-A-P." One signalman, Vic Gibson, told a colleague who was holding a blinker gun, "If you don't want them shooting at us, you'd better send them J-A-P." Nothing doing. The signalman felt that a response that like was as likely to invite gunfire as forestall it. The *Helena*'s batteries were seconds from turning loose when a *San Francisco* signalman, on order from McCandless, blinked a message in Morse from the bridge. "c38 . . . c38 . . ."

Seeing this signal—a reasonable approximation of the *San Francisco*'s hull number, CA-38—Rodman Smith relaxed his grip on the firing key and the *Helena*'s gun captains stood down. "Thank God the *Helena* accepted that," Jack Bennett said. "Captain Hoover, may he live forever, took a second look before letting us have it," McCandless wrote. The sad news quickly followed via the flashlight that the *San Francisco* was bereft of its senior leadership. On hearing this, Gil Hoover signaled that he would take command of the remnant of Task Force 67 for the journey home.

By 3:45 a.m., in the company of the *Fletcher* (untouched despite the numerological odds against her), Hoover's survivors cleared Sealark Channel. The *O'Bannon* found them in the channel with her SG radar and took station ahead. In Indispensable Strait, between Guadalcanal and Malaita, the damaged *Sterett* joined up, her steersman struggling with a balky rudder that was urging the ship toward Guadalcanal's shoals. Then the *Juneau* appeared ahead to port. Hoover directed Captain Swenson's wobbly ship to fall in. Plying submarine-haunted waters, none of the ships was out of danger yet. Some of them were good candidates to sink even without further work by the enemy.

Simple navigation was a challenge for ships that had been through a bender such as the night action of November 13. Down twelve feet by the bow, listing slightly to port, the *Juneau* was swerving and skidding as if her long hull were jointed somewhere below. The swells crested near the gunwales, her one screw knocked from a bent shaft, water seeped through seams in the stress-fractured hull, and her auxiliary electrical generators were helpless to power all the pumps. By dawn her technicians had patched things together well enough. They even restored local control to one of her five-inch mounts. Swenson decided to press on south for Espiritu Santo.

Through the last hours before dawn, bearing the burden of 83 dead and 106 seriously wounded sailors, the *San Francisco* tailed the *Helena*'s dim silhouette ahead. "I hung on, occasionally calling her by blinker gun and steering for the answering flash of light," McCandless wrote. The *San Francisco*'s engines were good for twenty-eight knots, but steering the damaged ship was a more serious problem. In Sealark Channel, between Guadalcanal and Florida Island, Bennett relieved McCandless and quickly noticed that his quartermaster Rogers was having to repeat his orders over the sound-powered phones. The other quartermaster, Higdon, had gone to the smoky emergency steering compartment below, where the helm orders were being manually executed. Seeing the sluggish response from steering, Bennett suspected Higdon was woozy from smoke inhalation and told Rogers to keep him talking so he wouldn't pass out and leave the ship unnavigable.

When a lieutenant stationed in Sky Forward, Dick Marquardt, called down, "You're about to run aground on Malaita!" Bennett understood that he might be a little groggy himself, having lost sight of the *Helena* when she turned south while obscured in the island's silhouette. As he righted his course and fell in line again with Hoover, the decks heeled and a warning came from Bob Dusch, the damage-control whiz, that the rush of free surface water was wiping out the wooden shoring that held several critical mattress patches in place near the bow. When Bennett's relief finally arrived,

Bennett scrawled the zigzag plan in chalk on the conning tower door and handed the newcomer a watch that he had taken from one of Callaghan's slain staff officers. Then he went to look for Bruce McCandless.

Bennett found him in the captain's emergency cabin, sitting on the edge of the bunk, eyes glazed and with blood trickling down his face from shrapnel wounds in his forehead and ear. Bennett picked out as many bits of steel as he could before determining that McCandless didn't need emergency attention. He left him there, went down to the gun deck, and sprawled on the steel deck, using a Great War–era tin hat for "a wholly unsatisfactory pillow." There were no words for what they had just been through, and none for the fresh horrors they would find topside when sunrise came.

33

Atlanta Burning

THE NIGHT OF NIGHTMARES PASSED. AS THE SUN DREW BACK THE long shadows of Tulagi and Florida Island from Savo Sound, the remains of the night's struggle were revealed in all their ragged trauma.

Broken through the keel, her bow and stern drifting in different directions with the currents, the *Atlanta* lay dead in the water a few miles off Lunga Point. Still heavily afire, she was kept from breaking apart only by the latent tensile strength of her decks and the fickle mercy of a calm morning sea. Every heavy apparatus on the ship that was removable was jettisoned: an anchor and its chain, a whaleboat and its davits, four torpedoes found in the disabled port side tubes, and miscellaneous gear of all kinds—paravanes, gangways, smoke screen generators, depth charges.

By the first blush of dawn, Lloyd Mustin saw evidence of the astonishing volume of ordnance that flew over the ship that night. The mainmast near his aft air-defense station, only eight inches in diameter, was riddled with holes. All three forward turrets were knocked out, several of their six barrels sliced away. Like a cavern in a gray sea cliff, her forward engine room was a void. Filled with black water, it was a grave for a fine engineering department headed by Lieutenant Commander Arthur Loeser and chief machinist's mate Henry A. Wolfe. In the mess compartment above it, a heavy serving table had been "plastered flat against the overhead" by the force of the torpedo's blast.

A few rapid tugs on a flywheel spinner was all it took to get a gasoline-powered handy-billy pump growling. Dropped over the side, the inch-and-a-half-diameter suction hose could draw on a limitless supply of seawater to fight fires, with pressure enough to play a stream high into the superstructure, or anywhere else something was burning. On the *Atlanta* that morning, almost everything was burning.

"It is a matter of wonder to observe, at close hand, a steel warship on fire," wrote Bill McKinney, the electrician's mate. Having rushed topside up ladders and through compartments that were scorched and baking hot, he found that his rebreather expired much more quickly than the fifteen minutes it was rated for. Emerging on the main deck, he confronted a landscape aflame. The shipboard fires illuminated a bleak, steel-gray landscape that seemed deserted. "What is burning that makes the jagged edges around shell holes white hot?" he wondered. "Paint, other combustibles, but more possibly that the type of enemy shells contained thermite, contact with which makes almost anything burn." Ammunition didn't need help. Below, magazines full of rounds for the twenties were popping away, small heavy box by small heavy box, and so fiercely that they set the deck burning, melted right through it, spilled down into the compartment below, and set it on fire, too. It was unfortunate for the antiaircraft cruiser that she stored such a large volume of ammunition.

When the forward gun director was hit, the thick mass of wiring running down through the trunk was set aflame, another avenue for the fiery contagion. A locker containing pyrotechnics—flares and smoke markers—had taken a direct hit, too, producing a spectacular runaway blaze. As flames aspired to the top of the steel foremast, the fires devoured its base, melting through its thirty-inch diameter and felling the eighty-odd-foot-high tower to port, trapping men in the 1.1 clipping rooms. Damage-control parties managed to cut the foremast free, righting some of her starboard list.

According to McKinney, a terrified shipmate ran past him at one point shouting, "Get off. She's going to blow!" But the executive officer, Dallas Emory, had already countermanded an order to abandon ship, and McKinney was just as happy to stay aboard. "Better to be blown up than eaten up," he figured. Then McKinney happened upon "a bright idea": opening the fire main in his compartment and allowing seawater to flood the deck. He thought this would provide a buffer between the fires above and the magazine below. Emory, in his cabin writing a report by the light of a battle lantern, approved the request. "Just don't sink the ship," he advised. As McKinney opened the main, no one on board seemed to understand that the same free-surface effect that was plaguing the *San Francisco* could have cap-sized the *Atlanta* had the seas gotten rough.

Searching the ship for wounded, Raymond Leslie came upon a hole in the boat deck caused by an explosion from below. The steel plates, blown upward into a jagged rise, had to be carefully negotiated. Razor-edged hunks of steel, most of them the size of anvils, some as large as small cars, were scattered across the decks. In wreckage nearby, Leslie found two shipmates, both friends of his, trapped under some deck plating. He and the other rescuers set themselves close against the heavy steel, lifting with the legs. Their shipmates were pulled free and taken to an aid station. Later, after daylight, when Leslie and the others returned to the site, they would marvel that they had been able to move the plates at all. Joined by others, they tried again, just to sate their curiosity. They found now that they couldn't budge them.

McKinney and another electrician, Bob Tyler, "took a little time to get rid of some bodies that lay in the way of ship's work." According to McKinney, "I recall many corpses, badly torn up, but there was not a great deal of blood. Could the white-hot metal that killed them have had a cauterized effect? More probably the massive shock of death stopped the heart and no more blood was pumped." A particularly grisly place was gun number five, the hip mount on the starboard side. Trained aft, its entire left bulkhead had been torn open and lay nearly toppled over the side. Near the mess of charred metal they attempted to recover the body of a boatswain's mate, and it came in half in their arms. Another sailor, the mount's pointer, "hung out of his seat with his head gone from the nose up," McKinney wrote. "He was jammed in place by a jagged portion of the turret structure which had penetrated his back. We couldn't get him loose, so I entered the wrecked turret to push him from within. The remains of the Turret Captain hung over his booth railing like a large piece of burnt bacon." They finally got the pointer out of his seat and tumbled him overboard. As a young sailor walked to the lifeline to throw a dismembered arm overboard, he ate an apple with his free hand. Tyler explored the forward superstructure, which McKinney called "a horrifying spectacle of flesh and bone." Though most of the remains were beyond recognition, a hand was found wearing a Naval Academy ring engraved with the class year 1911. The navigator, Lieutenant Commander James Stuart Smith, sat in the starboard bridge chair, dead without a mark on him.

With the forward engine spaces gutted and the after boilers swamped, the ship was powerless to resist the currents that moved toward the beach. They threatened to carry the crippled *Atlanta* within range of Japanese artillery.

Commander Nickelson rallied a work party to lower the ship's remaining anchor to keep her from grounding near the Japanese-held section of the coast. Even with all hundred fathoms of heavy chain run out laboriously by hand, it still did not reach.

As the shoreward drift continued, Captain Jenkins sent Lloyd Mustin to the ship's armory to issue Springfield rifles to the crew. As daylight came, shots began ringing out all through the ship's topside spaces when the newly armed crewmen began firing on Japanese survivors paddling in the oil-drenched waters around the ship. "They were so deeply ingrained against capture that they wouldn't let us rescue them, for the most part," said Mustin. He ordered the snipers to stand down.

With more than half of her forty-five officers killed or wounded, and 153 of 700 enlisted men dead or missing, the *Atlanta* was ultimately fortunate to lie so close to Guadalcanal. From the auxiliary radio room, survivors called Naval Base Guadalcanal (a makeshift naval station and encampment commanded by the skipper of the late *Astoria*, Captain Bill Greenman, who adopted the title Commander, Naval Activities, Cactus-Ringbolt Area) and asked for small boats to take off the wounded. The sailors ashore responded swiftly, manning boats and venturing into the battle-littered sea. Bill Kennedy, a gunner's mate at the station, wrote, "The entire area was covered with a thick layer of oil; all kinds of debris was floating in it with survivors hanging on to whatever they could grab. They were all so black with oil that we had to come in close to see if they were ours or theirs. American survivors took precedence, of course; later in the day we went back out for the Japs but found very few. My boat didn't see any."

A small fleet of utility craft, known as "mike boats," began motoring out to the ship. Manned by marines, they pulled alongside and took off survivors. To Mustin's surprise, one of the boats turned out to have an unexpected crew. "As it came alongside where I was standing at the rail—the rail was not very far above the water at this point—here stood up in the boat a Japanese sailor. He had his white uniform jumper on. His boatswain's insignia were unmistakable. He was gesturing that he wanted some rags. He showed us that he had about six or eight men there who were wounded in various ways and all covered with oil. He was taking care of them. A couple of them were Japanese, and a couple of them were Americans. They were all immobile. They were perhaps unconscious. This one Japanese boatswain's mate had taken it upon himself to take care of all those sailors."

Retrieving the wounded from the clutches of the sea, *Atlanta* sailors had to content themselves with small victories. Thomas Carroll took a raft out and returned with the only survivor of turret five, a sailor named Stanley Hicks, who had been blown out the side of the gun house when it was hit. Hicks's reunion with his brother, Benjamin, was tearful.

To hold on to one's sanity, it helped, Bill Kennedy found, to see the horror in terms of simple physics. Kennedy wrote, "There were not very many parts, arms and legs, that is. I don't know why, but when arms and legs are blown off, they usually sink—but not the torso; it will float. Doc told us that the torso has cavities which retain and even produce gasses—like the lungs, stomach, bowels, etc. Makes sense." After several shuttle trips out to the *Atlanta,* the decks of Kennedy's boat were blackened with oil. "It took weeks of washing them down with gasoline, over and over again, to dissolve it. With a lot of sweat, we got the boats clean. That is, we got the oil and grime off. Funny thing about the blood stains; much of it remained until we repainted the boat."

As morning deepened, the risk of air attack returned. The *Atlanta*'s vulnerability was evident enough. Little remained of her formidable main battery. Her aftermost two five-inch mounts were the only ones that weren't disabled. But without steam, there were no generators working, and thus no power to train them. It was not an ideal state for repelling a fast-developing air attack. A tug working out of Tulagi, the *Bobolink,* came alongside, hooked up, and gingerly began towing her toward shore until her anchor, streaming at full extension, finally grabbed the seafloor, holding the ship a few miles off Lunga Point.

The senior assistant in the engineering department, Lieutenant Commander John T. Wulff, realized that the ship's 250-kilowatt diesel generator could be tied into the switchboard to supply the necessary power, but the superheated compartment needed to be made habitable first. Bill McKinney and others set up a portable blower to remove the tremendous heat from the partially flooded engine room. A submersible bilge pump was next, pumping the water level below the second-level gratings. Then, adjusting the switchboard to take power from the emergency generator, he connected one end of a cable to the 440-volt board, and threaded the other end down several decks to the emergency diesel room, where the generator was. Through trial and error, Wulff and his men got power flowing to turret eight, and soon its guns were barking at the sky as a single Japanese aircraft approached. Ten salvos quelled any ambitions the pilot might have had to finish the crippled vessel, and the plane veered away.

Close by the *Atlanta,* a larger ship circled like a shark. When she was first seen, "There was a general rush for the torpedo tubes," McKinney wrote.

They stood down when Lloyd Mustin determined that the stranger was the *Portland*. The men of that ship, too, had been struggling to peg the identities of the smashed ships around them. Seeing a destroyer standing to their north, they quickly identified it as an enemy and trained the ship's two forward turrets on her. This turned out to be the *Yudachi,* still dead in the water. Captain DuBose got on the intercom and invited anyone who wasn't busy serving the main battery to come topside and watch a firing squad by naval rifle. In the *Atlanta,* all damage-control work was stopped. "We stood, frozen at the life-lines, spectators to a kind of action rarely witnessed," McKinney wrote.

The *Portland*'s fire-control team quickly got comfortable with their ship's gyrations, drew on the target with their after director, and fired six salvos from 12,500 yards. Over. Short. Straddle. Straddle. There came then a report from Commander Shanklin that the Japanese destroyer was showing a white flag.

DuBose asked his gunnery officer what nationality the flag was. The gun boss said, "It's not in my registry."

"Sink the S-O-B," DuBose replied.

The next salvo struck the destroyer amidships, bringing a bright flash and a tower of black smoke. When it cleared, nothing remained. On the *Atlanta,* "We raised a cheer," McKinney wrote. "A sentimentalist near me croaked, 'Don't cheer fellows. The poor guys are dead. It could have been you.' All shared his observation, few his recommendation."

The next short chapter in the "battle of the cripples" belonged to the Japanese. The *Hiei,* lying north of Savo Island, outside the *Portland*'s line of sight, opened fire on the nearest American ship, the *Aaron Ward.* As he lolled in an opiate-addled haze, Bob Hagen watched the great splashes close by as the third and fourth two-gun salvos straddled the ship, compelling Captain Gregor to duck behind the pilothouse wheel. Seeing the frailty of that small installation relative to the towers of seawater raised by the salvo, and his holy terror of a skipper diving for cover, Hagen couldn't suppress a numb smile. The torment ended quickly for the *Aaron Ward* when some Marine Dauntlesses from Henderson Field, escorted by Wildcats, found the battleship.

Shortly after 7 a.m., when Master Technical Sergeant Donald V. Thornbury planted a thousand-pound bomb into the *Hiei*'s superstructure, it was the first of a rain of ordnance that would fall in a daylong deluge, seventy sorties in all. The *Hiei*'s assailants included nine Avengers from the *Enterprise*'s Torpedo Squadron 10, "the Buzzard Brigade," which attacked after 10 a.m. Led by Lieutenant Albert P. Coffin and Lieutenant MacDonald Thomp-

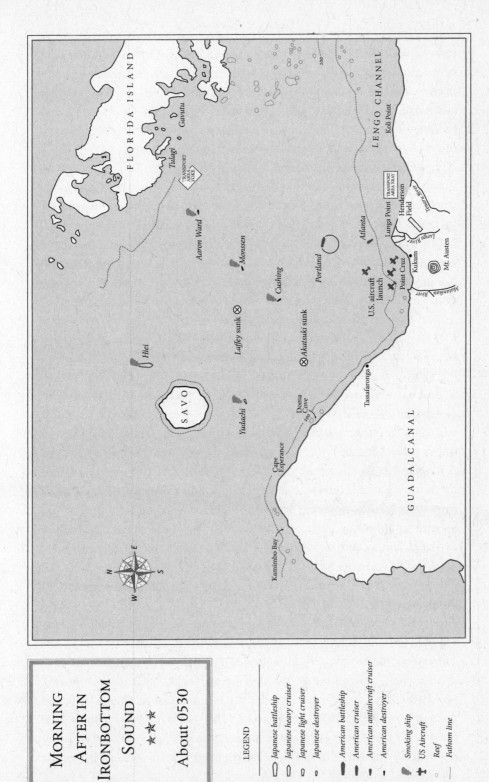

MORNING
AFTER IN
IRONBOTTOM
SOUND
★ ★ ★
About 0530

LEGEND

Japanese battleship
Japanese heavy cruiser
Japanese light cruiser
Japanese destroyer
American battleship
American cruiser
American antiaircraft cruiser
American destroyer
Smoking ship
US Aircraft
Reef
Fathom line

FLORIDA ISLAND

Tulagi
Gavutu

TRANSPORT
AREA (YOKE)

LENGO CHANNEL

Koli Point

Aaron Ward

Monssen

Atlanta

Lunga Point

TRANSPORT
AREA XRAY

Henderson
Field

Cushing

Portland

U.S. aircraft
launch

Point Cruz
Kukum

Mt. Austen

Laffey sunk ⊗

⊗ Akatsuki sunk

Hiei

Malanikau River

Matanikau River

Tenaru River

Lunga River

SAVO

Yudachi

Doma
Cove

100

Tassafaronga

Cape
Esperance

GUADALCANAL

N
E
W
S

Kamimbo Bay

100

100

son, the veterans of the action off Santa Cruz eased their big Grummans out of the cloud cover and dispersed to set up "anvil" torpedo attacks, converging on either bow. Zero fighter pilots flying from Rabaul, Buin, and the carrier *Junyo* were foiled by distance and heavy weather and could do little to protect the battleship. The Buzzard Brigade would claim three hits. Rearming at Henderson Field, they attacked again in the afternoon.

The *Hiei* still had a surprisingly deep reservoir of fight left in her. She was capable of ten or more knots, and as long as her crew remained ahead in the close race with floodwaters for control of the manual steering compartment, there was hope she might get away. By midmorning, the *Kirishima* received orders from Admiral Kondo to reverse course and return south to take the *Hiei* in tow. According to Japanese sources, however, an attack by a U.S. submarine, which landed two dud hits on the *Kirishima*, compelled Kondo to abandon the plan and recall the *Kirishima* to rejoin his Advance Force.

As American planes kept the struggling *Hiei* under siege, the tug *Bobolink* took the *Aaron Ward* under tow, handing her off to a patrol craft that brought her into Tulagi's harbor. The *Portland* aspired to get there, too, but her starboard sheer defied all efforts at navigation. Higgins boats pushed against her starboard bow. The ship's port anchor was cast out and streamed alongside. The crew fashioned large improvised sea anchors out of canvas and threw them overboard, hoping to drag enough water to pull the ship out of her circle. That, too, was to no avail. As the struggle continued, the *Portland* served as an emergency aid station for wounded sailors rescued from the sound. The cruiser's whaleboat, Higgins boats from Guadalcanal, and several floatplanes motoring around the surface brought some thirty-eight men aboard, most of them from the *Barton*. They were treated and sent on to Tulagi. Finally, the busy *Bobolink* nudged alongside and threw her powerful shoulder into the *Portland*'s starboard bow. Aided by the patrol boat *YC-236*, they got the heavy cruiser going in the right direction, creeping along at a walking speed.

At 10:20 a.m., disturbed by the persistence of the air attacks, which required the ship to keep moving and thus foiled flood-control efforts, Abe ordered the *Hiei*'s captain, Masao Nishida, to beach the ship on Guadalcanal. The flooding had conquered the steering compartment, and as soon as it was abandoned, the ship was stuck circling northeast of Savo Island. But Nishida flatly refused the order, and in the face of his doggedness, Abe relented. If they could survive the day, they might have the liberty, under cover of darkness, to pump flooded compartments dry and get her under way again.

The return of the Buzzard Brigade at about two twenty-five that afternoon dashed these hopes. Fliers swooped down and planted a pair of torpedoes into the battleship's starboard side. The shoring that held the floodwaters out of the steering compartment finally yielded, and the ship became unnavigable. As Captain Nishida ordered the crew to abandon, he supervised them from a chair perched atop turret three aft. He stayed there even as Dauntless dive-bombers bore down on the ship. With the *Hiei* listing to starboard and down by the stern, Abe ordered Nishida forcibly taken from the ship. Flying his flag in the destroyer *Yukikaze*, standing by, Abe decided his old flagship was a total loss. Though Admiral Yamamoto intervened directly from Truk, instructing Abe that the *Hiei* not be scuttled, leaving her instead to lend support to Tanaka's transports as they approached Savo Sound in conjunction with a renewed attack by surface warships, Abe saw no hope in this. After dark, the *Hiei* sank unobserved, somewhere north of Savo Island. Yamamoto was reportedly furious with Abe for his resistance, and removed him from seagoing command.

WHEN THE PILOTS FROM the *Enterprise*'s Buzzard Brigade returned to Henderson Field, they were met by the surprised commander of the Cactus Air Force, Brigadier General Louis Woods, who declared, "Boys, I don't know where you came from, but you look like angels dropping out of heaven to us." Touching down on the airfield again near dusk, with their khakis still fresh and their faces clean-shaven, the carrier pilots found old friends from flight school among the Marine fliers and enjoyed the occasion to celebrate. They gained full membership in the Cactus Air Force by donating some torpedo fuel to the bar, run by Seabees, who always had a healthy supply of grapefruit juice on hand as a mixer. Assigned tents in a camp already crowded with survivors of the naval action, the tenants of Henderson Field raised their glasses and cheered.

34

Cruiser in the Sky

CAPTAIN HOOVER LED HIS SQUADRON OF SURVIVORS TOWARD ESPIRITU Santo, forced to limp at ten knots until temporary repairs let the *San Francisco* keep pace with the nimbler survivors. The *Helena* led her and the damaged *Juneau* south. As the shell-battered *Sterett* passed the *San Francisco* to take station ahead, forming a patchwork destroyer screen with the unscratched *Fletcher* and the lightly grazed *O'Bannon*, her crew beheld what the night had wrought on Dan Callaghan's flagship. The bridge was battered and charred; the after control tower, thoroughly put to the torch. They counted twenty-six holes in her port side.

On request from Bruce McCandless, the *Juneau* sent the *San Francisco* a medical officer, Lieutenant Roger W. O'Neil, and a trio of corpsmen to assist with the wounded. O'Neil was angry about being sent away from his ship. "I don't know why they sent us over here," he said, coming aboard. "You people are going to sink, and we are needed back on the *Juneau.*" In Captain Swenson's ship, a damage-control party was working to fortify her fractured keel.

Just before dawn, the *San Francisco*'s senior enlisted men reported topside to join a grim detail, conducting what was known as a body parts sweep. Such an effort was necessary following any battle action in which casualties occurred. Its purpose was to cleanse the ship of human remains. The crew picked up body parts and threw them overboard, and washed down the ship's steel surfaces of drying blood. As with abandoning ship, it wasn't something that could be realistically rehearsed ahead of time.

"The ship was just absolutely a shambles," said Joseph Whitt, a *San Francisco* sailor. "It was just like you were opening up your eyes in a nightmare. I walked amidships and the five-inch guns that I passed had been hit, just wrecked. I looked at the stack—and this is a sight that I shall never ever forget. There were holes in the stack from the shrapnel from those explosions, and there was blood from the top of that stack running down the side of it, where the body parts had been blown up there and splattered down the side of it. The way that smelled...it was just something that no one should ever go through."

Few new sailors were equipped to handle it. "Detailing the senior rates for this gruesome task was a good call," Don Jenkins wrote. All around the ship, the growling of handy-billy pumps swelled. Hoses were dropped overboard and streams of water set flowing against all surfaces. Slowly the stubborn knots of flesh clotting the ship's thousands of crooks and crevices, the drying splashes of blood, were washed away. All hands received a "ditty bag" and were ordered to identify the dead, remove their dog tags and personal effects, place a five-inch dummy shell down the front of their dungarees, cinch their belt tight, and ease the body over the side. The *San Francisco* had no chaplain aboard, so there was no ceremony to any of this. Lieutenant James I. Cone, who supervised the gathering of personal effects, collected far too many Annapolis class rings for his liking. Through this grimly determined effort, the ship returned to a tolerable state of habitability.

Littering the deck everywhere were small tubes of phosphorous, detritus of the incendiaries fired by the Japanese battleships. "Fellows were picking them up and putting them in their pockets as souvenirs," Joseph Whitt remembered. It was a bad move. Some of the dud incendiary elements were still doing a slow burn. "One guy had one in his hip pocket, and before he tore his pants off, this thing really blistered him," Whitt said. "Water wouldn't put the fire out."

The sickbay was too small to handle all the wounded. They had to be carried to the hangar deck. Don Jenkins recalled, "I never will be able to erase from my mind the utter feeling of helplessness and sorrow one feels as each time you deliver another wounded to the hangar. The moans and screams of pain, and many of the badly wounded calling out to their mothers." In the admiral's cabin, the doctor from the *Juneau,* Lieutenant O'Neil, donned a mask to assist in emergency surgery on Captain Cassin Young. His wounds were mortal, and there was no saving him.

As the ships passed through Torpedo Junction, it was clear to everybody, most of all Captain Hoover, that they were a vulnerable group. The crews of

Wasp, the *North Carolina,* the *O'Brien,* and the *Saratoga* had been no less diligent than they were, and had enjoyed far more protection than Hoover's threadbare destroyer screen offered now. The *O'Bannon's* sonar was out of commission. The *Sterett's* stack was working, but the ship had no depth charges, having jettisoned them as the fires raged aft. She was able to steer only with her engines. The *Fletcher* was in good shape. But a single fully functional destroyer was a weak deterrent to submarine attack. Hoover called SOPAC air command to request aerial coverage and hoped for the best.

In the *Helena's* pilothouse, all talk was of the battered flagship, steaming on the port quarter. The helmsman, George A. De Long, thought the *San Francisco* would be lucky to reach Espiritu Santo. McCandless placed her fighting efficiency at 25 percent. Though the *Juneau* was four feet down by the bow, she looked considerably healthier as she made seventeen knots on the *Helena's* starboard quarter.

The radio, meanwhile, carried hopeful tidings—the excited transmissions from U.S. pilots as they swarmed a Japanese battleship, the *Hiei,* dead in the water near Savo Island. The running report was vastly entertaining for sailors who had just finished their own turn in the battle zone and had had a hand in leaving the aviators this first-class prize.

It was about 11 a.m. when a lookout noticed a disturbance on the surface of the sea to port. He said at first that it resembled "the usual eruption made by a porpoise." Then a *Helena* gunner on a port side mount spotted it, a thin wake and a fin breaching the surface, just inside the wake of the *Sterett,* riding on the *Helena's* port bow. A torpedo. He watched as it passed astern. The navigator shouted, "Hard right rudder, De Long!"

On the *San Francisco,* a bridge lookout, speechless, grabbed Lieutenant Commander Schonland by the shoulder and pointed at no fewer than four wakes approaching the ship's port bow. Schonland ordered, "Full right rudder, emergency full ahead." Seeing the white wakes burning toward the ship, Joseph Whitt starting running aft to escape the explosion. Leaping over a large gash in the deck, he caught his foot and went sprawling. He gathered himself quickly and looked forward to find the wake. The torpedo passed under the ship on the starboard side. He found himself looking directly at the *Juneau.*

There was no way to send warning to Captain Swenson's ship. With all of the *San Francisco's* steam lines broken, she could not give voice to her siren or her whistle, and with her flag bags burned, her TBS transmitter out, signal halyards cut, and all but one large searchlight wrecked, it was impossible to raise an effective alarm. Fate had placed Hoover's formation in the periscope crosshairs of the submarine *I-26*, the same boat that had hit the *Saratoga* in August. Lying along the eastern flank of the column's southerly line of travel, the IJN boat had three torpedo tubes flooded and ready.

As the *Helena* came right, De Long watched the *Juneau* through a porthole but soon lost her to the shifting line of sight. Then, unexpectedly, the navigator hollered, "Hard left rudder!" De Long reversed the helm, and the ship shuddered for several seconds and slowly came back. That was when the ocean shivered.

A *Helena* signalman was watching his counterpart on the *Juneau* through a glass, taking a blinker signal. One moment the man on the *Juneau* was standing there, sending Morse, the next he was gone, snatched up from the field of view as if by a giant hand. Removing the glass from his eye, the *Helena* man saw his counterpart hurtling through the air.

Joseph Whitt in the *San Francisco* heard a "loud *crrrrrack,* like a lightning strike nearby." On the bearing that the antiaircraft cruiser once occupied, all the *Helena*'s George De Long could see was a large cloud swelling low on the water. "Where is she? Where is she? Where is she? I don't want to ram her!" he said. No one remained in the *Helena*'s pilothouse. Everyone had raced out onto the bridge wing. A sailor ducked back into the pilothouse and said, quietly, "De Long, she ain't no more."

Even after the unprecedented blooding of the previous night, never had anyone witnessed a blast such as this. Bruce McCandless wrote, "The *Juneau* didn't sink—she blew up with all the fury of an erupting volcano. There was a terrific thunderclap and a plume of white water that was blotted out by a huge brown hemisphere a thousand yards across, from within which came the sounds of more explosions." As Hoover would report to Admiral Turner, "Debris fell to such extent and volume as to cause belief of high level bombing attack."

What fraction of the *Juneau*'s steel plates and hardened armor belts were launched skyward and fell back to earth in shards is anyone's guess, but the shrapnel rain was heavy and voluminous. As Schonland, McCandless, Wilbourne, and Lair looked on stunned from the *San Francisco*'s flag bridge, the officer-of-the-deck, Jack Bennett, noticed an object hurtling toward them through the air. "Scatter!" he shouted as a rectangular plate of steel plating wobbled in and smashed into the superstructure just a few feet from where they stood. It bounced across the deck and fell overboard. One of the

Juneau's twin five-inch mounts arced through the bright sky and splashed down not a hundred yards astern the *Fletcher.*

"As we got up even with it—the pall of smoke had begun to rise up from the water—there was a gigantic explosion under the water," Joseph Whitt said. "They said it was probably the boilers blowing up. She came up just like a big whale. You've seen pictures of them as they come up and breech and go back down. It was a big, huge bubble. In that bubble of water was part of the hull of that ship. I mean it was eerie."

As witnesses struggled to believe, an ocean swell some thirty feet high crested into the *San Francisco* from the starboard side. "Our ship rapidly keeled over to port until the outboard portion of the well deck was under-water," Don Jenkins wrote. "One had to hold on for dear life to keep from tumbling across the well deck into the sea. The ship slowly came back to an even keel and then we found that all our shoring and caulking had been knocked out of the waterline shell holes and sea water was pouring in by the thousands of gallons."

On a day of terrible visions, the sudden death of the *Juneau* may have been the worst of all. Few witnesses could imagine there were any survivors. The suddenness with which more than six hundred men perished had no analog in other types of combat. The single blast offered none of the emerging trauma of an eroding front line or a sundered and faltering flank. It was an apocalyptic accident, random and undeserved, and paid in a single shocking stroke. Chick Morris observed, "No one moved or spoke.... A man needs some kind of mental and physical reserve to accept such a disaster when not prepared for it, and we had exhausted our reserve during the night.... Many a man aboard *Helena* walked the decks for the following few hours in a kind of trance, brooding and frightened."

Robert Howe said, "We often talked about getting hit by a torpedo so we could go back to the States for repairs. Never again after seeing the *Juneau* disappear under a cloud of smoke." It was still Friday the thirteenth. "The rest of the day I don't think anyone took their eyes off the water."

GIL HOOVER TOOK the *Juneau's* loss hard. Her captain, Lyman Knute Swenson, had been a Naval Academy classmate and a close friend. Now he was either gone or, worse, alive, wounded and in urgent need of rescue. Untold scores of the antiaircraft cruiser's survivors floated on the swells in Torpedo Junction. Though many witnesses professed to see no survivors, they were assuredly there. The crew of an aircraft that happened by later counted at least sixty of them, their lives spared by freak accidents of physics that kept the gusting remains of the ship from breaking their bodies as they flew into the sea.

As Hoover judged it, the logic of the situation required him to foreclose any thought of saving them, or his friend. With just a single undamaged destroyer to chase submarines, with the responsibility to get heavily damaged ships and badly wounded men to base on his shoulders, with an adeptly commanded enemy submarine still at large, he decided he couldn't risk stopping to search for survivors. Earlier that morning he had ordered the *O'Bannon* to steam away to the north to transmit a report of the previous night's engagement to Nouméa. When maintaining radio silence, ships departed formation before transmitting their messages to avoid betraying the group's location to radio snoopers. The *O'Bannon* wasn't due to rejoin him until midafternoon.

Few naval commanders understood the delicate work of rescue at sea as well as Hoover. As commander of Destroyer Squadron 2, he had escorted the *Lexington* when she was sunk in the Coral Sea, and had received the Navy Cross for the manner in which his destroyers pressed in close, braving repeated heavy explosions and flames, to recover the carrier's survivors. Hoover's award citation stated, "The intrepid and seamanlike way that these officers handled their vessels about the listing and burning *Lexington* without regard for the flames and explosions emanating from her, was in accord with every fine tradition of our Navy and of the sea, and undoubtedly contributed to the rescue of many survivors who might otherwise have been lost." Circumstances now were vastly different. Still, he would write that the decision to continue south "was not made without much effort."

At eleven twenty-one, a B-17 Flying Fortress arrived from Espiritu Santo, as Hoover had requested, to provide air cover. To preserve radio silence, Hoover refrained from radioing Turner or Halsey about the incident. Instead, he had one of his signalmen blinker to the bomber overhead: "JUNEAU TORPEDOED DISAPPEARED LAT 10–32 LONG 161–02 AT 1109 X SURVIVORS IN WATER REPORT COMSOPAC." The plane acknowledged receipt of the message with a visual signal, and Hoover repeated it. He could only hope the pilot would appreciate the tremulous state of the survivors in the water, many of whom had to be severely wounded. The plane acknowledged receipt of the second transmission and zoomed off toward Henderson Field. Joseph Wylie, the exec of the *Fletcher*, would call Hoover's decision to press on to Espiritu Santo "probably the most courageous single decision I've ever seen a man make, because everybody's instinct is to go after survivors." Wylie felt that instinct strongly, but when Hoover signaled the *Fletcher* that he had reports of three more Japanese submarines lurking along their route, he felt mollified.

Shortly after noon, the destroyer *Buchanan* joined Hoover's group; the *O'Bannon* rejoined them at three thirty. As Hoover continued on, bringing his wounded ships home, the *Juneau*'s brown pall receded over the horizon behind them.

THE *ATLANTA* LAY AT ANCHOR a few miles from Lunga, seeping to death through her holes and broken seams. Jack Wulff, the assistant engineering officer, had hoped for a time that his crews would get the after fire room pumped down to where the burners could make steam. If the inboard screws got turning again, they could limp to Tulagi and make repairs in the shelter of a cove. Now, as the water levels rose, he saw the futility in it. With a fourth consecutive sleepless night approaching for the crew, the bucket brigades were up against their limits. When Dallas Emory, the exec, concurred that the ship couldn't be saved, Captain Jenkins radioed the *Portland* that he could not check flooding and would have to scuttle his ship. DuBose, as the senior officer present, approved. As boats from Guadalcanal took off the crew, a demolition charge was placed in the diesel engine room. When it blew, the *Atlanta* went quickly with all hatches open, revealing as she rolled over to port the grievous extent of her torpedo wound; it stretched from its impact point below the port side waterline across the keel and into the starboard bottom of the hull. "If we had tried to steam that ship," Lloyd Mustin said, "she might have opened in half.... If she had run into heavy weather, she would never have made it."

As night fell over Ironbottom Sound again, the *Portland* was still struggling toward Tulagi. Near midnight, those troubles were supplemented by the arrival of other combatants eager to throw themselves into the fracas in the sound: American PT boats. The first sign of their presence was a radio transmission Captain DuBose picked up over the TBS. "*Here comes a bear. Give him two fish.*"

The small boats were stalking a "bear"—a target. DuBose came to understand that the ship in question was his own. A bizarre parley ensued between the cruiser captain and the PT boat officers, with DuBose declaring his identity in plain English and his stalkers discussing among themselves what to do with the large stranger. *"This is the American cruiser* Portland. *This is Captain DuBose speaking. There is a tug standing out from Tulagi to assist us. The name of her captain is Lieutenant Foley. We are not—repeat not—a Japanese."* The PT boat skippers, having heard reports of crippled targets about, must have been skeptical of this silver-tongued, English-speaking enemy officer trying to talk his way out of a well-deserved spread to the midsection. The damaged heavy cruiser, struggling to keep a heading at three knots and unable to steer, was at the tiny boats' mercy.

Nervous lookouts scanned the waters for torpedo wakes. In the ambient light of the moon and star field overhead, here they came: two white bubbling lines in the deep, passing ahead. The PT skippers had evidently overestimated their target's speed, perhaps seeing the vigorous churn of her counter-turning screws but not appreciating its waste.

The commander of the PT boats in the area, Lieutenant Commander Alan P. Calvert, saw the absence of heavy U.S. ships in Savo Sound that night as an opportunity for his command.

According to Charles Melhorn of the PT-44, he gave the briefing to the "Peter Tares" that night, and it amounted to: "There is a Japanese task force due in about midnight, and we may have a battleship task force due in about midnight. Go out and get the Japs." Until that moment, when they emerged as the lone U.S. naval force in Savo Sound, they had been held on a leash, skirmishing indecisively with Tokyo Express destroyers now and then, but ordered to stay in their base as the November 13 battle approached.

Melhorn saw right away how it could be suicide, in such a vulnerable craft, to issue the standard blinker challenge to an unidentified ship. "If you challenge the wrong group, that's the end of you," he said. That may be why one of the boats, *PT-48,* dispensed with diplomacy and sent four fish churning toward the U.S. cruiser.

The gunners on DuBose's ship didn't appreciate the attention and according to Melhorn returned fire at their harassers. "We thought that was pretty dirty pool," Melhorn said. It was no dirtier than anything else a ship's crew might do at night, when friend and enemy alike are skulking phantoms.

The drama of the PT boat encounter passed. After midnight, in the first hours of November 14, the *Portland* reached Tulagi and anchored in thirty-nine fathoms. The steep drop-off near shore allowed them to tie up to a palm tree and run a gangway from the ship to the shore. They camouflaged the ship with netting to prevent being spotted from the air. "Then we all dropped in our tracks and fell asleep," Harold L. Johnson said. "We had been at general quarters over fifty hours by this time."

The peace would last for only about an hour. With the remnants of the American cruiser force limping away toward Espiritu Santo, the way was open for the Imperial Japanese Navy once again.

35

Regardless of Losses

ADMIRAL ISOROKU YAMAMOTO, LIKE HIS STAFF AND COMMANDERS throughout the South Seas fleet, was shocked by the savagery of Abe's fight with Callaghan. The grinding of steel tooth and nail was like nothing they had seen from the U.S. Navy. The Americans weren't known to be such fighters. At Cape Esperance in October, Goto had lost a cruiser but gave, in death, nearly as good as he got en route to accomplishing his larger mission, unleashing two battleships against Henderson Field. A month later now, Callaghan had done what his Navy had not been able to do thus far in the war. He had crippled a battleship, the *Hiei,* and left her to Henderson Field's vultures. The 36,600-ton warship was to the Imperial Japanese Navy something like what the HMS *Hood* had been to the Royal Navy before her loss in May 1941: older, smaller, and less powerful than the state-of-art newcomers to whom she played second chair, but an object of nostalgic affection because of her link to the Imperial palace. Hirohito himself had sailed in the *Hiei.* Her loss was a heavy blow.

After Callaghan thwarted Abe on the night of November 12–13, inflicting the loss of the *Hiei* and two destroyers, the *Akatsuki* and *Yudachi,* Henderson Field was assured of staying in business at least one more day. Accordingly, Yamamoto knew it was folly to allow Tanaka's eleven irreplaceable troop transports to proceed to Guadalcanal. Postponing plans to land the convoy until the fourteenth, he ordered it to withdraw to Shortland Island at the head of the Slot and await further orders. Yamamoto then turned his attention to renewing the effort to bring the Cactus Air Force under his fleet's big guns.

The battleship *Kirishima,* which had left the fracas with Callaghan and company largely unscathed, would be the centerpiece of another powerful bombardment sortie. When Yamamoto ordered Admiral Kondo to take her back to Guadalcanal for another attack, Kondo gathered up two newcomers to the fight in the Slot, the heavy cruisers *Atago* and *Takao,* to join her. The light cruisers *Nagara* and *Sendai* were attached as well, leading nine destroyers. Yamamoto had only reluctantly approved the scuttling of the *Hiei.* Vengeance would belong, if at all, to the ship that sailed with her that night, the *Kirishima.* The IJN's developing failure of nerve was now manifest. As the *Kirishima* headed back toward Guadalcanal under Admiral Kondo, it was telling that she was not joined by her mighty sister ships, the *Kongo* and *Haruna,* which Kondo left behind to screen the carriers. Committing battleships was the final gamble. Yamamoto chose to send just one of his three into the next fight.

Admiral Halsey would take a very different approach. Knowing from dispatches that another major naval attack was gathering, the SOPAC commander decided he could no longer play it safe with his sole remaining carrier, the *Enterprise,* and her powerful accompaniment of battleships. The men on Guadalcanal needed the fleet now more than ever before.

After the beating Callaghan had taken, Halsey knew that his cruiser striking force didn't have much left to offer. His sole remaining carrier, the *Enterprise,* didn't, either. When she was ordered north from Nouméa toward Guadalcanal, the carrier still had a crew of eighty-five repair technicians aboard, working to fix the disabled forward elevator. She trailed an oil slick. "This was the tightest spot that I was ever in during the entire war," Halsey would write.

"If any principle of naval warfare is burned into my brain, it is that the best defense is a strong offense—that, as Lord Nelson wrote in a memorandum to his officers before the Battle of Trafalgar, 'No Captain can do very wrong if he places his Ship alongside that of an Enemy.'" Now there were few other options. Willis Lee's battleships were his "only recourse." Their long days of steaming as sentinels, protecting other ships instead of attacking the enemy, were over. Shortly before 5 p.m. on November 13, Halsey broke every lesson he'd learned at the Naval War College. He decided to send in his battleships. He directed Admiral Kinkaid, commanding the *Enterprise* task force, to turn loose his big boys to enter the fight.

When Willis Lee received the signal via blinker light from the *Enterprise* to detach his heavy combatants from Task Force 16 and run north, and further learned that Halsey expected him to arrive off Guadalcanal by early morning on the fourteenth, Lee broke radio silence to inquire, *"What do you think we have—wings?"* Lee was in no position to get there so soon. When the *Washington* and *South Dakota,* joined by the four destroyers that happened to have the most fuel—the *Preston, Gwin, Walke,* and *Benham*—left the *Enterprise* task force at sunset and set a northward course, they were about 150 miles farther south than Halsey thought they should be.

This was the consequence of Kinkaid misunderstanding the orders from Halsey that directed him where to operate. When he was instructed to keep his task force near a particular line of latitude, Kinkaid understood the line as a limit on his northern movement and stayed well south of it. Having paid a high cost for Halsey's bold, some would say reckless, employment of the precious carriers at Santa Cruz—a cost that included not only the *Hornet,* but also his own reputation among aviation admirals, who felt he needlessly delayed launching a strike after the enemy was spotted—Kinkaid was probably in a mood for caution now.

The direction of the wind was another problem. With a southerly prevailing wind, Kinakid had to reverse course 180 degrees and head south, into the wind, in order to generate a headwind strong enough to launch or recover aircraft. This was one of the reasons Task Force 16 was farther south than many thought it should have been.

When a SOPAC staff officer, Charles Weaver, informed Halsey and Miles Browning that Lee could not reach the battle area on the night of November 13–14, he was met with a furious response. "You can well imagine the blast I got from my seniors who were sure that Lee was in a good position to intercept." Having pledged to Vandegrift that he would support the marines and soldiers on Guadalcanal with everything he had at his disposal, Halsey was chagrined to be forced to notify the general that neither his battleships nor any American naval units would be on hand that night to defend Guadalcanal from naval attack.

At the survivor camp on Guadalcanal that night, Bill McKinney, the *Atlanta* electrician, was resting underneath a tent he had been given by the Marines. He was too exhausted to celebrate with the victorious pilots, too exhausted even to set up his tent. So he used it as a blanket. He was awakened once when the heavy rains leaked underneath the canvas, turning the ground to mud. Around 2 a.m. he was awakened again, this time by a rain of fire. Two heavy cruisers, the *Suzuya* and *Maya,* arrived offshore that night to shoot up the airfield.

Men were shouting, running everywhere, as heavy explosions rolled in from the sound. Those who had endured the shelling by battleships a month earlier would say this one paled in comparison, but a bombardment from the sea was always terrifying. A sailor who had survived the sinkings of the *Wasp* and the *Barton* came sprinting into a bunker during the bombardment, mute with terror. McKinney took the assault by the two Japanese cruisers personally. "I had the feeling that they knew where we were and planned to finish us off," he said. He could see the "little winking pinpoints of blue light as their salvos thundered toward us. It was a fearful experience."

The closest large U.S. warship at hand in Savo Sound that night was Captain DuBose's *Portland,* tied up and concealed near Tulagi's shore across the sound as her crew worked on repairs. DuBose spotted the two enemy ships as their searchlights explored the anchorage off Lunga. Every faithful hand in the *Portland* prayed the lights would not find them. DuBose knew there was no way he could tackle two fully primed opponents with his ship barely navigable. So he watched the searchlights and instructed Commander Shanklin to fire only if they fixed in his direction. In due course Calvert's PT boats threw their weight at the Japanese cruisers, making several torpedo runs to no effect.

Firing five hundred shells apiece in an unmolested half hour, the *Maya* and *Suzuya* destroyed eighteen planes and damaged thirty-two more on Henderson Field. Frightful though it was, this bombardment paled with what the *Hiei* and *Kirishima* might have wreaked, and underscored the significance of Callaghan's sacrifice.

WHEN THE MORNING ROSE on Savo Sound on November 14, it was still Friday the thirteenth in Washington. The first dispatches of the events off Guadalcanal the previous night traveled quickly by radio from Nouméa to Pearl Harbor to the Navy Department and the Joint Chiefs of Staff. "The tension I felt at that time was matched only by the tension that pervaded Washington the night before the landing in Normandy," James Forrestal would write. Later, when a Japanese invasion force was reported in the Slot, President Roosevelt began to think the island was lost. But from Washington the president did not have contemporaneous knowledge of what the Cactus Air Force was doing. Japan's most important effort to send troops to the island was under way and now, thanks to the success of Callaghan and the failure of Abe, was exposed to daylight air attack. The most important day in the illustrious history of the Cactus Air Force was at hand.

At first light on Henderson Field, the ground crews of the 1st Marine Air Wing began a long day of work fueling and arming planes to strike at enemy targets in the Slot. The pace was so desperate that all hands from the mess tents were pressed into service. There would be time aplenty to eat after more pressing appetites had been sated. Soon the pilots were scouring the waters within two hundred miles of the island. The *Enterprise,* steaming two hundred miles south-southwest of Guadalcanal, was delayed in launching her dawn search, thanks to squalls. But most of the *Enterprise*'s sixty-two planes, including twenty-three Dauntlesses and nine Avengers, got in on the attack.

Winging north and west with varied responsibilities for search and strike, they found the ships that had hit them the previous night southwest of Rendova Island, New Georgia. The *Suzuya* and *Maya,* which had rendezvoused with the heavy cruisers *Chokai* and *Kinugasa,* were set upon violently. A flight of Dauntlesses led by Marine major Joseph Sailer fell on the *Kinugasa,* which was trailing oil from torpedoes hits landed by Marine Avenger pilots shortly after first light. The *Enterprise* Dauntlesses hit her hard, damaging her grievously with a heavy bomb. Two *Enterprise* pilots, Ensign Richard M. Buchanan and Lieutenant (j.g.) Robert D. Gibson, delivered the coup de grâce, leaving the *Kinugasa* to capsize and sink later that morning, taking down fifty-one men. Ensign Paul M. Halloran of the *Enterprise*'s Bombing Squadron 10 dove on the *Maya* but missed with his bomb. As he pulled out, the wing of his Dauntless struck the cruiser's mainmast, spilling gasoline into the superstructure. The resulting fires killed thirty-seven sailors. Halloran was never seen again.

But the pilots' principal objective was Tanaka's lightly defended transport force. Slugging south on Saturday morning, passing between New Georgia and Santa Isabel, the troop carriers were set upon by Cactus Air Force and *Enterprise* planes around the same time the Japanese cruisers were coming under attack. Tanaka's transports scattered, turning in slow circles to avoid the fall of bombs and torpedoes. By midafternoon, seven of the eleven transports had been sunk, along with all of their cargoes and a great many of their men.

Amid the catastrophe of these terrible losses to their amphibious capability, Admiral Tanaka salvaged what he could. In a remarkable feat of improvisational seamanship, he brought his destroyers alongside the foundering transports and transferred thousands of soldiers on the fly.

As they did so, Rear Admiral Kondo, riding in the light cruiser *Nagara,* took command of a makeshift but powerful bombardment force—the

Kirishima, joined by the heavy cruisers *Atago* and *Takeo*, the light cruisers *Nagara* and *Sendai*, and nine destroyers. They moved south again to lay their guns on Henderson Field, quickly overtaking Tanaka's four surviving transports and taking station ahead of them. Owing to the intensity of the air attacks directed at the Japanese cruisers and transports that day, the *Kirishima* and her consorts avoided detection from the air.

THE SURVIVING SHIPS OF Task Force 67 arrived at Espiritu Santo on the afternoon of November 14. Entering the channel, the *San Francisco* followed the *Helena* closely. A monument to the danger of haphazard navigation stood for all to see: the wreck of the luxury-liner-turned-troop-transport *President Coolidge*, which several weeks earlier had blundered out of the safety of the channel into the harbor's defensive minefield.

As the *San Francisco* came into the harbor, she passed, port-side-to-port-side, four other cruisers anchored in a line, the *Minneapolis, New Orleans, Pensacola,* and *Northampton.* "It was pretty awe-inspiring," Jack Bennett said. The crews of the anchored ships manned the rail and offered three rousing cheers to the battle-scarred counterpart. "Hip, hip hooray—three times, that was something emotional," Bennett said. "The greatest accolade you can get is from your comrades in arms."

In the harbor, the *Helena* went alongside a tanker to refuel. A sailor on the oiler surveyed the shrapnel-pocked light cruiser and hollered over the rail, "What happened?" A wag on the *Helena* replied, "Termites." Schonland refused an instruction to go alongside a tanker to refuel and requested an anchorage instead. With the flag lowered to half-mast, the *San Francisco* was assigned a berth, and as she eased in, the ships nearby gave her a hero's welcome. Ship whistles blew loud and long. Schonland arranged with Hoover for the *Helena*'s band to come aboard, and for her chaplain to conduct a funeral service on the *San Francisco*.

The mobile base hospital at Espiritu Santo was crowded. Ship's doctors, seeing the facilities available ashore, lamented the butchery they had been forced to perpetrate in the battle area: amputations, crushing tourniquets, dressings soaked through and dried into open wounds. In combat, you did your best with what you had. With his legs shot through with more than 130 shrapnel wounds, the *San Francisco*'s Cliff Spencer was taken to a wardroom full of wounded sailors and marines. "I wasn't near anyone I knew and at that moment I had never felt so sad and alone," he wrote. "Next to me on the opposite tier bunk lay a muscular young sailor. He was crying. I tried to strike up a conversation with him and asked, 'What ship are you off of?' He said the *Atlanta*. . . . As we talked the corpsman came to dress his wounds. He threw back the blankets and lifted about an eight-inch stub of his right leg. It had been amputated above the knee and had not been surgically closed, just a raw cut covered with a large bandage. He shocked me by almost screaming, 'The sons of bitches on the *San Francisco* did this! How can I ever work the farm with this bloody stump?'

"Needless to say I didn't volunteer the name of my ship."

The tribalisms of a naval force were still producing raw feelings. "There were some real hard feelings between the *Helena* and *San Francisco* when they got into port," a sailor recalled. It seems there were *Helena* sailors who thought the flagship had turned and run at the height of the engagement, and that "the *Helena* had to stay there and do the job—or whatever."

As the *San Francisco* underwent temporary repairs, Schonland was relieved as acting commander by Captain Albert F. France, from Halsey's staff. The personal effects taken from the dead were turned over with an inventory to the supply officer for shipment home to the relatives whose photos had adorned stateroom bulkheads, sat framed on small metal desks, and become shattered and scattered by the many impacts of the fight. The good order of the flagship was returning.

Turner sent a message to the ships of Task Force 67 that amply reflected his feelings toward the battered ships of his command.

Task Force 67 is hereby dissolved. In dissolving this temporary force I express the will that the number 67 be in the future reserved for groups of ships as ready for high patriotic endeavor as you have been. I thank you for your magnificent support of the project of reinforcing our brave troops in Guadalcanal and for your eagerness to be the keen edge of the sword that is cutting the throat of the enemy.

I was well aware of the odds which might be against you in your night attack on November 12 but felt that this was the time when fine ships and brave men should be called upon for their utmost. You have more than justified my expectations in taking from the enemy a toll of strength far greater than the strength you have expended.

With you I grieve for long cherished comrades who will be with us no more, and for our lost ships whose names will be enshrined in history. No medals however high can possibly give you the reward you deserve. With all my heart I say God bless the courageous men, dead and alive, of Task Force 67.

The Cactus Air Force's devastating attacks against the transports on the morning of the fourteenth would never have happened without their sacrifice. The deaths of Callaghan and his staff were the final blow to Ghormley's original SOPAC command. With their passing, and that of Norman Scott, the Navy simultaneously cashiered the folly of the old and some of the promise of the new. The winding course between victory and defeat off Guadalcanal offered a series of object lessons that future leaders would study and profit by. The tuition in that brutal school was steep.

But one more collision of giants remained to decide who would control Savo Sound. The next costly lesson would follow the very next night with another collision of the exhausted fleets.

At Pearl Harbor, monitoring the reports of more major Japanese naval units approaching Guadalcanal, Admiral Nimitz sent a broadcast to all task force commanders, bracingly stating the obvious: "LOOKS LIKE ALL OUT ATTEMPT NOW UNDERWAY TO RECAPTURE GUADALCANAL REGARDLESS LOSSES."

"The turret whips around but it is the guns themselves that seem to live. They balance and quiver almost as though they were sniffing the air. . . . Suddenly they set and instantly there is a belch of sound and the shells float away. The tracers seem to float interminably before they hit. And before the shells have struck the guns are trembling and reaching again. They are like rattlesnakes poising to strike, and they really do seem to be alive. It is a frightening thing to see."

—John Steinbeck, "A Destroyer," November 24, 1943

36

The Giants Ride

THE BATTLESHIPS *WASHINGTON* AND *SOUTH DAKOTA* PUSHED THROUGH the sea with an implacable ease. Halsey well understood the risks of sending Willis Lee's two big ships to set an ambush in Savo Sound. "The plan flouted one of the firmest doctrines of the Naval War College," Halsey would write. "The narrow treacherous waters north of Guadalcanal are utterly unsuited to the maneuvering of capital ships, especially in darkness." But the big ships were all he had left.

The *Washington* (the second and last ship of the *North Carolina* class), and the *South Dakota* (the first of a newer breed) were not sisters but close cousins, part of the surge in new major ship construction that followed the expiration of the 1930 London Naval Treaty's five-year-long "building holiday." The construction of the big new ships was politically risky for President Roosevelt during the pinchpenny, isolationist-minded years after the Great Depression. He waited until after the 1936 elections to authorize the *Washington*'s construction.

The Navy's General Board never seemed sure what it was willing to sacrifice in order to meet the limits imposed by treaty limitations on battleship displacement. Its preferred designs changed as frequently as its membership did. In the end, Lee's two battleships were the product of a decision to emphasize superior firepower. The two ships each carried a sixteen-inch main battery that fired a twenty-seven-hundred-pound projectile. More than ten times the weight of the eight-inch round fired by a heavy cruiser, these heavier weapons changed the calculus of warship architecture and, in turn, tactical doctrine as well. Though it was customary to design battleships to withstand hits from their own projectiles, the *Washington* did not have armor stout enough to defeat the heavy new sixteen-inch ordnance. The *South Dakota*'s side armor could take such a hit from beyond twenty thousand yards (or 11.4 miles), but only because her designers had compromised her ability to survive torpedoes. Rushed to the South Pacific soon after their commissionings, neither ship was put through the usual round of sea trials prior to deployment. But there was widespread confidence in them nonetheless, and the ships were more than a match for Japanese battleship such as the *Kirishima,* with a fourteen-inch main battery.

Aside from the short time they had operated together with the *Enterprise* task force, the *Washington* and the *South Dakota* had never been in each other's company. While Admiral Lee repeatedly drilled his gunnery and director crews in aiming their guns and finding targets, neither ship had much experience actually firing her big weapons. The *Washington* had only fired her main battery twice at night, both times in January 1942. Nighttime gunnery experience was scanter still on the *South Dakota*. She had fired her main battery three times, but never at night. Though the ships were state of the art, the state of their live-fire experience was far less than that of the old battleships sidelined on the West Coast: The *Colorado* conducted ten main-battery live-fire exercises between July and November. Lee's four destroyers had never operated together either.

The first time the *South Dakota*'s main battery was tested with a full nine-gun broadside, the wave of blast pressure pushed through the passageway where Captain Thomas Gatch was standing, tearing his pants right off him. The vast power of the sixteen-inch guns required a perfect physical apparatus to ensure not only their working order but also the safety of the ship. The bomb that exploded atop turret one during the air attacks of October 25 had gouged two barrels of turret two, which jutted out over the bomb's impact point. A lieutenant junior grade who served in the turret, Paul H. Backus, said, "As you can imagine, we made all kinds of measurements and sent messages back to the Bureau of Ordnance in Washington, describing these gouges, their depth, their length, and asked the question, 'Can we shoot these barrels?' We never did get an answer that we could live with." Finally word came back that turret two's center and left guns were not to be fired.

This powerful but patchwork group, Task Force 64, was Lee's first seagoing flag command. What he may have lacked in combat experience, he had made up for through the rigorous study of the practical problems of combat in the radar age. Having served as director of fleet training just before the war, he was one of the first naval officers to build a career on the wonkery of modern wave physics. The lingo of transmitters, receivers, double-lobe systems, and ring oscillators was like speaking in tongues to most officers. Imperturbable and capable of solving multiple lines of variables as they shifted, Lee was reputed to know the intricacies of radar systems better than their own operators did.

According to Admiral Kinkaid, a close friend and classmate, "He was not what you would describe as a 'military figure.' He was without the straight, taut carriage that that description would imply. Lee walked pigeon-toed and was hard of sight. At Annapolis he fretted the physical examination, memorizing the first two lines of the eye chart."

A native of Owen County, Kentucky, he was known back home as "Mose" but would acquire a more worldly nickname, "Ching," for his fondness for the Asiatic theater. According to Ernest M. Eller, a subordinate of Lee's at the Fleet Training Division, "He looked like an Arkansas farmer, a little like Will Rogers. He had a wrinkled, freckled face. You wouldn't have known he was very astute until you talked to him a while and learned what he knew. . . . He had a very mathematical, ingenious mind, and at the same time he talked very simply and very easily."

Lee matched his fluency in the language of science with a generous dose of Appalachian common sense. Early in his career, a destroyer he commanded suffered from a rat infestation. Tired of seeing the rodents scurrying across the wardroom's overhead beams, Lee fashioned a trap consisting of a solenoid mechanism and an armature attached to a meat cleaver. Delighted with the contraption, his officers diverted themselves with this minor blood sport, competing to see whose reflexes were quick enough to pull the lever and chop the stowaway rodents in two.

Lee's understanding of gunnery was world-class. In 1907, at age nineteen, he became the only American at the time to win both the U.S. National High Power Rifle and Pistol championships in the same year. In April 1914, during the U.S. intervention in Vera Cruz, Mexico, his landing force from the battleship *New Hampshire* came under fire. Wielding a borrowed rifle, Lee assumed a sitting position out in the open, drawing fire to locate enemy muzzle flashes, and killed three enemy snipers at long range. After such a performance in combat, the Olympics were hardly a test of nerves. At the age of thirty-two, he was a member of the U.S. rifle team that won seven medals, including five golds, at the 1920 Antwerp summer games.

Lee understood the powerful weapons of a battleship not as specialized naval instruments, but as extensions of the universal laws of ballistics that he had wholly absorbed by the time he took command. Most surface officers were obsessive students of gunnery, but few adapted their expertise to an age of new technology. Lee did so by conducting fire-control drills under odd conditions, sometimes requiring turrets be manned by relief crews instead of the first team, and throwing unexpected twists at them, randomly cutting out electrical connections to the mounts and scrambling their links to the fire-control radars, forcing his men to rely on backup systems or local control. Afterward, he gathered with Captain Glenn B. Davis; his gunnery officer, Commander H. T. Walsh; and a coterie of young officers, where his principal theorist, Ed Hooper, would run through the mathematics late into the night. "His conversation was so loaded with calculi and abelian equations," a historian wrote, "that sometimes Commander Walsh and Captain Davis would begin to look slightly helpless." That said a lot, seeing as Davis had served as the "experimental officer" at the Dahlgren Naval Proving Grounds, testing guns, armor, powder, and projectiles, and later served as chief of the gun section at the Bureau of Ordnance.

Lee knew that the key to victory lay not only in terms of engineering or mathematics, but in a crew's ability to adjust psychologically to the unexpected. Said Lloyd Mustin, "It doesn't take long to learn these things, a few hours. Learn the basics in a few hours and then start thinking in those terms day in and day out. Not everyone seemed able or willing to take the time." Willis Lee, like Norman Scott, took the time. He worked endlessly, late into the night, before unwinding with a few pages from a detective novel and falling asleep in his clothes a few hours before breakfast.

News of an inbound battleship force commanded Lee's attention. Late in the afternoon on November 14, he received a report that the submarine *Trout* had sighted large enemy units, southbound about 150 miles north of Guadalcanal. The Tokyo Express, though operating with changing rosters of ships and commanders, was keeping to its well-established timetable of midnight arrivals. While the Cactus Air Force was preoccupied with hammering Tanaka's transports that afternoon, Kondo's heavy surface force—the *Kirishima* joined by the heavy cruisers *Atago* and *Takao*—had avoided daylight air attack. It would be up to Lee's surface task force to stop them. Halsey had given him complete freedom of action after his arrival in the waters off Guadalcanal.

Japanese search planes had sighted Lee when he was still a hundred miles south of Guadalcanal, but failed to recognize his principal vessels as battleships. They reported Task Force 64 as composed of two cruisers and four destroyers. Later Kondo dismissed a report of a carrier and possibly some battleships some fifty miles south of the island, on grounds that they were not in position to intercept him that night. Like the men in Tanaka's transport force, Kondo was confident that the bombardment by the cruisers *Suzuya* and *Maya* the previous night had put down the Guadalcanal aviators. He had little idea what was in store for him.

As Task Force 64 approached the island's western shore, the captain of the *Washington,* Glenn Davis, walked into the chart house and pressed the button on the ship's intercom. "This is the captain speaking. We are going into an action area. We have no great certainty what forces we will encounter. We might be ambushed. A disaster of some sort may come upon us. But whatever it is we are going into, I hope to bring all of you back alive. Good luck to all of us." After the epic dustups of the previous two nights, the men on the islands around Savo Sound had learned to expect fireworks after dark. Willis Lee slugged north toward collision, aiming to oblige them.

SAVO SOUND WAS QUIET. Off the port bows of Lee's ships, the skies and calm waters were gently lit by flashes on the horizon—the gunfire from Tanaka's transport group as it resisted the last wave of aircraft from Henderson Field. As night fell, a quarter moon reclined overhead and the orange glow of fires warmed the western horizon, the fires of burning ships— trophies for the busy pilots of the Cactus Air Force.

None of this soothed the battleship sailors as they cruised at eighteen knots, prows easing through the sea. The sight of land nearby kept their nerves on edge. Appreciating the need for operating space, Lee had arranged his destroyers—the *Walke* leading the *Benham, Preston,* and *Gwin*—nearly three miles ahead of the battleships, which themselves were separated by nearly a mile. The men in the big ships craved sea room. "All we can do is trust in God and our surveys, and the surveys are not much good," wrote a *South Dakota* chaplain, James V. Claypool. He tried to play chess with another officer but found he couldn't concentrate. He read from a book titled *How to Keep a Sound Mind* but didn't get very far.

Lee checked in with Guadalcanal's radio station, known as "Cactus Control," for the latest dope. His own radio department had heard Japanese voices on the air, but couldn't translate them for want of an interpreter on board. Indeed, the intelligence setup was one of the continuing weaknesses of the SOPAC command. No reliable coordination yet existed between the commanders on the island and the naval forces they relied on for defense.

Neither Captain Greenman, the "Commander of Naval Activities," nor General Vandegrift was regularly apprised of the movements of friendly ships. As Lee awaited a reply from Cactus Control, there came a mysterious dispatch from an unidentified sender—one that Captain DuBose of the *Portland*, still moored to a palm tree in the shadows of Tulagi, would have understood all too well.

"There go two big ones, but I don't know whose they are." The intercepted words belonged to the skipper of a PT boat, lurking in shadow.

Order of Battle—The Battleship Night Action
(November 14–15, 1942)

U.S.
TASK FORCE 64
Rear Adm. Willis Lee

Washington (BB) (flagship)	*Benham* (DD)
South Dakota (BB)	*Preston* (DD)
Walke (DD)	*Gwin* (DD)

Japan
ADVANCED FORCE
Vice Adm. Nobutake Kondo

Bombardment Unit	*Screening Unit*
Vice Adm. Kondo	Rear Adm. Susumu Kimura
Kirishima (BB)	*Nagara* (CL)
Atago (CA) (flagship)	*Shirayuki* (DD)
Takao (CA)	*Hatsuyuki* (DD)
	Teruzuki (DD)
	Samidare (DD)
	Inazuma (DD)
	Asagumo (DD)

Sweeping Unit	*Reinforcement Unit*
Rear Adm. Shintaro Hashimoto	Rear Adm. Raizo Tanaka
Sendai (CL)	Four transports, nine destroyers
Uranami (DD)	
Shikinami (DD)	
Ayanami (DD)	

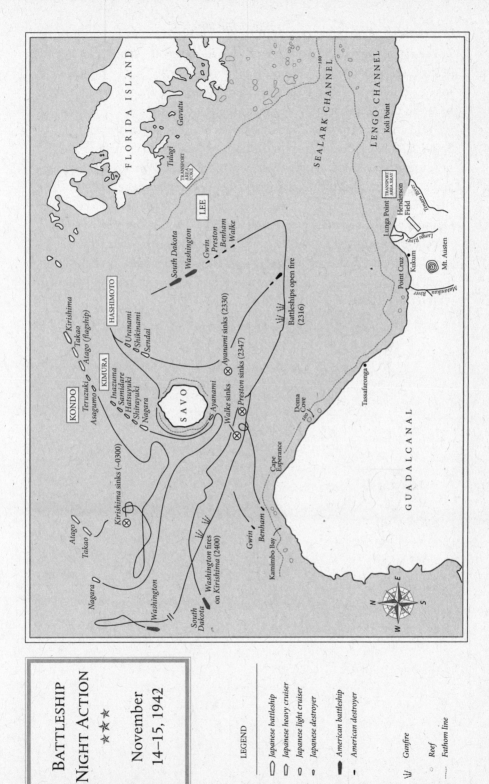

BATTLESHIP
NIGHT ACTION
★ ★ ★
November
14–15, 1942

LEGEND

∅ Japanese battleship
∅ Japanese heavy cruiser
∅ Japanese light cruiser
∅ Japanese destroyer
◆ American battleship
▬ American destroyer

⚡ Gunfire
∘ Reef
‒‒‒ Fathom line

FLORIDA ISLAND

Tulagi
Gavutu

TRANSPORT AREA YOKE

SEALARK CHANNEL

LENGO CHANNEL

Koli Point

LEE

South Dakota
Washington
Gwin
Preston
Benham
Walke

TRANSPORT AREA XRAY
Lunga Point
Henderson Field
Point Cruz
Kukum
Mt. Austen
Matanikau River
Lunga River

HASHIMOTO

KONDO
Teruzuki
Asagumo
KIMURA
Inazuma
Samidare
Hatsuyuki
Shirayuki
Nagara

Kirishima
Takao
Atago (flagship)
Uranami
Shikinami
Sendai

SAVO

Ayanami
Walke sinks
Preston sinks (2347)
Ayanami sinks (2330)

Battleships open fire
(2316)

Doma Cove

Tassafaronga

GUADALCANAL

Cape Esperance

Gwin
Benham

Kamimbo Bay

Washington fires
on Kirishima (2400)

Kirishima sinks (~0300)

Atago
Takao

Nagara

Washington

South Dakota

N E S W (compass rose)

Lee raised Guadalcanal again and warned them off. *"Refer your big boss about Ching Lee; Chinese, catchee? Call off your boys!"* The warning seemed to register. Another episode like the near torpedoing of the *Portland* would have had dire consequences for the mosquito boat drivers.

By ten thirty, Lee was cutting a clockwise arc about twenty miles north of Savo Island. With his sweeping radar beams revealing no contacts, he passed near the grave site of the *Hiei*, over the wrecks of the *Vincennes*, the *Quincy*, and the *Astoria*, then reentered Savo Sound, to cruise over the seafloor where the *Atlanta* lay. As the task force came around to a westerly heading and steamed toward Cape Esperance, the navigators and helmsmen of the task force noticed that their magnetic compass needles were twitching and spinning. Magnetic interference was straightforward enough an explanation. Some thought the dead ships of Ironbottom Sound were reaching out with an inscrutable message.

37

The Gun Club

FAITHFULLY MOTORING IN CIRCLES AS IT CAST ITS TEN-CENTIMETER microwaves, the *Washington*'s SG radar spied the enemy ships to the north of northwest, as they left the cover of Savo Island making twenty-one knots. The radars watched the enemy vessels for several minutes at a range of eighteen thousand yards, sharing their data on human wavelengths via the PPI scope, and to the mechanical fire-control computer that delivered calculus to the gun turrets, before losing track of the contacts because of interference from land.

The radars were sketching a picture, definite in range and bearing if indistinct in composition, of two groups of enemy ships north of Savo Island. Admiral Lee and Captain Davis had designed the *Washington*'s fire-control procedures around the fact that this type of data was essential to everything. They made sure that their radar plot officer did not operate the traditional way, communicating through a sailor who served as his "talker." Instead, he was wired up with his own headset to speak directly to the gunnery officer, the main battery plotting room officer, and the trainers in each of the gun director stations, all at the same time. In this way, he could describe the appearance of the scope and designate targets directly to all stations with a need to know, with less confusion.

With a Philip Morris hanging from his lips, Willis Lee said to Davis, "Well, stand by, Glenn, here they come." In every compartment of the *Washington*, an electronic bell gave two short rings, signaling a warning that a salvo was imminent. Hydraulic hoists trundled twenty-seven-hundred-pound projectiles up from the magazines to the turrets. The powder cars whisked up silk cylindrical bags filled with explosive propellant. The projectiles were eased mechanically onto the heavy bronze breech-loading trays and the powder bags laid in behind them, as many as eight per load depending on the range to the target. After the breech had been rammed and locked, the gun captain hit the ready light indicating the gun was ready to fire.

Admiral Kondo had arrayed his force in three groups. Consisting of the *Kirishima* and the cruisers *Atago* and *Takao,* his Bombardment Unit was his centerpiece. Ahead of those large ships went his Screening Unit, the light cruiser *Nagara* leading six destroyers, commanded by Rear Admiral Susumu Kimura. Off to the east steamed a separate Sweeping Unit made up of the light cruiser *Sendai* and three destroyers under Rear Admiral Shintaro Hashimoto. It was this latter group that Lee's radars detected first as the *Washington* and *South Dakota* plunged along on their westerly heading, tracing a course south of Savo Island. On the radar scope, the *Washington*'s radar plot officer watched the light echoes separate from the mass of Savo Island, "then separate into 'drops' similar to the effect of planes taking off from a carrier."

The *Washington*'s turrets trained to starboard and fixed on Hashimoto's group as it approached on the east side of Savo Island, sliding aft relative to the battleships as they moved west. At 11:13 p.m., when Main Battery Control reported to Lee that the narrowcasting fire-control radars had found targets and were yielding ranges, Lee hailed Gatch over the TBS and gave the *South Dakota* permission to open fire. It was not until the enemy vessels were spotted visually, at 18,500 yards, that the *Washington,* followed closely by the *South Dakota,* let loose. For the second time in three nights, Savo Sound erupted in thunder and light.

Ensign Robert B. Reed of the *Preston* watched the mighty flagship astern. As the corona of the *Washington*'s first broadside faded, he could follow the nine red tracers as they flew away, "grouped together for all the world like a flight of airplanes," he said. Reed watched the salvo disappear up into the low-hanging clouds, then reemerge ten miles downrange. When the fire-control radar received echoes that showed the first salvo had landed "over," beyond its target, the plotting officer checked his headphone chinstrap—the concussion of the big guns sent more than a few headsets clattering to the deck—then instructed the gunnery officer, Commander H. T. Walsh, to "spot down," lowering the elevation of the gun. The second salvo, fired forty-five seconds later, registered a "straddle." The officers watching the radars knew their fire was on target when they saw the radar image of the target flicker at the moment of impact.

After the two battleships commenced fire, radio snoopers in the *South Dakota* heard a cacophony of Japanese voices, "excited and very numerous." They counted at least thirteen stations on this frequency at one time. Though the *South Dakota*'s main battery was hamstrung, with just four guns working in her two forward triple turrets, she continued her cannonade until her forward turrets, swinging aft to remain on target, bumped up against the stops that kept her from firing into her own superstructure. The after turret, with no such restraints, kept firing, however, and as it trained straight aft the wash of fire from her barrels set fire to her two floatplanes, fantail-mounted on catapults. The small bonfires raged briefly before the next salvo blew them right off the ship.

The light cruiser *Sendai* and the destroyers *Shikinami* and *Uranami* were the objects of this large-caliber fury. Though Hashimoto's small squadron was engulfed in that maelstrom, not one of his ships was actually hit. The Sweeping Unit commander, the first Japanese naval officer to take fire from sixteen-inch guns, ordered his captains to lay a smoke screen—of little benefit against a radar-guided foe—and reverse course to seek other opportunities to "sweep." Surrounded by towering splashes, the captains of the Japanese ships, making smoke, beat a high-speed retreat.

The *Washington*'s secondary battery cracked ferociously away as well, with the two forward five-inch mounts shooting at the main battery's targets, and the next two mounts aft firing on a cruiser that appeared to be illuminating the *South Dakota*. The after dual five-inch mount lofted star shells. The intense flash of the five-inch fusillades blinded his main battery director operators and turret captains as they looked out through their night scopes. But fighting by eyesight was the old way of war. Now the human senses were an auxiliary system. "Radar has forced the Captain or OTC to base a greater part of his actions in a night engagement on what he is told rather than what he can see," Lee would write. Coolly deciding which directors would control which turrets, and switching them as the geometry of the engagement shifted, Willis Lee became the first naval commander to manage a gunfight mostly by radar remote control.

Using the picture his radar provided him, Lee could see his four destroyers ahead and monitor the shifting geometry of the landmasses around him. He had a fine view of the naval landscape. What he did not have, owing to an oversight in ship design, was an electronic picture of the situation to his rear. With his radar transmitters bolted to the front side of the tower foremast, he could register no returns through a sixty-degree arc astern. The *South Dakota* was in that blind spot. Without visual contact with the other battleship, he was susceptible to the same uncertainty that clouded the view of Scott and Callaghan in the previous surface engagements in Savo Sound. Lee could no longer be completely sure that large targets on his radar were hostile.

Lee's battleships were the first ships that night to make their powerful presence felt, but in short order the destroyers in his van were grappling with the enemy—and suffering the consequences of the collision. At about 11:30 p.m., the lead vessel, the *Walke,* located a target on her starboard beam at fifteen thousand yards. It was a lone enemy ship, the destroyer *Ayanami,* which had strayed from Hashimoto's formation and was winding a course west of Savo Island, alone. As the ship closed on their starboard hand, the *Walke* opened fire with her five-inch guns. Five minutes later, lookouts in Commander Max Stormes's *Preston,* third in line, spotted the *Nagara* ahead, leading four destroyers of the Screening Unit, and opened fire on her at seventy-five hundred yards. The *Walke* and the *Benham, Preston,* and *Gwin* turned their fire on these ships ahead.

The *Walke*'s captain, Thomas E. Fraser, had a hard time seeing his target, the *Ayanami,* given how closely the enemy destroyer was hugging Savo's shore. His radar could see the target only when it was far enough from land to return a separate echo. The *Ayanami*'s captain had no plans to allow that to happen. From the cover of the dark shoreline, around eleven thirty, he fired torpedoes at the American van and reversed course away from the action. The torpedoes were on their way. Enemy gunfire was faster in arriving.

By the light of a setting quarter moon flirting with low clouds, the *Preston* opened fire on another ship, the light cruiser *Nagara,* in the loom of Savo Island. Steaming at twenty-three knots, Stormes's ship found a hitting range at nine thousand yards when she was struck hard by a pair of 5.5-inch shells that plunged into her machinery spaces from the starboard side, killing everyone in her two fire rooms. The blast propelled a filthy cloud of firebrick and debris out of the stacks that settled all across the amidships area. Shattered torpedo warheads leaked TNT that quickly caught fire. The ship's after stack fell across a searchlight installation, knocking it over onto the starboard torpedo tube. A heavier hit followed as a strange ship—which the *Preston*'s officers would speculate was a Japanese heavy cruiser—approached from the port side of the American column and fired on the destroyer. One large shell entered the engine room, exploding against the electrical generators. Another hit near the number three gun, and a third was a direct hit on the number four. The blast was so great that it jammed guns one and two all the way forward. Aft of the stacks, the *Preston*'s decks were a blazing ruin. Captain Stormes was forced to give the order to abandon ship almost immediately.

However, to the executive officer of the *South Dakota*, Commander A. E. Uehlinger, and another officer, Henry Stewart, it was clear that the *Preston* was a victim of friendly fire. "I saw the *Washington* open fire to her starboard," Stewart said. "To us it looked as if the *Washington*'s fire had caused the accident." The action reports would lend credence to the idea that even Willis Lee was susceptible to making deadly mistakes in the heat of battle.

As the *Preston* coasted to a stop, the *Walke* was hit, too. Captain Fraser was working to set up a torpedo solution at a large target to starboard when the enemy fish arrived. One struck the *Walke* forward of the bridge, lifting the forward half of the ship "bodily out of the water," the action report read. As the destroyer crashed back into the sea without a bow forward of the bridge superstructure, one of the ship's magazines detonated and its explosion ruptured forward fuel oil tanks and tore holes in the superstructure decks. A few seconds later, several medium-caliber warheads slammed into the ship, blowing away a swath of her forecastle and forward superstructure decking. Across the main deck surged a flood of fuel oil several inches deep. Flames roared through the forward compartments. Very quickly it became clear that the *Walke* was going down by the bow. When machine-gun ammunition started popping and the forward bulkhead of the fire room finally buckled, Fraser decided to abandon ship. The severed bow floated on as the stern sank. Minutes later the survivors in the water were rocked by an undersea blast as the ship's depth charges exploded, to grievous effect in their company. The dead included Captain Fraser. The *Walke*'s dead would number eighty-two men, including six of her officers.

The *Benham*, behind the *Walke*, briefly took the lead before a shell plunged into her fire room. Then a torpedo struck, a Type 90 fish probably fired by the *Ayanami*. It carried away about fifty feet of the *Benham*'s bow below the main deck. The blast produced no fatalities but sent a tall column of hot seawater soaring toward the stars. When it came back down, it washed heavily over the length of the ship, causing injuries topside and carrying a man overboard. Then another shower fell on the *Benham*: oil and debris from the explosion on board the *Preston* ahead. The *Benham* continued along at ten knots. The *Gwin*, riding in the van's rear, popped star shells, illuminating the coast of Savo, where flashes of gunfire were visible. Her torpedo crew had a solution on a cruiser but a short circuit caused a torpedo to fire prematurely, well out of range. Then the *Gwin,* too, started absorbing shells, taking a hit in the engine room. A failure in her safety circuits caused three torpedoes to release from their tubes and slide harmlessly overboard. The *Gwin* came right to avoid the dying *Preston* and continued on her westerly course.

The *Benham*'s captain, Lieutenant Commander John B. Taylor, saw the trouble ahead and decided to steer clear of the damaged ships and the churn of enemy gunfire. Turning hard right, he made a half circle and steadied up, heading east until the *Washington* passed on an opposite course. Circling back around, Taylor, seeing the burning *Walke* and *Preston,* planned to stop and recover survivors. When the two cripples came under fire again, he elected, however, to withdraw.

It was around this time, at about 11:33 p.m., that the *South Dakota* suffered an appalling systems failure. Her after turret had just lashed out at a target off the starboard bow when Captain Gatch's ship was seized as if by an aneurysm, a short circuit in her main switchboard. As the breakers tripped out in the switchboards that served her secondary battery, only to find that they had been tied down by the chief engineer, the overload surged to other switches, creating a collapsing house of cards within the ship's power grid. In an instant the great battleship went dark. Gone were her gyros and all her fire-control equipment. As the battleship's main battery fell silent, there was nothing Gatch could do to his enemy but curse.

When the *Washington* turned left and passed the burning destroyers on their disengaged side, hidden from the enemy by their fires, she entered waters dense with flotsam and survivors. Making twenty-six knots through the debris field of the stricken *Walke* and *Preston,* the battleship's sailors threw life rafts overboard. From the ranks of bobbing heads they heard cries of encouragement: "Get after'em, *Washington!*"

Captain Gatch in the *South Dakota* tried to follow the *Washington* as she passed on the disengaged hand of the destroyers, but when a wreck of a destroyer loomed, threatening collision, he was forced to turn the other way, conning sharply right, passing between the *Walke* and *Preston* and the enemy. The maneuver placed his blinded warship in an unfortunate tactical position, silhouetted by the burning wrecks and plainly visible to an enemy hungry for targets. Three minutes after her switchboard failure, power returned to the ship. The outage was long enough to disorient one of the two most powerful ships in Savo Sound that night. And the confusion that reigned led to a tactical error in shiphandling that would draw concentrated enemy attention in the coming minutes.

The heavy toll inflicted on the four leading ships of the American column was the pattern set by previous engagements. Destroyers, always expendable, had sacrificed themselves in faithful adherence to duty. Seeing the plight of his leading foursome, Willis Lee excused his van from battle, ordering the *Benham* and the *Gwin* to retire. The *Washington* and *South Dakota* would carry this fight alone.

In the *Washington,* the detonation of the *Walke*'s depth charges could be felt like a speed bump under tread. The battleship, whose five-inch guns helped batter the *Ayanami* to a powerless, burning hulk, had to cease firing her secondary battery now for fear of hitting friendly destroyers.

For his part, Kondo was eager to send his two smaller groups to tangle with the Americans, but he was cautious and hesitant with his more powerful Bombardment Unit. He received a report from Commander Eiji Sakuma, captain of the *Ayanami,* taking credit for the grievous damage inflicted on the American destroyer van. The elation on the *Atago*'s bridge was squelched when word arrived from Admiral Hashimoto in the *Sendai* that the *Ayanami* had been terribly hit herself. Adrift northwest of Savo Island, she would finally sink when spreading fires detonated her torpedo battery, breaking her in two.

As his widely roaming forces circled and sparred with Lee, Kondo seemed torn between two objectives. Keenly aware that his mission was to suppress the airfield so as to give Tanaka's transports, steaming well to his north, a chance to land without further interference from the Cactus Air Force, Kondo kept the *Kirishima* and his two heavy cruisers interposed between Lee and the transports. Even as lookouts in the *Atago* and *Takao* insisted they had seen an American battleship among their opponents, Kondo discounted the possibility. He let his light forces carry the fight while awaiting his opportunity to throw the *Kirishima* at Henderson Field.

Having learned from his destroyers that the fight was going well against the U.S. "cruisers," Kondo ordered Hashimoto to assist the damaged *Ayanami*. As Hashimoto turned north to comply, he encountered Admiral Kimura's destroyers, compelling them into a full circular turn to avoid a collision. Kondo's unwieldy task force organization thus turned and bit him. As the Bombardment Force—the *Kirishima* and the two cruisers—finally turned south to close on Henderson Field, both Kimura and Hashimoto found themselves out of the fight.

Kondo had barely settled into his new heading when his lookouts spotted the *South Dakota* and identified her as a cruiser. At the same time, the *Nagara* reported seeing two enemy battleships near Cape Esperance. The *Atago*'s lookouts corrected their error in short order, announcing the presence of battleships. But it was only after his flagship's searchlights swept over the compact and powerful form of the forty-two-thousand-ton *South Dakota* that Kondo himself finally grasped the nature of his opponent. All at once both the admiral and his flagship's commanding officer, Captain Matsuji Ijuin, began shouting orders to engage.

Fixed by searchlights, the U.S. battlewagon drew the immediate violent attention of every major ship in Kondo's force. The Japanese flagship *Atago* and her sister ship, the *Takao,* struck the *South Dakota* especially hard, repeated scoring with eight-inch fire from five thousand yards. From the *Atago,* the *Nagara,* and four destroyers, thirty-four Long Lances splashed into the sea. The *Kirishima* fired on Gatch's ship with her fourteen-inch battery from eleven thousand yards, scoring with a hit at the base of her great after turret. The blast turned the surrounding deck planks into a storm of chips, incinerated the canvas gun bloomers, and cast fragments up and down the deck. A loader on the left gun inside the turret heard officers on the phones, wondering about the extent of the damage and whether the gun would still fire with an Olympian dent in her barbette. "Our turret commander was certainly a cool-headed duck," he recalled. "He said, 'Never mind how bad we're hit. I don't give a damn if the guns blow up. I'm going to fire.'" There came a double buzz followed by a long buzz, indicating the turret was about to discharge. The expectant seconds passed, but the great guns remained silent. With the main battery out, paralyzed by the electrical failure, Gatch was able to respond only with his secondary battery. The battleship's five-inch guns jackhammered fiercely in local control, but were hardly a deterrent to heavy cruisers and a battleship.

Topside, the *South Dakota* was taking the same kind of punishment that had turned the *San Francisco*'s decks into a killing field two nights before. The wash of shrapnel made a sizzling sound as it sliced into cables, gun shields, and steel decking. Well protected though the engineering compartments were deep within the vital "armored box," no battleship's topsides stations were proof against such firepower. More often than not, the armor-piercing rounds fired by Kondo's ships penetrated and passed through the superstructure plating without exploding. Still, the fires raged so fiercely that some enemy observers became convinced she was a goner. The barrage of hits to the *South Dakota*'s superstructure shattered steam pipes going to

Yard workers at Mare Island tend to the *Portland*'s massive torpedo wound.

The battleship *Hiei*, shown in dry dock in 1942.

Vice Admiral Nobutake Kondo led Japanese forces against Admiral Callaghan in the Cruiser Night Action, November 13, 1942.

The *Juneau* alongside the *Aaron Ward* in New York shortly after their commissionings, March 19, 1942.

Captain Lyman K. Swenson, commander of the *Juneau*, was among more than 700 lost when she was torpedoed on November 13.

Captain Cassin Young (right) replaced Charles H. McMorris as commander of the *San Francisco*. He had received the Medal of Honor from Admiral Nimitz in April 1942.

Four of the Sullivan brothers were killed when the *Juneau* exploded. George died later at sea.

the five Sullivan brothers
"missing in action" off the Solomons

THEY DID THEIR PART

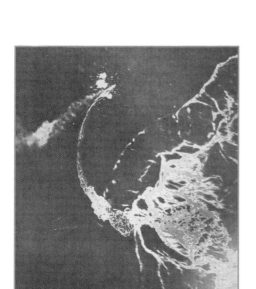

Damaged after battle with Callaghan's force, the *Hiei* burns and bleeds oil while evading attack from B-17 bombers the following day. She limped toward home but disappeared that night.

The *Cushing* led Callaghan's column—and paid the price.

The *Laffey* battled the *Hiei* at point blank range.

The *Aaron Ward* was heavily damaged the night of Friday the 13th.

Recruits at Bainbridge, Maryland, undergo testing, 1943.

New sailors at Naval Air Station Corpus Christi, October 9, 1942.

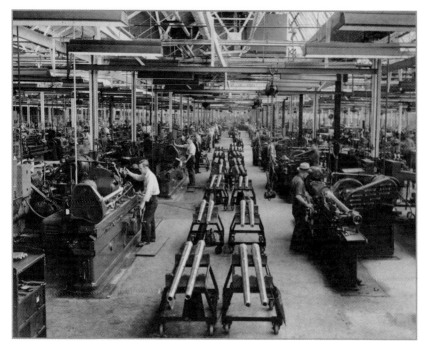

Metalworkers at a Chrysler plant in Detroit turn out 40 mm gun tubes.

The battleship *Washington* off New York City, preparing to leave for the Pacific, August 1942.

Willis A. Lee reports to the USS *Washington* at Tongatabu, September 14, 1942.

The *South Dakota*, July 1942.

The *South Dakota*'s secondary battery roars.

The *South Dakota* took a beating from Japanese cruisers on the night of November 14 but returned as a legend, hailed in the press as "Battleship X."

Note the effects of the blast, and the patches in the hull below the large hole.

A 14-inch shell from the *Kirishima* splintered the *South Dakota*'s deck and disabled turret three.

The *Walke* was one of three destroyers sacrificed in the cause of Willis Lee's victory.

The *Barton,* shown on her commissioning day at Boston Harbor, May 29, 1942.

South Dakota sailors bow their heads in memory of sailors lost in the Battleship Night Action, November 14–15, 1942.

Halsey said it was Scott's and Callaghan's bravery that got him his fourth star. He takes the oath from his chief of staff, Captain Miles Browning.

The Japanese transport *Kinugawa Maru*, beached on Guadalcanal after attack by Cactus Air Force fliers on November 15.

Nearly sunk in the Battle of Cape Esperance and with her bow bearing a large patch, the *Boise* returns to Philadelphia for repairs, November 20, 1942.

Captain Edward J. "Mike" Moran (right) hosts Admiral King aboard the *Boise*.

A *Boise* sailor inspects heavy splinter damage to a bulkhead.

Her proud crew claimed six enemy ships.

Captain Moran stands in front of the *Boise*'s battle-worn gun barrels.

Battle damage to the *San Francisco*'s hangar area, looking slightly aft from port to starboard.

The battered *San Francisco* enters San Francisco Harbor, December 11, 1942.

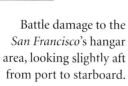

Glimpsed through a shell hole in a gun shield, Admiral Nimitz comes aboard the *San Francisco*.

Nimitz inspects the damaged bridge with Lieutenant Commander Herbert E. Schonland.

Lieutenant Commander Bruce McCandless received the Medal of Honor for conning the *San Francisco* after her senior officers were killed.

McCandless comforts the father and aunt of Admiral Callaghan.

The heavy cruiser *New Orleans*, her entire bow shorn away by a Long Lance torpedo, undergoes temporary repairs at Tulagi after the November 30 Battle of Tassafaronga.

Exuberant *San Francisco* sailors meet the press.

The *PT-109* heads for shore with 94 survivors of the *Northampton*. In the background, the *New Orleans*, with the *Maury* standing by, fights for her life. John F. Kennedy would take command of the PT boat in April 1943.

Admiral Arthur J. Hepburn conducted the official inquest into the causes of the defeat at Savo Island. Scapegoats were duly found.

Eugene Tarrant, photographed March 5, 2007 in San Francisco, served as captain's cook in the *San Francisco*.

The *New Orleans* returns to Pearl Harbor with a false bow and her forward eight-inch guns removed.

What victory looks like: Guadalcanal boasts a new wharf and several cranes to assist in unloading supplies.

Ghormley with Eleanor Roosevelt at Pearl Harbor, 1943. Ghormley's relief was wrongly thought the consequence of the defeat at Savo Island. Nimitz believed he was having a nervous breakdown.

GIVE US **LUMBER** FOR MORE PT'S

The sailors of the PT boat fleet fought gallantly in the Solomons, but the press still felt the need to sensationalize their capabilities.

After a taste of victory, the Navy learned how to play the PR game. Captain Gatch of the *South Dakota* confers with journalist Sidney Shallet in July 1943.

Lieutenant Hugh M. Robinson (left) and Lieutenant John M. Searles (right) display the scorecard for Motor Torpedo Boat Squadron 3: thirteen hits on Japanese ships in four months of work.

the ship's whistle, and gusts of steam scalded many sailors in those exposed spaces. In Battle Two, the executive officer, Commander A. E. Uehlinger, refused to abandon station after it was engulfed in steam. In the end, the battleship's high foremast superstructure was poor shelter. It was a death trap.

The chaplain, James Claypool, recalled hearing men praying. Some were so scared they couldn't remember the words to the Lord's Prayer. "At such times everything you do is a prayer," a chief petty officer said. "Even your cuss words are prayers."

The *South Dakota* was designed for a different kind of fight, conducted at distances to the horizon and beyond, where her huge guns could kill at standoff range. At close ranges, the variables were too many to manage and the risk was great. When an eight-inch shell exploded near an ammunition hoist, flashing through the opening and igniting some life jackets, a fire rose in a passageway adjacent to a handling room serving the five-inch battery. This small fire was a dangerous one. But it and the rest of the *South Dakota*'s belowdecks fires were quickly extinguished, and a disastrous secondary explosion was forestalled. It was Gatch's good fortune especially that none of the many torpedoes fired his way struck his ship, as her design was vulnerable below the waterline. Several Long Lances exploded prematurely on the way in. Topside, the flames danced.

WILLIS LEE IN THE *Washington* had been patiently tracking a large target on his starboard hand, but since he had lost track of the *South Dakota,* owing to his blind spot astern, he dared not turn loose his big guns on this bogey, the *Kirishima,* until her identity could be verified. When the Japanese opened their searchlight shutters on the *South Dakota,* however, he had his answer. Lee's flagship enjoyed momentary concealment as she slid behind the burning *Walke* and *Preston,* which blinded Kondo to his presence. Here was an hour of truth, and the truth was this: Willis Lee was the contemporary master of radar fire control, and *Washington*'s SG system gave him a clear electronic view of the oceanic battlefield under almost any circumstances.

While sailors in open-air stations saw the horror of naval combat in the machine age with their own senses—steaming through the debris fields of the sunken destroyers, shouting out to sailors bobbing on rafts nursing ghastly wounds, smelling the sweet tang of burned flesh—inside, officers with access to a radar image watched an abstract painting of the battlescape unfurl in a remorseless electric light. It was a picture cleansed of horror and emotion. Lee knew how to operate by it. He trained one group of his starboard side five-inch dual mounts on the *Atago,* and his main battery and the other group of five-inch mounts on the larger blip on his scope, the *Kirishima.* The *Washington's* unblinking electronic eyes nudged the main battery on target. From eighty-four hundred yards—"body punching range," as a *Washington* lieutenant put it—the South Pacific's battleship gunslinger emerged from the cover of his burning destroyers and turned loose with everything he had. Naval engineers who designed protective armor schemes for battleships calculated from the need to stop large-caliber direct gunfire from around twenty thousand yards. But at close ranges, stopping a sixteen-inch projectile was hopeless. One of the *South Dakota's* turret officers, Paul Backus, exclaimed, "Throwing fourteen-inch and sixteen-inch shells at that kind of range—Jesus." Willis Lee had won the draw on the *Kirishima.*

The last time Lee had held night spotting and gunnery practice was in January 1942. But since then, he had drilled his crews in target selection and fire-control procedures so thoroughly that it did not really matter whether it was night or day. An ensign named Patrick Vincent, stationed in the *Washington's* armored conning tower, said, "I was amazed at how well Captain Davis and Admiral Lee could function on the bridge with all the noise and blasting pressure from the guns. The racket was unbelievable. Even in the conning tower, it was almost impossible to communicate. The pressure from the gunfire spurting through open ports was knocking men down." It was nothing like what a battleship experienced on the receiving end of that fury.

It had been just six minutes since the *Kirishima's* gunners had lost a solution on the *South Dakota* and checked their fire. Lookouts on the *Atago,* spotting the *Washington,* shouted, "There is another ship forward of the first, a big battleship!" Short seconds later the lookouts were crying, "*Kirishima* is totally obscured by shell splashes!" According to Lee, the *Washington's* fire control and main battery "functioned as smoothly as though she were engaged in a well-rehearsed target practice." The first salvo probably hit, and the second one certainly did.

Ashore, roused from sleep by the heavy hammering of main batteries in the sound, Bill McKinney was among a team of *Atlanta* electricians stationed on a searchlight installation that stood watch over Guadalcanal's northern coast. Defended by a detachment of marines, the facility consisted of a tower of sixty-inch searchlights with a diesel generator and a remote-control director station. It was inoperable because its power cable had been slashed by overzealous foxhole diggers. Now, awakened, they were seized by the sight of battle. There was no telling who was friend or foe. It was like watching a baseball game without lineup cards, with everyone in the same colorless uniform. Ships revealed themselves suddenly with long gouts of flame and the bright parabolas of tracer rounds lazing through the night. The luminous red globes that seemed to float across the water knew no nationality. A few of them seemed to hover and disappear into the silhouette of a large ship, which stopped firing.

The *Kirishima* took a frightful battering from the *Washington*. The first hit destroyed the forward radio room located at the base of the foremast pagoda, below the main deck. Shells smashed into the barbettes of her two forward fourteen-inch turrets, starting fires that threatened the magazines. The battleship's assistant gunnery officer, Lieutenant Commander Horishi Tokuno, ordered a forward powder magazine flooded to prevent fires. The rush of water caused the ship to list slightly to starboard. Another projectile hit the steering machinery room, flooding it and leaving the rudder jammed to starboard. After this, only the ship's inboard shafts were working, making it impossible to steer by reversing the outboard shafts. When hydraulic pressure failed in the after part of the ship, her two after main gun turrets were left inoperable.

Heat and smoke from topside fires, sucked into the ship by ventilation turbines, forced the evacuation of the engine rooms. A pair of thirty-foot holes yawning in her deck amidships were the scars of this massive assault. On the *Kirishima*'s bridge, Lieutenant (j.g.) Michio Kobayashi noticed the ship slowing and turning in a circle.

The *Kirishima*'s main battery managed to roar several times in return. The commanding officer, Captain Sanji Iwabuchi, thought his first salvo scored two hits, one of them blowing off the bridge of his target. "At least ten hits were made upon them, but the enemy could not be finished off," he said. It was the familiar optimism of a warrior lost in a battle larger than he can comprehend. The fourteen-inch armor-piercing rounds passed like giant subway cars over the *Washington*'s rigging. "They must have been mighty close," a *Washington* sailor said, "but an inch is as good as a mile." Ed Hooper's remorseless radars would have allowed no escape, even if the enemy ship retained the ability to maneuver. As the radar automatically lay the big rifles, the *Washington*'s gun trains kept rolling and the night rained murderously with heavy metal. The U.S. flagship's rapid-firing secondary battery popped five-inch rounds into the *Kirishima*'s pagoda foremast, stacks, and superstructure, causing untold loss of personnel.

When the officer in Main Battery Control ordered the guns to cease fire, based on an erroneous report that his target had sunk, Captain Iwabuchi tried futilely to conn the *Kirishima* away from the *Washington*, but "we couldn't make way at all," he said. "In the meantime, the engine rooms became intolerable because of the increased heat, and most of the engineers were killed though they had been ordered to evacuate. Only the central engine could make the slowest speed. Fires brought under control gained strength again, so that the fore and aft magazines became endangered. Orders to flood them were then issued."

Ninety seconds later, Captain Davis ordered his main battery, "If you can see anything to shoot at, go ahead," and the great guns opened up again on the *Kirishima*, whose gunners were able to respond with only her after tur-ret. "More hits obtained," the action reported declared.

More than two hundred sailors lay dead in the *Kirishima*, victims of a stem-to-stern pummeling by at least twenty sixteen-inch shells from the *Washington*. Lieutenant Kobayashi believed the ship took half a dozen torpedoes as well, but these were most likely underwater hits. Many of the great twenty-seven-hundred-pound American projectiles struck short but plowed under the sea on flat trajectories to strike below the waterline. Admiral Lee, seeing their splashes, most likely counted these as misses. But they did, by far, the greatest damage to the *Kirishima*, all along her length. These underwater hits were Willis Lee's answer to the Long Lance torpedo.

After midnight, Kondo ordered his battered Bombardment Unit onto a westerly course. Only the *Atago*, lightly damaged, and the *Takao*, unhit, could comply. The *Washington*'s radars tracked the Japanese ships as they withdrew—a light cruiser was fixed for the forward turrets, and a destroyer for the after turret. But Lee, unsure of the *South Dakota*'s location, would not allow the main battery to fire.

Captain Gatch was fortunate to escape with a seaworthy battleship. The *South Dakota* had taken twenty-six hits, including eighteen by eight-inch projectiles and one by a fourteen-incher. The damage wrought to the upper works was serious. With all of the ship's lights out, working parties operated by feel as they searched for the dead in the darkened foremast tower. They would not soon forget the things they found.

Having lost track of the *Washington*, Gatch decided that his night was over. His battered ship, alone, was unable to carry the fight any longer. He elected to retire. This decision came as a relief to Willis Lee, who had pursuit on his mind and didn't need a wounded compatriot to worry about. The last report from Cactus Control at 7 p.m. put five Japanese transports dead in the water about fifteen miles north of the Russell Islands, and four more limping northwest with a small combat escort.

His big rifles not yet cool, Lee steered a course to intercept them the next day. The *Washington* had come through virtually unscratched by enemy fire. A five-inch hole in her giant "bedspring" air-search radar transmitter was her only wound. She took a much worse thrashing from the blast of her own guns: bulkheads caved in, compartments violently tossed, and a floatplane left in ruins, suitable only for parts. Her only human casualties were a punctured eardrum and an abrasion to the back of a hand. She was the most powerful ship in these waters, but any ship alone is a vulnerable one.

Shadowed by several of Kondo's destroyers, Glenn Davis rang the *Washington*'s engine room to make emergency power, and his raging boilers piped enough steam to whistle up the four shafts to nearly twenty-seven knots. At that speed, the 44,500-ton battleship, accelerating through a turn, cleaved wakes from her bow and stern that, in collision, generated wave peaks high enough to register on radar and spook her plotting officers that enemy ships were close in pursuit. When the *Washington*'s radar registered real phantoms—small blips, presumably destroyers, on the starboard bow—and when a smoke screen was sighted ahead, Captain Davis turned sharply right to avoid contact with a torpedo-wielding enemy; he continued turning until the flagship was headed south, on course to retire. As he did so, large explosions raised great columns of water in her wake. He had turned away just in time.

The battered *Kirishima* would not be saved. The light cruiser *Nagara* was nearby and Captain Iwabuchi requested a tow, but it was refused. The captain sent a radio message to Admiral Yamamoto, requesting that he order *Nagara* to tow the ship, but there was no time for intervention from Truk. The big vessel's list was just too severe. "An attempt to prevent the flooding of the steering gear room also failing, the ship became hopeless," Iwabuchi said. The ship alternated listing to left and to right, as the free-surface effect of floodwaters pulled her from side to side. Finally the ship listed to starboard so badly as to make it impossible to stand on the bridge. Iwabuchi ordered Lieutenant Kobayashi to use a flashlight to signal the destroyers *Asagumo* and *Teruzuki* to come alongside, one to starboard, the other to port, to remove survivors. Officers in the wrecked and burning ship performed the earnest rituals of defeat—lowering the ensign to shouted banzais, transferring the emperor's portrait to the *Asagumo*. As eleven hundred souls were taken off the colossal wreck, the list was so severe that Iwabuchi had no choice but to scuttle her. His engineers opened the Kingston valves, attached to the bottom of her fuel tanks to enable cleaning, and the sea flooded in.

Lieutenant Kobayashi had scarcely hopped over to the *Asagumo* when the *Kirishima* rolled hard and unexpectedly to port. The *Asagumo* freed her lines and pulled safely away. The captain of the *Teruzuki* had to order an emergency back full to avoid being capped by the turtling battleship's superstructure. With about three hundred men still on board, the *Kirishima* joined the boneyard in Ironbottom Sound shortly after 3 a.m. on November 15, about eleven miles west of Savo Island. "My men fought well and displayed the noble spirit of servicemen," Iwabuchi said. "My only regret is that we could not sink the enemy in exchange for our ship." Before the two fleets parted ways and returned home, the *Atago* tried one final time to grapple with the American battlewagons. Captain Ijuin's ship launched a dozen torpedoes in three salvos, but these, fired at a poor angle astern their retiring target, never had a chance. The cruiser opened fire with her eight-inch main battery on the *Washington* from fifteen thousand yards, but this was a halfhearted final gesture from a force that had spent its fighting energies. Ijuin ordered a smoke screen and turned away to the north. The *Washington*'s fire-control specialists tracked the *Atago* and observed the flashes of her gunfire, but Admiral Lee and Captain Davis had had enough for one night, too. They set course south and departed the battle area.

Lee had good reason to be satisfied with his night's work. Beyond the hammer blows he had landed on the *Kirishima*—the only battleship that would be sunk by another, one on one, during the entire Pacific campaign[*]—he knew that the Japanese troop transports, wherever they were, were too far away to reach Guadalcanal before sunrise, when Henderson Field's pilots, spared a thrashing from the sea, would be ready with a savage greeting. Lee directed the *Gwin* and the limping *Benham* to head for Espiritu Santo, but the *Benham* would not make it. Her fractured hull put her at risk of floundering and losing her entire crew. The *Gwin* scuttled her that night.

Finally locating the *South Dakota*, which greeted them with the signal, "I AM NOT EFFECTIVE," Lee and Davis formed up with Gatch. Following behind, the *Washington* plowed seas tainted with the *South Dakota*'s bunker oil all the way back to Nouméa. Shorn of the company of destroyers, the victorious American battlewagons, one riddled like a can on a stump, with thirty-nine fatalities, the other completely unscathed, rode beam-to-beam toward the comfort of their tropical home.

---

[*] The IJN battleships *Yamashiro* and *Fuso*, sunk during an engagement with U.S. battleships in Surigao Strait on the night of October 24–25, 1944, were done in mostly by destroyer torpedoes.

Later the *South Dakota*'s captain would marvel at the fact that the battleships hadn't been hit by torpedoes. Gatch credited the destroyers for this. He
thought they had "indirectly deceived" the Japanese; judging by the swarms
of torpedoes Kondo's escorts had fired at his van, Davis thought Kondo had
mistaken the U.S. destroyers for more lucrative targets. "This probably saved
the battleships being hit by torpedoes," he observed. When Lee asked Gatch
afterward whether he felt the use of his destroyers had been proper in light
of their near total loss, Gatch told him, "As things turned out, I thought it
was." This was cold testimony to the expendability of the destroyer force,
which lost more than two hundred men on the night of November 14–15.
Lee appreciated their sacrifice. "In breaking up the enemy destroyer attack,
our destroyers certainly relieved the battleships of a serious hazard and
probably saved their bacon," he wrote.

At Nouméa, the crews of the two battleships were far less generous with
each other. Until the *South Dakota* departed for a stateside overhaul, they
had more than a week to fight out the question of her combat performance
in the bars and lockups. "War was declared between the two ships. It was that
simple," a *Washington* sailor said. Furious, Lee finally called a truce, issuing a
special Order of the Day that stated, "One war at a time is enough!" and
arranging for the two battleships to stagger their liberties ashore.

Halsey's decision to throw his two battleships into the breach was vindi-
cated by victory. It was the sort of risk that Nimitz had implicitly counseled
against, and that Fletcher had forsworn with his carriers. "Our battleships,"
Lee wrote, "are neither designed nor armed for close range night actions
with enemy light forces. A few minutes intense fire, at short range, from secondary battery guns can, and did, render one of our new battleships deaf,
dumb, blind and impotent through destruction of radar, radio and fire control circuits." Halsey would say of his decision to send in Lee's battleships:
"How are all the experts going to comment now? The use we made of them
defied all conventions, narrow waters, submarine menace, and destroyers at
night. Despite that, the books, and the learned and ponderous words of the
highbrows, it worked." Naval tacticians would find it tempting to undervalue
what Lee accomplished that night, saying the *Washington* did what any
modern battleship should do to a smaller specimen of the previous generation. But his victory was anything but an anticlimax foretold in a war lab—
especially to the men who were there. Had Lee not confronted Kondo, the
airfield would have been a feast for the IJN that night and perhaps into the
next morning. If Henderson Field had been neutralized, the *Enterprise*
would have been the only source of U.S. airpower left in the combat area,

and a feeble one at that: When the carrier retired south, she had only eighteen Wildcat fighters on board. Her entire complement of Avengers and Dauntlesses had gone to operate with the Cactus Air Force at Henderson Field.

With the battle of giants over, Rear Admiral Tanaka turned the broad prows of his four navigable transports southward. (Several of their damaged cohorts would lie dead in the water near the Russell Islands, soon to fall victim to pilots from Guadalcanal.) Yamamoto himself endorsed Tanaka's plan to run the ships aground. It was around 4 a.m. when they beached themselves near Tassafaronga. Though they brought one last load into "Starvation Island," they took themselves out of the war. These ships would be easy targets for attacks from air, land, and sea. Set upon by the forces of nature in the ensuing decades, the wreckage of the transports would stand as symbols of Japan's futile determination to hold the southern Solomons. From a force of more than twelve thousand soldiers that Tanaka had originally embarked at Rabaul, only about two thousand straggled ashore, along with 260 cases of ammunition and fifteen hundred bags of rice. Every one of more than fifty-five hundred men Turner had transported to the island that week arrived safely. The numbers would spell victory.

38

The Kind of Men
Who Win a War

THAT MORNING ON GUADALCANAL, IN THE AFTERMATH OF THE battle in the sound, the outcome was still in doubt. Word went around to everyone holed up on the north shore that if the Japanese had prevailed, their troops would be storming ashore before dawn. The news passed like a current among the electricians working to repair the power cables serving the remote-control searchlight battery. "This ruled out any further sleep," Bill McKinney wrote. When the familiar throaty rumble of U.S. PT boats rolled in from the sound, it was safe to presume a victory. And when a report came in from the waterfront of enemy corpses floating in the water—uncountable multitudes of them—a sense of reassurance spread about the outcome. McKinney and his pals returned to work splicing cable, "like ladies in a sewing circle."

There were more than a few Americans out there on the swells. Survivors from the *Walke* and the *Preston* were among the oil-soaked throng revealed by the sunrise. Fighters on the morning patrol dipped down for a closer look, buzzing them to indicate their location to rescue boats. More than once, the pilot of an Army P-400 Airacobra bore down on a cluster of bobbing heads with his finger tensed on the trigger in case the survivors were enemy. The Guadalcanal campaign marked the onset, as far as U.S. servicemen were concerned, of "total war." Marine Raider units among others were slaughtering prisoners rather than hauling them around. At sea and in the air, the same brutal ethic prevailed, no matter what the international accords required. These sailors breathed considerably easier after noon, when the destroyer *Meade* arrived from Tulagi, lowered boats, and began taking them aboard. A pair of floatplanes left behind by Callaghan's cruisers puttered around, inviting survivors to grab a pontoon strut for a ride to safety. Taken to the *Meade,* they fouled the destroyer's well-kept wardroom, now a triage, with their blood.

But the worst traumas of November reached waters far from Savo Sound. Most of the American sailors who were still missing in action at that time were beyond the reach of helping hands from Guadalcanal. An appreciation of the ordeal suffered by the survivors of the USS *Juneau* would be gained only in retrospect, when nothing remained to be done for them. The fact that as many as 140 men had lived through the ship's sudden loss to a submarine torpedo on the morning of the thirteenth would surprise all who had witnessed her loss. The detonation of the *Juneau's* powder magazine killed nearly everyone in her forward sections. Almost all those who survived were stationed in the after part of the ship. The survivors may have been spared by the fractured keel, whose wobbly state might have dissipated the blast wave as it flowed aft along the ship's spine.

Spared was the wrong word for most of the men. Beneath a cloud of fuel oil vapors and powder smoke, they hit the waters in a squall of shattered steel, flying hatch covers, and tumbling gun barrels and radar antennae, the hard gore of a warship that tore flesh and broke bone. One *Juneau* survivor would estimate that two-thirds of his surviving shipmates who hit the water alive had received serious wounds. According to Allen Heyn, "Some of them were in very bad shape. Their arms and legs were torn off. And one of them, I could see myself his skull. You could see the red part inside where his head had been split open you might say torn open in places." The next morning, Heyn noticed that "his hair had turned gray just as if he was an old man."

Shortly after the *Juneau's* loss that morning, Gilbert Hoover had signaled her final coordinates to the pilot of a B-17 Flying Fortress that happened by overhead, with a request to relay the information to Nouméa. The pilot counted some sixty souls in the water and dropped a balsa life raft. His message to Halsey, however, took untold hours to be decoded, read, and acted upon. It was these sailors' vast misfortune to be cast adrift at a time when the Navy was gathering its resources for Lee's fight with Kondo. Search planes were scouring not the northern Coral Sea but the approaches to Guadalcanal. All available ships had been pressed into service either as convoy escorts or in a task force.

And so the *Juneau's* survivors bided their time. Addled by fatigue and exposure, some of them let go of the raft and swam below to search their ship's passageways for something dry to eat. They quarreled and contended with sharks. One of these survivors, George Sullivan, paddled around calling out for his four brothers, long gone. The oldest and highest-ranked Sullivan must have felt he had let his little brothers down. For his other shipmates, suffering the agonies of brine-swollen tongues, sunburned shoulders, bloated limbs, delirium, and the predations of sharks, he did what he could. When George found some survivors who were unrecognizably fouled in bunker oil, he swiped the faces with gobs of toilet paper, looking for the familiar facial features of his kin beneath layers of drying fuel.

Allen Heyn, on the raft with Sullivan, fought to overcome a powerful impulse to swim to the ship that he thought he sensed hovering below. He recovered in time to save another man from this delirium. Heyn held on to him for a time, long enough for the man to give up all struggles. He was preparing to surrender the deceased man to the sea when he found himself standing athwart the fierce resolve of the Irishman from Waterloo, Iowa. "You can't do that," Sullivan said. "It's against all regulations of the Navy. You can't bury a man at sea without having official orders from some captain or somebody like that."

These words were spoken with the unshakable certitude of a scrambled mind. Heyn was considering his argument, holding on to the corpse, half on the raft and half in the sea, when a shadow moved below the surface; the dead man lurched and one of his legs was carried away, ending the argument. George Sullivan was left on the cusp of uncharted oblivion, still calling for his brothers, his fevers and delusions a merciful sedative to grief. That night, four days after his ship had been turned to particles, he left the company of his shipmates. Stripping off his clothes, he said he was going to take a bath, then floated away, paddling to the place where another deep shadow rose, mercifully ending the nightmare.

EARLY ON THE MORNING of November 15, four transports arrived at Espiritu Santo with wounded sailors and marines from Guadalcanal. One of the transports, the *President Jackson,* carried seven seriously burned men from the *San Francisco* who did not survive the trip. Admiral Turner's *McCawley* was among this newly arrived group, too. Shortly after his arrival, he sent an aide to summon the acting commander of the *San Francisco.* Lieutenant Commander Schonland took the *Helena*'s motor whaleboat to the *McCawley* and was met at the gangway by Turner's flag lieutenant, who promptly told Schonland that his superior wanted to see not him, but the officer who was on the *San Francisco*'s bridge during the battle. The boat returned to the cruiser and came back with McCandless, who met with Turner and tendered his report.

The *San Francisco* continued to Nouméa, where Admiral Halsey came aboard to inspect the damage and give tribute to his men. Schonland met him at the top of the gangway. The damage-control officer must have recovered some of the pride he had lost after Kelly Turner's rebuff when Halsey gripped him by the shoulders and said, "Men like you, Schonland, are going to win this war."

Chick Morris, the young officer from the *Helena*, went into Nouméa town, "a quaint place, small and very French, but to us it was a metropolis," he wrote. "We did the shops, where under the Cross of Lorraine, the insignia of the Free French Government, you could buy almost anything American. We strolled past little movie houses. But what we wanted most was to look at the flowers and the small French houses with their tiny backyard gardens. And so before long we were outside the town proper and climbing a hill that overlooked the harbor.

"It was damned good to be walking on solid ground again. You went slowly, appreciating every step, almost tasting the earth with your feet through the soles of your shoes. All those days, weeks, months of ocean, and now something brown and firm that you could pick up in your fingers and look at—that you could feel and smell. And because it wouldn't last, you have the most aching desire to keep walking, walking, walking, just to feel it under your feet.

"The flowers were lovely. The little cottages with their gay little yards were lovely. The sun and the warmth and even the sight of the sea from the top of the hill were lovely. We soaked it up in silence."

Morris thought of a girl in Boston and his folks in New Hampshire. He then found a small Catholic church high on a hilltop. He wasn't a deeply religious man, but as he studied how the sun played on an old stained-glass window, he was moved to go inside.

The sanctuary was dimly lit, barely revealing the cobwebs in the hand-hewn wooden rafters. The basso tones of an old wheezing organ gently vibrated in the floor. An old lady knelt praying at the altar, where candles burned. Morris took a seat in a pew and lost track of time. "Down below in the harbor our ship lay quietly at anchor after slugging her way through a large part of the Japanese fleet, and we owed it to her and ourselves, I felt, to kneel for a moment and say thanks.

"How long I stayed there I don't remember. Not long, probably. I prayed, I think. I knelt and thought of guns thundering in the dark, of ships burning and men shouting as they leaped into the oily water. A prayer of thanks and gratitude was hidden somewhere in those thoughts, if not put into words. And I was on my knees, whether praying or not, when I became aware of the sunlight again.

"The sun had fingered a row of windows which before had been in darkness, and now in bright golden bars it filled the church with warmth and light. I looked up at the windows, and one in particular held my attention. You looked at it because you had to—because in a strange way it beckoned." From where Morris sat, "the streaming sunlight clearly illuminated the inscription on the glass, beneath a haloed figure whose face and outstretched hands shimmered with light. It read: 'St. Helena.'"

MEN LIKE THIS WOULD win the war, and Admiral Halsey appreciated it. But as he reviewed the circumstances of the *Juneau*'s loss, he found his anger rising: Why hadn't Captain Hoover stopped to rescue survivors? Halsey was arriving at some severe conclusions about the *Helena* skipper's suitability to command. He ordered him to report to his headquarters.

Hoover's decorations included two Navy Crosses, with a third (a second gold star) to follow after the events of Friday the thirteenth were duly considered. His destroyers had braved massive explosions at Coral Sea to save survivors of the sinking *Lexington*. His ship had been instrumental in two naval victories. But when Halsey got wind of what had happened, not even the sympathy and concurrence of Admiral Nimitz himself would save him.

"Despite this officer's magnificent combat record...I questioned him very thoroughly in the presence of Miles Browning and a VA [vice admiral] and my opinion that he had made an error in judgment was strengthened. I later visited his ship and thought I sensed a deterioration of morale. I called a conference of a VA and RA [rear admiral] and my chief of staff and discussed this matter. They concurred in the opinion I had formed, in that this cruiser skipper was no longer fit for command in his then condition. I accordingly detached him from his ship and ordered him to report to CinCPac."

So wrote Halsey in a manuscript draft of his memoirs, at least. In the eventual published version, he took less ownership of this decision. In the revised and published account, it was no longer he who interrogated Hoover. That job fell to his advisers—Jake Fitch, Kelly Turner, and Bill Calhoun, he said. They determined that Hoover had done wrong and recommended his detachment. "Reluctantly, I concurred," Halsey wrote. "I felt that the strain of prolonged combat had impaired his judgment; that guts alone were keeping him going; and that his present condition was dangerous to himself and to his splendid ship. In this conviction, I detached him with orders to CINC-PAC."

But the difference between draft and publication is interesting as an illustration either of the state of Halsey's memory, of the genuineness of his regret, or of his candor regarding his approach to leadership. The sympathetic concern Halsey professed for the captain's well-being was not borne out by the severity of his remedy. Halsey would regret that remedy soon enough.

WHEN THE *JUNEAU*'S LAST RAFT was finally located on the open sea, it contained but a single survivor, Allen Heyn. He was built like a weight lifter, a strapping young man with a broad face and black hair and a gap between his front teeth. Brought aboard the seaplane tender *Ballard*, he didn't need long to regain his senses and tell his grim story, though a shark had done its best to remove all witnesses, taking a fist-sized bite out of his left buttock. Three more survivors, Joseph Hartney, Victor James Fitzgerald, and Lieutenant (j.g.) Charles Wang, found by a seaplane, had the good fortune to reach San Cristóbal under propulsion of a heavy squall that had foiled several attempts by Catalina flying boats to land and retrieve them.

With Wang severely wounded and delirious, Hartney and Fitzgerald had sustained themselves with good seamanship, by singing Irish folk songs, and by the imperative to tend faithfully to their gravely wounded shipmate. When their raft entered a lagoon on San Cristóbal, they scarcely had the strength to paddle ashore. At ebb tide they grounded themselves on a coral ledge, and slept. When they awoke, the tide was carrying them the rest of the way in, and on the white sand beach where they landed was a freshwater stream that literally saved their lives. Found by natives, they passed into the care of a German-born copra planter who had no love for the Japanese.

On the nineteenth, a Catalina pilot reported ten men in a raft at 11–13 South, 11–59 East. Several ships were sent for them, and six men were rescued from rafts that originally held thirty. The final tally of *Juneau* survivors stood at ten after the sinking, not including O'Neil and the three corpsmen transferred to the *San Francisco*. Killed or forever missing were 683 men of a crew of almost seven hundred. As a Navy Department official would explain to a bereaved relative, "Efforts consistent with the paramount tactical necessities of the time were made to rescue as many survivors as possible. That these efforts were not successful in the case of many gallant officers and men is deeply regretted by the Navy."

FOR THE JAPANESE, it was becoming increasingly clear that Guadalcanal had become their Stalingrad. That was the opinion of Matome Ugaki, and though all such comparisons are inexact, there was no denying that in their zeal to advance the Japanese had stretched themselves beyond the nourishment of their supply train and exposed themselves against an enemy who was proving to be absolutely implacable in defense. The extent of the disaster of the previous two nights was now in full view.

When Kondo's procession of cripples returned to Truk harbor on November 17, Ugaki was watching from the decks of the *Yamato*. "It was lonely indeed that we couldn't see *Hiei* and *Kirishima* among them," he wrote in his diary. When Hiroaki Abe came on board the *Yamato,* he looked crestfallen. With a bandage swathing his lower jaw, he sorrowfully reported the loss of two ships. As Ugaki saw it, "He seemed to suffer especially for his sunken *Hiei*. He even confided that he thought he would have been better to have gone down with *Hiei*. I can well appreciate how he felt." A fiction, however, was concocted to keep spirits up. "Morale was lifted as it became almost certain, as a result of an investigation conducted by the advance force, that two or three enemy battleships had been sunk," Ugaki wrote in his diary. For the first time, a pattern was set: The proud IJN was reduced to consoling itself with fantasy. Ashore, the marines would learn that their Japanese opponents had been informed that New York and San Francisco had fallen to Japanese invasion forces.

The *Juneau*'s survivors were still fighting the descent into madness at sea when Kelly Turner wrote Halsey to recommend a posthumous Medal of Honor for Dan Callaghan, who "by his daring, determination and tactical brilliance prevented [the Japanese] from accomplishing their mission." Turner wanted the slain admiral decorated "for distinguishing himself conspicuously by gallantry and intrepidity at the risk and cost of his life above and beyond the call of duty." Similar recommendations, duly acted on in time, were made for Bruce McCandless and Herbert Schonland for bringing the *San Francisco* through the maelstrom that night. Turner wrote that "THE BEHAVIOR OF THE SHIP'S

COMPANY IS BEYOND PRAISE, NOT ONLY FOR BRAVERY BUT ALSO FOR EFFEC-
TIVENESS. FOR FIGHTING THEIR SHIP WELL AND EFFECTIVELY, FOR BRAVERY
BEYOND THE CALL OF DUTY. AND FOR OUTSTANDING PERFORMANCE IN ACTION
ON NOVEMBER 12–13, I RECOMMEND THAT THE *SAN FRANCISCO* BE THE FIRST VES-
SEL IN THE NAVY TO RECEIVE THE CITATION ANNOUNCED BY ALNAV 238* FOR
OUTSTANDING SHIP."

Navy Secretary Frank Knox wrote to Halsey two days later, "SPEAKING
FOR THE NAVY AS A WHOLE, I WANT TO EXPRESS TO YOU THE FEELING OF
PRIDE AND SATISFACTION THE ENTIRE SERVICE FEELS IN THE GREAT VICTORY
WON BY YOU AND YOUR MEN. . . ." Halsey replied, "MY DEEP THANKS FOR YOUR
INSPIRING MESSAGE. I AM PASSING IT ON TO THE HEROIC MEN WHO DID OUR
FIGHTING. SOPAC OFFICERS AND MEN OF THE ARMY, NAVY AND MARINE
CORPS RECOGNIZE NO DIVISION INTO SEPARATE SERVICES. WE ARE ALL IN
THE UNITED STATES SERVICE HERE. AS COMMANDER OF THAT SERVICE IN THIS
AREA I GRATEFULLY ACCEPT YOUR TRIBUTE TO ITS HEROES WITH A SENSE OF
HUMILITY FOR MYSELF AND GREAT PRIDE FOR THEM."

Nimitz wrote, "WE HAVE ADMIRATION BEYOND EXPRESSION FOR THE
UNSWERVING OFFENSIVE SPIRIT OF YOUR FIGHTING FORCES AND THEIR ABIL-
ITY TO STRIKE DOWN THE ENEMY WHILE ABSORBING HIS BLOWS. WE REGRET
DEEPLY THE LOSSES YOU HAD TO TAKE BUT THEY WERE GLORIOUSLY NOT IN
VAIN." For the marines on the 'Canal, Frank Jack Fletcher's decision to with-
draw the carriers seemed a lifetime ago. The Marine Corps' final verdict on
the fighting Navy's importance to the campaign was rendered by the general
who stood with his men since the first landings, Archie Vandegrift. "WE
BELIEVE THE ENEMY HAS SUFFERED A CRUSHING DEFEAT. WE THANK LEE FOR
HIS STURDY EFFORT LAST NIGHT. WE THANK KINCAID [*SIC*] FOR HIS INTER-
VENTION YESTERDAY. OUR OWN AIRCRAFT HAVE BEEN GRAND IN ITS RELENT-
LESS POUNDING OF THE FOE. THOSE EFFORTS WE APPRECIATE BUT OUR
GREATEST HOMAGE GOES TO SCOTT, CALLAGHAN AND THEIR MEN WHO WITH
MAGNIFICENT COURAGE AGAINST SEEMINGLY HOPELESS ODDS DROVE BACK
THE FIRST HOSTILE STROKE AND MADE SUCCESS POSSIBLE. TO THEM THE
MEN OF CACTUS LIFT THEIR BATTERED HELMETS IN DEEPEST ADMIRATION."
The Navy had earned nothing less. When it was all said and done at Guadal-
canal, three sailors would die at sea for every infantryman who fell ashore.

In a speech to the *New York Herald Tribune* Forum on November 17,
President Roosevelt lamented the loss of his former naval aide Dan
Callaghan. "During the past two weeks," FDR said, "we have had a great deal

---

* "All Navy" bulletin.

of good news and it would seem that the turning point in this war has at last been reached."

On the nineteenth, Major General Alexander M. Patch, the commander of the U.S. Army's Americal Division and the successor to General Vandegrift, arrived on Guadalcanal and delivered the best gift the 1st Marine Division ever received during their tenure in the South Pacific: the news that their tour of duty was near an end.

39

On the Spot

ON BOARD THE SAN FRANCISCO, HALSEY DECORATED MANY OF THE crew who had distinguished themselves, Jack Bennett among them. As the lieutenant junior grade's name was called, Halsey said into the standing mike, "Step closer, son." The words reverberated through the public-address system. When Halsey fixed the Navy Cross onto his shirt, its sharp pin stuck into Bennett's flesh, and Bennett was keenly aware of the microphone inches from his mouth. "I knew that any sound of pain I uttered would also boom out over the speakers," Bennett wrote. "I was already scared and now I had to grit my teeth and remain silent as the admiral continued trying to close the clasp, finally giving up when he saw the blood seeping through my shirt."

The repair supervisors at Nouméa, determining that the *Sterett* needed structural work, made plans to send her back to Pearl. "No sooner had the repair team left," Cal Calhoun wrote, "than we were told that Admiral Halsey himself was coming aboard to inspect our damage." No one could have failed to recognize the bushy eyebrows, the strong chin, or the direct gaze that bespoke confidence and strength. "He shook hands with each of us," Calhoun wrote, "and asked to be shown all of our battle damage." Halsey listened intently as Captain Coward cataloged the cost, human and material, extracted by each hit. "From time to time he simply shook his head as we described events," Lieutenant Calhoun wrote. By the end of the briefing, Halsey had tears in his eyes. In a low voice, he told Coward and his senior officers how proud he was of them.

"I wish I could recall his exact words," Calhoun wrote, "but I do remember some of his thoughts—he regretted that he had to send destroyers against battleships but was sure that the small ships would do their utmost; he was amazed that any destroyer could absorb eleven shell hits (three of which were fourteen-inch projectiles) and still steam away from the action under her own power; he was profoundly moved by the many stories of heroism, and by the mute but eloquent evidence of punishment and sacrifice that was apparent at every turn as he toured the ship. Finally he thanked us, with a sincerity that added a special quality to his words, and said, 'God bless you!' We stood there filled with admiration, respect, and pride and watched him climb into a waiting jeep and drive off. It was an unforgettable, once-in-a-lifetime occasion. To those of us who witnessed it, Admiral Halsey's name will always lead the list of inspirational combat leaders of World War II."

ON NOVEMBER 22, Admiral Halsey shared his thinking with Nimitz concerning his decision to relieve Gil Hoover:

> After analysis of the situation presented, I consider that the commanding officer, *Helena*, senior officer present in the task group, committed a serious and costly error in the action which he took; specifically:
>
> a) He should have made radio report of the torpedoing at once. Radio silence, as a measure of concealment, had ceased to be effective since the enemy was in contact. Only positive action to keep him submerged could be expected to delay his report.
>
> b) He should have instituted offensive action, together with, or closely followed by, rescue operations, utilizing at least one of his destroyers.
>
> His failure to take prompt action on the above lines was further aggravated by lack of any follow-up to insure that senior commands were informed of the *Juneau*'s loss. Commander South Pacific was first apprised of this fact as a result of his own inquiry into *Juneau*'s status when she was not included in the arrival report of the group.
>
> . . .
>
> In view of the above circumstances, I have this date relieved Captain G. C. Hoover of his command of the USS *Helena*, and ordered him by dispatch to proceed by the first available government air transportation and report to Commander-in-Chief for reassignment.

Canny, cautious, and discerning, Admiral Spruance picked up on an assumption that underlay Halsey's censure—that Hoover had had the means at hand to attack the enemy submarine. He asked Hoover for comment, asking specifically whether his two destroyers had functioning sonar systems. Hoover conceded that both the *Fletcher* and *Sterett* had working sound gear, though the latter was badly damaged. He added that he felt the need to bring damaged ships safely home outweighed the uncertain gain of searching for survivors of a vessel that had exploded so violently. Hoover emphasized the dangerous nature of the waters he was transiting, pointing to the dispatch the *Juneau* sent him that morning, notifying him of the threat of enemy aircraft and urging him to ask for prompt support from the *Enterprise* task force. He mentioned that neither the *Helena* nor the *San Francisco* had planes on board to hunt submarines.

But the merits of arguments no longer mattered. The fix was in. According to Bin Cochran of the *Helena,* the brawling and ill-tempered Captain Miles Browning, Halsey's chief of staff, had argued fiercely for Hoover's relief and later bragged about having Hoover sacked. Cochran, like most of his shipmates, held Hoover in high esteem for the coolheaded manner in which he had led the ship through two ferocious actions. Browning impressed people less.

Even Chester Nimitz's moderating voice couldn't overcome the damning effect of Halsey's memo. As reports and memoranda proceed up the Navy's chain of command, commanders are given the chance to add their own comments, or "endorsements," for the benefit of higher-ups. In his December 4 endorsement to Admiral King's copy of the memo, Nimitz acknowledged the difficult trial Hoover faced, confronted with a hard decision in perilous waters. He stated that the failure of the B-17 to report the loss of the *Juneau* in time was not Hoover's fault. Referring to sighting reports Hoover had received of enemy carriers, surface ships, and submarines nearby, he wrote, "Under these conditions the situation confronting Captain Hoover was one in which the necessity for getting his damaged ships back to a base was balanced against the natural instinct of every naval officer to go to the rescue of officers and men in distress and danger. Whatever may be the opinion of Captain Hoover's decision in this matter, he was the responsible officer on the spot and, from his war record, which includes two important night engagements, his courage may not be questioned." Breaking with Halsey, Nimitz recommended that King give Hoover "a suitable command at sea" after some time to rest.

It didn't matter. In the competitive, political world of the admiralty, written criticism from an area commander was inerasable, a terminal act. Halsey's impulsive disgust could not be unwritten, not by the Pacific Ocean Area commander in chief, and not even by Halsey himself after he later admitted that he had acted unjustly and in haste. The variances in Halsey's written accounts of his evaluation of Hoover's performance are curious. In his memoirs he offered "a confession of a grievous mistake. . . . I concluded that I had been guilty of an injustice." The draft manuscript of his memoirs offers a fuller discussion of these events than appears in the published version.

> CinCPac was in disagreement with me on my judgment, wondering if I had done an injustice to a man who had had a magnificent combat record. I was finally convinced that this man at the time in question was suffering from an aggravated case of combat fatigue and that his guts alone had kept him going. In modern warfare guts are not always enough—a man's brain must be clear. I wrote an official letter stating my belief that this officer had been suffering from combat fatigue at that time and that I had possibly committed an error of judgment in detaching him under such drastic circumstances. I requested that he be given a combatant command and stated that I should be delighted to have him in such a position under my command. I am afraid that my late action in attempting to clear this officer of the stigma that resulted from my detaching him had not been successful although it most certainly alleviated his feelings. I am deeply regretful of the whole incident. I have already acknowledged my mistake to him and to the Navy Department, and here I acknowledge it publicly. It is a tribute to the caliber of this officer that our personal relations are excellent.

In the published version, Halsey added that "Hoover's decision was in the best interests of victory," even as he removed the mea culpa about the tardiness of his change of heart and recast his role, in his account of how the original judgment was reached, from skeptical lead inquisitor to reluctant rubber-stamper of a staff recommendation.

In Nimitz's careful handling of the Hoover question, Halsey must have eventually seen the virtue of restraint in second-guessing combat commanders.* Still, the Navy felt the need to arbitrate questions of culpability

---

* Less than two years after impulsively sandbagging Hoover, Halsey himself benefitted from Nimitz's restraint when accusations flew after the Leyte Gulf campaign that he had handled his task force carelessly. See Hornfischer, *The Last Stand of the Tin Can Sailors*, pp. 126–131.

for defeat, even during wartime. Just as the Guadalcanal campaign was turning its way, it was preparing to launch an investigation into the causes of the fiasco that was the Battle of Savo Island.

DAN CALLAGHAN AND Norman Scott, in death, had shown an aggressive style that would carry the Navy's surface forces to victory. Willis Lee continued in that spirit, refining the state of the art with his battleships. They and their fighting sailors had stopped the Tokyo Express cold in November. Still, there was plenty of fodder for recrimination, for the surface fleet's first victories were won despite many avoidable errors.

Admiral Pye, from his billet as president of the Naval War College, criticized Callaghan's preparations and dispositions. "Orders such as 'Give them hell' and 'We want the big ones' make better newspaper headlines than they do battle plans. . . . A study of the naval actions so far in this war gives the impression that such successes as we have had have been largely due to the individual excellence of our ships and their crews, and not to exceptionally good use made of them by the commanders." Sharp words flew about what commanders did and should have done, but in death Scott and Callaghan were spared the indignity of inquiry. Concerning Callaghan's performance, Pye finally concluded, "There is no telling 'what might have been.' In this case we seem to have got some of the breaks of luck that the enemy got in the Battle of Savo Island. On the other hand, we seem to have repeated some of the errors—even exaggerated them—made a month earlier in the Battle of Cape Esperance."

The victories of November added new complexity to the arguments in Washington about where America's principal worldwide axis of effort should lie and opened up new avenues of possibility to take the offensive against the Japanese. Nimitz and MacArthur would long argue how best to exploit these. On October 24, as the Battle of Santa Cruz was looming, President Roosevelt had said a diversion of resources to hold Guadalcanal was needed to "take advantage of our success." Pressured by both Admiral King and General Marshall not to neglect the Pacific—"We cannot permit the present critical situation in the Southwest Pacific to develop into a second Bataan," they wrote—Roosevelt agreed to a cutback of forces flowing to England. As Major General Thomas T. Handy of the U.S. Army General Staff confided to General Marshall, "our main amphibious operations in 1943 are likely to be in the Pacific" and called the argument about Germany-first or Japan-first "largely academic."

Now one of the Army's foremost strategists, Lieutenant General Stanley Embick, provided a forceful rationale for abandoning the worldwide strategy long held to, at least in name, by the American and British commands. He pointed out on November 20 that under the prewar ABC-1 agreement, Britain was supposed to take first responsibility for the Far East theater while the U.S. fleet diverted Japan by threatening its flank. In reality, of course, those two roles were inverted. In line with the realities of geography and heavy industry, the Americans had taken the lead in their western ocean. And the fact of that leadership, Embick believed, changed everything. "Having assumed this commitment the U.S. must therefore maintain their position as a first charge," he wrote.

With even Army leaders advocating a Pacific-first strategy, the state of joint strategic planning was tenuous at best. Far from solving any problems, the diverse opinion within the Army allowed the old arguments among the services, and among the Allies, to gain new fervor. The lack of a consensus within American ranks effectively left Germany-first to exist only in the minds of politicians. The numbers spoke for themselves: At the end of 1942, the United States would field nearly 25 percent more combat troops in the Pacific than it did in England and North Africa, 464,000 to 378,000. The gap between Roosevelt's words and his military's work caused Britain's service chiefs to lament the very idea of combined planning with their Atlantic cousins. Their best insurance against America pursuing a full-on Pacific-first strategy was Churchill's friendship with Roosevelt. If Japan was traumatized by the bulldog savagery of the American defense of Guadalcanal, the British didn't care much for its implications, either.

ON THE MORNING OF November 23, Halsey wrote to his commanders to describe the array of new naval forces flowing into the South Pacific. The *Saratoga* was coming back. With the antiaircraft cruiser *San Juan* and a squadron of destroyers, she would re-form the nucleus of Task Force 11. The *Enterprise,* with the antiaircraft cruiser *San Diego* and Hoover's old Desron 2, would continue to comprise Task Force 16. Lee, shorn of the *South Dakota* now but soon to be given two more fast battleships, the repaired *North Carolina* and the brand-new *Indiana,* flew Task Force 64's flag in the *Washington.* With the fuel oil bottleneck finally easing, two older battleships, the *Maryland* and *Colorado,* would come south as Task Force 65 under Rear Admiral Harry W. Hill.

Rear Admiral Thomas Kinkaid, whom Halsey relieved of command of

Task Force 16 because a better-qualified aviation man, Rear Admiral Frederick C. Sherman, was available, would take the cruiser striking force, Task Force 67, with the heavies *Northampton, Pensacola, New Orleans,* the light cruisers *Honolulu* and *Helena,* and six destroyers. Task Force 66 came into being as well, with eight destroyers.

Five days later, Halsey announced their new strategic objective, Rabaul. He wrote MacArthur saying that New Guinea couldn't be secured until the Japanese strongpoint in the Bismarcks was under American control. He also staked the Navy's claim to the job, arguing that the attack against Rabaul "must be amphibious along the Solomons with New Guinea land position basically a supporting one only. I am currently reinforcing Cactus position and expediting means of operating heavy air from there. It is my belief that the sound procedure at this time is to maintain as strong a land and air pressure against the Japanese Buna position as your lines of communication permit, and continue to extract a constant toll of Japanese shipping, an attrition which if continued at the present rate he can not long sustain." The attrition wasn't easy on the Americans, either. Even with the new naval units on hand, Halsey's plan to surge toward Rabaul, much like MacArthur's similar concept earlier that year, seemed ambitious with the limited amphibious resources he had immediately at hand.

In late November Halsey received his fourth star, elevating him from vice admiral to admiral. When it was discovered that Nouméa was short of four-star pins for his epaulets, the Navy obtained a pair of two-star pins from a Marine major general and had them reconfigured by a repair ship's welding shop. After Vice Admiral William L. Calhoun presented Halsey with the makeshift four-star insignia, Halsey turned in his three-star pins and said, "Send one of these to Mrs. Scott and the other to Mrs. Callaghan. Tell them it was their husbands' bravery that got me my new ones."

Whatever else could be said of William F. Halsey, no one would complain that he didn't lead from the front. He had felt the concussion of Japanese gunfire. And as November came to an end, the Japanese would demonstrate that they had a few good salvos left in them. They had not yet given up on Jack London's least favorite island.

40

The Futility of Learning

AFTER THE STEEL-MAULING BATTLES OF NOVEMBER, BOTH FLEETS were left to improvise. The night of November 30–December 1 saw the first attempt by the Tokyo Express to deliver supplies using drums lashed together with ropes. Destroyers would steam in close to shore, then drop the drums overboard for small craft to retrieve for the troops. Rear Admiral Raizo Tanaka was the architect of the new approach.

In the face of the daily distress calls from the supply-straitened Japanese garrison on Guadalcanal, the officers of Destroyer Squadron 2 were resigned to the new role forced upon them. Tanaka's chief of staff, Commander Yasumi Toyama, lamented bitterly, "*Ahhh,* we are more a freighter convoy than a fighting squadron these days. The damn Yankees have dubbed us the Tokyo Express. We transport cargo to that cursed island, and our orders are to flee rather than fight. What a stupid thing!" For the crews of fighting ships, the life of the blockade runner was "a strenuous and unsatisfying routine."

On November 27, Tanaka steamed south from the Shortlands on a high-speed convoy run. Their sortie was not long a secret. Quickly the American patrol planes spied them from above the clouds: eight destroyers, six serving as transports, laden with supplies, magazines at half capacity, carrying eight torpedoes instead of the usual sixteen, to save on weight.

Planning for its reception was well along. As Tanaka was leaving Rabaul, Rear Admiral Thomas Kinkaid was sitting down to apply the knowledge the surface fleet had purchased with the lives of more than four thousand men to date. He was rewriting Task Force 67's operations plan. Op Plan 1–42 applied recent experience methodically. The confusions of early battles would be banished by forethought. Ship captains would know what to do automatically. Certain procedures would be established and used by default. The task force would be organized and deployed to reflect a best-practices approach to battle. Norman Scott's improvised doctrine of night battle would be refined, encoded as doctrine, and circulated for general use.

Except for the use of the radar, whose virtues were now well recognized, the new doctrine sounded a lot like what the Japanese had been doing from the start. As the enemy was scouted by radar (the Japanese used ship-launched floatplanes to the same end), the destroyers would surge forward independently at first contact to make a surprise torpedo attack. Then, as the time of their impact came, the cruisers, till then standing off at more than twelve thousand yards, would open fire while their aircraft lazed overhead dropping flares. If targets were lost, star shells could be used, but searchlights were strictly forbidden. All that was needed to turn the plan to a victory were more good ships and another cast of sailors willing to risk their lives to put ordnance on target first.

As the ships most recently assigned to Task Force 67 licked their wounds and headed home for repair, as new steel plates replaced those shattered in battle, a new task force came together at Espiritu Santo. Its haphazard nature was, once again, a reflection of the perpetual emergency besetting Admiral Halsey. He would refer to its composition as "a compromise dictated by necessity." Cruisers were borrowed from carrier task forces, destroyers from convoy assignment. They would be the same men who had lined the rails at Espiritu Santo and given the *San Francisco* a thunderous cheer. They came together at the end of November as a reconstituted Task Force 67 and made ready to fend off the Tokyo Express once again.

At Naval Base Guadalcanal, Lloyd Mustin and his operations team were working on the fly, too, trying to find a way to better use the daring but undisciplined PT boat force assigned to the area. The squadron now had fifteen boats, up from just four a few weeks earlier. But given the fluid and occasionally slipshod organization at Tulagi, Mustin found it hard to coordinate their sorties with the other naval forces in the area. Some destroyer commanders resisted involving their tin cans with the "hooligan Navy," mainly out of fear that it would be difficult to keep from stepping on one another's toes. "I thought we had better improve that," Mustin said, "or somebody was going to get hurt." Having seen the value of the intelligence that PT skippers acquired during their patrols in Savo Sound, Mustin chose, in the name of better cooperation, a PT boat man as his assistant operations officer. They figured out how many boats were available nightly, determined how frequently they could be used, set up patrol schedules, and began innovating new approaches to attacking the Japanese submarines and destroyers in the waters off Guadalcanal. Finding that Japanese destroyers could catch and run down PT boats on a clear night, he settled on a game of cat and mouse. The young PT boat officers learned to avoid being silhouetted in open water while avoiding flat water that would show their wakes, and to attack using diversions, with some boats working as decoys while boats closer to shore rushed in. As they changed their schemes, the Japanese did, too.

On the night of November 30, however, the PT boats were ordered to stay put at Tulagi. Something larger than they were cut out for was brewing that night. It was another run of the Tokyo Express, eight destroyers under Rear Admiral Tanaka. A large American force was gathering at Espiritu Santo to intercept him.

True to form, the Navy, on the eve of the mission, replaced Kinkaid with a new commander. Kinkaid balked at his reassignment from a carrier task force and wanted no further part of the South Pacific. And so, as Dan Callaghan had supplanted Norman Scott, as Cassin Young and Joe Hubbard had relieved Charles McMorris and Mark Crouter on the *San Francisco,* Rear Admiral Carleton Wright now became the officer in tactical command of Task Force 67. Long of service in the South Pacific but new to surface combat, Wright flew his flag in the newly arrived *Minneapolis,* leading a scratch team of four other cruisers—the *New Orleans, Pensacola, Honolulu,* and *Northampton.*

These newcomers to the Ironbottom Sound surface striking force, most of them reassigned from carrier escort duty, were a bit like replacement troops going forward to the front lines from rear-area antiaircraft battalions. They wore the same uniforms and wielded the same weapons, but they weren't wise in the bitter discipline of close combat. None of the four cruisers had had any part in the four surface actions fought in Savo Sound to this point. It could not be said, either, that they were commanded by the officer best equipped to prepare them for that new type of fight. The only surface-force flag officer alive who had fought and beaten the Japanese Navy, Willis Lee, was back in port with his squadron, tending to the *Washington* at

Nouméa. Though both were veteran cruiser commanders, neither Kinkaid nor Wright had fought a night action before, nor executed a tactical plan such as they were now designing.

They departed Espiritu Santo's Segond Channel anchorage at 11:30 p.m. on November 29, following a van composed of the destroyers *Fletcher, Drayton, Maury,* and *Perkins.* When they reached the eastern entrance to Lengo Channel at nine forty the next night, Wright's task force encountered some friendly transports. Augmenting his tag team, Halsey ordered two of their escorts, the *Lamson* and *Lardner,* to fall in astern the *Northampton.* And so another pickup squad with fresh leadership and big ideas headed north toward its destiny.

The *Fletcher,* with its modern SG radar, rode at the head of the line. If this was an improvement over Callaghan's approach two weeks before, the urge to hesitate would once again rise as a plague. According to the *Fletcher*'s executive officer, Lieutenant Joseph C. Wylie, "About the last visual dispatch we got before dusk settled in were instructions stating not to commence firing without permission."

Wylie was on the radar when strange contacts began to register. The first one appeared to the radar officer in the *Minneapolis* like "a small wart on Cape Esperance which grew larger and finally detached itself from the outline of the land mass." As Tanaka's force steamed within range of the American microwaves, Wylie reported their bearing, course, and speed to the other destroyers. With torpedoes ready, he radioed Wright, "REQUEST PERMISSION TO FIRE TORPEDOES." Wylie would call the task force commander's response "the most stupid thing that I have ever heard of." It was a single word: "NO." Wright deemed the range too long.

For four critical minutes Wright mulled the black night from the bridge of the *Minneapolis.* When he finally granted permission to the destroyers to fire their torpedoes, the radar showed that their targets had already passed them abeam, leaving the American missiles to pursue them from astern, a fruitless waste of fighting power. When Wright ordered the cruisers to open fire less than a minute after the destroyers had let fly, surprise became a casualty of impulsiveness, and what ensued was another confused free-for-all. As cruiser gunfire obliterated the senses, Wright lost sight of his targets behind the walls of water raised in front of them by American guns.

The spectacle was familiar to men observing from the beach. Lloyd Mustin and the others at Captain Greenman's headquarters saw great flashes of light that were too large to be mere gun discharges. They didn't know whose ships were out there bursting into flames, and there would be no knowing till morning. Suddenly and anticlimactically, Mustin's radio went silent. The sober messages that trickled in to Radio Guadalcanal over the next couple of hours told the story. From the *Minneapolis* came a dispatch before dawn that she had been torpedoed and was under way for Lunga at half a knot. The *Pensacola* weighed in with a similar report. Then Admiral Wright raised Greenman, asking: "CAN YOU SEND BOATS TOWARD SAVO?" The implications of the request were clear enough. Mustin instructed the *Bobolink* and four PT boats to sweep the sound, while Wright's second in command, Rear Admiral Mahlon S. Tisdale, ordered the destroyers to assist damaged cruisers northwest of Lunga Point. Wright then passed along a fuller report of the shattering damage inflicted on his task force and asked him to send it to Halsey.

The news of the rout was shocking to anyone who believed the fleet was at last on the path to victory. Wanting a clearer picture, Captain Greenman ordered Mustin to go up as an airborne observer to survey the sound. Racing to Henderson Field at dawn, the *Atlanta* survivor climbed into the rear seat of a Dauntless. The Marine pilot checked him out on the dive-bomber's twin-mounted Brownings, and they took to the skies.

Gaining altitude over Ironbottom Sound, Mustin could see no ships anywhere. He raised the PT boat headquarters at Tulagi, but the mosquito fleet didn't know much, either. Several long turns over the waters south of Savo yielded no clues until the morning sun reached the proper angle to the water, and then he saw it: a wide sprawling oil slick trailing away to the west with the friction of an eight-knot wind. It marked the resting place of yet another American ship in what some would call the Savo Navy Yard, or Ironbottom Sound. Her identity would be established soon enough. It was the *Northampton,* gutted by torpedoes fired by Tanaka's surprised but quick-triggered destroyer commanders.

When Wright's cruisers opened fire, they erred in concentrating on a single ship, the destroyer *Takanami,* riding ahead of Tanaka's group as a picket. As American projectiles straddled her and she returned fire, the cruisers' salvos, drawn to the light, converged in earnest. With memories still haunting the Japanese of what the *Washington* and *South Dakota* had wrought fifteen days before, it was easy for Tanaka to believe the American force included battleships.

Surprised but resilient, Tanaka ordered all commanders, *"Belay supply schedule! All ships, prepare to fight!"* The crews cast loose as many supply drums as they could when they brought their batteries to bear. Shielded by the flames of the *Takanami,* much as the *Washington* had been masked by the burning destroyers a few weeks before, Tanaka accelerated to full speed and ordered a course reversal that brought his column running parallel to his targets. His destroyers proceeded to let loose with one of the most lethal torpedo salvos of the war.

From on high in the rear seat of a Dauntless, Mustin could see the evidence of the swarm of fish that had beset Task Force 67. Washed up on Guadalcanal's northern beaches and Savo Island, their long forms lay at angles on the sand. Many were shiny and new, recently run aground. A great many more, of both American and Japanese origin, had decayed to rust, long of residence ashore. Their numbers spoke to the great volume of underwater ordnance loosed in both directions in these waters over the past few months.

Amid the flotsam on the sea below, Mustin could make out the workaday paraphernalia of U.S. Navy shipboard life: powder cases, wooden shoring, life rafts, donut rings, and wreckage of varied kinds. There were a great many sailors in the water, too, and many more waved from the shores of Savo. The PT boats were soon among them. Tulagi's "splinter fleet" puttered about, joining the *Fletcher* and *Drayton* in rescue duty.

Turning to pass over Tulagi, Mustin finally saw some large American ships. The *Minneapolis* and *New Orleans* were tied up close to shore, in the triage unit for wounded U.S. cruisers, mangled and nearly unrecognizable. The *New Orleans* had had her forecastle, about 150 feet of hull, removed clear back to her second turret by a single Long Lance. Its blast had triggered an adjoining magazine full of aircraft bombs and a large demolition charge, throwing a tower of flames and sparks twice as high as the foremast and turning the surrounding sea into a mass of flame. One hundred and eighty-two men, including the entire crew of turret two, died by shock. As the ship turned right, a fifty-yard length of the ship's own bow and forecastle tore away to port. One end of this heavy wreckage subducted under the keel, and the other bounced along the port side of the hull, tearing holes and wrecking the port inboard propeller. Sailors stationed aft believed they were running over the sinking carcass of the *Minneapolis* ahead.

Confronted with this cataclysm, Captain Clifford H. Roper passed the order to abandon ship. However, the exec, Commander Whitaker F. Riggs, canceled the order from his station in the rear of the ship, and ordered the crew to "lighten ship" with an eye toward saving her. And that's just what they did.

As the *New Orleans* nodded under by the bow, her broken nose plowing up a pile of foam, open to the sea, the damage-control officer, Lieutenant

Commander Hubert M. Hayter, and two subordinates, Lieutenant Richard A. Haines and Ensign Andrew L. Forman, remained at their post deep below in Central Station as it filled with toxic gas. When the air became unbreathable, Hayter gave his gas mask to an enlisted man who was suffering, then ordered all hands to evacuate. Two avenues of escape were available. One, a trunk that led from Central Station to the main deck, was blocked by flooding above, and Commander Hayter knew this. The other was a narrow, three-foot-diameter steel tube that led upward to the wardroom. The plotting room crew scurried up through it, but when Hayter's turn came, he found that his shoulders were too broad to fit through the opening to the tube, which was reinforced with a thick steel collar. Ordering "Small men first," he returned to his desk and resumed his damage-control duties. Haines and Forman remained with him in their increasingly untenable station until all three were asphyxiated. "I wondered what he thought about in those final minutes," the ship's chaplain, Howell M. Forgy, would write, "but I knew one thing: he was not afraid."

Forward, at the site of the magazine explosion, a sailor named Gust Swenning, shipfitter second class, dove beneath the rising waters to locate and wrestle closed an open watertight hatch that was causing the ship's sickbay compartment to flood. Badly injured in the initial explosion, and struggling against heavy fumes, Swenning plunged into the dark, dangerous void at least five times, groping around until he finally closed the hatch. He remained on duty through most of the next day until, lungs poisoned by noxious elements, he died of pulmonary edema.

Tied up to Tulagi's shore, the shattered hull of the *New Orleans,* truncated like a barge, lay draped in vegetation and cargo nets to hide it from enemy planes. It was an inglorious state for the ship whose chaplain, Commander Forgy, had coined the immortal phrase "Praise the Lord and pass the ammunition" while exhorting his ship's antiaircraft gunners under attack at Pearl Harbor. The *Minneapolis* was alongside her, too, similarly coiffed, the tug *Bobolink* serving as a pump house to keep her leaks from pulling her under. The crews of the broken ships hauled logs out of Tulagi's jungle to use as shoring for the forward compartments, and arranged with the Marine chaplain ashore to bury the dead.

The *Pensacola* was lucky to survive a battering by Long Lances. One of them shattered a full oil tank forward of turret three, tore the deck open above it, and splashed a fiery wave of oil all over the after part of the ship, topside and belowdecks. With the after fire main destroyed, her crew fought severe oil fires through the night, spreading carbon dioxide and foam compounds by hand as the ship was concussed by the deep cadence of eight-inch rounds detonating, one by one, all 150 of them, in the after magazine.

Wright might have expected better of his task force, given that he had surprised Tanaka by radar at long range. Three of his cruisers (all but the *Pensacola* and *Northampton*) enjoyed the superb sight picture provided by the advanced SG radar. But Wright understood little of the combat capability of his enemy. In his December 9 after-action report, he concluded that the torpedoings of the *Pensacola* and *Northampton* had been lucky shots from submarines. "The observed positions of the enemy surface vessels before and during the gun action makes it seem improbable that torpedoes with speed–distance characteristics similar to our own could have reached the cruisers." Of course, Wright's torpedoes were nothing like those of the Japanese.

Nearly a year into the war, and four months into a bitter campaign against Japanese surface forces, it seems incomprehensible that an American cruiser commander could be unaware of the enemy advantage in torpedo warfare. Norman Scott had called it specifically to Admiral Halsey's attention in October. The reports were there to be read. Before he rode to his death in the naval campaign for Java, the captain of the heavy cruiser *Houston*, Captain Albert H. Rooks, turned over to a colleague in Darwin an analysis he had written three weeks before the Pearl Harbor attack. It discussed at length Japan's prowess in torpedo combat and described their aggressively realistic night battle training. Their mastery of this specialty had been recommended to them by their experience in the Russo-Japanese War. When their diplomats agreed to constrain the size of their big-gun fleet at the Washington Conference, the Japanese, like other navies, emphasized construction of their light forces. Rooks's prewar report, which was based substantially on existing work of the Office of Naval Intelligence, never found its way into the battle plans. Not even Halsey grasped the superiority of Japanese surface-ship torpedoes. After Tassafaronga he endorsed Wright's view that the outcome had to have been the result of submarines. Norman Scott's October victory over a surprised Japanese force that failed to get its torpedoes into the water might have led the Americans to underestimate the weapon and place undue importance on gunnery.

The reward for this ignorance was to see four proud ships, two of them fitted with the new radar that had proven decisive in more capable hands, "picked off like mechanical ducks in a carnival shooting gallery," as Samuel Eliot Morison would put it. Only the *Honolulu*, a sister ship to the *Helena*, had been able to avoid the burning wrecks ahead and zigzag clear of the torpedo water. The *Minneapolis, New Orleans,* and *Pensacola* were put out of action for almost a year.

Generous in defeat, Wright recommended all five of his cruiser captains for the Navy Cross, writing speciously that each had "contributed greatly to the destruction of all enemy vessels within range." He made the wildly inaccurate claim that Task Force 67 had sunk two light cruisers and seven destroyers and praised the *Northampton*'s captain for the speed with which his crew abandoned ship. The award to Captain Roper of the *New Orleans* would puzzle survivors of that ship—"He did nothing heroic in any sense," one would write. Having crushed Wright's force, Tanaka faced a predicament comparable to the one his countryman Mikawa had faced in August. As he regrouped fifty miles from Guadalcanal's beach, he found that his ships were low on torpedoes. With only two destroyers fully loaded, he decided he was no longer in shape to risk another fight. He gave the order to return to Rabaul. Though his reputation was high among Americans, Tanaka would take lumps at home for declining to exploit his victory by delivering his supplies to the island. Here as in August, the Americans, for all their failings, could interpret a ghastly result as a win.

Order of Battle—Battle of Tassafaronga
(November 30, 1942)

U.S.	Japan
TASK FORCE 67	**REINFORCEMENT UNIT**
Rear Adm. Carleton H. Wright	Rear Adm. Raizo Tanaka
Minneapolis (CA) (flagship)	*Naganami* (flagship)
New Orleans (CA)	*Takanami* (DD)
Pensacola (CA)	*Oyashio* (DD)
Northampton (CA)	*Kuroshio* (DD)
Honolulu (CL)	*Kagero* (DD)
Fletcher (DD)	*Makinami* (DD)
Drayton (DD)	*Kawakaze* (DD)
Maury (DD)	*Suzukaze* (DD)
Perkins (DD)	
Lamson (DD)	
Lardner (DD)	

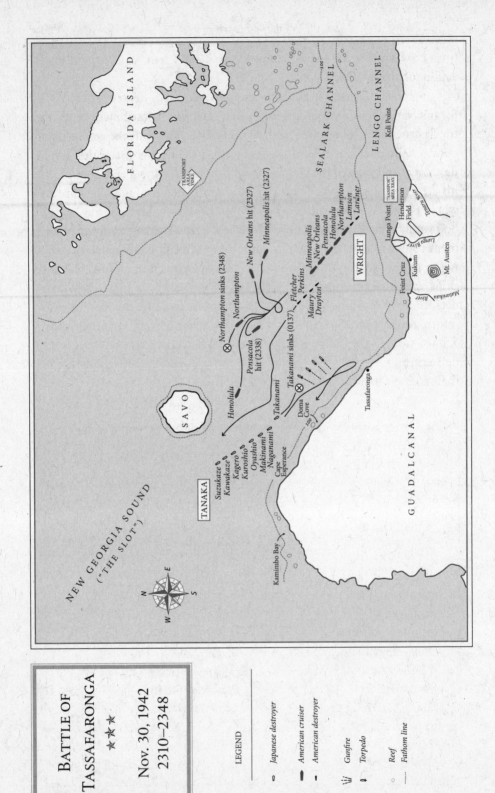

BATTLE OF
TASSAFARONGA
★ ★ ★
Nov. 30, 1942
2310–2348

LEGEND

∘─ Japanese destroyer

━ American cruiser

╵ American destroyer

🔥 Gunfire

↑ Torpedo

⌇ Reef

— Fathom line

FLORIDA ISLAND

NEW GEORGIA SOUND
("THE SLOT")

SAVO

TANAKA

Suzukaze
Kawakaze
Kagero
Kuroshio
Oyashio
Makinami
Naganami
Cape
Esperance

Kamimbo Bay

TRANSPORT
AREA
YOKE

Honolulu

Pensacola
hit (2338)

⊗ Northampton sinks (2348)

Northampton

New Orleans hit (2327)

Minneapolis hit (2327)

Takanami

Doma
Cove

⊗ Takanami sinks (0137)

Fletcher
Perkins
Maury
Drayton
Minneapolis
New Orleans
Pensacola
Honolulu
Northampton
Lamson
Lardner

WRIGHT

Tassafaronga

SEALARK CHANNEL

LENGO CHANNEL

Koli Point

TRANSPORT
AREA XRAY

Lunga Point

Henderson
Field

Lunga River

Point Cruz

Kukum

Mt. Austen

Matanikau River

GUADALCANAL

N E S W

* * *

WITH THE IMPERIAL JAPANESE Army's transport force decimated, and attrition to his destroyers reaching critical levels, Yamamoto was hard-pressed to provision the Imperial Army on Guadalcanal. The Japanese soldiers ashore were nourished by a withering vine. Of the thirty thousand men serving there at the end of November, it was estimated that just forty-two hundred were fit to fight. One three-thousand-man regiment reportedly had just sixty to seventy men capable of service. Admiral Ugaki called the cargo load of supplies landed in the last week of November "just chicken feed for thirty thousand men." On December 3, fifteen hundred drums were delivered without heavy opposition from the American fleet, but only about a third of the drums were recovered by the troops. On December 7, the Tokyo Express ran again, eleven destroyers under Captain Torajiro Sato. Planes from Henderson harassed them, and eight PT boats roared in after them, too. It was an inconsequential skirmish, but the unexpected presence of enemy combat forces compelled the Japanese to withdraw.

As new American naval forces steamed toward the South Pacific, a decisive victory was no longer within Yamamoto's grasp. Only after it had slipped from his fingers would he recognize the opportunity he had had within his reach in September and October. The time for the battle had passed. It had been preempted, if not won, by Scott, Callaghan, Lee, and, in his way, Wright. The U.S. Navy's narrow victories of November allowed it to absorb a catastrophe like Tassafaronga. This defeat resembled the first one, the Battle of Savo Island, in that it shored up, at fearful cost, the position of the men on the island and allowed them to build up strength to fight in their own defense.

Tanaka's final "drum runs" in December provoked no further large naval battles. No significant American formations were mustered to meet him, but he met fierce resistance from Henderson Field's aviators and the PT boats from Tulagi, which inflicted incremental losses on the Tokyo Express and forced Yamamoto to begin diverting submarines from hunting ships to running the blockade. On the night of the ninth, a pair of PT boats caught a Japanese sub on the surface three miles off Kamimbo Bay, towing a barge full of ammunition, food, and medicine. They opened their throttles, rushed in, and sank the *I-3* with torpedoes. Credit for the kill went to the *PT-59*, captained by John M. Searles. "This was quite a feather in the cap of those PT boat boys," said Lloyd Mustin.

On December 11, Tanaka led what would be the final run of the Tokyo Express. The mosquito fleet intercepted his force of nine destroyers between Cape Esperance and Savo Island. Tanaka's flagship, the *Teruzuki*, took a torpedo that detonated her depth charge stowage, sinking her. Fewer than one in five of the twelve hundred drums thrown overboard reached the beach.

Victory did not come by way of a shattering decisive battle. It came through attrition, exacted relentlessly, night after night. Victory, when it came, did not march on parade. It announced itself more subtly, through a return to normalcy and a reemergence of human behaviors that tended to disappear in periods of emergency, when the urgent struggle for survival concentrated minds. At the ice plant within the Marine perimeter, some enterprising leathernecks made a robust black market selling a slushy grog made from papayas, limes, fruit juice, and a surplus of torpedo fuel. When the fresh and generously supplied men of the Americal Division arrived, veteran riflemen suckered them mercilessly, selling to credulous souvenir seekers counterfeit Japanese battle flags manufactured at the parachute loft. On Red Beach that December, discipline among the beachmaster's boat crews teetered on the brink of breakdown. Cargo ships carrying shipments of beer quickly found themselves swarmed by lighters jockeying to unload them. Nets swung from the booms of ammunition ships full of bombs and howitzer projectiles and machine-gun ammunition and canned pineapple, but few boats volunteered to take them. Beer received higher priority. Delighted to find a Liberty ship carrying thirty thousand cases, thieves loaded up their boats and spirited the suds up the beach to a secret depot that was quite secure from discovery owing to its location several miles behind Japanese lines—"a fiasco which would be rather deplorable if it weren't so humorous," Lloyd Mustin said. "The boat crews knew it too, but by George, they were going to land some beer in a private cache known only to them."

The new commanding officer of American ground forces on Guadalcanal, General Patch, let the whole thing slide. He reportedly allowed fantastic quantities of surplus to pile up for off-the-books requisition. Just one in six cases of beer ferried ashore reached the quartermaster dump. Much as the Army supply clerks might have protested, no complaints ever came from Patch, who seemed to regard the theft as a generous toast to his brothers in arms who had served so well since August.

Under Patch, Guadalcanal would begin its transformation to a rear-area base, a place dense with storage depots, hospitals, baseball games, fire trucks, and ration dumps with beer stacked higher than two men could stand. There would be automotive maintenance shops, chapels, water carnivals and regattas with clowns on surfboards, forestry companies, performances by Bob Hope and Jerry Colonna, gardens tended by Japanese POWs, kennel shows, and visits by Eleanor Roosevelt. An armed forces radio affiliate known as The Mosquito Network would flourish there. Its program supervisor, hired out of Hollywood, would create a musical segment called the "Atabrine Cocktail Hour," promoting faithful use of the anti-malaria medication. Troops coming ashore would do so now as rehearsals for landings farther north and westward.

The Imperial Japanese Navy had lost the ability to impose its will on the waters of Savo Sound. Ashore, the position of the 17th Army, desperately drawn in to hold small parts of the island's tangled and mountainous twenty-five hundred square miles, was about as precarious as the initial U.S. position. "The whole color of the war ashore on Guadalcanal was changing, and we could see it," said Lloyd Mustin.

41

Future Rising

IN THIS SEA OF DESTINY, A SPANISH PRIEST HAD ONCE SEEN BOTH THE scale and the pattern of the coming days. Men now living, the survivors of the inferno of 1942, could begin to see the shape of the future, too. It was a wide, islanded oceanic vista cut through now with markers for a trail that would become a path that would become a road. Extended and improved by other ships and other crews, it would lead all the way to Tokyo.

Some would say the victory at Guadalcanal led nowhere. After all, instead of setting sights on conquering Rabaul, the Navy and the Marines would bypass it, jumping north to Tarawa and pouring through the Central Pacific. MacArthur would carry the fight on a line to the west, following a parallel route along New Guinea's northern coast toward the Philippines. But the rights of way for all these roads were laid by the ships and men of the South Pacific Forces. If they had faltered, Australia and New Zealand would have stood alone and America's confidence to undertake a serious offensive anywhere at all might have been broken entirely. For the American veterans of the struggle in the South Pacific, another road lay before them, a road home for a brief respite, and then a return to the war that gave no permanent reprieves except to the dead.

For several days after the *Atlanta* went down, Robert Graff drifted in and out of consciousness in a Lunga Point foxhole. Effectively checked out of the campaign, he was unaware of the final dramas that raged in Savo Sound. The pillars of the earth shook beneath him, but he remained in his own world, bruised body and mind rallying to their own defense.

One night Graff was placed in a small boat and sent to a waiting cargo ship, and along with many other stretcher cases was taken to Espiritu Santo. There, in a series of operations in a medical hut, doctors removed chunks of shrapnel that had riddled him that night. That's where he first heard the whole story of the loss of his ship, and of the deaths of Admiral Scott and the others on the *Atlanta*'s bridge under heavy fire from friend and foe. It felt like a story told by a stranger from another world. He walled himself off from the experience, even as he couldn't quite shake his wonderment that he had survived it. He would reflect on the arbitrary randomness of his luck for the rest of his life. "People were killed all around me. It put me in a very, very deep emotional funk for years."

Graff was taken to Efate to recover. Most of the other medical evacuees were taken to Nouméa, where they were transferred to the "receiving ship," which was not a vessel but a transfer facility consisting of a large tent city on a scenic hillside, well populated with survivors of the *Hornet*, the *Atlanta*, the *Northampton*, and various sunken destroyers. In time they were gathered and transferred to the holds of a transport, the *President Monroe*, which ferried them to Auckland. Graff ended up in Auckland, too.

On arrival in the harbor, Graff heard strains of a military band playing its bouncing repertoire. Recent history started to catch up with him then. "I just cried my heart out," he said. "I could not get ahold of myself, whatever there was to hold onto." A nurse came into his hospital room once or twice and lulled, "*Shhh*, there's nothing to cry about, old man." But she couldn't know and he didn't tell her. "I just continued to cry." In time, and with struggle, he was able to rise and lift himself out of bed.

The *Atlanta* survivors got four days of "free gangway" in New Zealand's largest city. "This was a privilege seldom afford in the USN. It means 'beat it and don't come back until we sail,'" Bill McKinney wrote. Strolling the city streets by evening, the sailors were, he recalled, "literally engulfed by girls. It would have taken a leper to have wound up with less than a girl on each arm. They were quite frank and got to the point quickly. Many of them seemed to live alone and we were invited to move in during our stay in Auckland. They were so blunt that many a usually self-assured sailor was left open-mouthed."

The *Helena*, now under a new captain, Charles P. Cecil, was ordered from Nouméa to Sydney for some R&R. Entering the harbor, the light cruiser was saluted by the deep groans of tugboat whistles and cheering well-wishers waving from sailboats and pleasure craft. The city's iconic Harbour Bridge, silhouetted in a rosy red at twilight, was the backdrop for a celebration that spilled ashore into the oyster bars and Red Cross–sponsored dances and cocktail parties.

Such pleasures were a superficial salve. Graff's shipmate Jim Shaw wrote to his wife, Jane, of the new perspective on life the experience of battle had given them. "We hate the petty bickering of politics.... We hate the disunity between labor and capital. We look with a sort of contemptuous tolerance on such organizations as the USO. We eye askance and critically the opinions aired by the press. As for the 'military commentators' who learn their strategy out of books, we writhe in disgust at their positive statements as to how the actual combat should be carried on.... After the war is over the fighting man is going to demand a kind of peace and a kind of government that will be some slight remuneration for the blood and toil and anguish of the war."

For Leonard A. Joslin, a survivor of the *Quincy,* nighttime was forevermore a haunted place. "Years later I'd have nightmares, and dreams at night, and I would see the ship coming into port. I'd see men waving. I could see the signal bridge. I knew that I was supposed to be up there. But the ship would fade away. And I'd try to catch it at another port, and the same thing. I could see the men waving, the signal bridge; I knew I was supposed to be up there. But the ship would leave me, and the dream would fade. Many times, years later even, I would dream of this ship, and the men. And they're waving at me."

On the eleventh of December, Joslin's vision unfolded in real time for the survivors of Dan Callaghan's old flagship arriving in her namesake city. As the crew manned the rail, thousands of Bay Area residents greeted them, jamming the hillsides and promenades to have a look at the battered *San Francisco* entering the harbor. Eugene Tarrant remembers the cool weather that welcomed their homecoming, and the fog that held the Golden Gate Bridge like a midnight pall off Savo. It was a publicist's dream: the veterans of a hero ship, returning to the city where she had been built (Vallejo), right next door to the hometown (Oakland) of the admiral who had died in battle on her bridge.

When the ambulatory survivors were flushed out of the Oak Knoll Naval Hospital and bused downtown for a ticker-tape parade six days later, "They gave this city a strange feeling of humility and sadness, and at the same time its greatest thrill in many a year," a *San Francisco Chronicle* reporter wrote.

The procession of survivors stretched out for more than a mile, attended by a crowd of seventy-five thousand lining the street. However, the mood of the celebration was peculiar. "It was the quietest parade this city has ever seen. There was some cheering and applauding, but it didn't stick. For the most part, the thousands on the streets stared as they would at a sacred procession." Some of the marchers proceeded with canes and crutches, wearing hospital robes. None of them stayed thirsty for long on Market Street that week.

Admirals Nimitz and King were on hand to give medals. They decorated Bruce McCandless with the Medal of Honor in front of an audience that included his parents and his wife. The father of Dan Callaghan drove over from Oakland, but the late admiral's mother and widow stayed home. "They didn't think they could face it. They didn't think they could stand it," Dan Callaghan, Sr., told a reporter. In Washington, President Roosevelt himself had just given the same award to family representatives of Callaghan and Norman Scott. Herbert Schonland and the *San Francisco*'s heroic firefighter, Reinhardt J. Keppler, received the Medal of Honor as well.

For the rest of the *San Francisco*'s crew, there was acclaim to go around, though many of them understood it was excessive. "In the press we were lauded beyond all reason," Clifford Spencer wrote. Almost everyone knew that other ships, including the *Sterett, Monssen, Barton, Juneau,* and *Atlanta,* had suffered far heavier proportions of casualties but weren't able to return for ticker tape and free beer. Whenever he heard the *San Francisco* referred to as the Navy's "fightin'est ship," McCandless would insist that "polishing off a battleship is a community job."

The homecoming of damaged warships was a rare thing for the public. The lack of a fair perspective on their accomplishments was inevitable. The way Mike Moran's *Boise* was feted in Philadelphia would forever irk many *Helena* sailors, who had thrown at least as much ordnance the enemy's way and were now rewarded with obscurity for having taken less in return.* *The New York Times* reported as fact that the *Boise* "sank six Japanese warships in twenty-seven minutes." To the lasting chagrin of the *Washington*'s men, the *South Dakota* was immortalized in the press as "Battleship X," used out of concern for security. When the mask was finally lifted, the ship's name was cast in lights that her dubious battle performance did not seem to merit.

---

* The *Helena* would be sunk in the Solomons, a victim of torpedoes, in the Battle of Kula Gulf, on July 6, 1943. That event seems to live more powerfully in the memories of her veterans than the Guadalcanal battles do.

Nevertheless, Captain Gatch announced that his ship "sank three Jap cruisers and demonstrated there's no match for a battleship, except equally good battleships." When the *San Francisco* entered harbor, she was in the company of a fellow veteran of Ironbottom Sound, the *Sterett*. As the cruiser prepared for a public reception at Pier 16, the humble tin can went, unheralded as those expendable ships often are, to the yard at Mare Island.

None of these small injustices matched what Eugene Tarrant and his fellow steward's mates and cooks suffered when they went ashore. Cameramen from the Fox Movietone News Agency dwelled on the *San Francisco*'s crew until Tarrant's turn came. When he and his S Division shipmates began filing past, the motion-picture crews turned their cameras on other subjects.

AS THE *SAN FRANCISCO* was approaching the West Coast for her grand reception, an Imperial Army colonel returned to Tokyo from Rabaul after a fact-finding mission to the Southern Area front. Across all services at Japan's forward-most base, he told high command, there was a wholesale lack of confidence. With the destruction of their reinforcement convoys in November and their faltering hold on New Guinea, both naval and Army high command saw that the end of the struggle was near. The colonel's report urged the unthinkable: abandonment of Guadalcanal, and the evacuation of its garrison. In the discussion that followed, the concern arose that if word of an evacuation reached the island, the soldiers might take their own lives.

The Americans had their own setbacks to explore, and their own fact-finding missions to launch. Though victory was within its grasp, the Navy was looking back on the disaster that had nearly derailed it in the beginning with the losses of the *Vincennes, Quincy,* and *Astoria*. An old saying later popularized by a veteran of the Solomons naval campaign, John F. Kennedy, went, "Victory has a hundred fathers. Defeat is an orphan." What then of the parentage a defeat suffered within the context of a larger victory? The Navy seemed bent on isolating it like a cancer.

On December 20, Ernest King ordered an "informal inquiry into the circumstances attending the loss of these vessels." Its purpose, he would write, was "to find out exactly what caused the defeat, and second, to determine whether or not any responsible officers involved in the planning and execution of the operations were culpably inefficient." Three days later, the man who would conduct the investigation reported to King's headquarters in Washington. His name was Arthur J. Hepburn. The chairman of the Navy's General Board, a panel of senior admirals that advised the secretary of the

Navy, Hepburn was the U.S. admiralty's most senior man. He had served as commander in chief of the U.S. Fleet and had a deep expertise in the mysteries of the world's largest ocean. As an ensign, after the Spanish-American War, he had participated in the U.S. Exploring Expedition, an oceanographic survey of the entire vast Pacific. He was serious, dignified, and reserved. As Hanson Baldwin wrote in a 1936 *New York Times* profile, "He is not a colorful personality; there are no legends about him on his flagships, no mass of Hepburn anecdota in the fleet. His record speaks for him; he is respected and trusted." Hepburn served in another role, too, one that is seldom mentioned in the shadow of his other accomplishments: He was the Navy's director of public relations, the sea service's principal public affairs man. After reporting to King, Hepburn sat down with Vice Admiral Ghormley in Washington and interrogated him. Ghormley had been puzzled and perturbed since his relief that any specific fault might attach to him for the August 9 disaster off Savo Island. His interrogation by his former superior— Ghormley had been Hepburn's staff operations officer after his tour in command of the *Nevada*—opened that wound again. On January 2, 1943, Hepburn reported to CINCPAC headquarters in Hawaii. When illness forced Hepburn to the hospital for three weeks, his aide, Commander Donald J. Ramsey, began reviewing documents at the headquarters of CINCPAC.

WHILE HEPBURN WAS CONVALESCING in Hawaii, American intelligence analysts were starting to divine from movements of troops, aircraft, and ships that the Japanese might be shifting to the strategic defensive. But something in the radio traffic suggested otherwise. Stymied by a change in Japanese ciphers, they took what they could from the radio traffic. Again and again they heard references to something known as "Operation KE," evidently planned to take place somewhere in New Guinea or the Solomons.

Nimitz believed Yamamoto might still have plans to strike at and reinforce Guadalcanal. When Halsey's intelligence staff saw signs in the third week of January that at least three carriers, the *Zuikaku*, *Zuiho*, and *Junyo*, were at Truk, along with the super battleships *Yamato* and *Musashi*, there was good reason for vigilance. Confronted with the possibility of another major naval assault, Halsey resolved to finish the replacement of the warweary Marine units on Guadalcanal while things were still relatively quiet. He ordered transports to bring in the last of the Army's 25th Division and take off the marines. A powerful element of the South Pacific Area naval force was ordered to support them and cover the withdrawal.

In desperation, the Imperial General Headquarters had drawn up an even more ambitious plan. As forces gathered at the great naval base in the Carolines, Japan's service branches were regrouping to defend the central and northern Solomons—and preparing to throw their fullest effort into Operation KE. After five months of attrition, Halsey and his staff were blameless in thinking it was another reinforcement effort.

Emperor Hirohito was sensitive about the public's opinion of a campaign that had emerged as a showcase of the Japanese will to fight. In public he held to the view that an opportunity for victory lay for the taking in the Solomons. In an Imperial Rescript broadcast to the nation on December 26, the very same day that the Imperial General Headquarters decided to withdraw, the emperor declared that "dawn is about to break in the Eastern Sky" and announced that forces then gathering would head toward the Solomons for the decisive battle.

In a meeting with his high commanders a few days later, however, the Emperor decided to do what until then was unthinkable. The Imperial Army would not reinforce. It would withdraw. Compelling testimony of the morbid state of Japanese soldiers on the island came from diaries taken from the dead. In late December, when deaths by starvation were tolling at a rate of more than a hundred a day, a Japanese Army lieutenant estimated the life expectancy of his comrades as follows: "Those who can stand—30 days. Those who can sit up—3 weeks. Those who cannot sit up—1 week. Those who urinate lying down—3 days. Those who have stopped speaking—2 days. Those who have stopped blinking—tomorrow." The Japanese were finished throwing good men and machines into the grinder.

Yamamoto would borrow a page from a seldom-studied playbook: that of the Royal Navy at Dunkirk. Operation KE was an evacuation mission, and it would take place right under the noses of the pilots and ships and PT boats of the South Pacific Forces. Reluctantly approving the plans, Hirohito said, "It is unacceptable to just give up on capturing Guadalcanal. We must launch an offensive elsewhere." But what was acceptable—and possible— was no longer up to the divine prince. The U.S. Navy had a great deal more to say about it. In the Solomons and in New Guinea, as elsewhere, momentum was swinging its way.

Secrecy was Operation KE's byword. Its true purpose was concealed not only from the Americans, but also from the Japanese infantrymen who were its principal beneficiaries. It began the last week of January with the coordinated movement of troops to the coast near Cape Esperance. Avoiding pursuit and encirclement from General Patch's army, which now numbered more than fifty thousand men, they hauled the last of their starving selves toward the shore on Savo Sound, sparing the dignity of potential mutineers with the cover story that they were gathering for a final offensive.

American planes were ranging well up the Slot now, hammering targets from the air base at Munda to Rabaul itself. Japanese aircraft, meanwhile, were newly recommitted en masse to their months-old drill: to make the long flight down to Guadalcanal, suppress the Cactus Air Force, block the sea approaches to the island, and cover the evacuation. In this final spasm of violence in the southern Solomons, a group of U.S. warships was set upon by Japanese torpedo bombers.

They came in at twilight on the evening of January 30, a flight of thirty-one torpedo-armed Betty bombers, bearing down from the starboard hand of Task Force 18 as it slugged a northwesterly course at twenty-four knots. Under the command of a rookie to the Pacific theater, Rear Admiral Robert C. Giffen, steamed the heavy cruisers *Wichita, Chicago,* and *Louisville,* the light cruisers *Montpelier, Cleveland,* and *Columbia,* and six destroyers. The escort carriers *Chenango* and *Suwannee* slugged along to provide air cover.

Giffen had orders to rendezvous with four destroyers southwest of Guadalcanal and then patrol Savo Sound. To keep the rendezvous, and to escape a significant threat from submarines, he chose in favor of better speed and ordered the slow carriers to lag behind. At twilight on January 30, this force was fifty miles north of Rennell Island when air-search radars lit up with bogeys. Submarines had indeed been hunting him, not with their torpedoes, but with their snooping periscopes and radios. Though he had been sighted, Giffen, like Gilbert Hoover, was loath to break radio silence. He thus declined to transmit interception coordinates to the combat air patrol provided by the *Chenango* and *Suwannee,* standing off to the south.

Except for the fact that they arrived after sunset, it was a reprise of the November 12 air attack on Turner and Callaghan, with a twist. From the sky at dim twilight fell a kaleidoscope of burning colors, flares, expertly dropped to show the direction of the American force and color-coded to indicate its composition. The Japanese air forces were as much students of night warfare as their Navy, and the Americans were no less bewildered by this innovation than by the others the Japanese had employed. Still, shipboard antiaircraft gunnery was, as ever, very effective, aided by a technological wrinkle kept strictly secret: the use of "proximity fuzes" that used a radar transmitter in the shell to tell it when to explode. One of the burning Bettys fell through the night sky and passed ahead of the *Chicago,* crashing into the sea off her port bow.

The last group to bear the designation Task Force 18 had been the star-crossed unit containing the *Wasp, Vincennes,* and *Quincy,* all of them now lost. The *Chicago* was a blooded veteran of these waters, too, having served, on the night it all began, as the interim flagship of Rear Admiral Crutchley's southwestern cruiser screen. Her captain at the time, Howard D. Bode, had assumed temporary command when his British superior left station on August 9 to confer with Turner and Vandegrift about the sightings of Japanese ships and the imminent withdrawal of Fletcher's carriers. Making contact with a mysterious squadron, then taken under fire and torpedoed in the bow, Bode's ship had steamed away from the action, searching for phantoms as Gunichi Mikawa made his lethal run.

Now, under a new captain, the *Chicago* stood in harm's way again. The flames on the water from the fuel of the crashed Betty cast her as a lucrative silhouette for other pilots. They lined up on her and dropped. Two of their torpedoes struck the cruiser on the starboard side, collapsing compartments and stilling three of her four screws. The ship's crew labored to flood port side tanks to bring her back from a starboard list. The *Louisville* took her in tow.

The following morning, Task Force 18 huddled around the *Chicago* as relays of Wildcats from the two escort carriers, and the *Enterprise,* too, tried to shield her from follow-up attacks. But there was no denying the Japanese this prize. After an early-afternoon chess match between search planes from Rabaul and the American combat air patrol, Japanese strike aircraft found the *Chicago* again around 4 p.m. It was unfortunate that most of the other ships of the group had been ordered to withdraw to Efate. The *Chicago* needed help against the planes. The Japanese bombers put four more torpedoes into the stricken cruiser. She rolled over and sank within twenty minutes, taking sixty-two officers and men to their graves.

THE REMOVAL OF GIFFEN'S cruiser group from the order of battle on February 1 was a boon to Operation KE. That day a force of twenty destroyers under Rear Admiral Hashimoto, who had succeeded Raizo Tanaka as commander of the Reinforcement Unit and who had fought Willis Lee the night of November 14, departed from Shortland Island for the first run at evacuating Guadalcanal's garrison. Labeled by long habit, the Reinforcement Unit had a mission now that was quite the opposite of what its name suggested.

As Hashimoto plunged south, aircraft from Henderson Field spied him north of Vella Lavella in the early afternoon. Soon swarms of Cactus Air Force planes were slashing at his ships, ninety-two planes in two waves. A near miss smote the destroyer *Makinami,* forcing the detachment of two more destroyers to stand by her. A second destroyer was hit and forced to turn back as well. After nightfall, Tulagi's PT boats piled in. The remaining Japanese destroyers contended with eleven of them attacking in pairs and trios. Lieutenant John Clagett's *PT-111* was taken under fire by the destroyer *Kawakaze.* One shell struck home, and the boat exploded into flames that claimed two men. The *PT-37,* hit three times and set afire, went down with her entire crew save one. The *PT-123* was attacked by a Pete reconnaissance floatplane, which deftly planted a bomb on her fantail, sinking her in flames.

Despite the opposition, Hashimoto got six destroyers through to Cape Esperance, and six more to Kamimbo Bay. Small boats from the destroyers motored to shore to begin gathering the men of the 17th Army. This first evacuation run would recover 4,935 men, most of them emaciated and disease-ridden. On February 4, a second run extracted 3,921 more, including the three-star generals Harukichi Hyakutake and Masao Maruyama, the commanders of the 17th Army and the 2nd (Sendai) Division, respectively.

General Patch was thoroughly fooled by the deception. On the seventh, he announced that the two recent runs of the Tokyo Express had *landed* more troops—an additional regiment with supplies, he said. That same day Hashimoto got under way on a third evacuation run, this time with eighteen destroyers. The persistence of the Japanese destroyermen in withdrawal and retreat was as gallant as anything they had done in battle. This last effort yielded a diminishing but significant return, 1,796 men. The rescue of 10,652 souls from Starvation Island was a boost to morale and a gift of grace that no member of that ferociously Spartan Army had any reason to expect. Hitler gave his 6th Army no such reprieve, insisting they hold their position on the Volga River until, drained of fuel, food, and fighting will, they had no choice but to surrender, which they did on January 31.

Operation KE cost the IJN one destroyer sunk and three more badly damaged, as well as fifty-six aircraft. Weighing this with the American losses of the *Chicago,* the destroyer *DeHaven,* three PT boats, and fifty-three planes, the equivalent of two divisions of Japanese troops, it could be said, departed Guadalcanal with their dignity intact.

The Americans on Guadalcanal had long known their enemy was withering away. Now he seemed to vanish before their weary eyes. General Patch was deprived of the pleasure of a final rout of his foe. But on February 9,

1943, he had the satisfaction of sending a dispatch to the headquarters of the commander, South Pacific Forces, and Admiral Halsey had the equivalent satisfaction of reading it.

TOTAL AND COMPLETE DEFEAT OF JAPANESE FORCES ON GUADALCANAL EFFECTED 1625 TODAY.... AM HAPPY TO REPORT THIS KIND OF COMPLI-ANCE WITH YOUR ORDERS.... 'TOKYO EXPRESS' NO LONGER HAS TERMINUS ON GUADALCANAL.

42

Report and Echo

THE MEN CAME HOME, AS THE LUCKY ONES DO. THE WAR RAGED ON.

On New Year's Day, the *President Monroe* arrived in San Francisco with her complement of *Atlanta* survivors. It was just as well they missed the hoo-hah over the *San Francisco*'s arrival three weeks before. An *Atlanta* veteran, Robert Chute, was "full of the usual horror stories and equally full of scathing remarks for the *San Francisco*," Bettsy Perkins, the wife of one of the ship's officers, wrote. "Mind you, Mrs. Perkins," he said, "I ain't talking about this ship to no one but you, but a guy's gotta blow off some steam to someone and all this Hero Ship stuff is bunk."

Perkins was tearfully reunited with her husband, Van Perkins, but the reunion was short-lived. When his leave was up, the war still beckoned. He was reassigned to the light cruiser *Birmingham*. In the Philippines in 1944, Perkins was serving as the cruiser's damage-control officer when she went to the assistance of a damaged ship, the light aircraft carrier *Princeton*, struck by a bomb. Commander Perkins was supervising the *Birmingham*'s fire-fighters as they played their streams into the burning carrier. His ship was so close alongside, and the sea so heavy, that her superstructure took a beating from the overhang of the carrier's flight deck. When the *Princeton*'s maga-zines detonated, Perkins was killed instantly. He was buried at sea quickly and summarily, and not a shipmate from the *Atlanta* was there for him. They had gone to fight their own wars.

After the war, Bettsy married one of the few men on earth who would understand her loss, another officer from the *Atlanta,* Jim Shaw, himself a widower. In her memoirs, published decades later, her outlook on the romance of naval service would acquire a bittersweet complexity, torn between romantic reverie and cold-eyed pragmatism.

I now see that I had a love for the *Atlanta* like that you afford a human being and that ships are after all just floating offices and as warm as a dead fish. I will never forget the *Atlanta.* She taught me a lesson. I won't ever try to love another ship. I'll just take them for what they are worth which is nothing. The *Atlanta* is dead and buried. She got buried in my heart which was perhaps the wrong place for her, but she got there, and now I realized that she was unique and that I must not try to hold up other ships to her standards which means that I must become more tolerant towards other ships because I cannot judge all by the exceptional.

With the *Atlanta* left to be honored in memory only—and by a new homesake, the CL-104, serving with the fleet in 1945—the public never deeply registered the name. As Guadalcanal's naval veterans found other ships to fight the war in, they would find that few other vessels or crews would withstand any comparison with the past.

No sooner had Robert Graff returned fully to the world at Oak Knoll than he was surrounded by inquisitors. "As soon as I could talk, people would gather around my bed. What they wanted to know was, what was it like to fight? What are the particulars that make battle different from civilian life? How do we prepare? The people back in Washington, what did they know?

"The first thing I told them was to try to do their part in making the ship's company a fighting team. If you can do that, you've got half the battle won. That means that everybody feels a responsibility for everybody else. Everybody has a job to do and his task is to do his job correctly and well. Talk to the shipmates in your division as much as you can, not only to learn your job but to build up a sense of confidence, little by little, that if you get hurt, another guy's going to know how to help you. If you do those two things, you're a long way along."

Lloyd Mustin was appalled that it should take exposure to actual combat for the Navy to develop rudimentary tactical competence. "The requirement to be ready to execute simple tactics in the dark while engaging the enemy, I suppose, is one of the things that you'd expect naval officers would be taught from the time they become midshipmen.

"You could adduce a lot of crocodile tears and a lot of clichés that all these poor guys didn't have any time to train together, and so forth, and it's essential that they be working as a team and so on. Well, that's just so much balderdash.... They should be able to work together as a team on no advance notice whatsoever by virtue of working to a single uniform common U.S. Navy doctrine, a single common signal book which, of course, we've had for years and years."

Graff didn't believe books could ever teach a man to respond effectively to the sensation of a bulkhead shattering or a keel buckling underfoot. "Think creatively, imaginatively, about what combat is really like," he told his inquisitors, "and what would you do if you lost control over your survival. You have to talk like that with your shipmates.

"There are no secrets here, but what you find is that some people are constitutionally unable to perform that way. So then the game is to make sure that they're put in positions where they can use the talents they have when circumstances are horrific." Unless everybody does his job, and learns to do it under duress, "there can be no fighting ship."

After Graff had healed well enough to be reassigned, he reported to Philadelphia, where a new aircraft carrier, the *Monterey,* was preparing to get under way for the Pacific. When her captain, a naval aviator, heard that an *Atlanta* survivor was joining his wardroom, he appreciated what he had and was smart enough to ask him to a private lunch. "He wanted to know everything," Graff said. "He really just probed me and probed me." Combat veterans tended to be resilient and adaptable. One way or another, Graff adapted to being in high demand.

The way America handled its "first team" differed markedly from Japan's. The Americans brought them home after their inaugural experience under sustained fire and employed them to train the next wave. The Japanese left them on the front to fight until the inevitable happened, and saw their human assets waste away. It was a gilded luxury that the Marine Corps could send home its first fighter ace, the commander of one of the most decorated squadrons in the Solomons, Captain John L. Smith, give him his Medal of Honor, and refuse his requests to return to combat, "not until you have trained 150 John L. Smiths." A less dramatic case, but more typical of the system, was Edgar Harrison, a fire controlman from the *San Francisco.* He took his battle experience to the Navy's technical schools, becoming the first instructor on the new Mark 56 fire-control system, developed to repel attacks by kamikaze aircraft.

As Graff went to sea in the *Monterey,* the *Aaron Ward*'s radar officer, Bob Hagen, reported to Seattle-Tacoma to become the gunnery officer of a new destroyer, the *Johnston,* whose captain, Commander Ernest E. Evans, was a combat veteran who had been similarly recycled from a previous assignment. Jesse Coward and Roland Smoot, commanders of the *Sterett* and *Monssen,* respectively, would take command of destroyer squadrons and play important tactical roles in later campaigns, too. Tested and seasoned by adversity, all would acquire varying degrees of naval legend in the Leyte Gulf campaign in the Philippines in 1944.

The epic of the Pacific war found new chapters for everyone. The endless game of personnel-rotation musical chairs saw the continuous replacement of the experienced by the inexperienced, until, by the end, only the experienced remained.

JOE JAMES CUSTER, the war correspondent, had served in the South Pacific campaign's earliest days and witnessed the destruction firsthand. On board the *Astoria,* and later, recovering from eye surgery at Queen's Hospital in Honolulu, he had become close with men who had served in the inferno. He had looked into their eyes and seen right through into their minds and souls, and found reflections of pain in a blackness that he called "something new the psychiatrists were working on." Experience was important. It delivered benefits, and took a price, too. "They were ill, physically, mentally, spiritually; they had undergone agonies of body and mind that were impossible to contemplate except by those who had actually been there." The scale of violence was impossible to reckon with.

Custer's articles detailing the loss of the *Astoria,* published near the end of October in *The Seattle Times* and elsewhere, awakened in the families of many servicemen an urgency to understand what their loved ones had been through. Letters soon began arriving in Room 232 at Queen's Hospital. Until his eyes healed and he could read them himself, the nurses on duty had to do the honors for him.

One correspondent's brother, a lieutenant, had gone missing. "We have received news from Wash. of his reported death. I guess it's natural that I should wish to repudiate this, but I just don't feel Tom is gone. You say a cruiser was lost—was anybody on board saved? If I could come to you personally to talk it over with you I'm sure I could readily make you see how much the truth means to me, to all of us. My mother hasn't even been told as yet what we've heard. We're afraid what the shock might do to her.... In the name of Christian charity, and as a fellow countryman, can you see fit to write and answer me?"

"You may not care to bother with this letter but please do as it will probly relieve the heartaches of seven people who morn the loss of a dear Boy just 20 years old, who was on the ship *Astoria* in battle. this is his grandfather writeing you for more information. He was dearly loved by me and his grandmother who passed away on the night of August 9th 42." (All typos in quotations are *sic.*)

Another correspondent had a son on the *Quincy,* now missing in action. Could he have swum to land or been taken prisoner? "If he is in a hospital would they let him write home and tell me where he is? My son's wife is to have a baby some time this month. . . . We grasp at any opportunity to contact someone who may have known our boy. . . . We shall never tire of listening to anything connected with the last days of the life of the *Astoria.*"

Someone in the War Department got the idea to send veterans of America's first victorious campaign around the country to factories, bolstering morale. By 1943, absenteeism was becoming a serious problem in the war industries. With women pressed into full-time service in the workforce, adding to their responsibilities as homemakers, many found the dual commitments difficult to sustain. Edgar Harrison of the *San Francisco* was called to duty in this effort. A speech was written for him, and he went out to testify to his experiences.

"This young man could be any of your sons or husbands," the executive who introduced him at one event said. "He's going to tell you about a battle you just heard about on radio." The speeches were made as bloody as the mores of public presentation would allow. For three months Harrison traveled to the manufacturing plants of the Midwest and Northeast, doing four or five speeches a day, always hitting the shift changes when the audience was double. "Guys would walk up to me afterwards with tears in their eyes, shake my hand, and not say a word. Everybody knew somebody in the Army or Navy," he said.

One morning in early 1943, before a speech at the Cadillac plant in Cadillac, Michigan, he was escorted to a railroad siding behind a large building and asked to paint his name on a large piece of steel on a flatcar. Then he was invited to follow it through every manufacturing phase on the assembly line, until, three hours later, it was driven off the end of the line, part of a finished Sherman tank.

Tom and Alleta Sullivan, gold-star parents of the five boys from the *Juneau,* began a speaking tour in February that took them to Baltimore,

Philadelphia, New York, Newport, Hartford, and through the heartland, slated to end with the launching in San Francisco of a new destroyer named after their sons. At a whistlestop in Chicago several weeks along, a survivor from the ship, Allen Heyn, confided to them what had really happened to George, their oldest, during his ordeal at sea.

They would inspire untold thousands of people in more than two hundred appearances nationwide before they returned to Waterloo and the public eye wandered elsewhere. Back home, they would be left to contend with the smaller minds of their community who suspected the couple of cashing in on their sons' loss. They would never feel at home in Waterloo again. And it finally became too much. In San Francisco the first week of April, at the launching of the USS *The Sullivans,* Alleta broke a champagne bottle against the hull and smiled graciously for the cameras. Before the ceremony could end, however, her strength gave out. She buckled and fell to the ground sobbing.

EARLY 1943 WAS A TIME of many reckonings. Foremost among them, in the echoing halls of the Navy's culture of reputation at least, was Admiral Hepburn's inquisition into the failures that decided the Battle of Savo Island.

After recovering from his illness in Hawaii, he went quickly to work, inspecting Admiral Nimitz's files and then interrogating Commander H. B. Heneberger, the senior surviving officer of the *Quincy,* and Commander Elijah W. Irish, the navigator of the *Chicago.* He boarded the next available ship for Nouméa, where he met with Admiral Halsey. Then, on February 16, he took his inquiry to Australia.

Interservice niceties were needed to gain an audience with Admiral Crutchley, still serving under U.S. command but now with Douglas MacArthur's Southwest Pacific Forces. Hepburn found the British officer's account of the battle, filed in Brisbane, "the most complete and lucid report of the entire operation," though of course Crutchley was miles away when it took place. Perhaps out of the respect thus gained, Hepburn would write that he "conferred with" (rather than "interrogated") Crutchley in Melbourne, on board the vessel that had been excused from disaster on August 9, the cruiser *Australia.* At Canberra, Hepburn was received by Australia's governor-general and attended a meeting of the War Council. He returned to Nouméa to interrogate Admiral Turner, then flew home to Pearl Harbor to examine Captain Greenman and begin work on his report to Admiral King.

Only then, on April 2, did Hepburn fly back to the mainland to interrogate the two officers whose culpable inefficiency he was beginning to see most clearly: Captain Riefkohl of the *Vincennes* and Captain Bode of the *Chicago*. Shrewd interrogators will often save the most difficult sessions for last. Armed with deep knowledge of the facts, and with his report largely already drafted, Arthur J. Hepburn arrived in Corpus Christi and prepared for the final stage of his inquest.

43

The Opinion of
Convening Authority

SOME OFFICERS SAW SUCCESS AND FAILURE AS PRODUCTS OF TEAM-work. "No one man was responsible for our success in the Pacific," wrote Charles W. Weaver, Ghormley's assistant operations officer. "It was a team effort by many good men. Others, of lesser stature, are scrambling now in their memoirs to remind posterity that *they* won the war." The Navy was now well along chasing something else: accountability from those who had marred its successful campaign with an avoidable defeat in the Battle of Savo Island.

The fleet seemed to find it irresistible to refight the battle. Retrospectively, wisdom abounded as to what commanders should have done, what risks they should have embraced or avoided. It had always been so. As a Roman general, Lucius Aemilius Paulus, observed in 168 BC, "In every circle, and, truly, at every table, there are people who lead armies into Macedonia."

Admiral King's flag secretary, Captain George L. Russell, noted that the exercise was significantly academic in nature. "The deficiencies which manifested themselves in this action, with particular reference to communications and the condition of readiness, together with erroneous conceptions of how to conduct this type of operation, have long since been corrected," he wrote. Long after it had ceased to matter, the Navy would deliver a verdict on its failings. As salve for its own institutional pride perhaps, or for bereaved relatives still mourning their losses, Admiral Hepburn would find his "culpable inefficiency."

A critic could find a long list of candidates to blame for the many errors of the Guadalcanal campaign: Riefkohl for failure to keep watch and his mystifyingly persistent belief that Mikawa's cruisers were friendly. Turner for not understanding the limits of the radar he relied on. Crutchley for removing the *Australia* from her patrol station without communicating his intentions up or down the chain of command. McCain for failing to report the cancellation of a critical air search. Fletcher and his superiors for the inability to mediate, arbitrate, or otherwise control a serious disagreement about the use of the carriers on the eve of a critical operation. Ghormley for his absorption in detail and absence in body and spirit from the combat zone. Halsey for his spendthrift way with his carriers in October, and for his miscommunications with Kinkaid that prevented Willis Lee from moving north with the *Washington* in time to help Callaghan's cruisers on the night of November 13. Callaghan and Wright for not exploiting a radar advantage against a surprised foe. The journalist and critic I. F. Stone would call the state of mind that permitted the Pearl Harbor attack "sheer stodgy unimaginative bureaucratic complacency." That syndrome was at work on August 9, and the result was another virtuoso performance by the blitz-minded Imperial Japanese Navy.

The day before his relief by Halsey, Ghormley prepared a commentary that cast the defeat at Savo Island as a result of flawed battle doctrine. His preliminary conclusion was that Kelly Turner's instructions to Crutchley's screening force were "too indefinite in regard to what the units of that group were to do and how they were to accomplish their tasks." Though Turner had written to Hepburn, "I was satisfied with arrangements, and hoped that the enemy would attack," Ghormley observed that those arrangements were woefully inadequate. "No special battle plan was prescribed to cover the possibility of a surface ship night attack," he wrote, also observing that Turner's instructions to the two radar pickets, the destroyers *Blue* and *Ralph Talbot*, "were faulty in requiring them to 'shadow' an enemy force and report them frequently. Time and space did not permit the employment of tactics of this nature." Neither Turner nor Crutchley, Ghormley observed, had decided how the two cruiser groups on patrol that night might coordinate in the event of enemy contact.

Stickling and insistent in some matters, Hepburn was laissez-faire in others. He didn't worry about the lack of a battle plan: "Only one plan of battle was practicable, viz., bring batteries to bear as quickly as possible," he wrote in his fifty-four-page "informal inquiry." He continued, "In my opinion, the important causes of the defeat suffered in this action are to be found in reasons other than those discussed above, and which fall within the general category of 'Readiness for Action.'"

Turner would angrily rebut the accusation that he had been passive in the face of Mikawa's threat. "I have been accused of being and doing many things but nobody before has ever accused me of sitting on my arse and doing nothing," he would tell his biographer. "If I had known of any 'approaching' Jap force I would have done something—maybe the wrong thing, but I would have done something.... What I failed to do was to assume that the g.d. pilots couldn't count and couldn't identify and wouldn't do their job and stick around and trail the Japs and send through a later report. And I failed to assume that McCain wouldn't keep me informed of what his pilots were or were not doing. And I failed to guess that despite the reported composition of the force, and the reported course, and the reported speed, the Japs were headed for me via a detour, just like we arrived at Guadalcanal via a detour. I wouldn't mind if they said that I was too damned dumb to have crystal-balled these things, but to write that I was told of an 'approaching force' and then didn't do anything, that's an unprintable, unprintable, unprintable lie.

"Nobody reported an 'approaching force' to me. They reported a force which could and did approach, but they reported another kind of force headed another kind of way. It was a masterful failure of air reconnaissance and my fellow aviators."

When misfortune came, no one's career was safe from a sudden change in the weather. Gilbert Hoover lost his seagoing career in Halsey's storm. Even Admiral Raymond Spruance, Nimitz's chief of staff and widely considered one of the Navy's most capacious minds, had taken lumps for what some critics deemed his excessive caution in the Battle of Midway. The experience soured him on second-guessing: "I have always hesitated to sit in judgment of the responsible man on the spot, unless it was obvious to me at the time he was making a grave error in judgment. Even in that case I wanted to hear his side of the matter before I made any final judgment."

Hepburn acknowledged some of this. "There is generally a twilight zone lying between culpable inefficiency on the one hand and a more or less excusable error of judgment on the other." But when he released his report on May 13, five weeks after finishing his interrogations and resuming his duties as chairman of the General Board, Hepburn's conclusions shone like a harsh ray through that twilight.

"In my opinion the primary cause of defeat must be ascribed generally to the complete surprise achieved by the enemy," he began. It was in the specific reasons for this surprise that culpable inefficiency lay. In order of importance, those reasons were: an inadequate condition of readiness on all ships to meet a sudden night attack, a failure to understand the telltale presence of enemy planes beforehand, a misplaced confidence in the radar pickets, delayed reports of enemy contact, and a communications breakdown regarding the canceled air-search mission. As a "contributory cause," Hepburn cited Fletcher's withdrawal of the carriers on August 9, which made necessary Crutchley's departure to the conference, which enabled the confused command arrangement for the southern cruiser group.

Though Captain Riefkohl's leadership of the northern cruiser group was "far from impressive," plying a box-shaped patrol course that Hepburn deemed poorly conceived, "there is only one instance in the circumstances immediately attendant upon the Savo Island Battle in which censure is definitely indicated and in which the foregoing considerations"—about the "twilight zone"—"did not apply. That was in the action, or inaction, of the Commanding Officer of the *Chicago*."

Hepburn thought Howard Bode culpable on two counts: the decision to remain at the rear of the formation—"a severe indictment of his professional judgment"; and to steam away from the battle zone for thirty-five minutes—"unexplainable." Hepburn's criticism was oddly self-canceling. He allowed that "it would be difficult to sustain a charge that his decision, or lack of decision, resulted in greater damage than actually occurred." He also saw that the most likely result, had Bode made the choices that presumably Hepburn would have made, would have been largely the same—"the *Chicago* would have been sunk instead of the *Canberra*." Nonetheless, Bode in the end was the only officer deemed culpably inefficient by the Navy's lone inquisitor and judge.

Afterward, in his endorsement to Hepburn's report, King wrote to James Forrestal: "Granting that the immediate cause of our losses was the surprise attack, the question is whether or not any officer should be held accountable for failing to anticipate it. Considering that this was the first battle experience for most of the ships participating in the operation and for most of the flag officers involved, and that consequently it was the first time that most of them had been in the position of 'kill or be killed,' the answer to that specific question, in my judgment, must be in the negative. They simply had not learned how and when to stay on the alert." King specifically exonerated Turner and Crutchley for the way they had deployed the cruisers. Regarding Bode in particular, King was silent.

Captain Russell wasn't having any of it. Admiral King's flag secretary wrote, "It does not necessarily follow that because we took a beating, some-body must be the goat. The operation was undoubtedly hastily planned, and poorly executed, and there was no small amount of stupidity, but to me it is more of an object lesson in how not to fight than it is a failure for which some one should hang."

Bode didn't hang. He was assigned to command the 15th Naval District, headquartered at the Balboa Naval Station in the Panama Canal Zone. His transfer to such a backwater would brand him forever as having fallen short of the mark.

He had aspired to flag rank and had always seemed to carry himself as if he would get there. His strict and severe manner might have been an attempt at redemption for a lapse that marred his early career. As a midshipman at the Naval Academy, he had gotten into trouble with three other upperclass-men for hazing. It was a mild offense and typical of the time, but because Bode was caught at it shortly after the superintendent had issued a warning, Bode got a hundred demerits, was confined to academy premises, and lost the privilege of attending the Army–Navy football game. The episode and its aftermath were page-one news in the Sunday *New York Times* in the autumn of 1910.

From his first day in Panama, Bode "seemed to be under some sort of a strain, and it was very noticeable to me and to the officers," a reserve lieu-tenant commander said. "He talked a great deal about wondering why he had been sent here, and before he got out of the plane asked a number of questions as to what kind of a place he was coming to, and couldn't under-stand why he had been ordered here because he was a combat man."

"He told me a number of times that he did not contemplate being here very long, and shortly after he arrived, within a day or so, he told me he would be out in about two weeks." That was when Admiral Hepburn came calling, summoning him to Corpus Christi.

The interrogations, which took place on April 2–3, did not go well for Bode. No one saw him for about a week. When he came back, he had a much more sanguine outlook. He was conversational and seemed acclimated to his new assignment. He invited younger officers to visit him and enjoy some scotch. "It was one of the most pleasant talks I had had with him since he had been attached to the Station," the officer said. The only thing he saw fit to complain about was the speed with which his letters home were reaching his wife.

Bode knew from the tone of Hepburn's questioning that his conduct was under scrutiny. But an inquiry, if undertaken in the right frame of mind, can be a motivator to change and redemption. Guadalcanal was supposed to have been his chance to redeem the loss of the *Oklahoma* at Pearl Harbor. (Bode was blameless for being ashore that morning, but captains never fully escape their responsibility.) Now he needed redemption for Guadalcanal, too, a double dose.

After returning to Panama from Texas, Bode wrote to Hepburn twice, explaining his decisions that night in greater clarity than he had mustered in his stunned state during the interrogation. He had lost track of the *Chicago*'s course heading after maneuvering to avoid torpedoes, he said. He had thought he was standing out to the northwest and hoped to rendezvous with the *Vincennes* group and reengage the enemy to seaward. When he noticed the quiet night around him and suggested reversing course, his navigator advised against it. "Although there are probably other minor details which might promote a fuller understanding, I think the above will clarify the situation attending the two points of criticism. I do hope that your cold is better," he closed, "and that you had a comfortable trip from New Orleans."

In the quiet of his new command, Bode had the chance to reflect more deeply on the Guadalcanal campaign. His further ruminations led him to write Hepburn a third time on April 18. "Within the past two weeks, I have had an opportunity to read the analysis of the Savo Island battle. From it I perceived that I had committed a grievous error of judgment in the very beginning, although the decision (to continue the formation) seemed sound and logical at the time and has since until the logic of cool analysis throws a different light upon it. That error has just been brought to realization. Although I can find a great deal to justify that decision even now, I do feel that I acted with too great a degree of assurance of the correctness of my estimate of a general and specific situation."

Though he was never reputed to change his mind much, it was clear he had been changed by this ordeal. "Some time recently I had an opportunity to clarify by amplification of information, effectively and conclusively, I believe some other points, which for purposes of analysis clarified other phases of the situation. I have now carefully considered what my course of action should now be. I have decided that the only honorable course is to atone for my errors of judgment in the only way I can."

First thing the next morning, he checked his laundry, then asked after the morning paper. The steward on duty gave it to him. Bode took the paper to the restroom, and ten or fifteen minutes later the steward heard a *whoom*.

"I am writing a letter to be delivered to my wife," his April 18 letter to Admiral Hepburn continued, "which I hope you will forward as soon as practical. Although she is a very courageous and competent person she should have knowledge of the why and wherefore, or a reason for this totally unexpected tragedy descending upon her.

"I can find no expression to convey to you my regret that the District you command is to be hindered with the culmination of the unfortunate situation in which I find myself. But I am sure that you will be able to understand the reaction caused by a sudden reversal of the path of life and hope and achievement I had been following."

The cook asked two janitors if they had heard the noise. They said they had. He came back and checked the laundry and the bedroom door twice, then went downstairs again and asked the two boys again if they were sure they had heard a noise. "Don't be afraid, there are no bombs here," one of them said.

Knocking on doors, calling for the captain, the cook told one of the janitors to climb a ladder and look through the bathroom window. When he came down the janitor said there was a figure lying on the floor, a woman, he thought, because it was wearing a blue bathrobe. Next to the body was a .38 caliber round that had done its work and lay there, bent on the floor.

"I am sure that the affairs of the Station will progress smoothly and effectively as long as necessary for the arrival of a relief," Bode wrote to Hepburn. "With assurance of my deep gratitude for your uniformly courteous consideration and the pleasure of my brief service under you. I am sincerely, Howard Bode."

"It is the opinion of the convening authority," the commandant of the 15th Naval District would conclude, "that although all of Captain Howard D. Bode's conduct up to his last act indicated that he was entirely rational, his reaction to criticism of his professional judgment and conduct as commanding officer of the USS *Chicago* during the first night action off Savo Island, resulted in a depression and unbalanced mental condition which was the direct cause of his death."

The chief of the Bureau of Medicine and Surgery supported that conclusion in its endorsement to Admiral King. "This Bureau concurs with the opinion of the Convening Authority and the Judge Advocate General that the death of Captain Bode occurred as a direct consequence of a severe mental illness characterized by depression, and accordingly is of the opinion that it should be considered not the result of his own misconduct."

A notation at the end of his personnel file indicates, apropos of nothing in particular, "Not a war casualty."

44

Ironbottom Sound

"THE MAGNITUDE OF THE SOLOMONS CAMPAIGN HAS NEVER BEEN fully realized," Joe Custer wrote. "Some day its detailed, barbaric history will awe the civilized world. The clock had been turned back thousands of years, back to the primitive, on Guadalcanal."

That history was quickly in the writing. The surrender ceremony on board the USS *Missouri* was barely two weeks past when recriminations were flying in the papers. The Marine Corps, it seemed, was working to shape its preferred narrative of the campaign. By that account, the Marines had been left high and dry by the Navy and had to make do on their own.

In the fall of 1945, with the war just two weeks over, *The New York Times* ran an article in which "senior Marine Corps operations officers" claimed that Ghormley's secretiveness had been costly at Guadalcanal, early on. "The Australian government, which might have moved to aid Admiral Ghormley, was alienated by his refusal to disclose the nature of his operations, it is said. . . . If Admiral Ghormley had been less secretive his original force might have been at least doubled, it is said here, and the tremendous tax upon the Marines would have been materially diminished." Ghormley made an easy target. But with Nimitz strongly allergic to public displays of interservice discord, no one rose to dispute the criticism.

Out of concern for decorum, Nimitz would long conceal the real reasons for Ghormley's relief. When Ghormley's son wrote Nimitz after the war to inquire as to CINCPAC's rationale, the admiral wrote back: "Your father was relieved by Admiral Halsey because of my belief that he was on the verge of a nervous breakdown during the early days of our attempt to capture Guadalcanal from the Japanese. The dispatches he sent to me from his headquarters in Nouméa so alarmed my operations staff officers by their panicky and desperate tone that I decided to replace him with Admiral Halsey—who had been sent to the area for a lookaround.... We parted the very best of friends—and when he was returned to me for employment after he had had some leave at home he served most satisfactorily as Commandant of the 14th Naval District and Commander, Hawaiian Sea Frontier, and we were always on most friendly terms and I admired him and considered him to be my friend."

The war's psychological casualties, from Robert Ghormley to Howard Bode to Alleta Sullivan and on through the years, would never be counted. They were lost in the larger story, for November 1942 had brought the Allies a worldwide turning of the tide. The victories at Guadalcanal and in North Africa, broadly seen, were part of the same worldwide effort. The two major Axis nations could pursue their separate military ambitions, but "their hopes for a combined victory over their enemies still looked to a meeting in the Middle East and the Indian Ocean, which had been blocked for the Japanese at Midway and in the Solomons as it was blocked for the Germans in North Africa and the southern part of the Eastern Front," the historian Gerhard Weinberg observed. A *Collier's* editorialist saw this on the day after Christmas 1942: "We don't claim to be prophets, but we feel constrained to agree with the numerous prophets, analysts and commentators who are saying that the first two weeks of November, 1942, in all probability, were the turning point of the war."

Five months later, a contributor to the magazine wondered what had been gained. "We have not begun to penetrate more than Japan's outpost lines. In sixteen months of war we have taken one airfield and three jungle towns. Japan has captured an empire.... The Japanese could lose all of the Solomons and all of New Guinea and New Britain without endangering any vital point in their empire."

But the significance of the Guadalcanal campaign was never about just war matériel or real estate. Though the idea had haunted Yamamoto from the beginning that American victory was inevitable, the outcome was not foreordained by advantages in industry and war production. As the French Army's performance against Germany in 1940 had suggested, arms and matériel were not sufficient for victory. It had to be seized by men with an active will to fight. On that score Japan had misestimated the United States as, in Weinberg's words, "unwilling to pay the price in blood and treasure to retake islands of which they had never heard, only to be returned to allies for whose colonial empires they had only disdain."

An American defeat was strongly possible well into November. Had such a setback occurred, Ernest King, who two weeks after Pearl Harbor was appointed COMINCH in a major shakeup, would likely have fallen in another one. The campaign would have been written off as his signature folly, a haphazardly conceived fantasy. King's powerful rivals such as General Hap Arnold would have testified morosely, no doubt, to the folly of the Navy's ambitions in the war's secondary theater. That it ended differently is a testament to the fighting character of the fleet at the squadron level. The Navy wasn't ready for its light forces—its cruisers and destroyers—to be the primary weapons of a naval campaign. By the end of November 1942, it wouldn't need to use much else to finish the job in the southern Solomons.

At Guadalcanal from August through November, the Japanese saw for the first time the terrifying aspect of the American nation resolved to total war and bent to slaughter. The Imperial Japanese Navy, well blooded, seemed to lose some of its will to fight. In the decades before the outbreak of the war, Japan came to the negotiating table in Washington and again in London out of a conviction of its matériel inferiority to the Western navies. Despite its fleet's achievement in the early stages of the war, a powerful current within the IJN cast it as an underdog against the United States. It compensated for the perceived inferiority through a dedication to training and esprit de corps. After Guadalcanal, pessimism was preeminent again. Not until October 1944—and not in any of the significant amphibious invasions that took place from Tarawa to Peleliu—did Japan again commit heavy surface forces to battle. The reason appears to be the shattering effect of the Guadalcanal defeat on morale.

Though Japanese losses in planes, pilots, and aircrewmen were terrible at Guadalcanal, far worse than at Midway, the 8th Fleet chief of staff, Toshikazu Ohmae, would cite the U.S. Fleet's use of radar-controlled gunfire as "the outstanding feature in the Guadalcanal campaign." The IJN's first realization, after the Battle of Cape Esperance, that the United States held a meaningful technology advantage at night was "a bad influence upon the morale of the men," Ohmae wrote. "The once high morale of the Japanese destroyer crews participating in the so-called 'Tokyo Express'...soon suffered a letdown. This lack of confidence in night engagements" disclosed "physical and mental defects in the Japanese naval forces which participated in the Guadalcanal sea battle fought from 12th to 14th November." A Marine veteran of Guadalcanal who became a general and a historian as well, Samuel B. Griffith II, argued that the land fighting had a "decisive nature." The air and sea actions were "ancillary." This avoids the fact that if the seas were lost, no level of gallantry would have saved the marines ashore from starvation and attrition. Admiral Halsey drew a convincing parallel. "If our surface forces in this epic battle had been routed our land forces on Guadalcanal would have been in the same position as our forces in the Philippines were at the beginning of the war. Archie Vandegrift would have undoubtedly taken to the hills. Those who had fallen into the hands of the Japanese would have received the same horrible mistreatment our prisoners did on all occasions. Archie Vandegrift would have been the 'Skinny' Wainwright of Guadalcanal, and the Bataan Death March would have been repeated."

Raymond Spruance credited Kelly Turner foremost among those making courageous decisions prior to November 13. "There were many courageous decisions, from lowest to highest commands, and heroic actions without number. First place among them, however, belongs to the decision of Commander Task Force 67, well knowing the odds and possible destruction of his forces, to send his cruisers and destroyers against the Japanese battleship bombarding force, and the resolute manner in which our ships were led into the resulting battle. The night action of 12–13 November probably saved Henderson Field and made possible subsequent air operations from Guadalcanal."

Some would question the value of that sacrifice. The historian Richard B. Frank did not second-guess Callaghan's tactical decisions, but wrote that the so-called Battle of Friday the 13th (or the Cruiser Night Action) only "purchased one night's respite for Henderson Field" and "postponed, not stopped, the landing of major Japanese reinforcements." However, the aviation historian John B. Lundstrom called that melee between ships "the key to Allied success" given what Henderson Field's fliers were thereby allowed to wreak the following day. The pivotal air attacks on the transport force throughout the day on the fourteenth might not have occurred at all had Abe's battleships been permitted to work over the airfields. And the meager troop landings that did take place were a fraction of what they might have been had all eleven transports reached Guadalcanal.

In Admiral King's analysis, Callaghan's fight was a triumph, despite the aspersions many, including the president of the Naval War College, Admiral Pye, would cast. "We have come to expect, and to count on, complete courage in battle from officers and men of the United States Navy," King wrote. "But here, in this engagement, we had displayed for our lasting respect and admiration, a cool but eager gallantry that is above praise. Had this battle not been fought and won, our hold on Guadalcanal would have been gravely endangered."

Having confronted the Imperial Japanese Navy's skill, energy, persistence, and courage, Nimitz identified the key to victory: "training, TRAINING and M-O-R-E T-R-A-I-N-I-N-G," he wrote King in February. In June 1943, the Navy's light forces got a new playbook from which to train. Common tactical principles were spelled out in *Current Tactical Orders and Doctrine, U.S. Pacific Fleet,* known as PAC 10. Its standardization of basic maneuvers helped make possible the victories of 1943, from Kolombangara (July 13) to Empress Augusta Bay (November 1–2) and onward. They also got better weapons. Terrible mechanical problems afflicted U.S. torpedoes in the first year of the war. The scuttlings of the *Benham* and *Hornet* were cases in point; in both instances, American destroyers firing on static targets at point-blank range had embarrassing results. Only three of the first eight fired by the *Mustin* against the *Hornet* hit and exploded. None of the four that the *Gwin* fired at the *Benham* scored.

The emotional truth of battle was a deeper, more complex matter. Robert Graff had years to think about it, and years not to talk. After serving in three warships he returned to New York to pursue a career in broadcast journalism at NBC. He put the "inhuman existence" of his experiences on the *Atlanta* out of his mind.

"War is unlike life," he said. "It's a denial of everything you learn life is. And that's why when you get finished with it, you see that it offers no lessons that can't be better learned in civilian life. You are exposed to horrors you would sooner forget. A disconnect needs to be made to get yourself cleansed." His children were after him for thirty-five years to talk about it. "I refused. I said 'Read it in the history books. I can't do it justice.' We were closed up tight as a clam." He attended the reunions of the *Atlanta,* the *Monterey,* and the *Flint,* a sister ship to the *Atlanta,* only sparsely. Then the memberships aged, and their associations faded away.

Before Christmas in 1997, his son, age fifty-five, made him an offer that Graff wished on one level that he could have refused: a trip to Guadalcanal. They would fly there via Fiji and stay in a Japanese-owned hotel in Honaira about ten miles up the coast from Henderson Field. All the arrangements had been made for a five-day trip. Against his better judgment, and years of reflexive avoidance, he agreed to go. They flew out in November 1998.

"I couldn't stop crying for most of the five days," Graff said. "After that trip, it was like finally I'm back in life. Like so many people, I never opened my mouth for fifty years about all of this. Suddenly everything was open. Most people get to that stage only with the help of doctors."

They spent the first few days visiting battle sites. There were rusted hulks of trucks and tanks and memorials to fallen Americans and Japanese. The drive out to Cape Esperance took them over twenty-five miles of rough island roads.

One morning they chartered a dive boat and took it out into Savo Sound armed with bouquets of flowers and leis and a big floating raft. The skipper gave a signal when they arrived over the wreck, 421 feet below. Using the sonor, backing down once or twice and pulling the helm as if he were parking a car, the captain positioned the boat over the wreck, then, on Graff's request, cut the engines and shut down the air-conditioning system. "We're right over the *Atlanta*," the captain said. Graff wanted silence.

The *Atlanta* survivor went to the fantail with a Melanesian Episcopal padre who had helped them make the arrangements. The padre, Graff's son Christopher, and his grandson Kenneth, who was in his twenties, each said a few words. The grandson talked about how far away the war seemed now, and how it was hard to understand what it was all about because its veterans didn't like to talk. So far away, and so little to talk about, except the hulk of the ship right below them, lying on her side on a ridge in the mud, her remaining anchor still wedged in the bank to keep her from going aground.

Somebody read some Scripture, then, stepping onto a diving platform mounted just inches above the surface, Graff began his eulogy. He addressed it to his former shipmates, whom he could sense all around him. He said that he had come out with his family to honor them and that they were good people and would be always remembered. "From the waters surrounding us, millions of javelins, reflected rays of the sun, blind us with your memory and pierce our hearts." He wondered whether life had turned out as they all had hoped it would, and said he feared there might not be much to show for everybody's efforts. "We were the youthful hope of the nation and the promise of mankind. Taking the world as we found it, in our way and in our time, we tried to remake the world—more hope, more possibility, a much larger community for happiness. That is what, years ago, brought us to Guadalcanal."

The three men and the padre threw their leis onto the water, and then pushed the raft overboard with a copy of the text of the speech. "And we just stood there and everybody cried watching these float on the surface of the water away from the ship on the current. And then I remember when it was time to go, and the captain started the engine. I impulsively removed the Navy cap I brought with me and flung it into the water with the flowers. And I sat down in the corner of the upper deck and cried a little bit more.

"Finally we got back to shore, and that was that."

ACKNOWLEDGMENTS

In three years of research and two of writing, I've accumulated several file cabinets full of debts to acknowledge. It's always a pleasure to do so.

I am again indebted to Tracy Devine, senior editor at Bantam Books, for a thousand small things and maybe two dozen larger ones toward the rehabilitation of my first and second drafts into prime form. Richard B. Frank, the author of the Guadalcanal campaign's definitive history, reviewed a draft of this manuscript, generously applying his vast expertise to save me from a number of embarrassments. Any remaining errors are mine to own.

My sincerest thanks to Edward August and Channing Zucker of the U.S. Cruiser Sailors Association; Aileen Boyle; David J. Brouchoud; Evelyn Cherpak and Teresa Clements at the Naval War College; Robert J. Cressman; Jonathan Dembo, Martha Elmore, and Dale Sauter in the Special Collections Department at East Carolina University's Joyner Library; Rebecca Doolin of the Owen County (Kentucky) Public Library; Robert L. Ghormley, Jr.; Eric Hammel; Carl T. Hartzell; Shawn Hennessy; Richard "Chief Johnny" Johnson; Brent Jones; Janis Jorgensen of the U.S. Naval Institute; Don Kehn; Aileen Kern; Gene Kirkland; Cathy Lloyd, Edward Marolda, Timothy Pettit, and Paul Tobin of the Naval Historical Center; Kelly Sullivan Loughren; John B. Lundstrom; Gregory Mackenzie; Bruce McCandless II; Dave McComb; Helen McDonald and Floyd Cox of the National Museum of the Pacific War; Mike Matheson; Terry Miller at the National Association of Destroyer Veterans; Vincent O'Hara; Attilio Serafini; Sam Sorenson; Clifford C. Spencer; Paul Stillwell; Paul Terrill; Barrett Tillman; Anthony Tully; Jack Wallace; Frank Weimann; Greg Wilsbacher of the University of South Carolina Newsfilm Library; Steve Wiper; Hank Wristen; and John Wukovits.

Special thanks to my longtime champion at Bantam Books, Nita Taublib, and to Angela Polidoro, assistant editor; Virginia Norey, designer; Shona McCarthy, production editor; Maggie Hart, production manager; and to the entire publishing team at Random House.

This book is dedicated to Rear Admiral Charles D. Grojean. Anyone who knew the late, great submariner and executive director of the Admiral Nimitz Foundation in Fredericksburg, Texas, or who has visited the National Museum of the Pacific War there or attended one of the annual Nimitz Symposia, or ever had the chance to speak to this warm and inspiring man about almost any subject under the sun, will understand why.

Without the love and understanding of my family, and its commodore, fleet master chief and first lieutenant, Sharon, nothing would really be possible.

SHIPS AND AIRCRAFT TYPES OF
THE GUADALCANAL CAMPAIGN

Combat Aircraft

U.S.

Bell P-39/P-400 Airacobra	Fighter
Boeing B-17 Flying Fortress	Heavy bomber
Consolidated B-24 Liberator	Heavy bomber
Consolidated PBY Catalina	Flying boat
Douglas SBD Dauntless	Dive-bomber
Grumman F4F Wildcat	Fighter
Grumman TBF Avenger	Torpedo bomber

Japan

Betty (Mitsubishi G4M Type 1)	Medium bomber
Kate (Nakajima B5N Type 97)	Torpedo bomber
Mavis (Kawanishi H6K Type 97)	Flying boat
Val (Aichi D3A Type 99)	Dive-bomber
Zeke (Mitsubishi A6M Type 0)	Fighter
Rufe (Nakajima A6M2-N)	Zeke floatplane variant

Combat Ships

BB	Battleship		CVL	Light carrier
CA	Heavy cruiser		CVS	Seaplane carrier
CL	Light cruiser		DD	Destroyer
CLAA	Antiaircraft cruiser		DMS	Destroyer-minesweeper
CV	Aircraft carrier		PT	Patrol torpedo boat

NAVAL BATTLES OF
THE GUADALCANAL CAMPAIGN

AUGUST 9, 1942

The Battle of Savo Island

Allied losses: heavy cruisers *Vincennes, Quincy, Astoria,* HMAS *Canberra* sunk; heavy
  cruiser *Chicago,* destroyers *Patterson* and *Ralph Talbot* damaged
Japanese losses: heavy cruisers *Chokai* and *Aoba* damaged
Allied KIA: 1,077

AUGUST 24

The Battle of the Eastern Solomons

U.S. losses: carrier *Enterprise* damaged
Japanese losses: light carrier *Ryujo* sunk; light cruiser *Jintsu* damaged
U.S. KIA: 38

OCTOBER 11

The Battle of Cape Esperance

U.S. losses: destroyer *Duncan* sunk; heavy cruiser *Salt Lake City,* light cruiser *Boise,*
  and destroyer *Farenholt* damaged
Japanese losses: heavy cruiser *Furutaka,* destroyers *Fubuki, Murakumo,* and *Natsu-
gumo* sunk; heavy cruiser *Aoba* damaged
U.S. KIA: 163

OCTOBER 25

The Battle of Santa Cruz

U.S. losses: carrier *Hornet,* destroyer *Porter* sunk; carrier *Enterprise,* battleship *South Dakota,* heavy cruiser *Portland,* AA cruiser *San Juan,* destroyers *Smith, Hughes,* and *Porter* damaged

Japanese losses: carriers *Shokaku, Zuiho,* cruiser *Chikuma,* and four destroyers damaged

U.S. KIA: 262

NOVEMBER 13

Cruiser Night Action (First Naval Battle of Guadalcanal)

U.S. losses: AA cruiser *Atlanta,* destroyers *Cushing, Laffey, Barton,* and *Monssen* sunk; heavy cruisers *San Francisco* and *Portland* and destroyers *Aaron Ward* and *Sterett* damaged; AA cruiser *Juneau* damaged and later sunk

Japanese losses: battleship *Hiei,* destroyers *Akatsuki* and *Yudachi* sunk; three destroyers damaged

U.S. KIA: 1,439

NOVEMBER 14–15

Battleship Night Action (Second Naval Battle of Guadalcanal)

U.S. losses: destroyers *Walke, Preston,* and *Benham* sunk; battleship *South Dakota* and destroyer *Gwin* damaged

Japanese losses: battleship *Kirishima,* destroyer *Ayanami* sunk; heavy cruiser *Atago* damaged

U.S. KIA: 242

NOVEMBER 30

The Battle of Tassafaronga

U.S. losses: heavy cruiser *Northampton* sunk; cruisers *Minneapolis, New Orleans,* and *Pensacola* damaged

Japanese losses: destroyer *Takanami* sunk

U.S. KIA: 395

TOTAL NAVAL LOSSES AT GUADALCANAL

	Allied		Japanese	
	#	tonnage*	#	tonnage*
Battleships	0		2	73,200
Heavy cruisers	6	76,600	3	31,500
Light cruisers	2	16,800	1	5,700
Destroyers	14	22,815	11	20,930
Submarines	0		6	11,300
Aircraft carriers	2	44,600	1	12,700
TOTAL	24	160,815	24	155,330

Total U.S. Navy KIA**:	5,041
Total U.S. Marine/Army KIA:	1,592

* Full-load displacement.
** Includes air group losses on Guadalcanal, and miscellaneous losses August 1942–February 1943.

SOURCE NOTES

Unless otherwise indicated, all times mentioned in the narrative are local time on Guadalcanal, or GMT–11. American reports use three times zones variously, GMT, GMT–11, and GMT–12, which was local time in Fiji and New Zealand. Japanese reports use Tokyo time (GMT–9).

Note that 12 noon Greenwich Mean Time is 11 p.m. local (GMT–11) and midnight GMT–12.

Prologue: Eighty-two Ships   (pp. xvii–xx)

Battle lessons: USS *Salt Lake City,* "Report of Action of USS *Salt Lake City* Against Japanese Surface Naval Units, Night of October 11–12, 1942, Off Savo Island, Solomon Islands," 26; COMINCH, "Battle Experience, October 1942," 20–28. **"They will live a long time":** Michener, *Tales of the South Pacific,* 3.

PART I:
Sea of Troubles

1: Trip Wire   (pp. 3–15)

"The Pacific: Of itself": Courtney, "We Must Win the Pacific," 67. **Martin Clemens on Guadalcanal:** Lord, *Lonely Vigil,* 22–23. **"If I lose control":** Sears, "A Coast-watcher's Diary." **Pacific strategy:** Stoler, *Allies in War,* 79. **"The air is saturated":** London, "The Terrible Solomons," 78. **Geography of southern Solomons:** Commander, Naval Base Guadalcanal, "History of U.S. Naval Advanced Base Guadalcanal, 1942–1945," 19; Soule, *Shooting the Pacific War,* 52–53. **Characterization of Nimitz:** Ernest Eller, quoted in Elarco Productions, *The Nimitz Story.* **"Tell Nimitz":** Potter, *Nimitz,* 11. **"An unshared front":** Courtney, "We Must Win the Pacific," 15. **"One of the few people I know":** Larrabee, *Commander in chief,* 389. **"Go back and**

vote": Potter, *Nimitz*, 10. "You always wanted to command": Ibid., 11–12. "Sub-consciously he sought": Buell, *Master of Sea Power*, 11. "Sometimes my bark": Glover, *Command Performance with Guts*, 34. King's view of Fletcher: Butcher, "Admiral Frank Jack Fletcher," 73. "Undoubtedly these acts": King, "Target Practice on Whales and Other Marine Mammals," 1. "His greatest weakness": Baldwin, "Confidential Notes," January 25, 1944. "So tough he shaved": Graybar, "Admiral King's Toughest Battle," 39. "One thing that might help": Ferrell, *The Eisenhower Diaries*, 48, 50. "If only I could keep him tight": Larrabee, *Commander in Chief*, 356. "You are requested to read": Buell, *Master*, 177. "I will be lucky to last six months": Nimitz to Mrs. Nimitz, March 22, 1942. "It must be constantly reiter-ated": Stoler, *Allies and Adversaries*, 78. "The whole question of whether": Ibid., 85. "I sent an order to Admiral Nimitz": King to Edson, September 29, 1949, 2. "We would nowhere be acting": Stoler, *Allies*, 82. "We should turn to the Pacific": Ibid. "Stop the enemy": King to Edson, September 29, 1949, 2–4. "Turn our backs": Stoler, *Allies*, 82. "A lot of islands": Ibid., 85. "We failed to see": Buell, *Master*, 192. "Congressmen are receiving": *Newsweek*, "The Periscope" (column), January 12, 1942, 7. "King's war is": Stoler, *Allies*, 88.

2: A Great Gray Fleet (pp. 16–26)

"On calm days": Graff, "World War II Writings, Document 7." Launching of *Atlanta*: Leavelle, "The Log of the Mighty A," March 24, 1943; Mustin interview, 184–185. "With the same pride": Leavelle, "The Log," March 24, 1942. *Atlanta*'s radars: Mustin interview, 453–459. "A rather dull tableau": Leavelle, "The Log," March 25, 1943. "To my artist's eye" and "a glorious hoax": Shaw, *Beside Me Still*, 81–82. "I think the answer": Ibid., 97. "What he jammed": Vandegrift, *Once a Marine*, 18. "Absolutely essential to stop" and "King's reiteration of": King, *Fleet Admiral King*, 388. "Must be conducted": Ibid, 387. Boundary between SOPAC AND SOWESPAC: COMINCH to CINCPAC, July 3, 1942 (0221). "Three weeks ago": Buell, *Master of Sea Power*, 203. Repair of Task Force 1: Fuquea, "Task Force One," 709–714. Fuel usage: Ibid., 716–717. "We're up against a navy": Mustin diary, May 14, 1942. "What in the world": Weaver, "Some Reminiscences of the Pacific War." "The knowledge of the geography": Ghormley, "The Tide Turns," 1. "Since my arrival": Ghormley to Frank Knox, October 11, 1940, Ghormley Papers. "Every day I was in London": Ghormley, "The Tide," 3. "Dissatisfied, proud, grasping": Ibid., 6–7. "Robinson Crusoe should be required": Gardner interview, 2.

3: The First D-Day (pp. 27–43)

"We kept very quiet": Kinkaid, *Four Years of War*, 192–194. "We were conscious of": Tregaskis, *Guadalcanal Diary*, 8. "Loose talk is a stupid habit": Ghormley to SOPAC command, "Disclosure of Information," 1. "I have smiled many times": Soule, *Shooting the Pacific War*, 44. Changes to Japanese code groups: Showers, speech, Nimitz Symposium 2007; Frank, *Guadalcanal*, 38–41. "I informed him": Ghormley,

"The Tide Turns," 100–101. **"I had experienced"**: Jones, *The USS, Astoria (CA-34) and the Men Who Sailed Her,* 30. **"Monday, Monday, Tuesday"**: Hirama, "Japanese Naval Preparations," 66. **"I never could figure out"**: Custer, *Through the Perilous Night,* 94. **"You will be governed"**: Nimitz quoted in Hoyt, *How They Won the War in the Pacific,* 94. **Invasion rehearsals in 1939**: Larrabee, *Commander in Chief,* 178. **"I saw that its shore"**: Bennink, narrative, 2. **"From an intelligence point of view"**: Hough, *History of U.S. Marine Corps,* 242–243. **"Some of us were"**: Kinkaid, *Four Years,* 207. **"Neither sharp nor perspicacious"**: Loxton, *The Shame of Savo,* 18. **Carrier air support controversy**: Lundstrom, *Black Shoe Carrier Admiral,* 333–337; Turner to Hepburn, "Answers to Questionnaire," 6. **"My Dutch blood"**: Vandegrift, *Once a Marine,* 120. Richard Frank, annotation to author's draft ms., April 12, 2010; see also Lundstrom, *Black Shoe Carrier Admiral,* 373–374: "Fletcher envisioned another grim carrier battle soon.... Hindsight has obliterated the validity of Fletcher's prudence." **"Who is closely acquainted"**: Turner to King, "Strategic Deployment," 3. **"You son of a bitch"**: Loxton, *The Shame of Savo,* 71; Lundstrom, *Black Shoe,* 336. **"I sent Dan Callaghan"**: Ghormley to Nimitz, July 29, 1942, 3. **"At first there was a mast"**: Calhoun, *Tin Can Sailor,* 51. **Early U.S. South Pacific strategy**: Braisted, *The United States Navy in the Pacific, 1909–1922,* 522–523; SOPAC, "South Pacific Strategy," 7–8. **Logistics**: Ghormley, "The Tide Turns," 62. **"Pounded flat into baked mud"**: Crenshaw, *South Pacific Destroyer,* 43. **"Almost every French civilian"**: SOPAC, "South Pacific Strategy," 10. **"The war in our area"**: Ghormley to McCain, May 19, 1942, 3. **"I think our actual deficiencies"**: Ghormley to Nimitz, July 29, 1942, 2–3. **"If an enemy lay beyond"**: Hough, *History,* 4–5. **"God was with us"**: Smoot interview, 92. **"Vague, black and shapeless"**: Custer, *Through,* 104. **"Like a purple lump"**: Kittredge, untitled narrative, 11. **"What the hell"**: Custer, *Through,* 104. **"All hands man your battle stations"** and **disposition of cruiser screen**: Crutchley, "Operation Watchtower," 11–12 (Hepburn Report Annex, 65). **"The pervasive mud"**: Jones, *WW2,* 48. **"Amazing panorama"**: Lord, *Lonely Vigil,* 40. **"Under information you plan"**: Ghormley to Fletcher, August 2, 1942 (0240). *"Enemy strength is overwhelming"*: McGee, *The Solomons Campaigns,* vol. 2, 30. **Lieutenant Snell's flag**: Bureau of Naval Personnel, *Information Bulletin,* September 1942, 60.

4: Nothing Worthy of Your Majesty's Attention (pp. 44–49)

"It is nothing worthy": Hara, *Japanese Destroyer Captain,* 104. **Japanese reaction to landings**: Ohmae, "The Battle of Savo Island," 1260–1267; Ugaki, *Fading Victory,* 177. **"Absolutely no concern with the Solomons"**: Ohmae, "The Battle," 1267. **Japanese intelligence deficiencies**: Kotani, *Japanese Intelligence in World War II,* 155, 161–162. **"Magnificent curtain"**: Commander, Task Group 62.6 "Operation Watchtower—the Capture and Occupation by United Nations Forces of Tulagi and Guadalcanal," 18. *Be it ever so humble...* **"How can you beat"**: Custer, *Through the Perilous Night,* 123. **"Either these are Army pilots"**: Ibid., 118. **"How do you like that"**: Ibid., 121–122.

5: Fly the Carriers (pp. 50–55)

"Whenever he became disgusted": Jones, *The USS* Astoria *(CA-34) and the Men Who Sailed Her,* 48. **"I have seen him 'blow up'":** Dyer, *The Amphibians Came to Conquer,* 1165–1166. **"After dark, conditions"** and **"No small share"** and **"a failure on":** McGee, *The Amphibians Are Coming!* 19–20. **"This was the Koro conference":** Vandegrift, *Once a Marine,* 129. **"All knew that the enemy":** Ghormley, "The Tide Turns," 93. During carrier flight operations, speeds of twenty-five knots were necessary, according to Frank Jack Fletcher. ComCruPacFlt, "Preliminary Report— Solomons Islands Operations," September 9, 1942, 3. **"It is the opinion":** MacArthur to King, July 8, 1942 (1020). **"The withdrawal of the naval attached units":** King to Nimitz, July 2, 1942 (2154). **"Marines cannot be dislodged":** Lundstrom, *Black Shoe Carrier Admiral,* 383. HMAS *Australia* conference: Commander, Task Force 62, War Diary, 4; Kinkaid, *Four Years of War,* 233.

6: A Captain in the Fog (pp. 56–61)

"His officers were scared": Zarker interview. **"He was short and stocky":** Backus interview, 93–94. **Cruiser engineering performance:** Fleet Maintenance Office, "Material and Engineering Performance Bulletin, Cruisers, Pacific Fleet," 14. **"TAKE CHARGE OF PATROL":** Crutchley, "Explanatory Memorandum," 9. **"AIRCRAFT REPORTS 3 CRUISERS":** CINCPAC, "Grey Book," August 8, 1942 (1025). **"WE WILL PENETRATE SOUTH":** Ohmae, "The Battle of Savo Island," 1271–1272. **"The Eighth Fleet is going":** Ugaki, *Fading Victory,* 178. **"I was satisfied with arrangements":** Turner to Hepburn, "Answers to Questionnaire" (Hepburn Report Annex, 272). **"WARNING—WARNING—PLANE":** USS *Ralph Talbot,* "Preliminary Report of Action," 1. **Errors by USS *Blue* and *Chicago:*** LaCouture interview, 22; Bode, "Memorandum for Admiral Hepburn," 2–3; Zarker interview: "The [*Chicago*'s] radar officer himself told me this at one of our reunions." **"WARNING—WARNING—STRANGE SHIPS":** USS *Chicago,* "Action Against Enemy Forces...," 2; USS *Astoria,* Statement of Lt. Cdr. J. R. Topper, 1 (Hepburn Report Annex, 535). **"A good course":** Bode to Hepburn, April 8, 1943, 2 (Hepburn Report Annex, 303). **Damage to HMAS *Canberra:*** HMAS *Canberra,* Executive Officer's Report, August 12, 1943, 1–2 (Hepburn Report Annex, 337–338).

7: The Martyring of Task Group 62.6 (pp. 62–79)

Nimitz "ultra secret" warnings: Nimitz to Task Force Commanders, August 6, 1942 (2336) (Hepburn Report Annex, 670). **Turner's instructions to Crutchley:** Turner to Crutchley, August 8, 1942 (1920) (Hepburn Report Annex, 677). **"The search radar was operating":** USS *Quincy,* "Preliminary Report," 2. **"The more I insisted"** and **"The OOD and the":** Jones, *The USS* Astoria *(CA-34) and the Men Who Sailed Her,* 115–116. **"Great display of light":** USS *Vincennes,* "Report of Action Between" (Hepburn Report Annex, 399–400). **"I didn't know":** Jones, *The USS* Astoria, 179. **Explosions mistaken for depth charges:** USS *Astoria,* "Battle of Savo Island," 13

(Hepburn Report Annex, 488). **Contact between Japanese and U.S. ships:** Bates and Innis, "The Battle of Savo Island," 152. *"Action port! Load":* Statement of M. Dunkleberger, in USS *Astoria,* "Statements of Surviving Personnel" (Hepburn Report Annex, 581). **"Fire every damn thing you got!":** Statement of L. F. Hager, in USS *Astoria,* "Statements," (Hepburn Report Annex, 596). **"Who sounded the general alarm?":** Donald A. Yeamans, in Jones, *The USS* Astoria. **"It was there.... I was suddenly cool":** Custer, *Through the Perilous Night,* 125. **"Surprised to see":** Lt. Jack Gibson, in Jones, *The USS* Astoria, 131. **"A stupid set up":** Eldred E. Bloodworth, in Jones, *The USS* Astoria, 100–101. **"The** *Astoria* **was shuddering"** and **"One more crossing":** Lt. Jack Gibson, in Jones, *The USS* Astoria, 131–132. **Flammable conditions on cruisers:** COMINCH, "Battle Experience, September 1942," 11–15; Bureau of Ships, "USS *Quincy,* USS *Astoria* and USS *Vincennes,* Report of Loss in Action," 18; Akers interview, 1. **"In a few minutes":** Custer, *Through,* 132–135. **"An ideal torpedoman":** Tanaka, "Japan's Losing Struggle for Guadalcanal," part 1, 698. **"There were explosions everywhere":** Ohmae, "The Battle of Savo Island," 1275. **"Times in the above narrative":** Hepburn, "Report of Informal Inquiry," 16. **"There are men"** and **"blown clear through"** and **"I sat there and listened":** Jones, *The USS* Astoria, 94–95. **"A roar like an express train":** Ibid., 132. **"An overtone of muffled sounds":** Custer, *Through,* 126. **"A crushing explosion...Look out for my leg":** Ibid., 132–135. **"In flashes of light":** Jones, *The USS* Astoria, 132. **"Steel piercing steel":** Ibid., 103. **"A shambles":** USS *Quincy,* "Report of the Engagement," 8. **"I found it in a shambles":** Ibid., 2 (Hepburn Annex, 442). **"Gas jetted high":** Jones, *The USS* Astoria, 120, quoting article in *The Daily Astorian* from August 6, 1981. **"Our ship was blazing":** Robert H. Atchinson, in Jones, *The USS* Astoria, 98. **"All communications were shot away":** Jones, *The USS* Astoria, 132–133. **"He could not have been more":** Ibid., 146. **"We sat there while the fire roared":** Ibid., 133. **"One of our crew":** Ibid., 105. **Damage control on** *Astoria:* USS *Astoria,* Statement of Lt. Cdr. J. R. Topper, 7 (Hepburn Report Annex, 541). **"Hey, man, I just made chief":** Jones, *The USS* Astoria, 105–106.

8: Burning in the Rain *(pp. 80–92)*

"REPORT SITUATION....CHICAGO SOUTH OF SAVO": HMAS *Australia,* "Night Action Off Savo," 2. **"Its searing light revealed":** Soule, *Shooting the Pacific War,* 3. **"Huge balls of red fire":** Custer, *Through the Perilous Night,* 166–167. **"OUT ALL LIGHTS":** HMAS *Canberra,* Engineer's Preliminary Report, 3. **"I was greatly impressed":** Ohmae, "The Battle of Savo Island," 1278. **"To remain in the area by sunrise":** Ibid., 1276. **"We were all shocked":** Ibid., 1275. **"He was everywhere":** Custer, *Through,* 160. **"Men naturally responded":** USS *Astoria,* Report of Engineering Department, 22. **"The rescue of these three men":** USS *Astoria,* "Executive Officer's Memorandum," 4. **"I stood for a moment":** Jones, *The USS* Astoria *(CA-34) and the Men Who Sailed Her,* 133–134. **"Shaking with cold and fright":** Ibid., 129–130. **"Able-bodied men":** Custer, *Through,* 139. **"One of the most horrible sights":** Jones, *The USS* Astoria, 137. **"Off her slanting side":** Custer, *Through,* 142. **"The day was beautiful":** Jones, *The USS* Astoria, 189. **Sinking of** *Astoria:* USS *Astoria,* "Battle of Savo Island", 7–12. **"These were endless hours":** Ghormley, "The Tide

Turns," 104. **"Most of them were young kids"**: Bennink, narrative, 8. **"If the *San Juan* had been up there"**: Rivero interview, 125. **"I couldn't help but"**: Smoot interview, 98. **"Without information except"**: Kinkaid, *Four Years of War,* 279. **"Blackest day of the whole war"**: Lundstrom, *Black Shoe Carrier Admiral,* 398. U.S. fatalities were *Quincy:* 370, *Vincennes:* 332, *Astoria:* 216, *Canberra:* 85, *Ralph Talbot:* 11, *Patterson:* 8, *Chicago:* 2, per Newcomb, *The Battle of Savo Island,* 257. **"Look what we've got here"**: Custer, *Through,* 149–150. **"A sound that I felt"**: Ibid., 169. **"That body burned in my dreams"**: Jones, *The USS* Astoria, 105. **"When he got to me"**: Ibid., 50. **"Don't you say one word"**: Powell interview. **"The conceited British and Americans"**: Ugaki, *Fading Victory,* 181.

PART II:
Fighting Fleet Rising

9: A New Kind of Fight (pp. 95–108)

"We drank a cocktail toast": Nimitz to Mrs. Nimitz, August 10, 1942. **"Obsessed with a strong feeling"**: Turner, "Comment on Hepburn Report," 9–10. **Air search sectors**: Frank, *Guadalcanal,* 91. **"Could not be heard"**: Ghormley to King, "CTF 62 Communications During the Occupation of Tulagi and Guadalcanal" (Hepburn Report Annex, 644). **"Was completely uninformed"**: Task Force 18, War Diary, August 9, 1942. **"Had timely and accurate information"**: Kinkaid, *Four Years of War,* 284. **"The way these carriers operate"**: Mustin diary, August 8. **"Was always trying"** and **"Three times during the night"**: Weschler interview, 88. **"We had to be very careful"**: Wylie, NWC interview, 58–59. **"I can take any dumb son"**: Wylie, USNI interview, 28. **"Hey, Cap'n"**: Wylie, NWC interview, 66. **"They were highly motivated"**: Ibid., 60. **"The moon rose"**: Soule, *Shooting the Pacific War,* 37. **"The Nation has passed through"**: *Bureau of Navigation Bulletin,* "Information for Naval Personnel," February 1, 1942, 28. **Navy muster rolls statistics**: COMINCH, *First Official Report to the Secretary of the Navy,* March 1, 1944, 494. **"They go to war because"**: Hynes, quoted in *The War,* episode 1, first broadcast on PBS, September 23, 2007. **"I thought I was in a forest"** and **"Well, this doesn't make"**: Hagen, Nimitz interview, 3–5, 25–26. **"As a bunch"**: George T. Sullivan, undated letter, on display, NMPW. **Sullivan brothers' early life**: Satterfield, *We Band of Brothers,* 23–29; Associated Press, "Five Iowa Brothers," 10. **"I guess our minds are made up"**: Satterfield, *We Band,* 55. **"Magic box"**: Brown, *A Radar History of WWII,* 248. **"There wasn't any real training"**: Rivero interview, 104. **"A narrow man"** and **"Our flag officers"**: Baldwin, "The Naval Defense of America," 454–455. **"Neither I nor"**: Turner, "Comment on Hepburn Report," 7–8. **Operation of SG and SC radar**: Brown, *A Radar History of WW II,* 237, 248. **Radar in the *Aaron Ward***: Hagen 7, 10; Hagen, Nimitz interview, 6–7. **"It is to be hoped that"**: COMINCH, "Battle Experience: August and September 1942," 11-10–11-11. **"The war has been variously termed"**: Commander, Naval Base Guadalcanal, "History of U.S. Naval Advanced Base Guadalcanal," 137. **Preparation of Espiritu Santo**: Gardner interview, 2; Ghormley to King, "Advance Bases, South Pacific Area." **"A gleam in Ghormley's eye"**: Dyer, *The Amphibians*

Came to Conquer, 257. "**It was dry**": Eller interview, 578–579. "**There is going to be a**": Mustin diary, August 13. "**They're so goddamned scared**": Ibid., August 9. "**I wish to God**": Ibid., August 11. "**All their fleet**": Baldwin, "The Naval Defense of America," 455–456. "**Our planes had come**": Larrabee, *Commander in Chief,* 281. "**That night we went to bed**": Soule, *Shooting,* 81.

10: The Tokyo Express (pp. 109–113)

"**Our real enemy is Germany**" and "**We have gained**": Sherwood, *Roosevelt and Hopkins,* 622. "**Foresaw grave difficulties**": Tanaka, "Japan's Losing Struggle for Guadalcanal," part 1, 687, 690. **Combat on Guadalcanal:** Reeder, *Fighting on Guadalcanal,* 13; Merillat, *Guadalcanal Remembered,* 86. "**A housefly's attacking**": Tanaka, "Japan's Losing Struggle," part 1, 691. "**We watched these awful machines**": Tregaskis, *Guadalcanal Diary,* 125. "**We thought it was just**": Mangrum interview, 2.

11: A Function at the Junction (pp. 114–122)

"**Rough guess**": Wheeler, *Kinkaid,* 252. "**Indications point strongly**": Quoted in Prados, Combined Fleet Decoded, 371. "**Old *Lexington* and *Yorktown***": Morison, *The Struggle for Guadalcanal,* 92. "**First ones spotted**": Mustin diary, August 24, 1942. "**Men on other ships**": Leavelle, "The Log of the Mighty A," March 28, 1943. "**First plane missed**": Mustin diary, August 24. **Damage-control efforts on *Enterprise:*** Stafford, *The Big E,* 164. "**My worst fears**": Tanaka, "Japan's Losing Struggle for Guadalcanal," part 1, 693–694. "**Everyone is withdrawing but the Marines**": Merillat, *Guadalcanal Remembered,* 114. "**CONSIDER SITUATION CRITICAL**": Ghormley to Nimitz, August 25, 1942 (0330). "**WE HAVE MADE GOOD START**": Nimitz to King, August 25, 1942 (2241). "**UNTIL THE STRENGTH**" and "**FOR THE PRESENT**": Ghormley to Nimitz, August 29, 1942 (0310). On August 30, Vandegrift informed Ghormley that F4Fs were the only planes that could meet Japanese bombers effectively at altitude. He had just eight of them. Ghormley, "The Tide Turns," 18. "**Surface craft, unless heavily protected**": Ghormley to Stark, June 11, 1941. "**It is apparent that landing**": Ugaki, *Fading Victory,* 193. "**Greatest immediate threat to success**": Ghormley to MacArthur, August 25, 1942 (0320). "**Perfect failure**": Ugaki, *Fading,* 197. **Japanese reinforcements:** General Headquarters, Far East Command, Monograph No. 98, 17–19. "**Like a house in a severe earthquake**": Lundstrom, *Black Shoe Carrier Admiral,* 471–472. "**Sounds like there's a function at the junction**": Leavelle, "The Log," March 28, 1943. "**What saved Guadalcanal**": Merillat, *Guadalcanal Remembered,* 112.

12: What They Were Built For (pp. 123–134)

"**It seemed we were on the fringe**": Barham, *The 228 Days of the United States Destroyer* Laffey *(DD-459),* 56–57. **Cactus Air Force operations:** Smith interview, 3–4, 13; Mangrum interview, 9–10, 14. "**They come right up**": Fike interview, 12. "**Certainly the means**": Ibid., 6–7. "**So dumbfounding**": Tanaka, "Japan's Losing Struggle for Guadalcanal," part 1, 696. "**It was difficult**": Mangrum interview, 9–10. "**Let's give Cactus the wherewithal**": Nimitz to King, September 1, 1942 (2331). "**Appears enemy is building up**": Vandegrift to Turner, September 1, 1942 (2313). "**Leaves much to the initiative**" and "**Keep in mind that**": Ghormley to SOPAC task force commanders, September 9, 1942 (1018). "**I cling to the fond hope**": Mustin diary, September 9, 1942. "**A tremendous step forward**": Musicant, *Battleship at War,* 10. "**I have to spill this to somebody**": Ghormley to Nimitz, September 7, 1942, Ghormley Papers. "**What could I say**" and "**Jim, you've got a bad case**": Albion and Connery, *Forrestal and the Navy,* 105–106. "**Boys, I've got a surprise**": Halsey, *Admiral Halsey's Story,* 108. "**Criticism of basic concepts**": Hara, *Japanese Destroyer Captain,* 119. "**Unless Guadalcanal is settled**": Ugaki, *Fading Victory,* 200. "**SITUATION AS I VIEW IT TODAY**": Ghormley to Nimitz, September 11, 1942 (0516). **Battle of Edson's Ridge**: Frank, *Guadalcanal,* 237–241. "**Sharks were everywhere**": Richardson, "My War," unpaginated. "**They didn't want anybody to know**": Weschler interview, 101–102. "**I guess he and Captain Gatch**": Backus interview, 133–134.

13: The Warriors (pp. 135–144)

Norman Scott: U.S. Naval Academy, *Lucky Bag,* 1911. "**Made things so miserable**": Morison, *The Struggle for Guadalcanal,* 148 n. "**Kind of like a junior Halsey**": Graff interview. **Gunnery exercises**: Chief of Naval Operations to Commander, Battleships, Battle Force, January 19, 1942; Crenshaw, *South Pacific Destroyer,* 39–40. "**I did not know, from actual contact**": Ghormley, "The Tide Turns," 24. "**It was the way**": Morris, *The Fightin'est Ship,* 24–25. "**For the next two weeks**": Spencer, *The War Years: Hellfire and Glory,* 51–52. "**The best simulation of action**": USS *Salt Lake City,* "Offset Battle Practice." "**Outstanding development of the war**" and "**We are still not getting**": CINCPAC, "Gunnery Bulletin No. 2–42," June 6, 1942, 1–2. "**Quite a lot of technique**": Mustin interview, 456. **Internal gunnery communications**: USS *Salt Lake City,* "Report of Action, Night of October 11–12, 1942," 18. "**With a sickening *thump***": Spencer, *The War Years,* 53. "**In trying to give you an idea**": Ibid., 52. "**Quick and slick as precision machinery**": Morris, *The Fightin'est Ship,* 23. "**He'll be a *Helena* man**": Ibid., 25–26. "**We knew things were going**": Howe interview, 15. "**In his leather jacket**": Morris, *The Fightin'est Ship,* 27. "**The *Helena* craved action**": Ibid., 12. "**We want to be consistent**": Ibid., 2. "**Have you ever heard**": Ibid., 19–20. "**The whole ship is enveloped**": Ibid., 22–23. "**Too short a time to justify**": COMINCH, "Battle Experience: August and September 1942," 14–4. "**His training section was constantly**": Eller interview, 565–566. "**Had practically lapsed**": Ghormley, "The Tide Turns," 87. "**It is continually proved**": COMINCH, "Battle Experience: August and September 1942," 12–25. "**Scott had balls**": Graff interview.

14: The Devil May Care (pp. 145–149)

So this is war: Smoot interview, 95. **Nimitz court-martial**: Hoyt, *How They Won the War in the Pacific,* 39. "**My gunnery officer saw**": Smoot interview, 95. "**The sky was soon crisscrossed**": Thomason, quoted at www.destroyerhistory.org/benson-gleavesclass/ussmonssen/thomason_03.html. **Smoot and Puller:** Smoot interview, 101. When the first rescue boats were taken under heavy fire, a coxswain named Samuel B. Roberts volunteered to serve as a decoy. He steered his small craft directly toward the Japanese lines and drew their fire. His initiative was successful, and the marines were evacuated. But as Roberts was about to move beyond range of the enemy guns, his boat was hit and he was mortally wounded. Roberts was posthumously awarded the Navy Cross. The destroyer escort USS *Samuel B. Roberts* (DE-413) was christened in his honor. For more on that ship and its own epic story, see Hornfischer, *The Last Stand of the Tin Can Sailors.* **"As the first marines appeared":** Thomason, quoted at www.destroyerhistory.org/benson-gleavesclass/ ussmonssen/thomason_03.html. **Douglas Munro:** Hough, *History of U.S. Marine Corps Operations I,* vol. 1. 316–317. **"Everything we could do":** Smoot interview, 101–102.

15: The Visit   *(pp. 150–156)*

"Today, September is going to pass": Ugaki, *Fading Victory,* 221. *Laffey*'s **stores:** USS *Laffey,* Deck Log for March 31, 1942. **"So far removed from the critical area":** Nimitz to Ghormley, October 8, 1942, Ghormley Papers. **"We recognized the fact that":** Arnold, *Global Mission,* 322–323. **"It was obvious that":** Ibid., 340–342. **"I presented the need for aircraft":** Ghormley, "The Tide Turns," 126–127. **Combined Chiefs of Staff planning:** Hayes, *The History of the Joint Chiefs of Staff in World War II,* 183–186. **"Under constant pressure":** Hoyt, *How They Won the War in the Pacific,* 151–152. **"My God, what are we going to do":** Potter, *Nimitz,* 236. **"If the Japanese desired":** Ghormley, "The Tide," 126–127. **"I never saw an admiral before":** Hal Lamar, in Elarco Productions, *The Nimitz Story.* **"Planes are too expensive":** Hoyt, *How They Won,* 153. **"I feel that our present operations":** Ibid., 158. **"Such a blow cannot":** Ibid., 162. **"Satisfied in every way … It was just the kind of trip":** Trumbull, "Nimitz Confident After Pacific Trip," 6. **"When this war is over":** Vandegrift, *Once a Marine,* 171–172. **"HAVE STRIKING FORCE OPERATE":** Ghormley to Scott, October 5, 1942 (1202) (CINCPAC Command Summary II, 891).

16: Night of a New Moon   *(pp. 157–168)*

USS *San Francisco*'s **"scarlet letter":** Spencer interview. **"New-type heavy units"** and **"mystery ship":** Ghormley to MacArthur and Fitch, October 8, 1942 (1035). **"A steady, chattering stream":** Morris, *The Fightin'est Ship,* 32. **Japanese October dispositions:** Frank, *Guadalcanal,* 374–375. **"Battles can only be won":** USS *Quincy,* Action Report, 3 (Hepburn Report Annex, 443). **"Surface ships should be employed":** COMINCH, "Battle Experience: Solomon Islands Actions, August and September 1942," 12–47. **Surface battle doctrine:** Hone, "U.S. Navy Surface Battle Doctrine," 71–72. **Scott's battle plan:** Commander, Task Group 64.2, "Memorandum for Task Group 64.2," October 9, 1942, 1; see also Scott's Memorandum Number Two, October 10, 1942, and Scott to Ghormley, October 4, 1942 (0600). **"Any qualified watch officer":** Crenshaw, *South Pacific Destroyer,* 56. **"The two lines on the chart":** Morris, *The Fightin'est Ship,* 34. **"As grim as his guns"** and **"Captain** seem to be worried?": Ibid., 34–35. "We'll catch it sure" and "The Japs would strike": Ibid., 31. "We were moving west": Ibid., 36. *Pass the word from gun to gun:* Morris, *"Pick Out the Biggest,"* 36. "There was little to do": Morris, *The Fightin'est Ship,* 36. "Well, sir, these islands": www.usssanfrancisco.org. "**Dumpy and fat**": Morris, *The Fightin'est Ship,* 39. *"One large, two small vessels":* CTG 64.2, "Report of Night Action," 1. "**The only indication**": Weems, "Solomons Battle Log," 83. "**Exe-cute to follow**": USS *Salt Lake City,* Action Report, 6.

17: Pulling the Trigger (pp. 169–178)

"**Column left**": Commander, Task Group 64.2, "Report of Night Action," 3; Crenshaw, *Naval Shiphandling,* 179. *"Are you taking station":* McCalla, "Report of Action," TBS Log, 2. "**Do not rejoin**": CTG 64.2, "Memorandum for Task Group 64.2." "**Ships visible**": Morris, *The Fightin'est Ship,* 43. "**The night had been still**": Ibid., 46. "**The second never touched the water**": USS *Salt Lake City,* "Report of Action of USS *Salt Lake City* Against Japanese Surface Naval Units, Night of October 11–12, 1942, Off Savo Island, Solomon Islands," 8. "**Pick out the biggest**" and "**Daddy, I want to go home**": Morris, *"Pick Out the Biggest,"* 45. "**I felt a wildly exultant joy**": Weems, "Solomons Battle Log," 85. "**I am Aoba**" and *"Bakayaro!":* Ugaki, *Fading Victory,* 238. *"Cease firing, all ships":* USS *McCalla,* "Report of Action," TBS Log, 2; the *Salt Lake City* recorded, *"Cease firing, our ships."* "Report of Action," 7. *"Rapid fire, continuous.... Begging your pardon, Admiral":* Spencer interview. "**It took some time to stop**": CTG 64.2, "Report of Night Action," 3. "**Every time he could train**": Richardson, "My War," unpaginated. *"How are you?... Twelve is okay":* USS *Salt Lake City,* "Report of Action," 7. "**Stood there transfixed**": Richardson, "My War." "**Almost immediately she was observed**": USS *Duncan,* "Detailed Report of Action of USS *Duncan* During Engagement with Japanese Forces Off Savo Island, 11–12 October 1942," 4.

18: "Pour It to 'Em" (pp. 179–188)

"**Getting hotter than a Joe Louis fight**": Morris, *"Pick Out the Biggest,"* 52. "**Fired at *Boise* unopposed**": USS *Boise,* "Action Off Cape Esperance," 8. "**The fuze hasn't gone off**": Morris, *"Pick Out,"* 58–60. "The battle had been a game": Morris, *The Fightin'est Ship,* 53. "Take it easy, son": Ibid., 60. "Outta my way!": Morris, "Mike Moran's Men," part 1, 51. **Damage to *Salt Lake City:*** USS *Salt Lake City,* "Report of Action of USS *Salt Lake City* Against Japanese Surface Naval Units, Night of October 11–12, 1942, Off Savo Island, Solomon Islands," 16, 19, 23–24. "**The enemy was silenced**": Commander, Task Group 64.2, "Report of Night Action," 4. "**D491 v D456**": COMINCH, "Battle Experience: Solomon Islands Actions, October 1942," 20–27. *"Detail one of your boys":* USS *Salt Lake City,* "Report of Action," 12. "**Engaged enemy west of Savo**": Scott to Ghormley, October 11, 1942 (1528). "**And the navigator pushed**": McCandless letter, *Proceedings,* 123. "**Rather too sensitive... If we do not approve**": Ugaki, *Fading Victory,* 226. **Loss of *Furutaka:*** IJN *Furutaka,* "Action Record"; also Lacroix and Wells, *Japanese Cruisers of the*

Pacific War, 309. **"Bow end looked cooked"**: Lundstrom, *The First Team and the Guadalcanal Campaign,* 297. **"As we pulled into harbor"**: Barham, *The 228 Days of the United States Destroyer* Laffey *(DD-459),* 66. **"Little things, remembered now in detail"**: Morris, *The Fightin'est Ship,* 60. **"Crude night firing practices"**: CTG 64.2, "Report of Night Action," 7. **"The rapidity and accuracy"**: USS *Boise,* "Action Off Cape Esperance," 1. **"Throughout the 'Night Battle'"**: Japanese General Headquarters, Far East Command, Monograph No. 98, 35. **"Restrict telephone circuits"**: USS *Salt Lake City,* "Report of Action," 25–30.

PART III:
Storm Tide

19: All Hell's Eve (pp. 191–199)

"Admiral Ghormley treated me like a son": MacDonald interview, 203–204. **"The ship and crew members"**: Brodie, *A Guide to Naval Strategy,* 278. **11th Air Fleet strength**: Lundstrom, *The First Team and the Guadalcanal Campaign,* 293–294. *Damn that plane....***"Outside, a thousand rockets"**: Soule, *Shooting the Pacific War,* 111–112. **"The exploding gunfire"**: Kennedy, *Fearless Warrior,* 64. **"The air was filled"**: Lundstrom, *The First Team,* 301. **"Our single light bulb swayed"** and **"Again the earth heaved"**: Soule, *Shooting,* 111–112. **"It seemed as if all"**: Frank, *Guadalcanal,* 317. **"Daylight disclosed"**: Soule, *Shooting,* 113. **"But luckily the teleradio"**: MacKenzie, "Report on Coast-Watching," 21–22. **"The Marines at the airport"**: Wolfert, *Battle for the Solomons,* 64. **"It was the hopelessness"**: Halsey, *Admiral Halsey's Story,* 116. **"We don't know whether"**: Miller, *The Cactus Air Force,* 121. **"The situation is critical"**: Ghormley to Nimitz, October 14, 1942 (1410). **"It became immediately obvious"**: MacKenzie, "Report," 22. **"Security our position"**: Nimitz to King, October 15, 1942 (2235). **"I have resigned myself"**: Agawa, *The Reluctant Admiral,* 335. **"It now appears"**: Morison, *The Struggle for Guadalcanal,* 178. **"Can use no more aircraft"**: Fitch to Ghormley, October 15, 1942 (0921). **"The Japs have the run"**: Merillat, *Guadalcanal Remembered,* 181–182. **"I don't think we have"**: Lundstrom, *The First Team,* 311.

20: The Weight of a War (pp. 200–207)

"Call it what you will": Mustin diary, October 15. **"There were lots of lessons"** and **"He was the perfect example"**: Mustin interview, 515. **"Magnificently trained"** and **"They didn't come down"**: Ibid., 546. **"The Japanese must not be"**: Trumbull, "Nimitz Confident After Pacific Trip," 6. **"He was almost despairing."**: Baldwin interview, 344–345. **"Assume you will make Ghormley"**: King to Nimitz, "Grey Book," July 2, 1942 (2154). **"I think he had a premonition"**: Weaver, "Some Reminiscences," 9. **"The situation demands"**: Vandegrift to Ghormley, October 16, 1942 (0025). **"Urgently need this area"**: October 15, 1942 (0246). **"This appears to be all out"**: Ghormley to Nimitz, October 16, 1942 (0440). **"Overwhelming need for strength"**: Nimitz to Commander, Task Force 8, October 16,

1942 (2221). "One of the few times" and "The situation looked very dark": Eller interview, 585. "It was evident to all of us": Layton, *"And I Was There,"* 461. "Too immersed in detail": Nimitz to Mrs. Nimitz, October 17, 1942. "We wasted no time": Layton, *"And I Was There,"* 461–462. "IN VIEW GHORMLEY'S": Nimitz to King, October 16, 1942 (0937). "It was a sore mental struggle": Nimitz to Mrs. Nimitz, October 17, 1942. "APPROVED": King to Nimitz, October 16, 1942 (0245). "I fudged this": Baldwin interview, 349–350, 353–354. "Not once during the entire visit": *New York Times*, "Admiral's Tribute to Wounded," 3. "Dear Ghorm": Scott to Ghormley, October 22, 1942, Ghormley Papers. "They were just delighted": Mustin interview, 520.

21: Enter Fighting   (pp. 208–215)

"You will take command": Halsey, *Admiral Halsey's Story*, 109. "I have always insisted on": Ibid., 137. "We were absolutely elated": Musicant, *Battleship at War*, 88. "During wartime it's important": Graff interview. "The *Enterprise* is now operating": COMSOPAC, "Operational History of the South Pacific," 4. "A real old salt": U.S. Naval Academy, *Lucky Bag*, 1904. "We would take the top": Soule, *Shooting the Pacific War*, 122. "He was a fighting man": Custer, *Through the Perilous Night*, 43–44. "From the American admiral": Hoyt, *How They Won the War in the Pacific*, 165–166. *"Boiling oil."*..."You go to hell!" COMSOPAC, "Operational History," 3. "Brilliant in common sense": Mustin interview, 528. "The officers and chiefs": Halsey, *Admiral*, 140. "COMPLETE WITH BLACK TIE": Ibid., 139. "I would like to see it": Hoyt, *How They Won*, 172. "As I dug into my new job": Halsey, *Admiral*, 136. "The maximum possible urgency": Halsey to Vice OpNav, October 21, 1942 (0517). "You are well aware of": Hoyt, *How They Won*, 172. "What do we get in exchange?" and "We will continue to protect you": Halsey, manuscript, 369–370; Potter, *Bull Halsey*, 184; Schom, *The Eagle and the Rising Sun*, 408–410. "If we are defeated": Hayes, *The History of the Joint Chiefs of Staff in World War II*, 191. "Today—our Saturday": Nimitz to Mrs. Nimitz, October 24, 1942. "Tired, hungry": Nimitz to Mrs. Nimitz, October 24, 1942. "The view expressed": Hurd, "Pacific Command Shake-Up Is Laid to Guadalcanal Crisis," 1, 41. "What did I do that was wrong?": Nimitz to Robert L. Ghormley, Jr., January 27, 1961. "Complete lack of offensive use...I presume most of us": Hoyt, *How They Won*, 168. "When history is written": Weaver, "Some Reminiscences," 10. "My anxiety about the Southwest Pacific": Arnold, *Global Mission*, 355.

22: "Strike—Repeat, Strike"   (pp. 216–222)

"Something is in the air": Merillat, *Guadalcanal Remembered*, 226–227. "Smash anything we find": Mustin diary, October 25, 1942. Japanese forces: Frank, *Guadalcanal*, 374–376; Morison, *The Struggle for Guadalcanal*, 206–207. "The victory is already": Frank, *Guadalcanal*, 341–342. "2300 BANZAI!": Ibid., 354. "This settled everything": Ugaki, *Fading Victory*, 245. "Having inferior forces": Hoyt, *How They Won the War in the Pacific*, 171. "They began to echo": Halsey, *Admiral Halsey's*

Story, 116. **"Are we going to evacuate or hold?"** and **"I can hold":** Halsey, *Admiral,* 117. **"If Vandegrift had fired an arrow":** Richard B. Frank, email to author, September 24, 2009. **"Carrier power varies":** Halsey, *Admiral,* 120. **"STRIKE—REPEAT, STRIKE":** Lundstrom, *The First Team and the Guadalcanal Campaign,* 349.

23: Santa Cruz (*pp. 223–236*)

U.S. aircraft strength: Lundstrom, *The First Team and the Guadalcanal Campaign,* 353. **"PROCEED WITHOUT *HORNET*":** Moore, *The Buzzard Brigade,* 29. **"Drove the guns into the stops":** Grahn interview. **"It was beneath the dignity":** Claypool, *God on a Battlewagon,* 5; Backus interview, 126. Backus disputed Morison's description of the *South Dakota* as an "abominably dirty" ship, 200 fn. **"Forasmuch as the spirit":** Claypool, *God,* 7. **"In their borrowed clothes":** Ibid., 6–9. **"Men have to have something":** Ibid., 74. **"I wish we had as many carriers":** Nimitz to Mrs. Nimitz, October 27, 1942. **"Numerically or tactically"** and **"Considering the great superiority":** Hara, *Japanese Destroyer Captain,* 134.

24: Secret History (*pp. 237–242*)

Pilot and aircrew casualties: Scouting Squadron 3, "Report of Operations at Guadalcanal Island," 1–4. **"Have received most earnest attention":** Turner to Vandegrift, October 29, 1942. **King's lasciviousness:** Buell, *Master of Sea Power,* 78–79, which elaborates, "Women avoided sitting near him at dinner parties because his hands were too often beneath the table. King's interest in women led him into a number of extramarital affairs." **"Enemy offensives since September 15":** Halsey to Commander, Task Force 42, October 30, 1942. **Japanese supply requirements and capacity:** Parshall, "Oil and the Japanese Strategy in the Solomons." **"In the end, one side or":** Hurd, "Navies Manoeuvre for Big Stakes in Solomons," E3. **"We won":** Graybar, "Admiral King's Toughest Battle," 39. **"So far as I'm concerned":** McCormick, "King of the Navy," 20. *Chicago Tribune* **incident:** Toland, *The Rising Sun,* vol. 1, 427. **"So mismanaged was":** Graybar, "Admiral King's," 40. **"I spoke more frankly":** Baldwin interview, 356–359. The angry captain was Charles R. "Cat" Brown (see Samuel B. Griffith to Charles R. Brown, October 10, 1962, and Griffith to Hanson W. Baldwin, October 10, 1962, Baldwin Papers). **"The *Boise* fired on six targets":** USS *Boise,* "Report of Action," 1; Fox Movietone News, "Hero 'Battleship X' Revealed to Be the USS *South Dakota*" (newsreel). **"There was every reason to believe":** Graybar, "Admiral King's," 42–43. **"There was no one in Washington":** Baldwin interview, 361–362.

25: Turner's Choice (*pp. 243–252*)

"In the half dawn" and **"He couldn't thank us enough":** Leavelle, "The Log of the Mighty A," March 29, 1943. **November 4 naval bombardment:** USS *Helena,* "Report of Shore Bombardment," 1–3; Turner to Nimitz, November 7, 1942 (2358). **"I know we haven't got much":** Eller interview, 590. **"It wasn't the noise":** Halsey, *Admiral*

Halsey's Story, 123. "The gunners fired as though": Morris, *The Fightin'est Ship,* 67. "For operations against Jap light forces": Scott to Halsey, November 8, 1942 (0020). *Pensacola*'s problems: Holbrook, *The History and Times of the USS* Portland, 175. "He spent a great deal of time": Mustin interview, 523. Japanese plans: Frank, *Guadalcanal,* 429. U.S. estimates: Turner to Callaghan, "Letter of Instructions Concerning Future Operations of Task Force 67," quoted in COMINCH, "Battle Experience: November 1942," 27-17, 27-18. "It looks this time": Hoyt, *How They Won the War in the Pacific,* 182–183. "We must establish local naval superiority": Baldwin, "Lessons of the Solomons Campaign," 3.

26: Suicide *(pp. 253–262)*

"I heard about all the plans": Tarrant interview. Turner's order to Callaghan: Turner to Callaghan, November 12, 1942 (0133), quoted in Nimitz, "Preliminary Report of Action, 12–13 November 1942," 3. "He said to me, 'Yes' ": Tarrant interview. "The wind carried their voices": Bennett interview. "Calm, unemotional, resolute": Bennett, "Callaghan Was Calm…," 18. "We were all prepared to die": Whitt interview. "All hell seemed dancing": www.siprep.org/about/si_history _brief.cfm. Callaghan, Virgil, and Dante: Murphy, *Fighting Admiral,* www .microworks.net/pacific/library/fa-chapter1.htm. Joe Foss interception: SOPAC, "Naval Air Combat Intelligence Report," November 8–12, 1942; COMINCH, "Battle Experience: November 1942," 27-8. "An old-time cavalry deployment": McCandless, "The *San Francisco* Story," 37. "With this beautifully clear view": Mustin interview, 564. "Seemed to literally hammer them": COMINCH, "Battle Experience: November 1942," 28-8. "I just had time": Wallace quoted at www.modelwarships .com/features/words/Wallace/Wallace.html. "We heard them yelling": Morris, *The Fightin'est Ship,* 71. "To set his ship down" and Betty versus DD: Leavelle, "The Log of the Mighty A," March 30, 1943. "There was no comment": Jack Slack quoted in Parrent, *Third Savo,* 60. "Almost pathetically": Morris, *The Fightin'est Ship,* 72–73. "I got him over my shoulders" and "How he got into": Wallace, www.usssanfrancisco .org. "A delaying action": COMSOPAC, "Operational History of the South Pacific," 19. Turner wrote Callaghan, "At White Poppy (Nouméa) is Task Force 16. I have no knowledge as to its future movements." COMINCH, "Battle Experience: November 1942," 27-17, 27-18. "God's burning finger": Melville, *Moby-Dick,* 579. "This is suicide, you know": Hammel, *Guadalcanal: Decision at Sea,* 112. "You will not fear": Bible, Psalm 91, New International Version. "If Callaghan had had": Mustin interview, 571, 574. "Only to show disparity": Bennett interview. "You're in no condition": Bennett interview. "I was praying": Howe interview, 21.

27: Black Friday *(pp. 263–272)*

"A place of bitter struggles": Ugaki, *Fading Victory,* 255. Volunteer Attack Force usage: Dull, *Battle History of the Imperial Japanese Navy,* 256–257. "In all the years of" and "This blessed squall": Hara, *Japanese Destroyer Captain,* 138. "Small island" and "Prepare for gun": Ibid., 140. "A blackness so thick" and "Where in the hell": Hartney, "The Story of the *Juneau*," 2. **U.S. approach:** USS *Cushing*, "Report of Engagement," 1; USS *Helena*, "Action Off North Coast," 17. **"When we finally had":** Graff interview. **"As uncomplicated as":** Morris, *The Fightin'est Ship*, 84. **"We knew the bearing":** Hagen interview. **"Solution! Enemy course 107":** Calhoun, *Tin Can Sailor*, 75. *"I said a short prayer":* McKinney, *CL-51 Revisited*, 39. *"There is a ship crossing":* USS *Cushing*, "Report of Engagement," 1. *"What do you make of it":* USS *Helena*, Extracts from *Helena*'s TBS Log for 0142. **"SHALL I LET THEM HAVE":** Ibid., 1441 GCT. **"There in the starlight":** Mustin interview, 576. *"What are you doing, Sam?":* USS *Portland*, "Night Action Between Task Force 67.4 and Japanese Forces, November 13, 1942," 3. **Turn ninety degrees left:** The *Portland*'s action report states at 0146, "At about this time, column movement 90 degrees L to 270 degrees was believed ordered." The *Helena*'s TBS log indicates at 0149, "Changed course to left. Hard left rudder." **"PROBABLE ENEMY SHIPS IN SIGHT":** Frank, *Guadalcanal*, 440. **"There was a stampede":** Hara, *Japanese*, 141.

28: Into the Light   *(pp. 273–281)*

"The light seemed high": Cochran, "Recollections." **"Counter-illuminate!":** Graff interview; Morison manuscript, p. 6, has Nickelson ordering counter-illumination; but Graff, who was there, states that Jenkins ordered counter-illumination and that Nickelson exclaimed as indicated. See also Leavelle, "The Log of the Mighty A," March 31, 1943. *"Action port":* USS *Atlanta*, "Engagement with Japanese Surface Forces Off Guadalcanal," Encl. D, Paragraph 4. **"You couldn't help but see":** Mustin interview, 579. *"Odd ships commence fire":* USS *Portland*, "Night Action Between Task Force 67.4 and Japanese Forces, November 13, 1942," 3. **"A display of futility":** Mustin interview, 585. **"It was disorganized":** Becton, *The Ship That Would Not Die*, 9. **"A roar so constant":** Barham, *The 228 Days of the United States Destroyer* Laffey *(DD-459)*, 81–82. **"It was so close":** Hale, letter to author, 2. **"She was only about":** Barham, *228 Days*, 81–82. **"So close Hank could have":** Becton, *The Ship*, 9. **"The whole world suddenly"** and **"The *Laffey* was designed":** Barham, *228 Days*, 84. **"The next second":** Ibid., 84–85. **"I could see that":** Hale, letter to author, 2. **"The air was full":** Barham, *228 Days*, 89. **"I gulped":** Hara, *Japanese Destroyer Captain*, 114. **"A form of firecracker":** USS *Sterett*, "Report of Action on Night of November 12–13, 1942," 7. **"A ghostly gray":** Ibid., 4. **"Oh, you poor":** Calhoun, *Tin Can Sailor*, 78–79. **"It was as if a huge"** and **"The number-four handling room":** Parrent, *Third Savo*, 32. **Damage to** *Sterett:* USS *Sterett*, "Report," 2, 6. **Citations of** *Sterett*'s **crew:** Ibid., 11–15.

29: The Killing Salvo   *(pp. 282–289)*

"Should have sufficed": McCandless, "The *San Francisco* Story," 39. Callaghan may have realized that a close-range fight was the only way his cruisers could defeat battleships, but no evidence exists that this was his design. **"At least four bursts of flame":** USS *Portland*, "Night Action Between Task Force 67.4 and Japanese Forces, November 13, 1942," Encl. B, "Gunnery Officer's Report," 2. **"Practically all of our shots":** USS *Helena*, "Action Off North Coast Guadalcanal," 5. **"The tracers from fifteen guns":** Luehman interview, 6. **"Smoky orange bonfire":** Morris, *The Fightin'est*

Ship, 86. *"The* Atlanta's *turning left"* and "First I had to swing": McCandless, "The *San Francisco* Story," 40–41. "Swept out of line": Morris, *The Fightin'est Ship*, 87. "A tremendous *piiing*": Graff interview. "A monstrous column of water": Mustin interview, 583. Second torpedo hit on *Atlanta:* Ibid., 581. "Like a pendulum": Parrent, *Third Savo*, 47. "Stick a pillow in it": Shaw, *Beside Me Still*, 107. "It was absolutely deafening": Mustin interview, 582–583. *Atlanta's* final range reading: McKinney, *CL-51 Revisited*, 45. Identification of *San Francisco:* Morton, *Mustin*, 197. "Some alarm on the port side" and damage to *Atlanta:* Mustin interview, 590; Leavelle, "The Log Mighty A," April 1, 1943. *My God, they got Scott:* Graff interview. "Let's get below": Hammel, *Guadalcanal: Decision at Sea*, 255. "I hit, I'm pretty certain": Moredock, quoted in National Geographic Society, *The Lost Fleet of Guadalcanal*. "I don't know where I thought": Graff interview. "Illuminated the firing ship": Mustin interview, 588–589. "We were firing": Gibson, "As I Remember," 32. "Probably she drifted": McCandless, "The *San Francisco* Story," 41. The *Atlanta's* William B. McKinney added, "Two years later I met the officer who had been in charge of Turret 3 on that heavy cruiser. He acknowledged that they had pumped out three three-gun salvos at what they first thought was a Japanese ship. Also, in later years, Bob Tyler [EM1/c] served on the same ship with the former *San Francisco* gunnery officer who conceded that *all San Francisco*'s main battery turrets had fired three salvos at *Atlanta*" (McKinney, *CL-51*, 49). "You could measure them": Mustin interview, 590–591. "I continued to try our phones": McKinney, *CL-51*, 40. "The smoke was so thick": Ibid., 41. *"Cease firing own ships":* USS *Portland*, "Night Action," 4. *"What is the dope":* Ibid., 3. One naval historian has claimed that Callaghan "gave the [cease fire] order deliberately to conceal the approach of his cruisers" and "hoped to use the extreme darkness of that particular night to his advantage." See Hone, "Give Them Hell," 190. I have found no evidence of this. "We fired at so many targets": Harrison interview. "I watched, almost transfixed": Casten, *Our Ship: The* Helena, 60.

30: Death in the Machine Age (*pp. 290–298*)

"I drank coffee by the gallon": Halsey manuscript, 386–387; Halsey, *Admiral Halsey's Story*, 126. "The concussion could be felt": William Marshal Chaney, 1st Battalion, 147th Infantry RCT, quoted in Parrent, *Third Savo*, 24. "The star shells rose, terrible and red": Leckie, *A Helmet for My Pillow*, 116–118. "All you could see": Melhorn interview, 95. "Consciously or unconsciously": Jones, *WWII*, 54. *"Can we open fire":* USS *Helena*, "Action Off North Coast of Guadalcanal," Encl. B, TBS log, 1500 GMT (0200 GMT –11), 3. "The duel about to begin" and "Two four-gun salvos hit": McCandless, "The *San Francisco* Story," 41. "We just put a nine-gun": Hamilton interview. Hits claimed: USS *San Francisco*, "Action Report—Night Action—Nov. 12–13, 1942," 2. "With a pagoda-like superstructure": Spencer, *The War Years*, 76. "Just like a barroom brawl": Trumbull, "Mortally Wounded U.S. Destroyer Torpedoed Japanese Battleship," 5. "From bow to stern" and "Attempting to locate": USS *O'Bannon*, "Report of Engagement with Japanese Units on Morning of November 13, 1942," 3. "Seemingly everywhere": McCandless, "The *San Fran-*

cisco Story," 49. "The smell of burning flesh": Bennett interview. "That failure kept me alive": Arison, "A Battle to Remember." "One instant I was fine": Spencer, *The War Years: Hellfire and Glory,* 77. "I've lost steering control, sir!": McCandless, "The San Francisco Story," 41–42. Schonland's damage-control efforts: Schonland interview 1, 28–37. "This locker is too thin": Spencer, email to author, February 4, 2009. "Mangled red meat" and "Get off of me": Spencer, *The War Years,* 77. "Leaving Higdon" and "Against a midnight-blue": McCandless, "The San Francisco Story," 42–43. "Fighting by departments" and "We had good interior communications": Ibid., 44–46.

31: Point Blank *(pp. 299–310)*

Portland's torpedo hit and exchange with *Hiei:* USS *Portland,* "Night Action Between Task Force 67.4 and Japanese Forces, November 13, 1942," 4, 7, 8; Encl. B, gunnery officer's report, 3. "Other ships, blazing": Morris, *The Fightin'est Ship,* 87. "Wallowing there": Hartney, "The Story of the USS *Juneau,*" 3. "A weird, unforgettable pageantry": Ibid., 4–5. "Chief, just get me going": Barham, *The 228 Days of the United States Destroyer* Laffey *(DD-459),* 90. "My first reaction": Ibid., 95. "That these disasters": McCandless, "The San Francisco Story," 42. "Like a huge apartment building": Cook interview. "Don't cheer, men": Maclay, *The Life and Adventures of Jack Philip, Admiral, USN,* 254 n. Damage to *Hiei:* Tully, "Death of Battleship *Hiei.*" *Kirishima*'s withdrawal: Tokuno, USSBS interrogation, 2. "In the confused picture": USS *Portland,* "Night Action," 4. "Shell drunk" and "I hunched my back": Hara, *Japanese Destroyer Captain,* 149, 158. Damage to *Helena:* USS *Helena,* "Action Off North Coast of Guadalcanal," 17; Luehman interview. "We're going to take water": Schonland interview 1, 32. "Rogers couldn't see": Bennett interview. "We were the only game" and "You move like": Tarrant interview. "I am reluctant to compare": Becton, *The Ship That Would Not Die,* 9. "Exploded and simply disappeared": USS *Fletcher,* "Report of Action," 4. "The ship, broken in two": Hara, *Japanese,* 146. Damage to *Aaron Ward:* USS *Aaron Ward,* "Report of Action," 6; Hagen, Nimitz Museum interview, 20; author interview. "Hey Joe, aren't you glad": Wylie, NWC interview, 72.

32: Among the Shadows *(pp. 311–316)*

"Form 18. Course 092" and *"Unable raise other big boys":* USS *Helena,* "Action Off North Coast of Guadalcanal," Encl. B, TBS log, 4. "That sure looks like": Howe interview, 23. "It seemed like everyone": Heyn, "One Who Survived," unpaginated. "We'll fight her until": Calhoun, *Tin Can Sailor,* 80–81. "Bodies, mattresses and other debris": Parrent, *Third Savo,* 33. "We had not seen": Calhoun, *Tin Can Sailor,* 84. "H-I-S H-I-S": Gibson, "As I Remember," 33. "Driven from my mind": McCandless, "The San Francisco Story," 50. "If you don't want them shooting": Gibson, "As I Remember," 33. "Thank God the *Helena*": Bennett interview. "Captain Hoover, may he live forever": Morris, *The Fightin'est Ship,* 93. "I hung on": McCandless, "The San

Francisco Story," 51. **"You're about to run aground"**: Bennett interview, ECU. **"A wholly unsatisfactory pillow"**: Bennett, email to Johnny Johnson, April 2, 2005.

33: *Atlanta* Burning (pp. 317–325)

Efforts to save the *Atlanta*: USS *Atlanta*, "Action Report," Encl. C, Notes on Damage Control, Paragraph 12; Mustin interview, 602–610. **"Plastered flat"**: McKinney, *CL-51 Revisited*, 46. **"It is a matter of wonder"**: Ibid., 42. **"Get off. She's going to blow!"** Ibid., 40–41. **"Just don't sink the ship"**: Ibid., 43. **"Took a little time"**: Ibid., 51. **"A horrifying spectacle"**: Ibid., 55. **"They were so deeply ingrained"**: Mustin interview, 608. **"The entire area was covered"**: Kennedy, *Fearless Warrior*, 114. **"As it came alongside"**: Mustin interview, 605–606. **"There were not very many"**: Kennedy, *Fearless*, 114. **"There was a general rush"**: McKinney, *CL-51*, 44. **"It's not in my registry"**: Parrent, *Third Savo*, 43–44. **"We raised a cheer"**: McKinney, *CL-51*, 45. **Air attacks on *Hiei***: Lundstrom, *The First Team and the Guadalcanal Campaign*, 477–480; Frank, *Guadalcanal*, 454; Moore, *The Buzzard Brigade*, 68–69. **Decision to scuttle *Hiei***: Tully, "Death of Battleship *Hiei*"; Lundstrom, *First Team*, 482–483. **"Boys, I don't know"**: Moore, *Buzzard*, 70.

34: Cruiser in the Sky (pp. 326–334)

"I don't know why": Whitt interview; Satterfield, *We Band of Brothers*, 145. **Body parts sweep**: Spencer, *The War Years: Hellfire and Glory*, 71. **"The ship was just"**: Whitt interview. **"Detailing the senior rates"**: Jenkins, "A Real Belly Full," 2. **"Fellows were picking them up"**: Whitt interview. Lt. Cdr. S. Yunoki, the *Kirishima*'s main-battery fire-control officer, confirmed that bombardment ammo was fired on the U.S. ships. Interrogation of Lt. Cdr. S. Yunoki, 191. **"I never will be able"**: Jenkins, "A Real," 2. **"The usual eruption"**: USS *Helena*, "Report of Submarine Torpedo Attack on Task Unit and Sinking of USS *Juneau*," 2. **"Full right rudder"**: Schonland interview 1, 41–42. **"Loud *crrrrrack*"**: Whitt interview. **"De Long, she ain't no more"**: De Long, narrative, 1–2. **"The *Juneau* didn't sink"**: McCandless, "The *San Francisco* Story," 51. **"Debris fell to such extent"**: Hoover to Turner, November 14, 1942 (0001). **"As we got up even"**: Whitt interview. **"Our ship rapidly keeled"**: Jenkins, "A Real," 3. **"No one moved or spoke"**: Morris, *The Fightin'est Ship*, 95. **"We often talked"**: Parrent, *Third Savo*, 52. **"The intrepid and seamanlike way"**: Commander, Task Unit 17.5.4, "Report of Action in Coral Sea Area on May 8, 1942." **"JUNEAU TORPEDOED"**: USS *Helena*, "Action Off North Coast Guadalcanal," Encl. D. **"Probably the most courageous"**: Wylie, NWC interview, 79. **"If we had tried"**: Mustin interview, 610. **"Here comes a bear"**: Holbrook, *The History and Times of the USS Portland*, 195. **"This is the American cruiser Portland"**: Generous, *Sweet Pea at War*, 98. **"There is a Japanese task force"**: Melhorn interview, 98. PT boats seldom operated at the blistering speeds suggested by full-page ads in *Collier's* and the other weeklies. They were very heavily loaded, with four torpedoes, several gun mounts, smoke-making apparatus, and wooden hulls that became sodden with water (Mustin interview, 651). At speed, they tossed a high rooster-tail wake that was clearly visible at night. Their captains thus preferred to stalk. "We always idled in with the mufflers down and tried to get in a shooting position," said Charles Melhorn, whose boat, the *PT-44*, was in the posse that tangled with the *Portland* that night. "For the attack phase, the watchword was stealth" (Melhorn interview, 105). In *At Close Quarters*, 92, Bulkley referred to two PT boats being assigned to escort the *Portland* to Tulagi that night. No reference was made to a friendly fire incident with them. "**If you challenge the wrong group**" and "**We thought that was pretty dirty**": Melhorn interview, 99. The next morning, Captain DuBose sent an officer to talk with the skippers at the PT boat headquarters. The young officers there confirmed they had sortied but denied firing torpedoes at a friendly vessel. Years later, speaking at a reunion of PT boat sailors in New York, DuBose related this story, then offered that he must have been mistaken and that surely there were no torpedoes fired at the *Portland*. After a few beats, several of the old hands reportedly jumped to their feet and said, "Oh, yes there were!" It was not a tale that Admiral Halsey was eager to publicize. According to Heber A. Holbrook, a *San Francisco* veteran, "The only explanation for its absence from the official records is that DuBose, perhaps on orders from Admiral Halsey, ordered it suppressed" (Holbrook, *The History and Times of the USS* Portland, 194–196). "**Then we all dropped**": Parrent, *Third Savo*, 44.

35: Regardless of Losses (pp. 335–342)

"**This was the tightest spot**": Halsey manuscript, 383. "**If any principle of naval warfare**": Halsey, *Admiral Halsey's Story*, 128. **Halsey's orders to Kinkaid:** Commander, Task Force 16, "Operations of Task Force 16," 2. "***What do you think***" and "**You can well imagine**": Weaver, "Some Reminiscences," 11. "**I had the feeling**": McKinney, *CL-51 Revisited*, 58. "**The tension I felt**": Forrestal to Morison, October 22, 1948, quoted in Morison, *The Struggle for Guadalcanal*, 263. "**It was pretty awe-inspiring**": Bennett ECU interview. "**What happened?**": Cochran, "Recollections," 10. "**I wasn't near anyone**": Spencer, *The War Years: Hellfire and Glory*, 88–90. "**There were some real hard feelings**": Heiberg interview, 10–11. "**Task Force 67 is hereby dissolved**": Turner to Task Force 67, November 14, 1942 (2000). "**Looks like all out attempt**": Nimitz to CTFs, November 14, 1942 (0359), quoted in Lundstrom, *The First Team and the Guadalcanal Campaign*, 506.

PART IV:
The Thundering

Epigraph from Steinbeck, *Once There Was a War*, 172.

36: The Giants Ride (pp. 345–352)

"**The plan flouted**": Halsey, *Admiral Halsey's Story*, 128. **Battleship design and specs:** Friedman, *U.S. Battleships*, 282–283. **Gunnery practice:** Fuquea, "Task Force One," 732–733. "**As you can imagine**": Backus interview, 147; ComBatDiv 6 to USS *South Dakota*, November 8, 1942 (0210). "**He was not what you would**": Thomas C.

Kinkaid to Evan E. Smith, April 9, 1962, Papers of Thomas C. Kinkaid. **"He looked like an Arkansas farmer"**: Eller interview, 484–485. **Lee at the Olympics:** Houston, "Stand Aside, This Is Ching." **"His conversation was so loaded"**: Musicant, *Battleship at War,* 81–82. **"It doesn't take long"**: Mustin interview, 510–511. **"This is the captain"**: Musicant, *Battleship,* 114. **"All we can do"**: Claypool, *God on a Battlewagon,* 12. *"There go two big ones"*: USS *South Dakota,* "Action Report, Night Engagement 14–15 November 1942, with Japanese Naval Units, Off Savo Island," 4. *"Refer your big boss"*: Frank, *Guadalcanal,* 473.

37: The Gun Club   *(pp. 353–368)*

"Well, stand by, Glenn": Musicant, *Battleship at War,* 118. **"Then separate into 'drops'"**: USS *Washington,* "Action Report, Night of November 14–15, 1942," 21. **"Grouped together"**: Reed, "A Recollection," 7. **"Radar has forced"**: USS *Washington,* "Action Report," 29. **"I saw the *Washington* open fire"**: Lundgren, "The Battleship Action, 14–15 November 1942," 9, fn. 6. According to the *Walke*'s action report, the ship that hit the *Preston* was directly off her port beam. The *Washington*'s action report indicates that the battleship passed south of the sinking *Preston* at this same time, two hundred yards to the disengaged side, and that one of the *Washington*'s five-inch batteries, Mount 3 on the starboard side, had been "firing wild (training motor kicked out and the pointers were not matched). It was feared the mount might endanger own destroyers" (USS *Washington,* "Action Report," 9). However, the extent of damage to the *Preston* suggests that ordnance much heavier than five-inch hit her. **"Bodily out of the water"**: USS *Walke,* "Report of Surface Engagement with Japanese Forces, November 15, 1942," 2. **"Get after 'em, *Washington*!"**: Musicant, *Battleship,* 122. **Damage to and withdrawal of *Benham*:** USS *Benham,* "Report of Action," 3–4. **Power failure in *South Dakota*:** USS *South Dakota,* "Action Report," 5, 12. **Sinking of *Ayanami*:** Lundgren, "The Battleship Action," 12, fn. 11, citing postwar interview with Cdr. Eiji Sakuma. **"Our turret commander"**: Claypool, *God on a Battlewagon,* 17. **Damage to *South Dakota*:** USS *South Dakota,* "Action Report," 14; USS *South Dakota,* "Report of Gunfire Damage, Battle of Guadalcanal, 14–15 November 1942"; Backus interview, 141, 159. **"At such times"**: Claypool, *God,* 18. **"Body-punching range"**: Musicant, *Battleship,* 126. **"Throwing fourteen-inch"**: Backus interview, 153–154. Some naval historians consider the *Washington*'s duel with the *Kirishima* a foregone conclusion in favor of the U.S. ship. However, according to calculations by the naval weapons engineer Nathan Okun, at this close range the *Washington*'s twelve-inch armor belt was susceptible to penetration by a Japanese Type 91 armor-piercing projectile. The *Washington*'s sixteen-inch fire, in turn, had enough force to penetrate the *Kirishima*'s ten-inch belt, pass through the ship, and penetrate the belt on the other side going out, assuming the warhead did not detonate (Okun email to author, March 8, 2010). **"I was amazed"**: Musicant, *Battleship,* 126. **"There is another ship"** and **"*Kirishima* is totally obscured"**: Lundgren, "The Battleship Action," 18. **"Functioned as smoothly as"**: ComBatDiv 6 (Lee), "Report of Night Action, Task Force 64, November 14–15, 1942," 8. **"At least ten hits were made"**: Sanji Iwabuchi's report. **"They must have been mighty close"**: Musicant, *Battleship,* 128. **"We couldn't**

make way": Iwabuchi report. **"If you can see anything"**: USS *Washington,* "Action Report," 10. **Damage to *Washington:*** ComBatDiv 6 (Lee), "Report of Action," Encl. C, 2; USS *Washington,* "Action Report," 36. **Sinking of *Kirishima:*** Lundgren, "The Battleship Action," 24. **"My men fought well"**: Iwabuchi report. **"I AM NOT EFFECTIVE"**: ComBatDiv 6, "Report," Encl. C, 3–4. **"This probably saved the battleships"**: COMINCH, "Battle Experience: November 1942," 30–42. **"In breaking up"**: ComBatDiv 6, "Report," 7. **"War was declared"**: Musicant, *Battleship,* 137. **"Our battleships are neither"**: ComBatDiv 6, "Report," 8. **"How are all the experts"**: Hoyt, *How They Won the War in the Pacific,* 187. **Reinforcements landed:** Morison, *The Struggle for Guadalcanal,* 285; Frank, *Guadalcanal,* 490.

38: The Kind of Men Who Win a War   *(pp. 369–377)*

"This ruled out any further sleep": McKinney, *CL-51 Revisited,* 60–61. **"Some of them were"**: Heyn, "One Who Survived," unpaginated. **George Sullivan's end:** Satterfield, *We Band of Brothers,* 152–157. **"Men like you"**: Schonland interview 1, 50. **Chick Morris at Nouméa:** Morris, *The Fightin'est Ship,* 101–104. **"Despite this officer's"**: Halsey manuscript, 395–396. **"Reluctantly, I concurred"**: Halsey, *Admiral Halsey's Story,* 134. **Rescue of *Juneau* survivors:** Hartney, "The Story of the *Juneau,"* 11–12; Spruance to King, "Solomon Islands Campaign—Battle of the Solomons, 11–15 November 1942," 12. **"Efforts consistent"**: Cdr. A. C. Jacobs, USNR, to Mr. J. S. Taylor, July 27, 1944, NARA. **"It was lonely indeed"**: Ugaki, *Fading Victory,* 278. **"By his daring"** and **"THE BEHAVIOR OF"**: Turner to Halsey, November 16, 1942 (1038). **"SPEAKING FOR THE NAVY"**: Knox to Halsey, November 17, 1942 (1434). **"MY DEEP THANKS"**: Halsey to Knox, November 18, 1942 (1140). **"WE HAVE ADMIRATION"**: Nimitz to Halsey, November 15, 1942 (0103). **"WE BELIEVE THE ENEMY"**: Vandegrift to Halsey, November 15, 1942 (0318). **"During the past two weeks"**: Sherwood, *Roosevelt and Hopkins,* 656.

39: On the Spot   *(pp. 378–384)*

"Step closer, son": Bennett, www.usssanfrancisco.org/Bennet%20Jack%20CAPT .htm. **"No sooner had the repair team"** and **"I wish I could recall"**: Calhoun, *Tin Can Sailor,* 101–102. **"After analysis of the situation"**: Halsey to Nimitz, "Circumstances of Loss of *Juneau,"* November 22, 1942. **Hoover's response:** Hoover to Nimitz, "Circumstances of Loss of *Juneau,"* November 28, 1942, 2. **Browning's boast:** Casten, *Our Ship: The Helena,* C-4. **"Under these conditions"**: Nimitz to King, Third Endorsement of Halsey to Nimitz of November 22, 1942. **"A confession of a grievous mistake"**: Halsey, *Admiral Halsey's Story,* 133–134. **"CinCPac was in disagreement"**: Halsey manuscript, 395–396. **"Orders such as 'Give them hell'"**: U.S. Naval War College, Office of the President, "Comments on the Battle of Guadalcanal, November 11–15, 1942," 5. **"A study of the naval actions"**: Ibid., 8. **"There is no telling"**: Ibid., 5. **"Take advantage of our success"** and **"We cannot permit"**: Kimball, *Churchill and Roosevelt,* 611, quoting draft message Churchill, R-186/3, not sent. **"Our main amphibious operations"** and **"Having assumed this**

commitment": Stoler, *Allies and Adversaries*, 96. **U.S. troops in Pacific, Europe:** Ibid., 293 fn. 51. **Late-November naval dispositions:** Halsey to all SOPAC commanders, November 23, 1942 (0612); Morison, *The Struggle for Guadalcanal*, 291. **"Must be amphibious":** Halsey to MacArthur, November 28, 1942 (0145). **"Send one of these":** Halsey, *Admiral*, 132.

40: The Futility of Learning   (pp. 385–397)

"*Ahhh,* we are more": Hara, *Japanese Destroyer Captain*, 160. **"A compromise dictated by necessity":** Halsey to Nimitz, First Endorsement of Commander, Task Force 67, "Report of Action Off Cape Esperance, Night of November 30, 1942," 4. **"I thought we had better":** Mustin interview, 650. **Kinkaid's relief:** Lundstrom, *Black Shoe Carrier Admiral*, 492–494. Lundstrom compares the grounds for Kinkaid's relief with the grounds for Fletcher's and argues that Fletcher got a raw deal. **"About the last visual dispatch":** Wylie, NWC interview, 86. **"A small wart":** USS *Minneapolis*, "Action Report for 30 November–1 December 1942," Report of Radar Officer, 2. **"REQUEST PERMISSION"** and **"the most stupid thing":** Wylie, NWC interview, 86. **"CAN YOU SEND BOATS?":** Wright (CTF 67), "Report on Action Off Cape Esperance, Night of November 30, 1942," Compilation of TBS Transmissions, 5 (this message sent at 1620 Z); Mustin interview, 631–632. *"Belay supply schedule":* Hara, *Japanese*, 162. **Damage to *New Orleans:*** Wright, supplement to CTF 67 action report, 6; USS *New Orleans,* Report of the Executive Officer, action report, December 3, 1942, 1. *New Orleans* **abandon ship canceled:** Wristen, *History of the United States Navy Ship* New Orleans, 4–3. **Hayter, Haines, and Forman:** Brown, *Hell at Tassafaronga*, 131–132. **"I wondered what he thought about":** Forgy, *. . . And Pass the Ammunition*, 212–213; see also Hartzell and Wristen, *The USS* New Orleans, *An Amended History*, 21–25. **"The observed positions":** Wright, "Report on Action," 9–10. According to Ernest M. Eller, who served CINCPAC as assistant head of gunnery and antisubmarine training officer, "The real factor that defeated all of our training in anti-torpedo operations was its high speed at long range. These Japanese torpedoes would run at about 45 or 46 knots and could go, I believe, eleven miles at that rate. Of course, our torpedo at that speed would run only three miles. We operated on the assumption that if we stayed outside of 10,000 yards until we fired, then we could maneuver and avoid the torpedoes because at a longer range we could set our torpedoes at about 25 or 26 knots. In all the night actions in which we received damage—and most of them we received very serious damage— it was because of this fact that we didn't understand the torpedo and its capabilities." Eller interview, vol. 2, 614–615. **Submarine torpedoes at Tassafaronga:** Halsey to King, First Endorsement of Wright, "Report on Action," 1–2. **"Picked off like mechanical ducks":** Morison, *The Struggle for Guadalcanal*, 306. **"Contributed greatly to the destruction":** Wright, "Performance of Duty in Action with Enemy," 1–3. **"He did nothing heroic":** Wristen, *History*, 4–3. Wristen added, "The award is an example of the pre-war Navy where the captain *had* to be awarded a medal equal to the highest one earned by one of his crew." **Status of Japanese on Guadalcanal:** Ugaki, *Fading Victory*, 289, 301. **"This was quite a feather":** Mustin interview, 653–654. "A fiasco which": Ibid., 665–666. "The whole color of the war": Ibid., 666.

41: Future Rising (pp. 398–408)

Guadalcanal leading nowhere: "It had no geographical relation to the course the war would later follow, neither to Nimitz's central Pacific campaign nor to MacArthur's return to the Philippines." Larrabee, *Commander in Chief*, 257. "People were killed all around me" and "I just cried my heart out": Graff interview. "This was a privilege": McKinney, *CL-51 Revisited*, 69–70. "We hate the petty bickering": Shaw, *Beside Me Still*, 104. "Years later I'd have nightmares": Joslin, quoted in National Geographic Society, *The Lost Fleet of Guadalcanal*. "They gave this city a strange feeling": *San Francisco Chronicle*, "The San Francisco Heroes' Parade" 155, no. 155, 1. "They didn't think": O'Brien, Robert, "When the Proudest Veteran Came Home," unknown publication, in Spencer, *The War Years: Hellfire and Glory*, appendix. "In the press": Spencer, *The War Years*, 2:11. "Polishing off a battleship": Davies, "Cruiser San Francisco, Home," 1, 7. The *Boise* "sank six Japanese warships": *New York Times*, "Boise Captain Gives Credit," November 24, 1942. Gatch's statement: Fox Movie Tone News, "Hero 'Battleship X.'" "Victory has a hundred fathers": Keyes, *The Quote Verifier*, 234–235. "Informal inquiry into the circumstances": King to Forrestal, "Investigation of the Loss of the USS *Vincennes*, USS *Quincy*, USS *Astoria*, and HMAS *Canberra*," 2. "He is not a colorful personality": Baldwin, "A Sailor-Diplomat Runs Up His Colors," SM9. "Dawn is about to break": Morison, *The Struggle for Guadalcanal*, 317. "Those who can stand": Frank, *Guadalcanal*, 527. "It is unacceptable": Bix, *Hirohito and the Making of Modern Japan*, 461. Operation KE and evacuation statistics: Frank, *Guadalcanal*, 595. "Total and complete defeat": Patch to Halsey, February 9, 1943.

42: Report and Echo (pp. 409–415)

"Full of the usual horror stories": Shaw, *Beside Me Still*, 119. "I now see": Ibid., 155. "As soon as I could talk": Graff interview. "The requirement to be ready": Mustin interview, 513. "Think creatively" and "There are no secrets": Graff interview. "Something new the psychiatrists": Custer, *Through the Perilous Night*, 223. "We have received news": Ibid., 238–239. "You may not care": Ibid., 241. "This young man": Harrison interview. The Sullivans in Waterloo: Satterfield, *We Band of Brothers*, 199. "The most complete and lucid report": Hepburn, "Report of Informal Inquiry into the Circumstances Attending the Loss of the USS *Vincennes*, *Quincy* and *Astoria*, and HMAS *Canberra*, on 9 August 1942, in the Vicinity of Savo Island (Solomon Islands)," 37.

43: The Opinion of Convening Authority (pp. 416–422)

"No one man was responsible": Weaver, "Some Reminiscences," 14. "In every circle": Livy, Book 44, chapter 22. A typescript of a fuller version of this quotation is contained in the Ghormley Papers, box 15, folder u. ECU. **"The deficiencies which manifested"**: Russell to King, "Memo for Admiral," 2. In his command study of Admiral Fletcher, *Black Shoe Carrier Admiral,* John Lundstrom argues that Fletcher should not be criticized for deciding to withdraw Task Force 61 because the decision was announced at a conference in advance of its execution. The record establishes that neither Nimitz nor Ghormley managed to referee this important disagreement among their subordinates. **"Sheer stodgy unimaginative bureaucratic complacency"**: Stone, "Brass Hats Undaunted," September 8, 1945, in *The Best of I. F. Stone,* 90. **"Too indefinite in regard"** and **"No special battle plan"**: cited in Hepburn, "Report of Informal Inquiry into the Circumstances Attending the Loss of the USS *Vincennes, Quincy* and *Astoria,* and HMAS *Canberra,* on 9 August 1942, in the Vicinity of Savo Island (Solomon Islands)," Paragraph 79, 35. **"Were faulty in requiring them"**: Ibid., 35–36. **"Only one plan"**: Ibid., 41. **"In my opinion"**: Ibid., 44. **"I have been accused"**: Dyer, *The Amphibians Came to Conquer,* 372. **"I have always hesitated"**: Buell, *The Quiet Warrior,* 174–175. **"There is generally a twilight zone"** and **"In my opinion the primary cause"**: Hepburn, "Report," 52–53. **"Far from impressive"** and **"there is only one instance"**: Ibid., 54. **"It would be difficult"**: Ibid., 53. **"Granting that the immediate cause"**: King to Forrestal, September 14, 1943, 2. **"It does not necessarily follow"**: COMINCH, "Memorandum for Admiral," 4. **Bode's demerits**: *New York Times,* "Annapolis Hazers Punished," 1. **"Seemed to be under"** and **"He told me"** and **"It was one of the most pleasant"**: Commandant, 15th Naval District, "Record of Proceedings of a Board of Investigation Convened at the U.S. Naval Station Balboa, Canal Zone, in the Case of Howard D. Bode, Late Captain, U.S. Navy," Statement of Commander, USNR, April 20, 1943, 2–3. **"Although there are probably"**: Bode to Hepburn, April 8, 1943, 4 (Hepburn Annex, 305). **"Within the past two weeks"** and **"Some time recently"** and **"I am writing a letter"** and **"I can find no expression"** and **"I am sure that"**: Bode to Hepburn, April 18, 1943, 1–2. **"It is the opinion of"**: Commandant, 15th Naval District, April 24, 1943 1–2. **"This Bureau concurs"**: Chief of the Bureau of Medicine and Surgery, "Second Endorsement to JAG report dated July 13, 1943, July 17, 1943, 1—."

44: Ironbottom Sound   (*pp. 423–429*)

"The magnitude of the Solomons campaign": Custer, *Through the Perilous Night,* 223. **"Senior Marine Corps operations officers"**: Pope, "ANZACs Criticize Ghormley Tactics," 5. **"Your father was relieved"**: Nimitz to Robert L. Ghormley, Jr., January 27, 1961, Ghormley Papers. **"Their hopes for a combined victory"**: Weinberg, *A World at Arms,* 347–348. **"We don't claim to be prophets"**: *Collier's,* "The Idea Is to Win," 70. **"We have not begun"**: Lee, "How Japan Plans to Win," 74. **"Unwilling to pay the price"**: Weinberg, *World,* 344. **The IJN's perceived inferiority**: Hirama, "Japanese Naval Preparations for World War II," 63. **"The outstanding feature"**: Ohmae, "Japanese Commentary on Guadalcanal," 59. **Land fighting "decisive"; air and sea "ancillary"**: Samuel B. Griffith, II, to Hanson W. Baldwin, January 17, 1961, Baldwin Papers. **"If our surface forces"**: Halsey manuscript, 397. **"There were many courageous decisions"**: Spruance to King, February 18, 1943, 25. **"Purchased one night's**

respite": Frank, *Guadalcanal,* 461. **"The key to Allied success":** Lundstrom, *The First Team and the Guadalcanal Campaign,* 523. **"We have come to expect":** COMINCH, "Battle Experience: November 1942," 27–15. **"Training, TRAINING and M-O-R-E T-R-A-I-N-I-N-G":** Nimitz to King, "Solomons Island Campaign, 5th Battle of Savo," 16. **Issuance of** *Current Tactical Orders and Doctrine:* Hone, "U.S. Navy Surface Battle Doctrine," 72. **Robert Graff quotations and trip to Solomons:** Graff interview and Graff, "My Statement," Graff Papers.

BIBLIOGRAPHY

Key

NARA: National Archives and Records Administration (Archives II), College Park, Maryland
NHC: Naval Historical Center, Washington Navy Yard, Washington, DC
NMPW: National Museum of the Pacific War, Admiral Nimitz Foundation, Fredericksburg, Texas
NWC: Naval War College, Cushing Library, Newport, Rhode Island
USNI: United States Naval Institute, Annapolis, Maryland

Official Documents

15th Naval District, Commandant, "Record of Proceedings of a Board of Investigation Convened at the U.S. Naval Station Balboa, Canal Zone, in the Case of Howard D. Bode, Late Captain, U.S. Navy," April 20, 1943. NARA.

Bureau of Naval Personnel, Navy Department. *Information Bulletin,* 1942. NARA.

Bureau of Navigation, Navy Department. *Information for Naval Personnel,* 1942. NARA.

Bureau of Ships, Navy Department. "Summary of War Damage to U.S. Battleships, Carriers, Cruisers, and Destroyers, 17 October 1941, to 7 December 1942," September 15, 1943. NARA.

Commander, Battleship Division 6 (or Task Force 64, Lee). "Report of Night Action, Task Force 64, November 14–15, 1942." No serial, February 18, 1943. NARA.

Commander, Battleships–Cruisers, Pacific Fleet. General Administrative Files, Flag Files (Blue 361), 1942–45 (including ship materials and engineering reports, fleet gunnery bulletins, and reports of offset gunnery exercises, September–December 1942). RG 313, 370/A/45/1, Boxes 1–26. NARA.

Commander, Cruiser Division 5. "Report of Night Engagement of 30 November–1 December 1942." No serial, December 4, 1942. NARA.

Commander, Cruisers, U.S. Pacific Fleet (Fletcher). "Preliminary Report—Solomons Islands Operation." Serial 0039N, September 9, 1942. NARA.

Commander, Destroyer Division 9. "Action Report—Night of November 30, 1942–December 1, 1942, Off Savo Island." Serial 020-S. December 4, 1942. NARA.

Commander, Destroyer Squadron 10 (Stokes). "Engagement with Japanese Surface Units Off Savo Island, about 0200, November 13, 1942." No serial, November 15, 1942. NARA.

Commander, Destroyer Squadron 12 (Tobin). "Report of Action Off Savo Island, Solomons, Night of 11–12 October 1942." Serial 022, October 23, 1942. NARA.

———. "Report of Night Action Off Savo Island, November 13, 1942." Serial 0033, November 27, 1942. NARA.

Commander, Motor Torpedo Boat Flotilla 1 (A. P. Calvert). "Summary of Motor Torpedo Boat Combat Action in the Solomon Islands, 13 October, 1942, to 2 February, 1943." Serial 026, March 7, 1943. NARA.

Commander, Scouting Squadron 3 (VS-3). "Report of Operations at Guadalcanal Island," October 25, 1942. NARA.

Commander, South Pacific Area (COMSOPAC) (Ghormley). "Most Secret Letter to Admiral Nimitz," serial 0072, July 29, 1942. NARA.

———. "Preliminary Report, Watchtower Operation." Serial 0053, August 16, 1942. NARA.

———. "Advance Bases, South Pacific Area." Serial 0062, August 19, 1942. NARA.

———. "Commander Task Force 62 Communications During the Occupation of Tulagi and Guadalcanal" (First Endorsement of CTF 62, "Despatch Reports of Operations"). Serial 00626, September 6, 1942, NARA.

———. Administrative History Appendices, 1942. Operational Archives, NHC.

———. "Events Leading Up to U.S. Attack on Solomon Islands, Etc." (transcript of recording by Vice Adm. Ghormley). WWII Command File, January 22, 1943, Operational Archives, NHC.

———. "History of U.S. Naval Advanced Base Guadalcanal, 1942–1945," undated, WWII Command File, Shore Establishments, NHC, Box 417.

———. (compiled by Lt. D. C. Rudd, Flag Plot, ComSoPac staff). "Operational History of the South Pacific," undated (compiled in 1945), WWII Command File, Box 288. NARA.

Commander, Task Force 16 (USS *Enterprise*). "Operations of Task Force 16 in the Action for the Defense of Guadalcanal, 12–15 November 1942." Serial 0088, November 23, 1942. NARA.

Commander, Task Force 18 (USS *Wasp*), War Diary, August 1942. NARA.

Commander, Task Force 62 (Turner). "Despatch Reports of Operations During Occupation of Tulagi and Guadalcanal." Serial 0051, August 16, 1942. NARA.

————. War Diary, July–August 1942. NARA.

Commander, Task Force 67 (Wright). "Report on Action Off Cape Esperance, Night of November 30, 1942." Serial 06, December 9, 1942. NARA.

————. Operation Plan No. 1-42. Serial 01, November 27, 1942. NARA.

Commander, Task Group 62.6 (Crutchley). "Operation Watchtower—the Capture and Occupation by United Nations Forces of Tulagi and Guadalcanal." No serial, August 13, 1942. NARA.

————. "Explanatory Memorandum." No serial, February 21, 1943. Hepburn Report Annex.

Commander, Task Group 64.2 (Scott). "Memorandum for Task Group 64.2." Serial 0012, October 9, 1942. NARA.

————. "Memorandum Number Two." Serial 0013, October 10, 1942. NARA.

————. "Report of Night Action, 11–12 October 1942." Serial 0014, October 22, 1942. NARA.

Commander, Task Unit 17.5.4 (Destroyer Squadron 2), "Action in Coral Sea Area on May 8, 1942, Report of." Serial 080, May 18, 1942. www.ibiblio.org/hyperwar /USN/rep/Coral/ComDesRon2.html (last page view March 7, 2010).

Commander, Task Unit 67.2.3 (Tisdale). "Report of Action—Night of November 30–December 1, 1942." Serial 042, December 6, 1942. NARA.

Commander in Chief, U.S. Fleet (COMINCH) (King). Chart Room Collection of Dispatches and Related Records, South Pacific Action Dispatches, June 30–December 31, 1942. NARA, Records of the Chief of Naval Operations, RG 38, Entry NHC-53, Boxes 114–115.

————. "Battle Experience: Solomon Islands Actions, August and September 1942" (Secret Information Bulletin No. 2), March 1, 1943. WWII Command File, Box 260, Operational Archives, NHC.

————. "Battle Experience: Solomon Islands Actions, October 1942" (Secret Information Bulletin No. 3), March 15, 1943. WWII Command File, Box 260, Operational Archives, NHC.

————. "Battle Experience: Solomon Islands Actions, November 1942" (Secret Information Bulletin No. 4), March 25, 1943, written by R. S. Edwards, COMINCH chief of staff. WWII Command File, Boxes 260–261, Operational Archives, NHC.

————. "Memorandum for Admiral," July 31, 1943. NARA.

————. "Investigation of the Loss of the USS *Vincennes,* USS *Quincy,* USS *Astoria,* and HMAS *Canberra.*" No serial, September 14, 1943, NARA.

————. *First Official Report to the Secretary of the Navy,* March 1, 1944. Norwalk, Conn.: Easton Press, 2006.

————. "Comments by Fleet Admiral Ernest J. King, USN, on Chapter VI: Supporting the Guadalcanal Campaign," undated. NWC.

Commander in Chief, U.S. Pacific Fleet (CINCPAC) (Nimitz). Command Summary, "Grey Book" (operational orders), 2 vols. NHC, Operational Archives, Boxes 1–4.

——. "Gunnery Bulletin No. 2–42," June 6, 1942. NARA.

——. "Supply of Reinforcements to Continue Campaign in South Pacific." Serial 0164, July 17, 1942.

——. "Preliminary Report—Solomons Islands Operation." Serial 02576, August 23, 1942 (first endorsement to COMSOPAC report of August 16, 1942).

——. "Solomon Islands Campaign, Second Savo Island Action, 11–12 October 1942, Preliminary Report." Serial 03151, October 30, 1942.

——. "Future Operations in the Solomons Sea Area." Serial 0259, December 8, 1942.

——. "Solomon Island Campaign, Second Savo Night Action, Night of 11–12 October 1942." Serial 03791, December 26, 1942.

——. "Preliminary Report of Action, 12–13 November 1942," Serial 03812, December 28, 1942. NARA.

——. "Solomons Islands Campaign—Battle of the Solomons, 11–15 November 1942." Serial 00554, February 18, 1943. RG 38, Box 1728, NARA.

——. "Solomons Island Campaign, 5th Battle of Savo—November 30, 1942." Serial 00546, February 15, 1943. NARA.

——. "Solomon Islands Campaign from Fourth Battle of Savo, 30 November, 1942, to Munda Bombardment, 4–5 January, 1943." Serial 00599, March 9, 1943. NARA.

——. "Report of Night Action, Task Force 64—November 14–15, 1942, The Third Battle of Savo Island." Serial 00617, March 18, 1943. RG 38, Box 1728, NARA.

General Headquarters, Far East Command, Military Intelligence Section, General Staff, Allied Translator and Interpreter Section. Japanese Monograph No. 98, Southeast Area Naval Operations, Part I, May 1942–February 1943, Document No. 40427.

Hepburn, Arthur J. "Report of Informal Inquiry into the Circumstances Attending the Loss of the USS *Vincennes, Quincy* and *Astoria,* and HMAS *Canberra,* on 9 August 1942, in the Vicinity of Savo Island (Solomon Islands)," Serial 001965, May 13, 1943, with annexes, 3 vols. NARA, RG 38, Boxes 1727–1728.

HMAS *Australia.* "Night Action Off Savo Island," August 11, 1942. NARA.

HMAS *Canberra.* "Loss of the HMAS Canberra," August 12, 1942. NARA.

Imperial Japanese Navy, Action Records, IJN warships *Aoba, Atago, Chokai, Furutaka, Kinugasa, Kirishima,* August–November 1942. Records of Japanese Navy and Related Documents, Operational Archives, NHC, Box 55.

MacArthur, Douglas. *Reports of General MacArthur: The Campaigns of MacArthur in the Pacific,* 2 vols. Washington, DC: Government Printing Office, 1966 (originally published by General MacArthur's Tokyo headquarters, 1950).

MacKenzie, H. A. Lt. Cdr., RAN. "Report on Coast-Watching in the South Pacific Area Covering Period 1st June 1942 to 21st April 1943." SOPAC Administrative History Appendices, folder 34(19)(A), NHC.

Office of Naval Intelligence. "Guadalcanal and Tulagi Bases." WWII Command File, CNO Intelligence, Operational Archives, NHC, Box 118.

Turner, Richmond Kelly, to Ernest J. King. "Strategic Deployment in the Pacific Against Japan," March 26, 1942; secret note, March 27, 1942. NARA.

U.S. Naval War College, Office of the President (Adm. William S. Pye). "Comments on Action Reports Covering Activities in the Solomon Islands, August 7, 8, and 9, 1942." Serial 989, December 8, 1942. NARA.

———. "Comments on the Battle of Guadalcanal, November 11–15, 1942." Serial 2238, June 5, 1943. Ghormley Papers, Box 15, folder n.

———, Department of Analysis (Richard W. Bates and Walter D. Innis). *The Battle of Savo Island: Strategical and Tactical Analysis.* Newport, R.I.: U.S. Naval War College, 1950.

———. *Diagrams for the Battle of Savo Island: Strategical and Tactical Analysis.* Newport, R.I.: U.S. Naval War College, 1950.

U.S. Strategic Bombing Survey (USSBS). Interrogations of Japanese Officers. NHC.

> Masatake Okumiya, October 12, 1945 (USSBS No. 75)
> Hiroshi Tokuno, October 25, 1945 (USSBS No. 138)
> S. Yunoki, October 27, 1945 (USSBS No. 195)
> M. Matsuyama, October 31, 1945 (USSBS No. 255)
> Tadashi Yamamoto, November 20, 1945. (USSBS No. 467)
> Kikunori Kijima, November 27, 1945 (USSBS No. 464)

USS *Aaron Ward* (DD-483). "Report of Bombardment of Japanese Positions on Guadalcanal Island." Serial 001, October 18, 1942. NARA.

———. "Report of Action, Night of November 12–13, 1942." Serial 003, November 20, 1942. NARA.

———. "Recommendations Regarding Night Action of November 1213, 1942." Serial 007, December 30, 1942. NARA.

USS *Astoria* (CA-34). "Report of the Engineering Department of USS *Astoria* During and Subsequent to the Action with the Enemy at About 0200, August 9, 1942." No serial, August 18, 1942. NARA.

———, Executive Officer. "Night Cruiser Action Off Savo Island, Early Morning of 9 August 1942," August 19, 1942. NARA.

———. "Battle of Savo Island—Action Task Group 62.3, Early Morning August 9, 1942—Loss of USS *Astoria*." Serial 00500, August 20, 1942. NARA.

USS *Atlanta* (CL-51). "Engagement with Japanese Surface Forces Off Guadalcanal, Night of 12–13 November 1942, and Loss of the USS *Atlanta*." A-16–3, November 20, 1942. NARA.

USS *Bagley* (DD-386). "Night Engagement, August 9th, 1942, Tulagi-Guadalcanal Area." Serial 016, August 13, 1942. NARA.

USS *Barton* (DD-599). "Report of Action of November 12–13, 1942," November 26, 1942. NARA.

USS *Benham* (DD-397). "Report of Action, 14–15 November 1942." Serial 003, November 29, 1942. NARA.

USS *Blue* (DD-387). "Operations in Solomon Islands on Night of August 8th–9th, 1942." Serial 031, August 12, 1942. NARA.

USS *Boise* (CL-47). "Report of Action Off Cape Esperance on Night of 11–12 October 1942." No serial, undated advance copy. NARA.

USS *Chicago* (CA-29). "Action Against Enemy Forces, August 9th, 1942," Serial 099, August 12, 1942. NARA.

USS *Cushing* (DD-376). "Report of Engagement of Savo Island on November 13, 1942 and Destruction of USS *Cushing*." No serial, November 16, 1942. NARA.

———. "Loss of USS *Cushing*." No serial, November 19, 1942. NARA.

USS *Drayton* (DD-366). "Action Report, Night of 30 November–1 December, Off Northeast Coast of Guadalcanal." NARA.

USS *Duncan* (DD-485). "Detailed Report of Action of USS *Duncan* During Engagement with Japanese Forces off Savo Island, 11–12 October 1942." Serial 00735, April 26, 1943.

USS *Fletcher* (DD-445). "Report of Action." Serial S-1, November 15, 1942. NARA.

———. "Action Report." Serial S-3, December 3, 1942. NARA.

USS *Gwin* (DD-433). "Report of Night Action, 14–15 November 1942." Serial 047, November 16, 1942. NARA.

USS *Helena* (CL-50). "Report of Submarine Torpedo Attack on Task Unit and Sinking of USS *Juneau*." Serial 005, November 14, 1942. NARA.

———. "Report of Action Off North Coast of Guadalcanal, Early Morning of November 13, 1942." Serial 008, November 15, 1942. NARA.

———. "Report of Shore Bombardment, Koli Point, Guadalcanal Island, November 4, 1942." Serial 0012, November 15, 1942. NARA.

USS *Helm* (DD-388). "Report of Night Engagement Off Savo Island, Solomon Islands, August 9, 1942." Serial 129, August 14, 1942. NARA.

USS *Honolulu* (CL-48). "Action Report—Engagement Off Savo Island, Night of November 30th–December 1st, 1942." Serial 0142, December 4, 1942. NARA.

USS *Juneau* (CL-52). "Report of USS *Juneau* Activity from November 11 to 13, 1942, Inclusive." Serial 007, November 17, 1942. NARA.

USS *Laffey* (DD-459). "Battle Report of USS *Laffey*." No serial, November 14, 1942. NARA.

USS *Lamson* (DD-367). "Action Report, Night of 30 November 30–1 December 1942, Solomon Islands Area." Serial 00242, December 3, 1942. NARA.

USS *Lardner* (DD-487). "Report of Night Surface Action, November 30–December 1, 1942." No serial, December 8, 1942. NARA.

USS *Maury* (DD-401). "Report of Action with Japanese Surface Forces the Night of November 30–December 1, 1942, Off Savo Island." Serial 026, December 3, 1942. NARA.

USS *McCalla* (DD-488). "Report of Action Off Savo Island on Night of 11–12 October 1942." Serial 001, October 12, 1942. NARA.

USS *Minneapolis* (CA-36). "Action Report for 30 November–1 December 1942." Serial 0247, December 6, 1942. NARA.

USS *Monssen* (DD-436). "Report of Battle of November 13, 1942," November 16, 1942. NARA.

USS *New Orleans* (CA-32). "Action Report Covering Night Action November 30, 1942–December 1, 1942." Serial 637, December 4, 1942. NARA.

USS *Northampton* (CA-26). "Report of Action with Enemy." Serial 0109, October 31, 1942. NARA.

———. "Report of Action with the Enemy and Resultant Sinking of USS *Northampton*." Serial 06, December 5, 1942. NARA.

USS *O'Bannon* (DD-480). "Report of Engagement with Japanese Units on Morning of November 13, 1942." Serial 0134, November 17, 1942. NARA.

USS *Patterson* (DD-392). "Engagement with Enemy Surface Ships, Night of August 8th–9th 1942." Serial 001, August 13, 1942. NARA.

USS *Pensacola* (CA-24). "Report of Engagement with Enemy on the Night of November 30–December 1, 1942." Serial 0178, December 4, 1942. NARA.

USS *Perkins* (DD-377). "Report of Action, Night of November 30, 1942." Serial 01854, December 1, 1942. NARA.

USS *Portland* (CA-33), "Night Action Between Task Force 67.4 and Japanese Forces, November 13, 1942." Serial 073, November 21, 1942. NARA.

USS *Preston* (DD-379). "Report of Surface Engagement with Japanese Forces, November 15, 1942," November 30, 1942. NARA.

USS *Quincy* (CA-39), "Preliminary Report of Engagement the Night of 9 August 1942 Off Guadalcanal Island." Serial 004, August 12, 1942. NARA.

———. "Report of the Battle Off Guadalcanal Island, August 9, 1942" (by Lt. Cdr. John D. Andrew). No serial, August 15, 1942. NARA.

———. "Report of the Engagement the Morning of August 9, 1942, for Guadalcanal Island in Which the USS *Quincy* Participated" (by Lt. Cdr. Harry B. Heneberger). Serial 004, August 16, 1942. NARA.

———. "Additional Information in Regard to the ex-USS *Quincy,*" February 10, 1943. NARA.

USS *Ralph Talbot* (DD-390). "Preliminary Report of Action, August 8th–9th, 1942." Serial 03, August 11, 1942. NARA.

USS *Salt Lake City* (CA-25). "Offset Battle Practice," September 25, 1942. Records of the Commander, Cruisers, Pacific Fleet. NARA.

————. "Report of Action of USS *Salt Lake City* Against Japanese Surface Naval Units, Night of October 11–12, 1942, Off Savo Island, Solomon Islands." Serial 0140, October 19, 1942. NARA.

USS *San Francisco* (CA-38). "Action Report, Night Action, Nov. 12–13, 1942." Serial 067, undated, circa November 15, 1942, with battle damage report of Novmeber 20, 1942. NARA.

————. "Action Report —Loss of USS *Juneau,* November 13, 1942," November 15, 1942. NARA.

USS *South Dakota* (BB-57). "Action Report, Night Engagement 14–15 November 1942, with Japanese Naval Units, Off Savo Island." Serial 0165, November 24, 1942. NARA.

————. "Report of Gunfire Damage, Battle of Guadalcanal, 14–15 November 1942," undated. NARA.

USS *Sterett* (DD-407). "Report of Action on Night of November 12–13, 1942." Serial 005, November 20, 1942. NARA.

————. "Gunfire Damage, Battle of Guadalcanal, 13 November 1942," undated. NARA.

USS *Vincennes* (CA-44). "Report of Action Occurring Off Savo Island Area—Night of 8/9 August, 1942." Serial 0021, August 14, 1942. NARA.

————. "Report of Action Between USS *Vincennes* and Japanese Heavy Cruisers Near Savo Island on Night of August 8th–9th, 1942." Serial 0022, August 16, 1942. NARA.

————. "Additional Information Regarding Report of Action Off Savo Island Night of 8–9 August 1942." Serial 0029, September 5, 1942. NARA.

USS *Walke* (DD-416). "Report of Surface Engagement with Japanese Forces, November 15, 1942." Serial 00638, November 30, 1942. NARA.

USS *Washington* (BB-56). "Action Report, Night of November 14–15, 1942." Serial 0155, November 27, 1942. NARA.

USS *Wilson* (DD-408). "Report of Action Against Enemy Surface Ships Off Savo Island, Night of August 8th–9th, 1942." Serial 008, August 20, 1942. NARA.

Wright, C. H. to CINCPAC. "Performance of Duty in Action with Enemy." Serial P20–1, December 9, 1942. NARA.

Interviews

Akers, Frank (USS *Hornet*), interviewed September 10, 1942, by U.S. Navy, Bureau of Aeronautics. RG 313, Flag Files (Blue 361), Box 11, NARA.

Backus, Paul H. (USS *South Dakota,* turret officer), interviewed October 28, 1981, by Paul Stillwell. Naval Institute, Operational Archives Branch, NHC.

Baldwin, Hanson W. (journalist), interviewed June 16, 1975, by John T. Mason, Jr. Naval Institute, Operational Archives Branch, NHC.

Bennett, John E. (USS *San Francisco,* lieutenant junior grade), videotaped interview, December 1993. Courtesy of Johnny Johnson, USS *San Francisco* Association.

———, interviewed February 5, 1994, by Donald R. Lennon. Special Collections, Joyner Library, East Carolina University, Oral History Interview no. 138.

Berry, Joseph (USS *Helena,* supply department), interviewed March 23, 2007, by the author.

Clark, Gilbert H. (USS *Helena*), interviewed December 22, 2005, by Richard Misenhimer. NMPW.

Coates, Robert (USS *San Francisco,* radioman), interviewed February 4, 2009, by the author.

Cook, Jack (USS *Helena,* marine detachment, captain's orderly), interviewed December 14, 2006, by the author.

Davis, Glenn B. (USS *Washington,* captain), interviewed July 28, 1977, by Donald R. Lennon. Oral History Interview no. 46, Special Collections, Joyner Library, East Carolina University.

Egan, John (USS *San Francisco,* Marine detachment), interviewed March 5, 2007, by the author.

Eller, Ernest M. (CINCPAC staff), interviewed by John T. Mason, Jr., Naval Institute, August 25, 1977, October 18, 1977, and December 13, 1977. 2 vols. Operational Archives Branch, NHC.

Feindt, Donald J. (USS *President Adams*), interviewed May 2, 2003, by Richard Misenhimer. NMPW.

Fike, Charles L. (executive officer, Marine Air Group 23), interviewed by U.S. Navy, Bureau of Aeronautics, December 4, 1942. RG 313, Flag Files (Blue 361), Box 11, NARA.

Gardner, M. B. (COMAIRSOPAC chief of staff), interviewed January 13, 1943, by the Bureau of Aeronautics. Ghormley Papers.

Ghormley, Robert L., Jr., interviewed June 19, 2007, by the author.

Grahn, Alvin (USS *Hornet,* gunner's mate first class), interviewed by Tony Welch, http://carol_fus.tripod.com/navy_hero_alvin_grahn.html (last page view April 27, 2010).

Hagen, Robert C. (USS *Aaron Ward,* assistant communications and radar officer), interviewed February 8, 2007, by the author.

———, interviewed July 9, 2003, by Floyd Cox. NMPW.

Hamilton, William R. (USS *San Francisco,* gunner's mate first class). Interviewed March 19, 2007, by the author.

Harrison, Edgar (USS *San Francisco,* fire controlman first class), interviewed March 7, 2007, by the author.

Hechler, Ray (USS *Helena*), interviewed December 6, 2001, by William J. Alexander. NMPW.

Heiberg, Kristen F. (USS *Benham,* electrician's mate), interviewed October 6, 2000, by Phillip F. Reid. Naval Historical Foundation, Oral History Program, Operational Archives Branch, NHC.

Herndon, Charles K. (USS *San Francisco,* signalman third class). Interviewed February 1, 2009, by the author.

Howe, Robert M. (USS *Helena*), interviewed October 21, 2000, by William G. Cox. NMPW.

Johnson, Johnny (USS *San Francisco,* supply department), interviewed March 5, 2007, by the author.

LaCouture, John E. (USS *Blue,* gunnery officer), interviewed October 9, 2000, by David F. Winkler. Naval Historical Foundation, Oral History Program, Operational Archives Branch, NHC.

Lamar, Hal (CINCPAC staff), interviewed in "The Nimitz Story," Elarco Productions, the Admiral Nimitz Foundation, 1988. Arthur Holch, producer.

Luehman, Earl A. (USS *Helena,* turret officer), interviewed June 6, 1991, by Donald R. Lennon, Oral History Interview no. 129, Special Collections, Joyner Library, East Carolina University.

MacDonald, Donald J. (USS *O'Bannon,* executive officer), interviewed May 22, 1974 (1), July 23, 1974 (2), and August 5, 1974 (3) by John T. Mason, Jr., Naval Institute. Operational Archives Branch, NHC.

Mangrum, Richard C. (commander, VMSB-232), interviewed November 11, 1942, by the U.S. Navy, Bureau of Aeronautics. RG 313, Flag Files (Blue 361), Box 11, NARA.

Maysenhalder, Kenneth. (USS *Chicago,* store keeper second class). Interviewed July 9, 2007, by the author.

McClelland, James A. (USS *Helena*), interviewed March 20, 2003, by Richard Misenhimer. NMPW.

Melhorn, Charles M. (USS *Colhoun; PT-44*), interviewed September 1970 by Etta-Belle Kitchen, Naval Institute. Operational Archives Branch, NHC.

Mustin, Lloyd M. (USS *Atlanta,* assistant gunnery officer), interviewed twenty-one times between August 8, 1972, and August 8, 1973, by John T. Mason, Jr., Naval Institute. 2 vols. Operational Archives Branch, NHC.

Pearson, Tom (USS *San Francisco,* gunner's mate third class). Interviewed 2007 by the author.

Powell, John C. (USS *Astoria,* fire controlman first class), interviewed June 15, 2007, by the author.

Rivero, Horacio, Jr. (USS *San Juan,* assistant gunnery officer), interviewed November 1975 by John T. Mason, Jr., Naval Institute. Operational Archives Branch, NHC.

Schonland, Herbert E. (USS *San Francisco,* lieutenant commander and first lieutenant), interviewed October 1, 1983, by Karl Zingheim (Schonland 1) and November 1, 1984, by John T. Mason, Jr. (Schonland 2). Naval Institute. Unprocessed transcript.

Smith, John (commanding officer, VMF-223), November 10, 1942. RG 313, Flag Files (Blue 361), Box 11. NARA.

Smoot, Roland N. (USS *Monssen,* captain), interviewed November 1970–March 1971 by Etta-Belle Kitchen, Naval Institute. Operational Archives Branch, NHC.

Spencer, Clifford C. (USS *San Francisco,* Marine detachment). Interviewed September 24, 2008, by the author.

Stroop, Paul D. (COMAIRSOPAC, planning officer), interviewed September 14, 1969, by Etta-Belle Kitchen, Naval Institute. Operational Archives Branch, NHC.

Tarrant, Eugene (USS *San Francisco,* captain's cook), interviewed March 5, 2007, and April 11, 2007, by the author.

Ward, Alfred G. (USS *North Carolina,* fire-control officer), interviewed August 27, 1970, by John T. Mason, Jr., Naval Institute. Operational Archives Branch, NHC.

Weisenberger, Paul J. (USS *Helena,* machinist's mate first class), interviewed May 10, 2007, by the author.

Weschler, Thomas R. (USS *Wasp,* lieutenant), interviewed October 25, 1982, by Paul Stillwell, Naval Institute, Operational Archives Branch, NHC.

Whitt, Joseph V. (USS *San Francisco,* seaman first class), interviewed November 16, 2005, by Chris Rich. Clermont County Public Library.

———. Interviewed April 4, 2007, by the author.

Wylie, Joseph C. (USS *Fletcher,* executive officer), interviewed May 21, 1985, by Paul Stillwell, Naval Institute. Operational Archives Branch, NHC.

———, interviewed December 17, 1985, by Evelyn Cherpak. NWC.

Personal Papers

Baldwin, Hanson W. Manuscripts and Archives, Sterling Memorial Library, Yale University.

Ghormley, Robert L. Special Collections Department, Joyner Library, East Carolina University.

Graff, Robert D. Collection of Robert D. Graff.

King, Ernest J. NHC, Boxes 19–20.

Kinkaid Thomas C. NHC, Box 3.

Nimitz, Chester W. NHC, Boxes 1–4.

Unpublished and Privately Published Eyewitness Accounts

Arison, Rae E. (USS *San Francisco,* navigation officer). "A Battle to Remember." USS *San Francisco* newsletter, June 1994.

Baker, R. W. (ed). *History of the USS* Washington, *1941–1946.* New York: Robert W. Kelly Publishing Corp. Cruise book, undated.

Barham, Eugene Alexander (USS *Laffey,* engineering officer). *The 228 Days of the United States Destroyer* Laffey *(DD-459).* Robert Schneller, ed. Unpublished manuscript. 1988. NHC. Courtesy of Robert Schneller.

Bennett, John E. (USS *San Francisco,* lieutenant junior grade). www.usssanfrancisco.org/Bennet%20Jack%20CAPT.htm.

Bennink, Richard E. Untitled narrative. Undated. Collection of Richard E. Bennink and NWC.

Bergstrom, LeRoy W. (ed.). *The USS* Patterson: *Shipmates and Memories,* 2 vols. Collection of Carol and Mike McGregor.

Casten, Ray J. (USS *Helena,* lieutenant junior grade tactical plotting officer). *Our Ship: The* Helena. Privately published, 1991. Collection of Jack Cook.

Coates, Robert (USS *San Francisco*). Untitled personal narrative.

Cochran, D. Binion (USS *Helena,* ensign). "Recollections, Naval Battle of Guadalcanal, Cruiser Action, November 13, 1942." Unpublished manuscript, circa 1978. Collection of D. Binion Cochran.

De Long, George A. (USS *Helena,* helmsman). Untitled narrative, undated. Manuscript Collection 226, NWC.

Ghormley, Vice Admiral Robert L. "Events Leading Up to U.S. Attack on Solomon Islands, Etc.," January 22, 1943. WWII Command File, Box 288, NHC.

———. "The Tide Turns: Early History of South Pacific Force and South Pacific Area." Manuscript, undated. WWII Command File, NHC.

Gibson, Vic (USS *San Francisco,* signalman). "As I Remember," undated. Collection of Charles K. Herndon.

Halsey, William F. Draft manuscript of memoirs, pp. 366–404. Collection of John Wukovits.

Hartney, Joseph P. F. (USS *Juneau,* signalman second class), as told to Robert C. Fay. "The Story of the USS *Juneau:* A Survivor's Tale of Fate and of a Modern Miracle." www.geocities.com/pentagon/4072/hartney/hartney.html, scanned from the collection of Margo Riedel (last page view April 10, 2009).

Heyn, Allan Clifton (USS *Juneau,* gunner's mate second class). Statement in memorandum to Roger Pineau, Office of the CNO, from Head of the Navy's Casualty Branch, April 26, 1954. NARA.

Iwabuchi, Sanji (IJN *Kirishima,* captain). Untitled, undated report. Courtesy of Anthony Tully.

Jarman, James T. (P-39 pilot, USAAF). Letter to J. A. Walsh (USS *Walke*), January 17, 1981. www.destroyerhistory.org/goldplater/416walke_wilde10.pdf (last page view February 22, 2009).

Jenkins, Donald E. (USS *San Francisco*). "A Real Belly Full," undated. Collection of Charles K. Herndon.

Jones, Pat (ed.) (USS *Astoria*). *The USS* Astoria *(CA-34) and the Men Who Sailed*

Her. USS *Astoria* Reunion Association. Privately printed, 1992. Collection of John C. Powell.

Kinkaid, Thomas Cassin (Task Force 16, commanding officer). *Four Years of War in the Pacific,* chapter 7: "South Pacific—1942." Draft manuscript. NHC.

Kittredge, George W. (USS *Chicago,* turret officer). Untitled personal account, undated. Collection of Charles K. Herndon.

Luey, A. T., and H. P. Bruvold. *The 'Minnie' or, The War Cruise of the USS* Minneapolis, *CA-36.* Privately published, 1946.

McKinney, William B. (USS *Atlanta,* electrician's mate third class). *CL-51 Revisited.* Collection of Robert D. Graff.

Mustin, Lloyd. Diary, December 23, 1941–October 27, 1942. Collection of Robert D. Graff.

Parker, Edward N. (USS *Cushing,* captain). Untitled narrative, 1982 (revised 1985). www.destroyerhistory.org/goldplater/376cushing_wilde03.pdf> (last page view on February 8, 2009).

Reed, Robert B. (USS *Preston,* ensign). "A Recollection." www.destroyerhistory.org/goldplater/firstperson379.html> (last page view on February 21, 2009).

Richardson, Ford L. (USS *Farenholt,* seaman first class). "My War," undated.

Sayre, Frank (USS *San Francisco,* chaplain). "Farewell Frisco," October 31, 1959. Collection of Charles K. Herndon.

The Showboat: BB-55, USS North Carolina. Privately published cruise book, undated.

Spencer, Clifford C. (USS *San Francisco,* Marine detachment). *The War Years: Hellfire and Glory.* Ramona, Calif.: privately published, 2001.

The Story of the USS Salt Lake City, *1929–1946.* Privately published cruise book, undated.

Thomason, Chester C. (USS *Monssen,* electrician's mate third class). Personal narrative, undated. Courtesy of Chester C. Thomason. www.destroyerhistory.org/benson-gleavesclass/ussmonssen/thomason_03.html (last page view February 2, 2009).

Wallace, John G. (USS *San Francisco,* lieutenant junior grade). usssanfrancisco.org/Stories%20Of%20The%20Men.htm. (last page view March 4, 2010).

Weaver, Charles W., Jr. (SOPAC operations staff, lieutenant). "Some Reminiscences of the Pacific War," speech, Nashua Rotary Club, May 6, 1963. NWC.

Wilde, E. Andrew (ed.). *The USS* Aaron Ward *(DD-483) in World War II: Documents and Photographs.* Privately published, 1998; revised 2001. www.destroyerhistory.org/benson-gleavesclass/ussaaronward/research483.html (last page view January 24, 2009).

Wristen, Henry A. (ed.) (USS *New Orleans,* seaman first class). *History of the United States Navy Ship* New Orleans, *CA-32* (incorporating the ship's official reports).

Revised edition, September 10, 2007. Revised again by Carl Hartzell and Hank Wristen, under the title *An Amended History,* November 2009.

Books and Articles

Abend, Hallett. *Ramparts of the Pacific.* Garden City, N.Y.: Doubleday, Doran, 1942.

Agawa, Hiroyuki. *The Reluctant Admiral: Yamamoto and the Imperial Navy.* New York: Kodansha, 1982 (original Japanese edition 1969).

Albion, Robert Greenhalgh, and Robert Howe Connery, with Jennie Barnes Pope. *Forrestal and the Navy.* New York: Columbia University Press, 1962.

Aldrich, Robert. *France and the South Pacific Since 1940.* Honolulu: University of Hawaii Press, 1993.

Arnold, H. H. *Global Mission.* New York: Harper, 1949.

Associated Press. "Boise Captain Gives Credit to His Crew," *New York Times,* November 24, 1942, p. 8.

———. "Bridge Blasted from Battleship by U.S. Destroyer off Guadalcanal," *New York Times,* January 13, 1943, p. 1.

———. "Five Iowa Brothers Lost in Pacific Battle," *New York Times,* January 13, 1943, p. 10.

———. "5 Sullivans Died, Survivor Writes," *New York Times,* January 15, 1943, p. 7.

Baldwin, Hanson W. "A Sailor-Diplomat Runs Up His Colors" (Adm. Arthur J. Hepburn), *New York Times,* July 5, 1936, p. SM9.

———. "The Naval Defense of America," *Harper's,* April 1941, p. 449.

———. "Lessons of the Solomons Campaign," *New York Times,* October 24, 1942, p. 3.

———. "Handling of the News of the War," *New York Times,* November 23, 1942, p. 10.

——— (ed). *The Navy at War: Paintings and Drawings by Combat Artists.* New York: Morrow, 1943.

Ballard, Robert D., with Rick Archbold. *The Lost Ships of Guadalcanal: Exploring the Ghost Fleet of the South Pacific.* New York: Warner, 1993.

Bath, Alan Harris. *Tracking the Axis Enemy: The Triumph of Anglo-American Naval Intelligence.* Lawrence: University Press of Kansas, 1998.

Battle Stations!: Your Navy in Action. New York: William H. Wise, 1946.

Becton, F. Julian, with Joseph Morschauser III. *The Ship That Would Not Die.* New York: Prentice-Hall, 1980.

Bennett, John E. "Callaghan Was Calm and Collected at Guadalcanal," *Shipmate,* April 1996, p. 18.

Bergerud, Eric M. *Fire in the Sky: The Air War in the South Pacific.* Boulder, Colo.: Westview, 2001.

Bix, Herbert P. *Hirohito and the Making of Modern Japan.* New York: HarperCollins, 2000.

Braisted, William Reynolds. *The United States Navy in the Pacific, 1909–1922.* Austin: University of Texas Press, 1971.

Brodie, Bernard. *A Guide to Naval Strategy* (3rd edition). Princeton, N.J.: Princeton University Press, 1944.

Brown, Herbert C. *Hell at Tassafaronga: The History of the Heavy Cruiser USS* New Orleans *(CA-32).* Reston, V.: Ancient Mariners Press, 2001.

Brown, Louis. *A Radar History of World War II: Technical and Military Imperatives.* Philadelphia, Pa.: Institute of Physics, 1999.

Buell, Thomas B. *The Quiet Warrior: A Biography of Admiral Raymond E. Spruance.* New York: Little, Brown, 1974.

———. *Master of Sea Power: A Biography of Fleet Admiral Ernest J. King.* New York: Little, Brown, 1980.

Bulkley, Robert J., Jr. *At Close Quarters: PT Boats in the United States Navy.* Washington, D.C.: Government Printing Office, 1962 (Naval Institute reprint, 2003).

Butcher, M. E. "Admiral Frank Jack Fletcher, Pioneer Warrior or Gross Sinner?" *Naval War College Review,* Winter 1987, p. 69.

Calhoun, C. Raymond. *Tin Can Sailor: Life Aboard the USS* Sterett, *1939–1945.* Annapolis: Naval Institute, 1993.

Casey, Robert J. *Torpedo Junction!: With the Pacific Fleet from Pearl Harbor to Midway.* Indianapolis: Bobbs-Merrill, 1942.

Chafe, William H. *The Paradox of Change: American Women in the 20th Century.* New York: Oxford University Press, 1992.

Chambliss, William C. "Recipe for Survival," *Naval Institute Proceedings,* July 1944, p. 949.

Claypool, James V. "God on a Battlewagon," *Chicago Tribune,* May 7, 1944, May 9, 1944.

———. *God on a Battlewagon.* Philadelphia: John C. Winston, 1944.

Collier's, "The Idea Is to Win," editorial, December 26, 1942, p. 70.

Cook, Charles. *The Battle of Cape Esperance: Encounter at Guadalcanal.* New York: Thomas Y. Crowell, 1968.

Cooke, Alistair. *The American Home Front, 1941–1942.* New York: Atlantic Monthly, 2006.

Coombe, Jack D. *Derailing the Tokyo Express: The Naval Battles for the Solomon Islands That Sealed Japan's Fate.* Harrisburg, Pa.: Stackpole Books, 1991.

Courtney, W. B. "We Must Win the Pacific," *Collier's,* December 26, 1942, p. 15.

Crenshaw, Russell S., Jr. *Naval Shiphandling.* Annapolis: Naval Institute, 1955.

———. *The Battle of Tassafaronga.* Baltimore: Nautical & Aviation Publishing, 1995.

———. *South Pacific Destroyer: The Battle for the Solomons from Savo Island to Vella Gulf.* Annapolis: Naval Institute, 1998.

Custer, Joe James. *Through the Perilous Night: The* Astoria*'s Last Battle.* New York: Macmillan, 1944.

Davies, Lawrence E. "Cruiser San Francisco Home; Took 'Big Ones First' in Fight," *New York Times,* December 12, 1942. p. 1.

———. "Hero Gets Medal on San Francisco," *New York Times,* December 13, 1942, p. 3.

Davis, Kenneth S. *FDR: The War President, 1940–43.* New York: Random House, 2000.

Davis, Stephen F., Jr. "Perfect in Every Respect," *Naval History,* August 2008, p. 26.

DeBlanc, Jefferson J. *The Guadalcanal Air War: Col. Jefferson DeBlanc's Story.* Gretna, La.: Pelican, 2008.

Dillard, Nancy R. "Operational Leadership: A Case Study of Two Extremes During Operation Watchtower," February 7, 1997, Joint Military Operations Department, NWC.

Dull, Paul S. *A Battle History of the Imperial Japanese Navy (1941–1945).* Annapolis: Naval Institute, 1978.

Dyer, George C. *The Amphibians Came to Conquer: The Story of Adm. Richmond Kelly Turner.* Washington: Dept. of the Navy, 1972. www.ibiblio.org/hyperwar/USN/ACTC/index.html (last page view April 27, 2010).

Evans, David C. (ed. and trans.). *The Japanese Navy in World War II: In the Words of Former Japanese Naval Officers* (2nd edition). Annapolis: Naval Institute, 1986.

Ewing, Steve. *American Cruisers of World War II: A Pictorial Encyclopedia.* Missoula, Mont.: Pictorial Histories, 1984.

Farr, Scott T. "The Historical Record, Strategic Decision Making, and Carrier Support to Operation Watchtower." Master's thesis. U.S. Army Command and General Staff College, Fort Leavenworth, Kans., 2003. www.dtic.mil/cgi-bin/GetTRDoc?AD=ADA416432&Location=U2&doc=GetTRDoc.pdf (last page view October 30, 2009).

Feldt, E. A. "Coastwatching in World War II," *Naval Institute Proceedings,* September 1961, p. 72.

Felker, Craig C. *Testing American Sea Power: U.S. Navy Strategic Exercises, 1923–1940.* College Station: Texas A&M University Press, 2007.

Ferrell, Robert H. (ed.). *The Eisenhower Diaries.* New York: Norton, 1981.

Flynn, Thomas E. "Etajima, The Japanese Naval Academy," *Naval Institute Proceedings,* December 1943, p. 1597.

Forgy, Howell M., with Jack S. McDowell. *. . . . And Pass the Ammunition.* New York: D. Appleton-Century, 1944.

Forrestel, E. P. *Admiral Raymond A. Spruance, USN: A Study in Command.* Washington, D.C.: Naval Historical Center, Director of Naval History, 1966.

Frank, Richard B. *Guadalcanal: The Definitive Account of the Landmark Battle.* New York: Random House, 1990.

Friedman, Norman. *U.S. Cruisers: An Illustrated Design History*. Annapolis: Naval Institute, 1984.

———. *U.S. Battleships: An Illustrated Design History*. Annapolis: Naval Institute, 1985.

Fuquea, David C. "Task Force One: The Wasted Assets of the United States Pacific Battleship Fleet, 1942," *Journal of Military History* 61 (October 1997), p. 707.

Garvey, John. *San Francisco in World War II*. San Francisco: Arcadia, 2007.

Genda, Minoru. "Tactical Planning in the Imperial Japanese Navy," *Naval War College Review*, October 1969, p. 45.

Generous, William Thomas, Jr. *Sweet Pea at War: A History of USS* Portland. Lexington: University Press of Kentucky, 2003.

Gilbert, Alton Keith. *A Leader Born: The Life of Admiral John Sidney McCain, Pacific Carrier Commander*. Philadelphia: Casemate, 2006.

Glover, Cato D. *Command Performance with Guts*. New York: Greenwich Book Publishers, 1969.

Grace, James W. *The Naval Battle of Guadalcanal: Night Action, 13 November 1942*. Annapolis: Naval Institute, 1999.

Graybar, Lloyd J. "Admiral King's Toughest Battle," *Naval War College Review*, February 1979, p. 38.

Gunther, John. *Roosevelt in Retrospect: A Profile in History*. New York: Harper, 1950.

Hailey, Foster. "Destroyer at Savo Sold Life Dearly," *New York Times*, December 11, 1942, p. 10.

———. "With a Task Force in the Pacific," *New York Times*, November 5, 1944, p. SM8.

Halsey, William F., and J. Bryan III. *Admiral Halsey's Story*. New York: McGraw-Hill, 1947.

Hamilton, D. Lee. "Our Greatest Resource," *Naval Institute Proceedings*, April 1943, p. 509.

Hammel, Eric. *Carrier Clash: The Invasion of Guadalcanal and the Battle of the Eastern Solomons, August 1942*. St. Paul, Minn.: Zenith Press/MBI, 2004 (derived/adapted from *Guadalcanal: The Carrier Battles*, Crown, 1987).

———. *Starvation Island*. New York: Crown, 1987.

———. *Guadalcanal: Decision at Sea—The Naval Battle of Guadalcanal, November 13–15, 1942*. New York: Crown, 1988.

———. *Guadalcanal: The U.S. Marines in World War II, A Pictorial Tribute*. St. Paul, Minn.: Zenith, 2007.

Hara, Tameichi, with Fred Saito and Roger Pineau. *Japanese Destroyer Captain*. New York: Ballantine, 1961.

Harter, C. J. "Higher Education for Officers' Stewards and Cooks," *Naval Institute Proceedings*, March 1937, p. 321.

Hartney, Joseph P. F., with Robert C. Fay. "The Story of the *Juneau*," *Our Navy*, Mid-December 1943, p. 4.

Hastings, Max. *Nemesis: The Battle for Japan, 1944–45.* London: Harper, 2007 (published in the U.S. under the title *Retribution*).

Hayes, Grace Person. *The History of the Joint Chiefs of Staff in World War II: The War Against Japan.* Annapolis: Naval Institute, 1982.

Hayes, John D. "Admiral Joseph Mason Reeves, Part I," *Naval War College Review,* November 1970, p. 48.

Henderson, William C., Jr. *Escape from the Sea: The USS* Helena—*Pearl Harbor to Kula Gulf and Beyond.* Los Altos, Calif.: Henderson and Associates, 1995.

Hersey, John. *Into the Valley: A Skirmish of the Marines.* New York: Schocken, 1943.

Heyn, Allen Clifton. "One Who Survived," *American Heritage,* June 1956, p. 65. www.americanheritage.com/articles/magazine/ah/1956/4/1956_4_64.shtml. (last page view March 7, 2010).

Hirama, Yoichi. "Japanese Naval Preparations for World War II," *Naval War College Review,* Spring 1991, p. 63.

Holbrook, Heber A. *The History of the USS* San Francisco *in World War II.* Dixon, Calif.: Pacific Ship and Shore, 1978.

———. *The History and Times of the USS* Portland. Dixon, Calif.: Pacific Ship and Shore, 1990.

Hone, Thomas C. "The Effectiveness of the 'Washington Treaty' Navy," *Naval War College Review,* November–December 1979, p. 35.

Hone, Thomas C., and Trent Hone. *Battle Line: The United States Navy, 1919–1939.* Annapolis: Naval Institute, 2006.

Hone, Trent. "U.S. Navy Surface Battle Doctrine and Victory in the Pacific," *Naval War College Review,* Winter 2009, p. 67.

———. "'Give Them Hell!': The U.S. Navy's Night Combat Doctrine and the Campaign for Guadalcanal," *War in History* 13, no. 2 (2006), p. 171.

Hornfischer, James D. *The Last Stand of the Tin Can Sailors: The Extraordinary World War II Story of the U.S. Navy's Finest Hour.* New York: Bantam, 2004.

Hough, Frank O., Verle E. Ludwig, and Henry I. Shaw. *History of U.S. Marine Corps Operations in World War II,* vol. 1: *Pearl Harbor to Guadalcanal.* Washington, D.C.: Historical Branch, Headquarters, U.S. Marine Corps, 1958.

Hoyt, Edwin P. *How They Won the War in the Pacific: Nimitz and His Admirals.* New York: Weybright & Talley, 1970.

Hurd, Charles. "Pacific Command Shake-Up Is Laid to Guadalcanal Crisis," *New York Times,* October, 25, 1942, p. 1.

———. "Navies Manoeuvre for Big Stakes in Solomons," *New York Times,* November 1, 1942, p. E3.

Hutchinson, John A. *Bluejacket: In Harm's Way from Guadalcanal to Tokyo.* New York: Vantage, 1995.

Jacobsen, Philip H. "Intelligence Contributions to U.S. Naval Operations in the

Pacific." www.microworks.net/pacific/intelligence/stemming_tide.htm (last page view January 15, 2009).

Jersey, Stanley Coleman. *Hell's Islands: The Untold Story of Guadalcanal.* College Station: Texas A&M University Press, 2008.

Jones, James. *WWII: A Chronicle of Soldiering.* New York: Grosset & Dunlap, 1975.

Kennedy, Bill. *Fearless Warrior: A Gunner's Mate on the Beach at Guadalcanal.* Jefferson, N.C.: McFarland, 1991.

Keyes, Ralph. *The Quote Verifier: Who Said What, Where, and When.* New York: Macmillan, 2006.

Kilpatrick. *Night Naval Battles in the Solomons.* Pompano Beach, Fla.: Exposition, 1987.

Kimball, Warren F. (ed.). *Churchill and Roosevelt: The Complete Correspondence,* vol. 1: *Alliance Emerging, October 1933–November 1942.* Princeton, N.J.: Princeton University Press, 1984.

———. *The Juggler: Franklin Roosevelt as Wartime Statesman.* Princeton, N.J.: Princeton University Press, 1991.

King, Ernest J., and Walter Muir Whitehill. *Fleet Admiral King: A Naval Record.* New York: Norton, 1952.

Kotani, Ken. *Japanese Intelligence in World War II.* Translated by Chiharu Kotani. New York: Osprey, 2009.

Kurzman, Dan. *Left to Die: The Tragedy of the USS* Juneau. New York: Pocket, 1994.

Lacroix, Eric, and Linton Wells, II. *Japanese Cruisers of the Pacific War.* Annapolis: Naval Institute, 1997.

Lanier, William D., Jr. "The Tyranny of Red Tape," *Naval Institute Proceedings,* July 1942, p. 919.

Larrabee, Eric. *Commander in Chief: Franklin Delano Roosevelt, His Lieutenants, and Their War.* New York: Harper, 1987.

Layton, Edwin T. with Roger Pineau and John Costello. *"And I Was There": Pearl Harbor and Midway—Breaking the Secrets.* New York: William Morrow, 1985.

Lea, Homer. *The Valor of Ignorance.* New York: Harper, 1909.

Leavelle, Charles, with Lieutenant Edward D. Corboy (anonymously). "The Log of the Mighty A," *Chicago Tribune,* in fourteen serial installments, March 21–April 3, 1943.

Leckie, Robert. *A Helmet for My Pillow.* New York: Random House, 1957.

———. *Challenge for the Pacific: Guadalcanal—The Turning Point of the War.* New York: Doubleday, 1965.

Lee, Clark. "How Japan Plans to Win," *Collier's,* May 22, 1943, p. 15.

London, Jack. *South Sea Tales,* 1911.

Lord, Walter. *Lonely Vigil: Coastwatchers of the Solomons.* New York: Viking, 1977.

Loxton, Bruce, with Chris Coulthard-Clark. *The Shame of Savo: Anatomy of a Naval Disaster.* Melbourne, Australia: Allen & Unwin, 1994.

Lundgren, Robert. *"Kirishima."* Internet posting, NavWeaps Discussion Boards, May, 7, 2009. http://warships1discussionboards.yuku.com/topic/9460/t/Kirishima. html. (last page view January 27, 2010).

———. *"Kirishima* Sinks." Internet posting, NavWeaps Discussion Boards, May 8, 2009. http://warships1discussionboards.yuku.com/topic/9460/t/Kirishima.html (last page view January 27, 2010).

———. "The Battleship Action, 14–15 November 1942," June 19, 2009. www.navweaps. com/index_lundgren/index_lundgren.htm (last page view December 14, 2009).

———. *"Kirishima* Damage Analysis," June 26, 2009. www.navweaps.com/ index_lundgren/index_lundgren.htm (last page view December 14, 2009).

Lundstrom, John B. *The First Team and the Guadalcanal Campaign: Naval Fighter Combat from August to November 1942.* Annapolis: Naval Institute, 1993.

———. *Black Shoe Carrier Admiral: A Biography of Frank Jack Fletcher.* Annapolis: Naval Institute, 2006.

Maclay, Edgar Stanton. *The Life and Adventures of Jack Philip, Rear Admiral, USN.* New York: American Tract Society, 1904.

McCandless, Bruce, with George Creel. "Mr. McCandless Takes Over," *Collier's,* January 30, 1943, p. 13.

———. "The *San Francisco* Story," *Naval Institute Proceedings,* November 1958, p. 35.

———. Letter to the editor, *Naval Institute Proceedings,* May 1963, p. 120.

McCormick, Robert. "King of the Navy," *Collier's,* January 16, 1943, p. 18.

McDowell, John. "The Terrible Ordeal of the USS *Juneau,"* *Sea Classics,* March–April 1986, p. 18.

McGee, William L. *The Amphibians Are Coming: Emergence of the 'Gator Navy and Its Revolutionary Landing Craft* (*Amphibious Operations in the South Pacific in World War II,* vol. 1). Santa Barbara, Calif.: BMC, 2000.

———. *The Solomons Campaigns: Pacific War Turning Point,* vol. 2: *Amphibious Operations in the South Pacific in World War II.* Santa Barbara, Calif.: BMC, 2002.

McMahon, Morgan, Edward A. Sharpe (ed.). "Morgan McMahon and Radar," Southwest Museum of Engineering, Communications and Computation, Glendale, Ariz. www.smecc.org/mcmahon's_radars!.htm (last page view October 29, 2009).

McMillan, George. "I Served My Time in Hell," *American Heritage,* February 1966. www.americanheritage.com/articles/magazine/ah/1966/2/1966_2_10.shtml (last page view October 29, 2009).

Merillat, Herbert Christian. *Guadalcanal Remembered.* New York: Dodd, Mead, 1982.

Miller, John, Jr. *Guadalcanal: The First Offensive.* Washington, D.C.: U.S. Army, Center for Military History, 1949.

Miller, Thomas G., Jr. *The Cactus Air Force.* Fredericksburg, Tex.: Admiral Nimitz Foundation, 1990 (originally published 1969).

Millis, Walter (ed.), with E. S. Duffield. *The Forrestal Diaries.* New York: Viking, 1951.

Moore, Stephen L., with William J. Shinneman and Robert Gruebel. *The Buzzard Brigade: Torpedo Squadron Ten at War.* Missoula, Mont.: Pictorial Histories, 1996.

Morison, Samuel Eliot. *The Struggle for Guadalcanal, August 1942–February 1943,* vol. 5: *History of United States Naval Operations in World War II.* New York: Little, Brown, 1949.

————. *The Two-Ocean War: A Short History of the United States Navy in the Second World War.* New York: Little, Brown, 1963.

Morris, C. G., and Hugh B. Cave. *The Fightin'est Ship: The Story of the Cruiser Helena.* New York: Dodd, Mead, 1944.

Morris, Frank D. *"Pick Out the Biggest": Mike Moran and the Men of the* Boise. New York: Houghton Mifflin, 1943.

————. "First Lap on Tokyo" (2 parts), *Collier's,* October 3, 1942, p. 16; October 10, 1942, p. 17.

————. "Mike Moran's Men" (2 parts), *Collier's,* February 6, 1943, p. 18; February 13, 1943, p. 26.

Morton, John Fass. *Mustin: A Naval Family of the Twentieth Century.* Annapolis: Naval Institute, 2003.

Mullins, Wayman C. (ed). *1942: "Issue in Doubt."* Austin: Eakin, 1994.

Murphy, Francis X. *Fighting Admiral: The Story of Dan Callaghan.* New York: Vantage Press, 1952. www.microworks.net/pacific/library/fa-chapter1.htm (last page view May 28, 2009).

Musicant, Ivan. *Battleship at War: The Epic Story of the USS* Washington. New York: Harcourt Brace Jovanovich, 1986.

Newcomb, Richard F. *The Battle of Savo Island.* New York: Holt, Rinehart & Winston, 1961.

New York Times. "Report on Annapolis Hazing," October 14, 1910, p. 8.

————. "Annapolis Hazers Punished," October 16, 1910, p. 1.

————. "U.S. Discloses Bases in Fijis and Hebrides," October 13, 1942, p. 1.

————. "Foe Massing for Guadalcanal Attack; Loses All of 14 Bombers in One Raid; Three Japanese Cruisers Believed Hit," October 19, 1942, p. 1.

————. "Callaghan Killed Leading in Battle," November 17, 1942, p. 1.

————. "Japanese Victory Claimed by Tokyo," November 17, 1942, p. 5.

————. "Admiral N. Scott Killed in Battle," November 18, 1942, p. 9.

————. "Admiral's Tribute to Wounded," November 21, 1942, p. 3.

————. "Callaghan Praised by Battle Comrades," December 2, 1942, p. 8.

————. "Japanese on Guadalcanal Believed New York Taken," February 24, 1943, p. 8.

O'Hara, Vincent P. *The U.S. Navy Against the Axis: Surface Combat, 1941–1945.* Annapolis: Naval Institute, 2007.

Ohmae, Toshikazu. "Japanese Commentary on Guadalcanal," *Naval Institute Proceedings,* January 1951, p. 57.

―――. "The Battle of Savo Island," *Naval Institute Proceedings,* December 1957, p. 1263.

Parrent, Erik (ed.). *Third Savo: Battle at Guadalcanal.* Paducah, Ky.: Turner, 1995.

Parshall, Jonathan. "Oil and Japanese Strategy in the Solomons: A Postulate." www.combinedfleet.com/guadoil1.htm (last viewed January 15, 2009).

Parshall, Jonathan, and Anthony Tully. *Shattered Sword: The Untold Story of the Battle of Midway.* Washington, D.C.: Potomac, 2005.

Parsons, Robert P. *MOB 3: A Naval Hospital in a South Sea Jungle.* Indianapolis: Bobbs-Merrill, 1945.

Percival, Franklin G. "Wanted: A New Naval Development Policy," *Naval Institute Proceedings,* May 1943, p. 655.

Pogue, Forrest C. *George C. Marshall: Ordeal and Hope, 1939–1942.* New York: Viking, 1966.

Poor, Henry V., Henry A. Mustin, and Colin G. Jameson. *The Battles of Cape Esperance, 11 October 1942, and Santa Cruz Islands, 26 October 1942.* Washington, D.C.: Naval Historical Center, 1994 (originally published without attribution as *Combat Narratives: Solomon Islands Campaign* by the Office of Naval Intelligence, 1943).

―――. *The Battles of Savo Island and Eastern Solomons.* Washington, D.C.: Naval Historical Center, 1994 (originally published without attribution as *Combat Narratives: Solomon Islands Campaign* by the Office of Naval Intelligence, 1943).

Pope, Quentin. "ANZACs Criticize Ghormley Tactics," *New York Times,* September 18, 1945, p. 5.

Potter, E. B. "The Command Personality," *Naval Institute Proceedings,* January 1969, p. 18.

―――. *Nimitz.* Annapolis: Naval Institute, 1976.

―――. *Bull Halsey.* Annapolis: Naval Institute, 1985.

Potter, E. B., and Chester W. Nimitz (eds). *Triumph in the Pacific: The Navy's Struggle Against Japan.* Englewood Cliffs, N.J.: Prentice Hall, 1963.

Prados, John. *Combined Fleet Decoded.* New York: Random House, 1995.

Pratt, Fletcher. *The Navy's War.* New York: Harper, 1944.

―――. *The Fleet Against Japan.* New York: Harper, 1946.

Rasenberger, Jim. *America 1908: The Dawn of Flight, the Race to the Pole, the Invention of the Model T, and the Making of a Modern Nation.* New York: Scribner, 2007.

Reeder, Russel P., Jr. *Fighting on Guadalcanal.* Washington, D.C.: Government Printing Office, 1943.

Reynolds, David. *In Command of History: Churchill Fighting and Writing the Second World War.* New York: Basic, 2005.

Roosevelt, Eleanor. "To Care for Him Who Shall Have Borne the Battle," *Collier's,* November 28, 1942, p. 20.

Ruiz, C. Kenneth, with John Bruning. *The Luck of the Draw: The Memoir of a World*

War II Submariner, from Savo Island to the Silent Service. St. Paul, Minn.: Zenith, 2005.

Satterfield, John R. *We Band of Brothers: The Sullivans and World War II.* Parkersburg, Iowa: Mid-Prairie, 1995; second edition 2000.

Schom, Alan. *The Eagle and the Rising Sun: The Japanese-American War, 1941–1943.* New York: Norton, 2004.

Sears, Stephen W. "A Coastwatcher's Diary," *American Heritage,* February 1966. www.americanheritage.com/articles/magazine/ah/1966/2/1966_2_104.shtml (last page view, October 29, 2009).

Seno, Sadao. "A Chess Game with No Checkmate: Admiral Inoue and the Pacific War," *Naval War College Review,* January–February 1974, p. 26.

Shalett, Sidney. *Old Nameless* (about the USS *South Dakota*). New York: Appleton-Century, 1943.

Shanks, Sandy. *The Bode Testament* (fiction). Lincoln, Neb.: iUniverse, 2001.

Shaw, Elizabeth R. P. *Beside Me Still: A Memoir of Love and Loss in World War II.* Annapolis: Naval Institute, 2002.

Shaw, Henry I., Jr. *The First Offensive: The Marine Campaign for Guadalcanal* (Marines in World War II Commemorative Series). Quantico, Va.: Marine Corps Historical Center, 1992.

Sheehan, J. M. "The Wardroom Mess," *Naval Institute Proceedings,* June 1936, p. 842.

Sherwood, Robert E. *Roosevelt and Hopkins: An Intimate History.* New York: Harper, 1948.

Simpson, B. Mitchell, III. *Admiral Harold R. Stark: Architect of Victory, 1939–1945.* Columbia: University of South Carolina Press, 1989.

Smith, S. E. (ed.). *The United States Navy in World War II.* New York: Morrow, 1966.

Soule, Thayer. *Shooting the Pacific War: Marine Corps Combat Photography in WWII.* Lexington: University Press of Kentucky, 2000.

Stafford, Edward P. *The Big E: The Story of the USS* Enterprise. Annapolis: Naval Institute, 1962.

Steinbeck, John. *Once There Was a War.* New York: Viking, 1958.

Stevenson, Nikolai. "Four Months on the Front Line," *American Heritage,* October–November 1985. www.americanheritage.com/articles/magazine/ah/1985/6/1985_6_49.shtml (last page view October 29, 2009).

Stille, Mark. *USN Cruiser vs. IJN Cruiser.* New York: Osprey, 2009.

Stoler, Mark A. *Allies and Adversaries: The Joint Chiefs of Staff, the Grand Alliance, and U.S. Strategy in World War II.* Chapel Hill: University of North Carolina Press, 2000.

———. *Allies in War: Britain and America Against the Axis Powers, 1940–1945.* London: Hodder Arnold, 2005.

Stoler, Mark A., and Melanie S. Gustafson (eds). *Major Problems in the History of World War II.* Boston: Houghton Mifflin, 2003.

Stone, I. F., and Karl Weber (ed.). *The Best of I. F. Stone*. New York: Public Affairs, 2006.

Tanaka, Raizo. "Japan's Losing Struggle for Guadalcanal" (2 parts), *Naval Institute Proceedings*, July 1956, p. 687; August 1956, p. 815.

Ten Eyck, J. C. "Industrial War Power," *Naval Institute Proceedings*, May 1944, p. 557.

Thach, John S. "The Red Rain of Battle: The Story of Fighter Squadron Three," *Collier's*, December 5, 1942, p. 14.

Thomas, Lowell. *These Men Shall Never Die*. Philadelphia: John C. Winston, 1943.

Toland, John. *The Rising Sun: The Decline and Fall of the Japanese Empire, 1936–1945* (2 vols). New York: Random House, 1970.

Tregaskis, Richard. *Guadalcanal Diary*. New York: Random House, 1943.

Trumbull, Robert. "Nimitz Confident After Pacific Trip," *New York Times*, October 15, 1942, p. 6.

———. "Mortally Wounded U.S. Destroyer Torpedoed Japanese Battleship," *New York Times*, December 19, 1942, p. 5.

Tucker, Richard W., as told to Michael Stern. "The Ship That Wouldn't Die," unknown publication, p. 6.

Tully, Anthony P. "Death of Battleship *Hiei:* Sunk by Gunfire or Air Attack?" 1997. www.combinedfleet.com/atully03.htm (last page view October 29, 2009).

Ugaki, Matome. *Fading Victory: The Diary of Admiral Matome Ugaki, 1941–1945*. Translated by Masataka Chihaya. Donald M. Goldstein and Katherine V. Dillon, editors. Pittsburgh: University of Pittsburgh Press, 1991.

United States Naval Academy, *Lucky Bag* (yearbooks).

Vandegrift, A. A., with Robert B. Asprey. *Once a Marine*. New York: Norton, 1964.

Walker, Charles H. *Combat Officer: A Memoir of War in the South Pacific*. New York: Presidio, 2004.

Weems, Ensign George B., with additional text by Captain F. A. Andrews, USN. "Solomons Battle Log," *Naval Institute Proceedings*, August 1962, p. 80.

Weinberg, Gerhard L. *A World at Arms: A Global History of World War II*. Cambridge, U.K.: Cambridge University Press, 1994.

Wetterling, J. D. "The Most Furious Sea Battle," *Los Angeles Times*, May 28, 2001.

Wheeler, Gerald E. *Kinkaid of the Seventh Fleet*. Annapolis: Naval Institute, 1996.

Wilhelm, Donald. "Radar, the Supersleuth," *Collier's*, May 22, 1943, p. 16.

Wolfert, Ira. "Solomons Battle a Fiery Spectacle," *New York Times*, November 28, 1942, p. 6.

———. *Battle for the Solomons*. Boston: Houghton Mifflin, 1943.

Wooldridge, E. T. (ed.). *Carrier Warfare in the Pacific: An Oral History Collection*. Washington, D.C.: Smithsonian Institution, 1993.

Wukovits, John F. *Admiral "Bull" Halsey: The Life and Wars of the U.S. Navy's Most Controversial Commander*. New York: Palgrave Macmillan, 2010.

Other Sources

Elarco Productions. *The Nimitz Story: From Fredericksburg to Tokyo Bay.* Documentary. Produced by Arthur Holch. Narrated by Walter Cronkite. Fredericksburg, Tex.: Admiral Nimitz Foundation, 1988.

Fox Movietone News. "Hero 'Battleship X' Revealed to Be the USS *South Dakota*" (newsreel). Undated. Edited by Anthony Muto. Narrated by Lowell Thomas. University of South Carolina Newsfilm Library.

Houston, Floyd. "Stand Aside, This Is Ching," memorial speech, delivered to the U.S. Naval Academy Rifle Team, ca. August 2007. http://neveryetmelted.com/?p=2913 (last page view February 24, 2009).

National Geographic Society. *The Lost Fleet of Guadalcanal.* Video. Produced and directed by Robert Kenner. Written by Kage Kleiner. Madison Publishing, 1993.

The Dictionary of American Naval Fighting Ships, www.history.navy.mil/danfs/index.html.

The Imperial Japanese Navy Home Page, www.combinedfleet.com.

Naval History & Heritage Command, www.history.navy.mil/index.html.

The Naval Technical Board, www.navweaps.com/index_tech/index_tech.htm.

INDEX

ABC-1 agreement, 24, 383
Abe, Hiroaki, 111–12, 159,
        302
    and the IJN *Hiei*,
        324–25, 375
    Vanguard Force,
        111–12, 217, 223,
        224, 233–34
    Volunteer Attack Force,
        263–65, 270, 272,
        274–75, 277,
        282–83, 312
Adell, Cecil, 57, 60
Ainsworth, Walden L.
        "Pug," 88
aircraft (Japanese), 182
    Aichi D3A Val dive-
        bombers, 47, 182
    Guadalcanal Campaign,
        aircraft used in, 433
    kamikaze aircraft, 411
    Mitsubishi A6M Zero
        fighters, 47, 118, 124,
        192, 244–45, 255–56,
        324
    Mitsubishi G4M Betty
        medium bombers,
        46, 47, 48, 57, 118,

147, 192, 244–45,
        255–56, 257,
        405–6
    Nakajma B5N Kate
        torpedo bombers,
        192
    11th Air Fleet, 46–49,
        83, 159, 244
    See also under Santa
        Cruz, Battle of
aircraft (U.S.), 182
    B-17 Flying Fortress
        heavy bombers,
        96, 112, 118, 154,
        219, 223, 331, 370
    F4F Wildcat fighters,
        107, 111, 115–16,
        132, 147, 186, 198,
        255, 256–57, 322–23,
        324–25
    Guadalcanal campaign,
        aircraft used in, 433
    P-400 or P-39 Airacobra
        fighters, 182, 198,
        368
    PB2Y Coronado Flying
        Boat, 208
    PBY Catalina patrol

bombers, 96, 105,
        112, 115, 223
    SBD Dauntless dive-
        bombers, 105, 107,
        115, 132, 182, 198,
        237, 322–23, 324–25,
        339, 389
    shortages of, 107–8, 119,
        198
    TBF Avenger torpedo
        bombers, 105, 115,
        192, 339
    See also Henderson
        Field; *also under*
        Santa Cruz, Battle of
aircraft carriers (Japanese)
    aircraft aboard, 226–27
    See also Pearl Harbor
aircraft carriers (U.S.)
    aircraft aboard, 226
    as central to the fleet,
        11, 95, 106–7, 145
    Operation Watchtower,
        supporting, 34–35,
        41–42, 51–55, 81,
        95, 106–7
    Operation Watchtower,
        withdrawing from,

aircraft carriers (*cont'd*)
51–55, 81, 83,
97–98
two carriers, power of,
221
Aleutian Islands, 11
Alfred, Lord Tennyson, 307
Alhena (cargo ship), 146,
149
Alligator Creek, battle at,
110–11
Americal Division. *See*
U.S. Army, 164th
Infantry
Andrew, John D., 76
Anthony, Keithel P., 71,
90–91
Aola village (Guadalcanal
Island), 4, 5
Araki, Tsutau, 185
Arcand, Albert, 308
Arison, Rae, 261–62, 294,
306
Arnold, Henry H. "Hap,"
151–52, 202, 205
Australia, the sea-lanes to,
5, 6

Backus, Paul H., 134,
346, 362
Baird, Jim, 181
Baldwin, Hanson W.,
9, 103, 188, 202, 205,
239–41, 251–52, 403
Ball, Bill, 101
Barham, Eugene A., 277,
301
Barker, Seaman, 77
Bates, Walter, 84
Battleship Night Action
(Second Naval Battle
of Guadalcanal),
348–50, 352, 353–68,
436
Allied losses, 436

casualties, 357, 364, 436
friendly fire, victims of,
347
IJN *Kirishima*, hit and
scuttled, 363–64,
365–66
Ironbottom Sound,
magnetic inter-
ference from, 352
Japanese losses, 436
order of battle, **350**
PT boats and, 350, 352
survivors, 357, 369–70,
371–72
tactical error, 358–59
battleships (Japanese),
127, 131, 195
battleships (U.S.), 21–22,
89, 106, 127–28, 130,
137, 145
battleship sinking
battleship, 366
and fuel shortages, 22,
383
officer's dining facilities,
253
primacy of, 302
treaty limitations on,
345–46
Beckmann, Alcorn G., 176
Becton, Julian, 276, 277,
307
beer shipments, theft of,
396
Bell Labs, 102
Bennett, Jack, 254, 261–62,
291, 297, 304, 314,
315–16, 329, 340
Bode, Howard D., 29, 54,
56–58, 59–61, 80, 82,
89, 127, 406
and Hepburn's inquiry,
415, 420–21
Hepburn's report,
reaction to, 418,
419–22

suicide, 421–22
15th Naval District,
assignment to, 420
Boles, Warren, 142, 162,
181
Bonaparte, Louis-
Napoléon, 37
Bondsteel, Lynford, 306
Bougainville Island, 6
Bouterse, Matthew J., 73,
78–79, 90
Brown, Julian P., 212
Browning, Miles, 337, 373,
380
Buchanan, Richard M., 339
Bull, Cornelius, 242
Burke, Arleigh, 98

Calhoun, C. Raymond
"Cal," 268, 275, 279,
313, 374, 378–79,
384
Callaghan, Daniel, Sr., 401
Callaghan, Daniel J.,
24–25, 32
and the Cruiser Night
Action, 266–67,
268–70, 275, 283,
288, 295
death of, 298, 304
and Hepburn's inquiry,
417
and Operation Watch-
tower, 33–36, 41–42,
151, 191, 238, 244,
254–55
posthumous Medal of
Honor, 375
radar, distrust of, 266–67,
268–69, 310
and the *San Francisco*,
244, 246, 249, 253–
54, 254–55, 259, 260,
261–62, 269, 288,
295, 298

Saratoga conference,
33–36
and Task Force 67.4,
248–49, 250–51, 252,
254–55, 259
temperament, 382
Calvert, Alan P., 333
Cape Esperance, Battle of,
157–66, **165**, **167**,
168, 169–78, 179–88,
191–92, 205–6,
241–42, 435
after-action report,
241–42
Allied losses, 435
casualties, 435
friendly fire, victims of,
177–78, 186, 187
Japanese losses, 435
lessons learned,
187–88
loss of control, 172–78
map, **167**
Order of Battle, **165**
press and, 205
Scott's tactical error,
169–71
Carl, Marion, 154
Carlson, Evans, 215
Carroll, Lewis, 41
Carroll, Thomas, 320–21
Casten, Ray, 289
Cates, Clifton B., 110
Chicago Tribune, 240
Churchill, Winston, 12,
13, 383
Chute, Robert, 409
Clagett, John, 407
Claypool, James V., 234,
349, 361
Clemens, Martin, 4, 15,
41, 110
Cochran, Bin, 273, 284,
312, 380
Coffin, Albert P., 322
Cole, William, 310

Coleman, George L., 63
Coleridge, Samuel Taylor,
260
Collett, John A., 227
Collier's magazine, 1, 7, 240,
424
Colonna, Jerry, 397
Cone, James I., 298, 327
Cook, Jack, 301
Cook, James, 5
Coral Sea, Battle of, 11, 83,
92, 171, 373
Corboy, Edward, 17, 18,
116, 243
Coward, Jesse, 275, 278–80,
313, 378, 412
Cresswell, Lenard B.,
110–11
Crouter, Mark H., 259, 293
Cruiser Night Action (First
Naval Battle of
Guadalcanal),
263–70, 273–81,
282–89, 291–96,
297–98, 299–310,
311–16
accomplishment of,
426–27
Allied losses, 436
Atlanta burning,
317–21
casualties, 315, 320,
326–37, 375, 436
IJN *Hiei* and, 265, 268,
274–75, 276–78, 279,
283, 291–94, 297,
299–303, 322
IJN *Hiei*, burning and
scuttling, 293, 302,
324–25, 328, 335,
336
IJN *Hiei*, Torpedo
Squadron 10 ("The
Buzzard Brigade")
attack on, 322–23,
324–25, 335

Japanese losses, 436
map (morning after in
Ironbottom Sound),
323
map (Nov. 12–13), **271**
Naval Academy rings,
collecting, 319, 327
order of battle, **270**
and radar technology,
266–67, 268–69, 310
survivors, 330–32,
340–41, 373–74,
374–75, 379–82,
398–99, 409–11
and Torpedo Junction,
327–30
cruisers (Japanese), 179
cruisers (U.S.), 137,
155–59
fire-control system, **164**
officer's dining facilities,
253
Crutchley, Victor A. C.,
xxi, 40, 47, 49, 54,
57
the Battle of Savo
Island, 58, 59–60, 65,
80, 417
and Hepburn's inquiry,
414, 417, 418
Cummings, Damon M.,
298
Curtin, Daniel, 288
Custer, Joe James, 39, 40,
41, 47–48, 64–65,
68–69, 72, 81, 84,
85, 87, 90, 210, 412,
423

d'Argenlieu, Thierry, 212
Davidson, Lieutenant
Commander, 75
Davis, Arthur C., 117, 231
Davis, Clenroe W., 166
Davis, Elmer, 242

Davis, Glenn B., 201, 348, 349, 353, 362, 364, 365, 366–67
de Gaulle, Charles, 37
De Long, George A., 328–29
Dean (fire controlman), 77
Decatur, Stephen, *xx*
Dempsey, Jack, 102
"Destroyer, A" (Steinbeck), 343
destroyers (Japanese), 120, 123–25
destroyers (U.S.), 137, 144–49
value of, 120
Dietz, Gilbert G., 73
Doolittle, Jimmy, 11, 22, 28, 228
DuBose, Laurance T., 260, 283, 288–89 299–303, 322, 332–33, 338, 350
Duke, Irving T., 142
Dusch, Robert, 304, 315

Eastern Solomons, Battle of the, 114–18
Allied losses, 435
casualties, 435
Japanese losses, 435
Edson, Merritt, 132, 148, 154, 215
Edson's Ridge, Battle of, 132
Efate (New Hebrides), *xxi*
Egan, John, 296
Eisenhower, Dwight D., 9, 14, 23
El Alamein, victory at, 247
El Cid, 144
Eller, Ernest M., 105, 143, 203, 347
Emory, Dallas, 201, 318, 332
Empress Augusta Bay, Battle of, 427

England
U.S. combat troops in, 383
Espiritu Santo (New Hebrides), 104–15
Evans, Ernest E., 412
Evins, Thomas A., 269, 276, 301

Federal Shipbuilding and Drydock Company (Kearny, NJ), 17
Fiji Islands
Operation Watchtower rehearsal, 32–33
Fike, Charles L., 125
1st Marine Division (Guadalcanal), *xxi*, 19, 27, 51, 132
tour of duty ending, 377
Fitch, Aubrey W., 158, 198, 224
Fitch, Jake, 374
Fitzgerald, Victor James, 374
Fletcher, Frank Friday, 260
Fletcher, Frank Jack, *xxi*, 8–9, 24
aircraft carriers, protectiveness of, 51–55, 81, 83, 97–98, 122, 367, 418
Battle of Midway, 11
Battle of the Coral Sea, 11
Battle of the Eastern Solomons, 114–18
and Hepburn's inquiry and report, 417, 418
and Operation Watchtower, 33–36, 39, 49, 50–55, 112–13, 114–15, 121, 122

Saratoga conference, 33–36
and Turner, 33–34, 35–36, 51–55
Florida Island (Solomon Islands)
Japanese air attack on, 46–49
See also Guadalcanal, Battle of; Guadalcanal Island; Savo Island, Battle of; Tulagi Island
Fontana, Paul, 256
Forgy, Howell M., 391
Forman, Andrew L., 391
Forrestal, James, 128–29, 130, 338, 419
Foss, Joe, 194, 255, 256
Fowler, R. L., 177
Fox Movietone News Agency, 402
France, Albert F., 341
Frank, Richard B., 53, 221, 426
Fraser, Peter, 28
Fraser, Thomas E., 356
Friday the 13th, Battle of. *See* Cruiser Night Action
Furst, Vince, 85

Garver, C. C., 116
Gash, Russell W., 266
Gatch, Thomas, 128, 134, 233, 234–35, 346, 354, 358, 360, 364, 366–67
Gavutu Island, 42
Geiger, Roy, 196, 199, 219, 237
German Navy (ships)
Bismarck, 182
Tirpitz, 201
Germany first strategy

ABC-1 agreement, 24, 383
vs. Pacific first strategy, 11–15, 130, 151–53, 382–83
Ghormley, Robert L., *xxi*, 20, 23–25
capability and perseverance, questions concerning, 119–20, 129, 154–55, 200, 202–3
Commander, South Pacific Forces (COMSOPAC), 33, 36, 37–39, 41–42, 87, 88, 91n, 97, 104–5, 106, 107, 114, 119–20, 121, 126, 128–29, 132, 137, 143, 151, 152, 153, 158, 191, 197, 206
and Hepburn's inquiry, 403, 417
Hepburn's report, commentary on, 417–18
and "Island Warfare," 38–39
relieved as COMSOPAC, 204–5, 206, 209, 213–14, 423–24
Saratoga conference, absence from, 33
and secrecy, 28–29
strain of command, 128–29, 130, 132, 151, 153, 202–3, 209, 211
Gibson, Jack, 65, 67–68, 71–72, 77–78, 85
Gibson, Robert D., 339
Giffen, Robert C., 405
Gone with the Wind (Mitchell), 17
Gorman, Charles C., 86

Goto, Aritomo, 158–59, 166, 175, 179, 183, 187, 233, 335
Gould, Frank, 313
Graff, Christopher (son), 427–29
Graff, Kenneth (grandson), 428–29
Graff, Robert, 16, 136, 144, 267, 284, 286, 287, 398–99, 410, 411, 412, 427–28
return to the *Atlanta* site, 427–29
Grahn, Alvin, 228, 232
Grant, Ulysses S., 215
Great Lakes Naval Training Station, 100–101
Great White Fleet, 30, 31, 210
Greenman, William G., 31, 320, 350
the Battle of Savo Island, 62, 63–64, 72, 73, 74, 84, 85, 89–90
and Hepburn's inquiry, 414
Gregor, Orville F., 102, 308, 322
Griffith, Samuel B., II, 426
Guadalcanal campaign
aircraft carrier support, 34–35, 41–42, 51–55, 95, 97–98
aircraft losses, *xix*
Allied losses, 435–36
Battle for Henderson Field, 217–22, 223–24
Battle of Cape Esperance, 157–66, **165, 167,** 168, 169–78, 179–88, 191–92, 205–6, 241–42, 435
Battle of Edson's Ridge, 132
Battle of Santa Cruz,

224–30, **226,** 230–36, 251–52, 436
Battle of Savo Island, 58–59, 60–61, 62–76, **65, 66,** 76–79, 81, 82–83, 84–91, 95, 104, 106, 240–42, 435
Battle of Tassafaronga, 385–93, **393, 394,** 395–97
Battle of the Eastern Solomons, 114–18, 435
Battleship Night Action (Second Naval Battle of Guadalcanal), 348–50, **350, 351,** 352, 353–68, 436
beer shipments, theft of, 396
black market, 396
Cactus Control, 349–50, 364
casualties, *xix,* 89, 93, 435–36, 447. *See also* under separate battles
Cruiser Night Action (First Naval Battle of Guadalcanal), 263–70, **270, 271,** 272, 273–81, 282–89, 291–96, 297–98, 299–310, 311–16, 317–25, 326–34, 436
expeditionary force, 27–29, 31–32, 32–36, 29–43
Henderson Field. *See* Henderson Field
Ichiki's assault, 109–11
importance of, *xvii–xx,* 212–13

Guadalcanal campaign
(*cont'd*)
Japanese garrison, 11,
111, 120, 132, 197,
121, 132, 146–49,
155–56, 395
Japanese garrison,
attempts to reinforce,
120–21, 123–26, 132,
146–49, 155–56, 212,
244–45, 250
Japanese garrison,
bombardment and
air attacks on,
146–48, 206–7,
213, 246–47
Japanese garrison,
evacuation
(Operation KE),
402–8
Japanese losses, 435–36
Japanese naval
bombardment and
air attacks, 105–6,
123–24, 132, 147,
159, 192–99, 244–45,
246, 335–36, 337–38
landing, Japanese
resistance to, 42–43
logistics (fuel,
reinforcements, and
supplies), 22–23,
35–36, 50–51, 87–88,
89, 104–5, 157
medals and commen-
dations, 375–76,
378–79, 393, 400
Nagumo's Striking
Force, 58, 69, 111,
114, 125, 159, 217,
218, 219, 221, 236
naval losses, 435–36, 437
Nouméa (New
Caledonia), *xxi*, 37–
39, 104, 209–12, 230

as "Operation
Shoestring," 23
preparations, 19–20,
21–23, 23–25
press and, 205, 213,
237–42, 251–52, 401,
412–13
Saratoga conference,
33–36
the Slot (New Georgia
Sound), **26**, 137
submarine threat, 62,
121–22
U.S. Navy (August
1942), *xxi*
U.S. Navy (October 18,
1942), **214**
warship losses, *xix*
See also Operation
Watchtower; radar
technology
Guadalcanal Island
(Solomon Islands)
Australia, as the sea-
lanes to, 5, 6
expeditionary force
arrival at, 39–43
geography and history,
5–6
Henderson Field. *See*
Henderson Field
Japanese interest in, 5
Lever Brothers coconut
plantation, 6,
39–40, 42
Mosquito Network
(armed forces
radio), 307
New Georgia Sound
(the Slot), **26**,
137
transformation of,
396–97
See also Florida Island;
Guadalcanal, Battle
of; Savo Island,

Battle of; Tulagi
Island
Gunnery, naval
exercises conducted by
Norman Scott,
137–40, 157, 181,
187
fire-control systems
(cruiser), 164

Hagen, Bob, 100–101, 267,
307–8, 322, 412
Haines, Preston B., 29
Haines, Richard A., 391
Hale, Richard, 123, 186–87,
276, 278
Hall, Perry, 279–80, 313
Halligan (chief electrician),
74
Halloran, Paul M., 339
Halsey, William F., Jr.,
11, 24, 130–31,
208–12
Commander, South
Pacific Forces
(COMSOPAC),
208–12, 218, 220–22,
224, 238–39, 244,
246, 249–50, 251,
290, 336–37, 348–49,
367, 372, 373–74,
381n, 383, 386, 403,
408, 426
Henderson Field, visit
to, 245–46
and Hepburn's inquiry,
414, 417
and Hoover's ability to
command, 373–74,
379–81
informality and
management style,
210–12, 238, 245–46
Japanese, public
tauntings of, 210

and the *Juneau*
    survivors, 373–74,
    379–82
Nouméa reorganization,
    209–12, 230
Rabaul as new strategic
    objective, 384
relieves Ghormley,
    204–5, 206, 209,
    213–14, 423–24
Handy, Thomas T., 382–83
Hank, William E., 276–77
Hara, Tameichi, 111, 131,
    235, 264, 265, 272,
    278, 303, 307–8
Hardison, Osborne B., 231
Harmon, Leonard Roy,
    305–7
Harmon, Millard F., 221
Harper's magazine, 188
Harrison, Edgar, 289, 411,
    413
Hartney, Joseph, 265–66,
    300, 374
Hashimoto, Shintaro, 354,
    359, 406–7
Hayes, John D., 84, 86
Hayter, Hubert M., 390–91
Henderson, Lofton R., 105
Henderson Field (Guadal-
    canal Island), 102,
    107–8, 111, 186
    aircraft at, 192, 198
    aircraft shortages,
        107–8, 119, 132
    Battle of Edson's Ridge,
        132
    Cactus Air Force, 102,
        105, 107–8, 111,
        118, 120, 124–26,
        147, 153, 191–92,
        196–97, 198, 237,
        325, 338–40, 342,
        348–49, 359, 405
    Fighter One airstrip,
        132

fuel shortages, 198
Halsey's visit to, 245–46
IJN *Hiei*, Torpedo
    Squadron 10 ("The
    Buzzard Brigade")
    attack on, 322–23,
    324–25, 335
Japanese garrison,
    attacks by, 132, 224,
    237
Japanese garrison,
    offensive against,
    243–44, 246–47
Japanese garrison,
    supplying. *See* Tokyo
    Express
Japanese naval
    bombardment and
    air attacks, 105–6,
    123–24, 132, 147,
    159, 192–99, 238,
    239, 244–45, 246,
    254–59, 263–65,
    335–36, 337–38
Marine Bombing
    Squadron 232
    (VMSB-232), 107
Marine Corps Pioneers,
    51
Marine Fighter
    Squadron 223
    (VMF-223), 107,
    113
Nimitz's recommended
    improvements, 154
Henderson Field, Battle for,
    217–22, 223–24
    casualties, 224
Heneberger, H. B.
    and Hepburn's inquiry,
    414
Heneberger, R. G., 63
Hepburn, Arthur J.
    inquiry and report,
    402–3, 414–15,
    416–19

Heyn, Allen, 312, 370, 371,
    374, 414
Hicks, Benjamin, 321
Hicks, Stanley, 321
Higdon, Harry S., 294, 295,
    297, 315
Hill, Harry W., 383
Hirohito, Emperor, 44,
    263, 404
Hisamune, Yonejiro, 175
Hitler, Adolph, 12, 407
HMAS *Australia*, xxi, 27,
    49, 54, 57, 80, 88,
    414, 417
HMAS *Canberra*, 27, 49, 54,
    59, 60, 61, 64, 80,
    81–82, 127
    sinking of, 127, 435
HMS *Exeter*, 127
HMAS *Hobart*, 49, 88
HMS *Hood*, 182, 335
HMS *Prince of Wales*, 48
HMS *Repulse*, 48
Holcomb, Thomas, 219
Hollingsworth, Sam, 142
Hooper, Edwin B., 127, 209,
    348, 363
Hoover, Gilbert C., 140–41,
    143, 155, 162, 340
    Cruiser Night Action,
        171, 181, 241, 256,
        261, 267, 269, 273,
        289, 303, 311–13
    and the *Juneau*
        survivors, 330–32,
        370, 373–74, 379–82
    reassignment of,
        379–82, 418
    Task Force 67, taking
        command of,
        314–15, 326,
        327–32
    and Torpedo Junction,
        327–30
Hoover, Herbert, 141
Hope, Bob, 397

Howe, Robert, 141, 262, 311–12, 330

Hubbard, Joseph C., 259, 294–95

Hyakutake, Harukichi, 217, 224, 237, 407

Hynes, Samuel, 100

Ichiki, Kiyonao, 109–11

Ijuin, Matsuji, 360, 366

Imperial Japanese Army Guadalcanal garrison, 11, 111, 120, 132, 197, 121, 123–26, 155–56, 243–44, 246–47, 250

2nd Army, 155

2nd (Sendai) Division, 217–18, 219, 244, 407

17th Army, 45, 112, 124, 131–32, 148, 217, 239, 244, 407

38th Division, 217

Imperial Japanese Navy (IJN)

Combined Fleet, 11, 44, 111–12, 120, 131, 212, 221, 244–45, 250

fuel shortages, 131, 150, 258

IJ Army, competition with, 45, 131–32

IJN 8th Fleet, 45, 217

IJN 11th Air Fleet, 45, 244

loss of confidence, 425–26

night training, 392

Rabaul (New Britain), base at, 5, 19, 20, 46, 105

Tokyo Express, 109, 120–21, 126, 144, 146–49, 155–56,

158–59, 166, 196–97, 197–99, 212, 217, 238–39, 244–45, 254, 263, 283, 335, 342, 348–49, 368, 385, 387, 395, 396, 408, 425

Truk conferences, 45, 131

Truk naval base, 45, 59, 82, 83, 92, 111, 114, 227

Imperial Japanese Navy (Battle of Guadalcanal)

Advance Force, 111, 159, 217, 218, 219, 225, 227, 232, 250, 339, 349, **350**, 354–56

aftermath, 398–408

aircraft losses, *xxi*, 425

Battle for Henderson Field, 217–22, 223–24

Battle of Cape Esperance, 157–66, **165**, **167**, 168–78, 179–88, 191–92, 205–6, 241–42, 435, 425

Battle of Edson's Ridge, 132

Battle of Santa Cruz, 224–30, **226**, 230–36, 436, 251–52

Battle of Savo Island, 58–59, 60–61, 62–76, **65**, **66**, 76–79, 81, 82–83, 84–91, 95, 104, 106, 240–42, 435

Battle of Tassafaronga, 385–93, **393**, **394**, 395–97

Battle of the Eastern Solomons, 114–18, 435

Battleship Night Action (Second Naval Battle of Guadalcanal), 348–49, 349–50, **350, 351**, 352, 436, 353–61, 361–68

Bombardment Force, **270**, 324, 335–36, 354–56, 359–60, 364

captains dying with their ships, 185

casualties, *xix*, 425, 447

Cruiser Night Action (First Naval Battle of Guadalcanal), 263–70, **270, 271**, 272, 273–81, 282–89, 291–96, 297–98, 299–310, 311–16, 317–21, 436

Guadalcanal garrison, supplying. *See* Tokyo Express

Henderson Field, naval bombardment and air attacks on, 105–6, 123–24, 132, 147, 159, 192–99, 238, 239, 244–45, 246, 254–59, 263–65

importance of, 11, 121, 375, 398, 423, 424–29

intelligence failure, 44, 45

naval losses, 435–36, 437

Operation KE (Japanese Guadalcanal garrison evacuation), 402–8

operational code groups, 28–29, 45

Striking Force, 58, 69, 111, 114, 125, 159, 217, 218, 219, 221, 224, 229, 236

Tokyo Express, 109, 120–21, 126, 144,

146–49, 155–56,
158–59, 166, 196–97,
197–99, 212, 217,
238–39, 244–45, 254,
263, 283, 335, 342,
348–49, 368, 385,
387, 395, 396, 408,
425
Truk conferences, 45,
131
U.S. landing, response
to, 44–49
Vanguard Force,
111–12, 217, 223,
224, 233–34
Volunteer Attack Force,
263–65, 270, 272,
274–75, 277, 282–83
warship losses, *xix*
11th Air Fleet, 46–49
Imperial Japanese Navy
(ships)
Akatsuki, 273, 274, 293,
335
Amatsukaze, 264, 265,
272, 278, 303, 307
Aoba, 46, 59, 64, 75, 76,
82–83, 158, 166, 173,
175, 183
Asagumo, 292, 300,
365–66
Atago, 336, 340, 348–49,
354, 359, 360, 362,
364, 366
Ayanami, 356, 359
Chikuma, 230
Chitose, 159
Chokai, 46, 59, 64, 70,
75, 81, 82–83, 197,
250, 339
Fubuki, 166
Furutaka, 46, 59, 70,
82–83, 158–59,
166, 178, 183,
185–86
Fuso, 366n

Haruna, 159, 192, 195,
250, 263, 336
Harusame, 265, 268, 279
Hatsuyuki, 166
Hayashio, 263
Hiei, 83, 112, 131, 159,
217, 250, 265, 268,,
274–75, 276–78, 279,
283, 291–94, 297,
299–303, 322–23,
324–25, 335, 336,
375
Hiryu, 105
Hiyo, 159, 217, 233, 235
Ikazuchi, 274, 284
Inazuma, 274
Jintsu, 118
Junyo, 159, 217, 224,
231, 232, 250, 324,
403
Kako, 46, 59, 60, 64, 69,
70, 82–83, 91–92
Kawakaza, 112
Kinugasa, 46, 59, 64, 70,
75, 82–83, 159, 166,
180, 182, 186, 197,
250, 339
Kirishima, 83, 112, 131,
159, 217, 250, 265,
268, 272, 277, 291,
293, 300, 302–3,
312, 324, 336, 340,
346, 354, 359, 360,
361, 365–66, 375
Kongo, 159, 192, 195,
250, 263, 336
Kumano, 250
Makinami, 407
Maya, 198, 250, 337–38,
339, 349
Murasame, 292, 300
Musahi, 403
Mutsu, 112, 131
Mutsuki, 118
Myoko, 198
Nagara, 264, 265,

268, 275, 279, 336,
339–40, 354, 356,
360, 365
Nisshin, 159
Ryujo, 112, 114, 115,
118
Samidare, 292, 302
Sendai, 336, 354, 355,
359
Shiratsuyu, 120, 300
Shirinami, 355
Shoho, 11
Shokaku, 111, 115, 159,
217, 226, 228–30
Suzuya, 337–38, 339, 349
Takanami, 389
Takao, 336, 340, 348–49,
354, 359, 360, 364
Tenryu, 46, 59, 60, 76,
82–83, 245
Teruzuki, 366
Uranami, 355
Yamashiro, 366n
Yamato, 111, 127, 131,
218, 375, 403
Yubari, 46, 59, 70, 82–83
Yudachi, 265, 268, 270,
307, 308, 322, 335
Yugiri, 120
Yukikaze, 275, 325
Yunagi, 46, 59, 82–83
Yura, 218–19
Zuiho, 159, 217, 226,
226, 227, 230, 403
Zuikaku, 111, 115, 197,
217, 224, 226, 228,
233, 235, 403
See also aircraft carriers;
battleships; cruisers;
destroyers; motor
torpedo boats;
submarines;
torpedoes
Irish, Elijah W.
and Hepburn's inquiry,
414

"Iron Bottom Bay"
(Mahler), 93
Ironbottom Sound
magnetic interference
from, 352
morning after map, **323**
Irvine, Charles B., 226
Ishmael (fictional
character), 260
Iwabuchi, Sanji, 363–64,
365, 366

Jabberwock (Carroll), 41
Jackson, Andrew, 135–36
Jackson, Charles, 307
Jacobs, Randall, 100
Japan
U.S. attacks on, 11, 22,
28
U.S. landing on
Guadalcanal,
response to, 44–49
Japanese Navy. *See* Imperial
Japanese Navy
Jenkins, Don, 327, 330
Jenkins, John H., 277
Jenkins, Samuel P., 18,
106, 201, 206–7, 269,
273–75, 284, 285–87,
320, 332
Jenks, Henry P., 274
Johns, Wade, 72
Johnson, Harold L., 334
Johnson, Stanley, 240
Jones, James, 291
Jones, John Paul, *xx*
Joslin, Leonard A., 400
Jutland, Battle of, 102

Kawaguchi, Kiyotake,
121, 148
Kennedy, Bill, 193, 321
Kennedy, John F., 402
Kennedy, Joseph, 24

Keppler, Reinhardt J.,
305, 401
Kettering, Charles F., 10
Kikkawa, Kiyoshi, 270
Kimmel, Husband E., 8, 24
Kimura, Susumu, 264, 354,
359
King, Ernest J., *xxi*, 4–5, 31,
34, 88
Commander in Chief,
U.S. Fleet
(COMINCH),
12–14, 19–20, 53, 89,
119, 122, 129, 143,
202, 205, 382, 400,
425, 426–27
and Hepburn's inquiry
and report, 402–3,
414, 419
personality, 8–9, 238
and the press, 239–40,
241, 242
Kinkaid, Thomas, *xxi*,
27–28, 33, 89, 97,
117, 220, 221–22,
224, 227, 230, 233,
244, 252, 336, 337,
347, 383–84,
395–96, 387–88
Kittredge, George, 39
Knox, Frank, 7, 23, 214–15,
240
Kobayashi, Michio, 363,
364, 365–66
Koerner, Ozzie, 142
Kolombangara, Battle of,
427
Kondo, Nobutake, 111, 159,
361, 367, 375
Advance Force, 217, 218,
219, 225, 227, 232,
250, 339, 349, 350
Bombardment Force,
270, 324, 335–36,
354–56, 359–60,
364

Koro Island, 32
Kurita, Takeo, 195, 264

Laffan, John J., 173, 180
Lair, Rodney B., 298, 329
Lamar, Hal, 154
Lawrence, John E., 195
Layton, Edwin T., 204
Lea, Homer, *ix*
Leckie, Robert, 291
Lee, Willis, 144, 201,
218–19, 220, 222,
244, 245, 251, 252,
336–37, 397–88
Battleship Night Action,
345–49, **350**, 352,
354, 357, 359,
261–64, 366–67
gunnery expertise,
347–48, 361–62
and Hepburn's inquiry,
417
and radar technology,
347, 353, 355, 361
Task Force 64, 345–49,
350, 352
temperament, 382
LeHardy, Louis M., 298
LeHardy, Marcel, 36
Leslie, Dale M., 148
Leslie, Maxwell F., 116–17
Leslie, Raymond, 285, 319
Lever Brothers coconut
plantation, 6,
39–40, 42
Lincoln, Abraham, 215
Loeser, Arthur, 317
London, Jack, 5, 384
Loomer, F.C., 69
Lowe, Edward S., 298
Lucky (ship's mascot), 116
Luehman, Earl A., 283,
303
Lundstrom, John B., 426
Lunga Point, 40, 41

Lunga River, 43
Luttrell, Wyatt J., 84

Maas, Melvin J., 53–54
MacArthur, Douglas, 10,
    12, 19, 20, 31, 98,
    158, 212–13, 382,
    384, 398, 414
MacDonald, Donald, 191
MacKenzie (Australian
    coastwatcher), 195,
    198
Mahler, Walter A., 93
Mangrum, Richard C., 107,
    111, 125
Marco Polo Bridge
    Incident, 110
Marcus Island, 28
Marquardt, Dick, 315
Marshall, George, 5, 12,
    13–14, 19, 20, 151,
    382
Maruyama, Masao, 407
Maslo, Samuel, 163
Massachusetts Institute of
    Technology, 102
Mather, Major, 193
McCain, John S., *xxi*,
    33–36, 104, 115, 132,
    158, 158n
    and Hepburn's inquiry,
    417
McCandless, Bruce, 184–85,
    255, 261, 401
    commendations,
    375–76, 401
    Cruiser Night Action,
    283, 284, 287,
    291–92, 293, 294–95,
    297–98, 301, 304,
    314, 326, 329
McClellan, George B., 215
McCombs, Charles E.,
    308–9
McCullough, John, 298

McIntire, Ross, 249
McKinney, Bill, 268, 285,
    288, 318–22, 337–38,
    362, 399
McLaughlin, Ensign, 77
McMorris, Charles H., 155,
    157, 173, 175, 184,
    187, 246
Melhorn, Charles, 333
Merillat, Herbert, 198–99,
    218
Michener, James, *xx*
Midway Island
    battle of, *xix*, 11, 18,
    22, 28, 44, 45, 83,
    105, 418
    Japanese and, 11, 83,
    92, 115
Mikawa, Gunichi, 45, 46,
    58–59, 61, 65, 81,
    82, 127, 161, 168,
    197, 218, 250, 393,
    406
Mitchell, Margaret, 17, 18
Moby-Dick (Melville), 260
Moore, Bryant E., 157
Moore, Samuel N., 73, 76
Moran, Edward J. "Mike,"
    143, 155, 164, 170,
    173, 174, 175, 179,
    180, 181, 182, 184,
    186, 187
Moredock, Stewart, 286–87
Morison, Samuel Eliot,
    116, 392
Morris, C. G., 142
Morris, Chick, 137, 140–42,
    158–59, 162, 163,
    166, 172, 181, 187,
    247, 257, 258–59,
    267, 284, 300, 330,
    372–73
    and the St. Helena
    window, 373
Mosquito Network (armed
    forces radio), 307

motor torpedo boats, 129
Mount Austin, 43
Munro, Douglas A., 149
Murakami, Yonosuke, 125
Mustin, Lloyd M., 17–18,
    22, 97, 99, 103,
    106–7, 116, 138,
    200–201, 207, 217,
    248, 256, 261, 269,
    274, 285–88, 317,
    320, 322, 348,
    386–87, 388–90, 395,
    396, 410–11

Nagano, Osami, 44
Nagumo, Chuichi, 83,
    111–13, 182
    Battle of the Eastern
    Solomons, 114–18
    Striking Force, 58, 69,
    111, 114, 125, 159,
    217, 218, 219, 221,
    224, 229
"Naval Defense of America,
    The" (Baldwin), 188
Naval Research Laboratory,
    102
Nelson, Lord Horatio, 336
Nelson, Thomas C., 227
New Georgia Sound. *See*
    Slot, The
New Guinea, 98, 402
    as an U.S. objective,
    384
New York Times, 9, 57,
    155, 202, 205, 213,
    237–42, 251–52,
    401, 403, 423
Newsweek magazine, 14
Nickelson, William R. D.,
    Jr., 274, 285, 320
Nimitz, Catherine, 7, 95,
    205, 213, 235
Nimitz, Chester W., *xxi*,
    6–7, 99

Nimitz, Chester W. (*cont'd*)
  Commander in Chief,
    Pacific Fleet
    (CINCPAC), 7–8,
    9–10, 20, 21–23, 24,
    31–32, 34, 62, 89, 95,
    107, 125, 128–29,
    130, 151, 154–56,
    197, 198, 213, 235,
    301, 342, 367, 380,
    381n, 382, 400, 403
  and the *Decatur*,
    145–46, 155
  and Ghormley, 119–20,
    128–29, 130, 132,
    151, 153, 154–55,
    158, 202, 204–5,
    213–14, 423–24
  Halsey and, 211
  Pacific strategy, 11–12,
    35, 203–4, 220
  and the press, 155, 202,
    240
  work habits, 10
Nishida, Masao, 277, 324–25
North Africa campaign
  landing and battle, 23,
    130, 152, 153, 247,
    424
  U.S. combat troops in,
    383
Nouméa (New Caledonia),
    xxi, 37–39, 104
  Halsey reorganizing,
    209–12, 230
  logistical bottleneck,
    150–53, 211
Noyes, Leigh, *xxi*, 33–36,
    97–98, 122, 134

O'Beirne, Emmet, 298
O'Neil, Roger W., 326,
    327, 374
Ohmae, Toshikazu, 70, 82,
    83, 124

Operation KE (Japanese
    Guadalcanal garrison
    evacuation), 402–8
Operation Pestilence, 37
Operation Sledgehammer,
    12
Operation Torch (Oper-
    ation Gymnast), 11
Operation Watchtower
    (Invasion of
    Guadalcanal). *See*
    Guadalcanal
    campaign
Ozawa, Jisaburo, 236

PAC 10 (*Current Tactical
    Orders and Doctrine,
    U.S. Pacific Fleet*), 427
Pacific first strategy
  ABC-1 agreement, 24,
    383
  vs. Germany first
    strategy, 11–15, 130,
    151–53, 382–83
Pacific Fleet (CINCPAC), 7,
    10–11, 20, 21–23
  aircraft carriers, 11,
    34–35, 41–42, 51–55,
    145
  battleships, 21–22, 89,
    106, 127, 130, 137,
    145
  combat troops in, 383
  communication
    problems, 349–50
  cruisers, 137, 155–59
  destroyers, 137, 144–49
  fuel shortages, 22, 31,
    35–36, 130, 383
  Higgins boats, 147,
    148, 324
  intelligence weakness,
    349–50
  patrol boat YC-236, 324
  PT boats, 195–96,

    332–34, 350, 352,
    386, 389, 390, 395
  rescue at sea, 331–32,
    369–70
  role of, 123
  Scouting Force, 31
  ship armament, 17–18,
    142, 200, 243, 248,
    255
  submarines, 91, 91n,
    145, 324, 348
  See also radar techno-
    logy; torpedo warfare
Pacific Ocean area, map,
    xvi
Parker, Edward N. "Butch,"
    266–67, 268, 275,
    292
Patch, Alexander M., 377,
    396–97, 404, 407–8
Pearl Harbor
  attack on, 7–8, 18, 21,
    29, 141, 182, 235,
    247, 391
  espionage and, 18, 28,
    141
  investigation, 24
  Pacific Fleet (CINCPAC),
    7, 10–11
Peguod (fictional ship), 260
Perkins, Bettsy, 409–10
Perkins, Lewis W., 80–81
Perkins, Van, 409
Philip, Jack, 302
Philippines, 426
  espionage and attack
    on, 28
  Leyte Gulf campaign,
    412
Pollock, Edwin A., 110
Port Moresby (New
    Guinea)
  Japanese strategy
    concerning, 11
Posh (sailor on the *San
    Francisco*), 258–59

Powell, John C., 91
PT boats, 195–96, 332–34,
    350, 352, 386, 389,
    390, 395
    PT-37, 407
    PT-44, 333
    PT-48, 333
    PT-59, 395
    PT-111, 407
    PT-123, 407
Puller, Lewis B. "Chesty,"
    99, 103, 147–49, 174,
    219
Pye, William S., 24, 35, 91n,
    382, 426

Rabaul (New Britain)
    Japanese base at, 5, 19,
        20, 105
    as U.S. strategic
        objective, 384
    11th Air Fleet, 46–49
radar technology, 17, 88,
    102–4, 115, 138–39,
    170, 171, 228, 266,
    267, 347, 353,
    354–56, 386, 388, 425
    development of, 102
    distrust of, 63–64,
        103–4, 158, 266–67,
        268–69, 310
    and firing range, 173
    Mark 56 fire-control
        system, 411
    Plan Position Indicator
        (PPI) cathode
        display, 103
    SG ("Sugar George")
        microwave surface-
        search radar, 103–4,
        127–28, 158, 163–64,
        261
Radke, Royal, 64
Ramsey, Dewitt C., 121
Ramsey, Donald J., 403

RCA, 102
Reed, Robert B., 354
Richardson, Ford, 133,
    176–77, 187
Riddell, Robert E., 69
Riefkohl, Frederick, 49
    the Battle of Savo
        Island, 61, 62, 63,
        70, 75, 89
    and Hepburn's inquiry
        and report, 415,
        417, 418
    and Operation
        Watchtower, 96
Riggs, Whitaker F., 390
Rivero, Horacio, 88, 103
Robinson, Cecil S., 117
Rogers, Floyd A., 295, 297,
    304, 315
Rooks, Albert H., 392
Roosevelt, Eleanor, 397
Roosevelt, Franklin, *xix*, 7,
    12, 14, 23–24, 32, 109,
    130, 141, 152, 215,
    338, 345, 383, 401
Roosevelt, James, 215
Roosevelt, Theodore, 30,
    210, 215
Roper, Clifford H., 390,
    393
Russell, George L., 416
    Hepburn's report and,
        419–20

Sailer, Joseph, 339
St. Elmo's fire, 260
Saito, Hiroshi, 30
Sakuma, Eiji, 359
Samuelson, Allen B., 294,
    296
Sander, Carl, 64
Santa Cruz, Battle of,
    224–36
    aircraft involved in,
        226–34, 235

Allied losses, 436
    casualties, 235, 436
    Japanese in, **226**
    Japanese losses, 436
    press and, 251–52
    U.S. Combat Task
        Forces in the South
        Pacific (October 26,
        1942), **225**
Santa Cruz Islands, 19,
    105, 221
Santiago de Cuba, Battle of,
    302
Sato, Torajiro, 395
Saturday Evening Post, 10
Savo Island, 39
Savo Island, Battle of,
    62–79, 80–82, 84–89,
    89–91, 95, 106
    Allied losses, 435
    casualties, 89, 435
    Ghormley and, 204n
    Hepburn's inquiry
        and report on,
        402–3, 414–15,
        416–19
    Japanese losses, 435
    Japanese Navy and,
        58–59, 82–83, 104
    map, **66**
    Order of Battle, **65**
    press and, 240–42
    radar, distrust of, 63–64,
        158
    sighting of Mikawa's
        force, 58, 95, 97
    survivors, treatment of,
        91, 130
    See also Florida Island;
        Guadalcanal Island;
        Tulagi Island
Scanland, Francis W., 29
Schonland, Herbert E.,
    259, 294–95, 298,
    304, 328, 329, 340,
    341, 371–72

Schonland (*cont'd*)
   commendations,
      375–76, 401
Scott, Marjorie, 206, 384
Scott, Norman, 42, 47,
      88–89, 96
   and the *Atlanta*, 248,
      249, 259, 260, 286
   Battle of Cape
      Esperance, 157–66,
      165, 167, 169–78,
      179–88, 191–92,
      205–6, 283
   battle plan, 159–62, 162,
      168, 171
   cease-fire order, 175–76
   friendly fire, death from,
      286–87
   gunnery and night
      action exercises,
      137–40, 157, 181, 187
   misunderstood
      command, 169–71
   and Operation
      Watchtower, 136–40,
      143, 144, 196, 220,
      239, 244, 246,
      247–48, 392
   and Task Force 67.4,
      248–49, 259
   temperament, 382
   and the Tokyo Express,
      155–56, 158–62,
      166, 217, 247,
      283
Seabees
   Civil Engineer Corps
      and, 211
searchlights
   forbidding use of, 386
Searles, John M., 395
Seattle Times, 412
Seaward, Eugene T., 175,
      177
Shanklin, Elliott W., 283,
      299, 322

sharks
   and survivors in the
      water, 133, 197, 371
Shaw, Elizabeth, 18
Shaw, James C., 285, 400,
      410
Shaw, Jane, 400
Sherman, Forrest, 34, 97, 98
Sherman, Frederick C., 384
Shiloh, Battle of, *xx*
Shoup, Frank, 77, 84, 86, 90
Sinclair, George A., 85
Slot, The (New Georgia
      Sound)
   as battlefield, 137
   map, **26**
   submarines in, 91n,
      213
Small, Ernest G., 138–39,
      155, 182–83, 184
Smith, James Stuart, 319
Smith, John L., 107, 411
Smith, Milton Kimbro, 73
Smith, Rodman D., 142,
      162, 267, 273,
      313–14
Smith, William A., 117
Smoot, Roland N., 88, 145,
      146–49, 309, 412
Snell, Evard J., 43
Solomon Islands, 5
   Australia, the sea-lanes
      to, 5, 6
   See also Florida Island;
      Guadalcanal Island;
      Savo Island, Battle
      of; Tulagi Island
Soule, Thayer, 107–8,
      192–94
South Pacific
   survivors, sharks and,
      133, 197, 371
   U.S. Navy Combat Task
      Forces (October 26,
      1942), **225**
   U.S. Navy Combat Task

Forces (November
      12, 1942), **252**
   Western colonial
      ambitions and, 25
Spencer, Clifford C.,
      137–38, 140, 292,
      294, 296–97, 340,
      401
Sperry, Charles Stillman, 30
Spruance, Raymond A., 7,
      11, 236, 208, 241–42,
      380, 418, 426
Stalin, Joseph, 109
Stalingrad, 247
Stark, Harold, 9, 24
Steinbeck, John, 343
Sterrett, David S., 278
Stewart, Henry, 357
Stimson, Henry L., 130
Stokes, Thomas M., 269,
      274
Stone, I. F., 417
Stormes, Max, 356–57
Strong, Stockton B., 226
Stutt, William, 58, 97
submarines (Japanese), 62,
      121–22, 196, 259
   in The Slot, 213
   submarine *I-1*, 395
   submarine *I-19*, 133, 134
   submarine *I-26*, 121,
      166, 328–29
   Torpedo Junction,
      121–22, 243,
      327–30
submarines (U.S.), 91, 91n,
      145, 324, 348
   and fuel delivery, 198
   See also torpedo warfare
Sullivan, Alleta and Tom,
      101
   War Department
      campaign to bolster
      morale, 413–14
Sullivan, George, 312
   death of, 371, 414

Sullivan brothers, 101–2,
371
superstition, 260–61, 272,
307, 330
Sutherland, Richard K., 151
Suzuki, Masakane, 277
Swenning, Gust, 391
Swenson, Lyman Knute,
102, 232, 312, 315,
326, 328, 330

Takahashi, Sadamu, 228
Tanaka, Raizo, 69, 109,
110, 118, 120, 125,
159, 250, 263, 335,
339, 368, 387–90,
393, 395, 396
Tarrant, Eugene, 253–54,
305–7, 400, 402
Task Force 1, 22
Task Force 11, 383
Task Force 16, 18, 22–23,
28, 220, 223, **225**,
231, 252, 259, 383
Task Force 17, 220, 223,
225, 236
Task Force 18
Japanese torpedo
bomber attack,
405–6
Task Force 44, *xxi*
Task Force 61, *xxi*, 122, 126,
225
Battle of Santa Cruz,
224–30, **226**, 230–36,
436
Task Force 62, *xxi*, 48–49,
50–51, 88–89, 126
Task Force 62.6, 62–76,
126
Task Force 63, *xxi*, 126
Task Force 64, 126–27, 134,
136, 143, 206–7, 220,
225, 236, 237–38,
244, 252, 383

Battle of Cape
Esperance, 157–66,
165, 167, 168, 169–
78, 179–88, 191–92,
241–42, 435
Battleship Night Action
(Second Naval Battle
of Guadalcanal),
348–50, **350, 351**,
352, 353–68, 436
Task Force 65, 383
Task Force 66, 384
Task Force 67, 246, 250–51,
340–42, 384, 426
and the air attack on
Henderson Field,
254–59
Battle of Tassafaronga,
385–93, **393, 394**,
395–97
disbanding of, 341
operations plans,
rewriting, 386
Wright's inaccurate
claims, 393
Task Force 67.4, 248–49,
252, 260–62
Cruiser Night Action
(First Naval Battle of
Guadalcanal),
263–70, **270, 271**,
272, 273–81, 282–89,
291–96, 297–98,
299–310, 311–16,
317–25, 326–34,
436
and the number 13,
260–61, 272, 307,
330
Tassafaronga, Battle of,
385–93, 395–97
Allied losses, 436
casualties, 436
Japanese losses, 436
map, **394**
Order of Battle, **393**

PT boats and, 389, 390
and radar technology,
388
survivors, 390
torpedo warfare and,
392–93
Taylor, Edmund B., 176,
177, 178
Taylor, John B., 358
Terauchi, Masamichi, 274
Thomason, Chester C., 147,
148
Thompson, lieutenant, 71
Thompson, MacDonald,
322, 325
Thornbury, Donald V.,
322
Tisdale, Mahlon S., 389
Tobin, Robert G., 170,
171, 175, 176,
184, 267
Tokuno, Horishi, 363
Tokyo
B-25 raid against, 11,
22, 28, 228
Tokyo Express, 109,
120–21, 158–59,
166, 196, 212, 217,
238–39, 254, 335,
368, 385, 387, 395,
425
Cactus Air Force and,
146–49, 263, 342,
348–49, 359, 395
end of, 396, 408
Operation KE (Japanese
Guadalcanal
garrison
evacuation), 402–8
PT boats and, 395
U.S. Navy and, 144,
155–56, 244–45,
283
Tokyo Rose, *xix*
Tonga Islands, 21
Tongatabu, 18, 21

Topper, James, 74
torpedo warfare
danger of, 54, 229
run aground, 390
torpedo bombers, 231,
105, 115, 192,
226–27, 228, 231,
232, 243, 256, 339,
405
Torpedo Junction,
121–22, 243, 327–30
torpedoes, unreliably of,
xviii, 427
torpedo warfare (Japanese),
17, 55, 60, 69–70, 76,
133, 166, 205, 213,
229, 230, 233, 234,
237, 241, 265,
274–75, 278–79, 330,
356–58, 370, 388–89,
392–93, 401n, 406
Long Lance (Type 93
torpedo), 178,
284–85, 299–300,
307, 360, 361, 364,
390–91
motor torpedo boats,
129
surface-ship torpedoes
superiority of, 392
technical advantage of,
248, 299, 355, 392
See also submarines
torpedo warfare (U.S.),
91–92, 176, 233, 267,
268, 276, 283,
292–93, 310, 366n,
395, 396
mechanical problems
with, 355, 427
torpedo fuel as a
beverage, 325, 396
See also submarines
Touve, Norman R., 85
Toyama, Yasumi, 395
Trafalgar, Battle of, 336

Tregaskis, Richard, 111
Truesdell, William H.,
47–48, 64, 73–74
Tsukuhara, Nishizo, 244
Tulagi Island (Solomon
Islands), 4, 6, 19, 42
Japanese air attack on,
46–49
See also Florida Island;
Guadalcanal, Battle
of; Guadalcanal
Island; Savo Island,
Battle of
Turnbull (reporter), 155
Turner, Richmond Kelly,
xxi, 27, 30–31, 57
the Battle of Savo
Island, 58, 59–60, 80,
81–82, 85, 87, 90–91,
161, 417
and Fletcher, 33–34,
35–36, 51–55, 59–60
and Hepburn's inquiry,
414, 417
Hepburn's report,
rebuttal to, 418
and Operation
Watchtower, 47,
51–55, 89, 95, 96–97,
103, 132, 151, 153,
204, 220, 221, 238,
244, 246, 250–51,
254, 255, 259, 341,
368, 371–72, 374,
375–76, 426
and "the Pineapple
Fleet" (Hawaiian
Detachment), 31
Twining, Merrill B., 34
Tyler, Bob, 319
Tyndal, Bill, 181
Tyndal, Edward, 181

Uehlinger, A. E., 357, 361
Ugaki, Matome, 44, 59,

91–92, 120, 132, 150,
185, 218, 263, 375,
395
U.S. Army
Guadalcanal, forces in,
404–5
SOWESPAC (Southwest
Pacific Command),
19–20
U.S. Navy, competition
with, 11–12,
19–20
25th Division, 403
164th Infantry
("Americal"
Division), 157
U.S. Army Air Forces,
151–52, 192
U.S. Marine Corps
Marine Raiders, 215
personnel, 100
1st Marine Air Wing,
157, 339
5th Marine Regiment,
244
7th Marine Regiment,
219
8th Marine Regiment,
238
U.S. Marine Corps
(Battle of
Guadalcanal), 98
Henderson airstrip.
See Henderson
airstrip
Marine units, replacing,
403
U.S. Navy and, 132,
198–99, 225, 236,
243–44, 245, 297,
423–24
1st Battalion, 1st Marine
Regiment, 110–11
2nd Battalion, 1st
Marine Regiment,
110

1st Marine Division,
xxi, 19, 27, 51,
132, 377
2nd Marine Raiders,
215
U.S. Navy
aircraft carriers, 11,
34–35, 41–42, 106–7,
145
armament, 17–18, 142,
200, 243, 248, 255
battleships, 21–22, 89,
106, 137, 145
code breaking, 28–29,
45, 129, 240
Combat Task Forces in
the South
Pacific (November
12, 1942), **252**
Combat Task Forces in
the South
Pacific (October 26,
1942), **225**
commanders, confidence
in, 134, 137
communications,
96–97, 349–50
crew conflicts, 367
cruisers, 137, 155–159
destroyers, 137, 144–49,
157–58
at Guadalcanal (August
1942), *xxi*
at Guadalcanal
(October 18, 1942)
Higgins boats, 147, 148,
324
and "Island Warfare,"
38–39
intelligence weakness,
349–50
Japanese Navy,
chauvinism toward,
95–96, 98
logistics (fuel,
reinforcements, and
supplies), 22–23,
35–36, 89, 104–5,
130, 150–153
patrol boat YC-236, 324
personnel, 100
PT boats, 195–96,
332–34, 350, 352,
386, 389, 390, 395
recruits, training of,
98–102
rescue at sea, 331–32,
369–70
role of, 123
secrecy and espionage,
18, 28, 39
South Pacific Area
Command
(SOPAC), 19–20
submarines, 91, 91n,
145, 324, 348
and superstition,
260–61, 272,
307, 330
survivors, sharks and,
133, 197, 371
systemic problems,
96–97, 349–50
U.S. Army, competition
with, 11–12
See also Guadalcanal,
Battle of; Midway,
Battle of; torpedo
warfare; radar
technology
U.S. Navy (ships)
Aaron Ward (DD-483),
102, 104, 246, 267,
276, 278, 307–9, 322,
324
Alchiba (AK-23), 87, 238
American Legion
(AP-35), 90
Anderson (DD-411), 233
Argonne (AP-4), xxiii,
151, 191, 209, 220,
290
Arizona (BB-39), 18, 182
Astoria (CA-34), 27,
29–31, 40, 47, 49
the Battle of Savo
Island, 62, 63–65, 66,
66–69, 71–75, 91,
127
casualties, 412–13
Japan, returning
Hiroshi Saito's body
to, 30, 90–91
Japanese propaganda
and, 29–30
sinking of, 76–79, 81,
84–87, 320, 412–13
Atlanta (CL-51), 16–18,
21, 22, 103, 106, 115,
118, 123, 127, 128,
196, 200–201, 206–7,
218, 239, 246, 248,
249, 255–56, 257,
260
armament, 17–18,
142, 200, 243, 248
burning, 317–21
casualties, 320
Cruiser Night Action,
267, 269, 269,
273–75, 283,
284–88, 322
friendly fire, victim of,
341
reunions, 427
sinking of, 332, 398
survivors, 398–99,
409–11
torpedoing of, 284–88,
293, 299, 332
Augusta (CA-31), 99
Bagley (DD-386), 59,
60, 85, 88
Ballard (AVD-10),
374
Barnett (AP-11), 51
Barton (DD-599), 246,
257, 278

Barton (*cont'd*)
  survivors, 324
  torpedoing of, 307–10
Benham (DD-397), 337,
  427
  Battleship Night
    Action, 349, 356,
    357–58, 359, 366
Birmingham (CL-62),
  409
Blue (DD-387), 49, 60,
  88, 112, 168, 417
Bobolink (AT-131), 321,
  324, 389
Boise (CL-47), 143, 155
  armament, 248
  Battle of Cape
    Esperance, 156, 158,
    160, 164–65, 170,
    171, 173, 174, 175,
    179, 180–83, 184,
    186, 205, 241–42
  Philadelphia,
    reception at, 401
Breese (DM-18),
  139–40
Buchanan (DD-484),
  42, 86, 88, 161, 168,
  186, 246, 247, 257,
  333
Chenango (ACV-28),
  405
Chester (CA-27), 206,
  213
Chicago (CA-29), 27, 29,
  39, 40, 42, 49, 54,
  56–58, 80, 82, 88, 89,
  405
  Japanese attack on, 59,
    60–61
  sinking, 406, 407
Cleveland (CL-55), 405
Colorado (BB-45), 21,
  346, 383
Columbia (CL-56), 405
Copahee (ACV-12), 156

Crescent City (AP-40),
  21, 246
Cushing (DD-376), 246,
  247, 260
  Cruiser Night Action,
    266–67, 268, 269,
    275–76, 279, 292,
    293, 301
Decatur (DD-5),
  145–46, 155
DeHaven (DD-469), 407
Dewey (DD-349), 88
Drayton (DD-366)
  Battle of Tassafaronga,
    388, 390
Duncan (DD-485), 160,
  171, 176, 186
  friendly fire, victim of,
    177–78, 187, 268
Ellet (DD-398), 88
Enterprise (CV-6), *xxi*,
  11, 18, 21, 22–23,
  27, 34, 47, 48, 53,
  107, 121, 122,
  130–31, 137, 144,
  208, 209–10, 213,
  218, 221, 244, 251,
  290, 336, 367–68,
  383, 406
  aircraft from, 339
  Battle of Santa Cruz,
    224, 226–28, 230,
    231–34, 236, 236,
    245
  Battle of the Eastern
    Solomons, 115,
    114–18
  IJN *Hiei*, Torpedo
    Squadron 10 ("The
    Buzzard Brigade")
    attack on, 322–23,
    324–25
Farenholt (DD-491),
  133, 160, 170, 171,
  175–76, 184
  friendly fire, victim of,

  177–78, 186, 187,
    268
Fletcher (DD-445), 98,
  136, 246, 260–61
  Battle of Tassafaronga,
    388, 390
  Cruiser Night Action,
    267, 278, 307,
    309–10, 313, 314, 326,
    330, 331–32, 380
Flint (CL-97)
  reunions, 427
Fuller (AP-14), 238
George F. Elliott (AP-
  13), 48, 63
Gwin (DD-433), 246,
  337, 427
  Battleship Night
    Action, 349, 356,
    357–58, 359, 366
Helena (CL-50), 138,
  140–43, 206, 213,
  218, 237–38, 244,
  246, 256, 257, 261,
  340–41, 341, 384
  armament, 142, 248,
    255
  Battle of Cape
    Esperance, 155, 156,
    158, 160, 161, 166,
    171–72, 176, 181,
    184, 186, 205, 241
  and *Boise's* reception
    at, 401
  Cruiser Night Action,
    266, 268–69, 273, 274,
    283–84, 291, 296,
    300, 304, 311–12,
    313, 313–16, 326
  R&R in Sydney,
    399–400
  sinking, 401n
  and Torpedo Junction,
    328–30
Helm (DD-388), 62,
  70–71, 88

Henley (DD-391), 88, 112

Honolulu (CL-48), 384
  Battle of Tassafaronga, 387, 392–93

Hopkins (DD-249), 85–86

Hornet (CV-8), 11, 121, 132, 137, 196, 201, 213, 218, 221, 337, 427
  Battle of Santa Cruz, 224–25, 228–30, 231–33, 236, 245
  and Doolittle's raid on Tokyo, 11, 22, 28, 228
  survivors, 399

Houston (CA-30), 32, 127

Hull (DD-350), 88

Hunter Liggett (AP-27), 51, 80

Idaho (BB-42), 22

Indiana (BB-58), 383

Jarvis (DD-393), 48

Johnston (DD-557), 412

Juneau (CL-52), 17, 89, 102, 127, 128, 232, 246, 248, 261
  casualties, 375
  Cruiser Night Action, 265–66, 269, 278, 296, 300–301, 312, 315, 326
  survivors, 330–32, 370–71, 373–74, 374–75, 375, 379–82
  torpedoing of, 330, 331, 328–30

Kansas (BB-21), 210

Laffey (DD-459), 123, 160, 171, 184, 186, 186–87, 246, 260
  Cruiser Night Action, 269, 276–78, 279, 293

  onboard inventory, 150
  torpedoing of, 299, 301

Lamson (DD-367)
  Battle of Tassafaronga, 388

Lardner (DD-487), 246
  Battle of Tassafaronga, 388

Lexington (CV-2), 11, 53, 116, 134, 331, 373

Long Island (ACV-1), 107

Louisville (CA-28), 405, 406

McCalla (DD-488), 161, 168, 174, 186, 246

McCawley (AP-10), *xxi*, 27, 47, 54, 96–97, 157, 246, 371–72

Maryland (BB-46), 21–22, 383

Maury (DD-401)
  Battle of Tassafaronga, 388

Meade (DD-602), 370

Meredith (DD-434), 197

Minneapolis (CA-36), 121, 123, 340
  Battle of Tassafaronga, 387, 388, 389, 390, 391, 393

Mississippi (BB-41), 22

Missouri (BB-63), 423

Monssen (DD-436), 39, 42, 88, 145, 146–49, 246, 278, 307, 308–10

Monterey (CVL-26), 411, 412
  reunions, 427

Montpelier (CL-57), 405

Mugford (DD-389), 47, 88

Mustin (DD-413), 233, 386, 427

Nevada (BB-36), 24, 29, 106, 403

New Hampshire (BB-25), 347

New Mexico (BB-40), 22

New Orleans (CA-32), 115, 123, 249, 340, 384
  Battle of Tassafaronga, 387, 390–91, 391, 393

North Carolina (BB-55), 21, 22–23, 28, 103, 115, 118, 123, 126, 127, 128, 133, 133–34, 137, 205, 241, 383

Northampton (CA-26), 228, 230, 232, 340, 384
  Battle of Tassafaronga, 387, 388, 389, 392, 393
  sinking of, 393

O'Bannon (DD-450), 191, 246, 260, 261
  Cruiser Night Action, 267, 269, 276, 292–93, 304, 308, 311, 314, 326, 331

O'Brien (DD-415), 133, 134

Oglala (CM-4), 141

Oklahoma (BB-37), 29, 57, 106

Panay (PR-5), 30

Patterson (DD-392), 59, 60, 81–82, 88

Pennsylvania (BB-38), 21–22, 141

Pensacola (CA-24), 136, 246, 248, 384
  Battle of Tassafaronga, 387, 389, 391–98, 393

Perkins (DD-377)
  Battle of Tassafaronga, 388

Porter (DD-356)
sunk, 230, 234
Portland (CA-33), 21,
22, 118, 123, 246,
249, 260, 261,
338
Cruiser Night Action,
267, 269, 270, 283,
288, 288–89, 295–96,
299–303, 311, 332,
350
PT boats and, 332–34
uncontrolled circling,
299–300, 303, 324
President Adams (AP-
38), 21, 246
President Coolidge, 340
President Hayes (AP-39),
21
President Jackson (AP-
37), 21, 89–90, 246,
259, 371
President Monroe (AP-
104), 399, 409
Preston (DD-379), 231,
246, 337
Battleship Night
Action, 349, 354,
356–58
burning, 361
friendly fire, victim of,
357
survivors, 369–70
Princeton (CVL-23),
409
Quincy (CA-39), 21, 27,
40, 49, 160, 173, 406
the Battle of Savo
Island, 62, 63, 64, 65,
71, 73, 74, 75–76, 82,
91, 127
casualties, 413
survivors, 400
Ralph Talbot (DD-390),
49, 60, 88, 417
S-44, 91, 91n

Salt Lake City (CA-25),
123, 138, 155, 156,
201
Battle of Cape Esper-
ance, 158, 160,
161, 166, 168, 170,
172–73, 178, 179,
182–83, 184, 185,
186, 187 88, 205
San Diego (CL-53), 383
San Francisco (CA-38),
21, 123, 155, 156,
201, 206, 213, 218,
220, 237–38, 244,
246, 249, 253–54,
254–55, 257, 260,
261, 340–41
Battle of Cape Esper-
ance, 157–58, 160,
163, 166, 168, 170,
171, 173, 174, 175,
176, 180, 183,
184–85, 186, 205,
255, 371–72
body parts sweep,
326–27
collision with the
Breese, 139– 40
Cruiser Night Action,
267, 269, 274, 283,
284, 287–88, 291–96,
297–98, 302, 302–3,
313–16
damage-control,
303–7
feelings against, 341,
409
fires and hits on,
258–59, 293–94,
300, 319, 326
and friendly fire, 341
friendly fire, Scott's
death by, 286–87
officer's com-
mendations,
375–76

San Francisco,
reception at,
400–401
and Torpedo Junction,
328–30
San Juan (CL-54), 21,
42, 47, 60, 88–89,
103, 136, 231, 383
Saratoga (CV-3), *xxi*, 21,
27, 34, 35, 47, 48, 53,
107, 114, 118, 119,
121, 122, 127, 137,
237, 383
Watchtower
conference, 33–36
Selfridge (DD-357), 88
Shaw (DD-373), 246
Smith (DD-378), 231
Solace (AH-5), 90
South Dakota (BB-57),
89, 127, 128, 134,
137, 213, 231, 232,
233, 236, 245, 337,
366
armament, 346
armor, 346
attack on, 360–61,
364
Battleship Night
Action, 345, 347,
358–59, 360–61, 364
burial at sea, 234–35
casualties, 364
as a hard-luck ship,
128, 164
power failure, 358, 364
reception of, 401–2
Washington, crew
conflicts with, 367
Sterett (DD-407), 36,
143, 244, 246, 260
Cruiser Night Action,
268, 269, 275, 276,
278–80, 292–93, 293,
301, 313, 314, 326,
380

courage of the crew,
280–81
Halsey's visit, 378–79
reception of, 402
Suwannee (ACV-27),
405
Tennessee (BB-43),
21–22
Trout (SS-202), 348
Truxtun (DD-14), 249
Vestal (AR-4), 259
Vincennes (CA-44), 21,
27, 40, 49, 96, 127,
173, 406
the Battle of Savo
Island, 61, 62, 64,
65, 69–70, 71, 73,
75, 91
Walke (DD-416)
Battleship Night
Action, 349, 356
burning, 361
casualties, 357
friendly fire, victim of,
357–58
survivors, 357, 369–70
Washington (BB-56), 21,
89, 127–28, 143, 151,
196, 200, 201, 201–2,
206, 218, 219–20,
220, 236, 245, 337,
383, 397–88
armor, 346
Battleship Night
Action, 345, 349,
353–56, 358, 361–64,
365
and friendly fire, 347
and the IJN *Kirishima*,
363–64, 365–66
and radar technology,
353, 355, 361–63,
365
reception of, 401–2
South Dakota, crew
conflicts with, 367

Wasp (CV-7), *xxi*, 21,
27, 34, 53, 107, 114,
118, 119, 121, 406
survivors, 134, 141
torpedoed, 132–34,
137, 240
West Virginia (BB-48),
262
Wichita (CA-45), 405
Wilson (DD-408), 62,
70–71, 81, 86, 88
Yorktown (CV-5), 11, 53,
115, 116, 171
Zeilin (AP-9), 157

Valley Forge, Battle of, *xx*
Valor of Ignorance, The
(Lea), *ix*
Vandegrift, Alexander
Archer, *xxi*, 19, 20,
23, 27, 194, 198, 203,
337, 377, 426
and Operation Watch-
tower, 33–36, 42,
54, 60, 89, 107,
110, 125–26, 132,
154, 219, 220–21,
237, 243, 244, 245,
250, 350
Saratoga conference,
33–36
Vincent, Patrick, 362
Vose, James E. "Moe,"
229
Vouza, Jacob, 41

Wake Island, 28, 35
Walker, Frank R., 60
Wallace, John G., 256,
258–59
Walsh, H. T., 348, 354
Wang, Charles, 374
Ward, Alfred G., 103
Watkins, C. C., 84

Weaver, Charles W., 202,
215, 337, 416
Weems, George B., 168,
174
Weschler, Thomas R., 97,
98, 134
Whitt, Joseph, 327, 328,
329–30
Widhelm, William "Gus,"
229
Wiggens (gun captain),
175–76
Wilbourne, William W.,
262, 292, 298, 329
Wilkinson, E. R., 292–93
Wintle, Jack, 298
Wirth, Turk, 260
Wolfe, Henry A., 317
Wolverton, Tom, 173, 179
Wood, Hunter, 231
Woods, Louis, 237, 325
World War II
the Blitz, 23–24
France, invasion of, 12,
14
Germany first vs. Pacific
first strategy, 11–15,
130, 151–53, 382–83
Germany's U-boat
campaign, 22
Japanese surrender,
423
Marco Polo Bridge
Incident and, 110
North Africa campaign,
23, 130, 152, 153,
247, 424
Operation Sledge-
hammer, 12
Operation Torch
(Operation Gym-
nast), 11, 23
recruits, training of,
98–102
Russian front, 12, 109,
215, 247

World War II (*cont'd*)
War Department
campaign to bolster
morale, 413–14
See also Pearl Harbor;
Tokyo Express
Wright, Carleton H., 123,
134, 387–88, 392
and Hepburn's inquiry,
417
inaccurate claims, 393

Wulff, John T., 321, 332
Wylie, Joseph C., 98–99,
103, 136, 261, 308,
310, 331–32, 388

Yamamoto, Isoroku, 11,
20, 30, 44–45, 111,
112–13, 120, 121,
124, 131, 159, 185,
192, 195, 196, 198,
212, 218, 250, 255,
325, 335–36, 365,
368, 395, 403, 404
Yeamans, Donald, 74
Yokota, Minoru, 121, 166
Young, Cassin, 246, 254,
259, 261, 291, 295,
297–98, 327

Zarker, Raymond, 56

PHOTO CREDITS

TITLE PAGE

Admiral Ernest J. King (Fox Movietone News, © University of South Carolina)

PART OPENERS

Part I   Vice Admiral Robert L. Ghormley (U.S. Navy)
Part II   Rear Admiral John S. McCain (U.S. Navy)
Part III   Captain Frederick L. Riefkohl (U.S. Navy)
Part IV   Captain William G. Greenman (U.S. Navy)

PHOTO INSERT I

Page 1   Admiral Ernest J. King (Fox Movietone News, © University of South Carolina)
Admiral Chester W. Nimitz (U.S. Navy)
Vice Admiral Robert L. Ghormley (U.S. Navy)
Rear Admiral Frank Jack Fletcher (U.S. Navy)

Page 2   Rear Admiral Richmond Kelly Turner (U.S. Navy)
Rear Admiral John S. McCain (U.S. Navy)
An F4F Wildcat prepares to launch (U.S. Navy)

Page 3   The heavy cruiser *Vincennes* opens fire (Royal Australian Navy/Collection of
    Brent Jones)
Captain Frederick L. Riefkohl (U.S. Navy)
The *Astoria* (Royal Australian Navy/Collection of Brent Jones)

Page 4   *Astoria* gunners in drills (U.S. Navy)
Captain William G. Greenman (U.S. Navy)
The *Astoria*, shown in Hawaiian waters (U.S. Navy)

Page 5   The last photo of the *Quincy* (U.S. Navy)
Rear Admiral Gunichi Mikawa (National Archives)

Page 5   Captain Samuel N. Moore (U.S. Navy)
The *Quincy* in the South Pacific (U.S. Navy)

Page 6   Two U.S. destroyers, the *Blue* and the *Patterson* (U.S. Navy)
Chicago sailors cut away damaged bow plating (U.S. Navy)
Captain Howard D. Bode (U.S. Navy)

Page 7   Lloyd M. Mustin (Naval Historical Center) ·
Admiral Isoroku Yamamoto (Official portrait by Shugaku Homma, Naval
    Historical Center)
Rear Admiral Norman Scott (Collection of Michael Scott)

Page 8   The light cruiser *Boise* (U.S. Navy)
Captain Robert G. Tobin receives the Navy Cross from Admiral William
    F. Halsey (U.S. Navy)
The antiaircraft cruiser *Atlanta* maneuvers with four destroyers (U.S. Navy)

Page 9   The destroyer *Farenholt* (U.S. Navy)
Radar (U.S. Navy)
The SG radar (U.S. Navy)

Page 10   Major Joseph Foss (U.S. Navy)
Major General Alexander A. Vandegrift, USMC (U.S. Navy)
Marine tanks prowling near Alligator Creek (U.S. Navy)

Page 11   Lieutenant Colonel Lewis B. "Chesty" Puller (National Archives)
Nimitz with Vandegrift (Fox Movietone News, © University of South Carolina)
The SBD Dauntless (U.S. Navy)

Page 12   As the *Wasp* burns in the background, the destroyer *O'Brien* is torpedoed
    (U.S. Navy)
Rear Admiral Raizo Tanaka (National Archives)
The *Wasp* sinks (U.S. Navy)

Page 13   The destroyer *Laffey* brought hundreds of *Wasp* survivors home (U.S. Navy)
A Japanese plane takes a plunge while the *Enterprise* takes a bomb (U.S. Navy)

Page 14   The damaged *Hornet* under tow from the *Northampton* (U.S. Navy)
Chaplain James Claypool presides over burials at sea (U.S. Navy)

Page 15   Daniel J. Callaghan (U.S. Navy)
Newly outfitted *Helena* (U.S. Navy)
The *Atlanta* (U.S. Navy)
Captain Gilbert C. Hoover (U.S. Navy)

Page 16   The *Portland* (U.S. Navy)
Captain Laurance T. DuBose (U.S. Navy)
Captain Samuel P. Jenkins (U.S. Navy)
Lieutenant Robert D. Graff (Courtesy of Robert D. Graff)

PHOTO INSERT II

Page 17   Yard workers tend to the *Portland*'s massive torpedo wound (U.S. Navy)
The battleship *Hiei* (Courtesy of Anthony Tully)
Vice Admiral Nobutake Kondo (National Archives)

Page 18   The *Juneau* alongside the *Aaron Ward* (U.S. Navy)
Captain Cassin Young (U.S. Navy)
Captain Lyman K. Swenson (U.S. Navy)

Page 19   The Sullivan brothers (U.S. Navy)
The *Hiei* burns and bleeds oil (National Archives)
The *Cushing* (U.S. Navy)

Page 20   The *Laffey* battled the *Hiei* at point blank range (U.S. Navy)
The *Aaron Ward* (U.S. Navy)

Page 21   Recruits at Bainbridge, Maryland (U.S. Navy)
New sailors at Naval Air Station Corpus Christi (U.S. Navy)

Page 22   Metalworkers turn out 40 mm gun tubes (National Archives)
The battleship *Washington* (U.S. Navy)

Page 23   Willis A. Lee (U.S. Navy/Special Collections, Joyner Library, East Carolina
University)
The *South Dakota* (U.S. Navy)
The *South Dakota*'s secondary battery roars (Fox Movietone News, ©
University of South Carolina)

Page 24   The *South Dakota* took a beating but returned as a legend (U.S. Navy)
Damage to the *South Dakota* (U.S. Navy)
A 14-inch shell from the *Kirishima* splintered the *South Dakota*'s deck
(U.S. Navy)

Page 25   The *Walke* (U.S. Navy)
The *Barton* (U.S. Navy)
South Dakota sailors bow their heads (U.S. Navy)

Page 26   Halsey takes the oath from his chief of staff (U.S. Navy)
The Japanese transport *Kinugawa Maru* (U.S. Navy)
The *Boise* returns to Philadelphia (U.S. Navy)

Page 27   Captain Edward J. "Mike" Moran hosts Admiral King aboard the *Boise* (Fox
Movietone News, © University of South Carolina)
A *Boise* sailor inspects damage to a bulkhead (U.S. Navy)
The *Boise*'s proud crew (Fox Movietone News, © University of South Carolina)

Page 28   Captain Moran in front of the *Boise*'s battle-worn gun barrels (U.S. Navy)
Battle damage to the *San Francisco*'s hangar area (U.S. Navy)

Page 28   The battered *San Francisco* (Fox Movietone News, © University of South
            Carolina)
          Closeup with sailors (Fox Movietone News, © University of South Carolina)

Page 29   Admiral Nimitz comes aboard the *San Francisco* (U.S. Navy)
          Nimitz inspects the damaged bridge (U.S. Navy)
          Lieutenant Commander Bruce McCandless (Fox Movietone News, ©
            University of South Carolina)
          McCandless comforts the father and aunt of Admiral Callaghan (U.S. Navy)

Page 30   The heavy cruiser *New Orleans,* her entire bow shorn away, undergoes
            temporary repairs (U.S. Navy)
          Exuberant *San Francisco* sailors meet the press (Fox Movietone News,
            © University of South Carolina)
          The *PT-109* (US Navy)

Page 31   Admiral Arthur J. Hepburn (U.S. Navy)
          Eugene Tarrant (James D. Hornfischer)
          The *New Orleans* returns to Pearl Harbor (U.S. Navy)
          Guadalcanal boasts a new wharf and several cranes (U.S. Navy)

Page 32   Ghormley with Eleanor Roosevelt at Pearl Harbor, 1943 (U.S. Navy)
          The sailors of the PT boat fleet fought gallantly, but the press still felt the need
            to sensationalize their capabilities (U.S. Navy)
          Captain Gatch of the *South Dakota* confers with journalist (U.S. Navy)
          Lieutenant Hugh M. Robinson (left) and Lieutenant John M. Searles (right)
            (Courtesy of Gene Kirkland and George Brooks)

PHOTO: © MARK MATSON

JAMES D. HORNFISCHER, a native of Massachusetts, is the author of *Ship of Ghosts* and *The Last Stand of the Tin Can Sailors,* which won the Samuel Eliot Morison Award for Naval Literature and was chosen by *The Wall Street Journal* as one of the five best books on "war as soldiers know it." A graduate of Colgate University and the University of Texas at Austin, he lives with his wife and their three children in Austin, Texas.

www.jameshornfischer.com